THE PHYSIOLOGICAL BASIS OF MEMORY
Second Edition

CONTRIBUTORS

Georges Chapouthier
J. Anthony Deutsch
C. R. Gallistel
Robert D. Hawkins
Susan D. Iversen
Robert A. Jensen
Joe L. Martinez, Jr.
James L. McGaugh
Mary Plough
David Quartermain
Allen M. Schneider
Peter E. Simson
Larry R. Squire
Stuart Zola-Morgan

THE PHYSIOLOGICAL BASIS OF MEMORY

Second Edition

Edited by

J. ANTHONY DEUTSCH

Department of Psychology
University of California, San Diego
La Jolla, California

1983

ACADEMIC PRESS
A Subsidiary of Harcourt Brace Jovanovich, Publishers
New York   London
Paris   San Diego   San Francisco   São Paulo   Sydney   Tokyo   Toronto

ACADEMIC PRESS, INC.
111 Fifth Avenue, New York, New York 10003

United Kingdom Edition published by
ACADEMIC PRESS, INC. (LONDON) LTD.
24/28 Oval Road, London NW1 7DX

Library of Congress Cataloging in Publication Data

Main entry under title:

The Physiological basis of memory.

   Includes bibliographical references and index.
   1. Memory–Physiological aspects. I. Deutsch,
J. Anthony, Date
QP406.P49   1983   612'.82   83-11747
ISBN 0-12-213460-5 (alk. paper)

PRINTED IN THE UNITED STATES OF AMERICA

83 84 85 86   9 8 7 6 5 4 3 2 1

84-4345 MCL

CONTENTS

Chapter 3.   Cellular Neurophysiological Studies of Learning
Robert D. Hawkins

Chapter 4.   Spreading Depression: A Behavioral Analysis
Allen M. Schneider and Peter E. Simson

Chapter 5.   Brain Lesions and Memory in Animals: A Reappraisal
Susan D. Iversen

Chapter 10. **The Role of Catecholamines in Memory Processing**
David Quartermain

CONTRIBUTORS

Numbers in parentheses indicate the pages on which the authors' contributions begin.

GEORGES CHAPOUTHIER (1), *Département de Psychophysiologie, Centre National de la Recherche Scientifique, Gif-sur-Yvette, France*

J. ANTHONY DEUTSCH (367), *Department of Psychology, University of California, San Diego, La Jolla, California 92093*

C. R. GALLISTEL (269), *Department of Psychology, University of Pennsylvania, Philadelphia, Pennsylvania 19104*

ROBERT D. HAWKINS (71), *Center for Neurobiology and Behavior, College of Physicians and Surgeons, Columbia University, New York, New York 10032*

SUSAN D. IVERSEN (139), *The Psychological Laboratory, Department of Experimental Psychology, University of Cambridge, Cambridge CB2 3EB England*

ROBERT A. JENSEN (49), *Department of Psychobiology, School of Biological Sciences, University of California, Irvine, Irvine, California 92717*

JOE L. MARTINEZ, JR.[1] (49), *Department of Psychobiology, School of Biological Sciences, University of California, Irvine, Irvine, California 92717*

[1]Present address: The Salk Institute, La Jolla, California 92037.

JAMES L. MCGAUGH (49), *Department of Psychobiology, School of Biological Sciences, University of California, Irvine, Irvine, California 92717*

MARY PLOUGH[2] (351), *Department of Psychology, Swarthmore College, Swarthmore, Pennsylvania 19081*

DAVID QUARTERMAIN (387), *Department of Neurology, Physiology, and Biophysics, New York University–School of Medicine, New York, New York 10016*

ALLEN M. SCHNEIDER (121, 351), *Department of Psychology, Swarthmore College, Swarthmore, Pennsylvania 19081*

PETER E. SIMSON (121), *Department of Psychology, New York University, Washington Square, New York, New York 10003*

LARRY R. SQUIRE (199), *Veterans Administration Medical Center, San Diego, California 92161, and Department of Psychiatry, University of California School of Medicine, La Jolla, California 92093*

STUART ZOLA-MORGAN (199), *Veterans Administration Medical Center, San Diego, California 92161, and Department of Psychiatry, University of California School of Medicine, La Jolla, California 92093*

[2]Present address: School of Medicine, University of Miami, Miami, Florida 33136.

PREFACE TO THE FIRST EDITION

This volume represents an attempt to collate in one source important information concerning the physiological substrate of memory and learning. The book should be useful to researchers and interested students alike. It has been written to be comprehended by an attentive reader even if he lacks previous background in the subject. The contributors have not merely been content to catalogue a series of facts. Findings and theories are critically evaluated so that the reader is given a realistic appraisal of the status of the field.

After the early, somewhat uncritical enthusiasm which ushered in the vast spate of work on the physical basis of memory, intense skepticism, disappointment, and disillusionment set in among many. However, a careful reading of the book will reveal that continuous progress is being made in the field and that the mood of self-doubt has actually produced a needed increase in sophistication. This heightening of intellectual refinement is necessary though perhaps not yet adequate to solve one of nature's most difficult and intriguing problems.

PREFACE TO THE SECOND EDITION

This second edition covers much the same ground as the first, being a review of many areas of research that shed light on the physiological basis of memory. Although the advances have been much less publicized than those that preceded the first edition, progress in these areas has in many cases been remarkable, and an updated book is now in order. In some areas, such as the exploration of mnemonic function through the use of electroconvulsive shock and the use of spreading depression, unforeseen complexities have arisen. On the other hand, surprising simplifications have occurred in the area of memory facilitation. In neuropsychology, research on animal subjects has been forced into closer juxtaposition to that based on clinical observation. As a result, the chapters describing these two areas overlap much more than in the first edition, although the reader will note that the interpretation of the same facts can still differ widely.

In yet another area—the manipulation of synaptic transmission to test certain hypotheses of memory function—it is gratifying to see that hypotheses first proposed as a result of basic research on rats are now proving their value in enlarging our understanding of human cognitive deficit. Interesting developments have also occurred in the sophistication with which we are able to interpret learning produced by direct brain stimulation. Another very exciting development that has occurred since the publication of the first edition is the momentous discovery of the basis of associative learning at the cellular level. The second edition is therefore a chronicle of solid and exciting progress in an area that is of almost universal interest.

THE PHYSIOLOGICAL BASIS OF MEMORY
Second Edition

PROTEIN SYNTHESIS AND MEMORY[1]

GEORGES CHAPOUTHIER

Département de Psychophysiologie
Laboratoire de Physiologie Nerveuse
Centre National de la Recherche Scientifique
91190 Gif-sur-Yvette, France

[1]We wish to thank Dr. M. Le Moal and Dr. B. Soumireu-Mourat for their suggestions and Dr. Dian Ellis for her help in translating the manuscript.

THE PHYSIOLOGICAL BASIS OF MEMORY   1

I. INTRODUCTION

The achievement of molecular genetics has produced considerable evidence that hereditary information is stored in a chemical code, the DNA molecule. Because innate information can be stored in chemical form, many authors since Monné (1948) and Katz and Halstead (1950) have postulated that acquired information might also be stored chemically.

The problem of acquisition of information by the brain brings us to a preliminary discussion of the concepts of learning and memory. There is no general agreement among psychologists about a definition of these terms. It does not seem necessary here, however, to discuss these definitions in depth, and, in the context of the study of the molecular approach which follows, we could simply define these concepts by the use of the term information. In this sense, learning could appear as "acquisition and retention of information" by the nervous system (Ungar, 1970a), and memory, as the sum of all the information stored in the brain (Chapouthier & Matras, 1982).

Only a few types of molecules have an information content high enough to code all the information required for the rather complex processes of learning and memory. Those most likely to be involved in such a role are nucleic acids and proteins. Investigations of this hypothesis have been undertaken in recent years, and I should like to summarize the most important of them. Of the nucleic acids studied, most attention in investigations concerning memory has been directed toward RNA, since DNA is known to be involved in genetics. It is interesting, however, to note that some authors (Gaito, 1961; Griffith & Mahler, 1969; Reinis & Lamble, 1972) have suggested a possible role of DNA in acquired information.

All the studies dealt with in this chapter have attempted to discover a correlation between behavioral modifications occurring during learning and macromolecular changes. However, the authors disagree on the precise nature of these modifications. Some investigators assume that it has been clearly proven that acquired information is stored in macromolecules and that a "molecular code of memory" exists. Many others are skeptical of this point of view and are more prone to assign nucleic acids and proteins a limited nonspecific role in learning. These positions will be discussed and a general view of the present state of this important controversy will be given in this chapter.

The studies to date can be divided into four main areas of investigation: (1) the study of chemical changes associated with learning, (2) the study of the effect of inhibitors of RNA and protein synthesis on learning, (3) the search for a molecular code of memory, and (4) the modern conception of the role of proteins in learning.

II. CHEMICAL CHANGES ASSOCIATED WITH LEARNING

The simplest method for investigating the role of nucleic acids and proteins in learning and memory is to look for the quantitative or qualitative changes in these substances in the nervous system following learning. The principle is simple, but its application is not always easy. It is probable that only a comparatively small number of neurons are activated by a given learning situation, and the resulting chemical changes are sometimes difficult to distinguish from the metabolic processes correlated with the activity of the nervous system.

A. Classical Data

The first studies in this field were carried out by Hydén (1959) on brain RNA in rats. By means of sophisticated microtechniques, Hydén and his colleagues were able to measure the quantity and the base ratio of RNA in a single nerve cell (Hydén & Egyhazi, 1962; Hyden & Lange, 1965). From the results obtained, Hydén concluded that RNA base ratio can be modified by learning processes (Hydén, 1959, 1967). Other investigators used a more indirect method: if a radioactive precursor of RNA is administered to rats before training and if training increases RNA synthesis, radioactivity should be found in RNA after learning. This technique has been used with rats by Glassman's group (Glassman, 1969), who used uridine as precursor, and by Bowman and Strobel (1969), who used cytidine. Shashoua (1968) studied learning in fish which had been injected with labeled orotic acid, a common precursor of both uridine and cytidine; he found that the uridine–cytidine ratio was modified during acquisition of new swimming skills. In planarians Corning and Freed (1968) showed changes in labeled RNA turnover after conditioning.

In the case of protein synthesis, Hydén and Lange (1968) found that the incorporation of tritiated leucine in rats was increased after learning. Similar results were obtained by Beach, Emmens, Kimble, and Lickey (1969). In chicks Bateson, Horn and Rose (1969) showed increased incorporation of labeled lysine after imprinting. Finally, Bogoch (1968, 1974), after various studies of glycoproteins in pigeon brain, discovered modification of some of them after learning. He insists upon the important role played by glycoproteins in information processing in the brain.

For further details on this problem, the reader is referred to reviews by Bogoch (1974), Gaito (1974), Uphouse, McInnes, and Schlesinger (1974), and Ungerer (1975).

B. Discussion

Despite many promising results, the interpretation of this type of experiment remains difficult. First, it is extremely difficult to draw a general conclusion from the results obtained in this field because, in the various experiments, too many conditions vary widely. The animals used were either the usual laboratory animals or, in some cases, unusual ones, such as chicks (Bateson *et al.*, 1969), pigeons (Bogoch, 1968), goldfish (Shashoua, 1968), or even planarians (Corning & Freed, 1968). The animals were trained in the following tasks: motor learning (Hydén & Lange, 1965, 1968; Shashoua, 1968), discrimination (Bogoch, 1968; Bowman & Strobel, 1969), avoidance (Beach *et al.*, 1969; Glassman, 1969; Gold, Altschuler, Kleban, Lawton, & Miller, 1969), or classical conditioning (Corning & Freed, 1968). Numerous differences also exist in the chemical methods which can be carried out on nucleic acids and proteins, either directly on the substances after learning (Bogoch, 1968; Hydén, 1959, 1967, 1969) or by a more indirect way such as the study of the incorporation of a nucleotide or its precursor (Bowman & Strobel, 1969; Glassman, 1969; Shashoua, 1968) or an amino acid (Bateson *et al.*, 1969; Beach *et al.*, 1969). This chemical analysis itself may be done on various quantities of nervous tissue, from a single neuron (Hydén, 1959; Hydén & Egyhazi, 1962), to parts of the brain (Beach *et al.*, 1969; Bowman & Strobel, 1969; Glassman, 1969; Hydén & Lange, 1968), to the whole brain (Bogoch, 1968; Shashoua, 1968).

A second difficulty in the interpretation of this type of experiment is that it is not easy to distinguish between the chemical changes occurring in the brain after learning and the ones occurring after stimulation without learning (Ungar, 1970a). Increase in RNA and protein synthesis and even changes in RNA base ratio have been shown to occur in the brain after various types of stimulation without learning (Debold, Firschein, Carrier, & Leaf, 1967; Grampp & Edström, 1963; Rappoport & Daginawala, 1968). In this last study, the authors tried various olfactory stimuli on the isolated head of the catfish. Some stimuli, certainly new to the fish (such as morpholine or amyl acetate), caused changes in the RNA base ratio, but similar effects were caused by extracts of shrimp, certainly familiar to the animal. Moreover, some other new stimuli, such as camphor, had no effect. It is possible that, even in the experiments including a control group of animals submitted to stimulation without learning, chemical changes following learning could result from quantitative differences rather than from qualitative ones. This could mean that a stimulation followed by retention needs a more active metabolism than a stimulation without retention (Ungar, 1970a).

Among the methods used to date, only two could prove the existence of qualitative changes during learning: DNA–RNA hybridization (Machlus & Gaito, 1969) and production of specific antibodies (Jankovic, Rakic, Veskov, &

Horvat, 1968; Mihailovic & Jankovic, 1961; Rosenblatt, 1970). These methods, however, are still at a very early stage.

C. Modern Data

In recent investigations of the molecular changes occurring after learning, attention has been given to the phosphorylation of proteins. Radioactive phosphate was administered to rodents; after conditioned avoidance training, radioactivity was increased, as compared to proper controls, both in nuclear proteins and in synaptosomal proteins (Dunn, Entingh, Entingh, Gispen, Machlus, Perumal, Rees, & Brogan, 1974; Routtenberg, Ehrlich, & Rabjohns, 1975). Here the phosphate is covalently bound to the proteins, and the radioactivity increase seems to appear mainly in phosphoserine. Especially the phosphorylation of synaptosomal proteins (Perumal, Gispen, Glassman, & Wilson, 1977), which has also been shown to appear during extinction (Gispen, Perumal, Wilson, & Glassman, 1977), seems to be of a great importance in the processing of information in the brain. According to Perumal *et al.* (1977), such a phosphorylation could alter the conformation of proteins in a way that may be essential for the formation of new pathways mediating memory storage. This new approach to molecular changes occurring after learning therefore seems to be a promising one.

III. EFFECTS OF INHIBITORS OF RNA AND PROTEIN SYNTHESIS ON LEARNING

Numerous drugs are known to have an effect—either facilitating or decreasing—on learning (see Chapters 2 and 9). Some results of drugs acting either on RNA synthesis or on protein synthesis will be summarized here. The main drugs used in the study of RNA synthesis are 8-azaguanine, actinomycin D, and camptothecin, all of which inhibit the transcription of DNA into RNA; however, other studies involving RNase and precursors of nucleic acids provide results compatible with the above ones. In the study of protein synthesis the main drugs used are puromycin (which blocks the peptide chain elongation in the ribosomes in combining with the forming peptide to give a peptidyl-puromycin), cyclohex-imide, acetoxycycloheximide, and anisomycin (which block the amino acid transfer from tRNA to peptide).

A. 8-Azaguanine, Actinomycin D, and Camptothecin

The three above-mentioned drugs act on RNA synthesis. The first experiment in this field, the well-known study of Dingman and Sporn (1961), was done with 8-azaguanine. The authors trained rats to escape from mazes filled with water. Using 8-azaguanine, Dingman and Sporn showed that this substance can impair learning when injected before training, but has no effect when injected afterward. Although, in the authors' opinion (Dingman & Sporn, 1964), this experiment was not conclusive in itself, it can be considered the first attempt to affect learning by a substance acting on RNA synthesis.

A few attempts have been made using actinomycin D in rodents. The earlier studies (Barondes & Jarvik, 1964; Cohen & Barondes, 1966) were difficult to interpret because of the high toxicity of the drug. More recently both the position discrimination experiments on mice by Squire and Barondes (1970) and the appetitive learning task in rats by Daniels (1971) showed memory impairment by temporal administration of actinomycin D. As noted by Squire and Barondes, however, the results might have been due to an indirect action of actinomycin D producing necrosis or electrical abnormality in the brain. Arguments in favor of this interpretation can be found in the studies on rats by Goldsmith (1967), who used a passive avoidance task, and by Nakajima (1969), who employed position discrimination learning. Goldsmith (1967) explained the performance impairment observed by a brain damage in the limbic system. Nakajima (1969) showed that injection of actinomycin D in the hippocampus resulted in spike discharges in that area and that these discharges should be responsible for the learning deficit observed. In chicks, Codish (1971) was able to impair retention of imprinting by injection of actinomycin D in the hippocampus. Agranoff, Davis, Casola, and Lim (1967) found that intracerebral actinomycin D could impair memory consolidation in the goldfish, but did not affect long-term memory. These results are similar to those obtained by Agranoff's group with puromycin in the goldfish (Section III,C). Oshima, Gorbman, and Shimada (1969) injected homing salmon with actinimycin D. This treatment was able to inhibit olfactory discrimination by the animals between home water and other types of natural water. It was suggested by Oshima's experiments that inhibition of RNA synthesis could interfere with long-term olfactory memory in the homing salmon.

Evidence was produced by Glassman, Henderson, Cordle, Moon, and Wilson (1970) of the effects of actinomycin D in impairing the learning ability of headless cockroaches. The learning task for the animals was to keep their legs raised to avoid an electric shock (Horridge, 1962). It has been shown by Glassman's team that actinomycin D can impair the acquisition of this avoidance behavior. The mechanisms of this action remain, however, unclear, and further work is still needed. The main difficulty in the use of 8-azaguanine and actinomycin D in studies on the role of RNA synthesis on learning is still the toxicity of these substances (Deminière & Cardo, 1971; Warburton & Russell, 1968).

Promising results have been obtained by Neale, Klinger, and Agranoff (1973) with camptothecin in goldfish. Camptothecin injected after conditioned avoidance learning produces a sharp performance decrease in the animals when tested 8 days later. This drug seems to have reversible effects on RNA synthesis without the toxic properties of actinomycin D. It provokes a 65–70% inhibition of RNA synthesis for 2 hours and a secondary protein synthesis inhibition of only 30% after 4 hours. Since the latter percentage of protein synthesis inhibition seems to be too slight to have any effect on memory, camptothecin could provide a good tool for future work on the effect of RNA synthesis in learning which is still poorly understood.

B. Effects of RNase and of RNA Precursors

RNase is not an inhibitor of RNA synthesis but an enzyme catalyzing the degradation of RNA. It is, however, interesting to compare the results obtained with antibiotics to some results obtained with RNase. This enzyme was used by Corning and John (1961) to suppress retention after regeneration in planarians (Section IV,A,2). More recently, Jaffard and Cardo (1968, 1969) showed that RNase injected into the brain was able to suppress some retention, but not when learning was strongly consolidated. This observation could explain the negative results obtained with RNase by Stevens and Tapp (1966) in a pattern discrimination task; in such a difficult learning task, where the consolidation requires a large number of trials, RNase appears to be without effect once the animal has reached criterion.

If learning can be impaired by RNA synthesis inhibition or by RNA degradation, it would be logical to expect that facilitation of RNA synthesis would facilitate learning. Evidence for this facilitation has been provided by the work of Ott and Mathies (1973a, 1973b) in brightness discrimination experiments in rats. These authors showed that intrahippocampal injection of an RNA precursor, uridine monophosphate, 30 minutes prior to onset of training, can delay extinction of the acquired behavior (Ott and Mathies, 1973a). In a further study (1973b), using a one-way avoidance task in rats, they showed that when uridine monophosphate was administered together with an antibiotic, cycloheximide (Section III,D), the impairing effect of cycloheximide on retention was able to block the beneficial effect of uridine monophosphate.

For more detailed information on this question, the reader is referred to the reviews by Glassman (1969), Ungerer (1969a), Cohen (1970), Chapouthier and Ungerer (1973), and Barraco and Stettner (1976).

C. Puromycin

Studies on the effect of puromycin were undertaken using mice, birds, and fish as experimental animals. The first results in this field were obtained in Flexner's laboratory with mice. The task used was a right–left discrimination in a Y maze involving an avoidance criterion; the animals had to choose the correct arm within a few seconds. They were trained to a criterion of 9/10 correct choices. The injection of puromycin was intracerebral, since subcutaneous injections have been shown not to inhibit protein synthesis sufficiently to impair memory. Temporal injections of 90 µg each of puromycin impaired memory in animals trained 24 hours previously (J. B. Flexner, Flexner, & Stellar, 1963; L. B. Flexner, Flexner, Roberts, & De la Haba, 1964). This was correlated with a marked inhibition of protein synthesis in the temporal area. If the injections are given 3 to 6 days after training, temporal injections alone are ineffective. To affect memory at this time, it is necessary to use six injections in various parts of the cerebral cortex (two temporal, two ventricular, and two frontal injections. L. B. Flexner thinks that for 3 to 6 days there is a kind of short-term memory localized in the temporal region, but, after this time, there appears a longer term memory having no precise localization in the cortex. Deutsch (1969), however, pointed out that other explanations of this effect were possible, especially differences in the dose necessary to suppress memory either 24 hours or several days after learning; the small dose present in the cortex after temporal injections could be sufficient to suppress recently acquired memory, but a higher dose, requiring several injections, would be necessary to erase many-day-old memory.

L. B. Flexner, Flexner, and Roberts (1967) have made interesting observations with this preparation: puromycin was without effect on overtrained animals, and successive injections of puromycin became rapidly ineffective. The reasons for this are not clear. L. B. Flexner explains the second point by a more rapid elimination of puromycin from the brain, perhaps due to vascular changes.

J. B. Flexner and Flexner (1967) found that intracerebral injection of isotonic NaCl solution was able to suppress the amnesic effect of a prior injection of puromycin. This effect of saline injections was interpreted to be due to a washing off by saline of the abnormal peptides produced by puromycin. Later, J. B. Flexner and Flexner (1969) found that not only NaCl, but also other chlorides, an ultrafiltrate of blood serum, or even water alone could produce the same effect and restore memory after puromycin injection. The question remains whether this effect can really be interpreted as a washing off of abnormal peptides, or if a more indirect mechanism, such as the action of ions on cerebral electrical activity (Cohen, Ervin, & Barondes, 1966), could not partially interfere with the memory process.

Barondes's group trained mice in the same right–left discrimination. Their results are in agreement with Flexner's, but they also throw a new light on some aspects of the work. According to Barondes, puromycin does not impair the early stage of retention, but is highly effective a few hours after injection (Barondes & Cohen, 1966).

Whereas these results were obtained in a maze-learning task with negative reinforcement, Ungerer (1969b, 1971, 1975) tried puromycin on mice trained in an instrumental learning situation with positive reinforcement. She was able to show that puromycin, which had been effective in erasing a maze-learning task, was completely ineffective in an instrumental situation in which a mouse was to learn to press a lever to obtain food, even though the drug was injected in the same places in the brain and in the same quantity as in the former experiments. If the instrumental learning task involves a discrimination, however (between lit and an unlit light), puromycin is able to impair retention. Similarly, Ungerer and Chapouthier (1975) showed that puromycin can impair retention of a conditioned avoidance learning task in a shuttle box. Together with Ungerer's (1975) behavioral analysis of Flexner's maze discrimination task these data tend to show that puromycin only impairs retention in learning situations involving discrimination.

Agranoff and Klinger (1964) devised in goldfish a conditioned avoidance to light in a shuttle tank. When learning is achieved in a session of 20 trials in 1 day, the score of the animal in a session 3 days later can be used as a measure of retention of learning. Puromycin, injected intracranially in doses from 90 to 210 μg during the 30 minutes following the first session, can impair retention, but there is no effect if the puromycin is injected more than 60 minutes after the first session (Agranoff, Davis, & Brink, 1965, 1966). If puromycin is injected before training, it does not affect it, but the retention shows impairment 3 days later. Agranoff's conclusion is that puromycin does not affect immediate memory during learning or long-term memory (60 minutes after learning), but that the drug can inhibit consolidation. Similar results seem to have been obtained by action of electroconvulsive shock immediately after learning (Davis, Bright, & Agranoff, 1965).

The effect of puromycin in the goldfish was confirmed by Potts and Bitterman (1967). These authors emphasized the fact that puromycin seems to suppress specifically conditioned fear; in an experiment with positive reinforcement, puromycin was without effect. It can be pointed out, however, that since the appetitive situation and the conditioned avoidance situation differ by many parameters, other explanations of the difference of effect of puromycin could be possible. As suggested by Deutsch (1969), a strongly consolidated training (as a task with positive reinforcement could be) would show less susceptibility to puromycin. In this aspect, the work of Potts and Bitterman with goldfish could be compared with the study of Ungerer (1969b) with mice.

Evidence was produced by Oshima et al. (1969) of the ability of puromycin to inhibit olfactory discrimination of the homing salmon. This result is similar to the one obtained by the same authors with actinomycin D (Section III,A).

Using birds as experimental animals, puromycin has been tested by Gervai and Csanyi (1973) in imprinting in chicks and by Mayor (1969) in a discrimination learning between green and red stimuli in the Japanese quail. Gervai and

Csanyi showed that puromycin was able, in some experiments, to impair performance in the imprinting situation, and Mayor showed that the drug can provoke memory deficit in the Japanese quail.

Studies on fish support the idea that puromycin acts on memory through its known function as protein synthesis inhibitor. Concerning mice and birds, however, many authors have questioned this interpretation and proposed that puromycin action on learning could be due to indirect side effects other than its proper effect on protein synthesis. As will be discussed later (Section III,D), puromycin might produce abnormal peptides (peptidyl-puromycin) which could interfere with memory (J. B. Flexner & Flexner, 1967; L. B. Flexner & Flexner, 1968). According to Mayor (1969), this could explain why puromycin is able to produce retention deficits in some situations in which other antibiotics are inactive (see Section III,D). Cohen et al. (1966) showed that puromycin also produces a strong depression of electrical cortical activity in the temporal area of the brain. Puromycin also seems to produce occult seizures: intracerebral injections of puromycin in mice increase their susceptibility to seizures after subconvulsive doses of pentylenetetrazol; conversely, an anticonvulsivant improves retention after puromycin treatment (Cohen & Barondes, 1967).

Finally, drugs that are known to enhance the noradrenaline level in the brain, such as imipramine, d-amphetamine, or tranylcypromine, improve retention in puromycin-treated mice. Taking these data into account, R. B. Roberts, Flexner, and Flexner (1970) have suggested that puromycin action on memory may be due to the blocking of adrenergic sites.

The question of the precise mechanism of action of puromycin on memory still remains open; beyond this, the various secondary effects of this drug make the interpretation of the results in terms of protein synthesis inhibition alone difficult. More clear-cut results have been obtained with the antibiotics discussed in Sections III,D and E.

D. Cycloheximide and Acetoxycycloheximide

Acetoxycycloheximide and cycloheximide have been applied either intracerebrally or subcutaneously in a variety of situations and a variety of animal species. Unlike puromycin, these two drugs do not provoke important side effects that could explain their amnesic effects. The only side effects known to result from these two antibiotics are modifications in the motor activity level of the subjects, but these modifications do not seem able to explain their action on memory. It has been shown (Segal, Squire, & Barondes, 1971; Squire & Barondes, 1972) that isocycloheximide, which has the same effect on motor activity as cycloheximide but no effect on protein synthesis, does not impair memory. Gutwein, Quartermain, and McEwen (1974) used two different cycloheximide dosages in a passive avoidance task; both doses acted on locomotor activity, but only the higher dose modified memory. For all these authors, these two drugs, unlike puromycin, offer clear examples of memory impairment due to protein synthesis inhibition.

Acetoxycycloheximide was used by Flexner's group in mice trained in the same right–left discrimination task as was used for the puromycin experiments. According to these authors, although acetoxycycloheximide produces a strong inhibition of protein synthesis, it seems to be without effect on either short-term or long-term memory. Moreover, simultaneous injections of acetoxycyclohex-imide and puromycin are also without effect on memory. Acetoxycycloheximide seems to "protect" memory from the action of puromycin (L. B. Flexner & Flexner, 1966). Similar results have been obtained by Barondes and Cohen (1967a) who made simultaneous injections of cycloheximide and puromycin with no effect on memory.

One of the many hypotheses attempting to explain this phenomenon postu-lates that the action of puromycin is due to the synthesis of abnormal peptides (peptidyl-puromycin) which could interfere with memory; the formation of these peptides could be suppressed by acetoxycycloheximide (J. B. Flexner & Flexner, 1967; L. B. Flexner & Flexner, 1968). Reinis (1969) claimed to have shown the presence of such peptides by their effect on behavior, whereas Ungerer, Spitz, and Chapouthier (1969), using the same learning situation as Flexner, were unable to find them.

Barondes and Cohen (1967b) considered that Flexner's criterion of nine correct responses out of ten was too severe and might mask the effect. To test this hypothesis, they submitted one group of mice to prolonged training (criterion 9/10) another to short training (criterion 3/4). Intracerebral injections of acetoxy-cycloheximide were able to impair memory for 3 hours to 7 days after injection in the animals submitted to short training, but not in the animals submitted to prolonged training. The criterion of 9/10 correct responses in such an easy learning task as left–right discrimination creates a kind of "overtraining" in the animals, which become resistant to acetoxycycloheximide.

In other experiments (Barondes & Cohen, 1968), it was shown that acetoxycycloheximide is able to suppress memory even in mice trained to the 9/10 correct response criterion in the case of a light–dark discrimination. Bar-ondes' group assumed that, since light–dark discrimination is a more difficult and less "natural" task for mice, there could be "less active stimulation of protein synthesis in the appropriate neural pathways" on each exposure to the cues, thus preventing the "overtraining" effect found with a 9/10 criterion in a left–right discrimination task.

Many recent studies have confirmed and extended the results of these initial experiments. They have shown, as has been stressed by Ungerer (1975), that (1) retention seems more sensitive to cycloheximide or acetoxycyclohex-imide if the learning task is more difficult or, for a given task, if training is shorter, and (2) duration during which memory retention can be impaired by the two drugs varies with the animal species or the learning task used.

The first point has been confirmed by numerous studies (Flood, Bennett, Rosenzweig, & Orme, 1972; Geller, Robustelli, & Jarvik, 1971; Schmaltz & Delerm, 1974; Squire & Barondes, 1972). Flood *et al.* (1972), for example, analyzed with precision the parameters able to affect the degree of amnesia in cycloheximide-treated mice (shock intensity, shock duration, original latency to enter the shock compartment, retention interval), in a one-trial, step-through, passive avoidance task. According to Flood *et al.* (1972), when these parameters are measured and controlled, highly consistent amnestic effect can be obtained. Finally, they showed that overtrained animals are no more sensitive to cycloheximide-induced amnesia.

As far as the second point underlined by Ungerer (1975) is concerned, again the discrepancy of results between rodents and fish must be emphasized. Barondes (1970) showed that to inhibit retention in mice, cycloheximide or acetoxycycloheximide must be administered immediately before or immediately after learning (depending on the learning task). Agranoff *et al.* (1966) found in goldfish, however, that acetoxycycloheximide, like puromycin (Section III,C), was able to inhibit the consolidation of a conditioned avoidance response when it was injected up to 1 hour after training.

It is difficult to compare the other results obtained with very different animal species. In chicks, Gervai and Csanyi (1973) found no effect of cycloheximide on the retention of imprinting, and in the Japanese quail Mayor (1969) found no effect of acetoxycycloheximide on the retention of a color discrimination task. Since both groups found effects with puromycin (Section III,C), they concluded that the action of puromycin was indirect and not related to its effect on protein synthesis. Mayor (1969) noted that since only puromycin inhibits memory, the basis for its effect seems more likely to be mediated by the action of peptidyl-puromycin rather than by the quantitative inhibition of macromolecular synthesis. From this point of view, the negative results obtained with acetoxy-cycloheximide can be considered arguments in favor of the nonspecific role of puromycin. Similar results to those obtained with actinomycin D and puromycin (Sections III,A and C) were obtained by Oshima *et al.* (1969) for the homing salmon. In insects, B. M. Brown and Noble (1967) and Glasmann *et al.* (1970) were able to impair with cycloheximide the learning ability of headless cockroaches. These results are similar to those obtained by Glassman *et al.* (1970) with actinomycin D (Section III,A).

An interesting study by Andry and Luttges (1972) examined the relationship of cycloheximide and electroconvulsive shock (ECS) in producing amnesia. These authors showed that combined cycloheximide and ECS treatments produced amnesia at times when neither alone did. Their data provide evidence in favor of a dual trace hypothesis of memory storage: a short-term memory (which could be disrupted by ECS) and a long-term memory (which could be disrupted by cycloheximide); such a dual mechanism has been criticized however by authors such as Deutsch (1969, see Section III,C).

E. Anisomycin

Anisomycin has the great advantage of inhibiting protein synthesis as strongly as the other antibiotics with no toxic effect (Flood, Bennett, Rosenzweig, & Orme, 1973). Anisomycin has a depressive effect on spontaneous locomotor activity, but Squire and Barondes (1974) were able to show that this effect is clearly distinct from the effect on protein synthesis and on memory. If injected subcutaneously every 2 hours, anisomycin maintains a protein synthesis inhibition level in the brain of more than 85%, as long as the injections continue. Results obtained by Flood *et al.* (1973) in a one-trial passive avoidance task in mice suggest that memory impairment is a direct function of the duration of protein synthesis inhibition. This result is, to date, the most convincing argument in favor of the role of protein synthesis inhibition in amnesia. If the delay between two of the regular injections is increased (and therefore protein synthesis inhibition reduced for a short time), it has been shown by Flood, Bennett, Orme, and Rosenzweig (1975b) that the longer the interruption of protein synthesis inhibition, the better the retention.

Anisomycin exerts identical effects on memory as cycloheximide (Flood *et al.*, 1973; Squire & Barondes, 1974). Even combined injections of anisomycin and acetoxycycloheximide are able to block retention in an active avoidance training task in mice in the same way as anisomycin alone (Flood, Bennett, Orme, & Rosenzweig, 1975a).

Interesting investigations have been undertaken by Flood, Bennett, Orme, and Jarvik (1977) on the relationship between anisomycin and ECS in producing amnesia. These studies confirm and enlarge upon the previous work by Andry and Luttges (1972, Section III,D). Flood *et al.* (1977) studied the action of anisomycin treatment on the amnesic effects of ECS in both passive and active avoidance tasks in mice. It should be recalled here that ECS given to an animal just after a training session leads to performance impairment in a memory test later on. The longer the delay between the end of the training session and the ECS treatment, the slighter the impairment. This is what is called the ECS amnesic gradient. Flood *et al.* have studied the effect of protein synthesis inhibition by anisomycin on this ECS gradient. They showed that protein synthesis inhibition following ECS could delay the ECS gradient. The longer the duration of protein synthesis inhibition following ECS, the longer this delay. The data cannot be explained by direct action of ECS on protein synthesis, which could be "added" on to action of anisomycin. It is true that ECS can impair protein synthesis (Dunn, Giuditta, Wilson, & Glassman, 1974), but in Flood's experiments, the protein synthesis inhibition produced by combined ECS and anisomycin treatment does not differ greatly from the inhibitory effect occurring after anisomycin alone. The most logical explanation is that the amnesic gradient of ECS is *dependent* on protein synthesis: as soon as protein synthesis resumes, even after hours of inhibition, the ECS gradient effect reappears.

F. Discussion

It is difficult to draw general conclusions from all these studies since many parameters differ from one to another. First, an attempt could be made to compare those studies which used the mouse or the goldfish as the experimental animal, despite all the discrepancies previously noted between these two studies. It might then be possible to relate Agranoff's "long-term" memory, on which the antibiotics are ineffective, to the overtraining situation in Flexner and Barondes' studies and to the strongly consolidated situation in some of Ungerer's experiments. Thus, it is possible to delimit three stages in retention: first, immediate memory, on which the antibiotics had no effect; second, a stage of memory consolidation during which the antibiotics were effective; and, third, an "overtraining" situation insensitive to antibiotics. Various memory stages have been recently proposed, however, as a result of the data obtained for chicks. Using Cherkin's (1969) paradigm, Watts and Mark (1971) trained chicks in a one-trial avoidance task. Chicks have a tendency to peck. If, in a learning trial, they encounter a chrome bead coated with a chemical aversant, they will tend to avoid pecking in a subsequent pecking test. In studying the action of various drugs on this very clear-cut memory model, Watts and Mark put forward the hypothesis that there are two stages in the formation of memory: a labile memory phase which can be disrupted by sodium pump inhibitors such as ouabain, followed by a long-term memory, which can be disrupted by antibiotics. The same group has reported an earlier memory stage, called "short-term memory," situated within 10 minutes after training and before the beginning of labile memory; this early phase could be disturbed by administration of KCl or LiCl (Gibbs & Ng, 1977). If these arguments are taken into consideration, both short-term memory and labile memory, as defined by these authors, should be included in what we earlier called "immediate" memory. Further work is still needed, however, to define the exact stages of memory formation, since some recent data have provided evidence that, at least in some cases, antibiotics can also impair short-term memory. Quartermain and McEwen (1970) investigated cycloheximide-induced amnesia in a passive avoidance task in mice. They found that with high-voltage electric shock, amnesia appeared a few hours after learning; whereas with low-voltage electric shock, amnesia appeared immediately. An "antibiotic-resistant stage" of memory would seem, therefore, to depend largely on the level of consolidation of the task. In studying cycloheximide effects on two inbred strains of mice, Randt, Barnett, McEwen, and Quartermain (1971) found almost equal memory impairment in both strains, despite the fact that one of them supposedly had only short-term memory. These data tend to suggest that even short-term memory can be impaired by antibiotics treatment; they are in agreement with Deutsch's (1969) thesis that there are no such things as successive "stages" of qualitative nature in memory, but rather that a quantitative change of a continuous nature occurs as memory becomes older.

A second point that should be emphasized is that, for most of the antibiotics used, the mechanism of action on learning remains unclear. Some authors, such as Deutsch (1969), have pointed out that antibiotics might act on retention in a way more indirect than by direct inhibition of protein synthesis. As we have seen, the most convincing data in favor of involvement of protein synthesis in memory have been obtained with anisomycin. However, results of experiments on improvement of learning by drugs facilitating protein synthesis are less convincing. The effects on learning of tricyanoaminopropene (Chamberlain, Rothschild, & Gerard, 1963; Egyhazi & Hydén, 1961; McNutt, 1967) and of magnesium pemoline (Beach & Kimble, 1967) still remain controversial. Some authors (Gaito, 1963; Uphouse et al., 1974) have analyzed the possible effect of protein synthesis on gene regulation, which would explain how the "trained neuron" differs from the neuron before training. According to Uphouse et al. (1974), this gene regulation could lead to permanent changes in cell metabolism in such a way that the transmission characteristics of the cell are altered. However, such a model remains hypothetical.

IV. THE SEARCH FOR A MOLECULAR CODE OF MEMORY

The principle of biological assay is to detect, not by biochemical but by biological effects, the chemical modifications that occur in animals. In the particular bioassay to be discussed below, "donor" animals are submitted to a certain type of training, then an extract of their nervous system is prepared and injected by various routes to "recipient" animals. The performance of these recipients in the task learned by the donors is then tested and compared with the performance given in the same task by control recipients (usually injected with an extract of "naive" nervous system). If successful, this method has the advantage of demonstrating the possibility of specific transfer of information, but, like all bioassays, it is a delicate technique and often a source of many artifacts (Gaddum, 1953). Because the test of the recipients is behavioral, the variability of responses is often even larger and the probability of error even greater than for ordinary bioassays. Compared with the procedures discussed in the two preceding sections: (1) the probability of error is much greater than in the direct analysis of chemical changes associated with learning because of the variability of the behavioral test and (2) the possibility of artifacts is much greater than in the study of the effect on learning of a known single substance, such as an antibiotic drug, because the bioassay is used to test unknown and impure substances in the presence of several others. Therefore, this method involves the use of a large number of animals, and the experiments must be replicated many times under different conditions. Even so, most of the evidence provided to date still remains highly controversial.

A. Experiments on Planarians

The first experiments of this type were done on planarians in McConnell's laboratory. Because of the importance this category of experiments subsequently acquired, we would like to describe the principal results obtained in this field. The work of McConnell and colleagues (McConnell, Jacobson, & Kimble, 1959; McConnell, Jacobson, & Maynard, 1959; McConnell, Shigehisha, and Salive, 1968) can be studied at three levels: the possibility of learning in planarians, the retention of learning after regeneration, and the "memory transfer through cannibalism" effect. This work has been criticized at all three levels of the phenomena that McConnell claimed to have demonstrated.

1. Learning in Planarians

Before McConnell's results appeared, some authors had already observed phenomena resembling learning in planarians. Thompson and McConnell (1955) devised a method of "classical conditioning" of these animals. It is known that planarians are sensitive to light. After determination of the level of responses by planarians to light, the method consisted in the association of a light (conditioned stimulus) and electric shock (unconditioned stimulus). Thompson and McConnell showed that, after training, the experimental animals responded more to light than did the controls. Their conclusion was that the animals had been able to associate light to electric shock, that is, to be conditioned. Some authors (Bennett & Calvin, 1964; Halas, James, & Knutson, 1962) were unable to replicate this classical conditioning of planarians. Halas *et al.* showed that, in the planarian *Dugesia tigrina,* it was difficult to find a significant difference between the animals submitted to paired light and shock and some of the control groups. They concluded that McConnell's results did not show learning phenomena, but rather a general sensitization to light caused by some kind of manipulation of the animals. More recently, attempts have been made to demonstrate classical conditioning in two European species; the results were that only one of them showed an effect resembling classical conditioning (Chapouthier, Legrain, & Spitz, 1969). According to McConnell (1967), it is possible that some species, and even some strains in the same species, are refractory to classical conditioning.

The possibility of discrimination learning was shown in planarians by several authors. J. B. Best and Rubinstein (1962), Chapouthier, Pallaud, and Ungerer (1968), and Corning (1964) showed that it was possible to induce in planarians an elementary right–left discrimination. Other types of discrimination were used by Humphries (1961), Griffard and Pierce (1964), and Block and McConnell (1967). Discrimination learning by planarians leads to an important problem: following the learning phase (during which the animal begins to choose significantly the "correct" arm of the maze and to avoid the arm where it receives punishment), a phase of rejection occurs (during which the animals paradoxically choose the "wrong" arm of the maze) (J. B. Best & Rubinstein, 1962; Chapouthier et al., 1968; Corning, 1964).

Some authors have reported positive results in complex operant conditioning in planarians (Lee, 1963; Seydoux, Girardier, Perrin, Ruphi, & Posternak, 1967), but these experiments are of such importance that much more replication in a number of laboratories is needed.

2. Retention of Learning after Regeneration

When cut in two, planarians are able to regenerate into two complete individuals. This peculiarity was used by McConnell, Jacobson, and Kimble (1959), who proved that after regeneration both sections of the animal show equal retention of classical conditioning. The same effect was observed by McConnell, Jacobson, and Maynard (1959) in the second generation of regenerated planarians. All these experiments caused McConnell to postulate, according to Hyden's work, that memory could have a molecular basis, possibly RNA. Experiments involving the action of RNase (Section III,B) seemed to confirm this hypothesis.

This observation was criticized by H. M. Brown, Dustman, and Beck (1966a, 1966b). These authors claimed that the greater responsiveness to light of regenerated worms comes from the fact that the regenerated animals are smaller than the original one, and it has been proved that smaller animals tend to be more responsive to light. This criticism, however, does not explain the fact that, in McConnell's experiments, the control group (regenerated and therefore smaller animals) responded significantly less than did the experimental animals. The interpretation of H. M. Brown et al. (1966b) can explain a comparison with animals before regeneration, but not with controls after regeneration. Moreover, many authors have shown different kinds of retention after regeneration. Westerman (1963) showed a retention of habituation and Ernhardt and Sherrick (1959) and Corning (1966) a retention of discrimination after regeneration.

3. Transfer of Memory through Cannibalism

When hungry, planarians are capable of cannibalizing other individuals of the same species cut up into suitably sized pieces. McConnell fed trained planarians to naive ones; this method was the equivalent of a crude injection of the supposed information-carrying molecule. The ability of the recipients of trained animals to respond to light was then tested and compared to the responses of recipients of naive animals in the same situation. The results of these experiments were positive, and McConnell (1962) claimed to have obtained a transfer of memory through cannibalism. An experiment of the same type using purified RNA instead of fragments of planarians was carried out by Jacobson, Fried, and Horowitz (1966); their results were also positive: the classical conditioning paradigm seemed able to be transferred by injection of trained RNA into the digestive cavity of naive animals.

The interpretation of this type of experiment remains difficult because it must be postulated that RNA is not degraded by planarians. Moreover, although believing that classical conditioning can occur in planarians, some authors were not able to show a specific transfer of memory by cannibalism in these animals. Hartry, Keith-Lee, and Morton (1964) showed that not only cannibals of trained animals showed a greater ability to respond to light, but cannibals of some control groups also showed the same ability. Their interpretation is that experimental conditions in trained and in some control groups produce in the cannibalized animals the appearance of a general activating factor which makes the cannibals more sensitive to light. More recently we have shown that some physiological conditions such as hunger can increase the response level of planarians to light (Chapouthier, 1967a). For the transfer of memory by cannibalism itself, we found that cannibals of some control groups (animals submitted to light alone) exhibited an increased responsiveness to light intermediate between that of the cannibals of naive planarians and the cannibals of trained planarians (Chapouthier, Legrain, & Spitz, 1969). In such a situation, it was difficult to choose experimentally between the hypothesis of transfer of memory through cannibalism (McConnell, 1967) and the hypothesis of activating substance (Hartry et al., 1964).

To answer this type of objection, McConnell (1966) tried to transfer discrimination learning. His results were positive, and he claimed to have clearly demonstrated the specificity of the effect. Negative results, however, were obtained by Picket, Jennings, and Wells (1964) and by G. Chapouthier (unpublished results).

In summary, there apparently are phenomena resembling learning in planarians, and some retention after regeneration exists. The results of the bioassay methods, however, mostly using classical conditioning situations, are not sufficiently clear. The only proof of specific transfer of information in planarians would be the transfer of learned discrimination. These experiments will have to resolve the problem of the rejection phase (Section IV,A,1). Such an important question needs more evidence produced by experiments from various laboratories. For more detailed information, the reader is referred to the reviews by Chapouthier, Legrain, and Spiz (1969), Corning and Riccio (1970), and McConnell and Shelby (1970). The experiments on planarians have been extended by more clear-cut studies in vertebrates.

B. Experiments on Vertebrates

The first experiments in this field were published in 1965, almost simultaneously, by four groups of workers (Babich, Jacobson, Bubash, & Jacobson; Fjerdingstad, Nissen, & Røigaard-Petersen; Reinis; and Ungar & Oceguera-Navarro). They were followed by a great controversy and many publications, some of them reporting negative results, some of them positive ones. Since then considerable evidence has been accumulated on the validity of the findings, and different laboratories have published positive results. Most of the negative results, obtained largely in the early stages of research in the field, can be explained in the light of the positive findings.

It is not possible here to review separately all the relevant publications. Systematic discussions have been published by Rosenblatt (1970), Ungar (1971), Ungar and Chapouthier (1971), Smith (1974), and Chapouthier (1978b). We would like, however, to discuss a few aspects of this question, especially (1) the possible reasons for failure to replicate some positive results, (2) the type of training situation used, (3) the problem of the specificity of the bioassay, and (4) the question of the chemical identification of the responsible factors.

1. Reasons for Failure to Replicate the Bioassays

Difficulty in replication has always been one of the most vulnerable points of criticism of these experiments. Some of the unsuccessful attempts during the early stages of this research can be partially understood today.

a. Chemical Composition. The first probable reason for inability to reproduce the positive experiments is the chemical composition of the extract used. Among the four original groups of workers, two (Babich, Jacobson, Bubash, & Jacobson, 1965; Fjerdingstad *et al.*, 1965) claimed to have obtained their results with an RNA preparation. Since it is now known (Ungar & Fjerdingstad, 1971) that the active factors are linked with RNA, but are not RNA, it can be understood how some investigators, using crude RNA preparations, have been able to obtain positive results although others, using more purified RNA, were unable to replicate them. Most of the negative results were obtained with RNA preparations, while the authors using crude extracts obtained positive results more easily (see Ungar & Chapouthier, 1971).

b. Dose. The clearest results were obtained with a high dose of extracts (Chapouthier & Ungerer, 1969; Ungar, 1967a, 1967b; Ungar & Irwin, 1967). In these experiments each recipient received the equivalent of many times his brain weight. Moos, Levan, Mason, Mason, and Hebron (1969) and Rosenblatt (1969), however, obtained positive results with very small doses. Their results could perhaps have been caused, in the experiment of Moos *et al.*, by a peculiar type of training situation (acquired aversion to saccharine) and, in Rosenblatt's case, by a different route of administration of the extracts (intravenous).

    c. Interval between Injection and Testing of the Recipients.   Most of the positive results were obtained when a sufficient interval was allowed between injection and testing of the recipients. The effect often only appears a few days after the injection. In many of the negative publications (Byrne, Samuel, Bennett, Rosenzweig, Wasserman, Wagner, Gardner, Galambos, Berger, Margules, Fenichel, Stein, Corson, Enesco, Chorover, Holt, Schiller, Chiappeta, Jarvik, Leaf, Dutcher, Horovitz, & Carlson, 1966; Gordon, Deanin, Leonhardt, & Gwynn, 1966; Gross & Carey, 1965; Lambert & Saurat, 1967; Luttges, Johnson, Buck, Holland, & McGaugh, 1966), all the tests were done within 24 hours after the injection, which was too soon. It can be pointed out that the positive experiments which have used such a schedule were extremely difficult to replicate (Babich, Jacobson, & Bubash, 1965; Babich, Jacobson, Bubash, & Jacobson, 1965).

    d. Duration of Donor Training.   It seems necessary not only to bring the donors to a certain criterion of training, but also to keep them at criterion for several days, probably to allow sufficient time for the active material to accumulate (Chapouthier & Ungerer, 1969; Ungar, 1967a, 1967b). In some cases, however, an excess of training seem to decrease the effect (Ungar, 1967a).

    e. Other Factors.   There are many other factors which can interfere with the assay, and many are interrelated. For example, the route of injection (which can be intraperitoneal, intravenous, or intracerebral) does not seem to be of considerable importance, but it is possible that intraperitoneal administration requires higher doses than other types of injection. As for the known factors, keeping the extracts at low temperature remains an elementary precaution. Animals which are either too young or too old do not seem to produce any effect when used as recipients (Adam & Faiszt, 1967). Food deprivation of recipients seems, according to Reinis (1965), to be important when donors are trained under the same conditions. More recently, Golub, Masiarz, Villars, and McConnell (1970) found that rest periods interposed during training of the donors significantly increase the performance of the recipients. There remain, of course, unknown parameters, and there is no general rule guaranteeing a positive effect. Complete success in replicating the experiments is still not assured today. Even in a recent study using pure material, for example, Misslin, Ropartz, Ungerer, and Mandel (1978) found an effect only one time out of three. This permanent difficulty in replicating the data makes the interpretation of the results in terms of "information transfer" difficult as well.

2. Types of Training in Positive Experiments

Many types of learning situations have been attempted with positive results. The principal ones are as follows:

1. Habituation to sound (Ungar & Oceguera-Navarro, 1965)
2. Habituation to a sound producing audiogenic seizure (Daliers & Rigaux-Motquin, 1968)
3. Habituation to air puffs (Ungar, 1967b)
4. Avoidance (Albert, 1966; Kleban, Altschuler, Lawton, Parris, & Lords, 1968)
5. Escape in a water maze (Essman & Lehrer, 1966)
6. Dark avoidance (Fjerdingstad, 1969b; Gay & Raphelson, 1967; Golub, Epstein, & McConnell, 1969; Ungar, Galvan, & Clark, 1968; Wolthuis, 1969)
7. Conditioned avoidance (Adam & Faiszt, 1967; Chapouthier, Pallaud, & Ungerer, 1969; Chapouthier & Ungerer, 1969; Cohen, 1969; Faiszt & Adam, 1968; Fjerdingstad, 1969c; Rosenblatt & Miller, 1966; Ungar, 1967a, 1967b)
8. Left–right discrimination (Essman & Lehrer, 1967; Krylov, Kalyuzhnaya, & Tongur, 1969; Rosenblatt & Miller, 1966; Ungar, 1967a, 1967b; Ungar & Irwin, 1967)
9. Discrimination between two compartments (Jacobson, Babich, Bubash, & Goren, 1966; Rosenblatt, 1969)
10. Choice of the lighted alley in a maze (Fjerdingstad et al., 1965; Gibby, Crough & Thios, 1968; Røigaard-Petersen, Nissen, & Fjerdingstad, 1968; Ungar, 1967a, 1967b; Ungar & Irwin, 1967; Wolthuis, Anthoni, & Stevens, 1968)
11. Acquired avoidance of saccharine (Moos et al., 1969; Revusky & De Venuto, 1967)
12. Conditioned avoidance of drinking (Weiss, 1970)
13. Learning of a detour by chicks (Rosenthal & Sparber, 1968)
14. Wire climbing (Gibby & Crough, 1967)
15. Color discrimination in goldfish (Zippel & Domagk, 1969)
16. Black and white discrimination (Dyal & Golub, 1967)
17. Alimentary conditioned reflexes (Reinis, 1965, 1968)
18. Instrumental learning in a Skinner box (Byrne & Hughes, 1967; Byrne & Samuel, 1966; Chapouthier, Pallaud, & Ungerer, 1969; Dyal & Golub, 1968; Dyal, Golub, & Marrone, 1967; Golub et al., 1970; Golub & McConnell, 1968; McConnell, Shigehisha, & Salive, 1968; Rosenblatt, Farrow, & Herblin, 1966; Rosenblatt, Farrow, & Rhine, 1966; Rosenblatt & Miller, 1966)

19. Alternation in a Skinner box (Fjerdingstad, 1969a)
20. Conditioned approach (Babich, Jacobson, & Bubash, 1965; Babich, Jacobson, Bubash, & Jacobson, 1965; Jacobson, Babich, Bubash, & Jacobson, 1965; McConnell *et al.*, 1968)
21. Fixation of postural asymmetry (Giurgea, Daliers, & Mouravieff, 1970)

It should be noted that some situations always lead to negative results. This seems to be the case in the choice of the dark alley of a maze (Chapouthier & Ungerer, 1968, 1969; Luttges *et al.*, 1966; Ungar, 1967a; Ungar & Irwin, 1967). Most of the publications cited above report experiments done on rodents (rats or mice). One (Rosenthal & Sparber, 1968) used chicks, and a few (Fjerdingstad, 1969c; Zippel & Domagk, 1969) used goldfish. Experiments with other animal groups would be useful.

Braud (1970) claimed that even extinction could be transferred by brain extracts in goldfish. In his experiment, recipients were injected with brain extracts prepared from donors that had acquired and then extinguished a conditioned avoidance response in shuttle tank; the recipients extinguished the response significantly faster than the controls. These results, if they are confirmed, would suggest the possibility that both acquisition and extinction are active processes, correlated with the synthesis of molecules. This had already been suggested in a different situation by some experiments of Jacobson, Fried, and Horowitz (1966) in planarians. In their experiments, however, there was no transfer of extinction, but on the contrary, extracts prepared from extinguished planarians produced a positive transfer effect; this would suggest that in the extinguished donors the "positive" molecules remain present but are inhibited by some other substance. Chapouthier (1967b) showed that, taking into account this similarity of active mechanisms, it could be possible to construct a mathematical theory explaining many peculiarities of learning phenomena. More experimental work is still needed in the field, for such a new conception of extinction needs much more proof than is supplied in these two studies.

For more detailed information relating to the entire problem the reader is referred to reviews by Rosenblatt (1970), Ungar (1971), Ungar and Chapouthier (1971), Smith (1974), and Chapouthier (1978b).

3. Specificity of the Bioassay

The question of the specificity of the bioassay and of the limits of this specificity is certainly one of the most important problems in this field. It is important to stress that among the several authors claiming positive results, most have used a procedure of testing the recipients with reinforcement. In this case, the only thing that can be proved is a facilitation of learning in the animals injected with trained brain extract, but not a specific transfer of information.

Arguments in favor of a relative specificity of the extracts are the results published by Ungar (1967a, 1967b), who has performed "cross transfer" experiments between habituation to two different stimuli and between two types of avoidance tasks. Ungar showed that donor brains obtained from sound-habituated donors could not facilitate recipient habituation to air puffs and that, conversely, donor brains obtained from air puff-habituated donors could not facilitate recipient habituation to sound. Similar results were produced by the two avoidance tasks. These experiments suggest that the extract of donor brains trained in a certain situation has a specific effect on recipients tested in the same situation. Other arguments in favor of the specificity of the bioassays have been provided by experiments on goldfish (Ungar, Galvan, & Chapouthier, 1972; Zippel & Domagk, 1969). It is possible to train goldfish in a shuttle tank to discriminate between two colored stimuli. When brain extracts of these color-trained fish are administered to recipients, these recipients tend to show color preferences similar to those acquired by the donors. Since the color preferences of the recipients are measured without any reinforcement, these data were assumed to be one of the most convincing proofs of the specificity of the bioassays. They can, however, be criticized in the sense discussed in Section IV,C,1.

4. Chemical Identification of the Active Material; the Possibility of a Molecular Code of Memory

Because of the influence of Hyden's and McConnell's experiments, many authors have thought, as already stated, that the substance responsible for transfer effects was RNA. This idea is at the origin of many negative results. Others, with no preconceived ideas, began with crude extracts and proposed the hypothesis that small molecules, probably peptides, were responsible for the effects (Chapouthier, 1968; Fjerdingstad, 1969b; Giurgea et al., 1970; Rosenblatt, Farrow, & Herblin, 1966; Ungar & Oceguera-Navarro, 1965). It has been proved by Ungar and Fjerdingstad (1971) that the RNA preparations were active because of the presence of peptides linked to RNA. This complex can be dissociated at low pH and, after separation from the active peptide, the RNA has no transfer activity.

The first active peptide, isolated from brains of rats trained to avoid a dark box (Ungar et al., 1968), has been completely purified and identified (Ungar, Desiderio, & Parr, 1972). It was found that it was a peptide composed of 15 amino acids having the following sequence: H-Ser-Asp-Asn-Asn-Glu-Glu-Gly-Lys-Ser-Ala-Glu-Gln-Gly-Gly-Tyr-NH$_2$. More recently, Ungar (1976) proposed another form of the peptide: H-Ser-Glu-Gly-Lys-Ser-Ala-Gln-Gln-Gly-Gly-Tyr-NH$_2$.

Ungar's group has also isolated further peptides: "ameletine" has been isolated from the brain of rats which had learned not to startle to a sound stimulus; its sequence is pGlu-Ala-Gly-Tyr-Ser-Lys-OH (Burzynski, 1976).

Two "chromodiopsins" have been isolated from the brain of fish trained either to avoid a blue stimulus and to choose the green (chromodiopsin B → G) or to avoid the green one and to choose the blue (chromodiopsin G → B). The sequences of these two peptides are (Tate, Galvan, & Ungar, 1976) *p*Glu-Ile-Gly-Ala-Val-Phe-Pro-Leu-Lys-Tyr-Gly-Ser-Lys-OH (chromodiopsin B → G), *N*-Ac-Lys-Gly-Glu-Ile-Ala-Val-Phe-Pro-Leu-Lys-Tyr-Gly-Ser-OH   (chromodiopsin G → B).

Recently another group (Guttman & Cooper, 1975) has provided evidence for a peptide which plays a role in the control of step-down avoidance called "catabathmophobin." Purification is still in progress.

According to Ungar, a great number of such peptides are synthesized in the brain in various situations and are able to elicit various types of behavior when injected into recipients. These peptides would therefore represent a molecular memory code (Ungar, 1969, 1970a,b, 1976). A few speculations have already been made on the possible mechanisms of such a coding in the brain. Most theories postulate that molecules could direct the traffic of nerve impulses along neural pathways through an appropriate chemical coding of the synapses (R. M. Best, 1968; Rosenblatt, 1967; Szilard, 1964; Ungar, 1968). In these theories, therefore, the chemical code is understood as a complement to the structural and electrical codes of the nervous system. These bold conceptions remain, however, highly controversial. In a general review of the transfer phenomenon, Smith (1974) concluded that both nonspecific (arousal factors) and specific (acquired information) transfers could be assumed. However, many authors still believe that only the nonspecific results have substance, i.e., the peptides isolated only modify learning ability and a "molecular code of memory" has yet to be found. Their arguments will be presented in the following sections.

C. Critical Approach to the Above Studies

1. Critical Approach to the Behavioral Test

The most striking results in favor of the specificity of the transfers are based on color discrimination in goldfish (see Section IV,B,3). Two groups of donors are trained to choose opposite colors in a shuttle tank; recipients of brain extracts from trained animals tend to choose the same colors as had been learned by the donors. In order to be convincing, however, the behavioral test would have to show that both colors have the same spontaneous effect on the fish. This is far from the case.

For example, it is possible to show (Chapouthier, 1978a) that fish have very strong spontaneous color preferences. The consequence is that two donor groups which are trained to respond to different colors differ in the time needed to reach learning criterion. Therefore, they also differ in the quantity of stress received, and this may have an effect on the recipients. Second, in the "color preferences'' the respective effects for color itself and for luminance were not properly analyzed. Chapouthier (1973) showed that in changing luminance of the source slightly, the "transfer effect" disappeared, despite the persistence of the "color." This can be achieved by adding a neutral filter to one of the colored sources, which would slightly modify the luminance of this source during the test of the recipients; as soon as the neutral filter was added, the recipients seemed unable to make the proper response. A more logical explanation of the results would be a nonspecific modification of the light and/or color preferences of the recipients by stress factors.

2. Nonspecific Interpretation of the Effects of Scotophobin

Most of the peptides isolated by the bioassay method must still be thoroughly studied and their precise effects on behavior analyzed. Scotophobin, however, has been submitted to a wide range of investigations, and its action mechanism is known in part.

Experiments proving that artificial scotophobin or scotophobin-like peptides modify behavior have been widely replicated (Bryant, Santos, & Byrne, 1972; De Wied, Sarantakis, & Weinstein, 1973; Guttman, Matwyshyn & Warriner, 1977; Malin, 1974; Miller, Small, & Berk, 1975; Thinès, Domagk, & Schonne, 1973). Many of the above investigators doubt, however, that scotophobin has the specific function proposed by Ungar. De Wied et al. (1973) showed that scotophobin-related peptides could modify behavior in avoidance situations but were inactive in a light–dark preference test. Miller et al. (1975) found that the transfer effect only takes place when the recipients are in a state of stress. Moreover, the same authors studied the way the donor rats master the "avoidance of the dark" test. They discovered that these donors continue to avoid the dark box even after it has been illuminated like the light compartment. According to Miller et al. (1975), this indicates that animals learned to avoid cues other than, or in addition to, darkness. The specificity of "dark" avoidance seemed therefore far from clear. Some authors have even criticized the scotophobin design on purely behavioral grounds. In order to bring out the dark avoidance effect more clearly in the treated recipients, Ungar selected populations of recipient mice according to an inborn dark preference criterion. According to Wojcik, Mitros, Jastreboff, and Zielenski (1975), such selection is meaningful only when this inborn reaction is quite stable. These authors noticed fluctuations in the dark box time in populations of mice selected for their preference to the dark which could partially explain some of Ungar's results. They also found a link between time spent in the dark compartment and motor activity, suggesting that "nonspecific factors may influence motor activity" and shorten the time spent in the dark.

A more precise explanation of the mechanism of action of scotophobin was recently given by Misslin et al. (1978). Using an open-field test, these authors found differences in the emotionality of the scotophobin-treated animals: treated subjects showed less emotional reactivity than the controls. According to Misslin *et al.* (1978), since more emotional animals spent more time in the darkened compartment the effect of scotophobin which reduces the emotional reactivity could explain the shortening of the time spent in the dark box. Moreover, since Ungar's experiments were carried out on subjects selected for their dark preference, which also happen to be more emotional subjects, the effect on emotional reactivity is even stronger. This is certainly the most convincing nonspecific interpretation of the effects of scotophobin presented to date. Should it be confirmed, it would mean that the peptide acts on behavior through an effect on emotionality.

3. Discussion

It would, of course, be useful to have studies similar to that carried out on scotophobin on the effects of the other peptides. As far as ameletin is concerned, Lackner and Tiemann (1974) and Weinstein, Bartschot, Cook, Tam, and Guttman (1975) reported that the synthetic peptide had slightly different effects than the natural one. The authors assumed, therefore, that the sequence of the natural product is not perfectly known. However, no data are available concerning a possible nonspecific effect of ameletin or of the other peptides of this category.

Whatever results may be obtained in the future, the evidence provided to date on the "transfer of color" in goldfish (Section IV,C,1) or on the effects of scotophobin (Section IV,C,2) strongly suggest that these peptides act on learning in a nonspecific manner. From this point of view they present a promising family of behaviorally active chemicals, but do not provide, however, a convincing answer to question of the "molecular code of memory."

V. MODERN CONCEPTIONS OF THE ROLE OF PROTEINS IN LEARNING

A. Paradoxical Sleep, Learning, and Memory

Recent investigations on the role of paradoxical sleep provide indirect evidence for the function of protein synthesis in learning and memory. It has been shown that deprivation of paradoxical sleep impairs learning both in mice (Fishbein, 1971) and in rats (Leconte & Bloch, 1970). Conversely, following a learning phase, paradoxical sleep duration seems to be increased in the rat (Leconte & Hennevin, 1971; Lucero, 1970). Paradoxical sleep [or rapid eye movement (REM) sleep] seems, therefore, to be an important phase in the treatment of previously acquired information. For more detailed information on this problem, the reader is referred to reviews by Hennevin and Leconte (1971) and Fishbein and Gutwein (1977).

Because the numerous studies analyzed next show that REM sleep is strongly linked with protein synthesis, it can be assumed that protein synthesis plays an important role in memory.

Numerous investigations have provided evidence for a relationship between protein synthesis and paradoxical sleep. Pegram, Hammond, and Bridgers (1973) have studied the effect of subcutaneously injected cycloheximide on paradoxical sleep in mice; they could show that the injections were followed by a reduction in the amount and frequency of paradoxical sleep. Stern, Morgane, Panksepp, Zolovick, and Jalowiec (1972) studied the modifications of REM sleep in cats following puromycin or cycloheximide injection, either intraventricularly or intraperitoneally. They discovered a decrease in REM sleep on the day of the drug administration in most cases. However, for the group administered cycloheximide intraventricularly alone, they found an increase in REM sleep during the days following that of drug administration, a result which might be linked to the recovery from inhibition of protein synthesis. With another antibiotic, chloramphenicol, Petitjean, Sastre, Bertrand, Cointy, and Jouvet (1975) obtained a decrease in REM sleep in cats, as did as Kitahama and Valatx (1975) in mice. Rojas-Ramirez, Aguilar-Jimenez, Posadas-Andrews, Bernal-Pedraza, and Drucker-Colin (1977) investigated the effects of various antibiotics on paradoxical sleep in rats. They found that three of them (anisomycin, chloramphenicol, and vincristine) were able to decrease REM sleep without affecting slow-wave sleep. Finally, more direct work by Bobillier, Sakai, Seguin, and Jouvet (1974) has provided evidence that experimental deprivation of REM sleep in rats leads to decrease in protein synthesis.

Growth hormone has provided related data. Growth hormone (GH) is known to act on protein synthesis (Korner, 1965; Tata, 1968) and has also been shown to be produced during slow-wave sleep (Sassin, Parker, Mace, Gotlin, Johnson, & Rossman, 1969; Takahashi, Kipnis, & Daughaday, 1968). Since slow-wave sleep preceded REM sleep, the question was raised whether GH plays a role in the occurrence of REM sleep. Stern, Jalowiec, Shabshelowitz, and Morgane (1975) found that in cats given GH intraperitoneally REM sleep was increased during the 3 hours following injection. Drucker-Colin, Spanis, Hunyadi, Sassin, and McGaugh (1975) sutdied the effect of GH and anisomycin on sleep in rats. They found that GH increased and anisomycin inhibited REM sleep. If both drugs were administered together, GH was able to compensate the effects of anisomycin. All these data confirm the link between protein synthesis and REM sleep.

Other studies have used bioassay-like methods to discover which REM sleep factors from donor animals could influence the sleep patterns of the recipients. The question of brain factors able to transfer sleep is an old one. As early as 1913, Legendre and Pieron discovered that a sleep-promoting factor, called "hypnotoxin," could be extracted from the cerebral spinal fluid of sleep-deprived dogs. Two groups have provided data on such sleep-promoting factors. Monnier, Koller, and Graber (1963) investigated the effects of sleep in two rabbits linked by a vascular bridge which allowed the blood of a donor to reach a recipient. When electrographic sleep patterns are artificially induced in the donor by brain stimulation, the same patterns appear in the recipient, showing the existence of a blood factor. Schoenenberger, Cueni, Hatt, and Monnier (1972) have isolated a small peptide from the donor blood which seems to be the active factor. This peptide has been shown to have the sequence Trp-Ala-Ser-Gly-Glu, and has been called delta sleep-inducing peptide (DSIP) (Monnier, Dudler, Gachter, & Schoenenberger, 1975). The artificially synthesized peptide can induce sleep both in rodents and in cats (Kafi, Monnier, & Gallard, 1979; Monnier, Dudler, Gachter, & Schoenenberger, 1977; Nagasaki, Kitahama, Valatx, & Jouvet, 1980; Polc, Schoenenberger, & Haefely, 1978). On the other hand, Pappenheimer, Miller, and Goodrich (1967) were able to transfer to rats and cats a sleep-promoting factor from the cerebrospinal fluid of sleep-deprived goats. Additional data also provide evidence that this is a small peptide (Fencl, Koski, & Pappenheimer, 1971). Furthermore, Nagasaki *et al.* (1980) have discovered a sleep-promoting substance (SPS) in the rat. All the above studies have worked with sleep-promoting factors, but not especially those which promote REM sleep. Other investigators have, however, shown the existence of specific paradoxical sleep-inducing proteins.

Employing a push–pull cannula technique, Drucker-Colin, Spanis, and Rojas-Ramirez (1977) were able to study the effects on sleep of midbrain reticular formation perfusates in cats. They found that perfusates obtained during sleep from donors were able to induce sleep in recipient cats. Nagasaki, Iriki, Inove, and Uchizono (1974) confirmed these data in rats, showing that a sleep-promoting substance exists in brainstem homogenates. By means of polyacrylamide-gel electrophoresis the rate of proteins in perfusate during the various states of sleep and wakefulness can be compared. Using this method, Drucker-Colin, Spanis, Cotman, and McGaugh (1975) found that peak increase of proteins corresponded to periods of REM sleep. These results, according to the authors, suggest that proteins are intimately rerelated to the physiological processes regulating REM sleep (Drucker-Colin *et al.*, 1977). Further characterization of the proteins showed them to be rather large polypeptides (Spanis, Gutierrez, & Drucker-Colin, 1976). For review of recent developments concerning the effects of these peptides as well as other non-brain-derived peptides, see Riou (1981).

B. Peptides and Memory

Two groups of peptides have been shown to act on learning and memory: hypothalamoneurohypophyseal peptides, on the one hand, enkephalins and endorphins, on the other. We would like to summarize the main results obtained with these peptides, which, in turn, will enable us to discuss the present state of the relationship between memory and protein synthesis. For a review of the whole field, see Martinez, Jensen, Messing, Rigter, and McGaugh (1981) and Koob and Bloom (1982).

1. Hypothalamic Peptides and Memory

The examination of the effects of hypothalamic peptides on learning and memory was begun by De Wied and his colleagues in Netherlands. They turned their attention first to ACTH, an hypophyseal hormone which stimulates liberation of corticoids when the organism is under stress. The hormone was studied for its possible effect on memory. De Wied and his group (De Wied, 1976; De Wied, Witter, & Greven, 1975) were able to show that ACTH not only can restore normal learning abilities in hypophysectomized rats, but it can also inhibit extinction of a learned task in normal subjects. Most of the learning tasks used by De Wied group were avoidance tasks. ACTH being a 39 amino acids protein, it was interesting to learn which part of the sequence acts upon behavior. De Wied and his colleagues were able to show that the fragment 4–10 of the molecule and, even more specifically, portion 4–7 (De Wied et al., 1975), the sequence of which is H-Met-Glu-His-Phe-OH, were able to act upon learning in the same way as the total molecule.

The authors were able to modify the 4–10 fragment of ACTH either by replacing an amino acid by another or by replacing an L-amino acid by its D-isomer. They obtained a modified 4–10 fragment of ACTH that had either the opposite effect (facilitating extinction) or a much stronger effect (one molecule is one thousand times more active than the natural product).

Many other hypothalamic peptides have been shown to act on learning and memory (De Wied, 1965): α-MSH, β-MSH (melanocyte-stimulating hormone) and vasopressin (ADH). This is hardly surprising for α-MSH and β-MSH (both produced by the intermediate lobe of the hypophysis), since both include the 4–10 portion of ACTH. α-MSH even duplicates the 1–13 part of ACTH. But vasopressin, a hormone from the posterior hypophysis known for its vasopressor and antidiuretic effects, has similar effects, although it is biochemically very different from the ACTH-like peptides. The effects of vasopressin are even stronger than those described for ACTH: a single administration is sufficient, whereas repetitive administrations of ACTH-like peptides were needed (Bohus, Gispen, & De Wied, 1973; De Wied, 1971). Both vasopressin and vasopressin-like peptides, such as desglycinamide lysine vasopressin (DG-LVP), have the same behavioral effects, but DG-LVP does not possess the vasopressor or antidiuretic functions (Lande, Witter, & De Wied, 1971; De Wied, Greven, Lande, & Witter, 1972). It must, therefore, also be assumed here that these peptides act upon behavior by a direct effect on the nervous system. Recently Alliot and Alexinsky (1982) and Sara, Barnett, and Toussaint (1982) have shown facilitation by vasopressin in positively reinforced tasks. These authors raise the question of whether the effect is truly on memory or on other, nonspecific, behaviors, such as a vasopressin-induced tendency to persevere.

The precise mechanism of action of these peptides is not understood, nor is the zone of the brain they are acting in known. As far as the mechanism of action is concerned, data provided by Schotman, Gispen, Jansz, and De Wied (1972) and by Reith, Schotman, and Gispen (1974) have shown that pituitary peptides have an effect on protein synthesis: hypophysectomized rats synthesize protein in the brain at a decreased rate, whereas ACTH-like peptides increase the incorporation of labeled leucine in brain proteins. The precise site of action of these peptides still remains to be found, but ACTH analogues seem to act on limbic structures (De Wied *et al.*, 1975). Furthermore, it has recently been demonstrated that lesions of the rostral septal area and of the dorsal hippocampus abolish the consolidating effect of vasopressin on avoidance behavior (Bohus, Van Wimersma-Greidanus, Urban, & De Wied, 1977). These structures seem, therefore, to play a role in the action of the peptides. For further discussion of the role of limbic structures in memory, see Chapouthier and Matras (1982).

Bohus, Kovacs, Greven, and De Wied (1978) have provided evidence that another hormone, oxytocin, has the inverse effect of vasopressin: in a one-trial passive avoidance task in rats, oxytocin seems to attenuate consolidation, whereas vasopressin enhances it. Studies of the effects of fragments and analogs of these two molecules have shown that the basis for the consolidating effect of vasopressin is located in the covalent ring structure of this molecule (called pressinamide), while that for the opposite effect of oxytocin is located in the tocinamide ring structure. The line peptide chain of these molecules seems to have an effect on retrieval of memory rather than on consolidation itself. Very promising work is being carried out in this field, and it is expected that, in coming years, precise action of defined molecular structures will be able to modify different stages of information processing in the brain.

2. Effects of Enkephalins and Endorphins on Learning

The study of the effects of enkephalins and endorphins upon learning is still at a very early stage. Following the discovery of brain receptors for morphine, it was discovered that natural peptides, enkephalins and endorphins, could interact with these receptors (Cox, Goldstein, & Li, 1976; Hughes, Smith, Kosterlitz, Fothergill, Morgan, & Morris, 1975; Lazarus, Ling, & Guillemin, 1976). With the exception of the enkephalins, all these peptides are parts of a common molecule β-lipotropin (β-LPH). For the history of the discovery of the enkephalins and endorphins, see Rossier and Chapouthier (1982). Various portions of β-LPH as well as β-LPH itself have been shown to facilitate avoidance learning in the rat (De Wied, 1977; De Wied, Bohus, Van Ree, & Urban, 1978; Rigter, Shuster, & Thody, 1977); among the active portions are the fragment 61–76 (α-endorphin) and the fragment 61–91 (β-endorphin).

As far as the smaller pentapeptides (leucine-enkephalin, methionine-enkephalin) are concerned, there is now evidence that they also act on learning. Kastin, Scollan, King, Schally, and Coy (1976) demonstrated that Met-enkephalin and some analogs could facilitate acquisition of a twelve-choice maze-learning task with food reward by hungry rats. They verified that differences in appetite, thirst, olfaction, or general activity could not explain the results. Since some of the analogs have no opiate activity, this action on learning might go through another channel than opiate receptors. Other results (Rigter, 1978; Rigter, Greven, & Van Riezen, 1977) show that both Leu-enkephalin and Met-enkephalin are able to reduce carbon dioxide-induced amnesia in an avoidance task in rats. Since naloxone, a potent antagonist of morphine, has no effect of on this reduction, the authors conclude once again that the antiamnesic activity of the enkephalins is not mediated through opiate receptors. Related results have been obtained by Belluzi and Stein (1977), who showed that in a single-trial step-down learning task in rats, intraventricular administration of Met-enkephalin or even morphine could facilitate retention. De Wied, Bohus, Van Ree, and Urban (1978) also found that the specific opiate antagonist naltrexone could not prevent α- and β-endorphin-induced delay of extinction.

The question is far from clear, however; other investigators, for example, Messing, Jensen, Martinez, Vasquez, Soumireu-Mourat, and McGaugh (1979), have found results which apparently oppose the preceding ones. Using a one-trial inhibitory step-through avoidance task, these authors analyzed the effect of both intraperitoneally injected morphine and its antagonist naloxone. They found that morphine inhibited retention and naloxone enhanced it. These data, opposite in effects to the preceding ones, also differ concerning the action of naloxone, which had no effect in some of the studies described above. Despite these contradictory results, which may be due to type of training used or to routes of injection of the drugs, all the authors agree that opiate mechanisms are clearly involved in memory storage process. Further studies will be needed to clarify the apparent discrepancies.

One of the most striking results in this field is probably the discovery by De Wied, Kovacs, Bohus, Van Ree, and Greven (1978) that γ-endorphin (corresponding to the 61–77 part of β-LPH) facilitates extinction both in a pole jumping avoidance behavior task and in a passive avoidance task, an effect exactly opposite to those of α-endorphin, β-endorphin, β-LPH 61–69, and Met-enkephalin. A similar effect can be obtained with a reduced version of the molecule des-Tyr^1-γ-endorphin, which might be considered a kind of inborn neuroleptic (De Wied, 1979; Kovacs, Telegdy, & De Wied, 1982).

Despite this striking result, the precise effect of peptides on learning still remains to be studied in detail. Some authors have already suggested that the interpretation of the data is not as simple as that provided by De Wied and his colleagues. Recent work by Le Moal, Koob, and Bloom (1979) for example, showed that α- and γ-endorphins have differential actions in two different learning situations. In a pole-jump avoidance task, α-endorphin inhibited and γ-endorphin facilitated extinction, a result confirming De Wied's data. In a runway task for water, however, both peptides increased resistance to extinction. According to the authors, the results make any simple interpretation in terms of neuroleptic activity difficult to accept. More work is still needed in order to know if the peptides really act on learning mechanisms or on other behavioral variables affecting performance.

Data obtained in our own laboratory with mice (Prado de Carvalho, Chapouthier, & Rossier, 1982) suggested that des-Tyr-γ-endorphin acted not on learning itself, but on emotional reactivity. This indirect action on emotionality may well account for the contradictory results obtained in learning tasks. The extent to which emotional responses are implicated in the task may determine the direction of the effect (Rossier & Chapouthier, 1982).

As far as the site of action of these endorphins is concerned, evidence has been provided by De Wied, Bohus, Van Ree, and Urban (1978) that β-endorphin injected intraventricularly is able to induce a shift from lower to higher frequencies of hippocampal theta rhythm during paradoxical sleep. Gamma-type endorphins also seem to be acting on limbic brain structures (Kovacs *et al.*, 1982). This again stresses the role of midbrain limbic structures in the action of these neuropeptides (Chapouthier & Matras, 1982). Site of action is, however, not the only common point between ACTH-like and morphine-like peptides.

Mains, Eipper, and Ling (1977) and J. L. Roberts and Herbert (1977a, 1977b) have shown that both ACTH and β-lipotropin have a common precursor, called proopiocortin by Rubinstein, Stein, and Udenfriend (1978) and now known as pro-opio-melano-cortin (see Rossier & Chapouthier, 1982). Wiegant, Gispen, Terenius, and De Wied (1977) could show that the pharmalogical properties of the two groups of peptides are similar. According to these authors, ACTH fragments antagonize morphine binding to opiate-binding sites; when administered intraventricularly, both ACTH-like and morphine-like drugs can produce excessive grooming in rats, which can in turn be blocked by naloxone administration. This recent study suggests that there is a common denominator for the pharmacological action of these two types of drugs. Should this idea be confirmed at the behavioral level, the number of peptide categories involved in learning would be raised to four: (1) bioassay ("transfer") peptides, (2) REM sleep peptides, (3) vasopressin-like peptides, and (4) ACTH or morphine-like peptides.

VI. CONCLUSIONS

The principal results obtained to date concerning the role of nucleic acids and proteins in learning and memory bring us to the following conclusions:

1. It is possible to show by chemical methods that there are quantitative and qualitative differences in the RNA and protein contents of the brain in naive and trained animals. It is difficult, however, to determine whether these changes result from the learning itself or from a nonspecific increase in brain metabolism.

2. RNA and protein synthesis play a role in the early stage of memory consolidation. This phenomenon can be altered by various inhibitors of RNA and protein synthesis, whose mechanism of action has not yet been clearly defined.

3. Bioassay methods are used to provide evidence for a macromolecular code of memory. These methods have shown that brain peptides in trained animals are able to alter the behavior of recipient animals when administered to them in sufficient doses. This behavioral effect seems to be nonspecific, however, and not directly related to memory coding.

4. Protein synthesis is increased during REM sleep, which represents an important stage of information processing in the brain.

5. Various brain peptides seem to facilitate learning. Besides the bioassay peptides already mentioned, the most attention today has been directed to ACTH-like, vasopressin-like, and morphine-like peptides. Further work is, however, needed to know if this facilitation is specific to learning or due to nonspecific variables acting on performance.

The two last approaches provide new ways of studying the biochemistry of memory. It can be assumed that the combined development of these two methods will produce, in the coming years, long-awaited answers to the question of the role of proteins in memory.

REFERENCES

Adam, G., & Faiszt, J. Conditions for successful transfer effects. *Nature (London)*, 1967, *216*, 198–200.

Agranoff, B. W., Davis, R. E., & Brink, J. J. Memory fixation in goldfish. *Proceedings of the National Academy of Sciences of the U.S.A.*, 1965, *54*, 788–793.

Agranoff, B. W., Davis, R. E., & Brink, J. J. Chemical studies on memory fixation in goldfish. *Brain Research*, 1966, *1*, 303–309.

Agranoff, B. W., Davis, R. E., Casola, L., & Lim, R. Actinomycin D blocks formation of memory of shock avoidance in goldfish. *Science*, 1967, *158*, 1600–1601.

Agranoff, B. W., & Klinger, P. D. Puromycin effect on memory fixation in the goldfish. *Science*, 1964, *146*, 952–953.

Albert, D. J. Memory in mammals: Evidence for a system involving nuclear ribobucleic acid. *Neuropsychologia*, 1966, *4*, 79–92.

Alliot, J., & Alexinsky, T. Effects of postrial vasopressin injections on appetitively motivated learning in rats. *Physiology and Behavior*, 1982, *28*, 525–530.

Andry, D. K., & Luttges, M. W. Memory traces: Experimental separation by cycloheximide and electroconvulsive shock. *Science*, 1972, *178*, 518–520.

Babich, F. R., Jacobson, A. L., & Bubash, S. Cross-species transfer of learning: Effect of ribonucleic acid from hamsters on rat behavior. *Proceedings of the National Academy of Sciences of the U.S.A.*, 1965, *54*, 1299–1302.

Babich, F. R., Jacobson, A. L., Bubash, S., & Jacobson, A. Transfer of a response to naive rats by injection of ribonucleic acid extracted from trained rats. *Science*, 1965, *149*, 656–657.

Barondes, S. H. Is the amnesic effect of cycloheximide due to specific interference with a process in memory storage? In A. Lajtha (Ed.), *Protein metabolism of the nervous system* (pp. 543–553). New York: Plenum Press, 1970.

Barondes, S. H., & Cohen, H. D. Puromycin effect on successive phases of memory storage. *Science*, 1966, *151*, 594–595.

Barondes, S. H., & Cohen, H. D. Comparative effects of cycloheximide and puromycin on cerebral protein synthesis and consolidation of memory in mice. *Brain Research*, 1967, *4*, 44–51 (a).

Barondes, S. H., & Cohen, H. D. Delayed and sustained effect of acetoxycycloheximide on memory in mice. *Proceedings of the National Academy of Sciences of the U.S.A.*, 1967, *58*, 157–164 (b).

Barondes, S. H., & Cohen, H. D. Effect of acetoxycycloheximide on learning and memory of a light–dark discrimination. *Nature (London)*, 1968, *218*, 271–273.

Barondes, S. H., & Jarvik, M. E. The influence of actinomycin D on brain RNA synthesis and on memory. *Journal of Neurochemistry*, 1964, *11*, 187–195.

Barraco, R. A., & Stettner, L. J. Antibiotics and memory. *Psychological Bulletin*, 1976, *83*(2), 242–302.

Bateson, P. P. G., Horn, G., & Rose, S. P. R. Effects of an imprinting procedure on regional incorporation of tritiated lysine into protein of chick brain. *Nature (London)*, 1969, *223*, 534–535.

Beach, G., Emmens, M., Kimble, D. P., & Lickey, M. Autoradiographic demonstration of biochemical changes in the limbic system during avoidance training. *Proceedings of the National Academy of Sciences of the U.S.A.*, 1969, *62*, 692–696.

Beach, G., & Kimble, D. P. Activity and responsivity in rats after magnesium pemoline injections. *Science*, 1967, *155*, 698–701.

Belluzi, J. D., & Stein, L. Enkephalin- and morphine-induced facilitation of long-term memory. *Society for Neuroscience Abstracts*, 1977, *3*, 230.

Bennett, E. L., & Calvin, M. Failure to train planarians reliably. *Neurosciences Research Program Bulletin*, 1964, *2*, 3–24.

Best, J. B., & Rubinstein, I. Maze learning and associated behavior in planaria. *Journal of Comparative and Physiological Psychology*, 1962, *55*, 560–566.

Best, R. M. Encoding of memory in the neuron. *Psychological Reports*, 1968, *22*, 107–115.

Block, R. A., & McConnell, J. V. Classically conditioned discrimination in the planaria *Dugesia dorotocephala*. *Nature (London)*, 1967, *215*, 1465–1466.

Bobillier, P., Sakai, F., Seguin, S., & Jouvet, M. The effect of sleep deprivation upon *in vivo* and *in vitro* incorporation of tritiated amino-acids into brain proteins in the rat at three different age levels. *Journal of Neurochemistry*, 1974, *22*, 23–31.

Bogoch, S. *The biochemistry of memory*. London & New York: Oxford University Press, 1968.

Bogoch, S. Glycoproteins and brain circuitry: The "sign-post" theory in normal memory function and in the regressive states of brain tumors and psychoses. *Biological Psychiatry*, 1974, *9*(1), 73–88.

Bohus, B., Gispen, W. H., & De Wied, D. Effect of lysine-vasopressin and ACTH 4–10 on conditioned avoidance behavior of hypophysectomized rats. *Neuroendocrinology*, 1973, *11*, 137–143.

Bohus, B., Kovacs, G. L., Greven, H., & De Wied, D. Memory effects of arginine-vasopressine (AVP) and oxytocin (OXT): Structure requirements. *Neuroscience Letters*, Supplement, 1978, *1*, S80.

Bohus, B., Van Wimersma Greidanus, T. B., Urban, T., & De Wied, D. Hypothalamoneurohypophyseal hormone effects on memory and related functions in the rat. In R. R. Drucker-Colin & J. L. McGaugh (Eds.), *Neurobiology of sleep and memory* (pp. 333–345). New York: Academic Press, 1977.

Bowman, R. E., & Strobel, D. A. Brain RNA metabolism in the rat during learning. *Journal of Comparative and Physiological Psychology*, 1969, *67*, 448–456.

Braud, W. G. Extinction in goldfish: Facilitation by intracranial injection of RNA from brains of extinguished donors. *Science*, 1970, *168*, 1234–1236.

Brown, B. M., & Noble, E. P. Cycloheximide and learning in the isolated cockroach ganglion. *Brain Research*, 1967, *6*, 363–366.

Brown, H. M., Dustman, R. E., & Beck, E. C. Experimental procedures that modify light response frequency of regenerated planaria. *Physiology and Behavior*, 1966, *1*, 245–249. (a)

Brown, H. M., Dustman, R. E., & Beck, E. C. Sensitization in planarian. *Physiology and Behavior*, 1966, *1*, 305–308. (b)

Bryant, R. C., Santos, N. N., & Byrne, W. L. Synthetic scotophobin in goldfish: Specificity and effect on learning. *Science*, 1972, *177*, 635–636.

Burzynski, S. R. Sequential analysis in subnanomolar amounts of peptides. Determination of the structure of a habituation-induced brain peptide (ameletin). *Analytical Biochemistry*, 1976, *70*, 359–365.

Byrne, W. L., & Hughes, A. Behavioral modification by injection of brain extract from trained donors. *Federation Proceedings, Federation of American Societies for Experimental Biology*, 1967, *26*, 676.

Byrne, W. L., & Samuel, D. Behavioral modification by injection of brain extract prepared from a trained donor. *Science*, 1966, *154*, 418.

Byrne, W. L., Samuel, D., Bennett, E. L., Rosenzweig, M. R., Wasserman, E., Wagner, A. R., Gardner, R., Galambos, R., Berger, B. D., Margules, D. L., Fenichel, R. L., Stein, L., Corson, J. A., Enesco, H. E., Chorover, S. L., Holt, C. E., III, Schiller, P. H., Chiappeta, L., Jarvik, M. E., Leaf, R. C., Dutcher, J. D., Horovitz, Z. P., & Carlson, P. L. Memory transfer. *Science*, 1966, *153*, 658–659.

Chamberlain, T. J., Rothschild, G. H., & Gerard, R. W. Drugs affecting RNA and learning. *Proceedings of the National Academy of Sciences of the U.S.A.*, 1963, *49*, 918–924.

Chapouthier, G. Taux de réponse à la lumière en relation avec le cannibalisme chez la planaire *Dugesia lugubris*. *Comptes Rendus Hebdomadaires des Seances de l'Academie des Sciences, Serie D*, 1967, *265*, 2047–2050. (a)

Chapouthier, G. Esquisse d'une théorie moléculaire de la mémoire et de l'oubli. *Revue du Comportement Animal*, 1967, *4*, 1–9. (b)

Chapouthier, G. Le transfert de molécules de mémoire chez les vertébrés. *Annee Biologique*, 1968, *7*, 275–285.

Chapouthier, G. *Essais de transfert par voie chimique d'informations acquises par le cerveau: Etude critique*. Thèse de Doctorat ès-Sciences, Université Louis Pasteur, Strasbourg, 1973.

Chapouthier, G. Critique de la spécificité des transferts par voie chimique d'informations acquises par le cerveau: La discrimination de couleurs chez le poisson. *Psychologie Française*, 1978, *23*(1), 27–32. (a)

Chapouthier, G. Discussion critique des transferts par voie chimique d'informations acquises par le cerveau. In J. Delacour (Ed.), *Neurobiologie de l'apprentissage* (pp. 72–83). Paris: Masson, 1978. (b)

Chapouthier, G., Legrain, D., & Spitz, S. La planaire en taut qu'animal de laboratoire dans les recherches psychophysiologiques. *Experimentation Animale*, 1969, *1*, 269–280.

Chapouthier, G., & Matras, J. J. *Introduction au fonctionnement du système nerveux*. Paris: Editions Medsi Publ., 1982.

Chapouthier, G., Pallaud, B., & Ungerer, A. Relations entre deux réactions des planaires face à une discrimination droite-gauche. *Comptes Rendus Hebdomadaires des Seances de l'Academie des Sciences, Serie D,* 1968, *266,* 905–907.

Chapouthier, G., Pallaud, B., & Ungerer, A. Note préliminaire concernant l'effet sur l'apprentissage des broyats de cerveau conditionné. *Revue du Comportement Animal,* 1969, *3,* 55–63.

Chapouthier, G., & Ungerer, A. Effet de l'injection d'extraits de cerveau conditionné sur l'apprentissage. *Comptes Rendus Hebdomadaires des Seances de l'Academie des Sciences, Serie D,* 1968, *267,* 769–771.

Chapouthier, G., & Ungerer, A. Sur l'effet de certains extraits de cerveau conditionné sur l'apprentissage. *Revue du Comportement Animal,* 1969, *3,* 64–71.

Chapouthier, G., & Ungerer, A. Bases biochimiques de l'apprentissage et de la mémoire. *Encephale,* 1973, *62,* 408–426.

Cherkin, A. Kinetics of memory consolidation: Role of amnesic treatment parameters. *Proceedings of the National Academy of Sciences of the U.S.A.* 1969, *63,* 1094–1101.

Codish, S. D. Actinomycin D injected into the hippocampus of chicks: Effects upon imprinting. *Physiology and Behavior,* 1971, *6,* 95–96.

Cohen, H. D. Learning, memory, and metabolic inhibitors. In G. Ungar (Ed.), *Molecular mechanisms in memory and learning* (pp. 59–70). New York: Plenum Press, 1970.

Cohen, H. D., & Barondes, S. H. Further studies of learning and memory after intracerebral actinomycin D. *Journal of Neurochemistry,* 1966, *13,* 207–211.

Cohen, H. D., & Barondes, S. H. Puromycin effect on memory may be due to occult seizures. *Science,* 1967, *157,* 333–334.

Cohen, H. D., Ervin, F., & Barondes, S. H. Puromycin and cycloheximide: Different effects on hippocampal electrical activity. *Science,* 1966, *154,* 1557–1558.

Corning, W. C. Evidence of a right–left discrimination in planarians. *Journal of Psychology,* 1964, *58,* 131–139.

Corning, W. C. Retention of a position discrimination after regeneration in planarians. *Psychonomic Science,* 1966, *5,* 17–18.

Corning, W. C., & Freed, S. Planarian behavior and biochemistry. *Nature (London),* 1968, *219,* 1227–1229.

Corning, W. C., & John, E. R. Effect of ribonuclease on retention of conditioned response in regenerated planarians. *Science,* 1961, *134,* 1363–1365.

Corning, W. C., & Riccio, D. The planarian controversy. In W. L. Byrne (Ed.), *Molecular approaches to learning and memory* (pp. 107–149). New York: Academic Press, 1970.

Cox, B. M., Goldstein, A., & Li, C. H. Opioid activity of a peptide, β-lipotropin-(61–91), derived from β-lipotropin. *Proceedings of the National Academy of Science of the U.S.A.,* 1976, *73,* 1821–1823.

Daliers, J., & Rigaux-Motquin, M. L. Transfer of learned behaviour by brain extracts. I. Audiogenic seizure. *Archives Internationales de Pharmacodynamie et de Therapie,* 1968, *176,* 461–463.

Daniels, D. Effects of actinomycin-D on memory and brain RNA synthesis in an appetitive learning task. *Nature (London),* 1971, *231,* 395–397.

Davis, R. E., Bright, P. J., & Agranoff, B. W. Effects of ECS and puromycin on memory in fish. *Journal of Comparative and Physiological Psychology,* 1965, *60,* 162–166.

Debold, R. C., Firschein, W., Carrier, S. C., III, & Leaf, R. C. Changes in RNA in the occipital cortex of rats as a function of light and dark during rearing. *Psychonomic Science,* 1967, *7,* 379–380.

Deminière, J. M., & Cardo, B. Activité unitaire corticale chez la souris après injection locale d'actinomycine-D. *Physiology and Behavior,* 1971, *6,* 663–665.

Deutsch, J. A. The physiological basis of memory. *Annual Review of Psychology,* 1969, *20,* 85–104.

De Wied, D. The influence of the posterior and intermediate lobe of the pituitary and pituitary peptides on the maintenance of a conditioned avoidance response in rats. *International Journal of Neuropharmacology*, 1965, *4*, 157–167.

De Wied, D. Long term effect of vasopressin on the maintenance of a conditioned avoidance response in rats. *Nature (London)*, 1971, *232*, 58–60.

De Wied, D. Hormonal influences on motivation, learning, and memory processes. *Hospital Practice*, 1976, *11*(1), 123–131.

De Wied, D. Peptides and behavior. *Life Sciences*, 1977, 20, 195–204.

De Wied, D. Schizophrenia an inborn error in the degradation of β-endorphin—a hypothesis. *Trends in NeuroSciences*, March 1979, *2*, 79–82.

De Wied, D., Bohus, B., Van Ree, J. M., & Urban, I. Behavioral and electrophysiological effects of peptides related to lipotropin (β-LPH). *Journal of Pharmacology and Experimental Therapeutics*, 1978, *204*, 570–580.

De Wied, D., Greven, H. M., Lande, S., & Witter, A. Dissociation of the behavioural and endocrine effects of lysine vasopressin by tryptic digestion. *British Journal of Pharmacology*, 1972, *45*, 118–122.

De Wied, D., Kovacs, G. L., Bohus, B., Van Ree, J. M., & Greven, H. M. Neuroleptic activity of the neuropeptide β-LPH 62–77 (des-Tyr^2-γ-endorphin; DTγE). *European Journal of Pharmacology*, 1978, *49*, 427–436.

De Wied, D., Sarantakis, D., & Weinstein, B. Behavioral evaluation of peptides related to scotophobin. *Neuropharmacology*, 1973, *12*, 1109–1115.

De Wied, D., Witter, A., & Greven, H. M. Behaviourally active ACTH analogues. *Biochemical Pharmacology*, 1975, *24*, 1463–1468.

Dingman, W., & Sporn, M. B. The incorporation of 8-azaguanine into rat brain RNA and its effects on maze learning by the rat: An inquiry into the chemical basis of memory. *Journal of Psychiatric Research*, 1961, *1*, 1–11.

Dingman, W., & Sporn, M. B. Molecular theories of memory. *Science*, 1964, *144*, 26–29.

Drucker-Colin, R. R., Spanis, C. W., Cotman, C. W., & McGaugh, J. L. Changes in protein levels in perfusates of freely moving cats: Relation to behavioral state. *Science*, 1975, *187*, 963–965.

Drucker-Colin, R. R., Spanis, C. W., Hunyadi, J., Sassin, J. F., & McGaugh, J. L. Growth hormone effects on sleep and wakefulness in the rat. *Neuroendocrinology*, 1975, *18*, 1–8.

Drucker-Colin, R. R., Spanis, C. W., & Rojas-Ramirez, J. A. Investigation of the role of proteins in REM sleep. In R. R. Drucker-Colin & J. L. McGaugh (Eds.), *Neurobiology of sleep and memory* (pp. 303–319). New York: Academic Press, 1977.

Dunn, A., Entingh, D., Entingh, T., Gispen, W. H., Machlus, B., Perumal, R., Rees, H. D., & Brogan, L. Biochemical correlates of brief behavioral experiences. In F. O. Schmitt & F. C. Worden (Eds.), *The neurosciences: Third study program* (pp. 679–684). Cambridge MA: MIT Press, 1974.

Dunn, A., Giuditta, A., Wilson, J. E., & Glassman, E. The effect of electroshock on brain RNA and protein synthesis and its possible relationship to behavioral effects. In M. Fink, S. Kety, J. McGaugh, & T. A. Williams (Eds.), *Psychobiology of convulsive therapy* (pp. 185–197). New York: Wiley, 1974.

Dyal, J. A., & Golub, A. M. An attempt to obtain shifts in brightness preference as a function of injection of brain homogenates. *Journal of Biological Psychology*, 1967, *9*(2), 29–33.

Dyal, J. A., & Golub, A. M. Further positive transfer effects obtained by intraperitoneal injections of brain homogenates. *Psychonomic Science*, 1968, *11*, 13–14.

Dyal, J. A., Golub, A. M., & Marrone, R. L. Transfer effects of intraperitoneal injection of brain homogenates. *Nature (London)*, 1967, *214*, 720–721.

Egyhazi, E., & Hydén, H. Experimentally induced changes in the base composition of the ribonucleic acids of isolated nerve cells and their oligodendroglial cells. *Journal of Biophysical and Biochemical Cytology,* 1961, *10,* 403–410.

Ernhardt, E. N., & Sherrick, C. *Retention of a maze habit following regeneration in planaria* (D. maculata). Paper presented at meeting of the Midwestern Psychological Association, St. Louis, Missouri, 1959.

Essman, W. B., & Lehrer, G. M. Is there a chemical transfer of learning? *Federation Proceedings, Federation of American Societies for Experimental Biology,* 1966, *25,* 208.

Essman, W. B., & Lehrer, G. M. Facilitation of maze performance by "RNA extracts" from maze-trained mice. *Federation Proceedings, Federation of American Societies for Experimental Biology,* 1967, *26,* 263.

Faiszt, J., & Adam, G. Role of different RNA fractions from the brain in transfer effect. *Nature (London),* 1968, *220,* 367–368.

Fencl, V., Koski, G., & Pappenheimer, J. R. Factors in cerebrospinal fluid from goats that affect sleep and activity in rats. *Journal of Physiology (London),* 1971, *216,* 565–589.

Fishbein, W. Disruptive effects of rapid eye movement sleep deprivation on long-term memory. *Physiology and Behavior,* 1971, *6,* 279–282.

Fishbein, W., & Gutwein, B. M. Paradoxical sleep and memory storage processes. *Behavioral Biology,* 1977, *19,* 425–464.

Fjerdingstad, E. J. Chemical transfer of alternation training in the Skinner box. *Scandinavian Journal of Psychology,* 1969, *10,* 220–224. (a)

Fjerdingstad, E. J. Chemical transfer of learned preference. *Nature (London),* 1969, *222,* 1079–1080. (b)

Fjerdingstad, E. J. Memory transfer in goldfish. *Journal of Biological Psychology,* 1969, *11*(2), 20–25. (c)

Fjerdingstad, E. J., Nissen, T., & Røigaard-Petersen, H. H. Effect of ribonucleic acid (RNA) extracted from the brain of trained animals on learning in rats. *Scandinavian Journal of Psychology,* 1965, *6,* 1–5.

Flexner, J. B., & Flexner, L. B. Restoration of memory lost after treatment with puromycin. *Proceedings of the National Academy of Sciences of the U.S.A.,* 1967, *57,* 1651–1654.

Flexner, J. B., & Flexner, L. B. Further observations on restoration of memory lost after treatment with puromycin. *Yale Journal of Biology and Medicine,* 1969, *42,* 235–240.

Flexner, J. B., Flexner, L. B., & Stellar, E. Memory in mice as affected by intracerebral puromycin. *Science,* 1963, *141,* 57–59.

Flexner, L. B., & Flexner, J. B. Effect of acetoxycycloheximide and acetoxycycloheximide-puromycin mixture on cerebral protein synthesis and memory in mice. *Proceedings of the National Academy of Sciences of the U.S.A.,* 1966, *55,* 369–374.

Flexner, L. B., & Flexner, J. B. Studies on memory: The long survival of peptidyl-puromycin in mouse brain. *Proceedings of the National Academy of Sciences of the U.S.A.,* 1968, *60,* 923–927.

Flexner, L. B., Flexner, J. B., & Roberts, R. B. Memory in mice analyzed with antibiotics. *Science,* 1967, *155,* 1377–1383.

Flexner, L. B., Flexner, J. B., Roberts, R. B., & De la Haba, G. Loss of recent memory in mice as related to regional inhibition of cerebral protein synthesis. *Proceedings of the National Academy of Sciences of the U.S.A.,* 1964, *52,* 1165–1169.

Flood, J. F., Bennett, E. L., Orme, A. E., & Jarvik, M. E. Protein synthesis dependent gradient of ECS retrograde amnesia. *Behavioral Biology,* 1977, *21,* 307–328.

Flood, J. F., Bennett, E. L., Orme, A. E., & Rosenzweig, M. R. Effects of protein synthesis inhibition on memory for active avoidance training. *Physiology and Behavior,* 1975, *14,* 177–184. (a)

Flood, J. F., Bennett, E. L., Orme, A. E., & Rosenzweig, M. R. The relation of memory formation to controlled amounts of brain protein synthesis. *Physiology and Behavior*, 1975, *15*, 97–102. (b)

Flood, J. F., Bennett, E. L., Rosenzweig, M. R., & Orme, A. E. Influence of training strength on amnesia induced by pre-training injections of cycloheximide. *Physiology and Behavior*, 1972, *9*, 589–600.

Flood, J. F., Bennett, E. L., Rosenzweig, M. R., & Orme, A. E. The influence of duration of protein synthesis inhibition on memory. *Physiology and Behavior*, 1973, *10*, 555–562.

Gaddum, J. H. Bioassays and mathematics. *Pharmacological Reviews*, 1953, *5*, 87–134.

Gaito, J. A biochemical approach to learning and memory. *Psychopharmacological Review*, 1961, *68*, 288–292.

Gaito, J. DNA and RNA as memory molecules. *Psychological Reviews*, 1963, *70*, 471–480.

Gaito, J. A biochemical approach to learning and memory: Fourteen years later. *Advances in Psychobiology*, 1974, *2*, 225–239.

Gay, R., & Raphelson, A. "Transfer of learning" by injection of brain RNA: A replication. *Psychonomic Science*, 1967, *8*, 369–370.

Geller, A., Robustelli, F., & Jarvik, M. E. Cycloheximide induced amnesia: Its interaction with detention. *Psychopharmacologia*, 1971, *21*, 309–316.

Gervai, J., & Csanyi, V. The effects of protein synthesis inhibition on imprinting. *Brain Research*, 1973, *53*, 151–160.

Gibbs, M. E., & Ng, K. T. Psychobiology of memory: Towards a model of memory formation. *Biobehavioral Reviews*, 1977, *1*, 113–136.

Gibby, R. G., & Crough, D. G. RNA-induced enhancement of wire climbing in the rat. *Psychonomic Science*, 1967, *9*, 413–414.

Gibby, R. G., Crough, D. G., & Thios, S. J. RNA-enhancement of a single discrimination task. *Psychonomic Science*, 1968, *12*, 295–296.

Gispen, W. H., Perumal, R., Wilson, J. E., and Glassman, E. Phosphorylation of proteins of synaptosome-enriched fractions of brain during short-term training experience: The effects of various behavioral treatments. *Behavioral Biology*, 1977, *21*, 358–363.

Giurgea, C., Daliers, J., & Mouravieff, F. Pharmacological studies on an elementary model of learning: The fixation of an experience at spinal level. *Abstracts, International Congress of Pharmacology, 4th, 1969*, 1970, pp. 291–292.

Glassman, E. The biochemistry of learning: An evaluation of the role of RNA and protein. *Annual Review of Biochemistry*, 1969, 38, 605–646.

Glassman, E., Henderson, A., Cordle, M., Moon, H. M., & Wilson, J. E. Effect of cycloheximide and actinomycin D on the behavior of the headless cockroach. *Nature (London)*, 1970, *225*, 967–968.

Gold, M., Altschuler, H., Kleban, M. H., Lawton, M. P., & Miller, M. Chemical changes in the rat brain following escape training. *Psychonomic Science*, 1969, *17*, 37–38.

Goldsmith, L. J. Effect of intracerebral actinomycin D and of electroconvulsive shock on passive avoidance. *Journal of Comparative and Physiological Psychology*, 1967, *63*, 126–132.

Golub, A. M., Epstein, L., & McConnell, J. V. The effect of peptides, RNA extracts, and whole brain homogenates on avoidance behavior in rats. *Journal of Biological Psychology*, 1969, *11*(1), 44–49.

Golub, A. M., Masiarz, F. R., Villars, T., & McConnell, J. V. Incubation effects in behavior induction in rats. *Science*, 1970, *168*, 392–394.

Golub, A. M., & McConnell, J. V. Transfer of a response bias by injection of brain homogenates: A replication. *Psychonomic Science*, 1968, *11*, 1–2.

Gordon, M. W., Deanin, G. G., Leonhardt, H. L., & Gwynn, R. H. RNA and memory: A negative experiment. *American Journal of Psychiatry*, 1966, *122*, 1174–1178.

Grampp, W., & Edström, J. E. The effect of nervous activity on ribonucleic acid of the crustacean receptor neuron. *Journal of Neurochemistry*, 1963, *10*, 725–731.

Griffard, C. D., & Pierce, J. T. Conditioned discrimination in the planarian. *Science*, 1964, *144*, 1472–1473.

Griffith, J. S., & Mahler, H. R. DNA ticheting theory of memory. *Nature (London)*, 1969, *223*, 580–582.

Gross, C. G., & Carey, F. M. Transfer of learned response by RNA injection: Failure of attempts to replicate. *Science*, 1965, *150*, 1749.

Guttman, H. N., & Cooper, R. S. Oligopeptide control of step-down avoidance. *Life Sciences*, 1975, *16*, 915–924.

Guttman, H. N., Matwyshyn, G., & Warriner, G. H., III Synthetic scotophobin-mediated passive transfer of dark avoidance. *Nature (London), New Biol.*, 1977, *235*, 26–27.

Gutwein, B. M., Quatermain, D., & McEwen, B. S., Disociation of cycloheximide's effects on activity from its effects on memory. *Pharmacology, Biochemistry and Behavior*, 1974, *2*, 753–756.

Halas, E. S., James, R. L., & Knutson, C. S. An attempt at classical conditioning in the planarian. *Journal of Comparative and Physiological Psychology*, 1962, *55*, 969.

Hartry, A. L., Keith-Lee, P., & Morton, W. D. Planaria: Memory transfer through cannibalism reexamined. *Science*, 1964, *146*, 274–275.

Hennevin, E., & Leconte, P. La fonction du sommeil paradoxal. Faits et hypothèses. *Année Psychologique*, 1971, *2*, 489–519.

Horridge, G. A. Learning of a leg position by the ventral nerve cord in headless insects. *Proceedings of the Royal Society of London*, 1962, *157*, 33–52.

Hughes, J., Smith, T. W., Kosterlitz, L. A., Fothergill, B., Morgan, A., & Morris, H. R. Identification of two related pentapeptides from the brain with potent opiate agonist activity. *Nature (London)*, 1975, *258*, 577–579.

Humphries, B. Maze learning in planaria. *Worm Runner's Digest*, 1961, *3*(2), 114–116.

Hydén, H. Biochemical changes in glial cells and nerve cells at varying activity. *Biochemistry of the central nervous system* (vol. 3, pp. 64–89). Oxford: Pergamon, 1959.

Hydén, H. Behavior, neural function and RNA. *Progress in Nucleic Acid Research and Molecular Biology*, 1967, *6*, 187–218.

Hydén, H. Trends in brain research on learning and memory. In S. Bogoch (Ed.), *The future of the brain sciences* (pp. 265–279). New York: Plenum Press, 1969.

Hydén, H., & Egyhazi, E. Nuclear RNA changes in nerve cells during a learning experiment in rats. *Proceedings of the National Academy of Sciences of the U.S.A.*, 1962, *48*, 1366–1372.

Hydén, H., & Lange, P. W. A differentiation in RNA response in neurons early and late in learning. *Proceedings of the National Academy of Sciences of the U.S.A.*, 1965, *53*, 946–952.

Hydén, H., & Lange, P. W. Protein synthesis in the hippocampal pyramidal cells of rats during a behavioral test. *Science*, 1968, *159*, 1370–1373.

Jacobson, A. L., Babich, F. R., Bubash, S., & Goren, C. Maze preferences in naive rats produced by injection of ribonucleic acid from trained rats. *Psychonomic Science*, 1966, *4*, 3–4.

Jacobson, A. L., Babich, F. R., Bubash, S., & Jacobson, A. Differential-approach tendencies produced by injection of RNA from trained rats. *Science*, 1965, *150*, 636–637.

Jacobson, A. L., Fried, C., & Horowitz, S. D. Planarians and memory. *Nature (London)*, 1966, *209*, 599–601.

Jaffard, R., & Cardo, B. Influence de l'injection intracorticale de ribonucléase sur l'acquisition et la rétention d'un apprentissage alimentaire chez le rat. *Journal de Physiologie (Paris)*, 1968, *60*, Supplement 2, 470.

Jaffard, R., & Cardo, B. Influence de l'injection intracorticale de ribonucléase sur l'apprentissage d'une discrimination visuelle chez le rat. *Journal de Physiologie (Paris)*, 1969, *61*, Supplement 2, 322–323.

Jankovic, B. D., Rakic, L., Veskov, R., & Horvat, J. Effect of intraventricular injection of antibrain antibody on defensive conditioning reflexes. *Nature (London)*, 1968, *218*, 270–271.

Kafi, S., Monnier, M., & Gallard, J. M. The delta sleep inducing peptide (DSIP) increases duration of sleep in rats. *Neuroscience Letters*, 1979, *13*, 169–172.

Kastin, A. J., Scollan, E. L., King, M. G., Schally, A. V., & Coy, D. H. Enkephalin and a potent analog facilitate maze performance after intraperitoneal administration in rats. *Pharmacology, Biochemistry and Behavior*, 1976, *5*, 691–695.

Katz, J. J., & Halstead, W. D. Protein organizations and mental function. *Psychology Monographs*, 1950, *20*, 1–38.

Kitahama, K., & Valatx, J. L. Effets du chloramphenicol et du thiamphenicol sur le sommeil de la souris. *Comptes Rendus des Seances de la Societe de Biologie et de Ses Filiales*, 1975, *169*, 1522–1525.

Kleban, M. H., Altschuler, H., Lawton, M. P., Parris, J. L., & Lords, C. A. Influence of donor-recipient brain transfers on avoidance learning. *Psychological Reports*, 1968, *23*, 51–56.

Koob, G. F., & Bloom, F. E. Behavioural effects of neuropeptides: Endorphins and vasopressin. *Annual Review of Phsyiology*, 1982, *44*, 571–582.

Korner, A. Growth hormone control of biosynthesis of protein and ribonucleic acid. *Recent Progress in Hormone Research*, 1965, *21*, 205–238.

Kovacs, G. L., Telegdy, G., & De Wied, D. γ-Type endorphines attenuate passive avoidance behavior following microinjection into the nucleus accumbens. *Neuroscience, Supplement*, 1982, *7*, 121.

Krylov, O. A., Kalyuzhnaya, P. I., & Tongur, V. S. Possible conveyance of conditioned connection by means of a biochemical substrate. *Zhurnal Vysshei Nervnoi Deyatel'nosti imeni J. P. Pavlova*, 1969, *19*, 286.

Lackner, H., & Tiemann, N. Synthese eines verhaltensphysiologish wizksamen hexapeptids. *Naturwissenschaften*, 1974, *61*, 217–218.

Lambert, R., & Saurat, M. RNA et transfert d'apprentissage: Une réplique d'expérience. *Bulletin CERP*, 1967, *16*, 435–438.

Lande, S., Witter, A., & De Wied, D. Pituitary peptides: An octapeptide that stimulates conditioned avoidance acquisition in hypophysectomized rats. *Journal of Biological Chemistry*, 1971, *246*, 2058–2062.

Lazarus, L. H., Ling, N., & Guillemin, R. β-Lipotropin as a prohormone for the morphinomimetic peptides endorphins and enkephalins. *Proceedings of the National Academy of Sciences of the U.S.A.* 1976, *73*, 2156–2159.

Leconte, P., & Bloch, V. Déficit de la rétention d'un conditionnement après privation de sommeil paradoxal chez le rat *Comptes Rendus Hebdomadaires des Seances de l'Academie des Sciences, Serie D.*, 1970, *271*, 226–229.

Leconte, P., & Hennevin, E. Augmentation de la durée de sommeil paradoxal consécutive à un apprentissage chez le rat. *Comptes Rendus Hebdomadaires des Seances de l'Academie des Sciences, Serie D*, 1971, *273*, 86–88.

Lee, R. M. Conditioning of a free operant response in planaria. *Science*, 1963, *139*, 1048–1049.

Legendre, R., & Pieron, H. Recherches sur le besoin de sommeil consécutif à une veille prolongée. *Zeitschrift für allgemeine Physiologie*, 1913, *14*, 235–262.

Le Moal, M., Koob, G. F., & Bloom, F. E. Endorphins and extinction: differential actions on appetitive and adversive tasks, *Life Sciences*, 1979, *24*, 1631–1636.

Lucero, M. Lengthening of REM sleep duration consecutive to learning in the rat. *Brain Research*, 1970, *20*, 319–322.

Luttges, M., Johnson, T., Buck, C., Holland, J., & Mc Gaugh, J. An examination of "transfer of learning" by nucleic acid. *Science*, 1966, *151*, 834–837.

Machlus, B., & Gaito, J. Successive competition hybridization to detect RNA species in a shock avoidance task. *Nature (London)*, 1969, *222*, 573–574.

Mains, R. E., Eipper, B. A., & Ling, N. Common precursor to corticotropins and endorphins. *Proceedings National Academy of Science of the U.S.A.*, 1977, *74*, 3014–3018.

Malin, D. H. Synthetic scotophobin: analysis of behavioral effects in mice. *Pharmacology Biochemistry and Behavior*, 1974, *2*, 147–153.

Martinez, J. L., Jensen, R. A., Messing, R. B., Rigter, J. L., & McGaugh, T. L. (Eds). *Endogenous peptides and learning and memory processes*. New York: Academic Press, 1981.

Mayor, S. J. Memory in the japanese quail: effects of puromycin and acetoxycycloheximide. *Science*, 1969, *166*, 1165–1167.

Mc Connell, J. V. Memory transfer through cannibalism in planarians. *Journal of Neuropsychiatry*, 1962, *3*, Supplement 1, 42–48.

Mc Connell, J. V. New evidence for "transfer of training" effect in planarians. Symposium on the Biological bases of memory traces, XVIII International Congress of Psychology, Moscow, 1966.

McConnell, J. V. Specific factors influencing planarian behavior. In W. C. Corning & E. C. Ratner (Eds.), *Chemistry of learning; invertebrate research* (pp. 217–233). New York: Plenum Press, 1967.

McConnell, J. V., Jacobson, A. L., & Kimble, D. P. The effects of regeneration upon retention of a conditioned response in the planarian. *Journal of Comparative and Physiological Psychology*, 1959, *52*, 1–5.

McConnell, J. V., Jacobson, R., & Maynard, D. M. Apparent retention of a conditioned response following total regeneration in the planarian. *American Psychologist*, 1959, *14*, 410. (Abstract)

McConnell, J. V., & Shelby, J. M. Memory transfer experiments in invertebrates. In G. Ungar (Ed.), *Molecular mechanisms in memory and learning* (pp. 71–101). New York: Plenum Press, 1970.

McConnell, J. V., Shigehisha, T., & Salive, H. Attempts to transfer approach and avoidance responses by RNA injections in rats. *Journal of Biological Psychology*, 1968, *10*(2), 32–50.

McNutt, L. 1,1,3-Tricyano-2-amino-l-propene: A pharmacological attempt to enhance learning ability. *Proceedings of the American Psychological Association*, 1967, *2*, 77–78.

Messing, R. B., Jensen, R. A., Martinez, J. L., Jr., Vasquez, B. J., Soumireu-Mourat, B., & McGaugh, J. L. Naloxone enhancement and morphine impairment of memory. *Advances in Pharmacology and Therapeutics, Proceedings of the International Congress of Pharmacology, 7th, 1978*, 1979, p. 560.

Mihailovic, L., & Jankovic, B. D. Effect of intraventricularly injected anti-n. caudatus antibody on the electrical activity of the cat brain. *Nature (London)*, 1961, *192*, 665–666.

Miller, R. R., Small, D., & Berk, A. M. Information content of rat scotophobin. *Behavioral Biology*, 1975, *15*, 463–472.

Misslin, R., Ropartz, P., Ungerer, A., & Mandel, P. Non-reproducibility of the behavioral effects induced by scotophobin. *Behavioral Processes*, 1978, *3*, 45–56.

Monné, L. Functioning of the cytoplasm. *Advances in Enzymology and Related Subjects of Biochemistry*, 1948, *8*, 1–69.

Monnier, M., Dudler, L., Gachter, R., & Schoenenberger, C. A. Humoral transmission of sleep. IX. Activity and concentration of the sleep peptide delta in cerebral and systemic blood fractions. *Pflüegers Archiv*, 1975, *360*, 225–242.

Monnier, M., Dudler, L., Gachter, R., & Schoenenberger, G. A. Transport of the synthetic peptide DSIP through the blood brain barrier in rabbit. *Experientia*, 1977, *33*(12), 1609–1610.

Monnier, M., Koller, T., & Graber, S. Humoral influences of induced sleep and arousal upon electrical brain activity of animals with crossed circulation. *Experimental Neurology*, 1963, *8*, 264–277.

Moos, W. S., Levan, H., Mason, B. T., Mason, H. C., & Hebron, D. L. Radiation induced avoidance behavior transfer by brain extracts of mice. *Experientia*, 1969, *25*, 1215–1219.

Nagasaki, H., Iriki, M., Inoue, S., & Uchizono, K. The presence of a sleep-promoting material in the brain of sleep deprived rats. *Proceedings of the Japanese Academy*, 1974, *50*, 241–246.

Nagasaki, H., Kitahama, K., Valatx, J. L., & Jouvet, M. Sleep promoting effect of the sleep promoting substance (SPS) and delta-sleep-inducing peptide (DSIP) in the mouse. *Brain Research*, 1980, *192*, 276–280.

Nakajima, S. Interference with relearning in the rat after hippocampal injection of actinomycin-D. *Journal of Comparative and Physiological Psychology*, 1969, *67*, 457–461.

Neale, J. H., Klinger, P. D., & Agranoff, B. W. Camptothecin blocks memory of conditioned avoidance in the goldfish. *Science*, 1973, *179*, 1243–1246.

Oshima, K., Gorbman, A., & Shimada, H. Memory-blocking agents: Effects on olfactory discrimination in homing salmon. *Science*, 1969, *165*, 86–88.

Ott, T., & Matthies, H. Some effects of RNA precursors on development and maintenance of long term memory: Hippocampal and cortical pre- and post-training application of RNA precursors. *Psychopharmacologia*, 1973, *28*, 195–204. (a)

Ott, T., & Matthies, H. Suppression of uridine monophosphate induced improvement in long term by cycloheximide. *Psychopharmacologia*, 1973, *28*, 103–106. (b)

Pappenheimer, J. R., Miller, J. B., & Goodrich, C. A. Sleep-promoting effects of cerebrospinal fluid from sleep deprived goats. *Proceedings of the National Academy of Science of the U.S.A.*, 1967, *58*, 513–517.

Pegram, V., Hammond, D., & Bridgers, W. The effects of protein synthesis inhibition on sleep in mice. *Behavioral Biology*, 1973, *9*, 377–382.

Perumal, R., Gispen, W. H., Glassman, E., & Wilson, J. E. Phosphorylation of proteins of synaptosome-enriched fractions of brain during short-term training experience: Biochemical characterisation. *Behavioral Biology*, 1977, *21*, 341–357.

Petitjean, F., Sastre, J. P., Bertrand, N., Cointy, C., & Jouvet, M. Suppression du sommeil paradoxal par le chloramphenicol chez le chat. Absence d'effet du thiamphenicol. *Comptes Rendus des Seances de la Societe de Biologie et de Ses Filiales*, 1975, *169*, 1236–1239.

Picket, J. B. E., III, Jennings, L. B., & Wells, P. H. Influence of RNA and victim training on maze learning by cannibal planarians. *American Zoologist*, 1964, *4*, 411–412.

Polc, P., Schoenenberger, J., & Haefely, W. Effect of the delta sleep-inducing peptide (DSIP) on the sleep wakefulness cycle of cats. *Neuroscience Letters*, 1978, *9*, 33–36.

Potts, A., & Bitterman, M. E. Puromycin and retention in the goldfish. *Science*, 1967, *158*, 1594–1596.

Prado de Carvalho, L., Chapouthier, G., & Rossier, J. Effect of des-Tyr-gamma-endorphin on behavior in mice. *Neuroscience*, Supplement, 1982, *7*, 171.

Quartermain, D., & McEwen, B. S. Temporal characteristics of amnesia induced by protein synthesis inhibitors: Determination by shock level. *Nature (London)*, 1970, *228*, 677–678.

Randt, C. T., Barnett, B. M., McEwen, B. S., & Quartermain, D. Amnesic effects of cycloheximide on two strains of mice with different memory characteristics. *Experimental Neurology*, 1971, *30*, 467–474.

Rappoport, D. A., & Daginawala, H. F. Changes in nuclear RNA of brain induced by olfaction in catfish. *Journal of Neurochemistry*, 1968, *15*, 991–1006.

Reinis, S. The formation of conditioned reflexes in rats after the parenteral administration of brain homogenate. *Activitas Nervosa Superior*, 1965, *7*, 167–168.

Reinis, S. Block of "memory transfer" by actinomycin D. *Nature (London)*, 1968, *200*, 177–178.

Reinis, S. Indirect effect of puromycin on memory. *Psychonomic Science*, 1969, *14*, 44–45.

Reinis, S., & Lamble, R. W. Labeling of brain DNA by ^{3}H-thymidine during learning. *Physiological Chemistry and Physics*, 1972, *4*, 335.

Reith, M. E. A., Schotman, P., & Gispen, W. H. Hypophysectomy, ACTH-1–10 and *in vitro* protein synthesis in rat brain stem slices. *Brain Research*, 1974, *81*, 571–575.

Revusky, S. H., & DeVenuto, F. Attempt to transfer aversion to saccharine solution by injection of RNA from trained to naive rats. *Journal of Biological Psychology*, 1967, *9*(2), 18–22.

Rigter, H. Attenuation of amnesia in rats by systemically administered enkephalins. *Science*, 1978, *200*, 83–85.

Rigter, H., Creven, H., & Van Riezen, H. Failure of naloxone to prevent reduction of amnesia by enkephalins. *Neuropharmacology*, 1977, *16*, 545–547.

Rigter, H., Shuster, S., & Thody, A. J. ACTH, α-MSH and β-LPH: Pituitary hormones with similar activity in an amnesia test in rats. *Journal of Pharmacy and Pharmacology*, 1977, *29*, 110–111.

Riou, F. *Peptides et sommeil*. Thèse de doctorat de 3ème cycle, Université de Lyon I, 1981.

Roberts, J. L., & Herbert, E. Characterisation of a common precursor to corticotropin and β-lipotropin: Cell-free synthesis of the precursor and identification of corticotropin peptides in the molecule. *Proceedings of the National Academy of Sciences of the U.S.A.*, 1977, *74*, 4826–4830. (a)

Roberts, J. L., & Herbert, E. Characterisation of a common precursor to corticotropin and β-lipotropin: Identification of β-lipotropin peptides and their arrangement relative to corticotropin in the precursor synthesized in a cell-free system. *Proceedings of the National Academy of Sciences of the U.S.A.*, 1977, *74*, 5300–5304. (b)

Roberts, R. B., Flexner, J. B., & Flexner, L. B. Some evidence for the involvement of adrenergic sites in the memory trace. *Proceedings of the National Academy of Sciences of the U.S.A.*, 1970, *66*, 310–313.

Røigaard-Petersen, H. H., Nissen, T., & Fjerdingstad, E. J. Effect of ribonucleic acid (RNA) extracted from the brain of trained animals on learning in rats. III. Results obtained with an improved procedure. *Scandinavian Journal of Psychology*, 1968, *9*, 1–16.

Rojas-Ramirez, J. A., Aguilar-Jiminez, E., Posadas-Andrews, A., Bernal-Pedraza, J. G., & Drucker-Colin, R. R. The effects of various protein synthesis inhibitors on the sleep-wake cycle of rats. *Psychopharmacology*, 1977, *53*, 147–150.

Rosenblatt, F. Recent work on theoretical models of biological memory. In J. Tou (Ed.), *Computer and information sciences* (Vol. 2, pp. 33–56). New York: Academic Press, 1967.

Rosenblatt, F. Behavior induction by brain extracts: A comparison of two procedures. *Proceedings of the National Academy of Sciences of the U.S.A.*, 1969, *64*, 661–668.

Rosenblatt, F. Induction of specific behavior by mammalian brain extracts. In G. Ungar (Ed.), *Molecular mechanisms in memory and learning* (pp. 103–147). New York: Plenum Press, 1970.

Rosenblatt, F., Farrow, J. T., & Herblin, W. F. Transfer of conditioned responses from trained rats to untrained rats by means of a brain extract. *Nature (London)*, 1966, *209*, 46–48.

Rosenblatt, F., Farrow, J. T., & Rhine, S. The transfer of learned behavior from trained to untrained rats by means of brain extracts. I and II. *Proceedings of the National Academy of Sciences of the U.S.A.*, 1966, *55*, 548–555, 787–792.

Rosenblatt, F., & Miller, R. G. Behavioral assay procedures for transfer of learned behavior by brain extracts. Parts I and II. *Proceedings of the National Academy of Sciences of the U.S.A.*, 1966, *56*, 1423–1430, 1683–1688.

Rosenthal, E., & Sparber, S. B. Transfer of a learned response by chick brain homogenate fed to naive donors. *Pharmacologist*, 1968, *10*, 168.

Rossier, J., & Chapouthier, G. Brain opiates. *Endeavour*, 1982, *6(4)*, 168–176.

Routtenberg, A., Ehrlich, Y. H., & Rabjohns, R. R. Effect of training experience on phosphorylation of a specific protein in neocortical and subcortical membrane preparations. *Federation Proceedings, Federation of American Societies for Experimental Biology*, 1975, *34*, 293.

Rubinstein, M., Stein, S., & Udenfriend, S. Characterisation of pro-opiocortin, a precursor to opioid peptides and corticotropin. *Proceedings of the National Academy of Sciences of the U.S.A.*, 1978, *75*, 669–671.

Sara, S. J., Barnett, J., & Toussaint, P. Vasopressin facilitates acquisition of an appetitive discrimination task and impairs its reversal. *Behavioral Processes*, 1982, *7*(2), 157–167.

Sassin, J. F., Parker, D. C., Mace, J. W., Gotlin, R. W., Johnson, L. C., & Rossman, L. G. Human growth hormone release: Relation to slow-wave sleep and sleep-waking cycles. *Science*, 1969, *165*, 513–515.

Schmaltz, G., & Delerm, B. Effets du cycloheximide sur la mémorisation d'un apprentissage d'évitement chez le rat: Récupération mnésique. *Physiology and Behavior*, 1974, *13*, 210–220.

Schoenenberger, G. A., Cueni, L. B., Hatt, A. M., & Monnier, M. Isolation and physical-chemical characterization of a humoral, sleep inducing substance in rabbits (factor "delta"). *Experientia*, 1972, *28*, 919–921.

Schotman, P., Gispen, W. H., Jansz, H. S., & De Wied, D. Effects of ACTH analogues on macromolecule metabolism in the brain stem of hypophysectomized rats. *Brain Research*, 1972, *46*, 349–362.

Segal, D. S., Squire, L. R., & Barondès, S. H. Cycloheximide: Its effects on activity are dissociable from its effects on memory. *Science*, 1971, *172*, 82–84.

Seydoux, J., Girardier, L., Perrin, M. C., Ruphi, M., & Posternak, J. M. Essai de mise en évidence d'un conditionnement de type opérant chez la planaire *Dugesia lugubris*. *Helvetica Physiologica et Pharmacologica Acta*, 1967, *25*, 436–438.

Shashoua, V. E. RNA changes in goldfish brain during learning. *Nature (London)*, 1968, *217*, 238–240.

Smith, L. T. The interanimal transfer phenomenon: A review. *Psychological Bulletin*, 1974, *81*(12), 1078–1095.

Spanis, C. W., Gutierrez, M. C., & Drucker-Colin, R. R. Neurohumoral correlates of sleep: Further biochemical and physiological characterisation of sleep perfusates. *Pharmacology, Biochemistry and Behavior*, 1976, *5*, 165–173.

Squire, L. R., & Barondes, S. H. Actinomycin D: Effects on memory at different times after training. *Nature (London)*, 1970, *225*, 649–650.

Squire, L. R., & Barondes, S. H. Variable decay of memory and its recovery in cycloheximide-treated mice. *Proceedings of the National Academy of Sciences of the U.S.A.* 1972, *69*, 1416–1420.

Squire, L. R., & Barondes, S. H. Anisomycin, like other inhibitors of cerebral protein synthesis, impairs "long term" memory of a discrimination task. *Brain Research*, 1974, *56*, 301–308.

Stern, W. C., Jalowiec, J. E., Shabshelowitz, H., & Morgane, P. J. Effects of growth hormone on sleep-waking patterns in cat. *Hormones and Behavior*, 1975, *6*, 189–196.

Stern, W. C., Morgane, P. J., Panksepp, J., Zolovick, A. J., & Jalowiec, J. E. Elevation of REM sleep following inhibition of protein synthesis. *Brain Research*, 1972, *47*, 254–258.

Stevens, D. A., & Tapp, J. T. Effect of ventricular injections of ribonuclease on learned discrimination and avoidance tasks in the rat. *Psychological Reports*, 1966, *18*, 286.

Szilard, L. On memory and recall. *Proceedings of the National Academy of Sciences of the U.S.A.*, 1964, *51*, 1092–1099.

Takahashi, Y., Kipnis, D. M., & Daughaday, W. H. Growth hormone secretion during sleep. *Journal of Clinical Investigation*, 1968, *47*, 2079–2090.

Tata, S. R. Hormonal regulation of growth and protein synthesis. *Nature (London)*, 1968, *219*, 331–337.

Tate, D. F., Galvan, L., & Ungar, G. Isolation and identification of two learning-induced peptides. *Pharmacology, Biochemistry and Behavior*, 1976, *5*, 441–448.

Thinès, G., Domagk, G. F., & Schonne, E. The effect of synthetic scotophobin on the light tolerance of teleosts (*Carassius auratus* and *Tinca tinca*). In H. P. Zippel (Ed.), *Memory and transfer of information* (pp. 363–371). New York: Plenum Press, 1973.

Thompson, R., & McConnell, J. V. Classical conditioning in the planarian, *Dugesia dorotocephala*. *Journal of Comparative and Physiological Psychology*, 1955, *48*, 65–68.

Ungar, G. Transfer of learned behavior by brain extracts. *Journal of Biological Psychology*, 1967, *9*(1), 12–27. (a)

Ungar, G. Chemical transfer of acquired information. *Proceedings of the 5th International Congress of the Collegium Internationale Neuropsychopharmacologicum, 1967*, pp. 169–175. (b)

Ungar, G. Molecular mechanisms in learning. *Perspectives Biological Medicine*, 1968, *11*, 217–232.

Ungar, G. Molecular neurobiology: Reflections on the first ten years of a new science. *Journal of Biological Psychology*, 1969, *11*(2), 6–9.

Ungar, G. Molecular mechanisms in information processing. *International Review of Neurobiology*, 1970, *13*, 223–253. (a)

Ungar, G. Role of proteins and peptides in learning and memory. In G. Ungar (Ed.), *Molecular mechanisms in memory and learning* (pp. 149–175). New York: Plenum Press, 1970. (b)

Ungar, G. Chemical transfer of acquired information. *Methods in Pharmacology*, 1971, *1*, 479.

Ungar, G. Biochemistry of intelligence. *Research Communications in Psychology, Psychiatry and Behavior*, 1976, *1*, 597–606.

Ungar, G., & Chapouthier, G. Mécanismes moléculaires de l'utilisation de l'information par le cerveau. *Année Psychologique*, 1971, *1*, 153–183.

Ungar, G., Desiderio, D. M., & Parr, W. Isolation, Identification and synthesis of a specific-behavior-inducing brain peptide. *Nature (London)*, 1972, *238*, 198–202.

Ungar, G., & Fjerdingstad, E. J. Chemical nature of the transfer factors: RNA or protein? Proceedings of the Symposium on Biology of Memory (Tihany, Hungary, septembre 1–4, 1969). In G. Adam (Ed.), *Biology of memory* (pp. 137–143). New York: Plenum Press, 1971.

Ungar, G., Galvan, L., & Chapouthier, G. Evidence for chemical coding of color discrimination in goldfish brain. *Experientia*, 1972, *28*, 1026–1027.

Ungar, G., Galvan, L., & Clark, R. H. Chemical transfer of learned fear. *Nature (London)*, 1968, *217*, 1259–1261.

Ungar, G., & Irwin, L. N. Transfer of acquired information by brain extracts. *Nature (London)*, 1967, *214*, 453–455.

Ungar, G., & Oceguera-Navarro, C. Transfer of habituation by material extracted from brain. *Nature (London)*, 1965, *207*, 301–302.

Ungerer, A. Antibiotiques et mémoire: Rôle de l'ARN et de la synthèse protéique dans la fixation de la mémoire. *Revue de Comportement Animal*, 1969, *3*, 72–80. (a)

Ungerer, A. Effets comparés de la puromycine et de *Datura stramonium* sur la rétention d'un apprentissage instrumental chez la souris. *Comptes Rendus Hebdomadaires des Séances de l'Academie des Sciences, Serie D*, 1969, *269*, 910–913. (b)

Ungerer, A. Effets de la puromycine sur la rétention d'un apprentissage instrumental chez la souris. *Physiology and Behavior*, 1971, *7*, 811–814.

Ungerer, A. *Analyse des déficits mnésiques induits par les inhibiteurs de la synthèse protéique chez la souris*. Thèse de Doctorat ès-Sciences, Strasbourg, Université Louis Pasteur, 1975.

Ungerer, A., & Chapouthier, G. Shuttle box learning in mice after puromycin injections. *Folia Biologica (Krakow)*, 1975, *23*(1), 73–79.

Ungerer, A., Spitz, S., & Chapouthier, G. Sur les polypeptides toxiques impliqués par Flexner dans l'effacement de la mémoire par la puromycine. *Comptes Rendus Hebdomadaires des Seances de l'Academie des Sciences, Serie D,* 1969, *268,* 2472–2475.

Uphouse, L. L., McInnes, J. W., & Schlesinger, K. Role of RNA and protein in memory storage: A review. *Behavioral Genetics,* 1974, *4*(1), 29–79.

Warburton, D. M., & Russell, R. W. Effect of 8-azaguanine on acquisition of a temporal discrimination. *Physiology and Behavior,* 1968, *3,* 61–63.

Watts, M. E., & Mark, R. F. Separate actions of ouabain and cycloheximide on memory. *Brain Research,* 1971, *25,* 420–423.

Weinstein, B., Bartschot, R. M., Cook, R. M., Tam, P. S., & Guttman, H. N. The synthesis of a peptide having the structure attributed to a sound habituating material. *Experientia,* 1975, *31*(7), 754–756.

Weiss, K. P. Measurement of the effects of brain extract on interorganism information transfer. In W. L. Byrne (Ed.), *Molecular approaches to learning and memory* (pp. 325–334). New York: Academic Press, 1970.

Westerman, R. A. Somatic inheritance of habituation of responses to light in planarians. *Science,* 1963, *140,* 676–677.

Wiegant, V. M., Gispen, W. H., Terenius, L., & De Wied, D. ACTH-like peptides and morphine: Interaction at the level of the CNS. *Psychoneuroendocrinology,* 1977, *2,* 63–69.

Wojcik, M., Mitros, K., Jastreboff, P. J., & Zielinski, K. The variability of innate darkness preference in mice: An evaluation of Ungar's design. *Acta Neurobiologiae Experimentalis,* 1975, *35,* 285–298.

Wolthuis, O. L. Inter-animal information transfer by brain extracts. *Archives Internationales de Pharmacodynamie et de Therapie,* 1969, *182,* 439–442.

Wolthuis, O. L., Anthoni, J. F., & Stevens, W. F. Interanimal transfer of information by brain extracts. *Acta Physiologica et Pharmacologica Neerlandica,* 1968, *15,* 93.

Zippel, H. P., & Domagk, G. F. Versuche zur Chemischen Gedachtnisübertragung von farbdressierten Goldfischen auf undressierte Tiere. *Experientia,* 1969, *25,* 938–940.

CHAPTER

2

FACILITATION OF MEMORY CONSOLIDATION[1]

JOE L. MARTINEZ, JR., ROBERT A. JENSEN, and
JAMES L. McGAUGH

Department of Psychobiology
School of Biological Sciences
University of California, Irvine
Irvine, California

I. INTRODUCTION

Humans, animals, and other creatures are capable of modifying their behavior as a result of encounters with their environment during the normal course
of their existence. If the modified behavior is not due to innate response tendencies, normal development, or temporary states induced by drugs or other causes,

[1]The research reported in this chapter that was conducted by the authors was supported by
research grants MH 12526 and AG 00538 from the U.S. Public Health Service.

then we may infer that learning has taken place. Since learning is a unique property of the individual organism, it follows that some processes within the organism are modified as a result of experience. Most have considered learning to be an exclusive property of the central nervous system (see Rosenzweig & Bennett, 1976), although some have suggested that neuroendocrine systems may be involved as well (Levine, 1968).

Learning seems logically to involve at least three different functions. First, the organism has to acquire the altered behavior. Second, once acquired, the altered behavior may be exhibited for some period of time; therefore, it has to be stored. Third, if the altered behavior is acquired, stored, and periodically evident, then it must be retrieved from storage. Some who study this question consider acquisition to be the process and storage to be the product of acquisition. Thus, Thompson, Patterson, and Berger (1978) define an engram as the set of physical changes that occur in the brain during learning. However, there is extensive evidence to support the view (Müller & Pilzecker, 1900) that an experience is not permanently stored in memory for some period of time after it has occurred (see McGaugh & Herz, 1972). Thus, memory storage may require active processes continuing after the experience has occurred.

Early experimental evidence for this suggestion that memories are labile for a period of time following an experience was provided by studies in which rats were given electroconvulsive shock (ECS) shortly after training (Duncan, 1949). The ECS impaired retention. The degree of impairment was greatest with a short training–treatment interval. The gradient of retrograde amnesia is usually interpreted as indicating that the treatment interfered with time-dependent processes underlying memory consolidation (McGaugh, 1966). It should be noted that this interpretation has not gone unchallenged, and discussion of alternative interpretations appears elsewhere (McGaugh & Herz, 1972; Spear, 1973).

Retrograde amnesia is readily produced by a variety of treatments including electrical stimulation of the brain, drugs, and hormones (see Barraco & Stettner, 1976; Dunn, 1980; Squire & Davis, 1981). However, it is increasingly clear (Martinez, Jensen, & McGaugh, 1981) that many treatments that produce amnesia will also enhance memory under appropriate experimental conditions (Gold, Hankins, Chester, Edwards, & McGaugh, 1975; Gold & van Buskirk, 1976b; Martinez, Vasquez, Jensen, & McGaugh, 1977). The treatments do not simply enhance or impair memory. Rather, they modulate. It is within this broader concept of memory modulation that we arrive at the subject matter of this chapter, enhancement of memory consolidation.

II. PRETRAINING VERSUS POSTTRAINING
   TREATMENTS

Before we proceed to a discussion of other issues concerning memory it is important to consider when the experimental treatment is given relative to the

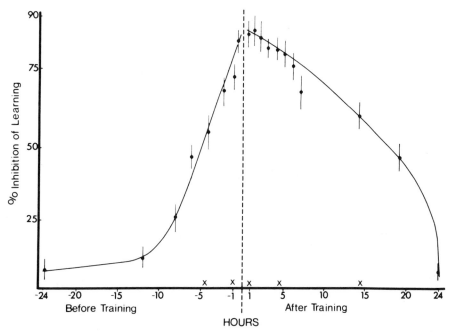

Figure 2.1. Inhibition of learning ($\pm$ SEM) following intraventricular injection of antiserum to brain gangliosides into groups of mice ($n = 12$) at varying time intervals before and after training on a step-through passive avoidance task. Control groups of mice injected with the antiserum previously absorbed with pure G_{M1} ganglioside to remove antibodies (X) demonstrated no inhibition of learning ($p < .01$). From Karpiak and Rapport, 1979.

training. As noted earlier, one can only infer that learning has been affected if the modified behavior is not due to a temporary state induced by drugs or other causes. If a drug is given before training, it cannot be known whether the drug affected learning by influencing performance through actions on other variables, such as attention, motivation, or arousal. Surprisingly little research has been directed to determining whether the effect on learning of a drug given pre- or posttrial is qualitatively different. In one such study Karpiak and Rapport (1979) administered antiserum to brain ganglioside intraventricularly to groups of mice at various time intervals either before or after training in an inhibitory avoidance task. The mice were tested for retention 7 days after training. It may be seen in Figure 2.1 that the antibody impaired retention performance whether it was administered before or after training. However, the nature of the curves obtained with pre- or posttrial administration are strikingly different and appear to be accelerated at different rates. Thus, one interpretation of these data is that different processes appear to be affected by pre- or posttrial injections, even though the behavioral outcome of impairment of retention performance was the same.

If an experimental treatment affects different processes when administered

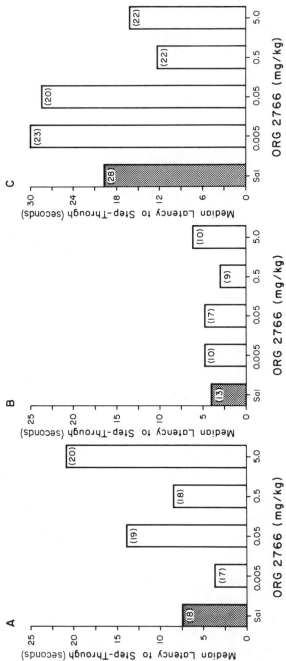

Figure 2.2. This figure demonstrates that 5.0 mg/kg ORG 2766 given 1 hour before training significantly ($p < .05$) facilitates acquisition of an inhibitory avoidance response in F344 rats (A). A 4-log unit dose range, 0.005–5.0 mg/kg ORG 2766, does not affect retention performance if it is administered either (B) immediately after training or (C) 1 hour before the retention test. However, an injection given before the retention test seems to be arousing, as all of the retention scores in this condition (C) are generally elevated and the saline control group in this condition differs significantly from the combined pre- and immediate posttrial saline control groups ($p < .01$). Note that the scale on the ordinate of (C) differs from (A) and (B). The numbers in parentheses, in each bar of the figure, are the number of animals in each experimental condition. From Martinez, Vasquez, Jansen, Soumireu-Mourat, and McGaugh, 1979.

before or after training, then there should be treatments that are only effective if given before or after training. For example, Martinez, Vasquez, Jensen, Soumireu-Mourat, and McGaugh (1979) administered a wide dose range of an ACTH(4–9) analog (Org 2766) to groups of rats either before or after training in an inhibitory avoidance task. The animals were tested for retention 24 hours after training. Figure 2.2 shows that a 5.0 mg/kg dose of Org 2766 given 1 hour before training significantly enhanced later retention performance, whereas a wide range of doses of Org 2766 given following training or before the retention test was without effect. The converse is also true. Martinez, Jensen, Vasquez, McGuinness, and McGaugh (1978) reported that a 1.0 mg/kg dose of methylene blue administered to rats enhanced retention of an inhibitory avoidance response only if it was given immediately after training and not 15 minutes before or 6 hours after training, or 15 minutes before retention testing. As before, one interpretation of these results is that different processes are affected by pre- or posttraining injections.

Taken together, the results of these studies suggest that those interested in studying memory consolidation should use posttraining treatments. Further, a posttraining treatment has the added advantage that the animal is in a normal state at the time of training and testing. It is important to recognize that performance is markedly influenced by the drug state of the animal at the time of training and testing. For discussion of this issue, see Colpaert (1977), Overton (1968, 1974), and Riccio and Concannon (1981).

III. TIME DEPENDENCY

As noted in Section I, the best evidence for the idea that memories are not permanently stored until some time after they occur is provided by demonstrations of time dependence. Further, if retrograde enhancement of memory is a form of memory modulation, and in a sense the opposite side of the coin of retrograde amnesia, then the effectiveness of an enhancing treatment should decrease as the training–treatment interval increases, as it does for memory-impairing treatments. Numerous studies have shown this to be the case. In one study, for example (McGaugh, 1968), mice were administered strychnine sulfate at various times after they were trained on a visual discrimination task. It may be seen in Figure 2.3 that retention was enhanced by strychnine administered only within 60 minutes following training. Thus, retrograde enhancement of memory is a time-dependent process as is retrograde amnesia produced by ECS or other amnestic agents.

Retrograde gradients of enhancement appear to be a general phenomenon that applies to rather diverse conditioning situations. Another example of this is provided by Destrade, Soumireu-Mourat, and Cardo (1973). They trained mice, which were implanted with chronic indwelling hippocampal electrodes, to learn

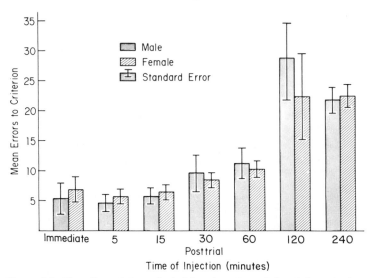

Figure 2.3. The effect of time of administration of strychnine (1.0 mg/kg ip) on visual discrimination learning in mice. From McGaugh, 1968.

an operant response for food reward. On the first day of training, the mice were given a continuous reinforcement schedule for a single 15-minute session. Following this, different groups of mice were given subseizure stimulation of the hippocampus at various intervals following the end of the training session. The number of bar presses the animals made during the first 5 minutes of a testing session on the following day may be seen in Figure 2.4. Stimulation given 30, 200, or 400, but not 600 seconds following training on Day 1 enhanced memory consolidation.

Examination of Figures 2.3 and 2.4 will reveal an important issue concerning the meaning of retrograde gradients of effectiveness. On one hand, the fact of time dependency of posttraining treatments suggests that memories are labile for a period of time following training. On the other hand, an examination of the range of times in which the posttrial treatment was effective, hours in the case of McGaugh (1968) and minutes in the case of Destrade *et al.* (1973), does not allow one to estimate the duration of memorial processes. In some experiments treatments affect memory when given 1 day or more following training (Mah & Albert, 1975). In a study of the amnestic effects of posttraining lesions on retention of an inhibitory avoidance task, Liang, McGaugh, Martinez, Jensen, Vasquez, and Messing (1982) found that lesions made up to 2 days following training produced retrograde amnesia. Thus, retrograde gradients of effectiveness do not give you precise information about the rate of consolidation. Some have suggested that this lack of time constancy precludes an understanding of the

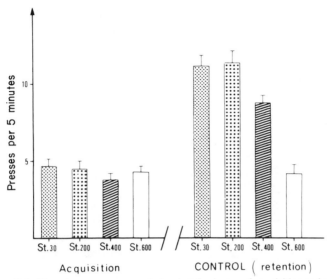

Figure 2.4. Mean lever press scores during last 5 minutes of acquisition and during first 5 minutes of control for the 30-, 200-, 400-, and 600-second posttrial stimulated groups (St.$_{30}$, St.$_{200}$, St.$_{400}$, St.$_{600}$) (means ± SEM). Sample size for each group = 10. From Destrade, Soumireu-Mourat, and Cardo, 1973.

physiological basis of memory consolidation (Chorover, 1976). Yet, even Chorover (1976) admits that "in a fundamental sense, the idea of consolidation is inescapable . . . and must necessarily be correct in outline [p. 563]." It is important to remember that retrograde gradients yield information about the interactive effects of a training experience with the nature and strength of the experimental treatment. If the relative effect of either of these components on the other is variable, then there is no reason to expect a time constant to emerge. In addition, a retrograde gradient is a global measure of susceptibility to change in a temporal sense of an experimental treatment that may affect one or more ongoing processes. If multiple processes are affected, then again, one would not expect a single time constant to emerge.

IV. MEMORY MODULATION

As noted earlier (Section I), a variety of experimental manipulations of CNS or endocrine functioning can modulate memory. Whether enhancement or impairment is observed depends primarily on the strength of the experimental treatment, the strength of the training experience, and the interaction between the experience and the treatment. This principle was first demonstrated by Bloch

(1970) who showed that posttraining stimulation of the brain can produce enhancement of memory as well as retrograde amnesia.

A good example of memory modulation is provided by the research of Gold and van Buskirk (1976b). In this study groups of rats were trained in an inhibitory avoidance task at different foot-shock intensities and given either 3 or 6 IU of ACTH immediately following training. The rats were given a retention test 24 hours later. Figure 2.5 below shows that at the lowest footshock level used (0.4 mA) both doses of ACTH-enhanced memory. At the next lowest level (0.5 mA) only the 3 IU dose was enhancing, and as the footshock was increased to 0.7 and 2.0 mA, both doses of ACTH produced retrograde amnesia. Thus, whether enhancement or impairment is observed with posttrial ACTH treatment depends on the level of the training footshock.

As noted above, it is also possible to observe enhancement or impairment, if only the dose or strength of the experimental treatment is varied. Gold and van Buskirk (1976a) using the same task and training procedures found, if different groups of rats are trained with a 0.7-mA footshock and given different doses of

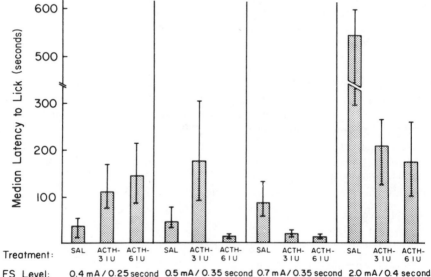

Figure 2.5. Median retention latencies (and interquartile ranges) of rats that were trained in an inhibitory (passive) avoidance task and received posttrial saline (SAL) of ACTH (3 or 6 IU) injections. Note that the 3-IU ACTH dose enhanced later retention of training with the two lowest footshock (FS) levels, but disrupted retention of training with the two highest footshock levels. The 6-IU ACTH injection significantly enhanced retention only of the lowest footshock level. This ACTH dose significantly impaired retention of training with all other footshock levels. From Gold and van Buskirk, 1976b.

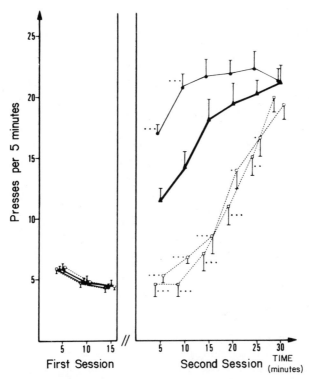

Figure 2.6. Performances registered during the first and second session for the different groups (10 animals by group). Statistical comparisons are made between each stimulated group and the nonstimulated group (xxx $p < .001$; xx $p < .01$; x $p < .02$). N.St. (▲- - -▲), no stimulation; N.HAD 80 (●———●), stimulation for 80 seconds that was one half of the amount needed to produce a hippocampal afterdischarge; HAD 4 (○- - -○) and HAD 8 (□- - -□), stimulation at threshold for hippocampal after discharge for 4 or 8 seconds, respectively. From Soumireu-Mourat, Destrade, and Cardo, 1975.

ACTH posttrial, that low doses (0.03 and 0.3 IU) enhance later retention performance and a higher dose of 3.0 IU impairs retention.

    Another example of this type of memory modulation was reported by Soumireu-Mourat, Destrade, and Cardo (1975), using the appetitive operant procedure described earlier (see Section III). In this case whether enhancement or impairment was observed depended on the current intensity of the hippocampal stimulation. The number of bar presses the mice made during the 15-minute acquisition session on Day 1 of their experiment may be found in the left panel of Figure 2.6. Following this acquisition session different groups of mice were given either no stimulation (N.St.), stimulation for 80 seconds that was one-half of the amount of current needed to produce a hippocampal afterdischarge

(N.HAD 80), or stimulation that was at the threshold for producing hippocampal afterdischarge activity for either 4 seconds (HAD 4) or 80 seconds (HAD 80). The right panel of Figure 2.6 shows that on Day 2 of the experiment, 24 hours after training and brain stimulation, enhanced retention performance was observed in the group that received subseizure hippocampal stimulation, and impaired retention performance was observed in the two groups that received supraseizure stimulation. Thus, manipulation of the strength of the reinforcing stimulus or the experimental treatment may lead to either enhancement or impairment. The outcome appears to depend on the interactive effects of the two variables.

Another important question that emerges from a discussion of memory modulation is whether experimental treatments alter retention by influencing processes involved in memory storage or whether they directly affect the neural substrate or storage. An analogy of this distinction is provided by considering a hypothetical process in which complex hydrocarbons may be combined under conditions of temperature and pressure to produce coal. Temperature and pressure may be altered so that the efficiency of coal production may be retarded or enhanced (mechanisms influencing memory storage) or the very nature of the end product itself is changed so that instead of coal, the process yields diamonds (substrate of storage). Memory modulation as presently conceived could be affecting memory at either level.

One interpretation of Duncan's (1949) experiment was that ECS produced retrograde amnesia by disrupting the substrate of storage. However, the concept of memory modulation suggests that even ECS under appropriate experimental conditions might produce retrograde enhancement of memory. Recently, Sternberg, McGaugh, and Gold (1981) reported that seizure-producing frontal cortex stimulation enhanced retention of an active avoidance task. In their study, groups of rats were given either a saline or propranolol (0.5 mg/kg) injection 30 minutes before receiving eight training trials on Day 1 of the experiment. All rats were given brain stimulation following training, and were given eight additional training trials on Day 2. The difference (Day 2 − Day 1) between the number of avoidances the animals made on the two days may be seen in Figure 2.7. Frontal cortex stimulation produced retrograde enhancement and, interestingly, this effect was blocked by propranolol, suggesting that antagonism of adrenergic systems may attenuate experimentally induced amnesia (see below).

At the level of the CNS and associated neuroendocrine systems, memory modulation may be thought of as different brain states. Each experimental treatment no doubt has a unique set of effects on brain functioning, and there are, no doubt, many kinds of specific changes in neurobiological functioning that will affect memory storage processes. Some brain states lead to amnesia and others lead to enhancement of memory. Memory modulation, according to this view, results from induction of brain states that are more or less optimal for memory storage.

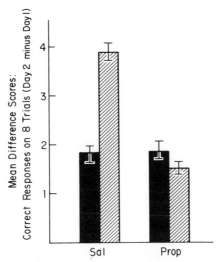

Figure 2.7. Low footshock and frontal cortex stimulation (5 mA/1 second). Frontal cortex stimulation (ECS) facilitates acquisition of a one-way active avoidance response in rats. The rats were given eight training trials on Day 1 and Day 2. The difference in the number of avoidances made on Day 2 − Day 1 is considered to be a measure of retention performance. Propranolol (Prop) (5.0 mg/kg, ip) given 30 minutes before training blocked the facilitating effect of frontal cortex stimulation. Sal, saline; ■, no stimulation; ▨, stimulation. From Sternberg, McGaugh, and Gold, 1981.

V. ATTENUATION OF EXPERIMENTALLY INDUCED AMNESIA

Most researchers wish to attenuate or reverse amnesia in order to specify which CNS or endocrine alteration produced by an amnestic agent is important for learning or memory. It should be possible to demonstrate, through the use of another agent or treatment, that the effect of an amnestic treatment is due to some specific mechanism.

For example, early research on this issue indicated that stimulant drugs, such as amphetamine and strychnine, attenuated amnesia induced by ECS (Bivens & Ray, 1966; McGaugh, 1968) or the protein synthesis inhibitor, cycloheximide (Barondes & Cohen, 1968). These findings suggested (Dawson & McGaugh, 1973) that the amnestic treatment interrupted memory consolidation processes and that the effect of the stimulant drug may be to restart consolidation. However, these results can be viewed somewhat differently. Martinez *et al.* (1981) noted that most treatments that attenuate amnesia will also enhance learning and memory in the absence of any amnestic treatment. Thus, treatments that make memory better might act in this manner when pitted against an amnestic agent.

This principle suggests that an experimental treatment may attenuate am-

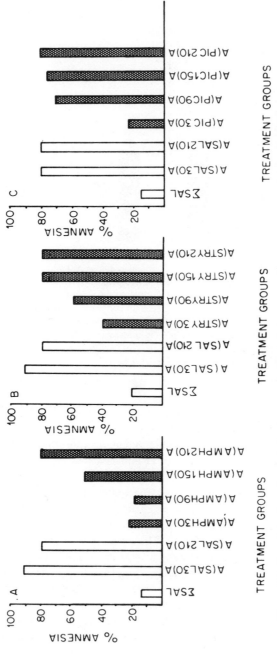

Figure 2.8. Time-dependent effects of stimulants on anisomycin-induced amnesia (N = 20/group). (A) d-Amphetamine blocked amnesia caused by anisomycin when given 30 or 90 minutes after passive avoidance training. d-Amphetamine failed to block amnesia when given 210 minutes after training. (B) Amnesia was blocked with a 30-minute posttraining injection of strychnine, and a slight effect was present with a 90-minute posttraining injection. Strychnine did not block anisomycin-induced amnesia when given 150 or 210 minutes after training. (C) Picrotoxin only blocked amnesia when administered 30 minutes after training. ΣSal, total saline; Anisomycin (drug and time)A. From Flood, Jarvik, Bennett, Orme, and Rosenzweig, 1977.

nesia even though its actions are unrelated to the primary effects of the amnestic agent. An experiment conducted by Flood, Jarvik, Bennett, Orme, and Rosenzweig (1977) illustrates this point. In this experiment groups of mice were trained in an inhibitory avoidance task; given the antibiotic protein synthesis inhibitor anisomycin both before and after training; given amphetamine, picrotoxin, or strychnine at various intervals following training; and tested for retention 1 week later. As may be seen in Figure 2.8, all three neural excitants were found to attenuate the amnesia induced by anisomycin if they were injected within 30 minutes of the training event, although none of these treatments significantly reversed the inhibition of protein synthesis induced by anisomycin. Thus, attenuation of amnesia may be understood in a general way as a form of memory modulation. Whether enhancement or impairment is observed depends on the strength of the training experience, the strength of the experimental treatments, and how these variables interact.

VI. ON THE NATURE OF SPECIFICITY

The most difficult problem faced in learning and memory research concerns the issue of specificity. This is true whether one investigates biochemical correlates of training (Dunn, 1976), neuroanatomical correlates of training (Greenough, 1978), neurophysiological correlates of training (Thompson et al., 1978), drug effects on training (Quartermain, 1976), brain lesions on learning and memory (Isaacson, 1976), or even simple invertebrate model systems (Davis, 1976). The problem is that a treatment or training experience has many effects. Which are the one(s) involved in learning and memory?

In studies of memory modulation, those interested in defining which neurobiological systems are involved in memory storage processes have relied on two basic strategies. The first involves the stimulation of restricted areas of the brain to determine which brain area, nucleus, or groups of cells modulate memory. The second involves the administration of drugs, which have well-characterized and limited actions, into the general circulation or restricted regions of the brain.

The first approach is of course a direct outgrowth of Duncan's (1949) study showing that ECS produces retrograde amnesia for an active avoidance task. It is reasonable to suppose that a treatment that causes amnesia by passing a seizure-inducing current through the brain may be producing its effect through stimulation of rather restricted areas of the brain. A search for those areas of the brain that will affect memory storage processes led to three interesting findings. First, it is apparent that posttrial stimulation of many brain areas, including amygdala (McDonough & Kesner, 1971), caudate nucleus (Thompson, 1958), entorhinal cortex (Martinez, McGaugh, Hanes, & Lacob, 1977), hippocampus (Wyers, Peeke, Williston, & Herz, 1968), thalamus (Mahut, 1964), midbrain reticular formation (Glickman, 1958), and substantia nigra (Routtenberg & Holzman, 1973), all produce retrograde amnesia (for review, see McGaugh & Gold, 1976). Second, in all of the studies cited above the effective stimulation was below seizure threshold, suggesting that the effect was initiated from the stimulated site. It is important to note, however, that even though an effect is initiated at a particular site, its effect on memory may be mediated locally, some distance away, or both. Third, in many instances localized stimulation of the brain was found to produce enhancement of memory (see, for example, Bloch, 1970; Gold *et al.*, 1975; Soumireu-Mourat *et al.*, 1975), which once again points out the modulatory nature of these treatments.

As noted above, other investigators strive to achieve specificity through the use of drugs with well-characterized actions. A good example of this approach is provided by Messing, Jensen, Martinez, Spiehler, Vasquez, Soumireu-Mourat, Liang, and McGaugh (1979). They trained groups of rats in an inhibitory avoidance task and administered the specific opiate antagonist naloxone ip at various doses immediately and 30 minutes following training. The animals were given a retention test 24 hours later. It may be seen in Figure 2.9 (left panel) that a total dose of 1.0 mg/kg was found to enhance memory. In order to test for specificity, other groups of rats were given the facilitating dose of naloxone (1.0 mg/kg) and a total dose of 30.0 mg/kg of the opiate agonist morphine. If the enhancing effects of naloxone were mediated through a specific action on opioid receptors,

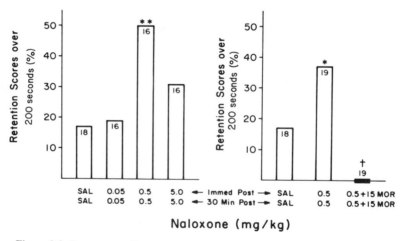

Figure 2.9. Percentage ceiling retention latencies of rats after naloxone or combined naloxone and morphine administration in a one-trial inhibitory avoidance task using 500-μA shock. †, $p < .1$; *, $p < .05$; **, $p < .01$ compared to the saline (SAL)-injected control group, using a χ^2 test ($df = 1$) with Yates' correction. MOR, morphine. From Messing, Jensen, Martinez, Spiehler, Vasquez, Soumireu-Mourat, Liang, and McGaugh, 1979.

then the morphine should block the effect of naloxone. As expected (Figure 2.9, right panel), the naloxone was again found to enhance memory, and this effect was blocked by morphine.

The results of the study by Messing *et al.* (1979) suggest that under appropriate experimental conditions, antagonism of opioid receptors leads to memory enhancement. Although specificity appears to be achieved by limiting the effect to opioid receptors, the fact that the drug was administered systemically, and was widely distributed in the body, precludes localization of the important receptors. In this regard, it is interesting that Gallagher and Kapp (1978) found that naloxone administered directly into the amygdala posttrial enhanced retention of an inhibitory avoidance response, and that the effect was blocked by the opiate agonist levorphanol. Thus, as with ECS, an effect of an experimental treatment that is widespread in nature may be reproduced by more local administration. This finding lends support to the suggestion that memory modulatory systems may be defined and characterized. However, it should be pointed out that if an experimental treatment attenuates amnesia, even though its actions are unrelated to the primary effects of the amnestic agent (Flood *et al.*, 1977), then the opposite may be true as well. Existence of attenuation of enhancement by an experimental treatment is not, considered alone, proof of specificity.

VI. PERIPHERAL MECHANISMS

Levine (1968) pointed out many years ago that neuroendocrine systems may be important for learning and memory. Others have suggested that certain peripheral hormones are not only important for learning and memory, but that they may be a part of the normal machinery of learning and memory (Martinez, 1982). In the normal course of environmental encounters, which may lead to learning, the hormonal responses of an animal or human *follow* the encounter. Thus, experimental procedures that administer a hormone, or a substance that acts in some way on a hormonal system, following a training experience, mimic a normal physiological process (Gold & McGaugh, 1977).

A study using this approach was described earlier (Section IV). Peripherally administered ACTH either enhanced or impaired memory depending on the dose of ACTH and the level of the training footshock (Gold & van Buskirk, 1976a, 1976b). Similarly, the hormones vasopressin (Bohus, van Wimersma Greidanus, Urban, & de Wied, 1977; van Wimersma Greidanus, Bohus, & de Wied, 1981), epinephrine, and norepinephrine (Gold & van Buskirk, 1975, 1976a) have all been reported to enhance retention of an inhibitory avoidance response.

In the case of epinephrine and norepinephrine, their memory modulatory actions are somewhat puzzling, as they are not thought to cross the blood–brain barrier in very great quantities, if at all. This suggests not only that peripheral hormonal systems may be involved in learning and memory, but that the primary site of action of these hormones may be in the periphery as well. ACTH, on the other hand, is known to have the adrenal cortex as its primary target, and the memory modulatory effects of ACTH may be mediated through glucocorticoids which are released by the adrenal cortex. However, de Wied (1974) suggested that many peptides hormones such as ACTH have a behavioral message encoded into certain of their amino acid sequences, as well as an endocrinological message. He proposed that sequences of ACTH such as ACTH(4–10) may be enzymatically freed from the whole ACTH molecule, and that it is these peptides that may be responsible for the behavioral actions of ACTH. This view is supported by evidence that fragments of ACTH [e.g., ACTH(4–10)] that do not affect the adrenal cortex influence learning and memory.

If peripheral hormonal systems are part of the normal machinery of learning and memory, it would not be surprising to find that some drug effects on learning and memory were mediated by these peripheral systems. There is extensive evidence that retention is enhanced by posttraining amphetamine administered ip (see McGaugh, 1973). However, Martinez, Jensen, Messing, Vasquez, Soumireu-Mourat, Geddes, Liang, and McGaugh (1980b) reported that a large dose range of d-amphetamine given intracerebroventricularly following training in an inhibitory avoidance task did not alter retention. This finding was paradoxical, as it was generally accepted that amphetamine affects learning and memory through an action on CNS catecholamine systems (see McGaugh, 1973). Additional studies suggested that the effect of amphetamine on memory was related to peripheral catecholamine function.

In these studies groups of rats were trained in an inhibitory avoidance task and were given posttrial one of several doses of either d-amphetamine or dl-4-hydroxyamphetamine, a form of amphetamine that crosses into the brain less freely than d-amphetamine (Martinez *et al.*, 1980b; Martinez, Vasquez, Rigter, Messing, Jensen, Liang, & McGaugh, 1980a). A retention test was given 72 hours following training. It was found that both amphetamines enhanced retention of the response at similar doses. The dose–response curve of the 4-hydroxyamphetamine may be found in Figure 2.10.

In order to determine which peripheral adrenergic system was involved in the amphetamine-induced enhancement of memory, further experiments were conducted using 6-hydroxydopamine, which produces a chemical sympathectomy, or adrenal medullectomy to remove important peripheral stores of catecholamines. Sympathectomy shifted the effective dose of both amphetamine and 4-hydroxyamphetamine to lower doses, whereas adrenal medullectomy abolished the enhancing actions of both amphetamines (Martinez *et al.*, 1980a; Martinez *et al.*, 1980b). Taken together, these studies indicate that

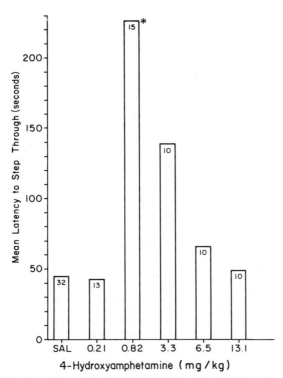

Figure 2.10. Immediate posttrial treatment (ip) with a 0.82 mg/kg dose of *dl*-4-hy-droxyamphetamine significantly (*p* < .01) enhances retention performance tested 72 hours following training in an inhibitory avoidance task (500 μA footshock for 1 second). The number of Sprague-Dowley rats used in each dose condition is shown in the bars. SAL, saline; *, p < .05. From Martinez, Vasquez, Rigter, Messing, Jensen, Liang, and McGaugh, 1980.

amphetamine may affect memory by acting primarily on the adrenal medulla (see Martinez, 1982), presumably by initiating release of its contents.

Others have also found that alteration of peripheral adrenergic systems may influence memory. Palfai and Walsh (1979) and Walsh and Palfai (1979), in two interesting studies, found evidence suggesting that the amnestic actions of reserpine are mediated through peripheral systems. They found that reserpine or the peripherally acting reserpine analogue, syrosingopine, administered to mice 2 hours prior to training produced a retention deficit for an inhibitory avoidance response. Either dopamine or norepinephrine, administered systemically, attenuated both the reserpine- and the syrosingopine-induced amnesia. Also, Sternberg and Gold (1980) found that phentolamine, an α-adrenergic antagonist with a limited ability to cross the blood–brain barrier, attenuated amnesia for an inhibitory avoidance response in rats induced by frontal cortex stimulation. These studies point out once again the principle that experimental treatment, in this case, treatment that appears to primarily affect peripheral systems, may attenuate amnesia, even though their actions may be unrelated to the primary effects of the amnestic treatment.

Today, most would agree that peripheral hormonal mechanisms influence the strength of a learned response (see Leshner, 1978). It is likely that the nature of the actions of hormones on memory is modulatory. Memory may be either enhanced or impaired depending on the conditions under which the learning experience occurred. It is also likely that these hormonal systems normally function in memory storage processes, but are not part of the substrate of storage. However, the necessity of these systems for memory has not been established. It may be that memory storage may proceed in the absence of peripheral influences, or it is possible that peripheral influences are necessary for memory storage to proceed.

VIII. CONCLUSIONS

Facilitation of memory consolidation appears to be a rather general phenomenon because it occurs in diverse conditioning situations with diverse experimental treatments. This fact suggests that memory storage is not a unitary process and reflects the simultaneous operation of many CNS and neuroendocrinological systems.

The time-dependent nature of memory enhancement suggests that memory storage is an active process and that it is susceptible to manipulation for a period of time after the training experience. However, retrograde gradients of enhancement have variable time courses, as do retrograde amnesia gradients. The variable time course appears to be the result of the interactive effects of the strength of the training experience and the nature and strength of the experimental treatment.

Experimental treatments such as ECS may either enhance or impair memory depending on the experimental conditions of the training experience. Thus, a more appropriate term for manipulation or CNS or endocrine functioning that leads to changes in the strength of a stored memory is modulation. Each set of changes may be viewed as a brain state. Some brain states lead to amnesia and others lead to enhancement of memory. We suggest that memory modulation results from the induction of brain states that are more or less optimal for memory storage.

Finally, peripheral hormonal mechanisms appear to be part of the normal physiology of learning and memory. It appears that the action of hormones on memory is modulatory in nature, and the strength of a learned response may depend on the action of one or more hormonal systems.

REFERENCES

Barondes, S. H., & Cohen, H. D. Arousal and the conversion of short-term memory to long-term memory. *Proceedings of the National Academy of Sciences of the U.S.A.*, 1968, *61*, 923–929.

Barraco, R. A., & Stettner, L. J. Antibiotics and memory. *Psychological Bulletin*, 1976, *83*, 242–302.

Bivens, L. W., & Ray, O. S. Effects of electroconvulsive shock and strychnine sulfate on memory consolidation. *In* H. Brill (Ed.), *Neuro-psycho-pharmacology* (pp. 1030–1034). Amsterdam: Mouton, 1966.

Bloch, V. Facts and hypotheses concerning memory consolidation. *Brain Research*, 1970, *24*, 561–575.

Bohus, B., van Wimersma Greidanus, Tj. B., Urban, I., and de Wied, D. Hypothalamo-neurohypophyseal hormone effects on memory and related functions in the rat. *In* R. R. Drucker-Colin & J. L. McGaugh (Eds.), *Neurobiology of sleep and memory* (pp. 333–346). New York: Academic Press, 1977.

Chorover, S. An experimental critique of "consolidation studies" and an alternative "model systems" approach to the biopsychology of memory. *In* M. R. Rosenzweig & E. L. Bennett (Eds.), *Neural mechanisms of learning and memory* (pp. 561–582). Cambridge, MA: MIT Press, 1976.

Colpaert, F. L. Drug-induced cues and states: Some theoretical and methodological inferences. *In* H. Lal (Ed.), *Discriminative stimulus properties of drugs* (pp. 5–21). New York: Plenum Press, 1977.

Davis, W. J. Plasticity in invertebrates. In M. R. Rosenzweig & E. L. Bennett (Eds.), *Neural mechanisms of learning and memory* (pp. 430–462). Cambridge, MA: MIT Press, 1976.

Dawson, R. G., & McGaugh, J. L. Drug facilitation of learning and memory. *In* J. A. Deutsch (Ed.), *The physiological basis of memory* (pp. 77–111). New York: Academic Press, 1973.

Destrade, C., Soumireu-Mourat, B., & Cardo, B. Effects of posttrial hippocampal stimulation on acquisition of operant behavior in the mouse. *Behavioral Biology*, 1973, *8*, 713–724.

de Wied, D. Pituitary-adrenal system hormones and behavior. *In* F. O. Schmitt & F. G. Worden (Eds.), *The neurosciences: Third study program* (pp. 653–666). Cambridge, MA: MIT Press, 1974.

Duncan, C. P. The retroactive effect of electroshock on learning. *Journal of Comparative and Physiological Psychology*, 1949, *42*, 32–44.

Dunn, A. Biochemical correlates of training experiences: A discussion of the evidence. In M. R. Rosenzweig & E. L. Bennett (Eds.), *Neural mechanisms of learning and memory* (pp. 311–320). Cambridge, MA: MIT Press, 1976.

Dunn, A. J. Neurochemistry of learning and memory: An evaluation of recent data. *Annual Review of Psychology*, 1980, *31*, 343–390.

Flood, J. F., Jarvik, M. E., Bennett, E. L., Orme, A. E., & Rosenzweig, M. R. The effect of stimulants, depressants, and protein synthesis inhibition on retention. *Behavioral Biology*, 1977, *20*, 168–183.

Gallagher, M., & Kapp, B. S. Manipulation of opiate activity in the amygdala alters memory processes. *Life Sciences*, 1978, *23*, 1973–1978.

Glickman, S. Deficits in avoidance learning produced by stimulation of the ascending reticular formation. *Canadian Journal of Psychology*, 1958, *12*, 97–102.

Gold, P. E., Hankins, L., Chester, J., Edwards, R. M., & McGaugh, J. L. Memory interference and facilitation with posttrial amygdala stimulation: Effect on memory varies with footshock level. *Brain Research*, 1975, *86*, 509–513.

Gold, P. E., & McGaugh, J. L. Hormones and memory. *In* L. H. Miller, C. A. Sandman, & A. J. Kastin (Eds.), *Neuropeptide influences on the brain and behavior* (pp. 127–143). New York: Raven Press, 1977.

Gold, P. E., & van Buskirk, R. B. Facilitation of time-dependent memory processes with post-trial epinephrine injections. *Behavioral Biology*, 1975, *13*, 145–153.

Gold, P. E., & van Buskirk, R. Effects of posttrial hormone injections on memory processes. *Hormones and Behavior*, 1976, *7*, 509–517. (a)

Gold, P. E., & van Buskirk, R. B. Enhancement and impairment of memory processes with post-trial injections of adrenocorticotrophic hormone. *Behavioral Biology*, 1976, *16*, 387–400. (b)

Greenough, W. T. Development and memory: The synaptic connection. In T. Teyler (Ed.), *Brain and learning* (pp. 127–145). Stamford, CT: Greylock, 1978.

Isaacson, R. L. Experimental brain lesions and memory. In M. R. Rosenzweig & E. L. Bennett (Eds.), *Neural mechanisms of learning and memory* (pp. 521–543). Cambridge, MA: MIT Press, 1976.

Karpiak, S. E., & Rapport, M. M. Inhibition of consolidation and retrieval stages of passive-avoidance learning by antibodies to gangliosides. *Behavioral and Neural Biology*, 1979, *27*, 146–156.

Leshner, A. I. *An introduction to behavioral endocrinology* (pp. 249–277). London & New York: Oxford University Press, 1978.

Levine, S. Hormones and conditioning. *In* W. J. Arnold (Ed.), *Nebraska symposium on motivation* (pp. 85–101). Lincoln: University of Nebraska Press, 1968.

Liang, K. C., McGaugh, J. L., Martinez, J. L., Jr., Jensen, R. A., Vasquez, B. J., & Messing, R. B. Posttraining amygdaloid lesions impair retention of an inhibitory avoidance response. *Behavioural Brain Research*, 1982, *4*, 237–249.

Mah, C. J., & Albert, D. J. Reversal of ECS-induced amnesia by post-ECS injections of amphetamine. *Pharmacology, Biochemistry and Behavior*, 1975, *3*, 1–5.

Mahut, H. Effects of subcortical electrical stimulation on discrimination learning in cats. *Journal of Comparative and Physiological Psychology*, 1964, *58*, 390–395.

Martinez, J. L., Jr. Conditioning: Modification by peripheral mechanisms. *In* C. D. Woody (Ed.), *Conditioning: Representation of involved neural functions* (pp. 601–623). New York: Plenum Press, 1982.

Martinez, J. L., Jr., Jensen, R. A., & McGaugh, J. L. Attenuation of experimentally-induced amnesia. *Progress in Neurobiology*, 1981, *16*, 155–186.

Martinez, J. L., Jr., Jensen, R. A., Messing, R. B., Vasquez, B. J., Soumireu-Mourat, B., Geddes, D., Liang, K. C., & McGaugh, J. L. Central and peripheral actions of amphetamine on memory storage. *Brain Research*, 1980, *182*, 157–166. (a)

Martinez, J. L., Jr., Jensen, R. A., Vasquez, B. J., McGuinnes, T., & McGaugh, J. L. Methylene blue alters retention of inhibitory avoidance responses. *Physiological Psychology*, 1978, *6*, 387–390.

Martinez, J. L., Jr., McGaugh, J. L., Hanes, C. L., & Lacob, J. S. Modulation of memory processes induced by stimulation of the entorhinal cortex. *Physiology and Behavior*, 1977, *19*, 139–144.

Martinez, J. L., Jr., Vasquez, B. J., Jensen, R. A., & McGaugh, J. L. Facilitation of reserpine in an inhibitory avoidance task in mice. *Behavioral Biology*, 1977, *21*, 139–144.

Martinez, J. L., Jr., Vasquez, B. J., Jensen, R. A., Soumireu-Mourat, B., & McGaugh, J. L. ACTH$_{4-9}$ analog (ORG 2766) facilitates acquisition of an inhibitory avoidance response in rats. *Pharmacology, Biochemistry and Behavior*, 1979, *10*, 145–147.

Martinez, J. L., Jr., Vasquez, B. J., Rigter, H., Messing, R. B., Jensen, R. A., Liang, K. C., & McGaugh, J. L. Attenuation of amphetamine-induced enhancement of learning by adrenal demedullation. *Brain Research*, 1980, *195*, 433–443. (b)

McDonough, J. H., & Kesner, R. P. Amnesia produced by brief electrical stimulation of the amygdala or dorsal hippocampus in cats. *Journal of Comparative and Physiological Psychology*, 1971, *77*, 171–178.

McGaugh, J. L. Time-dependent processes in memory storage. *Science*, 1966, *153*, 1351–1358.

McGaugh, J. L. Drug facilitation of memory and learning. *In* D. H. Efron, J. O. Cole, J. Levine, &
    J. R. Wittenborn (Eds.), *Psychopharmacology: A review of progress, 1957–1967* (pp.
    891–904). Washington, D.C.: U.S. Government Printing Office, 1968.
McGaugh, J. L. Drug facilitation of learning and memory. *Annual Review of Pharmacology,* 1973,
    13, 229–241.
McGaugh, J. L., & Gold, P. E. Modulation of memory by electrical stimulation of the brain. *In* M.
    R. Rosenzweig & E. L. Bennett (Eds.), *Neural mechanisms of learning and memory* (pp.
    549–560). Cambridge, MA: MIT Press, 1976.
McGaugh, J. L., & Herz, M. J. *Memory consolidation.* San Francisco: Albion Publishing Co., 1972.
Messing, R. B., Jensen, R. A., Martinez, J. L., Jr., Spiehler, V. R., Vasquez, B. J., Soumireu-
    Mourat, B., Liang, K. C., & McGaugh, J. L. Naloxone enhancement of memory. *Behavioral
    and Neural Biology,* 1979, *27,* 266–275.
Müller, G. E., & Pilzecker, A. Experimentalle beitrage zur lehre vom gedachtniss. *Zeitschrift fuer
    Psychologie,* 1900, *1,* 1–288.
Overton, D. A. Dissociated learning in drug states (state dependent learning). In D. H. Efron (Ed.),
    Psychopharmacology: A Review of Progress (pp. 918–930). Washington, D.C.: U.S.P.H.S.
    Publication # 1836, 1968.
Overton, D. A. Experimental methods for the study of state-dependent learning. *Federation Pro-
    ceedings, Federation of American Societies for Experimental Biology,* 1974, *33,* 1800–1813.
Palfai, T., & Walsh, T. J. The role of peripheral catecholamines in reserpine-induced amnesia.
    Behavioral and Neural Biology, 1979, *27,* 423–432.
Quartermain, D. The influence of drugs on learning and memory. In M. R. Rosenzweig & E. L.
    Bennett (Eds.), *Neural mechanisms of learning and memory* (pp. 508–518). Cambridge, MA:
    MIT Press, 1976.
Riccio, D. C., & Concannon, J. T. ACTH and the reminder phenomena. *In* J. L. Martinez, Jr., R. A.
    Jensen, R. B. Messing, H. Rigter, & J. L. McGaugh (Eds.), *Endogenous peptides and learning
    and memory processes* (pp. 117–142). New York: Academic Press, 1981.
Rosenzweig, M. R., & Bennett, E. L. (Eds.). *Neural mechanisms of learning and memory.*
    Cambridge, MA: MIT Press, 1976.
Routtenberg, A., & Holzman, N. Memory disruption by electrical stimulation of substantia nigra,
    pars compacta. *Science,* 1973, *181,* 83–86.
Soumireu-Mourat, B., Destrade, C., & Cardo, B. Effects of seizure and subseizure posttrial hippo-
    campal stimulation on appetitive operant behavior in mice. *Behavioral Biology,* 1975, *15,*
    303–316.
Spear, N. E. Retrieval of memory in animals. *Psychological Review,* 1973, *80,* 163–194.
Squire, L. R., & Davis, H. P. The pharmacology of memory: A neurobiological perspective. *Annual
    Review of Pharmacology and Toxicology,* 1981, *21,* 323–356.
Sternberg, D. B., & Gold, P. E. Effects of α- and β-adrenergic receptor antagonists on retrograde
    amnesia produced by frontal cortex stimulation. *Behavioral and Neural Biology,* 1980, *29,*
    289–302.
Sternberg, D. B., McGaugh, J. L., & Gold, P. E. Propranolol-induced attenuation of both memory
    facilitation and amnesia produced by frontal cortex stimulation. *Society for Neuroscience Ab-
    stracts,* 1981, *7,* 360.
Thompson, R. The effect of intracranial stimulation on memory in cats. *Journal of Comparative and
    Physiological Psychology,* 1958, *51,* 421–426.
Thompson, R. F., Patterson, M. M., & Berger, T. Associative learning in the mammalian nervous
    system. *In* T. Teyler (Ed.), *Brain and learning* (pp. 51–90). Stamford, CT: Greylock,
    1978.
van Wimersma Greidanus, Tj. B., Bohus, B., & de Wied, D. Vasopressin and oxytocin in learning
    and memory. *In* J. L. Martinez, Jr., R. A. Jensen, R. B. Messing, H. Rigter, & J. L. McGaugh

(Eds.), *Endogenous peptides and learning and memory processes* (pp. 413–427). New York: Academic Press, 1981.

Walsh, T. J., & Palfai, T. Peripheral catecholamines and memory: Characteristics of syrosingopine-induced amnesia. *Pharmacology, Biochemistry and Behavior,* 1979, *11,* 449–452.

Wyers, E. J., Peeke, H. V. S., Williston, J. S., & Herz, J. Retroactive impairment of passive avoidance learning by stimulation of the caudate nucleus. *Experimental Neurology,* 1968, *22,* 350–366.

CELLULAR NEUROPHYSIOLOGICAL STUDIES OF LEARNING

ROBERT D. HAWKINS

Center for Neurobiology and Behavior
College of Physicians and Surgeons
Columbia University
New York, New York

I. INTRODUCTION

In an influential review published in 1968, Kandel and Spencer surveyed the literature on the neurobiology of learning and concluded that there were at that time no preparations in which learning could be studied at a mechanistic level. They also suggested that the best approach to this problem would be to record the activity of single neurons and to relate that activity to behavior by establishing the neuronal circuit for the behavior. Learning could thus be shown to be due to a change in the properties of either the neurons or the connections in the circuit. Kandel and Spencer referred to this as the cellular-connection approach and contrasted it to the aggregate-field approach, which maintains that learning is a property of large ensembles of neurons and cannot be studied at the single cell level (e.g., Adey, 1965; John, 1967; Lashley, 1929; Pribram, 1971). Several studies had already shown that the activity of individual neurons could undergo changes which were analogs of various forms of learning (Bruner & Tauc, 1966; Kandel & Tauc, 1965a, 1965b; Pinsker & Kandel, 1967; von Baumgarten & Djahnparwar, 1967), but in none of those cases were the changes in neuronal activity related to changes in behavior.

Since 1968 the cellular-connection strategy has proven quite fruitful, and there are now a number of preparations in which changes in the properties of single neurons have been recorded accompanying learning. For two nonassociative forms of learning, habituation and sensitization, it has been possible to show a causal relationship between those changes and the change in behavior, and to explore their cellular mechanisms. Such an analysis has also been accomplished for classical conditioning in *Aplysia,* and there are several other preparations in which a cellular analysis of associative learning is either ongoing or seems possible in the near future. This chapter reviews the progress made since 1968 in applying the cellular-connection approach to the study of both nonassociative and associative learning. It is thus limited to those studies that have been able to combine single-cell recording and behavior and is not meant to be exhaustive. The interested reader is referred to Kandel (1977, 1978), Kandel and Schwartz (1982), and Thompson, Patterson, and Berger (1978) for other reviews.

II. NONASSOCIATIVE LEARNING: HABITUATION AND SENSITIZATION

Broadly speaking, learning can be defined as a "change in a subject's behavior to a given situation brought about by his . . . experiences in that situation [Hilgard & Bower, 1975, p. 17]." This definition includes nonassociative forms of learning, such as habituation and sensitization, and associative forms of learning, such as classical and operant conditioning. Habituation refers to a progressive decrease in response to a stimulus that is presented repeatedly. Thompson and Spencer (1966) listed nine parametric features of habituation that are commonly observed throughout the animal kingdom and include (1) recovery of the response with rest, (2) faster habituation with weaker stimuli and shorter intertrial intervals, (3) generalization to stimuli similar to the repeated stimulus, and (4) dishabituation, the rapid recovery of an habituated response following presentation of a different stimulus. Pavlov (1927) attributed habituation (which he referred to as extinction) to increased inhibition and dishabituation to disinhibition. Many later theorists (e.g., Konorski, 1967; Sokolov, 1963) have maintained this position on habituation. Groves and Thompson (1970), however, have argued that dishabituation is not due to the removal of habituation but is rather an instance of the independent process of sensitization, whereby presentation of one stimulus (usually strong, novel, or noxious) increases responsiveness to other stimuli. In this respect, sensitization is similar to classical conditioning. Sensitization differs from conditioning, however, in that the temporal relationship between the two stimuli is not critical.

Because habituation and sensitization are relatively simple behavioral processes, are observed in a wide variety of animals including those with simple nervous systems, and frequently occur in defensive reflexes that have simple neural circuitry, they have been the first types of learning to be explained successfully at the cellular level.

The earliest cellular studies of habituation and sensitization investigated those phenomena in the polysynaptic flexion reflex of acute spinal cats (Spencer, Thompson, & Nielson, 1966a, 1966b, 1966c). Subsequent studies of the monosynaptic gill-withdrawal reflex of the marine mollusc *Aplysia californica* have confirmed the basic findings from spinal cat and have carried them to a much greater level of detail; studies in other species with simple nervous systems, including crayfish and cockroach, have also produced similar results. Thus, it appears from these studies that the neuronal mechanisms of habituation and sensitization may have wide phylogenetic generality.

A. Habituation and Sensitization of Spinal Reflexes

Sherrington (1906) described decrement of the flexion reflex with repeated stimulation in spinal animals, and Prosser and Hunter (1936) showed that the decremented reflex could be restored by strong stimulation to another part of the body. Because of the relative simplicity and accessibility of the spinal cord (compared to the brain), Spencer, Thompson, and Nielson felt that this would be a good preparation for neurophysiological analysis. They first established the parametric features of habituation and dishabituation of the flexion response in acute spinal cats (Spencer *et al.*, 1966a). Electrical stimulation of the skin or of a cutaneous nerve of the hindlimb produces contraction of flexor muscles of that limb. If the stimulation is repeated at 1- to 10-second intervals, the response habituates. It recovers with rest, and it can be dishabituated by strong skin or nerve stimulation to another site (e.g., pinching the digits). Because (1) the dishabituated response is sometimes larger than the original (rested) response, (2) "dishabituation" can be produced without prior habituation, and (3) the response sometimes returns to the habituated level without further stimulation after brief dishabituation, Spencer *et al.* (1966a) argued that dishabituation is not a removal of habituation, but is rather a superimposed process of sensitization. Groves and Thompson (1970) subsequently showed that these arguments apply to habituation and dishabituation in intact animals as well.

Spencer *et al.* (1966a) next examined the locus of the change underlying habituation and dishabituation of the flexion reflex. Because these phenomena could be observed with stimulation of cutaneous nerves and recording of the volley in a ventral root, they argued that they must be due to changes in the CNS. When they recorded the response of motor neurons with intracellular electrodes, they found that the polysynaptic excitatory postsynaptic potential (EPSP) produced by cutaneous nerve stimulation became smaller during habituation and larger during dishabituation (Spencer *et al.*, 1966c). The excitability of the motor neurons (as tested either by stimulating muscle afferents or with intracellular current pulses) was unaltered during habituation, indicating that the locus of the change underlying habituation must be in the chain of interneurons presynaptic to them. Since decrement of the EPSP occurred normally in the presence of strychnine or picrotoxin, which block inhibitory transmission at many synapses, Spencer *et al.* (1966c) concluded that the most likely mechanism of habituation of the flexion reflex is homosynaptic depression of excitatory synaptic transmission in the interneuronal chain. During dishabituation, on the other hand, the excitability of the motor neurons was sometimes increased (Spencer *et al.*, 1966b), due in part to long-lasting depolarization of the motor neurons by synaptic bombardment (Spencer *et al.*, 1966c).

The next step in the analysis of habituation and dishabituation of the flexion reflex was recording from interneurons in the reflex pathway. The interneuronal circuit for the reflex has not been worked out, however, so it was necessary to make inferences by sampling interneurons without knowing their involvement in the reflex. Groves and Thompson (1970) described three types of interneurons on the basis of their response to cutaneous stimulation: (1) those whose response did not change with repeated stimulation, (2) those that had short latencies and showed a purely "habituating" response with repeated stimulation (type H), and (3) those with longer latencies which showed both "sensitizing" and "habituating" responses with repeated stimulation (type S). Groves and Thompson suggested that types H and S were excited in parallel and converged on later interneurons or motor neurons. In this model, habituation is due to homosynaptic depression in the type-H pathway, and sensitization is due to recruitment of the type-S neurons which increases the excitability of the type-H pathway either through prolonged synaptic bombardment, polysynaptic post-tetanic potentiation (PTP), or presynaptic facilitation.

Decreased responsiveness of type-H interneurons could be due to decreased excitation as suggested, or to increased inhibition. Groves and Thompson preferred the former because they found no interneurons that showed increased responsivity with repeated stimulation (as the hypothetical inhibitory interneurons should). On the basis of results from similar experiments, however, Wickelgren (1967a, 1967b) and P. D. Wall (1970) have made indirect arguments that an explanation in terms of increased inhibition is more likely. MacDonald and Pearson (1979a, 1979b) have also obtained evidence for increased inhibition during habituation of the flexion reflex in intact animals. Specifically, they found some interneurons, inhibition of which increases with repeated cutaneous stimulation, and they also found that strychnine (which blocks many inhibitory synapses) reduces behavioral habituation. The neuronal mechanisms for habituation and dishabituation of this reflex are thus still in dispute, largely because the interneuronal circuitry for the reflex has not been worked out. The difficulty of this task has encouraged researchers to seek preparations with simpler reflex circuitry, where a mechanistic level of explanation can be obtained.

B. Habituation of the *Aplysia* Gill-Withdrawal Reflex

Neurobiologists have been attracted to the higher invertebrates (annelids, arthropods, and molluscs) because they have relatively simple nervous systems, compared to vertebrates, but exhibit many complex behaviors including non-associative and associative learning. The central nervous system of the marine mollusc *Aplysia,* for instance, is estimated to consist of only 10,000 to 20,000 neurons, compared to an estimated 10^{12} for humans. Moreover, neurons of *Aplysia* (and other molluscs) are exceptionally large, making several types of electrophysiological and biochemical experiments on single neurons feasible. Finally, many of those neurons are unique individuals that can be identified in each member of the species and have characteristic biophysical and biochemical properties and synaptic connections (Frazier, Kandel, Kupfermann, Waziri, & Coggeshall, 1967; Koester & Kandel, 1977). For these reasons *Aplysia* and other higher invertebrates have seemed particularly suitable for the cellular-connection approach to studying the neural basis of behavior.

Probably the best-studied behavior of *Aplysia* is withdrawal of the gill and siphon (a fleshy spout which serves as the exhalant funnel for the gill) in response to tactile stimulation of the siphon or surrounding skin. This defensive reflex undergoes habituation if the stimulation is repeated at approximately 1-

minute intervals, recovers with rest, and can be dishabituated or sensitized by tactile or electrical stimulation to other parts of the body (Carew, Castellucci, & Kandel, 1971; Pinsker, Kupfermann, Castellucci, & Kandel, 1970). The neural circuit for the reflex is remarkably simple: a population of about 24 identified siphon mechanoreceptor neurons (Byrne, Castellucci, & Kandel, 1974; Castellucci, Pinsker, Kupfermann, & Kandel, 1970) make monosynaptic excitatory connections onto several identified gill and siphon motor neurons (Kupfermann, Carew, & Kandel, 1974; Kupferman & Kandel, 1969; Perlman, 1979). A few interneurons involved in a polysynaptic component of the reflex have also been identified (Hawkins, Castellucci, & Kandel, 1981a).

The locus of the neuronal change underlying habituation was therefore limited to one or more of the neurons or synapses in this circuit. Kupfermann, Castellucci, Pinsker, and Kandel (1970) recorded from gill motor neurons during habituation of the reflex in semiintact preparations and found that the number of spikes produced by siphon stimulation decreased, whereas the input resistance of the motor neurons remained unchanged (Castellucci *et al.*, 1970). These results indicated that the locus of the change underlying habituation was afferent to the motor neurons. Using a more reduced preparation, Byrne, Castellucci, Carew, and Kandel (1978) showed that repeated tactile stimulation of the siphon produced a constant number of spikes in the sensory neurons. Therefore the locus of habituation was either at the synapses between the sensory neurons and motor neurons or in the polysynaptic pathway. Castellucci *et al.* (1970) recorded the monosynaptic EPSP produced in gill motor neurons by intracellular stimulation of single sensory neurons in the isolated abdominal ganglion, and found that the amplitude of the postsynaptic potential (PSP) decreased with repeated stimulation at rates comparable to those used in the behavioral experiments. Moreover, this synaptic depression was still observed when the ganglion was bathed in a solution containing elevated concentrations of Ca^{2+} and Mg^{2+}, which raises the threshold of neurons and tends to block polysynaptic pathways.

These experiments therefore indicated that habituation of the gill-withdrawal reflex was due at least in part to homosynaptic depression at the synapses between the siphon mechanoreceptor neurons and the gill motor neurons. The next question was whether this depression was due to a presynaptic change in the amount of transmitter released or a postsynaptic change in the sensitivity of the receptors. Del Castillo and Katz (1954) had shown that this question could be addressed by a quantal analysis. At all synapses that have been studied, transmitter is released in discrete quanta of a few thousand molecules, which are thought to correspond to the contents of individual vesicles. Thus the size of the postsynaptic potential is equal to the number of quanta released times the potential produced by a single quantum. At low levels of release (for instance, in solutions containing low levels of Ca^{2+} and/or high levels of Mg^{2+}) the PSP can be seen to occur as integer multiples of a unit potential. It is thus possible to measure the size of the unit potential (that is, the potential produced by a single quantum of transmitter) and to calculate the average number of quanta released by each presynaptic action potential. Castellucci and Kandel (1974) performed a quantal analysis of depression at the sensory neuron–motor neuron synapses. They found that the potential produced by a single quantum remained constant, whereas the average number of quanta released by each action potential progressively declined with repeated stimulation. This result indicated that the locus of the change underlying habituation is presynaptic, in the terminals of the sensory neurons.

A decrease in the amount of transmitter released by each action potential in the sensory neurons could have several causes. The fact that it occurs at low levels of release indicates that it is not due to depletion of transmitter. It is known that Ca^{2+} is necessary for transmitter release, probably by allowing fusion of vesicles with the external membrane. A decrease in transmitter release could be due either to a decrease in the steady-state level of Ca^{2+} in the presynaptic terminal (perhaps because of increased buffering by mitochondria and/or smooth endoplasmic reticulum) or to a decrease in the amount of Ca^{2+} that enters the terminal when an action potential invades it. Nerve terminals and cell bodies have voltage-sensitive Ca^{2+} channels that participate in generation of the action potential along with the voltage-sensitive Na^+ and K^+ channels originally described for the action potential in the axon. Katz and Miledi (1969) and Horn and Miller (1977) found that the duration of the action potential in the presence of tetraethylammonium (TEA) is a sensitive index of the inward Ca^{2+} current in terminals and cell bodies. That is because TEA partially blocks the voltage-sensitive K^+ current that normally terminates the spike, allowing it to last much longer. Because the Na^+ current inactivates rapidly, inward current during the latter part of the spike in TEA is carried predominantly by Ca^{2+}.

Ideally, one would want to measure the Ca^{2+} current in the terminals of the sensory neurons, but this is not technically possible at the moment because the terminals are too small. Klein and Kandel (1978) measured the duration of the action potential in the cell bodies of sensory neurons in TEA solution and found that it decreased with repeated stimulation. Moreover, the change in duration of the action potential was well correlated with the change in amplitude of the PSP measured in a postsynaptic neuron. Klein and Kandel argued that changes in the currents measured in the cell body reflect similar changes occurring in the terminals, which would mean that the decrease in transmitter release underlying habituation is due to a decrease in the amount of Ca^{2+} entering the terminals of the sensory neurons during each action potential.

A decrease in Ca^{2+} influx could be due either directly to a decrease in conductance of the Ca^{2+} channels, or indirectly to an increase in conductance of the K^+ channels, which would have the effect of shortening the duration of the spike. In order to distinguish between these possibilities, Klein and Kandel performed a voltage-clamp analysis of the currents produced in sensory neurons by depolarizations mimicking action potentials (Klein, Shapiro, & Kandel, 1980). The advantage of the voltage clamp is that it permits the experimenter to hold the duration and amplitude of the depolarization constant in the face of changing currents. When Klein and Kandel blocked all of the currents except the Ca^{2+} current with ion substitutions and drugs, they found that the inward current still became progressively smaller with repeated depolarizations at 10-second intervals.

These results indicate that a mechanism of habituation of the gill-with-drawal reflex is a progressive decrease in the conductance of voltage-sensitive Ca^{2+} channels in the terminals of the sensory neurons. This decrease in conductance appears to be an extremely long-lasting form of inactivation that is intrinsic to the Ca^{2+} channels themselves. Whether it is caused by depolarization during the action potential, as is inactivation of Na^+ channels (Hodgkin & Huxley, 1952), or by the actual influx of Ca^{2+}, as is inactivation of some other Ca^{2+} channels (Tillotson, 1979), remains to be investigated.

The experiments described thus far have been concerned with the mechanism of habituation of the gill- and siphon-withdrawal reflex during a single session of repeated siphon stimulation. The reflex recovers its full amplitude in several minutes to 1 hour following such stimulation (Pinsker et al., 1970). However, if the stimulation is repeated on successive days, habituation is produced which lasts up to 3 weeks (Carew, Pinsker, & Kandel, 1972). An interesting question is whether this long-term form of habituation is merely an extension of the short-term form and has the same mechanisms or whether it involves an additional mechanism such as a morphological change (e.g., retraction of synapses). The answer to this question would be relevant to the more general question of how short-term memories are consolidated into long-term ones.

Castellucci, Carew, and Kandel (1978) examined the PSPs from siphon mechanoreceptor neurons to gill and siphon motor neurons in animals that had had long-term habituation training and in control animals. They found that whereas about 90% of sensory neurons made detectable PSPs in motor neurons in control animals, only about 30% did in long-term habituated animals. Thus the locus of the change underlying long-term habituation seems to be the same as that underlying short-term habituation: the sensory neuron–motor neuron synapses. Whether the mechanism is the same is under investigation. Carew, Castellucci, and Kandel (1979) found that transmission at sensory neuron–motor neuron synapses in long-term habituated animals could be restored in less than 2 hours by a strong sensitizing stimulus. This seems too fast for regrowth of retracted synapses, but it does not rule out more subtle morphological changes as the basis of long-term habituation. Bailey and Chen (1983) have obtained evidence for just such changes. Using serial reconstruction to analyze the fine structure of labeled sensory neurons, they found a decrease in the number of active zones (morphological specializations where vesicles are released) and a decrease in the number of vesicles per active zone in sensory neurons from long-term habituated animals, compared to sensory neurons from controls.

C. Sensitization of the *Aplysia* Gill-Withdrawal Reflex

The gill-withdrawal reflex can be sensitized by tactile or electrical stimulation of other parts of the body, including the mantle shelf, neck, and tail (Carew *et al.*, 1971; R. D. Hawkins & V. F. Castellucci, unpublished; Pinsker *et al.*, 1970). In experiments similar to those described above for habituation, Kupfermann *et al.* (1970) found that the locus of the neuronal change underlying sensitization is afferent to the motor neurons, and Castellucci *et al.* (1970) showed that stimulating the pleuroabdominal connectives (the pathways that carry input from the head, neck, and tail regions) produces facilitation of the sensory neuron–motor neuron EPSPs. Using a quantal analysis, Castellucci and Kandel (1976) found that this facilitation is due to an increase in transmitter release by the sensory neurons.

Because facilitation of the sensory neuron–motor neuron synapses is induced rapidly and lasts many minutes (Castellucci & Kandel, 1976; Castellucci *et al.*, 1970), it seemed likely that it involves some biochemical change. However, Schwartz, Castellucci, and Kandel (1971) found that this facilitation occurred normally when protein synthesis had been inhibited by 95%. Cedar, Kandel, and Schwartz (1972) next examined cAMP metabolism and found that prolonged nerve stimulation increased the rate of synthesis of cAMP in the abdominal ganglion. Similarly, Cedar and Schwartz (1972) and Levitan and Barondes (1974) found that adding serotonin, dopamine, or octopamine to the bath also increased the level of cAMP in the ganglion. Bernier, Castellucci, Kandel, and Schwartz (1982) dissected out single identified cells or small clusters after exposure of the ganglion to each of these transmitters, and found that only serotonin produced an increase in cAMP synthesis in the sensory neurons. Brunelli, Castellucci, and Kandel (1976) also tested each of these transmitters and found that serotonin, but not dopamine or octopamine produced facilitation at the sensory neuron–motor neuron synapses at concentrations as low as 10^{-6} M. Brunelli *et al.* found that facilitation could also be produced either by exposing the ganglion to dibutyryl cAMP (an analog that crosses cell membranes) or by injecting cAMP directly into sensory neuron cell bodies.

These results suggested the following model for the neuronal basis of sensitization of the gill-withdrawal reflex: sensitizing stimulation of the neck or tail excites serotonergic facilitating neurons which make synaptic connections on or near the terminals of the sensory neurons, causing stimulation of an adenylate cyclase and increased levels of cAMP in the sensory neurons. In turn cAMP enhances transmitter release from the sensory neurons, either by increasing the resting Ca^{2+} level or by increasing Ca^{2+} influx during action potentials in those neurons.

Klein and Kandel (1978) next examined the Ca^{2+} current during action potentials in sensory neurons, using the duration of the action potential in TEA solution as an assay. They found that connective stimulation, bath exposure to serotonin, and intracellular injection of cAMP all produce an increase in spike duration, indicating an increase in Ca^{2+} current in sensory neurons. As explained previously, a change in Ca^{2+} current could be due either to a direct action on the Ca^{2+} channels or to an indirect action on the K^+ channels. Using voltage-clamp techniques, Klein and Kandel (1980) found that serotonin does not produce any change in the inward (Ca^{2+}) current when all of the K^+ currents are blocked. Moreover, Siegelbaum, Camardo, and Kandel (1982) recorded the currents through single K^+ channels with patch clamp techniques, and found that serotonin causes a prolonged closure of those channels. It therefore seems that whereas habituation involves a direct decrease in Ca^{2+} conductance, sensitization involves a decrease in K^+ conductance. These results therefore support, at the biophysical level, the conclusion from mammalian spinal cord studies (Groves & Thompson, 1970; Spencer *et al.*, 1966c) that whereas habituation is due to an intrinsic decrease in excitation, sensitization is due to an independent and opposing excitatory process. Klein, Camardo, and Kandel (1982) analyzed the K^+ current which is modulated by serotonin and found that it is not one of the previously known types of K^+ current (fast K^+, delayed K^+, Ca^{2+}-dependent K^+, and muscarine sensitive K^+). They also showed that a decrease in this serotonin sensitive K^+ current can cause a prolongation of the action potential and hence an increase in the Ca^{2+} current and increased transmitter release.

Although these studies are extremely elegant, they rely on either connective stimulation or application of serotonin, the putative facilitating transmitter, to mimic the effects of natural sensitizing stimulation. Because these are crude procedures, it seemed desirable to identify neurons that mediate the effects of sensitizing stimuli and to see if stimulating those neurons would produce the same effects. Hawkins, Castellucci, and Kandel (1981b) identified three types of neurons in the abdominal ganglion, intracellular stimulation of which produces facilitation of PSPs in gill and siphon motor neurons. Further studies have concentrated on one of these, L29, which refers to a small group of electrically coupled neurons. Using a semi-intact preparation, Hawkins (1981a) found that these neurons are strongly excited by tactile or electrical stimulation of the tail similar to that used to produce sensitization. Hawkins (1981b) also found that intracellular stimulation of a single L29 neuron causes broadening of the spike in sensory neurons in TEA solution. Bailey, Hawkins, Chen, and Kandel (1981) have investigated the morphology of the L29 neurons and found that they make contact with the varicosities (which are the sites of transmitter release) of the sensory neurons, and that the L29 neurons contain dense core vesicles characteristic of aminergic neurons. Bailey, Hawkins, and Chen (1983) have also found that L29 neurons take up exogenous serotonin at a relatively low concentration (10^{-6} M), which is consistent with the idea that they are serotonergic. These experiments therefore support several aspects of the previously proposed model of the neuronal basis of sensitization.

This model is currently being extended to the molecular level. Kuo and Greengard (1969) have suggested that cAMP exerts all of its effects through protein phosphorylation. Many proteins exist in two states, phosphorylated and unphosphorylated, which may differ importantly in structure and function. Proteins are phosphorylated by a group of enzymes called protein phosphokinases, which have two components: a catalytic subunit and a regulatory subunit which may be sensitive to cAMP. When cAMP binds to the regulatory subunit, the catalytic subunit is freed and starts to phosphorylate substrate proteins. Castellucci, Kandel, Schwartz, Wilson, Nairn, and Greengard (1980) injected the purified catalytic subunit of cAMP-dependent protein kinase directly into sensory neurons and found that it caused facilitation of transmitter release and broadening of the spike in the sensory neurons in TEA solution. Moreover, injection of an inhibitor of the protein phosphokinase prevents serotonin from causing broadening of sensory neuron spikes in TEA solution (Castellucci, Nairn, Greengard, Schwartz, and Kandel, 1982). In addition, Paris, Kandel, and Schwartz (1980) have found that exposing the abdominal ganglion to either serotonin or dibutyryl cAMP stimulates phosphorylation of a 137,000-dalton membrane protein. These results indicate that serotonin-stimulated cAMP may cause increased transmitter release through phosphorylation of a specific membrane protein. It is attractive to think that that protein is either the K^+ channel or some protein associated with it. If this is true, the molecular basis of sensitization would be a change in conformation of a single type of molecule, perhaps the K^+ channel, leading to a decrease in K^+ current, an increase in spike duration, an increase in Ca^{2+} influx, and hence an increase in transmitter release from the sensory neurons.

The experiments described thus far have all been concerned with the mechanism of short-term sensitization. Like habituation, sensitization also has a long-term form. Whereas a single tactile or electrical stimulus produces sensitization lasting minutes to hours (Carew et al., 1971; R. D. Hawkins & V. F. Castellucci, unpublished; Pinsker et al., 1970), four strong stimuli a day for 4 days produce sensitization lasting weeks (Pinsker, Hening, Carew, & Kandel, 1973). The mechanism of long-term sensitization may simply be an extension of the short-term mechanism or it may involve some additional process such as induction of a new type of protein or synaptic growth (Kandel and Schwartz, 1982). Bailey and Chen (1983) have found that sensory neurons from long-term sensitized animals have more active zones and more vesicles per active zone than do sensory neurons from control animals, suggesting that these morphological changes may store the memory for the long-term behavioral change.

D. Habituation and Dishabituation in Crayfish

Like *Aplysia,* crayfish have been attractive subjects for cellular studies of learning because of the relative simplicity of their nervous systems. The behaviors that have been studied most thoroughly in crayfish are the two major responses of the animal to threatening stimuli: escape and defense. Both of these responses undergo habituation; interestingly, dishabituation has only been described for the defense response. The neuronal locus and mechanism of habituation of the escape response have been determined, but knowledge of the neural basis of plasticity of the defense response is less complete.

1. Habituation of the Escape Response

One of the responses of crayfish to threatening stimuli is backward swimming accomplished by a series of tail flips. This swimming can be initiated by three different neural systems, depending on the type of stimulation (Wine & Krasne, 1972). Phasic tactile stimuli (e.g., taps) to the anterior portion of the animal excite a pair of neurons, called the medial giants, which run the entire length of the nerve cord. Activity in these neurons produces a short-latency, stereotyped tail flip which propels the animal straight backward. Phasic stimuli to the posterior portion of the animal excite another pair of neurons called the lateral giants, which also run the entire length of the nerve cord (and actually consist of a series of electrically coupled segments). Activity of these neurons produces a different short-latency, stereotyped tail flip which produces a foreward somersault. Gradual stimuli (e.g., pinching) to either portion of the body can result in tail flips that are not mediated by either giant neuron system and have longer latencies and more variable topologies.

Wine, Krasne, and Chen (1975) described habituation of the lateral giant-mediated response in restrained, whole animals. They found that if taps to the side of the abdomen are repeated at 1- to 5-minute intervals, the probability of eliciting a tail flip progressively decreases, and that it takes more than 3 hours for the response to recover following such habituation. Moreover, the kinetics of habituation and recovery are basically the same if the nerve cord is transected rostrally, indicating that habituation is not due to an increase in descending inhibition but is rather intrinsic to the abdominal circuitry.

Krasne (1969) used an isolated abdomen preparation to study the neural basis of habituation of this response. He recorded the complex EPSP produced in lateral giant neurons by electrical stimulation of an afferent nerve root and found that the PSP has three components distinguishable by latency. If the stimulation is repeated at 1-minute intervals the first (α) component is relatively stabile, whereas the second (β) component becomes progressively smaller and eventually fails to initiate a spike. Krasne inferred that the β response is di- or trisynaptic on the basis of its latency, and noted that its amplitude tends to decrease in steps. This observation suggested that depression of the complex EPSP in the giant neuron (and by inference habituation of the escape response) is due to failure at synapses one or more steps afferent to the lateral giant. Since Krasne and Roberts (1967) had shown that depression of the PSP in the lateral giant occurs normally in the presence of picrotoxin, which blocks many inhibitory synapses in crayfish, he also concluded that habituation is probably due to an intrinsic decrease in excitation at those synapses.

Zucker carried out a more systematic analysis of the neural basis of habituation of the lateral giant-mediated response. He first worked out the basic neural circuitry for the reflex, which involves four layers of neurons (Zucker, 1972a; Zucker, Kennedy, & Selverston, 1971). Tactile stimulation of the abdomen excites a population of hair receptors on the abdominal carapace. These cells have electrical synapses with the lateral giant neurons that mediate the short latency (α) response in those neurons. The tactile hair receptors also make excitatory chemical synapses onto several identified sensory interneurons, which in turn have electrical synapses with the lateral giants. It is this pathway that produces the β component of the response in the lateral giants. The efferent limb of the circuit had been established previously, and consists of electrical synapses between the lateral giants and a population of fast flexor motor neurons and a motor giant neuron, both of which synapse on fast flexor muscles.

Zucker (1972b) next examined the mechanism of depression of the EPSP in the lateral giants. He found that activity in the sensory fibers did not change during repeated stimulation, ruling out receptor adaptation. The threshold and input resistance of both the lateral giant and the sensory interneurons also did not change, ruling out changes in the membrane properties of those neurons. On the other hand, the EPSP recorded in the tactile interneurons did show a strong depression with repeated stimulation. Because this depression occurred when only one sensory fiber was stimulated (with threshold stimulation of the root), Zucker concluded that it is homosynaptic. He also carried out a quantal analysis of depression of the EPSP in a tactile interneuron using the coefficient of variation (a statistical test that does not include any verification of its assumptions), and concluded that depression is due to a decrease in quantal content, that is, decreased release of transmitter by the sensory neurons.

Bruner and Kennedy (1970) observed low-frequency depression at another synapse in the neural circuit for the reflex: the neuromuscular junction between the motor giant neuron and the fast flexor muscles. The relevance of depression at this junction to behavioral habituation is obscure, however, because a single spike in a lateral giant neuron invariably produces a complete tail flip (Krasne &

Woodsmall, 1969). The mechanism of habituation of the crayfish escape response thus appears to be a progressive decrease in the amount of transmitter released by primary sensory neurons.

This mechanism presents the animal with a peculiar problem: water currents produced by its own tail flip movements stimulate the tactile hair receptors and should lead to maladaptive habituation of the reflex. However, Wine *et al.* (1975) found that lateral giant activity preceding tactile stimulation (as would happen during a spontaneous tail flip) prevents behavioral habituation in the intact animal, whereas giant activity after the tactile stimulation (as would happen during a reflexive tail flip) does not. Krasne and Bryan (1973; see also Bryan & Krasne, 1977a, 1977b) investigated this problem in the isolated abdomen preparation and obtained an analogous result. That is, stimulation of the lateral giant 10–100 msec before repeated stimulation of an afferent root prevents depression of the EPSPs in tactile interneurons. Krasne and Bryan found that lateral giant stimulation during the same interval also produces presynaptic inhibition of transmission at the sensory neuron to interneuron synapses. Because presynaptic inhibition at these synapses is thought to be due to shunting of the spike in the sensory neuron terminals (Kennedy, Calabrese, & Wine, 1974), lateral giant activity may prevent synaptic depression and maladaptive habituation of the reflex through this mechanism.

2. Habituation and Dishabituation of the Defense Response

The second common response of crayfish to threatening stimuli is to assume a defensive posture facing the threat, with the chelipeds raised and extended and the claws open. This response to repeated visual (Glantz, 1974a) or tactile (Hawkins & Bruner, 1981; Hoffmann, 1914) stimulation habituates and can be dishabituated by stimulation to other parts of the body. Glantz (1974b, 1977) has worked out part of the neural circuit for the visually triggered defense response and has determined points of plasticity in that circuit. Approaching visual stimuli excite motion detector interneurons which make monosynaptic excitatory connections onto command neurons for the defense response. With repeated stimulation the evoked response in both the visual interneurons and the command interneurons decreases, indicating that the site of neural plasticity underlying habituation of the reflex is at or afferent to the visual interneurons. Dishabituating stimuli or behavioral arousal increase the evoked response in the visual interneurons and also increase the motor response produced by command neuron stimulation, indicating that there are at least two sites of neural plasticity underlying dishabituation: at or afferent to the visual interneurons and efferent to the command interneurons. The mechanisms of these forms of neural plasticity have not been determined.

Hoffmann (1914) first described habituation of the claw-opening response to tactile stimulation (tapping the back or tail). Claw opening is produced by one muscle (the dactyl abductor) which is innervatd by only two motor axons, one excitor and one inhibitor, which run in different nerve bundles (Van Harreveld & Wiersma, 1937). During the course of studies that established the existence of peripheral inhibition in Crustacea, Hoffmann found that cutting the nerve bundle that contains the axon of the opener inhibitor for one claw abolished habituation of opening of that claw, whereas opening of the other (unoperated) claw habituated normally. Hoffmann's results have been cited (e.g., Schöne, 1961) as demonstrating that habituation of the claw-opening response is due to a buildup of peripheral inhibition.

Hawkins and Bruner (1981) investigated this hypothesis with more modern methods by recording the activity of the opener motor neurons during habituation. They found that with repeated stimulation evoked activity in the excitor motor neuron progressively decreases, whereas activity in the inhibitor remains unchanged. This result shows that habituation of this response is not due to a build-up of peripheral inhibition but rather to a decrease in excitation. This finding also indicates that the locus of the plasticity underlying habituation is at or afferent to the excitor motor neuron. Aréchiga, Barrera-Mera, and Fuentes-Pardo (1975) found that during repeated stimulation of the carapace, the evoked response of primary mechanoreceptor neurons remains constant while the response of mechanoreceptive interneurons decreases, suggesting that a locus of plasticity underlying habituation of the defense response is at the sensory neuron to interneuron synapses. Moreover, the response of the interneurons can be restored by arousing stimulation, suggesting that this may also be a locus of plasticity underlying dishabituation.

Unexpectedly, Hawkins and Bruner found three different peripheral mechanisms that contribute to dishabituation of the claw-opening response: an increase in evoked excitor activity, a decrease in evoked inhibitor activity, and PTP at the excitor neuromuscular junction following activation by the dishabituating stimulation. Together, these three mechanisms can quantitatively account for the observed increase in claw opening following dishabituation. Although it has often been proposed, this is the first demonstration that disinhibition can contribute to dishabituation. Jacklet and Rine (1977) suggested that neuromuscular PTP may also contribute to dishabituation of the *Aplysia* gill-withdrawal reflex.

E. Habituation of the Cockroach Escape Response

Cockroaches have a pair of tactile receptors, called cerci, on their posterior ends which are very sensitive to air currents made by approaching objects. Stimulation of these receptors produces a short latency escape response consisting of forward running that habituates with repeated stimulation (Roeder, 1948) and can be dishabituated or sensitized by stimulation to other parts of the body such as a leg (Zilber-Gachelin, 1966). Roeder described the neural circuit for this response: hair receptors on the cerci make monosynaptic connections onto giant and nongiant interneurons in the last abdominal ganglion, and these in turn make synaptic connections (which may be monosynaptic) onto leg motor neurons in the thoracic ganglion. Callec, Guillet, Pichon, and Boistel (1971) found that both the complex EPSP in the giant interneurons produced by air puffs to the cerci and the unitary EPSP produced by touching a single hair receptor undergo depression at relatively high frequencies of stimulation (>1 per second). Zilber-Gachelin and Chartier (1973a) showed that this depression occurs at lower frequencies of stimulation, paralleling behavioral habituation, and argued that it is presynaptic. They also found that transmission at the sensory neuron to interneuron synapses does not facilitate but that transmission at the interneuron to motor neuron synapses does, suggesting that this is the locus of plasticity underlying sensitization (Zilber-Gachelin and Chartier, 1973b).

F. Summary

In each of the cases reviewed, habituation and sensitization of defensive reflexes appear to be due to corresponding plasticity of synaptic connections. In the case of the cat flexion response it has not been possible to work out a wiring diagram of the reflex arc and to pinpoint loci of neural plasticity in that arc. This has been possible for each of the invertebrate reflexes discussed. These vary somewhat in the complexity of the circuits: the *Aplysia* gill-withdrawal reflex is partly monosynaptic, the cockroach escape response may be disynaptic, and the crayfish escape and defense responses to visual and tactile stimulation are at least trisynaptic. All of these, except the *Aplysia* gill-withdrawal reflex, involve giant "command" interneurons which have presumably evolved to minimize the latency of the response (and which are also inviting targets for neurophysiologists).

Habituation of all of the invertebrate reflexes appears to be due to a decrease in transmission at chemical synapses between primary sensory neurons and their target cells (sensory interneurons, command interneurons, or motor neurons), and, in those cases where it has been examined, this synaptic depression is presynaptic. Similarly, an analog of habituation in the frog spinal cord appears to be due to decreased transmitter release (Farel, Glanzman, & Thompson, 1973; Farel & Thompson, 1976; Glanzman & Thompson, 1979, 1980). Thus a progressive decrease in transmitter release may be a phylogenetically general mechanism of habituation. In *Aplysia* this synaptic depression has been shown to be due to a very long-lasting inactivation of a voltage-dependent Ca^{2+} conductance in the sensory neurons.

A variety of loci of plasticity underlying dishabituation or sensitization of the invertebrate reflexes have been described. For some (*Aplysia*-gill withdrawal and crayfish defense responses to visual and tactile stimulation), sensitizing stimuli increase transmission at the synapses between primary sensory neurons and their target cells. In the case of *Aplysia* this increase in synaptic transmission has been shown to be due to a decrease in a voltage-dependent K^+ conductance in the sensory neurons, perhaps caused by cAMP-dependent phosphorylation of the K^+ channels. For others (crayfish and cockroach escape responses), these synapses do not appear to be affected by sensitizing stimuli. Other loci and mechanisms which have been implicated in dishabituation are increased transmission between interneurons and excitor motor neurons (cockroach escape), decreased transmission between interneurons and inhibitory motor neurons (crayfish defense), and PTP at excitor neuromuscular junctions (crayfish defense and *Aplysia* gill withdrawal).

Although the exact locus and mechanism of plasticity underlying dishabituation may be different for different reflexes (and more than one may exist for the same reflex), in all cases where they have been adequately studied, both habituation and dishabituation have been found to be due to a change in the efficacy of transmission at preexisting synapses in the reflex arc. Thus these studies of nonassociative forms of learning have lent support to the cellular connection approach in general and have encouraged its application to the study of associative forms of learning.

III. ASSOCIATIVE LEARNING: INTRODUCTION

Classical and operant conditioning can be considered to be the next more complicated forms of learning after habituation and sensitization. Although it has been claimed that these are the only true forms of learning (e.g., Miller, 1967), it seems as reasonable to suppose that learning refers to a hierarchy of different but related processes, ranging from habituation to language acquisition, in which classical and operant conditioning occupy an intermediate position. The distinguishing feature of these associative forms of learning is that a specified change in behavior takes place only if two events (a conditioned stimulus and an unconditioned stimulus or a response and a reinforcement) occur in a specific temporal sequence. Like habituation and sensitization, classical and operant conditioning show many regularities across species and situations (see Kimble, 1961; Mackintosh, 1974).

The physiological mechanism of associative learning can be thought of as having three components: one that confers the requirement for temporal specificity and thus selects the information to be stored (which I will refer to as the association mechanism), one that is the physical store itself (which I will refer to as the engram), and one that permits retrieval of the information when it is needed. It is important to realize that these components are logically distinct and may have totally different loci and neural bases in the brain. Neuroscientists have so far concentrated their efforts on the search for the engram, but we will not truly understand the physiological basis of memory until we understand something about each of these three components.

If nonassociative and associative learning are related processes, then they may have some physiological mechanisms in common. This is easiest to consider in the case of sensitization and classical conditioning, which differ only in the requirement for temporal specificty. Obviously only classical conditioning involves an association mechanism, but these two forms of learning may both utilize the same type of engram (particularly since sensitization, like conditioning, can last weeks). Recent results on the neuronal mechanism of classical conditioning in *Aplysia* indicate that it is, in fact, simply an elaboration of the mechanism of sensitization. As more becomes known about the mechanisms of different types of associative learning in various species, it will be interesting to see to what degree they resemble those of habituation or sensitization, and in what ways they differ.

IV. VERTEBRATE STUDIES OF ASSOCIATIVE
LEARNING

Probably the single most influential idea for cellular research on vertebrate conditioning is Hebb's (1949) hypothesis concerning the neural basis of associative learning. More or less a priori, Hebb proposes that

> When an axon of cell A is near enough to excite a cell B and repeatedly or persistently takes part in firing it, some growth process or metabolic change takes place in one or both cells such that A's efficiency, as one of the cells firing B, is increased. [p. 62]

It is worth pointing out that this is a cellular-connection hypothesis because it states that the neural basis of learning is a change in the strength of synaptic connections between specific neurons. Hebb suggested that the most likely physical basis for this change is the growth of "synaptic knobs," although he allowed for other possibilities. Stent (1973), for instance, has proposed a mechanism whereby a change in the number of receptors could be the physical basis of Hebb's postulate. As stated, Hebb's hypothesis does not rule out the participation of other cells in changing the strength of the connection from A to B (for example, through presynaptic facilitation), although it is sometimes interpreted as doing so. If other cells are not involved, Hebb's postulate implies that the locus of the association mechanism and the engram are the same, but if other cells are involved these two components of learning may have different loci.

Hebb's hypothesis is basically a neuronal analog of behavior; that is, activity of cell A corresponds to the conditioned stimulus (CS) and activity of cell B corresponds to the conditioned response (CR) in classical conditioning. What distinguishes Hebb's model from other similar models (cf. Burke, 1966; Kupfermann & Pinsker, 1969) is the key role of an action potential in cell B.

Attempts to produce neural analogs of classical conditioning in identified invertebrate neurons have often been unsuccessful (e.g., Kandel & Tauc, 1965a; Wurtz, Castellucci, & Nusrala, 1967), but there have been successes in both invertebrates (von Baumgarten & Djahnparwar, 1967; von Baumgarten & Hukuhara, 1969) and vertebrates (Baranyi & Feher, 1981a, 1981b, 1918c; Levy & Steward, 1979; O'Brien, Wilder, & Stevens, 1977; Patterson, 1975; Patterson, Cegavske, & Thompson 1973). Although some of these studies appear to demonstrate that an action potential in the postsynaptic neuron plays a critical role in the neural plasticity (Baranyi & Feher, 1981a, 1981b, 1981c; O'Brien *et al.*, 1977), in none of them has the neural plasticity been related to corresponding behavioral plasticity. The simplest way that such a neural change might be related to behavioral conditioning would be if the CS caused activity of cell A and the CR was caused by activity of cell B. Hebb-type neural plasticity has also been proposed as the basis of adaptive plasticity of the vestibular-ocular reflex in a more indirect manner involving known cerebellar circuitry (Ito, 1972; Marr, 1969; Robinson, 1976). Recent cellular evidence, however, suggests that plasticity of this reflex may be due to a pairing-specific *decrease* in synaptic strength (Dufossé, Ito, Jastreboff, & Miyashita, 1978; Ito, 1982; Ito, Sakurai, & Tongroach, 1982), although this idea has also been challenged (Miles, Braitman, & Dow, 1980). Other synaptic mechanisms that have been proposed as the basis of conditioning include presynaptic facilitation and long-term potentiation (see Sections IV,D and V,E).

Probably the single most striking result of cellular research on vertebrate conditioning is the ubiquity of neural correlates of associative learning. These have been found throughout the vertebrate brain, including sensory areas (e.g., Gabriel, Saltwick, & Miller, 1975; Gibbs & Cohen, 1980; Oleson, Ashe, & Weinberger, 1975; Wall, Wild, Broyles, Gibbs, & Cohen, 1980), motor areas (Cegavske, Patterson, & Thompson, 1979; Gold & Cohen, 1981; Woody, 1970; Woody & Brozek, 1969), association areas (Krause & Disterhoft, 1982; Olds, Disterhoft, Segal, Kornblith, & Hirsh, 1972; Woody, Knispel, Crow, & Black-Cleworth, 1976), and limbic areas (Berger, Alger, & Thompson, 1976; Berger & Thompson, 1977; Gabriel, Miller, & Saltwick, 1977; Segal, Disterhoft, & Olds, 1972; Segal & Olds, 1972, 1973). These results have raised a question: which, if any, of these correlates represents the ''primary'' change underlying learning? One possibility is that the primary change is distributed throughout the brain. Thus, for instance, Oleson *et al.* (1975) have proposed that any unit driven by both the CS and the unconditioned stimulus (US) will show a conditioned effect, with the strength of the conditioning being proportional to the strength with which that unit is driven by the CS and US. Alternatively, one or more of the observed correlates represents the primary change, and the others are either derived from it or are epiphenomena not causally related to learning at all. Several rules have been proposed for deciding which correlates have a more

important relation to learning. Olds *et al.* (1972) proposed that the neural correlate with the shortest latency is likely to represent the primary neural change
underlying learning. The logic of this proposal is that the conditioned reflex arc
is a chain of neurons, so that an altered response in an early neuron in the chain
will affect the response of all later neurons. Gabriel (1976) criticized this idea by
pointing out that a change in the evoked response of a neuron early in the reflex
arc could be the result of tonic input from other brain regions, which would then
be primary. Thompson, Berger, Cegavske, Patterson, Roemer, Teyler, and
Young (1976) proposed that the site of the engram is the first locus that shows
changes during training, rather than the one with the shortest latency. However,
this requirement may be violated if there is more than one engram (e.g., short
term and long term).

These difficulties highlight one of the greatest problems of vertebrate
studies on the neural basis of learning. Although an abundance (perhaps an
overabundance) of cellular correlates have been found, demonstrating a causal
relation between any of these and behavior has proven extremely difficult. Three
vertebrate preparations (pigeon heart-rate conditioning and cat and rabbit eye-
blink conditioning) have been studied in sufficient detail that they seem closest to
this goal.

A. Pigeon Heart-Rate Conditioning

Aware of the difficulties of relating cellular events to behavior, Cohen
(1969) set out to develop a vertebrate preparation specifically suited for cellular
neurophysiological studies of learning. He chose pigeon heart-rate conditioning
because this behavior is acquired relatively rapidly and reliably in restrained
animals, making unit recording during acquisition practical. In the basic experimental arrangement (Cohen, 1969; Cohen & Durkovic, 1966; Cohen & Mac-
Donald, 1971), the CS is a 6-second presentation of diffuse white or colored light
that is immediately followed by 0.5 seconds of foot shock (the US). If this
sequence is repeated at approximately 5-minute intervals, within 20 to 30 trials
the CS comes to elicit cardioacceleration during the period preceding foot shock,
whereas it does not if the CS and US are repeatedly presented in an unpaired
fashion. Differential conditioning with, for instance, red and green light as the
differential stimuli can also be established. Following several days of training,
the conditioned response persists through at least 5 days of extinction.

Because Cohen (1969) felt that the best way to relate neural events to
behavior is to establish the neural circuit for the behavior, the fact that relatively
little was known about the neuroanatomy of the pigeon was a major disadvantage
of this preparation. In an extensive series of lesion studies, Cohen (1974) established the basic outline of the CS, US, and CR pathways for the conditioned
heart-rate change. Only recently has he begun to record neural activity during

conditioning. Gold and Cohen (1981) reported that light-evoked inhibition of vagal cardiac neurons (activity of which causes cardiac deceleration) increases during conditioning in paired animals, compared to unpaired controls. At the sensory end of the reflex arc, Gibbs and Cohen (1980) and J. Wall *et al.* (1980) have reported that the evoked activity of single units in the principal optic nucleus, nucleus rotondus, and ectostriatum (all visual areas) increases during conditioning in paired animals compared to unpaired controls, whereas retinal output remains unchanged. Moreover, units in each of the areas showing conditioned effects respond to the US (foot shock) as well as the CS (light). Gibbs, Cohen, Broyles, and Solina (1981) have found that units in the principal optic nucleus that show a conditioned effect are specifically those that initially respond to the CS with increased firing and to the US with decreased firing. The significance of this finding remains to be explored.

B. Cat Eye-Blink Conditioning

Charles Woody and his colleagues have spent more than a decade studying neural correlates of eye-blink conditioning in the cat. In the basic experimental arrangement (Woody & Brozek, 1969) a click (the CS) is followed 400 msec later by a tap (the US) to the glabella or the forehead of the animal. After four to six daily sessions of about 150 trials each, the click comes to elicit an eye blink on most trials, whereas it does not in animals that receive random presentations of the click and tap (Woody, Yarowsky, Owens, Black-Cleworth, & Crow, 1974). Furthermore, the conditioned eye-blink response can be extinguished by reversing the order of the CS and US for several sessions. Woody and Brozek (1969) found that the click-evoked response in the facial nucleus (a motor nucleus projecting to muscles involved in eye blink) increases during conditioning and decreases during extinction. They also found that application of KCl to the cortex blocks the conditioned response, indicating that the response is mediated (at least in part) by cortical pathways.

Woody (1970) next recorded click-evoked potentials in coronal-precruciate ("sensorimotor") cortex during conditioning. It seemed likey that this part of cortex mediated the conditioned response, because it has a click-evoked response with a latency appropriately shorter than the behavioral response, and stimulation of it produces contractions in muscles involved in eye blink. Woody found that the click-evoked potential in coronal-precruciate cortex, as in facial nucleus, increases during conditioning and decreases during extinction. In an extension of this analysis, Woody, Vassilevsky, and Engel (1970) recorded click-evoked unit activity extracellularly following training and found that it was greater in animals that had had paired training than in naive or extinguished animals. This effect was especially prominent with electrode placements where microstimulation produced contraction of the muscles involved in eye blink. Furthermore, the current threshold for producing eye blink with such stimulation was lower and the number of sites producing eye blink was higher in conditioned animals than in naive or extinguished animals. As controls, Engel and Woody (1972a, 1972b) found that neither of these effects was produced by training with a different CS (hiss) and a different US (air puff), which produces conditioned nose twitch.

Increased click-evoked unit activity in coronal-precruciate cortex implies some change in the reflex pathway at or afferent to those cortical neurons. A decreased microstimulation threshold implies some change at or efferent to coronal-precruciate cortex. Together, these results suggest that conditioning may produce a change in neural elements located in coronal-precruciate cortex, although changes in other loci are not ruled out (cf. Woody *et al.*, 1976, for similar results in auditory association cortex). Intracellular techniques are necessary to determine the exact nature of the observed neural changes. Using such techniques, Woody and Black-Cleworth (1973) and Brons and Woody (1980) found that units in coronal-precruciate cortex have a lower current threshold for spike initiation and a higher likelihood of producing excitation in eye-blink musculature in animals that have had paired training than in animals that have been trained with the CS alone. However, both of these changes are also produced by training with the US (glabella tap) alone. Thus they may be mechanisms involved in long-term sensitization, but their role in classical conditioning is still unclear.

C. Classical Conditioning in Rat

James Olds and his colleagues recorded the activity of single units in various regions of the brain during classical appetitive or aversive conditioning in rats. In an initial study Olds *et al.* (1972) used a conditioning procedure in which a food pellet was delivered to the rat 1 second after the onset of one of two tones (the CS^+), whereas the second tone (the CS^-) was presented unpaired with food. Training consisted of approximately 300 trials with each stimulus in one 15-hour session. The rats acquired a large conditioned response (general body movement) to the CS^+ and a smaller response to the CS^- in 30 to 40 trials (Segal & Olds, 1972). Olds *et al.* (1972) found that units in a variety of brain regions likewise developed a differential response to the CS^+. They were particularly interested in units that developed such a response with a latency of less than 20 msec after the tone onset, arguing that these were likely to be loci of the primary neural change underlying the conditioning. In this study they found such units in frontal and sensorimotor cortex and CA3 of hippocampus.

In subsequent studies, Olds and his colleagues concentrated on the activity of units in the hippocampus during similar conditioning procedures. Segal and Olds (1972) found that over the course of training conditioned unit responses appeared first in the dentate and then in CA3 and CA1 of hippocampus. Because the appearance of conditioned unit responses in CA3 and CA1 lagged behind the first appearance of a conditioned behavioral response over trials, their role as loci of the primary neural change underlying conditioning was brought into question. Segal and Olds next recorded unit activity in these areas during conditioning procedures in which either a tone was paired in alternate sessions with food or electric shock (Segal et al., 1972) or one tone was paired with food and a second tone was paired with shock (Segal & Olds, 1973). In either case, they found that units in the dentate developed a positive response to the tone paired with food and were inhibited by the tone paired with shock. This was similar to the conditioned behavioral response, which was activity with food and freezing with shock. Units in CA1 and CA3 of hippocampus, on the other hand, responded to the tone with increased activity regardless of whether it was paired with food or shock. These units also had a shorter response latency than did units in dentate (which has a major projection to CA3 and CA1), leading Segal and Olds to suggest that these three areas may be involved in a feedback circuit which is influenced by the nature of the reinforcement.

D. Rabbit Nictitating-Membrane Conditioning

Richard Thompson and his colleagues have undertaken a series of experiments on neural correlates of nictitating-membrane conditioning in the rabbit. They chose this preparation because relatively rapid and reliable conditioning could be obtained in restrained animals, making unit recording during acquisition possible, and because a great deal was already known about the behavioral properties of the conditioning (Gormezano, 1972). In the basic experimental arrangement (Thompson et al., 1976) the CS is a 350 msec tone, which terminates simultaneously with a 100 msec air puff to the eye (the US). Experimental animals received thirteen blocks of training per day for 2 days, with eight paired trials and one CS-alone trial per block. Control animals received a similar number of CS and US presentations, unpaired. Initially, animals showed no response to the tone, but by the end of the first training day experimental animals responded to it with movement of the nictitating membrane (which protects the eye) on about 90% of trials, and by the end of the second day they responded on almost 100% of trials. Control animals remained unresponsive to the tone (Berger & Thompson, 1978b). Furthermore, no conditioning was obtained in paired animals when the CS–US interval was 50 msec instead of 250 msec (Hoehler & Thompson, 1980).

Thompson and his colleagues (1976; Cegavske et al., 1979) first recorded multi-unit activity in the abducens nucleus (a motor nucleus that controls muscles involved in the nictitating membrane response) during conditioning. Not too surprisingly, they found a very good correlation between evoked activity in this nucleus and behavior. Because they doubted that this correlate represented a primary neural change underlying conditioning, however, they next wished to find correlates afferent to the abducens nucleus which might represent such a change. Instead of undertaking the laborious task of tracing the CS pathway from the ear to the motor nucleus, they decided first to investigate the hippocampus. Many previous studies (e.g., Milner, 1972; Segal et al., 1972; Segal & Olds, 1972, 1973) had implicated this structure as being important in learning and memory. Berger et al. (1976) and Berger and Thompson (1978b) recorded multi-unit and single-unit activity in the hippocampus during nictitating-membrane conditioning. They found that whereas units in CA1, CA3, and dentate showed no consistent response to either the CS or the US in naive or unpaired control animals, these units developed a response during the first block of trials in paired animals. This response appeared initially in the US (air puff) period of each trial, and with further blocks of training began appearing in the CS (tone) period, before the onset of the US. On average, the latency of the peak hippocampal-unit response was shorter than the latency of the behavioral response, and the development of the hippocampal response over trials paralleled or preceded the development of the behavioral response to the CS. Some individual units showed the pattern of results just described, whereas others showed no effect of the conditioning procedure. Berger and Thompson (1978a) categorized similar unit response data by cell type and found that 15 of 20 hippocampal pyramidal cells developed a conditioned response, whereas other cell types in the hippocampus ($N = 16$) did not.

Berger and Thompson (1977, 1978c) have obtained similar results from units in the lateral septum, but not the medial septum. These results implicate hippocampus and lateral septum as possible loci of the primary neural change underlying conditioning of the nictitating-membrane response. This idea has been challenged on the grounds that hippocampal lesions do not abolish the capability for conditioning (Schmaltz & Theios, 1972; Solomon & Moore, 1975), but Hoehler and Thompson (1980) suggest that these results can be reconciled by supposing that the hippocampus subserves "working" memory and that "reference" memory resides elsewhere. [McCormick, Clark, Lavond, and Thompson (1982) have recorded similar neural correlates of conditioning in cerebellum and have performed lesion studies that indicate that cerebellum may be the site of the primary memory trace for this type of learning.] A form of synaptic plasticity (long-term potentiation or LTP) that develops rapidly and can last hours or weeks has been described in dentate (Bliss & Gardner-Medwin, 1973; Bliss & Lømo, 1973) and hippocampus (Schwartzkroin & Wester, 1975). Berger and Thompson (1978b) have suggested that LTP may be the mechanism of the conditioned hippocampal unit responses. Exactly how LTP could produce the observed changes in unit responding and how those in turn are related to changes in behavioral responding during conditioning are not known.

E. Summary

Cellular studies of learning in vertebrates have revealed neural correlates in a wide variety of brain regions. This finding has raised the following questions of interpretation: (1) Which, if any, of these correlates are causally related to behavioral conditioning, and which are side effects of it? (2) Which, if any, represent "primary" neural changes, rather than being secondary consequences of changes in other brain areas that project to the recorded area? As was discussed earlier, neither of these questions can be resolved by simple rules based on latency or trials to criterion. The first question is essential, but the second may be misleading if it is taken to imply that only one brain area is primary. Indeed, the simplest (but by no means compelling) conclusion from the ubiquity of neural correlates is that the neural machinery for learning may be distributed in many brain regions. The fact that analogs of classical conditioning can be obtained in the isolated spinal cord (Patterson, 1975; Patterson *et al.*, 1973) supports the idea that the ability to develop conditioned responses is not the property of one specialized brain area.

It should be pointed out, however, that a distributed engram (if such is indeed the case) is not incompatible with the cellular-connection approach. In fact, the best way to tackle both of the questions raised above is with that approach. Causality can be demonstrated by establishing the neuronal circuit linking a given brain region to relevant receptor and effector organs, and primacy can be demonstrated by showing that the output of a region changes while its input remains constant. Unfortunately, these are very difficult tasks in the vertebrate brain, and in no case have both been accomplished. Neural correlates in higher brain areas such as hippocampus have not been causally related to behavior, whereas correlates in sensory and motor areas (which are plausibly related to behavior) have not been shown to be primary.

In addition to uncertainty about the locus of primary neural changes underlying learning, there is also almost complete ignorance about the mechanism of associative learning in vertebrates. Because in most cases correlates have been found in brain regions that are excited by the US as well as the CS (see, however, Gibbs *et al.*, 1981), Hebb-type synaptic plasticity is a possibility. In two cases in which neural correlates were found in motor nuclei (Cegavske *et al.*, 1979; Woody & Brozek, 1969), such a possibility is supported by the fact that direct stimulation of the motor neurons can serve as an effective US for behavioral conditioning (Black-Cleworth, Woody, & Niemann, 1975; Martin, Land, & Thompson, 1980). Furthermore, in naive animals the CS (tone) produces enhanced responsiveness of motor neurons, with the interval between the CS and maximum responsiveness being the same as the CS–US interval that produces optimal conditioning (Young, Cegavske, & Thompson, 1976). These observations are consistent with Hebb-type plasticity in the motor nucleus itself (assuming that the CS produces subthreshold depolarization of the motor neurons and the US produces superthreshold stimulation), but such plasticity has not been demonstrated in a brain area where a neural correlate of conditioning has also been recorded. Thus, despite the continued popularity of Hebb's hypothesis, there is as yet no evidence linking the plasticity he proposed to behavioral conditioning.

A quite different form of synaptic plasticity, LTP, has been proposed as the mechanism of neural correlates in the hippocampus (Berger & Thompson, 1978b). The details of this proposal are not clear, but one possibility is simple summation of CS and US inputs in neurons afferent to the synapse undergoing LTP. Although this mechanism is also still hypothetical, it has the advantage of invoking a type of synaptic plasticity known to occur in the same brain area as a neural correlate of behavioral conditioning.

V. INVERTEBRATE STUDIES OF ASSOCIATIVE LEARNING

Prior to 1968, there was only one invertebrate preparation that seemed particularly promising for a cellular analysis of conditioning (Horridge, 1962a, 1962b). The impetus for developing invertebrate preparations to study associative learning has been the same as for nonassociative learning: the relative simplicity of invertebrate nervous systems greatly facilitates cellular analysis and the relating of cellular events to behavior. In the past decade there has been a minor explosion of invertebrate preparations, several of which are described below. Studies of conditioning in these preparations have been aimed at answering two major questions: (1) To what degree does conditioning in invertebrates resemble conditioning in vertebrates and (2) What is the cellular mechanism of conditioning?

The first question is important because of its bearing on the second. That is, one would like to know whether the mechanism of learning in invertebrates is the same as the mechanism in vertebrates. This question can not be answered at present, but the more similar behavior is in invertebrates and vertebrates, the more likely it is that similar neuronal mechanisms are involved. A decade ago there was considerable doubt that many invertebrates were capable of conditioning at all. However, various forms of conditioning have now been demonstrated in several different invertebrates (e.g., Carew, Walters, & Kandel, 1981b; Crow & Alkon, 1978; Gelperin, 1975; Horridge, 1962a, 1962b; Lukowiak & Sahley, 1981; Mpitsos & Collins, 1975; Quinn, Harris, & Benzer, 1974; Walters, Carew, & Kandel, 1979), making it seem likely that the capability for conditioning is ubiquitous. Moreover, recent studies have shown that conditioning in invertebrates has higher order features such as second-order conditioning, Kamin blocking, a US preexposure effect (Sahley, Rudy, & Gelperin, 1981), and conditioned fear (Walters, Carew, & Kandel, 1981) characteristic of vertebrate conditioning. These findings enhance confidence that conditioning in vertebrates and invertebrates has the same underlying mechanisms and also open the possibility of studying the neural bases of these higher order features.

Progress on the second question has in most cases been limited to the recording of neural correlates of conditioning in motor neurons or interneurons. In two cases, however, fairly complete neuronal mechanisms of conditioning have been proposed (Alkon, 1979; Hawkins, Abrams, Carew, and Kandel, 1983). These involve basically the same type of engram (a long-lasting decrease in K^+ current due to cAMP-mediated protein phosphorylation) but different association mechanisms. As progress is made in the neuronal analysis of conditioning in other preparations, it will be interesting to see to what extent the mechanisms are similar and to what extent fundamentally different mechanisms of associative learning have evolved, both in different invertebrate species and for different tasks in the same species.

A. Leg-Position Learning in Locusts

Horridge (1962a, 1962b) published the first widely accepted report of associative learning in an invertebrate preparation amenable to cellular analysis. He suspended headless locusts or cockroaches over a saline bath with an electrode on the animal's leg so that when it relaxed and made contact with the bath the animal received an electric shock. Yoked control animals received an identical pattern of shock independent of their own leg movements. The experimental animals learned to keep the leg elevated and received progressively fewer shocks during a 45-minute training session. Moreover, during a second session 10 minutes later in which shock was contingent on leg position for all subjects, the experimental animals received fewer shocks than the control (previously yoked) animals, demonstrating savings from the previous training. Hoyle (1980) has shown that locusts and grasshoppers can also learn to perform a similar task to avoid a loud noise or to obtain food. Eisenstein and Cohen (1965) repeated Horridge's experiments with the prothoracic ganglion (which controls leg movement) isolated from the rest of the nervous system both anteriorly and posteriorly, and got results similar to those of Horridge. When they removed the ganglion, however, there was no longer a difference between experimental and control animals, indicating that the isolated prothoracic ganglion is both necessary and sufficient for learning of this task.

Hoyle (1965) carried the analysis to the next level by recording the activity of the single excitor motor neuron for the coxal adductor (a muscle that participates in leg lift) during learning. He found that the firing rate of this motor neuron could be conditioned directly; that is, if the animal was shocked when-

ever the firing rate fell below a certain level, the neuron increased its average rate
of firing for many minutes. A random pattern of shock did not produce the same
effect. Moreover, the learning did not seem to depend on proprioceptive feedback from leg position, since it still occurred if the tendon for the adductor was
cut. Tosney and Hoyle (1977) have replicated these results with a totally automated apparatus, and have been able to condition either an increase ("up"
training) or a decrease ("down" training) in firing frequency of the motor
neuron.

A change in firing frequency could be due either to a change in the intrinsic
pacemaker rhythm of the neuron or to a change in tonic synaptic input. Woolacott and Hoyle (1977) recorded the firing frequency of the excitor motor neuron
with the ganglion bathed in a high Mg^{2+}, low Ca^{2+} solution (which blocks
synaptic transmission) before and after training and found that it increased following "up" training and decreased following "down" training. However, the
changes observed were not as large as those seen in normal saline solution. These
results seem to indicate that both the pacemaker rhythm of the motor neuron and
tonic synaptic input onto it change as a result of training.

Woolacott and Hoyle (1976) reported that the input resistance of the motor
neuron (measured in normal saline) increases, and the amplitude of hyperpolarizing afterpotentials in it decreases following "up" training. These changes are
consistent with a prolonged decrease in a voltage-dependent potassium conductance in the motor neuron. Since a decreased potassium conductance would also
produce the observed increase in pacemaker rhythm of the motor neuron, this
could be the physical form of the engram or memory for the training (Hoyle,
1979). Presumably these changes in the motor neuron are triggered by activity in
other neurons. Which neurons those are and how they participate in the association mechanism remain to be investigated.

B. Taste-Aversion Learning in *Limax*

The gastropod molluscs are particularly attractive subjects for the cellular
analysis of associative learning for the same reasons that make them attractive for
the analysis of nonassociative learning: they have relatively few, large, and
individually identifiable neurons. One of the first gastropod preparations to show
convincing associative learning was the terrestrial slug, *Limax maximus*.
Gelperin (1975) found that if he fed slugs mushroom, which is normally a
preferred food, and then made them sick by gassing them with CO_2, they would
subsequently reject the mushroom but would ingest other foods (such as potato)
normally. The learning took one or two trials, and lasted several days. This
behavior is very similar to taste-aversion learning ("bait shyness") in mammals
(Garcia, McGowan, & Green, 1972).

Sahley, Gelperin, and Rudy (1981) modified the original procedure to make it more convenient for cellular analysis. They found that pairing food or a food odor with a bitter-tasting substance, such as quinidine sulfate, for only one trial also leads to subsequent avoidance of that food. Furthermore, they demonstrated differential conditioning by pairing one food (such as potato) with quinidine sulfate and exposing the animal to another (such as carrot) without the quinidine and then letting it choose between each food and rat chow. As expected, the animals usually avoided the food previously associated with quinidine but approached the other (foods were counterbalanced in this experiment).

Sahley, Rudy, and Gelperin (1981) have reported second-order conditioning with this procedure. That is, they first paired one food (e.g., carrot) with quinidine sulfate, and then paired a second food (e.g., potato) with the first food (carrot). Following this training, animals avoided the second food as well as the first, compared to controls. Moreover, Sahley, Rudy, and Gelperin reported two other forms of higher order conditioning (the Kamin blocking effect and a US preexposure effect) with this paradigm. In the blocking experiment, if carrot was first paired with quinidine and then a combination of carrot and potato was paired with the quinidine, the animals did *not* learn to avoid the potato, compared to controls. In the US preexposure experiment, if animals were given an exposure to quinidine 2 or 6 (but not 24) hours before a paired trial of carrot and quinidine, they also did not learn to avoid the carrot. Each of these effects has been reported for conditioning in mammals. These studies have thus demonstrated parallels between the learning abilities of slugs and mammals, and suggest that basic (and even higher order) learning phenomena may be similar throughout the animal kingdom.

As a first step toward the neural analysis of taste-aversion learning in *Limax,* Chang and Gelperin (1980) were able to reproduce the phenomenon in a preparation consisting of the isolated lips and central nervous system of the animal. In this preparation, application of a food substance to the lips elicits a recognizable "feeding motor program" of rhythmic activity in the buccal ganglion nerve roots (Gelperin, Chang, & Reingold, 1978). However, if a food substance is paired with a bitter-tasting substance (such as colchicine or nicotine) for one or two trials, it subsequently fails to elicit the feeding motor program for up to 6 hours, whereas other foods still reliably do so. Because it is possible to record the activity of neurons both extracellularly and intracellularly during learning in this preparation, it is a promising one for further neural analysis.

C. Aversive Conditioning in *Pleurobranchaea*

Of the gastropod molluscs, the most extensively studied subclass is the Opisthobranchia (hind-gilled) which includes *Pleurobranchaea, Hermissenda,* and *Aplysia.* These are all marine snails with reduced or absent shells. *Pleurobranchaea* and *Hermissenda* are carnivorous, whereas *Aplysia* is herbivorous.

One of the first opisthobranch preparations to demonstrate associative learning was *Pleurobranchaea*. Mpitsos and Davis initially reported conditioning of *Pleurobranchaea* in 1973, although that study has been criticized as having inadequate controls (Lee, 1976). In a subsequent study with better control procedures, Mpitsos and Collins (1975) established a conditioning paradigm which has been used since then. On each of ten training trials separated by 1 hour, experimental animals were presented with a standard solution of homogenized squid, which elicits approach and feeding responses in naives. If the animals exhibited feeding responses they immediately received 60 seconds of electric shock; if they did not feed or withdraw they received the shock after 3 minutes; and if they exhibited a sustained withdrawal response during the 3-minute period, they were not shocked at all. Matched control animals received the same amount of shock 30 minutes after each squid presentation. For over 5 days following this training experimental animals had a greater incidence of withdrawal responses to the squid and longer latencies and higher thresholds to elicit feeding responses than did the controls.

These findings have been extended in subsequent studies by Mpitsos, Collins, and McClellan (1978), who showed that random presentation of squid and shock does not produce the learned change in behavior, and that weaker but statistically significant learning can be obtained with a totally automated training procedure. W. J. Davis, Villet, Lee, Rigler, Gillette, and Prince (1980) have also demonstrated weak "differential" conditioning with (for instance) squid as the CS$^+$ and shrimp as the CS$^-$, although in each case no differential conditioning was obtained when the CS$^+$ and CS$^-$ were reversed.

W. J. Davis and Gillette (1978) have obtained a neural correlate of the basic conditioning procedure in *Pleurobranchaea*. They recorded the response of putative feeding "command" cells (Gillette, Kovac, & Davis, 1978) in the exposed nervous system of animals that had previously received paired, unpaired, or no training. Whereas these cells are excited by application of squid homogenate to the oral veil in naive animals (7 out of 16 cells tested) and in animals that have had unpaired training (10 out of 10 cells), they were inhibited in animals that had had paired training (9 out of 14 cells). Presumably, then, paired conditioning causes some change in the neural pathway from chemoreceptors in the oral veil to the putative feeding command cells. The exact nature of this change and the mechanism that produces it remain to be investigated.

D. An Associative Behavioral Change in *Hermissenda*

Alkon first reported associative training of *Hermissenda* in 1974, although in that study an unpaired control group did not differ from the paired training group. Crow and Alkon (1978) subsequently developed an automated procedure for associative training of *Hermissenda*. They placed the animals in glass tubes arranged radially on a turntable with a light bulb at the center of the turntable. Naive animals would normally locomote toward the light when it was turned on. However, if light was paired with rotation of the turntable 50 times a day for 3 days, the animals' latencies to approach the light significantly increased compared to their baseline scores and to those of animals that had had unpaired or random training. This effect was greatest when approach latencies were measured immediately after the end of training, but it could be retained for up to several days.

Light and rotation were chosen as the stimuli in these studies because of the simplicity of the relevant sensory structures in *Hermissenda*. Each eye of *Hermissenda* has five photoreceptors (of which two are type A and three are type B), each optic ganglion has 13 second-order visual neurons, and each statocyst has 12 hair cells. Moreover, the interactions between many of these neural elements have been characterized. Type A and type B photoreceptors inhibit each other, type B cells and caudal hair cells both inhibit "E" optic ganglion cells, and E cells excite B photoreceptors and inhibit caudal hair cells (cf. Alkon, 1979, 1980a).

Recent research has focused on the type B photoreceptors. These cells respond to a light step with a large depolarization during the light and a smaller, long-lasting depolarization (LLD) associated with an increased membrane resistance for many seconds after the light is turned off (Alkon & Grossman, 1978). Alkon (1979) has analyzed the ionic bases of these responses under voltage clamp, and has concluded that light induces three currents in the B photoreceptors: a transient Na^+ current, a transient K^+ current, and a sustained voltage-dependent Ca^{2+} current. The LLD is thought to be due to a continuation of the sustained Ca^{2+} current and a decrease in a resting K^+ current.

Crow and Alkon (1980) recorded the properties of B photoreceptors in nervous systems taken from animals that had just completed 3 days of either paired or random light and rotation training. They found that B cells in animals that had received paired training had higher rates of spontaneous firing in the dark (due to chronic, nonsynaptic depolarization) and higher input resistances than did cells from control animals. Farley and Alkon (1982) and West, Barnes, and Alkon (1982) have found that B cells also have increased evoked responses to light and larger LLDs, as well as higher input resistances in the dark 24 or 48 hours after paired training. These results are consistent with a persistent decrease in a K^+ conductance in B photoreceptors of paired animals. Alkon (1980a) has proposed that chronic depolarization of the B cells should lead to larger generator potentials in response to light because of (1) the voltage dependence of the light-evoked Ca^{2+} current and (2) inactivation of the transient, light-evoked K^+ current (Alkon, Lederhendler, & Shoukimas, 1982). Greater light-evoked activity of the B photoreceptors should in turn produce greater synaptic inhibition of the A photoreceptors, and hence decreased positive phototaxis.

Alkon (1979, 1980a) has proposed the following model to account for the chronic depolarization observed in B photoreceptors from animals that have had paired (but not random) light and rotation training. On each paired training trial, the combined activity of the B cells and the caudal hair cells produces strong inhibition of the E optic-ganglion cells and hence strong rebound excitation of the B photoreceptors when the light is turned off. This synaptic excitation is enhanced by the LLD in the B cells because of the increased input resistance associated with the LLD and in turn enhances it, presumably because of the voltage dependence of the LLD (Alkon, 1979; Alkon & Grossmann, 1978). The enhanced LLD lasts until the start of the next trial, causing a larger response to the light and an even larger and longer lasting LLD, etc. Thus enhancement of the LLD by pairing of light and rotation creates a positive feedback cycle of light and synaptically induced depolarization of the B photoreceptors, which builds up over trials.

In order to test this model, Alkon (1980b) measured the membrane potential of B photoreceptors during either paired or unpaired presentation of light and rotation in a semiintact preparation. He found that paired presentation of the stimuli produced larger LLD than did unpaired presentation (see also Alkon & Grossman, 1978). Moreover, membrane depolarization accumulated over two trials in preparations receiving paired training but did not in preparations receiving unpaired training, and could last more than 5 minutes following several training trials.

It is not clear how accumulation of membrane depolarization during training could lead to persistent depolarization lasting hours or days, however. An additional biochemical step might reasonably be involved. Neary, Crow, and Alkon (1981) have reported that a protein with a molecular weight of approximately 20,000 is significantly more phosphorylated in eyes from animals that have had 3 days of paired light and rotation training than in eyes from random control animals. Moreover, Alkon, Acosta-Urquidi, Olds, Kuzma, and Neary (1983) have found that intracellular injection of the catalytic subunit of cAMP-dependent protein phosphokinase produces an increase in membrane resistance and LLD and a decrease in K^+ current in B photoreceptors. It thus seems possible that the engram for light and rotation training in *Hermissenda* is a long-lasting decrease in a K^+ conductance in type B photoreceptors caused by cAMP-dependent protein phosphorylation. Alternatively, the decrease in K^+ conductance may be caused by Ca^{2+}–calmodulin-dependent protein phosphorylation triggered by an elevation in intracellular Ca^{2+} during training (Alkon, Shoukimas, and Heldman, 1982). More experiments are necessary to explore these ideas.

The model proposed for an associative behavioral change in *Hermissenda* has several weaknesses, most of which have to do with relating the observed cellular events to behavior. In particular, accumulation of depolarization in the type B photoreceptor has been observed *in vitro* for 2 (or in one case 10) trials and has been shown to last minutes, whereas the behavioral training consists of 50 trials a day for 3 days and is retained for days. Also, rotation often precedes light in the *in vitro* experiments, whereas in the behavioral experiments it follows it. Furthermore, there has as yet been no demonstration that the type B photoreceptors (or the eyes, for that matter) are necessary for learning, and there is no indication of how changes in photoreceptor activity might lead to the observed change in behavior (decreased locomotion). A great advantage of the model is that each of these points should be amenable to further cellular analysis.

E. Aversive Conditioning in *Aplysia*

Several early studies (Downey & Jahan-Parwar, 1972; Lee, 1969, 1970; Lickey, 1968) suggested that *Aplysia* are capable of associative learning. However, there has been no cellular analysis of the learning in these cases. Walters *et al.* (1979) used a paradigm similar to that described for *Pleurobranchaea* to demonstrate aversive classical conditioning in *Aplysia*. Experimental animals received a standard solution of shrimp homogenate (an initially neutral chemosensory stimulus) paired with 30 seconds of electric shock to the head three times a day for 2 days. When they were tested on the following day the animals showed no obvious reaction to the shrimp solution. However, if they received a mild electric shock to the tail in the presence of the shrimp solution, they exhibited significantly more escape locomotion than did control animals that had had unpaired shrimp and head shock training.

Walters *et al.* (1979) interpreted this result as evidence for conditioning of a motivational state analogous to fear in vertebrates. That is, following paired training with the shrimp solution and electric shock, presentation of the shrimp made the animals afraid in the sense that it enhanced their defensive responses. In order to test this hypothesis, Walters *et al.* (1981) measured several other defensive responses in the presence of the shrimp solution following similar training. They found that head withdrawal, inking, and siphon withdrawal were also enhanced by presentation of the shrimp in animals that had had paired training, compared to unpaired controls. Moreover, an appetitive response, feeding, was depressed in the presence of the shrimp. These results therefore support a conditioned fear hypothesis.

Carew, Walters, and Kandel (1981a) were able to record cellular correlates of the learning in motor neurons involved in several of these responses. One day after the end of training, animals were surgically opened under $MgCl_2$ anesthesia and their nervous systems exposed. The response of motor neurons involved in escape locomotion, inking, or siphon withdrawal to weak tail stimulation was then measured both with and without shrimp solution bathing the anterior tentacles. In all three cases tail stimulation produced a significantly larger response in the motor neurons in the presence of shrimp in animals that had had paired training, but not in control animals that had had unpaired training. However, application of the shrimp produced no change in the membrane potential or input resistance of the motor neurons. These results indicate that enhancement of these responses by the shrimp solution occurs at some stage in the reflex pathways prior to the motor neurons.

Although conditioning of a central motivational state in *Aplysia* is interesting from a comparative psychological point of view, it does not promise to be easy to analyze at the neuronal level, because the neural circuit for the learned behavior is not known and is probably quite complex. For this reason it seemed desirable to demonstrate conditioning of a simpler behavior, such as the gill- and siphon-withdrawal reflex, which has a relatively simple neural circuit that has been well described. There have been two reports of direct conditioning of the withdrawal reflex. First, Lukowiak and Sahley (1981) reported that if photo stimulation of the siphon was paired with tactile stimulation of the gill for 25 trials in a semiintact preparation, the photo stimulation came to elicit gill withdrawal (in 7 out of 10 preparations), but it did not if the two stimuli were presented in a random fashion. There has as yet been no neural analysis of this conditioning.

Second, Carew *et al.* (1981b) reported conditioning of the siphon-elicited withdrawal reflex, which has previously been used in extensive studies of the neuronal basis of habituation and sensitization (see Section II). They found that if mild tactile or electrical stimulation of the siphon (the CS) is paired with stronger electrical stimulation of the tail (the US) for 20 to 30 trials separated by 5 minutes in free or restrained animals, the siphon stimulation comes to elicit significantly larger gill and siphon withdrawals than if the two stimuli are presented in an unpaired or random fashion. This effect builds up during the training session and is retained for several days. Carew, Hawkins, and Kandel (1983) have demonstrated differential conditioning of this reflex with stimulation of the siphon and mantle shelf (a region anterior to the gill) as the discriminative stimuli. They obtained significant discriminative conditioning either 15 minutes or 24 hours after a single training trial, and stronger conditioning with 5 or 15 training trials. They also found that differential conditioning can be obtained with stimulation of two different sites on the siphon (rather than the siphon and mantle shelf) as the discriminative stimuli. Finally, they have begun to explore the interstimulus interval (ISI) function, and have obtained reliable conditioning when the CS precedes the US by 0.5 seconds (the standard ISI) but no conditioning when the US precedes the CS.

It was already known that the mechanism of sensitization of the withdrawal reflex is presynaptic facilitation of the siphon sensory neurons (see Section II). Because of the similarity of sensitization and classical conditioning, it was attractive to think that classical conditioning might also involve presynaptic facilitation as the mechanism for strengthening the CS pathway. This could work in two ways. First, the CS and US pathways might converge on facilitator neurons so that paired presentation of the CS and US would lead to greater firing of the facilitators and therefore greater presynaptic facilitation than unpaired presentation of the two stimuli. The results of the differential conditioning experiments made this mechanism seem unlikely, because it would require a separate facilitator for each site on the skin that can serve as a discriminative stimulus. Furthermore, Hawkins (unpublished) recorded from facilitator neurons in a semiintact preparation and found no unusual summation of the CS and US inputs.

Second, the CS and US might converge at the level of individual neurons in the CS pathway, with the US producing greater presynaptic facilitation of those neurons if it is temporally paired with spike activity in them. Hawkins *et al.* (1983) tested this possibility by attempting to facilitate differentially the synaptic transmission from two individual siphon sensory neurons in a semiintact preparation with a training procedure analagous to that used in the behavioral experiments. They found that tail shock produces significantly greater facilitation of the monosynaptic EPSP from a sensory neuron to a postsynaptic neuron if the shock is preceded by intracellularly produced spike activity in the sensory neuron than if it is either unpaired with spike activity or is presented alone. In this experiment facilitation of the EPSPs was measured 15 minutes after five training trials. The results were similar quantitatively as well as qualitatively with the results of behavioral experiments with the same protocol and parameters, indicating that this activity-dependent amplification of facilitation can account for behavioral conditioning of the reflex.

Activity-dependent facilitation could result from either a presynaptic or a postsynaptic mechanism. Because facilitation at these synapses underlying behavioral sensitization is presynaptic in origin and is due to broadening of the action potential which leads to an increase in Ca^{2+} influx in the sensory neurons (see Section II), Hawkins *et al.* (1983) investigated the possibility that this mechanism might also be involved in the activity-dependent amplification of facilitation underlying classical conditioning. They used the same experimental protocol as in the previous experiment except that they examined the duration of action potentials in the sensory neurons with the abdominal ganglion bathed in 50-mM tetraethylammonium. The differential training procedure produced a significantly greater increase in spike duration in paired than in unpaired sensory neurons, and this difference was maintained for at least 3 hours after training. Whether this same mechanism can account for memory lasting days remains to be investigated.

These experiments indicate that the mechanism of classical conditioning of the withdrawal reflex is simply an elaboration of the mechanism of sensitization of the reflex: presynaptic facilitation due to an increase in Ca^{2+} influx during each action potential in the sensory neurons. The pairing specificity characteris-

tic of classical conditioning results from the presynaptic facilitation being amplified by temporally paired spike activity in the sensory neurons. It is not yet
known which aspect of the action potential in a sensory neuron interacts with the
process of presynaptic facilitation to amplify it, or which step in the biochemical
cascade leading to presynaptic facilitation is sensitive to the action potential. An
attractive possibility is that the influx of Ca^{2+} with each action potential modulates the serotonin-sensitive adenyl cyclase in the sensory neuron so that the
cyclase subsequently produces more cAMP in response to serotonin (5-HT).
Alternatively, the adenyl cyclase, the regulatory protein (which couples the
cyclase to the 5-HT receptor) and the receptor itself, all of which are membrane-
associated proteins, may be modulated by the transmembrane voltage changes
that occur during an action potential. These and a number of other possibilities
remain to be investigated experimentally.

Activity-dependent amplification of presynaptic facilitation differs from
the mechanism proposed by Hebb (1949) in at least one important respect: Hebb
postulated a critical role for spike activity in the postsynaptic, rather than the
presynaptic neuron (see Section IV). Hawkins *et al.* (1983) tested the Hebb
postulate in their system and found that spike activity in the postsynaptic neuron
is neither necessary nor sufficient for conditioning to occur, because (1) in many
of their experiments the postsynaptic neuron was held at a hyperpolarized level
and did not fire any action potentials in response to the US, and (2) intracellular
stimulation of the postsynaptic neuron does not serve as an effective US. These
results indicate that conditioning of the withdrawal reflex is not due to Hebb-type
synaptic plasticity, but is rather due to activity-dependent amplification of presynaptic facilitation.

An attractive feature of activity-dependent amplification of facilitation is
that it is a mechanism of conditioning that could be very general. First, it requires
very little special circuitry, because the mechanism of pairing specificity is
intrinsic to neurons in the CS pathway. The minimum requirements of this model
are (1) a facilitatory system, such as the L29 neurons, which may project very
diffusely, and (2) differential activity in neurons which receive facilitatory input.
Thus, this mechanism may operate throughout the nervous system wherever
these two requirements are satisfied. Indeed, Walters and Byrne (1983) have
obtained similar results in another group of neurons in *Aplysia*. More spec-
ulatively, it is attractive to think that this mechanism may also operate in the
vertebrate nervous system, with the diffusely projecting aminergic or cholinergic
systems playing the role that the L29 neurons play in the abdominal ganglion of
Aplysia.

Second, the aspects of a mechanism of associative learning that are most
likely to be general phylogenetically are those at the fundamental molecular and
biophysical levels. Activity-dependent amplification of presynaptic facilitation
probably involves the same cascade of biochemical and biophysical processes

that mediate conventional presynaptic facilitation at the sensory neuron synapses: cAMP-dependent protein phosphorylation and decreased ionic conductances. These processes are widespread phylogenetically and seem to be highly conserved. If a step in that cascade has a voltage or ion sensitivity that makes it suitable as a mechansim of classical conditioning in *Aplysia,* it may very well have the same sensitivity, with the same consequences, in neurons of other species where it occurs.

F. Summary

Associative learning has now been demonstrated in several invertebrate preparations that are amenable to cellular analysis. In locust, *Limax,* and *Pleurobranchaea,* neuronal analysis of associative learning is thus far limited to correlates in motor or premotor neurons, whereas fairly detailed mechanisms have been proposed for the learning in *Hermissenda* and *Aplysia.* Despite the preliminary nature of some of this research, the available data seem to form a fairly consistent pattern. Associative training in both locusts and *Hermissenda* appears to produce a persistent decrease in a resting K^+ current in identified neurons. In the case of *Hermissenda,* there is evidence suggesting that this decrease in K^+ current may be caused by cAMP-dependent protein phosphorylation. There is also evidence indicating that both sensitization and associative learning in *Drosophila* may involve regulation of cAMP levels (Byers, Davis, & Kiger, 1981; R. L. Davis & Kiger, 1981; Dudai, Jan, Byers, Quinn, & Benzer, 1976; Duerr & Quinn, 1982). As was reviewed in Section II, more direct evidence indicates that sensitization of the gill-withdrawal reflex in *Aplysia* is due to a decrease in a voltage-dependent K^+ conductance caused by cAMP-dependent phosphorylation of a membrane protein. Studies of classical conditioning in *Aplysia* indicate that the neuronal mechanism of conditioning is simply an amplification of the mechanism of sensitization and therefore probably also involves cAMP-mediated protein phosphorylation leading to a decrease in K^+ conductance.

In each of these cases the component of mechanism being discussed is the store or engram. Thus the available evidence supports the notion that each of these types of learning (operant conditioning, classical conditioning, and sensitization) involves the same basic type of engram: cAMP-dependent protein phosphorylation leading to a persistent decrease in a K^+ current. What differs in each case is where this decrease in K^+ current occurs and thus what its consequences are: in locust it appears to occur in motor neurons, increasing pacemaker activity; in *Hermissenda* it appears to occur in photoreceptors, enhancing generator potentials; and in *Aplysia* it appears to occur in sensory neuron terminals, facilitating transmitter release.

There is less evidence regarding the association mechanism in most of these preparations. In *Hermissenda* the proposed association mechanism is somewhat complicated, but the crux of it may be considered to be summation of depolarization induced directly by light (the CS) and synaptically by offset of rotation (the US) in type B photoreceptors. In *Aplysia* the association mechanism is amplification of presynaptic facilitation of the sensory neurons by preceding spike activity in those neurons. The mechanism that is thought to underlie activity dependence of presynaptic facilitation is either voltage sensitivity or ion sensitivity of a cAMP-mediated decrease in K^+ conductance in the sensory neurons. If a similar mechanism occurred in different types of neurons it could account for the neuronal correlates of operant and classical conditioning observed in locust and *Hermissenda*. As reviewed above, conditioning in those preparations produces long-lasting decreases in K^+ current in motor neurons and photoreceptors, receptively. Those decreases in K^+ current may be cAMP mediated and could be triggered by (hypothetical) modulatory synaptic inputs produced by the reinforcing stimuli. If so, they might exhibit activity dependence similar to that seen in *Aplysia*. Thus, in the case of classical conditioning in *Hermissenda,* the modulatory input would be amplified if it was temporally paired with a generator potential in the photoreceptor. Similarly, in the case of positive operant conditioning in locust (Hoyle, 1979), the modulatory input would be amplified if it was temporally paired with spontaneous spike activity in the motor neuron. Several possible variants on this scheme might account for negative operant conditioning in locust, one of which would be to reverse the sign of the activity dependence.

Although these ideas are speculative, they offer the possibility of accounting for all of the cellular information on associative learning in invertebrates with a single mechanism: activity-dependent modulation of a cyclic nucleotide-dependent decrease in K^+ current. There is some evidence for a similar mechanism in vertebrates. Woody, Swartz, and Gruen (1978) found that iontophoresis of acetylcholine or injection of cyclic GMP produce longer lasting increases in membrane resistance in neurons of coronal-precruciate cortex if they are paired with intracellularly produced spike activity in those neurons than if they are not. This effect is implicated in eye-blink conditioning, because Brons and Woody (1980) recorded a prolonged increase in excitability of neurons in coronal-precruciate cortex of cats that had received such conditioning. It seems worth pointing out that this mechanism is different in several respects from the Hebb model which has guided much of the vertebrate research (see Section IV), and that in one case of conditioning (*Aplysia* withdrawal conditioning) in which the Hebb postulate has been directly tested, it has not been supported.

VI. CONCLUSIONS

Since Kandel and Spencer's review (1968), neuroscientists have made remarkable advances in understanding the neural bases of nonassociative learning (habituation and sensitization). These advances have come about largely through the development of invertebrate preparations that are well suited for the cellular-connection approach. In those preparations, habituation and sensitization have been shown to be due to changes in the efficacy of transmission at specific synapses, and in *Aplysia* that line of researh is now progressing to the molecular level. Although research on vertebrate preparations has been less conclusive, it also indicates that habituation and sensitization are due to changes in the properties of individual neurons and synapses. These results therefore support the cellular-connection hypothesis and the experimental approach it implies: studying the neural basis of learning on the level of single cells and their connections.

Until recently, progress in the analysis of associative learning has been less rapid. Cellular correlates of conditioning have been found in a number of vertebrate preparations, but have not yet led to any real understanding of the neural mechanisms of learning. One of the great problems of these preparations is in relating the observed neural events to behavior. It has been difficult to use the cellular-connection approach to this problem in vertebrates for several interrelated reasons: the complete neuronal circuit has not been worked out for any vertebrate learned behavior; vertebrate neurons are generally identifiable and seem to act only as members of classes and not as individuals; and technical problems have limited the use of intracellular recording and stimulation techniques. Some of these difficulties are currently being overcome by technological advances such as the development of the brain "slice" (e.g., Schwartzkroin & Wester, 1975). On the other hand, the invertebrate preparations most amenable to cellular analysis were thought not to be capable of associative learning only a short time ago. However, several "simple" invertebrate preparations have now been shown to be capable of associative learning comparable in many respects to that of vertebrates. Recent research on two of these (*Hermissenda* and *Aplysia*) has led to fairly detailed hypotheses about the neuronal mechanisms of classical conditioning. As the technical and behavioral advantages of invertebrate and vertebrate preparations converge, the cellular-connection approach should lead to continued progress in our understanding of the neural basis of associative learning.

REFERENCES

Adey, W. R. Electrophysiological patterns and cerebral impedance characteristics in orienting and discriminative behavior. *Proceedings of the International Union of Physiological Sciences, 23rd, 1965,* 1965, pp. 324–339.

Alkon, D. L. Associative training of *Hermissenda*. *Journal of General Physiology,* 1974, *64,* 70–84.

Alkon, D. L. Voltage-dependent calcium and potassium ion conductances: A contingency mechanism for an associative learning model. *Science,* 1979, *205,* 810–816.

Alkon, D. L. Cellular analysis of a gastropod (*Hermissenda crassicornis*) model of associative learning. *Biological Bulletin,* 1980, *159,* 505–560. (a)

Alkon, D. L. Membrane depolarization accumulates during acquisition of an associative behavioral change. *Science*, 1980, *210*, 1375–1376. (b)

Alkon, D. L., Acosta-Urquidi, J., Olds, J. Kuzma, G., & Neary, J. T. Protein kinase injection reduces voltage-dependent potassium currents. *Science*, 1983, *219*, 303–306.

Alkon, D. L., & Grossman, Y. Long-lasting depolarization and hyperpolarization in eye of *Hermissenda*. *Journal of Neurophysiology*, 1978, *41*, 1328–1342.

Alkon, D. L., Lederhendler, I., & Shoukimas, J. J. Primary changes of membrane currents during retention of associative learning. *Science*, 1982, *215*, 693–695.

Alkon, D. L., Shoukimas, J. J., & Heldman, E. Calcium-mediated decrease of a voltage-dependent potassium current. *Biophysical Journal*, 1982, *40*, 245–250.

Aréchiga, H., Barrera-Mera, B., & Fuentes-Pardo, B. Habituation of mechanoreceptive interneurons in the crayfish. *Journal of Neurobiology*, 1975, *6*, 131–144.

Bailey, C. H., & Chen, M. Morphological basis of long-term habituation and sensitization in *Aplysia*. *Science*, 1983, *220*, 91–93.

Bailey, C. H., Hawkins, R. D., & Chen, M. Uptake of [^{3}H]serotonin in the abdominal ganglion of *Aplysia californica*: Further studies on the morphological and biochemical basis of presynaptic facilitation. *Brain Research*, in press.

Bailey, C. H., Hawkins, R. D., Chen, M. C., & Kandel, E. R. Interneurons involved in mediation and modulation of gill-withdrawal reflex in *Aplysia*. IV. Morphological basis of presynaptic facilitation. *Journal of Neurophysiology*, 1981, *45*, 340–360.

Baranyi, A., & Feher, O. Intracellular studies on cortical synaptic plasticity: Conditioning effect of antidromic activation on test-EPSPs. *Experimental Brain Research*, 1981, *41*, 124–134. (a)

Baranyi, A., & Feher, O. Long-term facilitation of excitatory synaptic transmission in single motor cortical neurones of the cat produced by repetitive pairing of synaptic potentials and action potentials following intracellular stimulation. *Neuroscience Letters*, 1981, *23*, 303–308. (b)

Baranyi, A., & Feher, O. Synaptic facilitation requires paired activation of convergent pathways in the neocortex. *Nature (London)*, 1981, *290*, 413–415. (c)

Berger, T. W., Alger, B. E., & Thompson, R. F. Neuronal substrates of classical conditioning in the hippocampus. *Science*, 1976, *192*, 483–485.

Berger, T. W., & Thompson, R. F. Limbic system interrelations: Functional division among hippocampal-septal connections. *Science*, 1977, *197*, 587–589.

Berger, T. W., & Thompson, R. F. Identification of pyramidal cells as the critical elements in hippocampal neuronal plasticity during learning. *Proceedings of the National Academy of Sciences of the U.S.A.*, 1978, *75*, 1572–1576. (a)

Berger, T. W., & Thompson, R. F. Neuronal plasticity in the limbic system during classical conditioning of the rabbit nictitating membrane response. I. The hippocampus. *Brain Research*, 1978, *145*, 323–346. (b)

Berger, T. W., & Thompson, R. F. Neuronal plasticity in the limbic system during classical conditioning of the rabbit nictitating membrane response. II. Septum and mamillary bodies. *Brain Research*, 1978, *156*, 293–314. (c)

Bernier, L., Castellucci, V. F., Kandel, E. R., & Schwartz, J. H. Facilitatory transmitter causes a selective and prolonged increase in adenosine 3':5'-monophosphate in sensory neurons mediating the gill and siphon withdrawal reflex in *Aplysia*. *Journal of Neuroscience*, 1982, *2*, 1682–1691.

Black-Cleworth, P., Woody, C. D., & Niemann, J. A conditioned eye blink obtained by using electrical stimulation of the facial nerve as the unconditioned stimulus. *Brain Research*, 1975, *90*, 45–56.

Bliss, T. V. P., & Gardner-Medwin, A. R. Long-lasting potentiation of synaptic transmission in the dentate area of the unanaesthetized rabbit following stimulation of the perforant path. *Journal of Physiology (London)*, 1973, *232*, 357–374.

Bliss, T. V. P., & Lømo, T. Long-lasting potentiation of synaptic transmission in the dentate area of the anaesthetized rabbit following stimulation of the perforant path. *Journal of Physiology (London)*, 1973, *232*, 331–356.

Brons, J. F., & Woody, C. D. Long-term changes in excitability of cortical neurons after Pavlovian conditioning and extinction. *Journal of Neurophysiology*, 1980, *44*, 605–615.

Brunelli, M., Castellucci, V., & Kandel, E. R. Synaptic facilitation and behavioral sensitization in *Aplysia:* Possible role of serotonin and cAMP. *Science*, 1976, *194*, 1178–1181.

Bruner, J., & Kennedy, D. Habituation: Occurrence at a neuromuscular junction. *Science*, 1970, *169*, 92–94.

Bruner, J., & Tauc, L. Long-lasting phenomena in the molluscan nervous system. *Symposia of the Society for Experimental Biology*, 1966, *20*, 457–475.

Bryan, J. S., & Krasne, F. B. Protection from habituation of the crayfish lateral giant fibre escape response. *Journal of Physiology (London)*, 1977, *271*, 351–368. (a)

Bryan, J. S., & Krasne, F. B. Presynaptic inhibition: The mechanism of protection from habituation of the crayfish lateral giant fibre escape response. *Journal of Physiology (London)*, 1977, *271*, 369–390. (b)

Burke, W. Neuronal models for conditioned reflexes. *Nature (London)*, 1966, *210*, 269–271.

Byers, D., Davis, R. L., & Kiger, J. A. Defect in cyclic AMP phosphodiesterase due to the dunce mutation of learning in *Drosophila melanogaster*. *Nature (London)*, 1981, *289*, 79–81.

Byrne, J. H., Castellucci, V. F., Carew, T. J., & Kandel, E. R. Stimulus-response relations and stability of mechanoreceptor and motor neurons mediating defensive gill-withdrawal reflex in *Aplysia*. *Journal of Neurophysiology*, 1978, *41*, 402–417.

Byrne, J. H., Castellucci, V. F., & Kandel, E. R. Receptive fields and response properties of mechanoreceptor neurons innervating siphon skin and mantle shelf in *Aplysia*. *Journal of Neurophysiology*, 1974, *37*, 1041–1064.

Callec, J. J., Guillet, J. C., Pichon, Y., & Boistel, J. Further studies on synaptic transmission in insects. II. Relations between sensory information and its synaptic integration at the level of a single giant axon in the cockroach. *Journal of Experimental Biology*, 1971, *55*, 123–149.

Carew, T. J., Castellucci, V. F., & Kandel, E. R. An analysis of dishabituation and sensitization of the gill-withdrawal reflex in *Aplysia*. *International Journal of Neuroscience*, 1971, *2*, 79–98.

Carew, T. J., Castellucci, V. F., & Kandel, E. R. Sensitization in *Aplysia:* Restoration of transmission in synapses inactivated by long-term habituation. *Science*, 1979, *205*, 417–419.

Carew, T. J., Hawkins, R. D., & Kandel, E. R. Differential classical conditioning of a defensive withdrawal reflex in *Aplysia californica*. *Science*, 1983, *219*, 397–400.

Carew, T. J., Pinsker, H. M., & Kandel, E. R. Long-term habituation of a defensive withdrawal reflex in *Aplysia*. *Science*, 1972, *175*, 451–454.

Carew, T. J., Walters, E. T., & Kandel, E. R. Associative learning in *Aplysia:* Cellular correlates supporting a conditioned fear hypothesis. *Science*, 1981, *211*, 501–504. (a)

Carew, T. J., Walters, E. T., & Kandel, E. R. Classical conditioning in a simple withdrawal reflex in *Aplysia californica*. *Journal of Neuroscience*, 1981, *1*, 1426–1437. (b)

Castellucci, V. F., Carew, T. J., & Kandel, E. R. Cellular analysis of long-term habituation of the gill-withdrawal reflex of *Aplysia californica*. *Science*, 1978, *202*, 1306–1308.

Castellucci, V. F., & Kandel, E. R. A quantal analysis of the synaptic depression underlying habituation of the gill-withdrawal reflex in *Aplysia*. *Proceedings of the National Academy of Sciences of the U.S.A.*, 1974, *71*, 5004–5008.

Castellucci, V., & Kandel, E. R. Presynaptic facilitation as a mechanism for behavioral sensitization in *Aplysia*. *Science*, 1976, *194*, 1176–1178.

Castellucci, V. F., Kandel, E. R., Schwartz, J. H., Wilson, F. D., Nairn, A. C., & Greengard, P. Intracellular injection of the catalytic subunit of cyclic AMP-dependent protein kinase simulates facilitation of transmitter release underlying behavioral sensitization in *Aplysia. Proceedings of the National Academy of Sciences of the U.S.A.*, 1980, *77*, 7492–7496.

Castellucci, V. F., Nairn, A., Greengard, P., Schwartz, J. H., & Kandel, E. R. Inhibitor of adenosine 3′:5′-monophosphate-dependent protein kinase blocks presynaptic facilitation in *Aplysia. Journal of Neuroscience*, 1982, *2*, 1673–1681.

Castellucci, V., Pinsker, H., Kupfermann, I., & Kandel, E. R. Neuronal mechanisms of habituation and dishabituation of the gill-withdrawal reflex in *Aplysia. Science*, 1970, *167*, 1745–1748.

Cedar, H., Kandel, E. R., & Schwartz, J. H. Cyclic adenosine monophosphate in the nervous system of *Aplysia californica*. I. Increased synthesis in response to synaptic stimulation. *Journal of General Physiology*, 1972, *60*, 558–569.

Cedar, H., & Schwartz, J. H. Cyclic adenosine monophosphate in the nervous system of *Aplysia californica*. II. Effect of serotonin and dopamine. *Journal of General Physiology*, 1972, *60*, 570–587.

Cegavske, C. F., Patterson, M. M., & Thompson, R. F. Neuronal unit activity in the abducens nucleus during classical conditioning of the nictitating membrane response in the rabbit (*Oryctolagus cuniculus*). *Journal of Comparative & Physiological Psychology*, 1979, *93*, 595–609.

Chang, J. J., & Gelperin, A. Rapid taste-aversion learning by an isolated molluscan central nervous system. *Proceedings of the National Academy of Sciences of the U.S.A.*, 1980, *77*, 6204–6206.

Cohen, D. H. Development of a vertebrate experimental model for cellular neurophysiological studies of learning. *Conditional Reflex*, 1969, *4*, 61–80.

Cohen, D. H. The neural pathways and informational flow mediating a conditioned autonomic response. In L. V. DiCara (ed.), *Limbic and autonomic nervous system research*, (pp. 223–275). New York: Plenum Press, 1974.

Cohen, D. H., & Durkovic, R. G. Cardiac and respiratory conditioning, differentiation, and extinction in the pigeon. *Journal of the Experimental Analysis of Behavior*, 1966, *9*, 681–688.

Cohen, D. H., & MacDonald, R. L. Some variables affecting orienting and conditioned heart-rate responses in the pigeon. *Journal of Comparative and Physiological Psychology*, 1971, *74*, 123–133.

Crow, T. J., & Alkon, D. L. Retention of an associative behavioral change in *Hermissenda. Science*, 1978, *201*, 1239–1241.

Crow, T. J., & Alkon, D. L. Associative behavioral modification in *Hermissenda:* Cellular correlates. *Science*, 1980, *209*, 412–414.

Davis, R. L., & Kiger, J. A., Jr. Dunce mutants of *Drosophila melanogaster:* Mutants defective in the cyclic AMP phosphodiesterase enzyme system. *Journal of Cell Biology*, 1981, *90*, 101–107.

Davis, W. J., & Gillette, R. Neural correlate of behavioral plasticity in command neurons of *Pleurobranchaea. Science*, 1978, *199*, 801–804.

Davis, W. J., Villet, J., Lee, D., Rigler, M., Gillette, R., & Prince, E. Selective and differential avoidance learning in the feeding and withdrawal behavior of *Pleurobranchaea californica. Journal of Comparative Physiology*, 1980, *138*, 157–165.

Del Castillo, J., & Katz, B. Statistical factors involved in neuromuscular facilitation and depression. *Journal of Physiology (London)*, 1954, *124*, 574–585.

Downey, P., & Jahan-Parwar, B. Cooling as a reinforcing stimulus in *Aplysia. American Zoologist*, 1972, *12*, 507–512.

Dudai, Y., Jan, Y.-N., Byers, D., Quinn, W. G., & Benzer, S. Dunce, a mutant of *Drosophila* deficient in learning. *Proceedings of the National Academy of Sciences of the U.S.A.*, 1976, *73*, 1684–1688.

Duerr, J. S., & Quinn, W. G. Three *Drosophila* mutants that block associative learning also affect habituation and sensitization. *Proceedings of the National Academy of Sciences of the U.S.A.*, 1982, *79*, 3646–3650.

Dufossé, M., Ito, M., Jastreboff, P. J., & Miyashita, Y. A neuronal correlate in rabbit's cerebellum to adaptive modification of the vestibulo-ocular reflex. *Brain Research*, 1978, *150*, 611–616.

Eisenstein, E. M., & Cohen, M. J. Learning in an isolated insect ganglion. *Animal Behavior*, 1965, *13*, 104–108.

Engel, J., Jr., & Woody, C. D. Effects of character and significance of stimulus on unit activity at coronal-pericruciate cortex of cat during performance of conditioned motor response. *Journal of Neurophysiology*, 1972, *35*, 220–229. (a)

Engel, J., Jr., & Woody, C. D. Changes in unit activity and thresholds to electrical micro-stimulation at coronal-pericruciate cortex of cat with classical conditioning of different facial movements. *Journal of Neurophysiology*, 1972, *35*, 230–241. (b)

Farel, P. B., Glanzman, D. L., & Thompson, R. F. Habituation of a monosynaptic response in the vertebrate central nervous system: Lateral column-motoneurone pathway in isolated frog spinal cord. *Journal of Neurophysiology*, 1973, *36*, 1117–1130.

Farel, P. B., & Thompson, R. F. Habituation of a monosynaptic response in frog spinal cord: Evidence for a presynaptic mechanism. *Journal of Neurophysiology*, 1976, *39*, 661–666.

Farley, J., & Alkon, D. L. Associative neural and behavioral change in *Hermissenda:* Consequences of nervous system orientation for light- and pairing-specificity. *Journal of Neurophysiology*, 1982, *48*, 785–807.

Frazier, W. T., Kandel, E. R., Kupfermann, I., Waziri, R., & Coggeshall, R. E. Morphological and functional properties of identified neurons in the abdominal ganglion of *Aplysia californica*. *Journal of Neurophysiology*, 1967, *30*, 1288–1351.

Gabriel, M. Short-latency discriminative unit response: engram or bias? *Physiological Psychology*, 1976, *4*, 275–280.

Gabriel, M., Miller, J. D., & Saltwick, S. E. Unit activity in cingulate cortex and anteroventral thalamus of the rabbit during differential conditioning and reversal. *Journal of Comparative and Physiological Psychology*, 1977, *91*, 423–433.

Gabriel, M., Saltwick, S. E., & Miller, J. D. Conditioning and reversal of short-latency multiple-unit responses in the rabbit medial geniculate nucleus. *Science*, 1975, *189*, 1108–1109.

Garcia, J., McGowan, B. K., & Green, K. F. Biological constraints on conditioning. In A. H. Black & W. F. Prokasy (Eds.), *Classical conditioning. II: Current research and theory* (pp. 3–27). New York: Appleton-Century-Crofts, 1972.

Gelperin, A. Rapid food-aversion learning by a terrestrial mollusk. *Science*, 1975, *189*, 567–570.

Gelperin, A., Chang, J. J., & Reingold, S. C. Feeding motor program in *Limax*. I. Neuromuscular correlates and control by chemosensory input. *Journal of Neurobiology*, 1978, *9*, 285–300.

Gibbs, C. M., & Cohen, D. H. Plasticity of the thalamofugal pathway during visual conditioning. *Society for Neuroscience Abstracts*, 1980, *6*, 424.

Gibbs, C. M., Cohen, D. H., Broyles, J., & Solina, A. Conditioned modification of avian dorsal geniculate neurons is a function of their response to the unconditioned stimulus. *Society for Neuroscience Abstracts*, 1981, *7*, 752.

Gillette, R., Kovac, M. P., & Davis, W. J. Command neurons in *Pleurobranchaea* receive synaptic feedback from the motor network they excite. *Science*, 1978, *199*, 798–801.

Glantz, R. M. The visually evoked defense reflex of the crayfish: Habituation, facilitation, and the influence of picrotoxin. *Journal of Neurobiology*, 1974, *5*, 263–280. (a)

Glantz, R. M. Habituation of the motion detectors of the crayfish optic nerve: Their relationship to the visually evoked defense reflex. *Journal of Neurobiology*, 1974, *5*, 489–501. (b)

Glantz, R. M. Visual input and motor output of command interneurons in the crayfish defense reflex pathway. In G. Hoyle (Ed.), *Identified neurons and behavior of arthropods* (pp. 259–274). New York: Plenum Press, 1977.

Glanzman, D. L., & Thompson, R. F. Evidence against conduction failure as the mechanism underlying monosynaptic habituation in frog spinal cord. *Brain Research*, 1979, *174*, 329–332.

Glanzman, D. L., & Thompson, R. F. Alterations in spontaneous miniature potential activity during habituation of a vertebrate monosynaptic pathway. *Brain Research,* 1980, *189,* 377–390.

Gold, M. R., & Cohen, D. H. Modification of the discharge of vagal cardiac neurons during learned heart rate change. *Science,* 1981, *214,* 345–347.

Gormezano, I. Investigations of defense and reward conditioning in the rabbit. In A. H. Black & W. F. Prokasy (Eds.), *Classical conditioning II: Current Research and Theory* (pp. 151–181). New York: Appleton-Century-Crofts, 1972.

Groves, P. M., & Thompson, R. F. Habituation: A dual-process theory. *Psychological Review,* 1970, *77,* 419–450.

Hawkins, R. D. Identified facilitating neurons are excited by cutaneous stimuli used in sensitization and classical conditioning of *Aplysia. Society for Neuroscience Abstracts,* 1981, *7,* 354. (a)

Hawkins, R. D. Interneurons involved in mediation and modulation of gill-withdrawal reflex in *Aplysia.* III. Identified facilitating neurons increase Ca^{2+} current in sensory neurons. *Journal of Neurophysiology,* 1981, *45,* 327–339. (b)

Hawkins, R. D., Abrams, T. W., Carew, T. J., & Kandel, E. R. A cellular mechanism of classical conditioning in *Aplysia:* Activity-dependent amplification of presynaptic facilitation. *Science,* 1983, *219,* 400–405.

Hawkins, R. D., & Bruner, J. Activity of excitor and inhibitor claw motor neurones during habituation and dishabituation of the crayfish defence response. *Journal of Experimental Biology,* 1981, *91,* 145–164.

Hawkins, R. D., Castellucci, V. F., & Kandel, E. R. Interneurons involved in mediation and modulation of gill-withdrawal reflex in *Aplysia.* I. Identification and characterization. *Journal of Neurophysiology,* 1981, *45,* 304–314. (a)

Hawkins, R. D., Castellucci, V. F., & Kandel, E. R. Interneurons involved in mediation and modulation of gill-withdrawal reflex in *Aplysia.* II. Identified neurons produce heterosynaptic facilitation contributing to behavioral sensitization. *Journal of Neurophysiology,* 1981, *45,* 315–326. (b)

Hebb, D. O. *Organization of behavior.* New York: Wiley, 1949.

Hilgard, E. R., & Bower, G. H. *Theories of learning.* Englewood Cliffs, NJ: Prentice-Hall, 1975.

Hodgkin, A. L., & Huxley, A. F. The dual effect of membrane potential on sodium conductance in the giant axon of *Loligo. Journal of Physiology (London),* 1952, *116,* 497–506.

Hoehler, F. K., & Thompson, R. F. Effect of the interstimulus (CS–UCS) interval on hippocampal unit activity during classical conditioning of the nictitating membrane response of the rabbit (*Oryctolagus cuniculus*). *Journal of Comparative and Physiological Psychology,* 1980, *94,* 201–215.

Hoffmann, P. Über die doppelte Innervation der Krebsmuskeln. Zugleich ein Beitrag zur Kenntnis nervöser Hemmungen. *Zeitschrift fuer Biologie,* 1914, *63,* 411–442.

Horn, R., & Miller, J. J. A prolonged, voltage-dependent calcium permeability revealed by tetraethylammonium in the soma and axon of *Aplysia* giant neuron. *Journal of Neurobiology,* 1977, *8,* 399–415.

Horridge, G. A. Learning of leg position by headless insects. *Nature (London),* 1962, *193,* 697–698. (a)

Horridge, G. A. Learning of leg position by the ventral nerve cord in headless insects. *Proceedings of the Royal Society of London,* Series B, 1962, *157,* 33–52. (b)

Hoyle, G. Neurophysiological studies of "learning" in headless insects. In J. E. Treherne & J. W. L. Beament (Eds.), *The physiology of the insect central nervous system* (pp. 203–232). New York: Academic Press, 1965.

Hoyle, G. Instrumental conditioning of the leg lift in the locust. *Neuroscience Research Program Bulletin,* 1979, *17,* 577–586.

Hoyle, G. Learning, using natural reinforcements, in insect preparations that permit cellular neuronal analysis. *Journal of Neurobiology,* 1980, *11,* 323–354.

Ito, M. Neural design of the cerebellar motor control system. *Brain Research,* 1972, *40,* 81–84.

Ito, M. Cerebellar control of the vestibular-ocular reflex—around the flocculus hypothesis. *Annual Review of Neuroscience,* 1982, *5,* 275–296.

Ito, M., Sakurai, M., & Tongroach, P. Climbing fibre induced depression of both mossy fibre responsiveness and glutamate sensitivity of cerebellar Purkinje cells. *Journal of Physiology,* 1982, *324,* 113–134.

Jacklet, J. W., & Rine, J. Facilitation at neuromuscular junctions: Contribution to habituation and dishabituation of the *Aplysia* gill withdrawal reflex. *Proceedings of the National Academy of Sciences of the U.S.A.,* 1977, *74,* 1267–1271.

John, E. R. *Mechanisms of memory.* New York: Academic Press, 1967.

Kandel, E. R. Neuronal plasticity and the modification of behavior. In J. M. Brookhart & V. B. Mountcastle (Eds.), *Handbook of physiology* (Sect. 1, pp. 1137–1182). Bethesda, MD: American Physiological Society, 1977.

Kandel, E. R. *A cell-biological approach to learning.* Bethesda, MD: Society for Neuroscience, 1978.

Kandel, E. R., & Schwartz, J. H. Molecular biology of learning: modulation of transmitter release. *Science,* 1982, *218,* 433–443.

Kandel, E. R., & Spencer, W. A. Cellular neurophysiological approaches in the study of learning. *Physiological Review,* 1968, *48,* 65–134.

Kandel, E. R., & Tauc, L. Heterosynaptic facilitation in neurones of the abdominal ganglion of *Aplysia depilans. Journal of Physiology (London),* 1965, *181,* 1–27. (a)

Kandel, E. R., & Tauc, L. Mechanism of heterosynaptic facilitation in the giant cell of the abdominal ganglion of *Aplysia depilans. Journal of Physiology (London),* 1965, *181,* 28–47. (b)

Katz, B., & Miledi, R. Tetrodotoxin-resistant electrical activity in presynaptic terminals. *Journal of Physiology (London),* 1969, *203,* 459–487.

Kennedy, D., Calabrese, R. L., & Wine, J. J. Presynaptic inhibition: Primary afferent depolarization in crayfish neurons. *Science,* 1974, *186,* 451–454.

Kimble, G. A. *Hilgard and Marquis' conditioning and learning.* New York: Appleton-Century-Crofts, 1961.

Klein, M., Camardo, J., & Kandel, E. R. Serotonin modulates a specific potassium current in the sensory neurons that show presynaptic facilitation in *Aplysia. Proceedings of the National Academy of Sciences of the U.S.A.,* 1982, *79,* 5713–5717.

Klein, M., & Kandel, E. R. Presynaptic modulation of voltage-dependent Ca^{2+} current: Mechanism for behavioral sensitization. *Proceedings of the National Academy of Sciences of the U.S.A.,* 1978, *75,* 3512–3516.

Klein, M., & Kandel, E. R. Mechanism of calcium current modulation underlying presynaptic facilitation and behavioral sensitization in *Aplysia. Proceedings of the National Academy of Sciences of the U.S.A.,* 1980, *77,* 6912–6916.

Klein, M., Shapiro, E., & Kandel, E. R. Synaptic plasticity and the modulation of the Ca^{++} current. *Journal of Experimental Biology,* 1980, *89,* 117–157.

Koester, J., & Kandel, E. R. Further identification of neurons in the abdominal ganglion of *Aplysia* using behavioral criteria. *Brain Research,* 1977, *121,* 1–20.

Konorski, J. *Integrative activity of the brain: An interdisciplinary approach.* Chicago: University of Chicago Press, 1967.

Krasne, F. B. Excitation and habituation of the crayfish escape reflex: The depolarization response in lateral giant fibers of the isolated abdomen. *Journal of Experimental Biology,* 1969, *50,* 29–46.

Krasne, F. B., & Bryan, J. S. Habituation: Regulation through presynaptic inhibition. *Science,* 1973, *182,* 590–592.

Krasne, F. B., & Roberts, A. Habituation of the crayfish escape response during release from inhibition induced by picrotoxin. *Nature (London),* 1967, *215,* 769–770.

Krasne, F. B., & Woodsmall, K. S. Waning of the crayfish escape response as a result of repeated stimulation. *Animal Behavior,* 1969, *17,* 416–424.

Kraus, N., & Disterhoft, J. F. Response plasticity of single neurons in rabbit auditory association cortex during tone-signalled learning. *Brain Research,* 1982, *246,* 205–215.

Kuo, J. F., & Greengard, P. Cyclic nucleotide-dependent protein kinases. IV. Widespread occurrence of adenosine 3',5'-monophosphate-dependent protein kinase in various tissues and phyla of the animal kingdom. *Proceedings of the National Academy of Sciences of the U.S.A.,* 1969, *64,* 1349–1355.

Kupfermann, I., Carew, T. J., & Kandel, E. R. Local, reflex and central commands controlling gill and siphon movements in *Aplysia. Journal of Neurophysiology,* 1974, *37,* 996–1019.

Kupfermann, I., Castellucci, V., Pinsker, H., & Kandel, E. R. Neuronal correlates of habituation and dishabituation of the gill-withdrawal reflex in *Aplysia. Science,* 1970, *167,* 1743–1745.

Kupfermann, I., & Kandel, E. R. Neuronal controls of a behavioral response mediated by the abdominal ganglion of *Aplysia. Science,* 1969, *164,* 847–850.

Kupfermann, I., & Pinsker, H. Plasticity in *Aplysia* neurons and some simple neuronal models of learning. In J. Tapp (Ed.), *Reinforcement and behavior* (pp. 356–386). New York: Academic Press, 1969.

Lashley, K. S. *Brain mechanisms and intelligence: A quantitative study of injuries to the brain.* Chicago: Chicago University Press, 1929.

Lee, R. M. *Aplysia* behavior: Effect of contingent water-level variation. *Communications in Behavioral Biology,* 1969, *4,* 157–164.

Lee, R. M. *Aplysia* behavior: Operant-response differentiation. *Proceedings of the 78th Annual Convention of the American Psychological Association,* 1970, pp. 249–250.

Lee, R. M. Conditioning of *Pleurobranchaea. Science,* 1976, *193,* 72–73.

Levitan, I. B., & Barondes, S. H. Octopamine- and serotonin-stimulated phosphorylation of specific protein in the abdominal ganglion of *Aplysia californica. Proceedings of the National Academy of Sciences of the U.S.A.,* 1974, *71,* 1145–1148.

Levy, W. B., & Steward, O. Synapses as associative memory elements in the hippocampal formation. *Brain Research,* 1979, *175,* 233–245.

Lickey, M. Learned behavior in *Aplysia vaccaria. Journal of Comparative and Physiological Psychology,* 1968, *66,* 712–718.

Lukowiak, K., & Sahley, C. The *in vitro* classical conditioning of the gill withdrawal reflex of *Aplysia californica. Science,* 1981, *212,* 1516–1518.

MacDonald, J. F., & Pearson, J. A. Some observations on habituation of the flexor reflex in the rat: The influence of strychnine, bicuculline, spinal transection, and decerebration. *Journal of Neurobiology,* 1979, *10,* 67–78. (a)

MacDonald, J. F., & Pearson, J. A. Inhibition of spinal interneuronal activity by repeated cutaneous stimulation: A possible substrate of flexor reflex habituation. *Journal of Neurobiology,* 1979, *10,* 79–92. (b)

Mackintosh, N. J. *The psychology of animal learning.* New York: Academic Press, 1974.

Marr, D. A theory of cerebellar cortex. *Journal of Physiology (London),* 1969, *202,* 437–470.

Martin, G. K., Land, T., & Thompson, R. F. Classical conditioning of the rabbit (*Oryctolagus cuniculus*) nictitating membrane response, with electrical brain stimulation as the unconditioned stimulus. *Journal of Comparative and Physiological Psychology,* 1980, *94,* 216–226.

McCormick, D. A., Clark, G. A., Lavond, D. G., & Thompson, R. F. Initial localization of the memory trace for a basic form of learning. *Proceedings of the National Academy of Sciences of the U.S.A.,* 1982, *79,* 2731–2735.

Miles, F. A., Braitman, D. J., & Dow, B. M. Long-term adaptive changes in primate vestibuloocular reflex. IV. Electrophysiological observations in flocculus of adapted monkeys. *Journal of Neurophysiology,* 1980, *43,* 1477–1493.

Miller, N. E. Certain facts of learning relevant to the search for its physical basis. In G. C. Quarton, T. Melnechuk, & F. O. Schmitt (Eds.), *The neurosciences: A study program* (pp. 643–652). New York: Rockefeller University Press, 1967.

Milner, B. Disorders of learning and memory after temporal lobe lesions in man. *Clinical Neurosurgery,* 1972, *19,* 421–446.

Mpitsos, G. J., & Collins, S. D. Learning: Rapid aversive conditioning in the gastropod mollusk *Pleurobranchaea. Science,* 1975, *188,* 954–957.

Mpitsos, G. J., Collins, S. D., & McClellan, A. D. Learning: A model system for physiological studies. *Science,* 1978, *199,* 497–506.

Mpitsos, G. J., & Davis, W. J. Learning: Classical and avoidance conditioning in the mollusk *Pleurobranchaea. Science,* 1973, *180,* 317–320.

Neary, J. T., Crow, T., & Alkon, D. L. Change in a specific phosphoprotein following associative learning in *Hermissenda. Nature (London),* 1981, *293,* 658–660.

O'Brien, J. H., Wilder, M. B., & Stevens, C. D. Conditioning of cortical neurons in cats with antidromic activation as the unconditioned stimulus. *Journal of Comparative and Physiological Psychology,* 1977, *91,* 918–929.

Olds, J., Disterhoft, J. F., Segal, M., Kornblith, C. L., & Hirsh, R. Learning centers of rat brain mapped by measuring latencies of conditioned unit responses. *Journal of Neurophysiology,* 1972, *35,* 202–219.

Oleson, T. D., Ashe, J. H., & Weinberger, N. M. Modification of auditory and somatosensory system activity during pupillary conditioning in the paralyzed cat. *Journal of Neurophysiology,* 1975, *38,* 1114–1139.

Paris, C. G., Kandel, E. R., & Schwartz, J. H. Serotonin stimulates phosphorylation of a 137,000 dalton membrane protein in the abdominal ganglion of *Aplysia. Society for Neuroscience Abstracts,* 1980, *6,* 844.

Patterson, M. M. Effects of forward and backward classical conditioning procedures on a spinal cat hind-limb flexor nerve response. *Physiological Psychology,* 1975, *3,* 86–91.

Patterson, M. M., Cegavske, C. F., & Thompson, R. F. Effects of a classical conditioning paradigm on hind-limb flexor nerve response in immobilized spinal cats. *Journal of Comparative and Physiological Psychology,* 1973, *84,* 88–97.

Pavlov, I. P. *Conditioned reflexes* (G. V. Anrep, trans.). London: Oxford University Press, 1927.

Perlman, A. J. Central and peripheral control of siphon withdrawal reflex in *Aplysia californica. Journal of Neurophysiology,* 1979, *42,* 510–529.

Pinsker, H. M., Hening, W. A., Carew, T. J., & Kandel, E. R. Long-term sensitization of a defensive withdrawal reflex in *Aplysia. Science,* 1973, *182,* 1039–1042.

Pinsker, H. M., & Kandel, E. R. Contingent modification of an endogenous bursting rhythm by monosynaptic inhibition. *Physiologist,* 1967, *10,* 279.

Pinsker, H. M., Kupfermann, I., Castellucci, V., & Kandel, E. R. Habituation and dishabituation of the gill-withdrawal reflex in *Aplysia. Science,* 1970, *167,* 1740–1742.

Pribram, K. H. *Languages of the brain; experimental paradoxes and principles in neuropsychology.* Englewood Cliffs, NJ: Prentice-Hall, 1971.

Prosser, C. L., & Hunter, W. S. The extinction of startle responses and spinal reflexes in the white rat. *American Journal of Physiology,* 1936, *117,* 609–618.

Quinn, W. G., Harris, W. A., & Benzer, S. Conditioned behavior in *Drosophila melanogaster. Proceedings of the National Academy of Sciences of the U.S.A.,* 1974, *71,* 708–712.

Robinson, D. A. Adaptive gain control of vestibular ocular reflex by the cerebellum. *Journal of Neurophysiology,* 1976, *39,* 954–969.

Roeder, K. D. Organization of the ascending giant fiber system in the cockroach (*Periplaneta americana*). *Journal of Experimental Zoology*, 1948, *108*, 243–261.

Sahley, C., Gelperin, A., & Rudy, J. W. One-trial associative learning modifies food odor preferences of a terrestrial mollusc. *Proceedings of the National Academy of Sciences of the U.S.A.*, 1981, *78*, 640–642.

Sahley, C., Rudy, J. W., & Gelperin, A. An analysis of associative learning in a terrestrial mollusc. I. Higher-order conditioning, blocking, and a transient US pre-exposure effect. *Journal of Comparative Physiology*, 1981, *144*, 1–8.

Schmaltz, L. W., & Theios, J. Acquisition and extinction of a classically conditioned response in hippocampectomized rabbits (*Oryctolagus cuniculus*). *Journal of Comparative and Physiological Psychology*, 1972, *79*, 328–333.

Schöne, H. Complex behavior. In T. H. Waterman (Ed.), *The physiology of crustacea* (pp. 465–520). New York: Academic Press, 1961.

Schwartz, J. H., Castellucci, V. F., & Kandel, E. R. Functioning of identified neurons and synapses in abdominal ganglion of *Aplysia* in absence of protein synthesis. *Journal of Neurophysiology*, 1971, *34*, 939–953.

Schwartzkroin, P. A., & Wester, K. Long-lasting facilitation of a synaptic potential following tetanization in the *in vitro* hippocampal slice. *Brain Research*, 1975, *89*, 107–119.

Segal, M., Disterhoft, J. F., & Olds, J. Hippocampal unit activity during classical aversive and appetitive conditioning. *Science*, 1972, *175*, 792–794.

Segal, M., & Olds, J. Behavior of units in hippocampal circuit of the rat during learning. *Journal of Neurophysiology*, 1972, *35*, 680–690.

Segal, M., & Olds, J. Activity of units in the hippocampal circuit of the rat during differential classical conditioning. *Journal of Comparative and Physiological Psychology*, 1973, *82*, 195–204.

Sherrington, C. S. *The integrative action of the nervous system*. New Haven, CT: Yale University Press, 1906.

Siegelbaum, S. A., Camardo, J. S., & Kandel, E. R. Serotonin and cyclic AMP close single K^+ channels in *Aplysia* sensory neurones. *Nature*, 1982, *299*, 413–417.

Sokolov, E. N. Higher nervous functions: The orienting reflex. *Annual Review of Physiology*, 1963, *25*, 545–580.

Solomon, P. R., & Moore, J. W. Latent inhibition and stimulus generalization of the classically conditioned nictitating membrane response in rabbits (*Oryctolagus cuniculus*) following dorsal hippocampal ablations. *Journal of Comparative and Physiological Psychology*, 1975, *89*, 1192–1203.

Spencer, W. A., Thompson, R. F., & Nielson, D. R., Jr. Response decrement of the flexion reflex in the acute spinal cat and transient restoration by strong stimuli. *Journal of Neurophysiology*, 1966, *29*, 221–239. (a)

Spencer, W. A., Thompson, R. F., & Nielson, D. R., Jr. Alterations in responsiveness of ascending and reflex pathways activated by iterated cutaneous afferent volleys. *Journal of Neurophysiology*, 1966, *29*, 240–252. (b)

Spencer, W. A., Thompson, R. F., & Nielson, D. R., Jr. Decrement of ventral root electrotonus and intracellularly recorded PSPs produced by iterated cutaneous afferent volleys. *Journal of Neurophysiology*, 1966, *29*, 253–273. (c)

Stent, G. S. A physiological mechanism for Hebb's postulate of learning. *Proceedings of the National Academy of Sciences of the U.S.A.*, 1973, *70*, 997–1001.

Thompson, R. F., Berger, T. W., Cegavske, C. F., Patterson, M. M., Roemer, R. A., Teyler, T. J., & Young, R. A. The search for the engram. *American Psychologist*, 1976, *31*, 209–227.

Thompson, R. F., Patterson, M. M., & Berger, T. W. Associative learning in the mammalian nervous system. In T. Teyler (Ed.), *Brain and learning* (pp. 51–90). Stamford, CT: Greylock Publishers, 1978.

Thompson, R. F., & Spencer, W. A. Habituation: A model phenomenon for the study of neuronal substrates of behavior. *Psychological Review*, 1966, *173*, 16–43.

Tillotson, D. Inactivation of Ca conductance dependent on entry of Ca ions in molluscan neurones. *Proceedings of the National Academy of Sciences of the U.S.A.*, 1979, *76*, 1497–1500.

Tosney, T., & Hoyle, G. Computer-controlled learning in a simple system. *Proceedings of the Royal Society of London, Series B*, 1977, *195*, 365–393.

Van Harreveld, A., & Wiersma, C. A. G. The triple innervation of crayfish muscle and its function in contraction and inhibition. *Journal of Experimental Biology*, 1937, *14*, 448–461.

von Baumgarten, R. J., & Djahnparwar, B. Time course of repetitive heterosynaptic facilitation in *Aplysia californica. Brain Research*, 1967, *4*, 295–297.

von Baumgarten, R. J., & Hukuhara, T. The role of the interstimulus interval in heterosynaptic facilitation in *Aplysia californica. Brain Research*, 1969, *16*, 369–381.

Wall, J., Wild, J. M., Broyles, J., Gibbs, C. M., & Cohen, D. H. Plasticity of the tectofugal pathway during visual conditioning. *Society for Neuroscience Abstracts*, 1980, *6*, 424.

Wall, P. D. Habituation and post-tetanic potentiation in the spinal cord. In G. Horn & R. A. Hinde (Eds.), *Short-term changes in neural activity and behavior* (pp. 181–210). London & New York: Cambridge University Press, 1970.

Walters, E. T., & Byrne, J. H. Associative conditioning of single sensory neurons suggests a cellular mechanism for learning. *Science*, 1983, *219*, 405–408.

Walters, E. T., Carew, T. J., & Kandel, E. R. Classical conditioning in *Aplysia californica. Proceedings of the National Academy of Seiences of the U.S.A.*, 1979, *76*, 6675–6679.

Walters, E. T., Carew, T. J., & Kandel, E. R. Associative learning in *Aplysia:* Evidence for conditioned fear in an invertebrate. *Science*, 1981, *211*, 504–506.

West, A., Barnes, E., & Alkon, D. Primary changes of voltage responses during retention of associative learning. *Journal of Neurophysiology*, 1982, *48*, 1243–1255.

Wickelgren, B. G. Habituation of spinal motorneurons. *Journal of Neurophysiology*, 1967, *30*, 1404–1423. (a)

Wickelgren, B. G. Habituation of spinal interneurons. *Journal of Neurophysiology*, 1967, *30*, 1424–1438. (b)

Wine, J. J., & Krasne, F. B. The organization of escape behavior in the crayfish. *Journal of Experimental Biology*, 1972, *56*, 1–18.

Wine, J. J., Krasne, F. B., & Chen, L. Habituation and inhibition of the crayfish lateral giant fibre escape response. *Journal of Experimental Biology*, 1975, *62*, 771–782.

Woody, C. D. Conditioned eye blink: Gross potential activity at coronal-precruciate cortex of the cat. *Journal of Neurophysiology*, 1970, *33*, 838–850.

Woody, C. D., & Black-Cleworth, P. Differences in excitability of cortical neurons as a function of motor projection in conditioned cats. *Journal of Neurophysiology*, 1973, *36*, 1104–1116.

Woody, C. D., & Brozek, G. Changes in evoked responses from facial nucleus of cat with conditioning and extinction of an eye blink. *Journal of Neurophysiology*, 1969, *32*, 717–726.

Woody, C. D., Knispel, J. D., Crow, T. J., & Black-Cleworth, P. A. Activity and excitability to electrical current of cortical auditory receptive neurons of awake cats as affected by stimulus association. *Journal of Neurophysiology*, 1976, *39*, 1045–1061.

Woody, C. D., Swartz, B. E., & Gruen, E. Effects of acetylcholine and cyclic GMP on input resistance of cortical neurons in awake cats. *Brain Research*, 1978, *158*, 373–395.

Woody, C. D., Vassilevsky, N. N., & Engel, J., Jr. Conditioned eye blink: Unit activity at coronal-precruciate cortex of the cat. *Journal of Neurophysiology*, 1970, *33*, 851–864.

Woody, C., Yarowsky, P., Owens, J., Black-Cleworth, P., & Crow, T. Effect of lesions of cortical motor areas on acquisition of conditioned eye blink in the cat. *Journal of Neurophysiology,* 1974, *37,* 385–394.

Woolacott, M. H., & Hoyle, G. Membrane resistance changes associated with single identified neuron learning. *Society for Neuroscience Abstracts,* 1976, *2,* 339.

Woolacott, M. H., & Hoyle, G. Neural events underlying learning in insects: Changes in pacemaker. *Proceedings of the Royal Society of London,* Series *B,* 1977, *195,* 395–415.

Wurtz, R. H., Castellucci, V. F., & Nusrala, J. M. Synaptic plasticity: The effect of the action potential in the postsynaptic neuron. *Experimental Neurology,* 1967, *18,* 350–368.

Young, R. A., Cegavske, C. F., & Thompson, R. F. Tone-induced changes in excitability of abducens motoneurons and of the reflex path of nictitating membrane response in rabbit (*Oryctolagus cuniculus*). *Journal of Comparative and Physiological Psychology,* 1976, *90,* 424–434.

Zilber-Gachelin, N. F. Expériences de sensibilisation chez la Blatte. *Journal of Physiology (Paris),* 1966, *58,* 276–277.

Zilber-Gachelin, N. F., & Chartier, M. P. Modification of the motor reflex responses due to repetition of the peripheral stimulus in the cockroach. I. Habituation at the level of an isolated abdominal ganglion. *Journal of Experimental Biology,* 1973, *59,* 359–381. (a)

Zilber-Gachelin, N. F., & Chartier, M. P. Modification of the motor reflex responses due to repetition of the peripheral stimulus in the cockroach. II. Conditions of activation of the motoneurones. *Journal of Experimental Biology,* 1973, *59,* 383–403. (b)

Zucker, R. S. Crayfish escape behavior and central synapses. I. Neural circuit exciting lateral giant fiber. *Journal of Neurophysiology,* 1972, *35,* 599–620. (a)

Zucker, R. S. Crayfish escape behavior and central synapses. II. Physiological mechanisms underlying behavioral habituation. *Journal of Neurophysiology,* 1972, *35,* 621–637. (b)

Zucker, R. S., Kennedy, D., & Selverston, A. I. Neuronal circuit mediating escape responses in crayfish. *Science,* 1971, *173,* 645–650.

CHAPTER

4

SPREADING DEPRESSION: A BEHAVIORAL ANALYSIS[1]

ALLEN M. SCHNEIDER
Department of Psychology
Swarthmore College
Swarthmore, Pennsylvania

and

PETER E. SIMSON
Department of Psychology
New York University
New York, New York

[1]Preparation of this chapter was supported by Grant BNS-7924072 from the National Science Foundation.

I. INTRODUCTION

Potassium chloride (KCl) applied topically to a cerebral hemisphere produces a temporary depression of electrocortical activity which spreads over the stimulated hemisphere but does not spread interhemispherically (Bures & Buresova, 1960). Although this phenomenon, commonly referred to as spreading cortical depression, has been known for a number of years (Leao, 1944), it remained for Bures (1959) to recognize the potential for using the technique in behavioral research. Bures reasoned that if memory is stored in the form of a dual trace, one trace in each cerebral hemisphere (Sperry, 1964), then it should be possible to eliminate a trace in one of the hemispheres by depressing that hemisphere during training. Consistent with this prediction, Bures found that animals trained to avoid shock with one hemisphere depressed, retained the avoidance with the same hemisphere again depressed but did not retain the avoidance with depression shifted to the initially functional hemisphere(see Figure 4.1). Bures took these results as evidence that memory was confined to a single hemisphere. In his view the hemisphere that remained functional during training learned and stored information; the hemisphere that was depressed during training did not learn or store information.

Bures' experiment represents a pioneering effort. Nevertheless, the problem with the experiment, and for that matter any experiment using depression to study memory, is that it is difficult to draw a conclusion. Is depression affecting memory storage, as Bures surmised, or is it merely interacting with sensory and

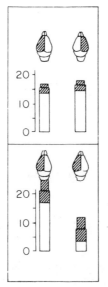

Figure 4.1. Comparison of number of trials to learn for animals trained and tested under opposite states of unilateral depression (top panel) with animals trained and tested under the same state of unilateral depression (lower panel). Savings occurred if the same hemisphere was depressed during training and testing, but no savings occurred if opposite hemispheres were depressed. Shading in hemispheres represents depression. After Bures, 1959.

motor processes to impair the animals ability to perform the response? The purpose of the present chapter is to answer these questions.

The chapter is divided into four sections. The first section describes the neural properties of depression. The second section considers the methodological requirements for using spreading depression in behavioral research. The third section is divided into two parts. The first part is concerned with the effects of depression on nonassociative processes (i.e., sensory and motor capacities). The second part is concerned with the effects of depression on associative processes (i.e., memory storage and retrieval). It should be emphasized that the non-associative and associative effects are not treated as mutually exclusive; rather, the nonassociative effects define the steps that must be taken to study the associative effects. The fourth section is a direct outgrowth of the data described in Section III and is concerned with reevaluating research on memory confinement and transfer in light of the nonassociative and associative effects of depression.

II. THE NEURAL PROPERTIES OF SPREADING DEPRESSION

When we study the behavioral effects of removing portions of the nervous system by means of surgery, we are limited by the fact that once central nervous system damage is produced it cannot be reversed. What is needed is a technique by which neural activity can be stopped and then reinstated, and the reversible properties of spreading depression seem to meet these needs.

Two bioelectric measures indicate that neural activity is arrested during spreading depression. First, Leao (1944) recorded EEG activity from a number of points on rabbit cortex and found that electrical stimulation of the cortex induced depressed EEG activity that spread at the rate of 2 to 6 mm per minute over the surface of the stimulated hemisphere. Second, depressed EEG activity is accompanied by both a negative shift in the steady potential (Leao, 1947) and an increase in the electrical impedance of the cortex (van Harreveld & Ochs, 1957).

Spreading depression can be triggered by a variety of chemical agents, including ACTH (Jakobartl & Huston, 1977b) and enkephalin (Sprick, Oitzl, Ornstein, & Huston, 1981), but the most commonly used chemical has been 25% KCl solution (Marshall, 1959). Applied to the cortex, KCl abolishes EEG activity for as much as 3 hours and induces repeated negative shifts in the steady potential for at least 90 minutes (Bures, 1959). Depression is also accompanied by temporary inhibition of protein synthesis (Bennett & Edelman, 1969; Ruscak, 1964) and an increase in turnover of norepinephrine (Schanberg, Schildkraut, Krivanek, & Kopin, 1968) and dopamine (Keller, Bartholini, Pieri, & Pletscher, 1972).

The boundaries that define the sphere of spread are under continual revision. Initially it was thought that depression of cortical activity in one hemisphere does not spread interhemispherically (Bures, 1959) or beneath the upper layers of the stimulated cortex (Ochs & Hunt, 1966). Crow, Petrinovich, and Carew (1973), however, found that KCl applied to one hemisphere not only induces depressed EEG activity in the cortex of the stimulated hemisphere but also induces depressed activity, although to a lesser extent and for a shorter time, in the cortex of the nonstimulated hemisphere.

Given the elaborate structural and functional connections between the cortex and subcortex, it is not surprising that cortical depression has extensive effects on subcortical activity. Specifically, cortical depression is accompanied by depressed activity in the hypothalamus (Shibata, Hori, & Kiyohara, 1981; Weiss & Fifkova, 1961), caudate nucleus (Bures & Buresova, 1963b), and amygdala (Fifkova & Syka, 1964) and increased activity in the bulbopontine reticular formation (Bures, Buresova, Fifkova, Olds, Olds, & Travis, 1961); tegmental activity also increases but returns to normal between shifts in the steady potential (Weiss, 1961). These effects of course make it impossible to specify any one anatomical site, or for that matter any group of sites, in the behavioral effects of cortical depression.

That spreading cortical depression can be temporarily blocked only by cuts in the upper cortical layers (i.e., apical dendrites) has been taken as evidence that the propagating mechanism is largely confined to the upper layers (Ochs, 1962). Moreover, the increase in electrical impedance of the cortex that accompanies spreading depression (van Harreveld & Ochs, 1957) has been taken to reflect a decrease in conducting properties of the intercellular space or, more specifically, an increase in membrane permeability to intercellular ions and water (van Harreveld & Schade, 1959). Furthermore, the uptake of intercellular material is thought to trigger the release of intracellular material, either potassium (Grafstein, 1956) and/or glutamic acid (van Harreveld, 1959), which in turn acts upon neighboring cells to excite depolarization in a chainlike reaction.

Although depression is a self-propagating phenomenon, the natural boundaries that define the extent of spread are subject to modification. For example, Weiss and Fifkova (1960) have elicited depression via cannulae directly in the hippocampus, the activity of which is not affected during cortical depression, whereas Bures and Buresova (1960) have found that cortical areas within the depressed hemisphere can be protected from spread if treated with magnesium or calcium chloride.

III. METHODOLOGICAL REQUIREMENTS FOR USING SPREADING DEPRESSION IN BEHAVIORAL RESEARCH

Using the technique of spreading depression in behavioral research requires two basic conditions: animals must have a smooth cortex to show depression reliably (Marshall, 1959), and animals must be free to move. The cortex

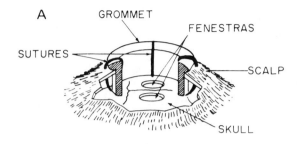

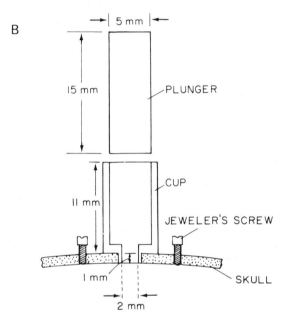

Figure 4.2. (A) The grommet preparation used by Schneider and Behar (1964), (B) The cup preparation employed by Russell and Ochs (1963).

problem is solved by using rats or rabbits. The movement problem is solved by one of several surgical preparations, all of which involve making an incision in the scalp and exposing the cortex through trephined openings. Each preparation provides a different way of reaching the trephined openings after the animals recover from surgery, thus making it possible for the animals to move with reasonable freedom.

In the original preparation (Bures, 1959), the trephined openings were reached simply by opening the sutures; the problem with this preparation is the irritation that ensues upon reopening the wound. Accordingly, subsequent preparations were designed to minimize contact with the wound (see Figure 4.2). One preparation used a rubber grommet centered over the trephined openings and secured with sutures to the scalp (Schneider & Behar, 1964). A second preparation used either small plastic cups (Russell & Ochs, 1963) or polyethelene tubing (Tapp, 1962), perforated at the base, fitted into the trephined openings, and secured with dental cement to anchoring screws. In all cases the exposed dura is kept moist between KCl treatments with either saline or Ringer's solution. Although the preparations were designed for long-term studies, their effectiveness is limited by bone regrowth and infection, both of which appear within 3 or 4 days after surgery (Ochs, 1966; Schneider & Ebbesen, 1967). Furthermore, histological analysis (Hamburg, Best, & Cholewiak, 1968) has shown that two or more applications of KCl to a single hemisphere result in lesions in the area exposed to KCl. In light of these effects, studies using KCl-induced depression must limit the time between surgery and termination of the experiment to 3 or 4 days, and either limit the number of KCl exposures to one treatment per hemisphere or equate the number of KCl exposures among groups.

IV. THE BEHAVIORAL EFFECTS OF SPREADING DEPRESSION

The spread of depression indiscriminately across the cortex of the stimulated hemisphere(s) introduces two behavioral spheres of influence, that of nonassociative and associative processes. Nonassociative processes are involved in detecting stimuli and executing responses; associative processes are involved in storing and retrieving learned information. Thus, differences between depressed and normal animals can result from differences in any one or combination of four factors: stimulus detection, response execution, and, in the case of conditioned responses, storage and retrieval. In the remainder of the chapter we will consider the effects of depression on each of these processes and then, to the extent that the behavioral analysis will permit, we will use these data to reevaluate studies on memory confinement and memory transfer.

A. Motor Behavior

Bures and his colleagues were the first to study the effects of depression on motor activity. Bures (1959) reported that bilateral depression impairs both the righting and placing reflex in rats, and Buresova, Bures, and Beran (1958) observed that unilateral depression impairs reaching for food with the paw contralateral to the depressed hemisphere. Consistent with Bures' findings that bilateral depression interferes with postural reflexes, Tapp (1962) observed that bilaterally depressed rats were impaired in their ability to balance on a rotating stick. The data are clear: depression does indeed produce impairment of coordination and posture-related reflexes. The interpretation is not clear: the depression-induced impairment may reflect interference with motor and/or sensory processes (e.g., visual, kinesthetic) for balance and coordination.

To further complicate these seemingly simple postural effects, Koppman and O'Kelly (1966) obtained evidence indicating that disruption of the subcortex, not the cortex, accounts for some of the results. Studying the effects of unilateral depression on choice responding in a T maze, they found that unilaterally depressed rats turned toward the side of the maze that corresponded to the unimpaired limbs, independent of the location of the reward. According to Koppman and O'Kelly, this type of ipsilateral effect is difficult to explain in light of the more commonly observed contralateral turning that occurs with lesion-induced paresis. They further note a parallel between the ipsilateral effect obtained with depression and that obtained with caudate lesions (Jung & Hassler, 1960). This similarity, taken together with the fact that cortical depression is accompanied by depressed activity in the caudate (Bures & Buresova, 1963b), suggests a possible link between the effects of cortical depression on turning behavior and caudate activity. The problem with this explanation is that there is no evidence that direct depression of the caudate produces ipsilateral responding. In fact, Weiss and Fifkova (1963) and later Jakobartl and Huston (1977a), found contralateral responding. The only reasonable conclusion then is that the ipsilateral responding produced by cortical depression is not the result of caudate depression.

The motor effects of depression are not limited to postural, righting, and turning reflexes. The effects have also been seen with behaviors involved in drinking and shock avoidance.

Schneider (1965) found that rats consume water at a slower rate under unilateral depression than under normal cortical conditions, but, given enough time, they consume the same amount under both conditions. That the difference in water consumption decreases as the time for drinking increases was taken as evidence that depression affects motor behavior. But here again a seemingly simple motor effect becomes complicated. Huston and Bures (1970) found that a single wave of spreading depression (produced by electrophoretic injections of KCl into the occipital cortex) elicited drinking and eating in otherwise satiated animals, a result which probably has more to do with the effect of depression on motivational than motor processes (Siegfried & Huston, 1977).

Schneider (1966, 1967) and Thompson and Hjelle (1965), in independent studies, examined the effects of depression on learned avoidance behavior and found that the disruptive effects correlated with the motor demands of the task. Depressed animals have more difficulty than normals in learning an active avoidance (moving between compartments), but are not different from normals in learning a passive avoidance (refraining from moving between compartments). The problem with these studies, or for that matter any study that uses a conditioning procedure to study motor effects, is that there are at least two interpretations.

The results might reflect differences in motor processes and/or associative processes, and it is difficult to decide among the alternatives.

Finally, there is evidence that some motor behaviors are neither impaired nor facilitated by depression. Eye blink and heart rate, for example, are not affected by depression when they are elicited by unconditioned stimuli. They are affected, however, when elicited by conditioned stimuli. Papsdorf, Longman, & Gormezano (1965) found that bilateral depression does not interfere with an eye blink elicited by infraorbital shock but does interfere with the same eye blink when conditioned to noise. Hendrickson and Pinto-Hamuy (1967) obtained similar results with heart-rate conditioning. Bilateral depression does not affect heart-rate deceleration to shock but does abolish conditioned deceleration to light. Although these results might be taken as evidence that depression disrupts associative processes, an alternative hypothesis would attribute the results to disruption of sensory processes, that is, to disruption of the animal's ability to detect the conditioned stimulus. In keeping with this alternative, we will now consider the effect that depression has on sensory processes.

B. Sensory Processes

The first indication that depression affects sensory processes came from a series of studies conducted in our laboratory. It was found that animals respond to depression as they would respond to any ordinary stimulus. First, they could learn to discriminate between different states of depression, that is, they could learn to press a lever for water with one hemisphere depressed and not to press with the other hemisphere depressed (Schneider & Kay, 1968). Second, the animal's ability to respond under depression varied along a stimulus generalization gradient, that is, as the state of depression became more similar between training and testing, responding became more similar. For example, animals trained and tested under bilateral depression showed better retention than animals trained under bilateral depression and tested normally (Schneider, 1967).

Results of follow-up studies have been mixed. Squire and Liss (1968) and later Mayes and Cowey (1973) failed to replicate the stimulus generalization effect. Greenwood and Singer (1974), on the other hand, replicated the effect using autonomic conditioning. Important, too, for the validity of the phenomenon are studies that have not only shown that depression has stimulus properties, but have identified what some of those properties may actually be.

C. Stimulus Properties of Depression

The simplest assumption is that depression affects stimuli related to motor behavior (i.e., stimuli that are kinesthetic in nature), and indeed there is evidence for this sort of hypothesis. It comes indirectly from a study by Ray and Emley (1964) who trained rats on a discrimination task with one hemisphere depressed and tested them with the opposite hemisphere depressed. Training consisted of reinforcing animals to respond to one arm of a maze with light on and to the other arm of a maze with light off. Testing consisted of the same procedure except reinforcement was omitted. The results were surprising. Instead of the animals making random choices during the test, as one would expect if depression disrupted retention, the animals almost always made incorrect choices. For example, if the animals learned to respond to the right arm with light on during training, they responded to the left arm with light on during testing. In short, they remembered the stimulus, but they reversed the response.

To explain these data we proposed a theory based on two assumptions (Schneider & Ebbesen, 1967). First, we assumed that depression produces paralysis or, equivalently, kinesthetic feedback in the limbs opposite the depressed hemisphere. Second, we assumed that during training the animals learn to use the paralysis to guide their choice of response. For example, an animal that is depressed in the right hemisphere and thus paralyzed in the left limbs, learns that a response to the left arm of the maze is a response toward the paralyzed side and a response to the right arm of the maze is a response away from the paralyzed side. Later during testing, when depression is shifted to the left hemisphere and the right side of the body is paralyzed, the animal, because it continues to use paralysis as a discriminative stimulus, responds to the right arm of the maze as if it were the left and the left arm as if it were the right. The result: correct responses during training become incorrect responses during testing.

A somewhat different perspective of the stimulus properties of depression comes from studies on shock sensitivity. Thompson and Enter (1967), for example, tested rats for shock sensitivity under bilateral depression, unilateral depression, and normal cortical conditions. The test consisted of subjecting rats to shock intensities that varied randomly from 0 to 0.9 mA and observing the frequency of both a flinch and locomotor response. The results indicated that unilateral and bilateral depression decrease sensitivity to shock (i.e., decrease responding) but to different degrees. Unilateral depression suppressed responding to shocks ranging from 0.1 to 0.7 mA, whereas bilateral depression suppressed responding to shocks ranging from 0.1 to 0.9 mA.

The effect of depression on shock sensitivity provides an important insight into seemingly contradictory results reported in the literature. Some investigators have found that bilateral depression prevents animals from learning an avoidance response to shock (Plotkin, 1967; Travis & Sparks, 1963), whereas others have found that it does not (Best, Orr, & Pointer, 1975; Schneider, 1966; Thompson & Enter, 1967). The successful studies used shock values equal to or greater than 0.8 mA; the unsuccessful studies used shock values equal to or less than 0.6 mA.

Interest in the stimulus properties of depression has been spurred by reports that depression itself is aversive. Winn, Kent, and Libkuman (1975) found that animals will avoid a taste previously associated with unilateral and bilateral depression, and Freedman and Whitman (1972) found that animals will avoid entering a particular quadrant of an open field previously associated with bilateral depression. That depression can be used to produce both taste and place aversion makes depression unique among aversive stimuli, for aversive stimuli ordinarily are effective in producing one but not both types of learning.

In conclusion, some basic rules regarding the stimulus properties of depression can be stated. First, depression has two effects on sensory input: it modifies existing input, such as kinesthetic feedback and sensitivity to shock, and it produces its own sensory input which is aversive in nature. Second, depression has two effects on conditioning: it conforms to stimulus generalization principles, and it acquires discriminative properties when used to signal reward. However, the effect of depression on conditioning is not limited to its stimulus properties; depression also effects conditioning by interfering with associative processes.

D. Associative Processes

The complexity of events underlying the associative process makes it essential to distinguish between the effects of depression on two processes. One is memory storage, the process by which learned information endures over time. The other is memory retrieval, the process by which learned information is accessed during recall. In the event that either process is disrupted, retention is lost, but the loss is different in each case. When storage is disrupted, the loss is nonrecoverable (permanent). When retrieval is disrupted, the loss is recoverable (temporary).

Studies examining storage and retrieval processes have, for the most part, used the same experimental design. In a typical experiment animals are trained under normal cortical conditions, are depressed either in the cortex or hippocampus at varied intervals after training, and are tested under normal cortical conditions the next day. By training and testing animals under normal cortical conditions, one eliminates nonassociative factors, and by depressing animals at varied intervals after training, one can trace the time-dependent effects of associative processes.

Evidence indicates that the sooner after training an animal is depressed, the greater the disruptive effects on subsequent retention. This result holds for both cortical and hippocampal depression, but there are differences.

Hippocampal depression disrupts retention either permanently (up to 21 days after training) or temporarily, depending on the interval between training and depression, 10 minutes or 24 hours, respectively. One explanation of this result is that hippocampal depression disrupts both storage and retrieval processes but at different intervals, storage 10 minutes after training, retrieval 24 hours after training (Kapp & Schneider, 1971).

Cortical depression, on the other hand, must be delivered in both hemispheres within 2 hours after training to disrupt retention (Bures & Buresova, 1963a), but, to our knowledge, the permanency of the disruption remains unspecified. There is also evidence that cortical depression elicited in a single hemisphere after training disrupts retention. In this case, however, the depression must be delivered within 15 minutes after training, and the disruptive effect is partial (Schneider, 1972). To explain this result we proposed that animals rely on duplicate memories, one in each hemisphere, to show retention and that depression of a single hemisphere after training disrupts one of those memories.

Depression has an entirely different effect on associative processes when it is administered during rather than after training. Instead of disrupting associative processes, it displaces them to new brain areas—areas outside the influence of depression. We base this conclusion on the following results. First, animals that are trained under bilateral depression, either cortical (Kukleta, 1966; Thompson, 1964) or hippocampal (Grossman & Mountford, 1964), can learn and thus store information under depression. Second, animals that are trained with depression in one cortical hemisphere and then bilaterally depressed immediately after training show partial retention, whereas animals that are trained under normal cortical conditions and then bilaterally depressed show no retention (Schneider, 1967). Apparently, when animals are trained with depression in one hemisphere, they store information in the subcortex of that hemisphere and the cortex of the functional hemisphere, and it is the subcortical storage that survives the amnesic effects of bilateral depression and produces partial retention.

Although these data indicate that during training the brain compensates for depression and stores information in new areas, the data reveal nothing about the location of those areas. The first step in determining the location should be directed at neural areas that are free from disruption during cortical depression (Carlson, 1967). Using this approach, Freedman, Pote, Butcher, and Suboski (1968) found that conditioning was significantly facilitated under bilateral depression if training trials were delivered between rather than during the steady potential shift that accompanies cortical depression. These data are revealing in at least two respects: first, they demonstrate that the electrical shifts in the cortex are reliable indices of neural susceptibility to associations; second, they identify the compensatory mechanism as either the cortex or subcortical structures, such as the tegmentum (Weiss, 1961), that undergo electrical shifts coincident with those in the cortex.

V. REEVALUATING THE BEHAVIORAL EFFECTS OF SPREADING DEPRESSION

Table 4.1 presents a summary of the behavioral effects of depression. Two points are noteworthy. The first is that depression has both associative and

TABLE 4.1
Summary of the Effects of Depression on Associative and Nonassociative Processes

Depression (timing)	Associative (storage and retrieval)	Nonassociative (sensory and motor)
During training	Displaces associative processes to the subcortex	Modifies existing sensory input, such as kinesthetic feedback and shock sensitivity
		Produces its own sensory input which is aversive in nature
		Impairs motor behavior, such as turning, running, and drinking
After training	Disrupts storage and retrieval depending on the site and time of depression	—
During testing	—	Same effect as during training

nonassociative effects. The second is that each of these effects can be further broken down, the associative effect into disruption of storage and retrieval processes, the nonassociative effect into disruption of sensory and motor processes. Thus, it is apparent that the behavioral effects of depression are multifaceted, and yet experiments have been marred by inadequate attention to these effects. A prime example are experiments that have used depression to study interhemispheric memory transfer.

A. Interhemispheric Memory Transfer

In the first such study Bures (1959) trained animals with one hemisphere depressed to avoid shock. The next day, he divided the animals into two groups and tested them for retention with either the same or opposite hemisphere depressed. He found that animals trained and tested with the same hemisphere depressed showed retention, whereas animals trained with one hemisphere depressed and tested with the opposite hemisphere depressed showed no retention. Bures took these data as evidence that memory was confined to the hemisphere that remained functional during training and, thus, laid the groundwork for studying memory transfer.

The question Bures (1959) asked was this: can a hemisphere that learned and stored information during training transfer that information to a hemisphere that had not learned during training? To find out, Bures repeated his original experiment, that is, he trained animals with one hemisphere depressed and tested them with the opposite hemisphere depressed, except before testing the animals he gave them a few training trials with both hemispheres functional. He reasoned that if transfer occurred, the animals should show retention, which they did. Soon after this study appeared, Russell and Ochs (1961, 1963) repeated Bures experiment with appetitive conditioning and found basically the same results, except they found that a single training trial with neither hemisphere depressed was sufficient to produce retention.

There have been two interpretations of these results. The original view proposed by Bures (1959) was that the brain does indeed have memory transfer properties, but in order for it to promote transfer from the trained to untrained hemisphere, both hemispheres must be activated simultaneously by a few training trials. The other view (Schneider, 1967) is that the brain does not have memory-transfer properties; rather, giving animals a few trials with both hemispheres functional produces learning, and the learned response generalizes to the test situation. In other words, what Bures took as evidence for a memory-transfer phenomenon, we took as a case for stimulus generalization.

Before pursuing the generalization hypothesis further, in fact in order to clarify it, it is important to add a comment about our view of memory confinement in general (Schneider, 1967). In our estimation the reason animals trained with one hemisphere depressed show no retention when tested with the opposite hemisphere depressed is not that one hemisphere stores memory and the other does not; rather, it is that depression has stimulus properties that are not the same during training and testing. Accordingly, giving animals a few training trials with both hemispheres functional makes the stimulus change produced by the shift in depression less severe and thus less disruptive.

We tested the generalization hypothesis in stages (Schneider & Ebbesen, 1967). We began by training animals to lever press for food with one hemisphere depressed and tested them with the opposite hemisphere depressed. We found, somewhat unexpectedly, that the animals showed a few lever presses during the retention test; that is, we found weak memory transfer, or in our view, weak stimulus generalization, even though the animals did not receive trials with both hemispheres functional.

We included two additional groups to identify the mechanism underlying the weak retention. Both groups were trained with one hemisphere depressed and were tested with the other hemisphere depressed. Both groups received a single reinforced trial between training and testing. One group received the trial with both hemispheres functional; the other group received the trial with one hemisphere depressed, the same hemisphere that later was depressed during testing. The results were clear. Animals that received the single trial with one hemisphere depressed showed stronger retention than animals that received the single trial with both hemispheres functional. The interpretation was also clear. The single trial produced learning, not memory transfer, and the depression during that trial, because it created a stimulus state similar to depression during testing, promoted stimulus generalization.

B. Challenging the Generalization Hypothesis

The stimulus-generalization hypothesis has not gone unchallenged. Resistance has come largely from two studies, one by Mayes and Cowey (1973) and the other by Albert (1966). Let us begin with the Mayes and Cowey experiment.

Mayes and Cowey reasoned that if the brain has memory-transfer properties that are stimulated by a few trials with neither hemisphere depressed, then cutting the corpus callosum, the neural circuits that presumably mediate transfer, should prevent the trials from producing retention. Consistent with this hypothesis, Mayes and Cowey found that animals with cut callosums and trained with one hemisphere depressed and tested with the opposite hemisphere depressed, showed no retention when given a single training trial with neither hemisphere depressed (i.e., interdepression training). Mayes and Cowey, however, neglected to consider one critical factor: cutting the corpus callosum has been shown to impair learning (Sperry, 1964). Thus, without a callosum, animals may fail to benefit from interdepression training not because they are deprived of transfer circuits, but because they are unable to learn quickly enough to benefit from a single training trial. Until this alternative is ruled out, no conclusion can be drawn.

More complex than Mayes and Cowey's experiment, but just as perplexing from a stimulus generalization point of view, is an experiment by Albert (1966). Albert repeated the conventional confinement–transfer procedure. He trained animals with one hemisphere depressed, gave them a few trials with neither hemisphere depressed, and tested them with the opposite hemisphere depressed. Albert centered his analysis on the time interval that ensued immediately after interdepression training. He found that the sooner after training he depressed a single hemisphere, the greater the amnesia the next day. Critical, however, was the hemisphere in which depression was initiated. Depression in the trained hemisphere (i.e., the hemisphere functional during initial training) had to be administered within the first minute after interdepression training to produce amnesia; depression in the untrained hemisphere (i.e., the hemisphere depressed during initial training) was effective up to 2 hours after interdepression training.

There have been two interpretations of these results. Albert took the results as evidence that interdepression training produces memory transfer and that depression of a single hemisphere after training disrupts the transfer process. Depression in the untrained hemisphere disrupts transmission of the trace (which takes 1 minute); depression in the nontrained hemisphere disrupts reception of the trace (which takes 2 hours).

On the other hand, we argued that interdepression training produces learning and that depression of a single hemisphere after training disrupts memory storage produced by that learning (Schneider, 1973). Moreover, to account for why memory storage is vulnerable for a longer period of time in the nontrained than trained hemisphere, we linked storage not only to interdepression training per se but to neural aftereffects that exist in the hemispheres during interdepression training. According to the theory, the untrained hemisphere, because it was depressed during initial training, has these aftereffects. The trained hemisphere, because it was functional during initial training, does not. Thus, during interdepression training when the animal learns and stores memory, one in each hemisphere, the storage in each hemisphere is different (i.e., is slower in the untrained than in the trained hemisphere) because the aftereffects are different. For lack of evidence, however, this hypothesis can only be considered highly tentative and remains a challenge for future research.

Obviously there is much more at stake here than Albert's results. The possibility that depression produces neural aftereffects undercuts the very feature of depression that researchers claim makes it ideally suited for behavioral research: its reversibility. One might argue that there is no reason for concern, especially since aftereffects have not been documented in EEG studies. However, researchers have demonstrated that EEG recordings, even under ideal conditions, are not as sensitive a measure of depression as is overt behavior. Carew, Crow, and Petrinovich (1970), for example, have found that EEG activity returns to normal at least 30 minutes before recovery of the placing reflex, and Teitelbaum and Cytawa (1965) report that KCl administered to animals that have recovered from lateral hypothalamic lesions, reinstates aphasia and adipsia for a period (3 days) that persists well beyond any EEG effects. So, in our opinion, aftereffects pose a real problem for depression research, but whether the findings require significant modification of the use of depression in behavioral research or merely reevaluation of a few experiments remains to be determined.

VI. CONCLUSION

We have argued that the technique of spreading depression has promised much more than it has delivered. Reviewing the literature and recounting some supportive evidence, we have seen that depression has pervasive effects both on behavior and on the nervous system. Nonetheless, depression still may be a useful tool in behavioral research: it can be confined to some degree to a single hemisphere, it disrupts memory storage when delivered after training, and it may be reversible. To utilize these distinctive features to maximum advantage, however, the overall range of effects must be taken into account. By explicating these effects, we have attempted to formulate guidelines for evaluating existing studies and generating new ones.

REFERENCES

Albert, D. J. The effect of spreading depression on the consolidation of learning. *Neuropsychologia*, 1966, *4*, 49–64.
Bennett, G. S., & Edelman, G. M. Amino acid incorporation into rat brain proteins during spreading cortical depression. *Science*, 1969, *163*, 393–395.

Best, P. J., Orr, J., & Pointer, J. E. Differential effects of cortical ablation and spreading depression on sensitivity to footshock: Implications for the role of the cortex in learning. *Physiology and Behavior*, 1975, *14*, 801–807.

Bures, J. Reversible decortication and behavior. In M. H. Brazier (Ed.), *Conference on the central nervous system and behavior* (pp. 207–248). New York: Josiah Macy, Jr. Foundation, 1959.

Bures, J., & Buresova, O. The use of Leao's spreading cortical depression in research on conditioned reflexes. *Electroencephalography and Clinical Neurophysiology, Supplement*, 1960, *13*, 359–376.

Bures, J., & Buresova, O. Cortical spreading depression as a memory disturbing factor. *Journal of Comparative and Physiological Psychology*, 1963, *56*, 268–272. (a)

Bures, J., & Buresova, O. Excitability changes in thalamus and caudate induced by cortical spreading depression. *Proceedings of the International Union of Physiological Sciences, International Congress, 22nd*, 1962, 1963, Abstracts, p. 1061. (b)

Bures, J., Buresova, O., Fifkova, E., Olds, J., Olds, M. E., & Travis, R. P. Spreading depression and subcortical drive centers. *Physiologia Bohemoslovenica*, 1961, *10*, 321–331.

Buresova, O., Bures, J., & Beran, V. A contribution to the problem of the dominant hemisphere in rats. *Physiologia Bohemoslovenica*, 1958, *7*, 29–37.

Carew, T. J., Crow, T. J., & Petrinovich, L. Lack of coincidence between neural and behavioral manifestations of cortical spreading depression. *Science*, 1970, *169*, 1339–1342.

Carlson, K. R. Cortical spreading depression and subcortical memory storage. *Journal of Comparative and Physiological Psychology*, 1967, *64*, 422–430.

Crow, T. J., Petrinovich, L., & Carew, T. J. Electrophysiological correlates of cortical spreading depression. *Behavioral Biology*, 1973, *8*, 219–226.

Fifkova, E., & Syka, J. Relationships between cortical and striatal spreading depression in rats. *Experimental Neurology*, 1964, *9*, 355–366.

Freedman, N., Pote, R., Butcher, R., & Suboski, M. D. Learning and motor activity under spreading depression depending on EEG amplitude. *Physiology and Behavior*, 1968, *3*, 373–376.

Freedman, N. L., & Whitman, R. D. Aversiveness of functional decortication and performance deficit. *Journal of Life Sciences*, 1972, *2*, 73–79.

Grafstein, B. Mechanism of spreading cortical depression. *Journal of Neurophysiology*, 1956, *19*, 154–171.

Greenwood, P. M., & Singer, J. J. Cortical spreading depression induced state dependency. *Behavioral Biology*, 1974, *10*, 345–351.

Grossman, S. P., & Mountford, H. Effects of chemical stimulation of the dorsal hippocampus on learning and performance. *American Journal of Physiology*, 1964, *207*, 1387–1393.

Hamburg, M. D., Best, P. J., & Cholewiak, R. W. Cortical lesion resulting from chemically-induced spreading depression. *Journal of Comparative and Physiological Psychology*, 1968, *66*, 492–494.

Hendrickson, C. W., & Pinto-Hamuy, T. Nonretention of a visual conditional heart-rate response under neocortical spreading depression. *Journal of Comparative and Physiological Psychology*, 1967, *64*, 510–513.

Huston, J. P., & Bures, J. Drinking and eating elicited by cortical spreading depression. *Science*, 1970, *169*, 702–704

Jakobartl, L., & Huston, J. Circling and consummatory behavior induced by striatal and neocortical spreading depression. *Physiology and Behavior*, 1977, *19*, 673–677. (a)

Jakobartl, L., & Huston, J. Spreading depression in hippocampus and neocortex of rats induced by ACTH 1-24. *Neuroscience Letters*, 1977, *8*, 189–192. (b)

Jung, R., & Hassler, R. The extrapyramidal motor system. In J. Field, H. W. Magoun, & V. E. Hall (Eds.), *Handbook of Physiology* (Vol. 2, pp. 863–927). Washington, D.C.: American Physiological Society, 1960.

Kapp, B. S., & Schneider, A. M. Selective recovery from retrograde amnesia produced by hippocampal spreading depression. *Science,* 1971, *173,* 1149–1151.

Keller, H. H., Bartholini, G., Pieri, L., & Pletscher, A. Effects of spreading depression on the turnover of cerebral dopamine. *European Journal of Pharmacology,* 1972, *20,* 287–290.

Koppman, J. W., & O'Kelly, L. I. Unilateral cortical spreading depression: A determiner of behavior at a choice point. *Journal of Comparative and Physiological Psychology,* 1966, *62,* 237–242.

Kukleta, M. Learning in functionally decorticate state and its transfer to normal state. *Journal of Comparative and Physiological Psychology,* 1966, *62,* 498–500.

Leao, A. A. P. Spreading depression of activity in the cerebral cortex. *Journal of Neurophysiology,* 44, *7,* 359–390.

Leao, A. A. P. Further observations on spreading depression of activity in cerebral cortex. *Journal of Neurophysiology,* 1947, *10,* 409–414.

Marshall, W. H. Spreading cortical depression of Leao. *Physiological Review,* 1959, *39,* 239–279.

Mayes, A. R., & Cowey, A. The interhemispheric transfer of avoidance learning: An examination of the stimulus control hypothesis. *Behavioral Biology,* 1973, *8,* 193–205.

Ochs, S. The nature of spreading depression in neural networks. *International Review of Neurobiology,* 1962, *4,* 1–64.

Ochs, S. Neuronal mechanisms of the cerebral cortex. In R. W. Russell (Ed.), *Frontiers in physiological psychology* (pp. 21–50). New York: Academic Press, 1966.

Ochs, S., & Hunt, K. Apical dendrites and propagation of spreading depression in cerebral cortex, *Journal of Neurophysiology,* 1966, *23,* 432–444.

Papsdorf, J., Longman, D., & Gormezano, I. Spreading depression: Effects of applying potassium chloride to the dura of the rabbit on the conditioned nicitating membrane response. *Psychonomic Science,* 1965, *2,* 125–126.

Plotkin, H. C. Role of the neocortex in the acquisition of avoidance conditioning. *Nature (London),* 1967, *13,* 1053–1054.

Ray, O. S., & Emley, G. Time factors in interhemispheric transfer of learning. *Science,* 1964, *144,* 76–78.

Ruscak, M. Incorporation of ^{35}S-methionine into proteins of the cerebral cortex *in situ* in rats during spreading EEG depression. *Physiologia Bohemoslovenica,* 1964, *13,* 16–20.

Russell, I. S., & Ochs, S. One-trial interhemispheric transfer of a learning engram. *Science,* 1961, *133,* 1077–1078.

Russell, I. S., & Ochs, S. Localization of a memory trace in one cortical hemisphere and transfer to the other hemisphere. *Brain,* 1963, *86,* 37–54.

Schanberg, S. M., Schildkraut, J. J., Krivanek, J., & Kopin, I. J. Effect of cortical spreading depression on norepinephrine-H^3 metabolism in brain stem. *Experientia,* 1968, *24,* 909–910.

Schneider, A. M. Effects of unilateral and bilateral spreading depression on water intake. *Psychonomic Science,* 1965, *3,* 287–288.

Schneider, A. M. Retention under spreading depression: A generalization decrement phenomenon. *Journal of Comparative and Physiological Psychology,* 1966, *62,* 317–319.

Schneider, A. M. Control of memory by spreading cortical depression: A case for stimulus control. *Psychological Review,* 1967, *74,* 201–215.

Schneider, A. M. Retrograde amnesic effects of unilateral spreading depression. *Physiology and Behavior,* 1972, *8,* 97–99.

Schneider, A. M. Spreading depression: A behavioral analysis. In J. A. Deutsch (Ed.), *The physiological basis of memory* (pp. 269–303). New York: Academic Press, 1973.

Schneider, A. M., & Behar, M. A chronic preparation for spreading cortical depression. *Journal of the Experimental Analysis of Behavior,* 1964, *7,* 350.

Schneider, A. M., & Ebbesen, E. Interhemispheric transfer of lever pressing as stimulus generalization of the effects of spreading depression. *Journal of the Experimental Analysis of Behavior*, 1967, *10*, 193–197.

Schneider, A. M., & Kay, H. Spreading depression as a discriminative stimulus for lever pressing. *Journal of Comparative and Physiological Psychology*, 1968, *65*, 149–151.

Shibata, M., Hori, T., & Kiyohara, T. Effects of cortical spreading depression on hypothalamic thermosensitive neurons and thermoregulatory behavior in the rat. *Neuroscience Letters, Supplement*, 1981, *6*, 41.

Siegfried, B., & Huston, J. Properties of spreading depression-induced consumatory behavior in rats. *Physiology and Behavior*, 1977, *18*, 841–851.

Sperry, R. W. The great cerebral commissure. *Scientific American*, 1964, *210*, 42–62.

Sprick, U., Oitzl, M. S., Ornstein, K., & Huston, J. P. Spreading depression induced by microinjections of enkephalin into the hippocampus and neocortex. *Brain Research*, 1981, *210*, 243–252.

Squire, L. R., & Liss, P. H. Control of memory by spreading cortical depression: A critique of stimulus control. *Psychological Review*, 1968, *75*, 347–352.

Tapp, J. T. Reversible cortical depression and avoidance behavior in the rat. *Journal of Comparative and Physiological Psychology*, 1962, *55*, 306–308.

Teitelbaum, P., & Cytawa, J. Spreading depression and recovery from lateral hypothalamic damage. *Science*, 1965, *147*, 61–63.

Thompson, R. W. Transfer of avoidance learning between normal and functionally decorticate states. *Journal of Comparative and Physiological Psychology*, 1964, *57*, 321–325.

Thompson, R. W., & Enter, R. Shock level and unconditioned responding in rats under sham unilateral, or bilateral spreading depression. *Journal of Comparative and Physiological Psychology*, 1967, *63*, 521–523.

Thompson, R., W., & Hjelle, L. Effects of stimulus and response complexity on learning under bilateral spreading depression. *Journal of Comparative and Physiological Psychology*, 1965, *59*, 122–124.

Travis, R. P., & Sparks, D. L. The influence of unilateral and bilateral spreading depression during learning upon subsequent relearning. *Journal of Comparative and Physiological Psychology*, 1963, *56*, 56–59.

van Harreveld, A. Compounds in brain extracts causing spreading depression of cerebral cortical activity and contraction of crustacean muscle. *Journal of Neurochemistry*, 1959, *3*, 300–315.

van Harreveld, A., & Ochs, S. Electrical and vascular concomitants of spreading depression. *American Journal of Physiology*, 1957, *189*, 159–166.

van Harreveld, A., & Schade, J. P. Chloride movements in cerebral cortex after circulatory arrest and during spreading depression. *Journal of Cellular and Comparative Physiology*, 1959, *54*, 65–84.

Weiss, T. The spontaneous EEG activity of the mesencephalic reticular formation during cortical spreading depression. *Physiologia Bohemoslovenica*, 1961, *10*, 109–116.

Weiss, T., & Fifkova, E. The use of spreading depression to analyse the mutual relationship between the neocortex and hippocampus. *Electroencephalography and Clinical Neurophysiology*, 1960, *12*, 841–850.

Weiss, T., & Fifkova, E. Bioelectric activity in the thalamus and hypothalamus of rats during cortical spreading EEG depression. *Electroencephalography and Clinical Neurophysiology*, 1961, *13*, 734–744.

Weiss, T., & Fifkova, E. The effect of neocortical and caudate spreading depression on "circling movements" induced from the caudate nucleus. *Physiologia Bohemoslovenica*, 1963, *12*, 332–338.

Winn, F. J., Kent, M. A., & Libkuman, T. M. Learned taste aversion induced by cortical spreading depression. *Physiology and Behavior*, 1975, *15*, 21–23.

CHAPTER

5

BRAIN LESIONS AND MEMORY IN ANIMALS: A REAPPRAISAL

SUSAN D. IVERSEN
The Psychological Laboratory
University of Cambridge
Cambridge CB2 3EB, England

I. INTRODUCTION

A great deal of time has passed since manuscripts were prepared for the first edition of *The Physiological Basis of Memory*, and it is timely to reexamine the questions raised at that time. In my contribution to that volume I reviewed the evidence suggesting that both frontal and temporal lobe lesions in monkeys result in behavioral changes which had been interpreted in terms of disorders of memory. An effort was made to define the contributions of these two cortical systems to the storage of information and to explore functional interactions between the two systems. Attention was also given to the possibility that the memory processes identified in experimental animals could be encompassed within a two-process model involving a short- and a long-term process to account for the properties of normal human memory. In particular that the frontal lobes mediate immediate or short-term memory, whereas the medial temporal lobes are involved in the long-term storage and retrieval of information; a thesis that has frequently appeared in the literature over the years. However, already at the time of the first edition of this treatise, a number of issues were raised that gave cause for concern, pointed out confusions in the way the terms were used, and questioned how clear the evidence was for the dissociation of short- and long-term memory in animals and the relevance of invoking two-process models. With hindsight and more recent experimental work, one can identify some of the reasons for the confusion.

First, although it had been established clearly in humans that medial temporal lesions interfered with long-term memory, it was not possible to replicate the findings in monkeys or rats. Indeed, on a number of the animal tests available both temporal and frontal lesions produced deficits, undermining further theories of an anatomical dissociation of short- and long-term memory. Difficulties of this kind arise for a number of reasons. One ought to be convinced at the outset that humans and the experimental animals have equivalent cognitive capacities. Furthermore, even when psychological deficits in humans have been defined, it is difficult to design equivalent tests for use in experimental animals. Finally, it takes time and experimentation to define the extent and limits of specific functional foci in the brain of the monkey and to match this information with the anatomical investigation of relevant clinical patients.

Second, it was not at all clear if frontal lesions in humans produced an immediate or short-term memory deficit, and thus there was reluctance to interpret the classical delayed response and delayed alternation impairments seen in monkeys after frontal lesions as proof of the involvement of this area of cortex in short-term memory.

The last decade has seen advances in all of these directions, and the new findings shed light on the problems raised in the earlier review.

II. THE NATURE OF THE MEDIAL TEMPORAL AMNESIA IN HUMANS

The evidence for an involvement of the medial temporal structures in memory rests principally on a single neurosurgical case, H.M., who at the age of 29, sustained a bilateral removal of the medial temporal lobe for the relief of intractable epilepsy. Postoperatively his IQ was found to be improved, but it quickly "became apparent that he now had a severe global amnesia." H.M. was, and remains, unable to form new permanent memories regardless of the sensory system involved in the reception of the information. Milner evaluated this case carefully and has continued to monitor his mnemonic and general cognitive capacities since that time (reviewed in Iversen, 1977). H.M. is able to recall events that occurred before his operation, his short-term memory is intact, and he is able to form new motor memories. Thus he appears to have a highly selective cognitive loss involving the processes required for the long-term storage of new information. There has been general agreement about the significance of H.M.'s deficit, demonstrating, as it does, that permanent memory can be disrupted in isolation, thus implicating a highly localized neural substrate in this aspect of memory function. Opinion has been more divided on the following issues: (1) what is the basic mnemonic process disturbed in amnesia and (2) what is the critical neuropathology associated with amnesia?

H.M. is, of course, a unique case, and his deficit has been viewed as a failure to translate information from short-term to long-term memory. Further isolated neurosurgical cases in which amnesia was seen after damage to the hippocampus or anatomically related substrates are cited in the literature. However, these earlier analyses did not direct attention to the fundamental nature of the anterograde amnesia. To study the dynamic properties of memory, groups of brain-damaged amnesic and control patients must be tested.

Korsakoff's psychosis is a well-defined condition that results in a range of emotional and cognitive dysfunction, including prominent amnesia. It is a relatively common condition, and in several laboratories this form of amnesia has been evaluated under a wide range of experimental conditions. Using such patients, Weiskrantz and Warrington initially recognized the importance of using a range of memory tasks. Their discovery that, contrary to expectation, amnesic patients show surprisingly good performance under certain test conditions and their interpretation of the significance of such findings have led to a reappraisal of the nature of the various forms of amnesia seen in brain-damaged patients. As Warrington (1976) comments: "These early quantitative studies tend to stress the global nature of the deficit both as regards the modality of stimulus and the method of testing. Perhaps the sheer density and apparent pervasiveness of the deficit led to the general acceptance of the failure of consolidation as an explanation of anterograde amnesia [p. 221]." It is to this question of whether or not amnesia does indeed reflect a failure of consolidation or some other aspect of information processing that Warrington and Weiskrantz have dedicated much attention in recent years. They were the first to test amnesics on a wide range of memory tasks capitalizing on the different kinds of memory paradigms to emerge from experimental studies of normal human memory. It is clear that amnesics perform very poorly in both recall and recognition tests. They studied forgetting rates in amnesic patients under a number of conditions, and one interesting fact, which has been verified repeatedly, emerged early on in their studies: notably that contrary to the usual finding in normal subjects where performance is better on recognition tasks than on recall, amnesics, despite their global impairment, perform relatively better on recall than on recognition. It was found that performance on recall tasks could be improved further by the use of cueing with partial information during learning and retention. Warrington and Weiskrantz (1968) devised a memory test using a graded series of fragmented line drawings of objects described by Gollin (1960). There were five versions of each drawing, the first being very incomplete, the fifth a complete representation, with three intermediate versions (Figure 5.1A). They found that normal subjects showed excellent retention of this material and reasoned that it might therefore provide a useful way of studying forgetting in amnesics. The test was prepared with ten sets of object drawings and for comparison a set of five-letter words chosen from the high frequency list in the Thorndike–Lorge Word Count. The words were prepared in four grades of fragmentation (Figure 5.1B). A group of amnesics (5 Korsakoff's psychosis, 1 temporal lobe case) and control patients with periperbal nerve lesions but matched IQ, were tested. The most incomplete drawing was presented first and then the succeeding versions, until a correct recognition or identification was achieved. The series was then repeated and the reduction in errors noted. Five trials were given on each series on each of 3 days. On each day in both amnesics and controls learning occurred over the five trials and marked retention was seen between days. Although learning was slower and retention poorer in amnesics, it was surprising to find such excellent performance in patients who show virtually no memory when pictorial or verbal information is presented for immediate recall or recognition (Warrington, 1974). These findings with cued recall were influential in the theoretical stance developed by Weiskrantz and Warrington to account for amnesia. They maintain that the pattern of results shown by amnesics is not explicable in terms of a basic deficit in consolidation and that the results with cued recall suggest that the impairment is due to interference resulting in retrieval difficulties. Successful memory depends on the elimination of irrelevant information, and this may be achieved both at the encoding stage or at the subsequent retrieval stage, when irrelevant responses are rejected. Interference is not dissipated in the amnesic, and thus irrelevant responses are made. Interference at the retrieval stage is thought to be particularly significant because it was found that cues given at the retrieval stage rather than during the initial learning or encoding phase are especially helpful to the amnesic. The interference hypothesis will account for the results with cued recall and the various effects of pro- and retroactive interference. The dissipation of interference is considered to be as important in the process of recognition, which will account for the severe recognition deficits also seen in amnesics.

One would expect old memories to be as susceptible to interference as new

Figure 5.1. (A) Fragmented line drawings of common objects after Gollin. (B) Fragmented form of words used by Weiskrantz and Warrington.

ones. The traditional view of amnesia is that old memories are normal despite the fact that new memories cannot be formed. However, Warrington disagrees with this normally held, but seldomly tested, view of amnesia. Amnesics are said to be able to remember personal events from the past. Such memories tend to concern notable family occasions and may through repetition achieve advantageous memory status. Additionally patients cannot be evaluated under standard conditions with such an approach. For this reason Sanders and Warrington (1971) extended a test of retrograde amnesia (Warrington & Silberstein, 1970) involving a questionnaire about past public events and a memory test of well-known faces. With this method a quantitative assessment of recent and remote events can be made. The long-term memory questionnaire consists of questions about finite events that were deemed to be of major importance, and reported in *The Times Review of the Year*. There were 9 sets of 12 questions, sampling events at intervals of 4 years, between 1930 and 1968. Two versions of the questionnaire, recall and multiple choice, were used. In the former the response was recorded by the experimenter, and in the latter version two alternatives, together with the correct answer, were presented. The subject was required to mark one as correct, guessing if necessary. The "well-known faces" test consists of photographs of personalities who were either well known at the time of testing or had been so in the past. There were 5 sets, each consisting of 15 faces, representing contemporary personalities of the early 1960s, late 1950s, and late 1940s, respectively. In the case of "remote" faces only those personalities who had faded from public life at a specified time in the past were included. On the "recall" version subjects were required to identify the faces by name, and on the multichoice version subjects were offered three alternative names and required to select one. The five amnesic patients showed negligible recall of events for all the time periods sampled. On the multiple choice version of the long-term memory questionnaire the normal subjects achieved high scores throughout the period tested, and under these conditions the performance of the amnesics is noticeably impaired, not deviating from the chance level obtainable by guessing. The same pattern of results emerged on the "well-known face" test, with no indication of any sparing of remote memories in the amnesics. If anything performance was slightly better (being above chance) on the test series involving contemporary figures.

These findings have a number of implications. First, the fact that remote events are not less impaired than recent events weakens consolidation as an explanation of amnesia. Second, the results suggest the duration of retrograde amnesia in such patients has been underestimated and does in fact span the subject's entire experience. Third, if this is so it is reasonable to propose a unitary functional disorder to account for both retrograde and anterograde memory defects.

This pattern of results undermines theories based on consolidation processes and adds further support to interpretations couched in terms of "interference and disinhibition phenomena." The cued-recall phenomenon in amnesics is robust, and Warrington and Weiskrantz (1970, 1974) have consistently interpreted it in terms of interference effects. They argue that irrelevant information in storage is not inhibited and dissipated normally, with the result that competing or irrelevant material interferes with retention of the correct response. Cued recall eliminates irrelevant responses. Equally paradigms can be developed that introduce irrelevant responses and thus enhance rather than reduce interference from prior learning experiences (Warrington & Weiskrantz, 1974,

1978). In a "reversal" experiment, the test stimuli were pairs of words selected because they were the only two words in Basic English that started with the same three letters (e.g., cyclone, cyclic; puddle, pudding; soft, sofa). The first of each pair formed List 1 and the second List 2. List 1 was declared by reading aloud the words presented sequentially on cards. The retention of List 1 was tested immediately by cued recall (first three letters presented). The second list was then learned under similar conditions and cued retention tested immediately. List 2 was presented for learning and retention four times in succession. Amnesics showed excellent retention of List 1 but no learning of List 2. At the end of the experiment the first three letters of each word type was presented and subjects were asked to generate two words. The controls generated significantly more words from List 2 (which had been learned and retained more often), but amnesics showed the reverse, recalling more words from List 1. Presumably the persistence of List 1 words interfered with the learning of the second list. Yet if response competition is the explanation for poor acquisition of List 2, it is difficult to account for the fact that amnesics and controls perform equally well on the first trial of List 2. Response competition should be maximal at this point. In a subsequent experiment (Warrington & Weiskrantz, 1978, Experiment II) pro- and retroactive interference were evaluated using the same kinds of word pairs. Although there was a tendency for the amnesics to show greater effects of interference, the effect was not striking. A final test of the competition response hypothesis capitalized on the fact that there are some words that are uniquely specified by their first three letters (e.g., juice, ankle, aisle), and for such stimuli response competition should be minimal. Two hundred such words were selected, and subjects were asked to generate words on being given the first three letters. The first 20 words "failed" were used for the learning task, together with 20 words correctly generated. The test words were written in capitals in a column, and the subject was required to copy out the list and read it out loud. Retention was tested 1 hour and 24 hours later by cued recall using the first three letters of the 20 learned words together with 20 words that had been successfully generated in the preliminary screening. At 1-hour retention amnesics performed as well as controls and significantly better than controls at 24 hours. As there were no alternative responses to be eliminated in this task, it cannot be argued that difficulty with competing responses provides a satisfactory explanation of amnesia. However, given that increased interference impedes amnesics further and the benefit to them of cued recall which works primarily at the stage of retention testing and not at the presentation stage (Warrington & Weiskrantz, 1970), a relationship between interference and retrieval would seem worth pursuing. According to Warrington and Weiskrantz (1978), "If an interference hypothesis is to be retained it would seem preferable at least to cast it in terms of slower extinction or slower long term forgetting of earlier material [p. 176]."

Gaffan (1976) has developed a closely argued but different explanation of the amnesic syndrome, which is also able to explain a number of the cardinal findings. He proposes that amnesics are able to form associations between stimuli and their consequences but lack the ability to discriminate which of two events is the more familiar. Thus the amnesic can generate responses adequately, but lacking a recognition memory has no means of checking whether the generated item is correct, i.e., they are unable to test the item for familiarity. On this theory memory tested with recognition methods (yes/no or forced choice) would be severely impaired, which is of course the case. If as Gaffan suggests, recognition is a subprocess of recall, memory tested with recall methods would also be impaired. The dramatic improvement with cued recall is easily explained, as the cues helped the subject to discriminate the familiar associations from the unfamiliar or act as replacement therapy to the normal recognition process that facilitates such discrimination.

In fact it is very difficult to distinguish between these hypotheses. Warrington (1976) questions the premise that recognition depends on familiarity discrimination and suggests that it is mediated by associative retrieval mechanisms. However, as it is not clear whether or not such a premise can be held regarding memory in normal humans, it is not possible to use the argument as a definitive one in evaluating theories of amnesia. It would seem that further breakthroughs in evaluating amnesia will occur hand in hand with studies of normal memory. However, the important thing is that the theoretical innovations of Warrington and Gaffan gave a much needed impetus to animal studies of temporal lobe amnesia.

As we shall see in Section III,E a number of novel tests of animal memory have been developed, and these stem largely from the theoretical positions taken by the clinical neuropsychologists. Thus for the first time we are beginning to present animals with tests appropriate to the assessment of memory rather than discrimination learning. It has been clear for a number of years that this was the barrier to progress in this area (Iversen, 1976).

We now turn to another area of controversy. This centers on the question of the critical damage in the limbic circuitry which results in global amnesia. H.M. sustained a radical bilateral medial temporal resection involving amygdala, hippocampus, overlying cortex, and encroachment on the white fiber bundles of the ventral temporal lobe (the so-called temporal stalk). In addition, a number of other elements of the circuitry may be presumed to have suffered dissociation as a consequence of the resection, for example, the fornical-mammillary body projections, septo-hippocampal interrelationships, amygdalofugal pathways in the stria terminalis. Scattered in the literature are isolated cases where the amnesia is related to damage in elements of Papez's limbic circuitry (reviewed in Iversen, 1977). Fornix section, mammillary body lesions, thalamic lesions, and cingulate lesions have been reported to disrupt mnemonic performance, although in a minor fashion compared with that seen in H.M. and in related cases. Bilateral amygdala damage was reported not to result in global amnesia. Different experts emphasize different aspects of the neuropathology of amnesia. Gaffan is impressed by the reports of amnesia after fornix section and considers this crucial pathology. In a provocative article Horel (1978) has emphasized that it may not be removal of the amygdalohippocampal substrate which is important, but rather the transection of the white fibers of the temporal stalk. Horel (1978) writes, "The possibility has rarely been seriously considered that it might be damage to some structure in the ventromedial gradient of the temporal lobe other than the hippocampus that is responsible for the amnesia. The amygdala and entorhinal area have been ruled out by both the human and animal data. However, the temporal stem is a likely possibility [p. 434]." He continues, "Any or all of the temporal lobe connections that lie within the injured stem could be responsible for the observed memory deficits but I chose to emphasize the connection to the medial magnocellular part of the medalis dorsalis nucleus because of the suggestion that pathology in this nucleus may be responsible for the amnesia of Korsakoff's psychosis [p. 435]." Traditional teaching has it that the cell loss in the mammillary bodies represents the central neuropathology in Korsakoff psychosis. However, in many patients the damage is far more extensive, involving hippocampus, amygdala, thalamus, and brainstem. Before death such patients invariably show gross intellectual deterioration in addition to amnesia, which suggests that they may not be the most useful cases to cite in any argument concerning the neuropathology of amnesia. Mair, Warrington, and Weiskrantz (1979) have been able to make a detailed neuropathological examination of two of their series of Korsakoff patients. These cases are valuable because they had been tested extensively on a memory battery and were known to have a selective amnesia and to be well preserved in other intellectual capacities. In both of these patients substantial cell loss in the medial nuclei of the mammillary bodies was observed together with gliosis on the medial aspect of the medial dorsal nucleus of the thalamus adjacent to the third ventricle. It is pointed out that the mammillary bodies are a narrow funnel through which connections from the midbrain and the hippocampus gain access to the thalamofrontal lobe circuitry. A lesion in the mammillary bodies, if severe enough, results in amnesia. However, a partial lesion may only impair memory if associated with abnormality in other parts of the limbic system, for example, the medial thalamus. Thus a mass action relationship may exist such that an extensive lesion at a specific site or a combination of diffuse lesions would be sufficient to produce amnesia. Such a hypothesis could account for the varied and discrepant reports in the literature on the neuropathology of memory. The problem has been confounded by the poor neuropsychological evaluation of the severity of memory disorders in many of the potentially interesting cases that have been reported. Rarely can one be convinced that selective amnesia existed. In the future this can be avoided by the introduction of an established pattern of memory tests to distinguish selective amnesia from general intellectual deterioration.

Although not disagreeing with the view that white fiber damage, particularly to the mammillary bodies and medial thalamic sites, may be associated with severe amnesia, Mishkin (1978) believes that we have too readily concluded that hippocampal and amygdala damage are not critical. He suggests that we missed the significant point by seeking a correlation between severity of amnesia and damage to either hippocampus or amygdala. In H.M. a bilateral lesion involving hippocampus and amygdala was made. Furthermore, in evaluating the histology of patients who showed amnesia after unilateral hippocampal damage, he is impressed that more severe amnesia is seen if there is unsuspected damage, not only to the intact hippocampus but also to amygdala. Mishkin's view is strongly supported, as we shall see later, by his observation that in monkeys combined amygdalohippocampal lesions result in profound memory disorders.

III. PRODUCTION OF TEMPORAL LOBE AMNESIA IN EXPERIMENTAL ANIMALS

In 1888, S. Brown and Schäfer made observations on the effects of bilateral temporal lobe lesions in monkeys; in one particular animal they reported:

> . . . his memory and intelligence seem deficient. He gives evidence of seeing and hearing and of possession of his senses generally, but it is clear that he no longer understands the meaning of sounds, sights and other impressions that reach him. Every object with which he comes in contact, even those with which he was previously most familiar, appear strange and is investigated with curiosity . . . and he will on coming across the same object accidentally a few minutes afterwards go through exactly the same process as if he had entirely forgotten his previous experiments. [p. 310–311]

Fifty years later Kluver and Bucy (1939) described the effects of temporal lobe removal in the monkey and again reported visual agnosia. However in both these cases the lesion was gross, involving temporal lobe association cortex together with underlying white fibers and removal or disconnection of all the major elements of the limbic system. Research then took off in two directions. Papez with the publication of his classic paper in 1937 had speculated on limbic activities (particularly hippocampus) in relation to disturbances of emotional behavior, and it was reasonably assumed that disruption of such a circuit would account for the emotional disturbances seen in the Kluver Bucy syndrome. Little attention was paid to the disorders of visual learning and memory seen in these same animals. The work and writings of Lashley (1950) had made it unfashionable to consider questions of localization of learning and memory functions.

Pursuing a meticulous research program over more than 30 years, Lashley was directed, on one hand, by the behaviorists postulating that psychological functions were the product of associations of conditioned reflexes. On the other hand were neurologists who saw, in clinical agnosias, a specific loss in such associative processes and suggested that the association cortex adjacent to the primary sensory areas might be the locus of such processes or, in other words, the permanent representation of an engram or memory.

Lashley considered the conditioned reflex as a relevant "psychological element" and sought its substrate. He found that the motor cortex was not vital for the execution of a learned response to a sensory stimulus, and although the sensory cortex was necessary for such behavior, every part of the sensory representation on the cortex was equally important. In turning to more complex responses that depend on the association of a variety of sensory inputs and responses, for example, maze learning or conditional reactions, Lashley found that the size of the lesion in the association cortex rather than its locus determined the severity of the loss of habit. A large number of such experiments on the rat led him to postulate that the engram of a habit, conceived as a product of conditioned reflex activity, did not occupy a specific locus in the nervous system. In reviewing his work in 1950 Lashley's contention was that, ". . . it is not possible to demonstrate the isolated localization of a memory trace anywhere within the nervous system. The complexity of the functions involved in reproductive memory implies that every instance of recall requires the activity of literally millions of neurones" and that his series of experiments "has discovered nothing directly of the real nature of the engram . . . they do establish limits within which concepts of its nature must be confined, and thus indirectly define somewhat more clearly the nature of the nervous mechanisms which must be responsible for learning and retention [p. 478]." Indeed it was from a much broader approach to the question of the neural mechanisms involved in learning processes that important lines of research were to develop.

To a great extent, specific technical developments are responsible for the upsurge of interest in questions of localization of function since the late 1940s, especially the following:

1. Experimental animals, and in particular subhuman primates, became more readily available.

2. Lesion techniques were developed and improved by, for example, the uses of subpial aspiration to remove cortical gray matter. This method unlike earlier knife incisions, made it possible to remove gray matter without producing unwanted damage to the underlying white fibers. The methods for stereotaxic surgery were introduced. These improved techniques together with the use of antibiotics to prevent postoperative infections made it possible to study animals with discrete brain lesions for long postoperative periods.

3. Experimental anatomical studies of the cerebral cortex were undertaken using strychnine neuronography (von Bonin, Garol, & McCulloch, 1942), elec-

trical stimulation (Petr, Holden, & Jirout, 1949), and more traditional staining methods for degeneration (Le Gros Clark, 1942; Mettler, 1935), in an effort to determine the cortico-cortical and cortico-subcortical interactions of the various cortical areas.

4. Special behavioral tests were designed. The precise details of such tasks were often dictated by controversial issues in learning theory but proved useful in assessing specific pyschological functions, for example, delayed response or alternation tasks to study memory, simultaneous discrimination in a Yerkes discrimination box or Wisconsin General Test Apparatus (WGTA) to study discrimination, and operant reinforcement schedules to study appetitive and aversive control of behavior.

5. Clinical cases with localized brain damage were investigated from a psychological rather than a purely neurological point of view, and the findings encouraged similar studies in experimental animals. This has been especially valuable in the case of the temporal lobe, where major advance in clinical work (reviewed in Section I) has occasioned similar investigations in animals.

A. Early Attempts to Study Amnesia in Animals

The description by Milner of global amnesia in H.M. generated a flurry of experimental interest. Older reports of the effects of temporal lobe lesions in animals were reread, and renewed attempts were made to produce amnesia in monkeys and other experimental animals.

In the mid-1950s, Brenda Milner had studied two series of patients with bilateral medial temporal lobe lesions. In one series, Scoville was the surgeon, and a direct bilateral lesion was made which was restricted to the medial temporal region and included the hippocampi. The other group were patients of Penfield's from the Montreal Neurological Institute who had sustained unilateral ventro-medial temporal lesions which also included the hippocampus. Electroencephalographic investigation subsequently revealed that the medial temporal structures of the unoperated side of the brain were abnormal and the patients had, in functional terms, bilateral medial temporal lesions. Milner (Penfield & Milner, 1958; Scoville & Milner, 1957) reported that both groups of patients showed extremely severe and specific memory difficulties. Despite the fact that their short-term memory, as assessed by observation and by more formal digit span measures, was intact, they appeared unable to form any new memories. One of the patients from the Scoville series (H.M.) was carefully and repeatedly studied over the first 12 years, and his mnemonic difficulties showed little improvement (Milner, Corkin, & Teuber, 1968). The impairment can be demonstrated in the visual, auditory, and tactile modalities in a variety of behavioral situations involving maze learning in the visual (Milner, 1965) and tactile mode (Corkin, 1965), recurring visual (Kimura, 1963) and auditory material (Milner,

1962), paired comparison of simple visual and auditory stimuli presented on the Konorski short-term memory paradigm (Prisko, 1963), and delayed matching from sample to visual stimuli (Sidman, Stoddard, & Mohr, 1968). Successful performance on all of the tasks involves storage of information over time, albeit in some cases a relatively short period.

These results raised the interesting possibility that the hippocampus (which appeared to be the most prominent structure damaged in both Scoville's and Penfield's cases) is critically involved in memory storage processes. It was apparent that the engram itself was not located in the hippocampus or adjacent temporal cortex because the patients who were unable to form new permanent memories after the operation showed only slight retrograde amnesia and could retrieve memories of long preoperative standing. This synthesis of the results is supported by dramatic demonstrations made during the preliminary stages of the operation when electrical stimulation of the cortex is employed to map the critical motor and speech areas in the vicinity of the intended lesion. Penfield noted that stimulation of temporal lobe cortex could evoke highly specific memories from the patient, memories that could still be elicited after the cortex itself had been removed (Penfield, 1965; Penfield & Perot, 1963). In a rather different series of experiments, Bickford, Mulder, Dodge, Svien, and Rome (1958) found that deep stimulation of the temporal lobe in human patients resulted in retrograde amnesia, the extent of which was related to the length of stimulation.

In pursuing these clinical findings, Orbach, Milner, and Rasmussen (1960) devised an ingenious set of behavioral tests for the monkey which they felt were behaviorally equivalent to the kinds of situations in which the hippocampal patients showed marked impairments. Monkeys with bilateral medial temporal lesions similar to those in the clinical patients were investigated on: (1) delayed response under various conditions, (2) delayed alternation, (3) visual and tactile discrimination, (4) object discrimination with widely spaced trials interposed with massed trials on irrelevant, visual discriminations, and (5) retention of operatively learned discrimination. The results were somewhat disappointing. Delayed alternation performance was impaired, as was visual and tactile discrimination performance, although to a lesser degree. However, there was no impairment on the distraction task (4) which had been designed to mimic the condition in which the clinical patients experience most difficulty. In discussing their results, the authors commented upon the difficulty of designing an adequate test of animal memory but also considered the possibility that the hippocampus in the monkey subserves a function other than memory, although they did not specify what the function might be.

> It is emphasized that the requirements of the tests applied to man are difficult to adapt to behaviour that is within the repertoire of the monkey. We may have been unsuccessful, and this source of discrepancy cannot be ruled out at the present stage of test analysis. Neither

can the possibility be ruled out of species differences in the organisation of temporal allocortical tissue. [Orbach et al., 1960, p. 248]

The last point seemed to be reinforced over the years as many endeavored and failed to demonstrate specific memory impairments after medial temporal lesions in monkeys (Cordeau & Mahut, 1964; Correll & Scoville, 1967), rats (Isaacson & Wickelgren, 1962; Kimble, 1968), and cats (Flynn & Wasman, 1960).

B. Studies of Temporal Lobe Association Cortex

The work was given new impetus by a suggestion of Weiskrantz. He pointed out that although hippocampal lesions did not seem to produce memory impairment in monkeys, bilateral lesions to the overlying temporal lobe association cortex result in severe deficits of associative learning. These impairments, he suggested, were perhaps the equivalent of the human amnesia syndrome. He went on to note von Bonin's claim that the temporal lobe undergoes considerable expansion during primate evolution with a concomitant expansion of lateral temporal cortex ventrally. This would reach its full extent in humans, and it would mean that the equivalent of the lateral temporal cortex in monkey is found more ventrally in humans. Temporal lobe association cortex has been studied both in humans and monkeys for a number of years, and it is relevant to see how this body of research relates to the direct attempts to produce amnesia with medial temporal lesions. Blum, Chow, and Pribram (1950) studied the effect of total temporal, total parietal, and combined temporal–parietal–preoccipital lesions on visual pattern discrimination, pattern string problems, visual conditional learning tasks, and auditory and tactile discrimination tasks. The parietotemporal lesioned animals were impaired on the visual and somaesthetic tasks, but the temporal animals only on visual tasks, and Blum et al. (1950) were forced to conclude that visual discrimination deficits were more likely to occur if the prestriate lesions extended into the ventral temporal lobe. At this time, Chow (1951) and Blum (1951) independently pursued the analysis of the visual and tactile deficits after various bilateral posterior cortex lesions. They eventually reported that lesions in the preoccipital region were more likely to produce visual discrimination deficits if the damage extended into the lateral temporal lobe cortex (Chow, 1951) and tactile discrimination deficits if the parietal cortex was involved in the lesion (Blum, 1951). These results were important because they suggested that modality-specific foci outside the primary sensory areas subserve sensory discriminative functions. Neither Chow nor Blum were willing to accept that these deficits reflected a purely associative dysfunction or "agnosia," as the lesions resulted in both sensory and discriminative loss. Indeed, they questioned the traditional dichotomy between sensory and discriminative function, and it is interesting to note that this problem has been largely avoided ever since.

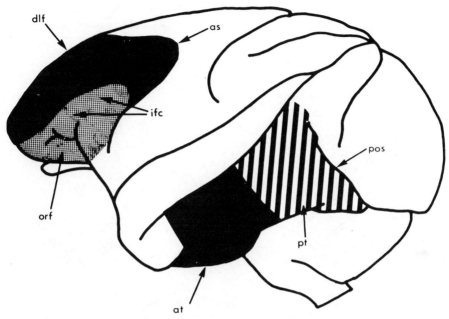

Figure 5.2. Lateral view of the brain of the rhesus monkey illustrating the extent of the posterior inferotemporal (pt), anterior inferotemporal (at), dorsolateral frontal (dlf), and orbitofrontal (orf) cortex. ifc, inferior frontal convexity; pos, posterior occipital sulcus; as, arcuate sulcus.

It seems that Lashley's students were uncertain whether to believe their own results in 1951. Chow, Blum, and Blum (1951) reported further experiments on the posterior cortex using sensory, discrimination, and short-term memory tasks, such as the delayed response. The spectrum of results led Chow *et al.* (1951) to suggest that "different foci of prime, though not exclusive significance for various functions exist within association areas, together with neuronal pools common to several functional categories [p. 59]." The historical contribution of these studies was to suggest that modality-specific areas existed in the posterior association cortex, and, in subsequent studies, it has been tacitly accepted that these deficits are of a "higher associative" nature and their basis has been sought within this framework.

The problem was pursued by Mishkin and Pribram (1954) and Mishkin (1954) who reported that bilateral lesions to the ventral temporal lobe cortex extending from the superior temporal sulcus to include the middle and inferior temporal gyri (inferotemporal cortex) impaired the postoperative retention and learning of visual pattern discriminations (Figure 5.2). Bilateral lesions to the superior temporal gyri, entorhinal cortex, or the hippocampus itself did not produce such an impairment. Subsequent behavioral studies involving electrical

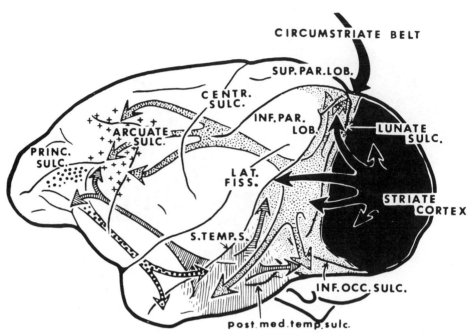

Figure 5.3. Summary diagram from Kuypers, Szwarcbart, Mishkin, and Rosvold (1965) illustrating the anterior projecting fibers from the striate cortex and visual circumstriate cortex to temporal and frontal cortex.

stimulation (Chow, 1961), epileptic foci (Stamm & Knight, 1963), and combination lesion studies (Mishkin, 1966), in addition to anatomical studies using the Nauta degeneration technique (Kuypers, Szwarcbart, Mishkin, & Rosvold, 1965) (Figure 5.3), have served to establish firmly that localized areas existed in the posterior association cortex concerned with "higher" levels of sensory and discriminative processes. Cortical areas concerned with visual processing, and presumably analogs of the inferotemporal cortex in the rhesus monkey and baboon, have been identified in the cat (Hara, 1962; Warren, Warren, & Akert, 1961) and less reliably in rats (Thompson, Lesse, & Rich, 1963). The auditory (Neff, 1961), tactile (Wilson, 1957), and olfactory (T. S. Brown, Rosvold, & Mishkin, 1963) modalities have similar higher processing areas in the posterior associative cortex of the monkey, although these areas have been identified in fewer species, and much less intensively studied. Mishkin (1979) has recently published a review comparing visual and somaesthetic organization in posterior cortex.

   The visual discrimination deficit localized by Mishkin and Pribram in 1954 had been extensively studied in the succeeding years in an effort to determine its basis. It had been shown to be modality specific in a classical double dissociation experiment by Wilson (1957) in which it was shown that lesions to the parietal cortex result in tactile and not visual deficits, whereas inferotemporal lesions produced the opposite results. In a series of experiments on inferotemporal lesioned monkeys, Chow (1952, 1954) found that certain visual discriminations, such as color, brightness, or objects, were more easily learned than form discriminations and that preoperative overtraining reduced the severity of the deficit (Orbach & Fantz, 1958). Several experiments demonstrated the apparent difference between primary sensory deficits following damage to the sensory projection areas and the "higher" or "associative deficits" after temporal cortical lesions (Mishkin & Hall, 1955; Wilson & Mishkin, 1959). However, most people were ready to accept that the deficit reflected impairment of a higher visual processing mechanism, and it seemed possible that the storage mechanisms necessary for learning were impaired. It was at this time, Weiskrantz suggested, that despite obvious differences in lesion site and testing methods, the monkey inferotemporal deficit might be related to the hippocampal impairment seen in Milner's patients. First, the animal tests involve the learning and retaining of visual tasks on the basis of 30 trials per day, and a monkey's inability to remember today what was learned yesterday would certainly result in slow acquisition. Second, the inferotemporal lesion does not include the hippocampus, but both the animal and clinical lesions include ventral temporal lobe cortex. This cortex has shown enormous enlargement during primate evolution according to the anatomist von Bonin (1941), which as mentioned earlier may well be accommodated by a progressive ventral migration of cortex in the temporal lobes, and if this is so the similarity between the clinical and animal lesions might be greater than it seems. We were therefore keen to test inferotemporal monkeys on visual memory tasks which (1) avoided the day-to-day acquisition problem referred to previously and (2) could be presented on paradigms similar to the interference situations in which the clinical cases showed the most severe memory difficulties (Iversen & Weiskrantz, 1970).

The test material consisted of object discrimination problems which inferotemporals are reported to be able to learn. A series of such problems of increased difficulty were presented on the following paradigms.

		Experiment 1		
Day 1	Object Problem A	Object Problem B		
Day 2		Object Problem B	Object Problem C	
Day 3			Object Problem C	Object Problem D	
Day 4				Object Problem D	Object Problem E

These essentially consisted of learning an object discrimination problem for example, B, and retaining it either after a 24-hour delay (Experiment 1), or after two successive 24-hour delays (Experiment 2), or after a 24-hour and further short delay (Experiment 3).

Experiment 3					
Day 1	Object Problem A	Object Problem B	Object Problem A		
Day 2		Object Problem B	Object Problem C	Object Problem B	
Day 3			Object Problem C	Object Problem D	Object Problem C	
Day 4				Object Problem D	Object Problem E	Object Problem D

The principal findings were that (1) inferotemporals have difficulty in learning the object problems on their first presentation but finally are able to reach criterion of 18/20; (2) inferotemporals require almost as many trials to relearn the problems when they are represented after a 24-hour delay (Experiment 1, Figure 5.4) and show little further improvement after another 24 hours (Experiment 2); and (3) a 24-hour delay is not necessary to produce this retention decrement. A 15-minute delay occupied with new visual learning (Experiment 3) was sufficient to impair retention. Results (2) and (3) were similar to the clinical findings, but it did not seem feasible to claim that they demonstrated categorically a memory impairment in view of the fact that the initial acquisition over a relatively short number of consecutive trials was also deficient. If these results were considered to reflect a unitary impairment, it seemed most reasonable to suppose that the basic deficit resulted in slow and inadequate acquisition, which in turn precluded adequate storage. However, it proved difficult to dissociate, experimentally, perceptual acquisition and memory. Both the temporal and normal animals reached the same criterion of acquisition, but the lesioned animals required more trials to do so. However, one may question what an arbitrary criterion of 18/20 represents. Performance at this level does not mean that both groups had acquired the same amount or kind of visual information. For example, if a tin soldier with a red hat, blue trousers, a gun, and six medals is used as an object discriminandum, noticing the red hat will suffice to distinguish this soldier from another with a green hat, red trousers, and no gun or medals, and, indeed, the criterion could be attained on this basis. However, noticing the blue trousers, the gun, and the six medals greatly increases the distinctiveness of the percept and would presumably serve to increase the probability that the stored impression of this particular object has sufficient distinctiveness to resist interference from another very similar soldier. To show impaired storage one would need to demonstrate that temporals learned a problem as easily as controls, and

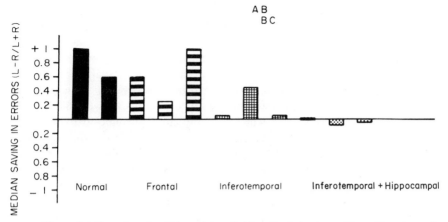

Figure 5.4. Retention after 24-hour delay of object discrimination problems (Experiment 1) in monkeys with lesions to dorsolateral, inferotemporal and deep inferotemporal/limbic cortex. A saving score of +1 indicates perfect retention and a score of 0 no retention. Reproduced from Iversen and Weiskrantz (1970).

yet showed poor retention. Even then, one could not be sure that during the initial perceptual analysis, occurring at the same rate, the amount or nature of the visual information analyzed by both groups was equally "meaningful" for storage processes, although one could aim to eliminate this difficulty by adjusting criterion levels to equate perceptual processes. However, such an approach lacks theoretical direction.

In the midst of this practical dilemma and consideration of the various indirect ways of trying to resolve the problem, evidence was presented showing that temporals are indeed deficient and abnormal in their perceptual processing abilities, irrespective of what their storage capacity might be. This advance was largely due to Butter who, with others, has reported impaired visual generalization (Butter, Mishkin, & Rosvold, 1965) and equivalence (Butter, 1968) performance in inferotemporal monkeys, which he considers "not due to a defect in coding perceptual features. Rather, the present findings suggest that their impairment may be due to a defect in sampling or attending to several aspects of stimuli [Butter, 1968, p. 38]."

In view of these findings it seemed prudent to relate our experimental findings to impaired visual categorization (Iversen & Weiskrantz, 1967). Even so, there remained, in the range of data, indications that storage capacity was deficient irrespective of difficulties on acquisition. In a later series of experiments, for example, the effects of interference and delay on retention were compared, and it was found in the inferotemporals that memory for object problems after visual interference was reduced, despite an insignificant impairment in initial acquisition (Iversen, 1970). More recently we have begun to understand why our data appeared to provide evidence both of impaired visual perception and of memory. The classical inferotemporal lesion extends from near the preoccipital sulcus to within 5 mm of the temporal pole and ventally from the superior temporal sulcus to include the medial and inferior temporal gyri (Figure 5.2). In some studies designed to dissociate the primary visual receiving area from the inferotemporal cortex, Mishkin and his collaborators studied various preoccipital lesions, and a careful analysis of the results showed that a small lesion in the preoccipital region which certainly failed anatomically to dissociate the two areas resulted in very severe visual discrimination deficits (Ettlinger, Iwai, Mishkin, & Rosvold, 1968). This observation was painstakingly pursued by Iwai and Mishkin (1967, 1969). Bilateral 5-mm strip lesions were made from the preoccipital sulcus to the anterior pole region, and it was found that animals with small lesions in the posterior interotemporal cortex had severe visual pattern discrimination deficits. The immediately anterior lesions did not result in such a severe deficit, but lesions yet more anterior in the temporal lobe again produced evidence of an impairment, although a less severe one than from the posterior lesion. These results indicated that two foci existed in the traditional inferotemporal lesion, and in later studies Iwai and Mishkin (1969) produced evidence that the basis of the visual deficits produced by the focal lesions may be different. The posterior focus severely impairs pattern discrimination, which is considered a sensitive test of perceptual analysis or categorization. The anterior focus impairs the concurrent learning of simple object discrimination problems, a task designed to challenge associative learning mechanisms. These foci and deficits are doubly dissociated in that the anterior lesions do not severely impair pattern discrimination nor the posterior lesion impair concurrent learning. It therefore seems likely that the higher levels of perceptual analysis are mediated by posterior temporal lobe cortex and that mechanisms vital for concurrent learning are subserved by related anterior cortex.

C. Further Specification of the Perceptual and Associative Deficits Associated with Inferotemporal Lesions

Several other groups have independently confirmed two functionally distinct areas in inferotemporal cortex. Cowey and Gross (1970) demonstrated dissociable deficits after anterior interotemporal lesions and more posterior lesions to an area they termed *foveal prestriate*. These latter lesions occupied the foveal representation of the striate cortex, notably of areas 4a and 4b of Zek (1974), and extended to include area 6 which lies in the ventral bank of the upper part of the superior temporal sulcus. Anatomical studies suggest that this lesion lies on the path by which visual information converges into the temporal lobe.
    Sahgal and Iversen (1978a, 1978b) later compared anterior inferotemporal

lesions with a more posterior lesion (termed *posterior inferotemporal*). The latter lesion did not include any of Zeki's prestriate foci but was confined anterior to the preoccipital sulcus and damaged a substantial part of strip lesions 0, I, and II defined by Iwai and Mishkin.

These animals were tested on delayed matching to sample of color and pattern stimuli. A testing apparatus with nine panels was used (Figure 5.5), and initially matching was studied using eight alternative stimuli at the sample and matching stages; that is, one of eight color stimuli appeared on the central panel and after a variable delay, appeared again on one of the eight surround panels together with seven nonmatch stimuli. This is a difficult task, and not surprisingly anterior and posterior inferotemporal produced a postoperative impairment. However, in a subsequent part of the study the task was modified in an effort to manipulate its complexity at the sample and match stages.

The task was presented either as a 7×4 (7 possible samples but only 4 stimuli at the match stage) or 4×8 task (4 possible samples but always 8 stimuli at the match stage). This modification represents an effort to tax, differentially, visual perceptual encoding as opposed to retrieval of encoded visual information.

Of course ideally one would like a selective test of these two aspects of visual processing, but this is impossible to achieve. How can one assess visual memory in the absence of presenting perceptually relevant information, and, on the contrary, how can perception be assessed without questioning the subject as to whether or not he saw and recognized the stimuli? All animal tests thus involve, to some extent, perceptual encoding and memory. The only strategy available to the experimenter is by experimental design to tax one of these aspects of visual processing relative to the other. Looking back to the tests used by Iwai and Mishkin in the original inferotemporal dissociation study, we can see that they did this. Simultaneous pattern discrimination in which the same visual stimulus is rewarded on every trial places little pressure on the processes of associative learning. If the patterns are similar, however, careful perceptual categorization will be required on every choice trial.

By contrast on the concurrent learning task, the junk objects are very easy to categorize at a glance, but the animal must learn that six different stimuli are associated with reward, and this on the basis of random presentation of the pairs of objects. Put in other words, the monkey can presumably see the difference between the objects easily but has difficulty in remembering which of them have been associated with reward.

It was with this problem in mind that Sahgal and Iversen designed their matching tasks. Comparing anterior and posterior inferotemporal lesions they showed that the anterior lesion produced a relatively more severe impairment on the 4×8 task, and the posterior lesion produced relatively more difficulty on the 7×4 task.

These lesion studies suggest that the prestriate cortex and posterior in-

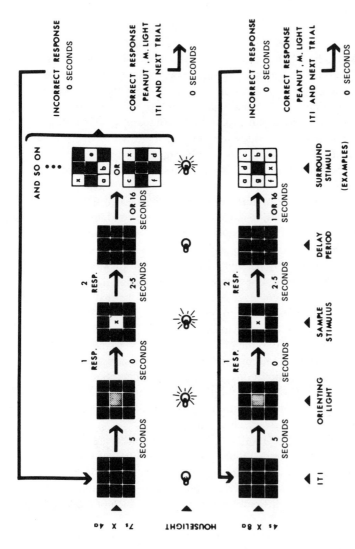

Figure 5.5. Diagram illustrating the testing panel and paradigm for the delayed matching to sample task used by Sahgal and Iversen (1978a). The X refers to a sample stimulus, which could be chosen with equal probability from 7 (7s × 4a) or 4 (4s × 8a) colors. (a) the 7s × 4a design. Red, orange, yellow, green, blue, purple and a grey stimulus served as the sample stimuli. The alternatives were chosen from within this range, with the constraint that, on any one stimulus slide, only 4 colors were present (one matching the sample, and 3 others chosen at random such that all possible stimuli were used an approximately equal number of times). In addition, each color appeared so that it was correct once in each of the 8 surround positions; thus 56 pairs of slides (samples and surrounds) were prepared. This task is schematically illustrated in the upper panel; note that, on any given presentation, only 4 panels were ultimately illuminated (the other 4 being blank), but that these varied trial to trial. (b) The 4s × 8a design. Red, yellow, green, and blue colors were selected as sample stimuli, but red, orange, yellow, green, blue, purple, white, and grey always appeared on the surround panels. Thirty-two pairs of slides were therefore prepared: The lower panel illustrates the nature of this task. The other letters refer to the matching stimuli. M.Light = food cup light. ITI = intertrial interval.

ferotemporal cortex are involved in perceptual analysis or categorization, whereas the area of anterior inferotemporal cortex to which they project serves processes by which reward strengthens the ability of certain visual stimuli to control behavior. We are now faced with the difficult task of trying to specify more precisely the nature of these two dissociable higher visual functions. Dean (1976) has suggested a number of different ways in which visual categorization could be affected (a) by a reduction in the animal's channel capacity so that fewer visual stimuli can be identified as different, (b) by using categories of lesser precision so that certain stimuli are classified as similar when they are really different, or (c) or by miscategorization so that stimuli which are the same are coded as different. It is very difficult to devise behavioral tests to distinguish these possibilities. Furthermore it may strike the reader that it is not obvious how some of these suggested impairments differ from changes in sensory thresholds. If the primary sensory cortex is damaged, animals do not receive sensory information and thus cannot resolve small differences between stimuli.

However it is clear that although lesions to the striate cortex reduce visual resolving power or activity, they do not impair the ability to differentiate visual dimensions, even dimensions that are very similar. Monkeys with large lesions to the striate cortex (visual I) and massive loss of visual resolving power can discriminate visual patterns as normal. By contrast inferotemporal lesions that result in no loss of visual acuity produce a devastating impairment on a circle/triangle discrimination. Presumably, they are able to resolve angles and curvature but lack the ability to focus on the relevant dimension. Likewise in the study of Sahgal and Iversen the posterior inferotemporal lesion produced animals that were capable of extremely fine color discriminations when trained with pairs of stimuli from a single color dimension, but at the same time those animals apparently were unable to categorize obviously dissimilar colors under the matching conditions.

A number of laboratories have turned to electrophysiological methods in an effort to understand further the functions of inferotemporal cortex.

Recognizing that the striate cortex and prestriate representations of the visual field are involved in trigger feature analysis of visual stimuli, it was assumed that neurons in the temporal lobe would respond to combinations of visual features. The acceptance of such hierarchical models of visual processing led to the search for "grandmother" cells in visual association cortex, a search which has not been successful. In the first study of its kind Gross, Rocha-Miranda, and Bender (1972) reported that a neuron in TE had been found which responded strongly to the silhouette of a monkey's hand. However this proved to be a rare neuron. There are, however, other properties of these neurons that give new insight into the role of anterior inferotemporal cortex.

The visual cortex (V1) receives information from the related nasal and temporal fields of the two eyes (i.e., left V1 receives input from the nasal field of left eye and the temporal field of the right eye). Zeki has described a number of specialized visual areas between the striate cortex and the temporal lobe (V1, V2, V3, V4a, V4b, V5, V6a, V6b). Each has its own trigger feature coding property, is topographically organized, and does not communicate (except on the vertical meridian) with its mirror image in the other hemisphere processing the opposite half of visual space. To be more precise if the image of a large object falls across the nasal fields of both eyes, half the image is processed in one hemisphere and half in the other. In the striate and the prestriate cortex there is minimal cross talk between the two cortical images. Thus one may reasonably ask if there are any neurons in the brain that receive a complete picture of an object regardless of where it happens to fall in the visual field or could compare the view of an object if it moved slightly or the eyes moved.

In either of these cases the visual image set up in sensory cortex would change, activating different trigger feature analyzers, yet we know from experience that we would go on seeing the same object. Visual constancy phenomena are well described in the literature, and it would appear that the TE neurons play a crucial role in these processes, which are essential for visual recognition and memory.

In discussing this issue in a recent review of visual processing mechanisms of brain, Cowey (1979) writes:

> What is the role of these unusual neurones? Gross and Mishkin (1977) have a proposal. We can recognize an object or pattern despite innumerable variations in its position, size, and orientation. Perhaps stimulus equivalence or visual constancy is a product of, or requires, neurones that receive convergent input from different visual areas and from all parts of those areas. This may help to explain why inferotemporal lesions impair visual discrimination learning in monkeys. An animal deprived of these neurones fails to recognize the equivalence of stimuli when they fall on fresh areas of the retina or in a different orientation—as must occur frequently during learning. Putting it baldly the animal may be learning a fresh discrimination each time it views the stimulus with a different part of the retina. [p. 8]

Cowey has investigated another aspect of visual processing that would seem to demand integration of information from a large area of the visual field. It is known that neurons in the visual cortex are binocular and respond to small local disparities in the image formed by a small object in the corresponding parts of the visual hemifields projecting to that hemisphere. Such neurons account for the excellent stereoacuity or depth perception seen in humans and animals when isolated targets are viewed. However, when viewing groups of objects or scenes the problem of relative depth judgment is clearly more complicated. The various objects will create innumerable retinal images, and one may ask how the brain matches a particular image in one eye with its correct partner in the other in order to evaluate the relative position in depth of a number of objects. We know that it is possible, and the random element stereogram devised by Julesz (1971) provides a useful experimental way of manipulating disparity and demonstrating the finesse of this aspect of global depth perception.

An array of randomly generated elements, which may be dots, lines, letters, shapes, or combinations of them, is presented to each eye separately, usually be projecting and viewing them through polarizing filters. As the two arrays overlap completely in the visual field only a single array is seen. The random elements in the surround of the display are identical and in register for each eye and we therefore see it in one plane. However, if an entire group of elements in the center of one array is shifted laterally, there is now horizontal disparity between each element of the central group and its corresponding element in the other eye. What we perceive is a central figure apparently hovering in front of the surround or lying behind it, depending on the direction of the shift. Each element seen by the left eye could be matched with not one but every one of a large number of dots in the other eye, and there are therefore many possible disparities or depth planes in a random element stereogram. What the brain seems to do is select that particular disparity where every image in one eye has a matching image in the other at that disparity, and to ignore all other less common disparities at which a proportion of the elements happen to match. We do not have a complete understanding of how this happens, but do know that TE neurons are essential for its success. Monkeys have been trained to make global stereopsis judgements, and bilateral inferotemporal lesions produced a severe impairment on this task (Cowey & Porter, 1979). By contrast, removal of the foveal representation of V1 and V2 severely reduces stereoacuity without affecting global stereopsis judgements (cited in Cowey & Porter, 1979).

The inferotemporal cortex is the last stage in the visual processing system which is still essentially concerned with the physical aspects of the stimulus rather than its meaning. The inferotemporal cortex has anatomical connections to the limbic areas of brain, and it is to these areas we must go to discover the processes by which certain visual events take a special significance and are thus memorized. The temporal lobe association cortex concerned with visual and auditory processing and the equivalent area concerned with tactile sensation in the parietal lobe show a common anatomical arrangement whereby multimodal convergence occurs at a number of successive sites in the association cortex. These areas of sensory convergence in turn project to areas associated with limbic structures or directly to limbic structures themselves.

D. Relationships between Temporal Lobe Cortex and the Limbic System

Van Hoesen *et al.* (1972) have shown multimodal convergence areas within posterior association cortex and from these areas projections to the entorhinal cortex overlying the hippocampus. Commenting on this input of highly integrated sensory information to the hippocampus, they comment ". . . the ventromedial portions of the temporal lobe are thought to contain structures vital for the higher-order functions of memory and the acquisition of new learning in Man. The striking memory deficits observed after damage to these regions of the brain are, perhaps, more understandable because the sensory information converging into these regions appears to be highly refined [Van Hoesen et al., 1972, p. 1473]." Later it was shown that the amygdala also receives a dense projection of integrated sensory information from temporal lobe. Using the anterograde lesion and degeneration technique (Turner, Mishkin, & Knapp, 1980) or the retrograde horseradish peroxidase tracing techniques (Aggleton, Burton, & Passingham, 1980), it has been shown that the multimodal convergence area of the superior temporal sulcus has strong connections with the basolateral nuclei of the amygdala.

The amygdala innervates the entorhinal cortex (Van Hoesen et al., 1972), and it seems likely that the amygdala is able to modulate the cortical influences impinging on the hippocampus via this connection to entorhinal cortex (Assaf, Iversen, & Thomas, 1980). From the various sectors of entorhinal cortex projections have been traced to the dentate gyrus and the pyramidal cells of the hippocampus. Using injections of tritiated amino acids, Rosene and Van Hoesen (1977) have also studied the intrinsic projection patterns of connections within the dentate gyrus and hippocampus and the efferent projections from hippocampus. Input to the hippocampus passes successively through the dentate gyrus and ammonic pyramidal subfields CA4–CA1 to the subiculum where the majority of hippocampal efferents, both cortical and subcortical, appear to originate. During primate evolution the subiculum increases in size, in parallel, it is suggested with the expansion of temporal lobe cortex. The subiculum projects via fornix to the septum and hence to the diencephalon, the hippocampal efferent pathway emphasized in earlier writings. However, in addition the subiculum has massive projections to the ventral temporal lobe, caudal cingulate cortex, and the mediobasal amygdaloid nucleus. Thus the hippocampus is projecting back to many of the areas from which it receives highly integrated sensory information.

The anatomical relationship between association cortex and the limbic system have been assumed to be concerned with the ultimate learning and memory of new information, but this proved a difficult hypothesis to validate on experimental animals despite the very clear evidence in humans that radical resection of the medial temporal structures results in profound disorders of learning and memory in all sensory modalities. Anatomical information of this kind clearly implies that there are functional relationships between temporal lobe cortex and the limbic system and suggests that it is reasonable to propose that sensory information is processed in temporal lobe by a sequential pathway facilitating progressively more complex associations. Mishkin maintained this view in the decade (1970–1980) when relatively little progress was made in demonstrating a role of medial temporal structures in the final associative processes required for memory. Specifically Mishkin proposed that following sensory analysis, a signal had to be associated with reward if learning was to occur. The projections from visual association cortex to the temporal pole cortex associated with the amygdala seemed to provide the crucial neural link for the formation of rewarded learned associations or in other words for events to acquire significance.

In the first attempt to pursue this problem Jones and Mishkin (1972) tested monkeys with amygdala, hippocampal, or orbital frontal lesions on object and spatial reversal tasks. The argument was that the repeated reversal of the relationship between one of the stimuli and reward would pressure the associative learning mechanism. In fact all the lesions impaired performance, and it was only by special pleading that the hypothesis could be upheld. Orbito-frontal lesions produced perseverative errors on both forms of reversal learning, but these were maximal in the early stages of the reversal. The hippocampal lesions impaired spatial but not object reversal because of a special significance in relation to the coding of spatial events. The amgydala lesion impaired performance on both forms of reversal learning, and the errors occurred throughout the period of reversal learning, suggesting that the deficits were indeed due to difficulty in forming new associations rather than response perserversations as in the case of the frontal lesions. It was thus suggested that the amygdala could account for the acquisition of learning through association with reward (or punishment, although this point has never been discussed adequately). It was proposed that ultimately the information would be handled by a memory storage process. Unfortunately for this pleasing sequential processing model only a handful of experiments (listed in Iversen, 1976) had been described in which monkeys could be said to demonstrate learning and mnemonic deficits after medial temporal damage, and yet in humans striking amnesia syndromes were seen after such lesions. Some critics found that this reflected a fundamental neurological discontinuity between humans and monkey (Passingham & Ettlinger, 1974); others questioned the involvement of the hippocampus in the human amnesia syndrome and suggested that we were studying the wrong lesion in experimental animals (Horel, 1978). A few remained optimistic that we had not yet devised for animals tasks equivalent to those that demonstrate the human amnesia syndrome dramatically (Iversen, 1976). It was clear that the few tasks impaired in monkeys after medial temporal lesions had some essential feature not present in repetitive discrimination learning, where the solution on every trial is the same and remains the same for the whole of the task.

E. The Development of Recognition Memory Tests in the Monkey

The important breakthrough in this area was made by Gaffan who, with an eye to the developing research on the human amnesia syndrome, was able to pinpoint the property of familiarity, which is germaine to the recognition tasks

severely impaired in human amnesics. In 1974 Gaffan proposed that two types of
memory could be distinguished: recognition memory by which he meant the
ability to judge familiarity, that is, to discriminate familiar from novel items, and
associative memory, which is the memory of what goes together with an item. In
animal memory tests differential reinforcement is commonly used to indicate to
an animal which stimulus is to be remembered. Gaffan devised two ingenious
tasks to assess these forms of memory. In the first, the monkey received five
trials on each of which he was required to displace a new object from a covered
food well and take the reward. On the subsequent retention trials the same five
objects appeared, in each case presented for a single trial in comparison with a
standard brass plaque covering the other food well. Five unfamiliar objects were
presented on the other five trials again each with the brass plaque. In this yes/no
recognition task, monkeys could remember the five previously presented items
either because the response tendency to them had been strengthened by their
previous reinforcement with food during the acquisition phase or because they
appear as familiar at retention. A second test was therefore devised in which all
the test objects were presented during acquisition and thus would be equally
familiar during retention. Half of them were rewarded during acquisition and
when these appeared at retention, the monkey was required to respond to the
brass plaque. Both tasks, which are illustrated in Figure 5.6, can be solved by
remembering the association of objects with food reward, but whereas familiarity
judgements can be used to advantage in the yes/no recognition task, this is not so
in the second task where all objects are equally familiar at retention. If associative mechanisms account for memory one would expect performance on the two
tasks to be equal. This is not what Gaffan (1974) found. Performance on the
yes/no recognition task was very much better than on the purely associative task,
emphasizing the facility of this form of recognition memory in monkeys.

Simultaneously Mishkin was considering the same problem. He was
puzzled by the fact that monkeys seemed unable to memorize visual objects or
events, although they are able to remember spatial events, for example, in
delayed response and delayed alternation tasks, very well. In delayed response
one or two discrete spatial events is presented and after a delay, the animal must
respond to that spatial location, whereas in delayed alternation he must remember the place just visited in order to go to the other location on the next trial. In
both tasks at the time of choice the cue is not present, and the animal must
remember if left or right was presented or responded to a few seconds before. If
instead we have two distinct visual objects (red cup versus blue comb) and
require the animal to respond on alternate trials to the cup and the comb, the task
becomes extraordinarily difficult for monkeys. Matching to sample is an example of another task involving memory of one of a subset of stimuli on each trial.
For example, with matching to sample of colors, the experiment might use four
distinct colors. On the same trial one color is presented and then, after a delay,
all four are presented and the animal is required to choose the color he has just

(A) Yes–no recognition		(B) Reward association	
Acquisition	Retention	Acquisition	Retention
a*	a*—R	a	b*—R
	f —R*	b*	a —R*
b*	b*—R	c*	d —R*
	c*—R	d	c*—R
c*	g —R*	e	g*—R
	h —R*	f	k*—R
d*	k —R*	g*	e —R*
	d*—R	h	f —R*
e*	e*—R	k*	m*—R
	m —R*	m*	h —R*

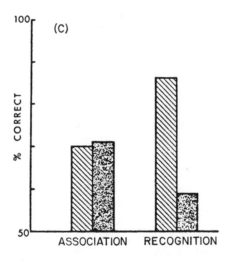

Figure 5.6. (A) and (B). Format for the recognition and reward association task. Letters refer to single objects during acquisition trials. R refers to brass plaque presented with objects during simultaneous discrimination retention trial. Asterisk refers to object or brass plaque rewarded on a given discrimination. (C). The effect of fornix section in monkeys on the recognition and reward association tasks. Hatched bars, controls; stippled bars, postoperative performance of lesioned monkeys.

seen. On any match trial the stimuli are identical, and so the only way to succeed on the task is to remember the specific stimulus seen immediately before or in other words the one seen most recently. Konorski described another form of matching or delayed comparison involving two stimuli (A and B). If the animal saw A followed by A, or B followed by B, a response was required but if A/B or B/A occurred no response was required. Again by the time the second stimulus occurs the task can only be solved if the immediately preceding stimulus is remembered. Memory of the preceding trials is of no use and indeed will be a source of interference. Monkeys learn the Konorski task with great difficulty. In pursuing this paradoxial feature of cognitive behavior in the monkey, Mishkin and Delacour (1975) devised a range of visual associative and memory tasks for the monkey to discover if this species is capable of nonspatial recognition memory. They noted that although memory was poor when some stimuli were repeated trial after trial, surprisingly good performance had been recorded in monkeys when using a new pair of objects on each successive memory problem, which consisted of one pretrial and a test trial (Harlow, 1944). Furthermore, the effectiveness of their memory became especially evident when the response rewarded on the test trial was to the novel object of the pair (nonmatch condition), that is the object that had not been presented on the pretrial (Mishkin, Prockop, & Rosovold, 1962). The effect was replicated in naive monkeys and four sophisticated monkeys comparing single trial match or nonmatch; the latter condition being acquired much more readily. After criterion was reached the match and nonmatch groups were transferred to the same task but using the same pair of stimuli; performance in both groups fell from 90 to 65%. In a second experiment it was found that nonmatching with repetitive stimuli can be acquired if the monkeys are first trained with a new pair of objects on each training session before being transferred to the final condition where a single pair of objects is used from session to session. These results suggest "that at least one form of non-spatial memory—recognition of a stimulus as familiar or novel—is highly developed in monkeys [Mishkin & Delacour, 1975, p. 333]." With this new insight into test methods, experimenters have returned to investigate the effect of medial temporal lesions on memory performance in the monkey.

First, Gaffan (1974) found that section of a major hippocampal efferent pathway, the fornix, resulted in severe impairment on the yes/no recognition task in monkeys but found no effect of the lesion on the reward association task (Figure 5.6). It has been found repeatedly that medial temporal lesions do not impair the ability to learn repetitive reward association tasks. Mishkin (1978) has used surgical removal of medial temporal structures, lesions more equivalent to those in humans. He reported that bilateral hippocampal or bilateral amygdala lesions result in an impairment, but a trivial one on the recognition memory tasks (such as that illustrated in Figure 5.7). However, if bilateral combined amygdala–hippocampal lesions are made, a very severe impairment is seen. It is interesting to note that in H.M. the amygdala and hippocampus were removed bilaterally. It has been reported in humans (reviewed in Iversen, 1977) that verbal and nonverbal memory impairments correlate with the extent of hippocampal damage in the left or right temporal lobe lesion. It would be interesting to

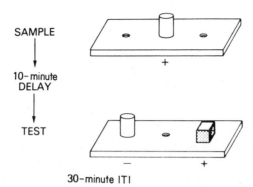

SAMPLE

10-minute
DELAY

TEST

+

_   +

30-minute ITI

Figure 5.7. Illustration of the one-trial object recognition task (delayed nonmatching to sample) devised by Mishkin (1978).

reevaluate this correlation looking for involvement of amygdala with hippocampus in the most severely impaired patients.

F. The Hippocampus and Memory in the Rat

As we have seen, the attempts of animal experimentalists to reconcile the effects of temporal lobe lesions in monkeys with global amnesia seen in humans has been a long and often frustrating process. If space permitted a similar consideration could be given to the equivalent experiments in the rat. Hippocampal lesions in the rat result in a wide range of behavioral deficits which have been listed and discussed over a number of years. Basically, in a wide range of tasks which involved inhibition of responding, hippocampal animals have been found deficient. Hippocampal rats lack behavioral flexibility and when required to alter their response strategy tend to repeat the previously relevant response. Originally, these observations were placed within a theoretical framework of response disinhibition by Douglas (1967) and Kimble (1968). In their review articles of human amnesia, Warrington and Weiskrantz (1978) have frequently commented upon the fact that their patients make many intrusion errors from previously presented material and have likened this error pattern to the disinhibition of responding seen in hippocampal lesioned rats. Their view is that amnesia is characterized by interference and disinhibition rather than by impairment of consolidation or recognition (Warrington, 1976) and thus the effects of hippocampal lesions in humans and rats are comparable.

Nadel and O'Keefe (1974), on the other hand, consider the ''response inhibition hypothesis a mere restatement of a portion of the behavioural defect consequent upon hippocampal damage which is vague enough so that any deficit can be interpreted post hoc as the inability to inhibit something [p. 379].'' According to their view a behavioral hypothesis of this kind should lead to the establishment of a theory. This would involve the progressive sharpening of the class of responses referred to and the construction of a model from the known anatomy and physiology of the hippocampus which could act as the theory required. This has not happened with the response inhibition hypothesis, because with a growing list of observations which do not fit the original hypothesis, it has become less rather than more specific. They themselves have investigated the hypothesis that the hippocampus is concerned with spatial functions and consider that the behavioral deficits seen in the rat after hippocampal lesions support such a hypothesis, and together with electrophysiological and anatomical data Nadel and O'Keefe (1974) have developed a theory that the hippocampus is essential for the generation of spatial cognitive maps of the world.

In rats spatial stimuli have a prepotent influence on discriminative behavior, and when problems can be learned on the basis of spatial stimuli, learning is rapid and performance accurate. When spatial stimuli are not available, position habits usually develop before responses are diverted to the correct discriminative stimulus. Furthermore Olton, Collison, and Werz (1977) have shown that the memory capacity for spatial information is substantial. Rats trained in an elevated radial arm maze are able to remember eight different spatial locations with great accuracy and can retain for 1 hour a single spatial location visited once. Lesions to the hippocampus impair behavior under the control of spatial cues. Olton, Walker, and Gage (1978) reported a lesion study employing the eight arm radial maze task validated behaviorally in earlier studies (Olton *et al.,* 1977). In this task the rat is faced with eight arms radiating from a central platform, and on every test trial one food pellet is located at the end of each arm. Rats learn to perform consistently well, averaging seven correct responses within the first eight choices on every test. Control experiments suggest that rats do not use response chains or intramaze cues to solve the problem, but, provided they are available, use extramaze cues to define the spatial location of each arm. In this lesion study the hippocampus sustained surgical disconnection in four different ways: (1) entorhinal cortex lesion, (2) fimbrial/fornix section, (3) septal lesion, (4) postcommissural fornix section. Deficits were found after all lesions.

O'Keefe, Nadel, Keightly, and Kill (1975) devised a rather different task with a circular runway placed in a room with a number of distinctive cues visible to the rat (Figure 5.8). The runway floor has eight floor holes where water can be obtained. The rat learns to locate the water hole in a particular position although the runway is rotated on every trial to ensure that a different hole is found at that point in space. The rat is required to visit the specified place and drink without investigating any of the other water holes. Successful performance is impaired by fornix section. Using the same apparatus, Winson (1978) reports that retention of a spatial memory is impaired by septal lesions which abolish hippocampal theta rhythm.

In monkeys hippocampal lesions have also been reported to impair spatial

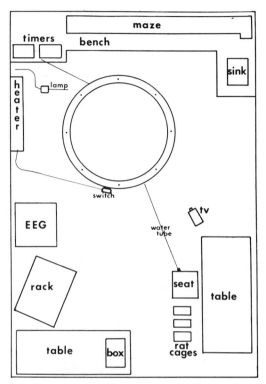

Figure 5.8. Illustration of the circular water hole apparatus described by O'Keefe, Nadel, Keightly, and Kill (1975) and subsequently used by Winson (1978). The position of the runway relative to a number of distinctive spatial cues in the room is illustrated.

behavior. It has been found consistently (Mahut, 1971; Mahut & Cordeau, 1963) that spatial reversal behavioral is impaired, whereas reversal behavior controlled by nonspatial cues (e.g., visual objects) remains unimpaired. Jones and Mishkin (1972) have verified this observation and emphasized the specific spatial nature of the hippocampal impairment by the finding that temporal pole cortex lesions or orbitofrontal lesions also impair reversal but under the control of both spatial and nonspatial cues. In these studies both in rat and monkey the perseverative nature of the impaired behavior is often commented upon, emphasizing that on spatial tasks, response disinhibition characterizes the behavior of the hippocampal-lesioned animal.

Electrophysiological results support the behavioral evidence for a spatial hypothesis. Three independent groups of workers (Hill, 1978; Olton, Branch, & Best, 1978; Ranck, 1973) have confirmed the observation of O'Keefe and Dostrovsky (1971) that the hippocampus contains neurons that are activated when rats are in a particular place in a spatially structured environment. In an open field apparatus neurons can be found that respond when the rat is in a particular corner and not when it is anywhere else. The neurons' activity was not correlated with any observed motor behavior, such as eating, drinking, exploring, or loco-moting. In subsequent experiments an elevated T maze apparatus with food in one arm was used (O'Keefe, 1976; O'Keefe & Conway, 1978). It was sur-rounded with black curtains and four distinctive extramaze cues were provided, one on each wall of the four walls of curtains. In this apparatus they were able to determine if a given neuron responded to one or more places in the environment and to determine which of the four controlling cues were essential for a place unit to fire. The most intuitively obvious relationship between places in the world and the hippocampus would be an isomorphic topographical one in which neighbor-ing cells in hippocampus code neighboring positions in space. Such an arrange-ment is seen in primary sensory cortex. The evidence suggests that this is not the case for hippocampal place cells, and neighboring CA1 cells are as likely to have fields widely separated in the environment as they are to have ones which are adjacent. It is not understood how widely distributed place cells are integrated to provide a coherent map of the world. Furthermore, it seems that a given neuron responds to more then one place in the environment, and thus a given environ-ment is not mapped by a unique group of hippocampal cells. This makes it difficult to determine how the maps are constructed. It would appear, however, that a place neuron is controlled by a constellation of cues, which includes reward functions. It is equally clear that "place cells fire in particular parts of an environment because the cues are available to the animal there and not primarily because of the animal's motives for going to that place, its past experience with rewards or punishments there, or its behaviour in that place [O'Keefe, 1979, p. 433–434].''

The radial maze has also been used for neurophysiological recording ex-periments (Olton, Branch, & Best, 1978) with similar outcome. Ninety percent of the units recorded had spatial correlates, some specific to one arm and some to more complex spatial contingencies. This quantitative study which employed strict neurophysiological criteria emphasizes that place cells constitute the major-ity of the cells in the hippocampus. They are more common in dorsal than in ventral hippocampus and have been found in the fascia dentata and pyramidal fields CA3 and CA1. It is not clear if the properties of the place cells differ in these locations, although the anatomical connections of the hippocampus would suggest that the detailed properties of CA1 place cells might be built up in stages via the dentate and CA3 field.

We still do not know if place is the only or even the major correlate of place cell firing. Certainly other classes of cells have been described like the theta or "displace" cells which respond only if there is a theta rhythm in the hippocampal EEG (indicative of reticular activating system involvement) and if the rat is moving and exploring the environment. Other cells seem linked with slow wave sleep states regardless of where the rat is in the environment. O'Keefe also suggested that novelty or change in the environment could be another crucial type of information coded by hippocampus. Such units have been studied by Vinogradova (1970) in the rabbit hippocampus. O'Keefe recognized that "it is possible that the firing of complex spike cells in a particular part of the environment is only part of the total repetoire of behavioural correlates of these cells and that a list of all these correlates might force us to postulate a function for the hippocampus which is even more abstract than the cognitive map theory [O'Keefe, 1979, p. 436]."

The extension of recording experiments to the behaving monkey is essential to determine if the theory of Nadel and O'Keefe (1974) can be generalized to the other forms of information processing implicated in the mnemonic processes mediated by hippocampus in primates. Although there appears to be little controversy about the existence of place cells in rat hippocampus, there is growing disagreement about what they are used for. Two competing theories have emerged, and both cite the theoretical writings of Tolman (1932) as their source. Both theories draw on the same electrophysiological findings. The proficient behavior of the rat on the radial eight-arm maze is crucial evidence for them both. Nadel and O'Keefe see this behavior as evidence for proficient spatial coding of the world, whereas Olton emphasizes the mnemonic capacity for handling sequences of spatial information (*working memory*) which is required for successful performance on such a task. Unlike associative memory, where a single item is reliably and repeatedly correlated with reward, on the radial maze a rewarded response to one arm is a unique, not to be repeated, response to a place in space. Working memory is a concept derived from studies of human memory where it can be shown that ordered lists of items can be committed and retrieved from memory. Olton suggests that spatially identified places (coded by place cells) represent items of the working memory and that as the rat visits place after place, a list of such items accrues. O'Keefe considers that Olton's deficit reflect a deficit in spatial coding, whereas Olton himself believes that impairment of the handling of spatial information by the working memory accounts for the impairments. In the earlier maze task, spatial coding and working memory are confounded. Recently, Olton and his collaborators have used tasks designed to dissociate spatial cognitive mapping and working memory. It proves difficult to devise tests which unequivocally dissociate these two processes (see O'Keefe's reply to Olton, Becker, & Handelmann, 1979). One such attempt is reported in Olton and Feustle (1981) where a four-arm elevated maze was used with distinctive cues provided within each arm. The maze was enclosed to eliminate extra-maze spatial cues. The rat was required to visit the four arms sequentially under three different testing conditions (1) arms with cues remaining in the same place (spatial coding or working memory possible); (2) arms rotated on each trial such that the relative position of the discriminative cues in space remained constant, for example, black and white next to diamond-patterned arm (spatial coding or working memory possible); (3) arms interchanged on each trial such that the relative position of the discriminative cues in space changed constantly (spatial coding precluded but working memory based on specific discriminative cues possible).

After fimbria–fornix lesions rats failed the task under all conditions. Olton argues that because an impairment was seen in the interchange condition, non-spatial working memory is impaired by the lesion, suggesting that working memory is more fundamental to the deficit than spatial coding.

Olton has made a further distinction between working and reference memory in the rat, which finds analogy in theories of human memory proposing episodic and semantic memory as different facets of long-term memory (Tulving, 1972). Episodic memory is used for recording unique events involving temporal/personal associations, whereas semantic memory is used for predictable regular relationships in the environment, for example, the rules governing performance on a task (turn over cards and place on table, pick up stylus and go to start, look ahead at target, etc.). Amnesic patients as we have seen show dramatically impaired episodic but largely intact semantic memory.

Olton and Papas (1979) have studied fornix–fimbria lesioned rats on a 17-arm radial maze in which 8 of the arms are baited and the rat is required to visit them systematically. Nine arms of the maze are unbaited and should not be visited. In this situation one can conceive that associative memory is used for the task rules (i.e., visit arms from central position and avoid consistently unrewarded arms), whereas working memory is essential if the baited arms are to be visited in an orderly fashion. Lesioned rats retain task rules and reacquire avoidance of unbaited arms but show a severe impairment on the spatial-strategy aspect of the task.

IV. THE FRONTAL LOBES AND MEMORY

Whereas observations of human patients gave impetus to the analysis of temporal lobe memory function, the reverse is the case as far as the frontal lobes are concerned.

Jacobsen (1936) was responsible for the upsurge of interest in this question. In the 1930s he set out to reexamine many of Lashley's ideas, using monkeys instead of rats as his experimental subjects. He believed in localization of function by historical conviction and politely justified his experiments by claiming that the rat may very well be different from the monkey. Lashley had previously reported that frontal lesions in the rat were no more devastating than posterior lesions on a variety of sensory/motor and complex maze tasks. Jacobsen, however, felt that some of the earlier reports of S. Brown and Schafer (1888) and Bianchi (1922) were indicative of highly specific psychological dysfunction after frontal lesions in the monkey, and from the beginning of his studies he favored an explanation of such deficits in terms of immediate or short-term memory.

Monkeys with large frontal lobe restrictions were found to be deficient on delayed response (Jacobsen, 1936) and alternation tasks, but the acquisition or retention of conditioned reflexes, discrimination habits, and puzzle box solutions were not affected. The delay tasks should be commented upon because, subsequently, they have been used extensively in neuropsychology, probably more so than any other tests. Jacobsen considered that a critical feature was the delay, and, hence, deficits were interpreted in terms of short-term memory. The tests thus became established as measures of short-term memory, and it has not always been fully recognized that they are, in fact, extremely complicated tasks, including a complex of behavioral parameters in addition to temporal delay. It is now accepted that animals may fail these tasks for many reasons and that failure after a certain brain lesion should not automatically imply the existence of a memory disorder. For example, spatial discrimination is intimately involved in the delayed response task, whereas the ability to inhibit repeatedly one response pattern in favor of another is demanded in the alternation task. Indeed, uncritical acceptance of the deficits on such tasks has retarded the development of a theory of frontal lobe function to such a degree that we are only just beginning to advance from Jacobsen's original ideas.

After Jacobsen's results were published, it was readily accepted that the frontal lobes were concerned in short-term memory processes. However, as neuropsychological work in primates became more widespread, an increasing number and variety of deficits were reported to be associated with frontal lobe lesions. For example, Harlow and his co-workers tested monkeys with large dorsolateral lesions on a range of complex visual discrimination tasks which included discrimination reversal (Harlow & Dagnon, 1942), responses to stimuli with multiple sign values (Harlow & Spaet, 1943), and contradictory reactions to similar and to identical stimuli (Settlage, Zable, & Harlow, 1948), and they were found to be deficient. Such findings immediately raised the question of modality specificity in relation to frontal deficits and their relationship to the sensory and discrimination deficits after posterior cortical lesions. At this relatively early stage of the investigation, the contention that the frontal lesions produced specific deficits in memory and discrimination tasks was challenged by studies of Chow, Blum, and Blum (1951) in which they investigated the effects of posterior and anterior cortical lesions, single or in combination, on a wide range of delay and discrimination tasks. They concluded that

> The data from this and other experiments tend to support the view that the neural substrate which is critical for retention or ready reacquisition of certain habits is organised into discrete centers specific to the functional category. The areas of concentration are supplemented by overlapping fringes of secondary significance. It appears likely that a cortical

region may have dual function, i.e., it may be focal for one ability and part of the fringe of another . . . destruction of associative areas (posterior and anterior association cortex) produces effects which are neither an aggregation of discrete symptoms, nor dependent solely on mass of tissue removed. [Chow, *et al.,* 1951, p. 70]

Clinical findings also failed to support the localization point of view. After lobectomy, leucotomy, or smaller lesions of the frontal lobe, general intellectual loss, affective changes, and sensorimotor deficits were reliably reported, but delayed response and alternation impairments were not seen (Teuber, 1964).

Despite these problems, the monkey experiments continued, and the task seemed to be (1) to prove that the frontal discrimination deficits were different from those produced by posterior lesions, (2) to identify the basis of the deficits, and (3) to seek a common unifying principle to explain the apparently different short-term memory and discrimination deficits in frontal animals.

As a consequence of further experimentation, it was established that the dorsolateral lesions which resulted in visual discrimination deficits also produced auditory (Weiskrantz & Mishkin, 1958) and tactile discrimination impairments (Iversen, 1967). The finding that a relatively small lesion could produce deficits in three modalities differentiated the frontal discrimination deficits from those following posterior cortical lesions where visual, auditory, and tactile discrimination deficits are associated with three separate and highly localized cortical areas.

Despite this important anatomical difference, it was still possible that both the frontal and posterior deficits reflected sensory discriminative disturbances. Weiskrantz and Mishkin (1958) favored a sensory explanation in discussing the auditory discrimination deficit they had demonstrated after dorsolateral frontal lesions and referred to the anatomical findings of Sugar, French, and Chusid (1948) showing a projection from the primary auditory cortex of the sylvian fissure to the dorsolateral frontal convexity. This view was upheld by Gross and Weiskrantz (1964), when in subsequent experiments it was shown that this auditory deficit was associated with dorsolateral lesions involving the arcuate sulcus, but not with damage to the sulcus principalis. These two selective lesions together constitute the total "dorsolateral" lesion usually studied (Figure 5.2).

However, others considered it more reasonable to suppose that the frontal discrimination deficits, which are not modality specific or associated with changes in sensory thresholds (Iversen & Mishkin, 1970), reflect a disorder different from those following posterior cortical lesions. The contention that anterior and posterior discrimination deficits differ is also supported by the interesting fact that frontals are less impaired on difficult than on simple discrimination tasks, whereas in posterior animals the opposite is true and the deficit more pronounced on difficult tasks (Chow, 1954), as would be predicted if sensory/perceptual mechanisms are involved. Few workers now doubt that these two groups of discrimination impairments reflect different underlying dysfunction; the question is what is the disorder in the case of frontal monkeys? The reports of frontal discrimination deficits have increased year by year, and the discussions of the papers invariably refer to Jacobsen's finding of delayed response and alternation impairments following similar lesions and to his interpretation in terms of short-term memory loss. In the absence of new ideas, parsimony proved popular, and a great many results were considered to concur, although loosely, with Jacobsen's ideas.

By the early 1960s it became necessary to accommodate a widely divergent body of data in the memory hypothesis, and serious misgivings began to be expressed. Indeed, it seemed to Rosvold and Mishkin (1961), reviewing the field at this time, that no unitary hypothesis that they could advance adequately accounted for all the results. Short-term memory difficulty could result in discrimination impairments if the animal failed to retain information from trial to trial, but it seems unlikely that retention would be satisfactory on a difficult simultaneous pattern discrimination but not on certain kinds of simple object discrimination tasks. This kind of synthesis of the data indicated that a memory hypothesis could not explain all the frontal deficits. Mishkin, Rosvold, and co-workers initiated specially designed object learning set experiments in frontals, and this contention was verified. The experiment was designed so that the animal's preferences were manipulated and controlled by first trial baiting of both objects on half of the problems and of neither object on the remainder. Analysis of the discrimination learning revealed that frontals showed impairment only on object problems when the first response was unrewarded, and, therefore, a change of response preference was required for solution. This experiment was developed in various ways and initial preference modified by a variety of prebaiting techniques. The range of results was consistent with the idea that the frontal's difficulty lay in reversing of response patterns and not in short-term memory; it did not seem reasonable to suppose than an animal could remember perfectly well which was the positive stimulus from the first to the subsequent trials when it was allowed to retain its preference and not when a change was required (Mishkin, 1964).

Shortly afterward the same workers extended their experiments to include animals with bilateral damage to the frontal cortex lying ventral to the traditional dorsolateral lesion. The effects of the two lesions were compared on a battery of short-term memory and discrimination tasks (Brutowski, Mishkin, & Rosvold, 1963), and unexpectedly it was found that the ventral or orbitofrontal lesions (Figure 5.2) resulted in more severe deficits that the dorsal lesions on almost all the discrimination tasks. Only on place reversal (delayed response was not included) were both groups equally impaired. These results suggested that the discrimination and short-term memory deficits might be dissociable to different parts of the frontal cortex, a possibility which had been indicated but not pursued in an earlier study (Gross & Weiskrantz, 1962). With this development, the

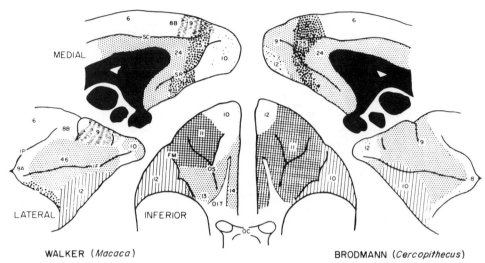

Figure 5.9. Cytoarchitectural maps of the frontal cortex of the rhesus monkey. On left according to Walker; on right according to Brodmann. The upper diagram shows the cortex of the medial wall of the hemisphere, the lower diagrams the lateral and inferior views of the frontal lobe.

theory of a frontal lobe memory impairment, which had lost its generality and with that its credence, was reborn. It is not relevant to continue a discussion of the frontal discrimination impairments, but for the sake of completeness it might be mentioned that lesions to Walker's cytoarchitectural Area 12 of the frontal cortex (Figure 5.9), which extends ventally from about 5 mm below the sulcus principalis to the lateral orbital sulcus and includes the inferior frontal convexity, produces a severe deficit on an auditory go/no go frequency discrimination task and a visual reversal task, without impairing auditory frequency threshold performance (Iversen & Mishkin, 1970). At least on this auditory task the impairment is greater than that produced by either medial orbital or dorsolateral frontal damage (Figure 5.10). This lesion (called inferior convexity lesion (IC) included cortex which in the past has been variously included in large dorsolateral lesions and damage to which is presumed to have been responsible for the variety of discriminative impairments seen after the traditional dorsal lesion. It remains to be shown that the restricted IC lesion produces discrimination deficits in all modalities. The equally important question which remains to be solved concerns the basis of such discrimination deficits. Response control and not discriminative capacity appears to be impaired, because, as Lawicka, Mishkin, and Rosvold (1966) have shown, the orbitofrontal animal has great difficulty with an auditory discrimination presented as go/no go tasks, but not if it is presented with a go left/go right response contingency. The orbital animal fails tasks in which trained or innate response bias must be changed (Butter, Mishkin, & Rosvold, 1963).

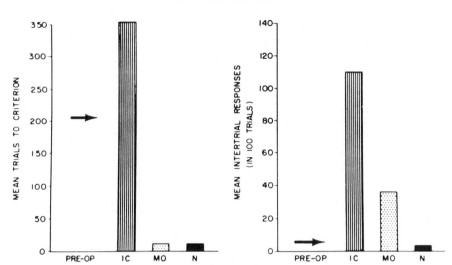

Figure 5.10. Preoperative acquisition (arrow indicates mean score for all monkeys preoperative) and postoperative retention of the auditory differentiation task after inferior convexity (IC) or
medial orbital (MO) lesions and unoperated controls (N). On the left the trials to criterion are shown
and on the right, the intertrial responses to the response box.

The observed response inflexibility could reflect dysfunction of motor or motivational control (Brutowski, 1964) or of some relationship between the two. It
would seem that these possibilities are not mutually exclusive but that the orbital
cortex includes foci modulating both of these responses. Iversen and Mishkin
(1970) have reported that although the IC lesion results in a severe go/no go
auditory discrimination impairment, a lesion to the remainder of the orbital
cortex [designated medial orbital (MO)] that does not impair learning scores on
this task (Figure 5.10) does disturb performance in a manner that may suggest
motivational disinhibition. The MO animals were observed repeatedly to open
the food box during the intertrial delays, a behavior pattern similar to that
reported by Brutowski and Dabrowska (1963) following lesions to the medial
surface of the frontal lobe in dogs, and ascribed by them to motivational disinhibition. On anatomical grounds it is not inconceivable that distinct areas of the
orbital cortex could modulate motor and hypothalamic systems via their connections with the extrapyramidal and subcortical limbic centers. This proves a
convenient point at which to leave the orbitofrontal deficit and return to the main
purpose of this discussion: memory deficits associated with frontal lesions.

The experiments of Lawicka *et al.* (1966) clarified part of the problem by
showing that deficits on certain discrimination tasks involving response control

followed orbital but not dorsolateral lesions, as was previously supposed. In demonstrating this she used both go/no go and go left/go right auditory discriminations and found that while restricted dorsolateral lesions which no longer included IC tissue did not impair the differentiation (go/no go) task, severe deficits were seen on the go left/go right task. Hence the original confusion dissipated only slowly. A more restricted dorsolateral lesion produces deficits on discrimination tasks but, again, not under all behavioral conditions. In the case of this deficit the go left/go right response pattern in relation to the discriminative cues would seem to be the critical behavioral pattern disorganized by the lesion. Extension of these experiments has shown that restricted dorsolateral frontal lesions, as indicated in Figure 5.10, produce delayed response, delayed alternation and go left/go right discrimination impairments, and the challenge is to find out if this group of deficits reflect a common dysfunction.

First, it is useful to identify any common features of these tasks. In delayed response and alternation, short-term intratrial and intertrial delays are striking properties, but they also occur in the go left/go right discrimination, as in all other successive or simultaneous discrimination tasks. Another prominent feature of all the three tasks is that they involve spatial information. In the delayed response task, a spatial cue has to be remembered and responded to; in a delayed alternation, the animals must remember a spatial position in order to be able to respond to the other position on the next trial, and in the discrimination task the auditory cues elicit responses to either the left or right side of the testing board. It is easy to describe such tasks and claim parsimony in the behavioral strategy required; in fact, it is much more difficult to validate such points. Konorski and Lawicka (1964) have done extensive studies with normal dogs on a great variety of such spatial and nonspatial tasks to evaluate the relative significance of stimulus as opposed to response elements in such performance. The paucity of such fundamental information has not prevented neuropsychologists from pursuing the frontal lobe problem, and the notion of spatial deficits and frontal lesions has received considerable attention recently. The restricted dorsolateral lesion that has been described includes the sulcus principalis, cortex dorsally to the midline, and laterally to 5 cm below the principalis and Area 8 of Brodmann in the limb of the arcuate sulcus (Figure 5.10). This latter cortex is called the frontal eye field, and Kennard (1939) reported some years ago that animals with lesion in this cortex exhibited aberrant visual search behavior indicative of transient hemianopia. This finding has been replicated since by Latto (1971) using a sensitive perimetry method devised by Cowey (1963) to determine the size, location, and permanence of field defects in monkeys. More recent behavioral work has tended to confirm that this cortex is involved in occulomotor functions, but the most compelling evidence for such a theory comes from stimulation studies in which Robinson and Fuchs (1969) have shown that in the monkey stimulation of neurons in Area 8 produces eye movements of a saccadic nature and from electrophysiological recording experiments of Bizzi (1967) showing that (in the unanaesthetized monkey) neurons in this area discharge only after initiation of eye movements. Teuber (1964) has reported changed visual search behavior in frontal patients, and similar impairments have been observed in monkeys with discrete bilateral lesions to Area 8 (Latto, 1981). This cortex projects to the superior colliculus (Kuypers & Lawrence, 1967) which electrophysiological and behavioral work implicates in processes concerned with the detection of events in visual space without being involved in the discriminative processes necessary to identify the sensory content of such events (Rosvold, Mishkin & Szwarcbart, 1958; Sprague, 1966; Sprague & Meikle, 1965). Most of these ideas are novel and lack adequate experimental proof, but evidence is accumulating that implicates Area 8 in the integration of responses to the spatial environment (Latto, 1981). Reasoning of this kin leads to the suggestion that it is damage to Area 8 in the restricted dorsolateral lesion that produces the go left/go right discrimination impairment and, possibly, the delayed response deficit, as both of these tasks are predominantly spatial in nature. The delayed alternation tasks also involves spatial information, but the animal responds in a regular manner to the two sides; a spatial strategy is required, rather than spatial discrimination on each trial, and the development and maintenance of such a strategy should be strongly influenced by the magnitude of the intertrial delay periods involved. Delayed alternation may therefore be the most relevant of the classical "frontal" tasks in relation to short-term memory.

All of these comments are rather speculative. Can the delayed response and auditory go left/go right deficits be anatomically dissociated from that on the delayed alternation task? This we do not know, as only a limited number of selective dorsolateral lesions have been studied (Goldman & Rosvold, 1970). If this hypothesis proves to be valid, it may be shown that at the end of this dissociation exercise only a small area in the frontal lobe remains which could be specifically related to short-term memory processes. The development of this line of research has been unfolded at such length to illustrate how, with a diversity of behavioral tasks and parcellation of a large lesion, an originally simple hypothesis may be lost only to be revived in a more precise form.

It now appears that the sulcus principalis and the surrounding tissue is involved in spatial memory tasks, but not because these tasks involve the discrimination of spatial cues. Thus it is claimed that the sulcus principalis is involved in short-term memory processing—but what does this term mean? It is understandable that two process theories of human memory have influenced our thinking. This matter was discussed at length in the first edition of this treatise. In the opinion of this author short-term memory in humans is largely, perhaps exclusively, related to audio-verbal processing and thus in animals finds no counterpart. Furthermore, in humans there is no evidence that frontal lesions impair short-term or primary audio-verbal memory. So we are dealing in the frontal lobes with some aspect of information processing which is likely to be complimentary to the temporal lobe memory process. However, it is proving very difficult to specify the essential feature of delayed spatial alteration dependent on frontal, as opposed to temporal, lobe processing, bearing in mind that both frontal and medial temporal lesions impair spatial alternation performance. It is regretable that we have been misled by the analogy with short-term audio-verbal memory in humans which led us to emphasize time as the crucial parameter rather than the nature of the information processing involved. In discussing frontal deficits in the 1930s, Jacobsen used interesting terms, such as defective synthesis, serializing, and organization and, unfortunately, also included the global term "immediate memory." This is the term that had impact, and has perhaps obscured the more dynamic properties of the tests in relation to frontal behavior, although it is well to remember that Jacobsen's ideas certainly were not confused. He states:

> Thus while we may grant synthesizing functions to the frontal area our problems now becomes one of stating under what connections and in what kinds of problems, synthesis or preferably behavior, is disrupted and ineffectual . . . adaptation is inadequate in those situations which require for their solution not only present sensory items but also elements of past experience which can be introduced only through the action of memory. [Jacobsen, 1936, p. 54]

And yet again

> This then appears to be the peculiar contribution of the frontal association areas, namely, recall of a particular past event which may be only in mediate association with some aspect of the present sensory environment and the integration and organisation of recalled elements with the organisms's stable habit systems. [Jacobsen, 1936, p. 56]

It is also worth recalling that these discoveries were not highly original. The pioneers of the brain lesion techniques in the nineteenth century, irrespective of their doctrinaire position either favoring or challenging ideas of localization of function, investigated almost all the areas of the cortex. Indeed, deficits in memory processing were described in these earlier studies to follow frontal and temporal lesions.

From his experiments and clinical observations Bianchi (1922) concluded that:

> Removal of the frontal lobes does not so much interfere with the perceptions taken singly, as it does disaggregate the personality, and incapacitate for serialising and synthesizing groups of representatives. The actual impressions, which serve to revive these groups, thus succeed one another disconnectedly under the influence of fortuitous external stimuli, and disappear without giving rise to associational processes in varied and recurrent succession. With the organ for the physiological fusion which forms the basis of association disappear also the physical conditions underlying reminiscence, judgement, and discrimination, as is well shown in mutilated animals. [Jacobsen, 1936, p. 6]

In the last decade there have been few breakthroughs in understanding the contribution of the frontal lobes to memory. One of the few was made by Pohl

(1973). He noted that posterior parietal and frontal cortex appear to process spatial information and attempted to define their unique contributions. The spatial alternation task involves at least three features; spatial discrimination, reversal, and delay. He introduced independent task measures of the former two functions with a "landmark" task and a visual object reversal task. In the landmark test the monkey faced two identical gray plaques to the left and right and was required to respond to the plaque closest to a cylindrical landmark. This task requires discrimination of the spatial relationships between the plaques and the landmark, and it will be appreciated that the spatial discrimination threshold can be determined with this testing procedure. Pohl suggests that this task demands the discrimination of relationships between externally presented spatial cues (*allocentric spatial coding* as Pohl defined this process). By contrast in the spatial alternation task the spatial cue (response to left or right) occurs briefly and is not available when the next decision to respond to the other place in space must be made. This Pohl suggests requires internal coding or representation of a spatial event relative to the individuals spatial location, which is then available to guide subsequent behavior, and he terms this *egocentric spatial coding*. Unlike the allocentric situation, the cues are not available in the external world but are held in some internal symbolic form. In the object reversal task the visual cues are always present, but reversal of the response is required periodically. Pohl studied bilateral parietal, temporal, or frontal lobe lesions (regrettably larger than we would now study) and found that the parietal lesions impaired allocentric discrimination, the frontal lesions, spatial reversal, and the temporal lesions, nonspatial visual reversal. He concluded that whereas the parietal lobe is concerned with the discrimination of spatial cues, the frontal cortex (perhaps one sector of it) mediates the interal representation of such information. More experiments are needed because Pohl's frontal lesion includes, in addition to sulcus principalis, the cortex of the arcurate sulcus, which is clearly involved in responses exploring visual space (Latto, 1981). Efforts must also be made to determine if the internal representation of nonspatial information also involves frontal cortex. It is interesting to note again that cognitive tasks involving spatial information have so far proved most useful for demonstrating frontal lobe memory function. I have previously noted (Iversen, 1976) that some of the most elegant biological demonstrations of animal memory involve the handling of spatial cues, for example, the radial maze task of Olton used for demonstrating working memory in rats, the food retrieval test used in chimpanzees (Menzel, 1973), and foraging behavior in the wild referred to in Olton *et al.* (1979).

Symbolic representation requires not only a record of the events themselves but also of their order and temporal relationships one to another. A number of investigators have commented on the importance of time cues for coding the order or sequence of events. Experiments by Yntema and Trask (1963) suggest that items in memory normally carry time tags which permit the discrimination of the more from the less recent, and frontal lesions could conceivably interfere with such a process. Unique or at least relative novelty would also be expected to enhance memory. These contentions are supported by experiments showing that frontal performance is greatly improved by certain behavioral manipulations which increase the information value of the relevant stimuli or introduce time markings to impose some structure on the incoming information, thus simplifying storage even for a normal animal. For example, Buffery (1964) reported that in frontal monkeys, impaired postoperative delayed matching from sample of color stimuli improved if novel colored stimuli were introduced into the experiment. Similarly Prisko (1963) found that frontal patients showed a deficit on a Konorski short-term memory tasks if colors, light flashes, or click stimuli were used, but showed normal performance if the stimuli were interesting nonsense patterns, each of which was unique. More recently, Pribram and Tubbs (1967) structured the delayed alternation task for frontal monkeys by demanding response in doublets (e.g., Right/Left delay, RL delay, RL delay, etc.) and reported improved performance. Such results suggest that both frontal monkeys and humans have difficulty if the task structure applies pressure to the short-term organization of incoming information, but the deficit envisaged does not concur with the traditional idea of short-term memory as a brief impression of the sensory environment that is ultimately transformed into a more permanent trace.

The theory has been verbalized in several ways, for example, in terms of an inflexible noticing order by analogy with the computer simulation model of human problem solving described by Newell, Shaw, and Simon (1958) and, more recently, in the more general terms of "proper programming—the parsing of the stream of stimulation to which the organism is subject" [Pribram & Tubbs, 1967, p. 1766]." Helpful as such theorizing is, it would seem that there is still a long way to go in our understanding of such frontal deficits. For example, is the impairment in "programming" most significant with respect to the organization of information bombarding the organism or with respect to the search strategies the organism may pursue in sampling the sensory environment? Indeed, it is pointless to ask such questions before the interdependence of such processes is established.

Thus, in conclusion, it seems possible that a very small part of the frontal cortex is involved in the "synthesizing or serializing" process that Jacobsen postulated. A range of impairments sharing this characteristic have been selected from the frontal literature, but many of them have been described only after the traditionally large frontal lesions. Further selective lesion studies will be necessary to discover if this small frontal region is critical for the structuring of incoming information demanded in certain tasks, which we have been encouraged to call short-term memory tests. However, it is fair to point out that although Jacobsen popularized the idea of immediate memory disorders following frontal lesions, he tried to prevent the too ready acceptance of the term with all its implications for psychological and physiological theories of memory.

In using the term immediate memory to designate the defect that follows injury to the
frontal areas we do so with little assurance that it is either sufficiently inclusive or descrip-
tively adequate for the phenomena in point. In some respects recognition memory and
recall appear to be better suited. It is obvious that use of any of these terms adds little to our
understanding of the essential physiological and psychological problems beyond a comfort-
able feeling of familiarity. For the present operational definition of the functions involved
may be a more satisfactory procedure. [Jacobsen, 1936, p. 53]

V. THE EFFECTS OF FRONTAL LESIONS IN HUMANS

In humans, as in animals, frontal lesions produce evidence of motivational
change, perseveration, and spatial disorientation. Faust (1966) reported that
orbital damage results in severe disorders of affect and motivation with strong
compulsive or disinhibited behavior. The anatomical evidence on the spatial
deficits also parallels the findings in the monkey. Lesions to Area 8 in both
monkey and humans produce a range of disorientation and "search" defects
which Teuber (1964) has convincingly described as manifesting a basic disorder
in the ability to "distinguish those changes in sensory input that result from his
own, self produced movements, and those that result from actual movement in
the environment [p. 439]."

The next task is to consider the behavioral basis of frontal impairments in
humans and to ask, as with the animal frontal literature, having demonstrated
impairment of response and spatial control, how strong is the independent evidence for a memory defect?

The fact that patients with frontal-lobe damage perform normally on a wide
variety of memory tasks has fostered the idea that they have no memory disorder.
They are not impaired on the delayed response or alteration tasks (Chorover &
Cole, 1966; Ghent, Mishkin, & Teuber, 1962), probably because it is difficult to
design a test equivalent to that used with animals, but also because such tasks
tend to be solved by sophisticated verbal coding strategies. However, a list of
human frontal impairments has emerged from the study of patients with focal
damage. Impairment after frontal lesions (greater after right than left) was found
on both a visual (Milner, 1965) and a tactile (Corkin, 1965) stylus maze, where
the subject is required to find the correct course by changing direction in response to a bell or the click of an error counter. Impairment is also seen on the
Konorski Paired Comparison task using clicks, flashes of light or colored lights
as stimuli. The subject is presented with the stimulus and shortly after with
another; if they are the same (A–A) one response is required, and if different
(A–B) another response is required. A few stimuli were paired and repaired
repeatedly in the test used by Prisko (1963), and cited in Milner and Teuber
(1968) suggesting that frontal lobectomy impairs the patients ability to keep the
different trials apart, so that they cannot distinguish between the most recently
presented stimulus and one shown some trials before. The stimuli themselves

have no meaning out of the context or structure of the task; stimulus A means something different depending on whether it follows A or B. A similar interpretation applies to the frontal impairment on the Wisconsin Card Sorting (Milner, 1963). Four sample cards are displayed and the subject requested to begin sorting a pile (128 cards) of test cards according to one of the three possible strategies; color, shape, or number (Figure 5.11). The tester has predetermined the order of sorting strategies required and says right or wrong to each sorting response. With this feedback subjects quickly adopt the required strategy. When nine constructive correct responses have been made, and without warning, the sorting strategy required is changed and the subject must find the next required strategy. Frontal patients are severely impaired on this task, particularly those with dorsolateral lesions (Milner, 1964). They perseverate their initial strategy achieving on average only 1.4 strategies compared with 4.7 in controls. Again in this task the subject must switch from one solution to another in response to verbal cues. However, if unable to keep a record of previous responses, the frontal patient would have difficulty in systematically trying sorting strategies until the correct one is found. Again the cards are very similar and easily confused. These results led Corsi to design a specific test of the ability to discriminate the order of events [described in Milner (1971)]. The recency test is presented in a verbal (line drawings of common objects) and nonverbal (abstract art pictures) form. The subject is presented with a deck of 184 test cards and is required to name or view each one before turning it over. From time to time, a test card appears, bearing a question mark between two test stimuli. The subject must indicate which of the stimuli on the card he saw most recently. Usually both stimuli have appeared before but sometimes one stimulus is new and on these trials recognition memory can be evaluated. The frontal patients perform poorly on the recency judgements but have excellent recognition scores. Thus they know what they have seen but not when they saw it.

It is interesting that if one can enhance the information content of repetitious stimuli, performance improves on frontal patients. For example, on recurring memory tasks frontal patients fail if visual nonsense figures or tactile wire shapes are used (difficult to discriminate and not very interesting), whereas if snatches of bird song are used as test stimuli, frontals perform normally. Temporal lobe lesions which produce a profound memory disturbance impair this task irrespective of the test stimuli used. The importance of the nature of the stimuli rather than the structure of the task is difficult to explain unless, as Milner and Teuber (1968) suggest, ''the short pause between stimuli or the likely and more interesting character of the birdsong material could compensate for the confusion engendered by the continuous recognition procedure [p. 348].'' Bearing in mind the frontal impairment on a tactile recurring figure task, visual and tactile finger mazes, and the paired comparison task employing repeated stimuli, it would seem that the frontal patient is impaired if pressure is put on the memory

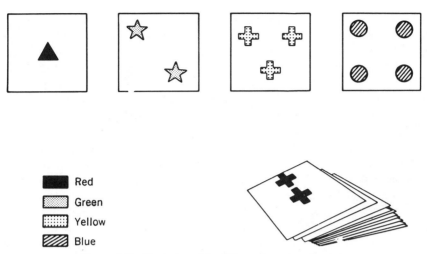

Red
Green
Yellow
Blue

Figure 5.11. Illustration of the Wisconsin card sorting task.

mechanism while it is handling easily confusable material. Either temporal structuring of the task to allow the mnemonic process to handle redundant material or increasing the information content of the material itself may significantly enhance performance. The notion of an impairment in monitoring and organizing the content of the memory does not have to be restricted to sensory input; indeed, there is every reason to suppose that memory processes constantly monitor both externally and internally initiated events, such as thoughts. Disorders of the organization of thought and planning are seen in frontal patients. Such a process could also be concerned with the monitoring of reafference, that is, the consequence of the response to input and, extended in this way, the explanation would account for the various spatial, response, and sorting impairments seen after frontal lesions.

Although the concept of planning both responses and thoughts has recurred in the frontal-lobe literature, the attempts to test the hypothesis have been piecemeal and generally not very successful. However cognitive psychology is beginning to make its impact in this domain and hopefully theoretical models of planning behavior (Norman & Shallice, 1980) will do for the frontal lobe what two process models of memory did for the temporal lobe.

Luria proposed a system for programming regulation and verification of responses, which is frequently referred to in describing frontal-lobe deficits. Unfortunately, frontal-lobe damage does not produce impairment on a range of tasks which at first sight are encompassed within Luria's theoretical framework. A more sophisticated model has been described by Norman and Shallice (1980) with separate control mechanisms for routine and nonroutine response programmes. Frontal lesions impair the latter function and on the tasks sensitive to such damage, although the operations used may be routine, which operations used and the order in which they are used is not routine. Shallice (1982) reported the effects of right versus left frontal lobe and posterior cortical damage on the Tower of London test in which three colored beads arranged in one order on three vertical sticks have to be arranged in a different specified order within a certain number of moves. Goal positions demand 2, 4, or 5 moves for solution. Left but not right anterior lesions impair this performance. In a similar vein Petrides and Milner, (cited in Milner, 1982) have been using a subject-ordered pointing task. Patients are presented with a stack of cards each displaying 6, 8, 10, or 12 stimuli in a regular array. On a given stack the number of items, the nature of the material and the spatial positions of the items remained constant. The subjects' task was to go through the stack, touching 1 and only 1 item on each card and taking care not to touch the same item twice. The subject himself initiated the programme and determined the order of responding. Four kinds of stimulus material were used (a) concrete high-imagery words (e.g., lemon, hammer), (b) abstract, low-imagery words (e.g., altitude, situation), (c) representational drawings, and (d) abstract designs. Patients with left frontal lesions were impaired on all the tasks, right frontal lesions on only the nonverbal tasks. In contrast on the recency tasks described earlier, right frontal lobe lesions resulted in more striking deficits than those in the left hemisphere. This partial dissociation of self ordered pointing to the left frontal lobe and temporal sequencing to the right, lead Milner (1982) to suggest that whereas the right frontal lobe is particularly concerned with monitoring sequences of *externally* ordered events, the left frontal lobe plays a major role in active planning and monitoring self-initiated responses.

VI. A FINAL SYNTHESIS

The posterior neocortex contains modality specific areas for processing sensory information. The next step in the anatomical pathway involves adjacent areas of association cortex which are also modality specific. The visual system has been studied in most depth, and it became clear from anatomical and lesion studies that visual information projects anteriorly in inferotemporal cortex, resulting, it was presumed, in progressively more complex analysis of the information. Finally an interaction with the underlying limbic structures was proposed enabling reward associations to be made prior to memory storage. The appeal of hierarchical models of this kind is obvious, but just as serial processing models have been challenged in sensory cortex by findings suggesting parallel as well as serial processing, so it would seem in association cortex.

Only recently with anatomical techniques have we been able to determine the projections from temporal lobe association cortex to and from limbic structures. The emphasis in this chapter is not anatomical, since many of the relevant findings in this context have been reviewed elsewhere (Iversen, 1976), but it is important to note how anatomical techniques are spearheading the advances in neuropsychology.

Highly integrated sensory information of posterior association cortex projects to multimodal areas of association cortex in parietal lobe and the depths of the superior temporal sulcus and hence to entorhinal cortex. The entorhinal cortex also receives input from the amygdala and orbitofrontal cortex (Van Hoesen *et al.*, 1972). The two subfields of entorhinal cortex project to dentate gyrus of hippocampus and from dentate gyrus information projects sequentially across the fields of pyramidal neurons CA4–CA1 (Rosene & Van Hoesen, 1977). Earlier views concerning the organizations of output from hippocampus have been reevaluated in rat, and comparative data on monkey are now available. Both the fimbria and the subiculum are sources of hippocampal efferents.

The subiculum projects widely to associative cortex as well as to the diencephalon, thus providing a reciprocal connection between association cortex and hippocampus. In the monkey, and even more so in humans, the subiculum is highly developed and has direct input from posterior association cortex (Van Hoesen, Rosene, & Mesulam, 1979), suggesting "the pivotal role of these areas in the potential interplay between the hippocampus formation and the association cortices [p. 608]."

Very recently it has been demonstrated that the amygdala also receives the highly integrated information of posterior association cortex via topographically organized pathway from the fundus of the superior temporal sulcus. Thus amygdala and hippocampus would appear to receive information in parallel to mediate the processes of associative learning and memory. The entorhinal cortex and the subiculum provide for rich interconnections between hippocampus and amydala. It remains a challenge to define the contribution of amygdala and hippocampus to learning and memory, but it is not unreasonable to suggest that the amygdala, with its strong connections to diencephalic and brainstem sites involved in the expression of emotion, is concerned with the affective component of learning and memory.

The frontal cortex also receives integrated sensory information from temporal lobe and in addition a rich input from the areas of parietal lobe coding spatial relationships of the external world and of the body. The peculiar contribution of the frontal lobe appears to be in the ordering of the incoming streams of information, but it is difficult at present to understand this proposed function in terms of the input to frontal cortex. Further definition of the contribution of the frontal lobe to memory remains a challenge to neuropsychology. One could imagine that the coding of an event involves at least four aspects of information processing:

1. Where did it happen?
2. When did it happen?

3. What was it?

4. Is it important to me?

Questions 1 and 2 provide the context of space and time, and it is suggested involve frontal cortex. Questions 3 and 4 provide the information about the event and its affective weighting and involve hippocampus and amygdala, respectively.

VII. SUMMARY

A number of questions have been posed throughout the chapter which may now be answered in summary.

1. Medial temporal lesions in humans result in severe global amnesia.

2. Other lesions to the brain areas related to the medial temporal cortex also result in amnesia, but on detailed neuropsychological evaluation it can be shown that these amnesias have different characteristics with regard to encoding, consolidation, rate of forgetting, and sensitivity to interference (Squire, 1981).

3. It therefore now seems unfruitful to attempt to draw together these various forms of amnesia with their varying neuropathology within a unitary theoretical framework. More useful will be attempts to relate the different features of the amnesia with particular profiles of neuropathological damage in cortex, thalamus, hippocampus, subiculum, fornix–fimbria, and diencephalon.

4. It seems that the classical case, H.M., and related cases with medial temporal damage involving amydala and hippocampus indeed have a defect of acquisition or consolidation (of the material itself or the cues laid down to facilitate subsequent retrieval) as originally suggested by Milner. Testing methods designed to facilitate encoding or retrieval would be predicted to improve such a deficit.

5. It is this clinical impairment which animal experimentalists have attempted to reproduce, initially with little success. In retrospect the design of the tasks and the lesion were inappropriate. With recently developed tests of recognition (episodic) memory and combined lesions of the amygdala and hippocampus or temporal cortex plus limbic damage, severe memory impairments in monkeys are seen. In the rat mnemonic processes seem to be dominated by the handling of spatial information, and in this species episodic spatial memory is impaired by surgical disconnection of the hippocampus. Nonspatial episodic memory also seems to be impaired suggesting that the impairment is not purely spatial.

6. A sector of frontal cortex contributes to certain aspects of memory which appear to involve coding the order and relationships between sequences of events and the responses to those events. Episodic memory for specific events is not impaired. This is clear both in monkeys and patients with focal frontal lesions. It remains impressive that on a number of tasks both hippocampal and

frontal lesioned animals and patients are impaired and that the residual behavior is characterized by perseveration. There are strong anatomical connections between limbic structures and the frontal lobes, and both areas project to similar brainstem sites (Nauta, 1964, 1971) which led Nauta to write, "This similarity could raise the suspicion that the prefrontal cortex affects the same general brainstem mechanisms which are also governed by neural discharge from the limbic forebrain. It could even be asked if the available anatomical data do not suggest that the prefrontal cortex is the isocortical representative of the same category of functions that is subserved by the limbic forebrain and its affiliated subcortical structures [Nauta, 1982, p. 405]." When these comments were made Nauta was no doubt considering the classical descending projections of limbic forebrain to brain stem. Recently, attention has focused on projections of limbic structures and frontal cortex to the forebrain subcortical sites, particularly the corpus striatum. Using modern anatomical tracing techniques, striking overlaps have been observed in the projections to striatum from frontal cortex, the amygdala and hippocampus, and the dopamine neurones of the ventral mesencephalon. There is every reason to believe that dopamine release in the striatum facilitates the integration of information from the cortical and limbic sites. Nauta (1982) suggested that these projections may serve as an interface between higher integrative functions and the motor system and thus provides the impetus for us to tackle, at the physiological level, the problem of how memory and thoughts organise responses.

Further studies are clearly required to attack this problem directly and define the unique but interrelated contributions of the temporal and frontal lobes to memory functions.

REFERENCES

Aggleton, J. P., & Mishkin, M. Recognition impairment after medial thalamic lesions in monkeys. *Neuroscience Abstracts,* 1981, *7,* 236.

Aggleton, J. P., Burton, M. J., & Passingham, R. E. Cortical and subcortical afferents to the amygdala of the rhesus monkey (*Macaca mulatta*). *Brain Research,* 1980, *190,* 347–368.

Assaf, S. Y., Iversen, S. D., & Thomas, S. R. Evaluation of synaptic transmission between the entorhinal cortex and the dentate gyrus of the rat during conditioned behaviour. *Physiological Society Abstract,* July 1980, p. 3.

Bianchi, L. *The mechanism of the brain and the function of the function of the frontal lobes* (J. H. MacDonald, trans.). Edinburgh: Livingston; 1922.

Bickford, R., Mulder, D. W., Dodge, H. W., Svien, H. J., & Rome, H.P. (1958). Changes in memory function produced by electrical stimulation of the temporal lobe in man. *Research Publications—Association for Research in Nervous and Mental Disease,* 1958, *36,* 227–247.

Bizzi, E. Discharge of frontal eye field neurons during eye movements in unanaesthetized monkeys. *Science,* 1967, *157,* 1588–1590.

Blum, J. S. Cortical organization in somaesthesis. Effects of lesions in posterior associative cortex on somato-sensory function in *Macaca mulata. Comparative and Psychological Monograph,* 1951, *20,* 219–249.

Blum, J. S., Chow, K. L., & Pribram, K. H. A behavioural analysis of the organization of the parieto-temporo-preoccipital cortex. *Journal of Comparative Neurology*, 1950, *93*, 53–100.

Brown, S., & Schäfer, E. A. An investigation into the functions of the occipital and temporal lobe of the monkey's brain. *Philosophical Transactions of the Royal Society of London, Series B*, 1888, *179*, 303–327.

Brown, T. S., Rosvold, H. E., & Mishkin, M. Olfactory discrimination after temporal lobe lesions in monkeys. *Journal of Comparative and Physiological Psychology*, 1963, *56*, 190–195.

Brutowski, S. Prefrontal cortex and drive disinhibition. In J. M. Warren & K. Akert (Eds.), *The frontal granular cortex and behaviour* (pp. 242–269). New York: McGraw-Hill, 1964.

Brutowski, S., & Dabrowska, J. Disinhibition after prefrontal lesions as a function of duration of intertrial intervals. *Science*, 1963, *139*, 505–506.

Brutowski, S., Mishkin, M., & Rosvold, H. E. Positive and inhibitory motor conditioned reflexes in monkeys after ablation of orbital or dorso-lateral surface of the frontal cortex. In G. P. Honik (Ed.) *Central and peripheral mechanisms of motor functions* (pp. 133–141). Prague: Czechoslovak Academy of Sciences, 1963.

Buffery, A. W. H. *The effects of frontal and temporal lobe lesions upon the behaviour of baboons.* Ph.D. thesis, University of Cambridge, 1964.

Butter, C. M. The effect of discrimination training on pattern equivalence in monkeys with inferotemporal and lateral striate lesions. *Neuropsychologia*, 1968, *6*, 27–40.

Butter, C. M., Mishkin, M., & Rosvold, H. E. Conditioning and extinction of a food rewarded response after selective ablations of frontal cortex in rhesus monkeys. *Experimental Neurology*, 1963, *7*, 65–67.

Butter, C. M., Mishkin, M., & Rosvold, H. E. Stimulus generalization in monkeys with inferotemporal and lateral occipital lesions. In D. J. Mostofsky (Ed.), *Stimulus generalization* (pp. 119–133). Stanford, CA: Stanford University Press, 1965.

Chorover, S. L., & Cole, M. Delayed alternation performance in patients with cerebral lesions. *Neuropsychologia*, 1966, *4*, 1–7.

Chow, K. L. Effects of partial extirpations of the posterior association cortex in visually mediated behaviour in monkeys. *Comparative Psychological Monograph*, 1951, *20*, 187–217.

Chow, K. L. Visual discrimination following temporal ablations. *Journal of Comparative and Physiological Psychology*, 1952, *45*, 430–437.

Chow, K. L. Temporal ablation and visual discrimination. *Journal of Comparative and Physiological Psychology*, 1954, *47*, 194–198.

Chow, K. L. Effect of local electrographic after discharge on visual learning and retention in monkey. *Journal of Neurophysiology*, 1961, *24*, 391–400.

Chow, K. L., Blum, J. S., & Blum, R. A. Effects of combined destruction of frontal and posterior "associative areas" in monkeys. *Journal of Neurophysiology*, 1951, *14*, 59–71.

Cordeau, J. P., & Mahut, H. Some long term effects of temporal lobe resections on auditory and visual discriminations in monkeys. *Brain*, 1964, *87*, 177–190.

Corkin, S. Tactually-guided maze learning in man; effects of unilateral cortical excisions and bilateral hippocampal lesions. *Neuropsychologia*, 1965, *3*, 339–352.

Correll, R. E., & Scoville, W. B. Significance of delay in performance of monkeys with medial temporal lobe resections. *Experimental Brain Research*, 1967, *4*, 85–96.

Cowey, A. A perimetric study of visual field defects in monkeys. *Quarterly Journal of Experimental Psychology*, 1963, *15*, 91–115.

Cowey, A. Cortical maps and visual perception. *Quarterly Journal of Experimental Psychology*, 1979, *31*, 1–17.

Cowey, A., & Gross, C. G. The effects of foveal prestriate and inferotemporal lesions on visual discrimination by rhesus monkeys. *Experimental Brain Research*, 1970, *11*, 128–144.

Cowey, A., & Porter, J. Branch damage and global stereopsis. *Proceedings of the Royal Society of London, Series B*, 1979, *204*, 399–407.

Dean, P. Effects of inferotemporal lesions on the behaviour of monkeys. *Psychological Bulletin,* 1976, *83,* 41–71.

Douglas, R. J. The hippocampus and behaviour. *Psychological Bulletin,* 1967, *67,* 416–442.

Ettlinger, G., Iwai, E., Mishkin, M., & Rosvold, H. E. Visual discrimination in the monkey following serial ablation of infero-temporal and preoccipital cortex. *Journal of Comparative and Physiological Psychology,* 1968, *65,* 110–117.

Faust, C. Different psychological consequences due to superior frontal and orbito-basal lesions. *International Journal of Neurology,* 1966, *5,* 418–421.

Flynn, J. P., & Wasman, M. Learning and cortically evoked movement during propagated hippo-campal after discharge. *Science,* 1960, *131,* 1607–1608.

Gaffan, D. Recognition impaired and association intact in the memory of monkeys after transection of the fornix. *Journal of Comparative and Physiological Psychology,* 1974, *86,* 1100–1109.

Gaffan, D. Recognition memory in animals. In J. Brown (Ed.), *Recall and recognition* (pp. 229–242). New York: Wiley, 1976.

Ghent, L., Mishkin, M., & Teuber, H. L. Short term memory after frontal lobe injury in man. *Journal of Comparative and Physiological Psychology,* 1962, *55,* 705–709.

Goldman, P. S., & Rosvold, H. E. Localization of function within the dorsolateral prefrontal cortex of the rhesus monkey. *Experimental Neurology,* 1970, *27,* 291–304.

Gollin, E. S. Developmental studies of visual recognition of incomplete objects. *Perceptual and Motor Skills,* 1960, *11,* 289.

Gross, C. G., & Mishkin, M. The neural basis of stimulus equivalence across retinal translation. In S. Harnard, L. Goldstien, R. W. Doty, J. Jaynes, & G. Krauthamer (Eds.), *Lateralization in the nervous system* (pp. 109–122). New York: Academic Press, 1977.

Gross, C. G., Rocha-Miranda, C. E., & Bender, D. B. Visual properties of neurons in inferotem-poral cortex of the macaques. *Journal of Neurophysiology,* 1972, *35,* 96–111.

Gross, C. G., & Weiskrantz, L. Evidence for dissociation between impairment on auditory discrimi-nation and delayed response in frontal monkeys. *Experimental Neurology,* 1962, *5,* 453–476.

Gross, C. G., & Weiskrantz, L. Some changes in behaviour produced by lateral frontal lesions in the Macaque. In J. M. Warren & K. Akert (Eds.), *The frontal granular cortex and behaviour* (pp. 74–98). New York: McGraw-Hill, 1964.

Hara, K. Visual defects resulting from prestriate cortical lesions in cats. *Journal of Comparative and Physiological Psychology,* 1962, *55,* 293–298.

Harlow, H. F. Studies in discrimination learning by monkeys. II. Discrimination learning without primary reinforcement. *Journal of General Psychology,* 1944, *30,* 13–21.

Harlow, H. F., & Dagnon, J. Problem solution by monkeys following bilateral removal of the prefrontal areas. 1. The discrimination and discrimination reversal problems. *Journal of Experi-mental Psychology,* 1942, *32,* 351–356.

Harlow, H. F., & Spaet, T. Problem solution by monkeys following bilateral removal of the prefrontal areas. IV. Responses to stimuli having multiple sign values. *Journal of Experimental Psychology,* 1943, *33,* 500–507.

Hill, A. J. First occurrence of hippocampal spatial firing in a new environment. *Experimental Neurology,* 1978, *62,* 282–297.

Horel, J. S. The neuroanatomy of amnesia. *Brain,* 1978, *101,* 403–445.

Isaacson, R. L., & Wickelgren, W. O. Hippocampal ablation and passive avoidance. *Science,* 1962, *138,* 1104–1106.

Iversen, S. D. Tactile learning and memory in baboons after temporal and frontal lesions. *Experi-mental Neurology,* 1967, *18,* 228–238.

Iversen, S. D. Interference and inferotemporal memory deficits. *Brain Research,* 1970, *19,* 277–289.

Iversen, S. D. Do hippocampal lesions produce amnesia in animals? *International Review of Neu-robiology,* 1976, *19,* 1–49.

194	Susan D. Iversen

Iversen, S. D. Temporal lobe amnesia. In C. W. M. Whitty & O. L. Zangwill (Eds.), *Amnesia* (pp. 136–182). London: Butterworth, 1977.

Iversen, S. D., & Mishkin, M. Perseverative interference in monkeys following selective lesions of the inferior prefrontal convexity. *Experimental Brain Research,* 1970, *11,* 376–386.

Iversen, S. D., & Weiskrantz, L. Perception of redundant cues by monkeys with inferotemporal lesions. *Nature (London),* 1967, *214,* 241–243.

Iversen, S. D., & Weiskrantz, L. An investigation of a possible memory defect produced by inferotemporal lesions in the Baboon. *Neuropsychologia,* 1970, *8,* 21–36.

Iwai, E., & Mishkin, M. *Two inferotemporal foci for visual functions.* Paper read at the Annual Meeting of the American Psychology Association, Washington, D.C. 1967.

Iwai, E., & Mishkin, M. Further evidence on the locus of the visual area in the temporal lobe of the monkey. *Experimental Neurology,* 1969, *25,* 585–594.

Jacobsen, C. F. I. The functions of the frontal association area in monkeys. *Comparative Psychological Monograph,* 1936, *13,* 1–60.

Jones, B., & Mishkin, M. Limbic lesions and the problem of stimulus reinforcement associations. *Experimental Neurology,* 1972, *36,* 362–377.

Julesz, B. *Foundations of cyclopean perception.* Chicago: Chicago University Press, 1971.

Kennard, M. A. Alteration in response to visual stimuli following lesions in the frontal lobe of monkeys. *Archives of Neurology and Psychiatry,* 1939, *41,* 1153–1165.

Kimble, D. P. The hippocampus and internal inhibition. *Psychological Bulletin,* 1968, *70,* 285–295.

Kimura, D. Right temporal lobe damage. *Archives of Neurology (Chicago),* 1963, *8,* 264–271.

Kluver, H., & Bucy, P. C. Preliminary analysis of functions of the temporal lobes in monkeys. *Archives of Neurology and Psychiatry,* 1939, *42,* 979–1000.

Konorski, J., & Lawicka, W. Analysis of errors by prefrontal animals on the delayed response test. In J. M. Warren & K. Akert (Eds.), *The frontal granular cortex and behaviour* (pp. 271–286). New York: McGraw Hill, 1964.

Kuypers, G. J. M., & Lawrence, D. G. Cortical projections to the red nucleus and the brain stem in the rhesus monkey. *Brain Research,* 1967, *4,* 151–188.

Kuypers, G. J. M., Szwarcbart, M. K., Mishkin, M., & Rosvold, H. E. Occipitotemporal cortico-cortical connections in the rhesus monkey. *Experimental Neurology,* 1965, *11,* 245–262.

Lashley, K. S. In search of the Engram. *Symposia of the Society for Experimental Biology,* 1950, *4,* 454–482.

Latto, R. Visual field defects after frontal eye-field lesions in monkeys. *Brain Research,* 1971, *30,* 1–24.

Latto, R. Visual perception and oculomotor areas in the primate brain. In D. J. Ingle, R. J. W. Mansfield, & M. A. Goodale (Eds.), *Advances in the analysis of visual behaviour* (pp. 671–691). Cambridge, MA: MIT Press, 1981.

Lawicka, W., Mishkin, M., & Rosvold, H. E. Dissociation of impairment on auditory tasks following orbital and dorsolateral frontal lesions in monkeys. *Congress of Polish Physiological Society Lectures, Symposia Abstracts of Free Communications,* 1966, p. 178.

Le Gros Clark, W. E. The visual centres of the brain and their connexions. *Physiological Review,* 1942, *22,* 205–232.

Mahut, H. Spatial and object reversal learning in monkeys with partial temporal lobe ablations. *Neuropsychologia,* 1971, *9,* 409–424.

Mahut, H., & Cordeau, J. P. Spatial reversal deficit in monkeys with amygdalohippocampal ablations. *Experimental Neurology,* 1963, *2,* 426–434.

Mahut, H., Moss, M., & Zola-Morgan, S. Retention deficits after combined amygdala-hippocampal and selective hippocampal resections in the monkey. *Neuropsychologia,* 1981, *19,* 201–225.

Mair, W. G. P., Warrington, E. K., & Weiskrantz, L. Memory disorder in Korsakoff's psychosis; a neuropathological and neuropsychological investigation of two cases. *Brain,* 1979, *102,* 749–783.

Menzel, E. N. Chimpanzee spatial memory organization. *Science,* 1973, *182,* 943–945.

Mettler, F. A. Corticofugal fiber connections of the cortex of Macaca mulatta. The occipital region. *Journal of Comparative Neurology,* 1935, *61,* 221–256.

Milner, B. Laterality effects in audition. In V. B. Mountcastle (Ed.), *Interhemispheric relations and cerebral dominance* (pp. 177–195). Baltimore: Johns Hopkins Press, 1962.

Milner, B. Effects of different brain lesions on card sorting *Archives of Neurology (Chicago),* 1963, *9,* 90–100.

Milner, B. Some effects of frontal lobectomy in man. In J. M. Warren & K. Akert (Eds.), *The frontal granular cortex and behaviour* (pp. 313–331). New York: McGraw Hill, 1964.

Milner, B. Visually guided maze learning in man: Effects of bilateral hippocampal, bilateral frontal and unilateral cerebral lesions. *Neuropsychologia,* 1965, *3,* 317–338.

Milner, B. Interhemispheric differences and psychological processes. *British Medical Bulletin,* 1971, *27,* 272–277.

Milner, B. (1982) Some cognitive effects of frontal-lobe lesions in Man. *Philos. Trans. Roy. Soc. London.* 298, 211–226.

Milner, B., & Teuber, H. L. Alterations of perception and memory in Man: Reflections on method. In L. Weiskrantz (Ed.), *Analysis of Behavioural Change* (pp. 236–375). New York: Harper and Row, 1968.

Milner, B., Corkin, S., & Teuber, H. L. Further analysis of the hippocampal amnesic syndrome: 14 year follow-up study of H.M. *Neuropsychologia,* 1968, *6,* 215–234.

Mishkin, M. Visual discrimination performance following partial ablations of the temporal lobe. II. Ventral surfaces vs. hippocampus. *Journal of Comparative and Physiological Psychology,* 1954, *47,* 187–193.

Mishkin, M. Perseveration of central sets after frontal lesions in monkeys. In J. M. Warren & K. Akert (Eds.), *The frontal granular cortex and behaviour* (pp. 219–237). New York: McGraw Hill, 1964.

Mishkin, M. Vision beyond the striate cortex. In R. W. Russell (Ed.), *Frontiers in physiological psychology* (pp. 93–119). New York: Academic Press, 1966.

Mishkin, M. Memory in monkeys severely impaired by combined but not in separate removal of amygdala and hippocampus. *Nature (London),* 1978, *273,* 297–298.

Mishkin, M. Analogous neural models for tactual and visual learning. *Neurophysiologia,* 1979, *17,* 139–151.

Mishkin, M., & Delacour, J. An analysis of short-term visual memory in the monkey. *Journal of Experimental Psychology, Animal Behavior Processes,* 1975, *1,* 326–334.

Mishkin, M., & Hall, M. Discrimination along a size continuum following ablation of the inferior temporal convexity in monkeys. *Journal of Comparative and Physiological Psychology,* 1955, *48,* 97–101.

Mishkin, M., & Pribram, K. H. Visual discrimination performance following partial ablation of the temporal lobe. I. Ventral vs. lateral. *Journal of Comparative and Physiological Psychology,* 1954, *47,* 14–20.

Mishkin, M., Prockop, E. S., & Rosvold, H. E. One trial object discrimination learning in monkeys with frontal lesions. *Journal of Comparative and Physiological Psychology,* 1962, *55,* 178–181.

Nadel, L., & O'Keefe, L. The hippocampus in pieces and patches: An essay on modes of explanation in physiological psychology. In R. Bellairs & E. G. Gray (Eds.), *Essays on the nervous system. A festschrift for Professor J. Z. Young* (pp. 367–390). London & New York: Oxford University Press (Clarendon), 1974.

Nauta, W. J. H. Some efferent connections of the prefrontal cortex in the monkey. In J. M. Warren & K. Akert (Eds.), *The frontal granular cortex* (pp. 397–407). New York: McGraw-Hill, 1964.

Nauta, W. J. H. The problem of the frontal lobe: A reinterpretation. *Journal of Psychiatric Research,* 1971, *8,* 167–187.

Nauta, J. W. H. Limbic innervation of the striatum. In Arnold J. Friedhoff and Thomas N. Chase (Eds.), *Gilles de la Tourette Syndrome* (pp. 41–47). New York: Raven Press, 1982.

Neff, W. D. Neural mechanisms of auditory discrimination. In W. A. Rosenblith (Ed.), *Sensory communication* (pp. 259–278). Cambridge, MA: MIT Press, 1961.

Newell, A., Shaw, J. C., & Simon, H. A. Elements of a theory of human problem solving. *Psychological Review*, 1958, *65*, 151–166.

Norman, D. A., & Shallice, T. (1980). Attention to action: Willed and automatic control of behaviour. Center for Human control of behaviour. Center for Human Information Processing Technical Report no. 90.

O'Keefe, J. Place units in the hippocampus of the freely moving rat. *Experimental Neurology*, 1976, *51*, 78–109.

O'Keefe, J. A review of the hippocampal place cells. *Progress in Neurobiology*, 1979, *13*, 419–439.

O'Keefe, J., & Conway, D. H. Hippocampal place units in the freely moving rats: Why they fire where they fire. *Experimental Brain Research*, 1978, *31*, 573–590.

O'Keefe, J., & Dostrovsky, J. The hippocampus as a spatial map. *Brain Research*, 1971, *34*, 171–175.

O'Keefe, J., Nadel, L., Keightly, S., & Kill, D. Fornix lesions selectively abolish place learning in the rat. *Experimental Neurology*, 1975, *48*, 152–166.

Olton, D. S., Branch, M., & Best, P. J. Spatial correlates hippocampal unit activity. *Experimental Neurology*, 1978, *58*, 387–409.

Olton, D. S., Collison, C., & Werz, M. A. Spatial memory and radial arm maze performance in rats. *Learning and Motivation*, 1977, *8*, 289–314.

Olton, D. S., Becker, J. T., & Handelmann, G. E. Hippocampus, spaces, and memory. *Behavioral and Brain Sciences*, 1979, *2*, 313–365.

Olton, D. S., & Feustle, W. A. Hippocampal function required for nonspatial working memory. *Experimental Brain Research*, 1981, *41*, 380–389.

Olton, D. S., & Papas, B. C. Spatial memory and hippocampal function. *Neuropsychologia*, 1979, *17*, 669–682.

Olton, D. S., Walker, J. A., & Gage, F. H. Hippocampal connections and spatial discrimination. *Brain Research*, 1978, *139*, 295–308.

Orbach, J., & Fantz, R. L. Differential effects of temporal neo-cortical resections on overtrained and nonovertrained visual habits in monkeys. *Journal of Comparative and Physiological Psychology*, 1958, *51*, 126–129.

Orbach, J., Milner, B., & Rasmussen, T. Learning and retention in monkeys after amygdala-hippocampus resection. *Archives of Neurology (Chicago)*, 1960, *3*, 230–251.

Papez, J. W. A proposed mechanism of emotions. *Archives of Neurology and Psychiatry*, 1937, *38*, 725–743.

Passingham, R. E., & Ettlinger, G. A comparison of cortical functions in man and other primates. *International Review of Neurobiology*, 1974, *16*, 233–299.

Penfield, W. Speech, perception and the uncommitted cortex. *Pontificiae Academiae Scientarum Scripta Varia*, 1965, *30*, 319–347.

Penfield, W., & Milner, B. Memory deficit produced by bilateral lesions in the hippocampal zone. *AMA Archives of Neurology and Psychiatry*, 1958, *79*, 475–497.

Penfield, W., & Perot, P. The brain's record of auditory and visual experience—A final summary and discussion. *Brain*, 1963, *86*, 595–696.

Petr, R., Holden, L. B., & Jirout, J. The efferent intercortical connections of the superficial cortex of the temporal lobe. (*Macaca mulatta*). *Journal of Neuropathology and Experimental Neurology*, 1949, *8*, 100–103.

Pohl, W. Dissociation of spatial discrimination deficits following frontal and parietal lesions in monkeys. *Journal of Comparative and Physiological Psychology*, 1973, *82*, 227–289.

Pribram, K. H., & Tubbs, W. E. Short-term memory, parsing, and the primate frontal cortex. *Science*, 1967, *156*, 1765–1767.

Prisko, L. H. *Short-term memory in focal cerebral damage.* Unpublished doctoral thesis, McGill University, 1963.

Ranck, J. B. Studies on single neurons in dorsal hippocampal formation and septum in unrestrained rats. *Experimental Neurology*, 1973, *41*, 461–555.

Ranck, J. B. Behavioural correlates and firing repertoires of neurons in the dorsal hippocampal formation and septum of unrestrained rats. In R. L. Isaacson & K. H. Pribram (Eds.), *The hippocampus* (Vol. 1, pp. 207–246). New York: Plenum Press, 1975.

Robinson, D. A., & Fuchs, A. F. Eye movements evoked by stimulation of frontal eye fields. *Journal of Neurophysiology*, 1969, *32*, 637–648.

Rosene, D. L., & Van Hoesen, G. W. Hippocampal efferents reach areas of cerebral cortex and amygdala in the rhesus monkey. *Science*, 1977, *198*, 315–317.

Rosvold, H. E., & Mishkin, M. Non sensory effects of frontal lesions on discrimination learning and performance. In D. Delfraysne (Ed.), *Brain mechanisms and learning* (pp. 555–567). Oxford: Blackwell, 1961.

Rosvold, H. E., Mishkin, M., & Szwarcbart, M. K. Effects of subcortical lesions in monkeys on visual discrimination and single alternation performance. *Journal of Comparative and Physiological Psychology*, 1958, *51*, 437–444.

Sahgal, A., & Iversen, S. D. Categorization and retrieval after selective inferotemporal lesions in monkeys. *Brain Research*, 1978, *146*, 341–350. (a)

Sahgal, A., & Iversen, S. D. The effects of foveal prestriate and inferotemporal lesions on matching to sample behaviour in monkeys. *Neuropsychologia*, 1978, *16*, 391–406. (b)

Sanders, H. I., & Warrington, E. K. Memory for remote events in amnesic patients. *Brain*, 1971, *94*, 661–668.

Scoville, W. B., & Milner, B. Loss of recent memory after bilateral hippocampal lesions. *Journal of Neurology, Neurosurgery and Psychiatry*, 1957, *20*, 11–21.

Settlage, P., Zable, N., & Harlow, H. F. Problem solution by monkeys following bilateral removal of the prefrontal areas. VI. Performance on tests requiring contradictory reactions to similar and to identical stimuli. *Journal of Experimental Psychology*, 1948, *38*, 50–65.

Shallice, T. Specific impairments of planning. *Philosophical Transactions of the Royal Society of London*, 1982, *298*, 199–209.

Sidman, H., Stoddard, L. T., & Mohr, J. P. Some additional quantitative observations of immediate memory in a patient with bilateral hippocampal lesions. *Neuropsychologia*, 1968, *6*, 245–254.

Sprague, J. M. Visual, acoustic and somaesthetic deficits in the cat after cortical and midbrain lesions. In D. P. Purpura & M. Yahr (Eds.), *The thalamus* (pp. 391–414). New York: Columbia University Press, 1966.

Sprague, J. M., & Meikle, T. H. The role of the superior colliculus in visually guided behaviour. *Experimental Neurology*, 1965, *11*, 115–146.

Squire, L. R. Two forms of human amnesia: Analysis of forgetting. *Journal of Neuroscience*, 1981, *1*, 635–640.

Stamm, J. S., & Knight, M. Learning of visual tasks by monkeys with epileptogenic implants in temporal cortex. *Journal of Comparative and Physiological Psychology*, 1963, *56*, 254–260.

Sugar, O., French, J. D., & Chusid, J. G. Corticocortical connections of the superior surface of the temporal operculum in the monkey (*Macaca mulatta*). *Journal of Neurophysiology*, 1948, *11*, 175–185.

Teuber, H. L. The Riddle of the frontal lobe in man. In J. M. Warren & K. Akert (Eds.), *The frontal granular cortex and behaviour* (pp. 410–441). New York: McGraw-Hill, 1964.

Thompson, R., Lesse, H., & Rich, I. Pretectal lesions in rats and cats. *Journal of Comparative Neurology*, 1963, *121*, 161–171.

Tolman, E. C. *Purposive behaviour in animals and man.* New York: Appleton-Century-Crofts, 1932.

Tulving, E. Episodic and semantic memory. In E. Tulving & W. D. Donaldson (Eds.), *Organization of memory* (pp. 381–403). New York: Academic Press, 1972.

Turner, B. H., Mishkin, M., & Knapp, M. Organization of the amygdalopetal projections from modality-specific cortical association areas in the monkey. (1980) *Journal of Comparative Neurology, 141,* 515–543.

Van Hoesen, G. W., Pandya, D. N., & Butters, N. Cortical afferents to the entorhinal cortex of the rhesus monkey. *Science,* 1972, *175,* 1471–1473.

Van Hoesen, G. W., Rosene, D. L., & Mesulam, M. M. Subicular input from temporal cortex in the rhesus monkey. *Science,* 1979, *205,* 608–610.

Vinogradova, O. S. Registration of information and the limbic system. In G. Horn & R. A. Hinde (Eds.), *Short and long term changes in neural activity and behaviour* (pp. 95–140). London & New York: Cambridge University Press, 1970.

Von Bonin, G. On encephalometry. *Journal of Comparative Neurology,* 1941, *75,* 287–314.

Von Bonin, G., Garol, H. W., & McCulloch, W. S. The functional organization of the occipital lobe. *Biological Symposia,* 1942, *7,* 165.

Warren, J. M., Warren, H. B., & Akert, K. Learning by cats with lesions in the prestriate cortex. *Journal of Comparative and Physiological Psychology,* 1961, *54,* 629–632.

Warrington, E. K. Deficient recognition memory in organic amnesia. *Cortex,* 1974, *10,* 289–291.

Warrington, E. K. Recognition and recall in amnesia. In J. Brown (Ed.), *Recall and recognition* (pp. 217–228). New York: Wiley, 1976.

Warrington, E. K., & Silberstein, M. A questionnaire technique for investigating very long term memory. *Quarterly Journal of Experimental Psychology,* 1970, *22,* 508–512.

Warrington, E. K., & Weiskrantz, L. New method of testing long-term retention with special reference to amnesic patients. *Nature (London),* 1968, *217,* 972–974.

Warrington, E. K., & Weiskrantz, L. Amnesic syndrome. Consolidation or retrieval. *Nature (London),* 1970, *228,* 628–630.

Warrington, E. K., & Weiskrantz, L. The effect of prior learning on subsequent retention in amnesic patients. *Neuropsychologia,* 1974, *12,* 419–428.

Warrington, E. K., & Weiskrantz, L. Further analysis of the prior learning effect in amnesic patients. *Neuropsychologia,* 1978, *16,* 169–177.

Weiskrantz, L., & Mishkin, M. Effects of temporal and frontal cortical lesions on auditory discrimination of monkey. *Brain,* 1958, *81,* 406–414.

Wilson, M. Effects of circumscribed cortical lesions upon somaesthetic and visual discrimination in the monkey. *Journal of Comparative and Physiological Psychology,* 1957, *50,* 630–635.

Wilson, M., & Mishkin, M. Comparison of the effects of inferotemporal and lateral occipital lesions on visually guided behaviour in monkeys. *Journal of Comparative and Physiological Psychology,* 1959, *52,* 10–17.

Winson, J. Loss of hippocampal theta rhythm results in spatial memory deficit in the rat. *Science,* 1978, *201,* 160–163.

Yntema, D. B., & Trask, F. P. Recall as a search process. *Journal of Verbal Learning and Verbal Behavior,* 1963, *2,* 65–74.

Zeki, S. M. The mosaic organisation of the visual cortex in the monkey. In R. Bellairs & E. G. Gray, (Eds.), *Essays on the nervous system* (pp. 327–343). London & New York: Oxford University Press (Clarendon), 1974.

CHAPTER

6

THE NEUROLOGY OF MEMORY: THE CASE FOR CORRESPONDENCE BETWEEN THE FINDINGS FOR HUMAN AND NONHUMAN PRIMATE[1]

LARRY R. SQUIRE AND STUART ZOLA-MORGAN

Veterans Administration Medical Center, San Diego, California and Department of Psychiatry, University of California, School of Medicine, La Jolla, California

"By next Friday evening they will all be convinced that they are monkeys."

THOMAS H. HUXLEY, 1861

[1]This work was supported by the Medical Research Service of the Veterans Administration and by NIMH Grant MH 24600.

I. INTRODUCTION

For nearly 100 years it has been recognized that damage in particular regions of the human brain can result in an amnesic syndrome, and that this syndrome can sometimes appear as a relatively circumscribed deficit (Bechterew, 1900; Korsakoff, 1887). The fact that a memory deficit can appear following localized brain lesions has taught us that the capacity for learning and remembering is to some extent a specialized function that depends crucially on the integrity of specific brain regions. It is this idea about memory that has encouraged its study as a separate entity.

If interest in the cerebral organization of memory is as keen today as ever, it is because the interdisciplinary efforts of neuroscience have connected questions about memory to the larger theme of neural plasticity. It is now possible to study nervous systems at the level of single cells and single synapses, and it has become reasonable to look to such diverse phenomena as visual deprivation, synaptic depression and facilitation, and denervation hypersensitivity for clues to the cellular mechanisms underlying learning and memory (Lund, 1978; McGaugh, Lynch, & Weinberger, 1983; Rozensweig & Bennett, 1976). In the case of certain favorable invertebrate species, it has been possible to work out the wiring diagram of simple forms of behavioral plasticity and to identify where the plasticity occurs (Hawkins, Abrams, Carew, & Kandel, 1983; Kandel, 1976; Kandel & Schwartz, 1982). In the rat, it is now possible to dissect out a thin slice of the hippocampal formation, that cerebral structure which the neuropsychological study of humans has most often linked to memory functions, and to study its capacity for plasticity in neurophysiological terms at the level of specific pathways and cell layers (Lynch & Schubert, 1980).

These developments in neuroscience bring to the subject of memory an awareness of how memory can be studied at different levels of analysis. Thus, careful neuropsychological study of cases of human memory dysfunction continues to inform us about memory at the global-structural level (for reviews, see Baddeley, 1982; Cermak, 1982; Hirst, 1982; Squire, 1982; Squire & Cohen, 1983; Stern, 1981; Weiskrantz, 1982), whereas experimental animals and specially devised preparations must be used to address questions about the synaptic changes that underlie memory. In many domains of biological science, animal models of clinical entities have proven useful. Animal models establish the necessary and sufficient conditions under which the clinical syndrome occurs and set the stage for more detailed biological study. For this reason an animal model of the human amnesic syndrome would appear to be a relevant if not vital step in developing a biology of memory.

The purpose of this chapter is to review attempts to develop a model of human global amnesia in the nonhuman primate, specifically in the rhesus and cynomolgus monkeys (*Macaca mulatta* and *M. fasicularis*). This effort has focused on two questions: (1) What are the specific brain structures in the monkey that when damaged produce amnesia? (2) What are the appropriate behavioral tasks for demonstrating amnesia in the monkey? Here we consider these two questions, suggest some reasons why efforts to produce the human amnesic syndrome in monkey has had a mixed success, and show how the human and monkey findings can now be brought into correspondence. To begin, we turn to the human cases upon which the work with monkeys is founded and review certain aspects of the amnesic syndrome in man that will become important as the findings with monkeys unfold. Accordingly, we (1) introduce the human amnesic syndrome; (2) identify two forms of amnesia: diencephalic and bitemporal; (3) consider the nature of the impairment in amnesia; and (4) review cliniconeuropathological information about which brain regions are affected.

II. DESCRIPTION AND ETIOLOGY OF AMNESIA

An amnesic syndrome can occur after temporal-lobe surgery, encephalitis, ischemic episodes involving the posterior circulation, traumatic head injury, electroconvulsive therapy (ECT), chronic alcohol abuse, tumors, and certain toxemias. Most of our systematic information about amnesia, however, comes from three sources: the Korsakoff syndrome, ECT, and well-studied single cases such as the noted patient H.M.

A. Korsakoff Syndrome

The best studied of the amnesias is the alcoholic Korsakoff syndrome, and a number of reviews are available concerning its neuropathological and neuropsychological aspects (Butters & Cermak, 1980; Talland, 1965; Victor, Adams, & Collins, 1971). The disease presents acutely as the Wernicke–Korsakoff syndrome. The Korsakoff syndrome refers to the chronic stage of the disease when the signs of Wernicke's encephalopathy have largely resolved and amnesia is the predominant remaining symptom. Extensive documentation of the neuropathology of the Wernicke–Korsakoff syndrome has indicated that the syndrome is associated with symmetrical brain lesions along the third and fourth ventricles, cortical atrophy, and cerebellar damage, together with less regular damage to the limbic system and lower brainstem. The mammillary bodies and dorsal medial nucleus of the thalamus are the most affected structures (Table 6.1), and these structures have been most often associated with findings of impaired memory (Brierley, 1977; Victor et al., 1971).

In the Korsakoff syndrome, patients are amnesic and sometimes confabulatory, but can perform normally on tests of general intelligence (Talland, 1965). Performance is also impaired on a number of cognitive tests (Oscar-Berman,

TABLE 6.1

Incidence of Involvement of Various Brain Regions in the Wernicke–Korsakoff Syndrome[a]

Region	No. of cases examined	No. of cases involved	Percentage involved
Hypothalamic nuclei			
Medial mammillary	47	47	100.0
Dorsal area	32	23	71.9
Thalamic nuclei			
Medial dorsal	43	38	88.4
Medial pulvinar	20	17	85.0
Lateral dorsal	25	17	68.0
Submedius/medial ventral	26	15	57.7
Parafascicular	34	17	50.0
Regions other than diencephalon or brainstem			
Cerebral cortex	51	29	56.9
Cerebellum	27	15	55.5
Hippocampus	22	5	36.4
Fornix	22	5	22.7

[a]From Victor, Adams, & Collins, (1971).

1980). The following observations of patient A.F. may be instructive (Zola-Morgan & Oberg, 1980). When A.F. was taken on a trip to the North Station in Boston, where he had been employed as a younger man, he expressed surprise and distress at the changes that had taken place there. About 6 months later he was taken there a second time. "At the station A.F. gave no sign of remembering our previous visit: he again showed extreme astonishment and disappointment at how different things were. He repeatedly assured us that he had not been in the area for years [Zola-Morgan & Oberg, 1980, p. 551]." During an interview 9 months later he recalled spontaneously some aspects of a visit to North Station, but always insisted that there had been only one such visit. After 9 additional months, at 2 years after the first trip, he was asked if "we ever went to Boston together," and he replied "I'm quite sure we never did." When asked about North Station, A.F. replied, "That's what has me confused, Doc. I would almost say that I'd been there. If I hadn't seen it how would I know it [was changed]. So as a matter of deduction I would say 'yes'. . . . I must have been there . . . and I think I was disappointed." When asked about how long ago the trip was, he said "Yesterday, or the day before; less than three days ago [Zola-Morgan & Oberg, 1980, p. 553]."

B. Electroconvulsive Therapy

Bilateral electroconvulsive therapy (ECT) is sometimes prescribed for the treatment of depressive illness, and amnesia is its major side effect (Squire, 1982c). The amnesia associated with ECT recovers to some extent after each treatment in a series and cumulates across treatments (Figure 6.1). Following a period of some 30–45 minutes, amnesia appears as a relatively circumscribed deficit in the absence of global confusion or change in general intellectual status. An advantage of ECT for the study of neuropsychological aspects of memory is that it permits before and after studies, whereby patients can be used as their own control subjects.

C. The Individual Case

Surely the best known of all the cases of human amnesia is patient H.M. (Scoville & Milner, 1957). In 1953 this individual sustained a bilateral resection of the medial temporal lobe in an attempt to relieve otherwise intractable epilepsy. The resection was accomplished in a single operative procedure and included the anterior two-thirds of the hippocampus, the parahippocampal gyrus, uncus, and amygdala (Figure 6.2). Following surgery, H.M. exhibited a marked inability to retain day-to-day events which has continued to the present time. Extensive formal testing has confirmed that H.M. has severely limited ability to acquire new verbal or nonverbal information, regardless of which sensory modality is used for acquisition (Milner, 1972). His memory for events that

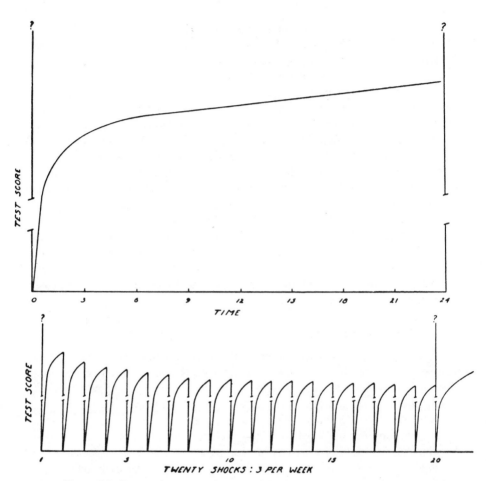

Figure 6.1. Course of recovery of memory functions during the hours following a single treatment with ECT, and between successive treatments, as hypothesized by Stone (1947). This view is now well supported by data (cf. Squire, 1982c).

occurred prior to his surgery (e.g., the 1930s and 1940s) is quite good (Marslen-Wilson & Teuber, 1975), though informal interviews have suggested that he may have a retrograde amnesia for events that occurred 1 to 3 years prior to surgery. He has considerable awareness of his memory defect. "Every day is alone in itself. . . . You see at this moment everything looks clear to me, but what happened just before? That's what worries me. . . . It's like waking from a dream. I just don't remember [Milner, 1970, p. 37]."

A second, well-studied patient is case N.A. (Teuber, Milner, & Vaughan, 1968). In 1960, at the age of 22, this individual sustained a stab wound to the

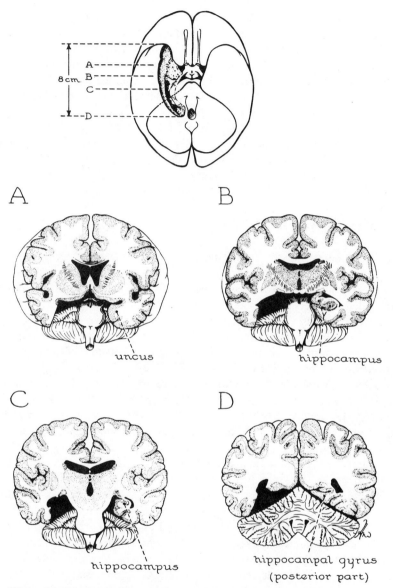

Figure 6.2. Drawings in cross section showing the estimated extent of removal in case H.M. Surgery was a bilateral, single-stage procedure but one side is shown intact here for illustrative purposes. (From Scoville & Milner, 1957.)

diencephalic region, as the result of a penetrating injury with a miniature fencing foil. Since his accident, N.A. has exhibited a marked amnesia, worse for verbal material than for nonverbal material. But N.A. recently achieved an I.Q. score of 124 and has surpassed control subjects in many perceptual and cognitive tests (Squire & Slater, 1978; Teuber *et al.*, 1968). In contrast his ability to acquire new verbal information is severely limited, and he has been unable to work since his accident. In 1978, computerized tomography (CT) scans identified a lesion in the left dorsal thalamic region (Squire & Moore, 1979).

N.A. describes his disorder as "not knowing whether I will remember something when I need to remember it." Or "The recording record doesn't let me know whether it's on the good side or the bad side. . . . sometimes I can remember and sometimes I can't [Kaushall, Zetin, & Squire, 1981, p. 385]."

III. TWO FORMS OF AMNESIA

With the variety of circumstances that can cause amnesia, one might suppose that there are many different kinds of amnesia, each impairing memory in a different way. For good reason, however, investigators and clinicians alike have tended until recently to view all amnesias as examples of the same underlying disorder. This is not to say that all amnesic disorders were thought to express themselves in behavior in exactly the same way. Patients with Korsakoff syndrome, for example, have a variety of cognitive deficits that have no obligatory relationship to amnesia (Moscovitch, 1982; Squire, 1982b). Zangwill has also expressed this view that ". . . other and more extensive psychological dysfunction must co-exist with amnesia for the classic picture of Korsakoff's syndrome to emerge [Zangwill, 1977, p. 113]." These differences in the outward appearance of the amnesias could be understood as the superimposition of various cognitive deficits upon a common "core" amnesia.

Surely one reason for supposing that all amnesias reflect the same underlying disorder is the fact that different amnesic groups do share many characteristics. Performance by different amnesic groups is often similar on standarized neuropsychological tests such as the Wechsler Adult Intelligence Scale (WAIS) or the Wechsler Memory Scale (WMS), and clinical impressions from patient interviews or mental status exams suggest a common underlying problem: difficulty in new learning (Figure 6.3), intact digit span or immediate memory, intact general intellectual capacity, and variable retrograde amnesia. A final reason for relating all the amnesias has been the possibility that they all reflect damage to brain structures that constitute an anatomical "circuit" (Papez, 1937).

Despite these reasons to group all the amnesias together, recent data provide a basis for distinguishing those amnesias associated with brain lesions of the diencephalic midline from those associated with brain lesions of the medial temporal region. This grouping was first suggested by Lhermitte & Signoret,

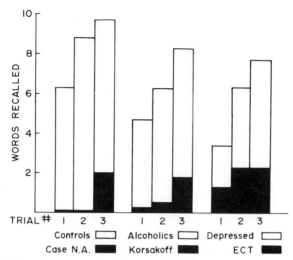

Figure 6.3. Impairment in paired-associate learning by three kinds of amnesic patients and appropriate control groups: case N.A., patients with alcoholic Korsakoff syndrome, and patients receiving bilateral ECT. Subjects were presented with ten noun–noun pairs on each of three successive trials. After each presentation they tried to recall the second word of each pair upon seeing the first word.

1972. Huppert and Piercy (1978, 1979) made the same suggestion following an analysis of forgetting in seven patients with Korsakoff syndrome, who have diencephalic lesions, and case H.M. who has bilateral damage to the medial temporal region. Through increased exposure, patients with Korsakoff syndrome were able to remember material 10 minutes after learning and then had a normal forgetting rate beyond that time. Case H.M., by contrast, seemed to exhibit rapid forgetting when tested by a similar procedure (Figure 6.4).

This analysis of forgetting has now been extended to case N.A., patients receiving ECT, and the San Diego Korsakoff population (Squire, 1981b). N.A. and patients with Korsakoff's syndrome exhibited a normal rate of forgetting across a 32-hour period, whereas patients receiving ECT exhibited rapid forgetting (Figure 6.5). Importantly, ECT and Korsakoff syndrome affected forgetting differently even when retention was identical in these two groups at 10 minutes after learning. These findings tend to distinguish N.A. and patients with Korsakoff syndrome, on the one hand, from H.M. and patients receiving ECT, on the other, a distinction based on the presumed neuropathology, diencephalic or medial temporal. Korsakoff syndrome and case N.A. are clear examples of diencephalic amnesia, whereas H.M. has bilateral damage to the medial temporal region. Although it is premature to speak of anatomy in the case of ECT, indirect evidence has also linked this amnesia to dysfunction of the medial temporal region (Inglis, 1970). Recent data suggest that this same distinction

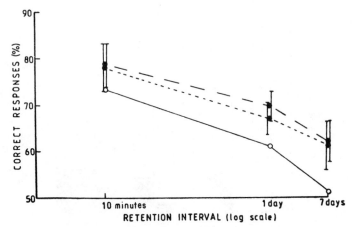

Figure 6.4. Patients with Korsakoff syndrome (●— —●) and patient H.M. (○———○) were given extra exposure to pictorial material in order to equate their recognition memory to that of control subjects at 10 minutes after learning. Patients with Korsakoff syndrome exhibited a normal rate of forgetting, whereas patient H.M. seemed to exhibit a more rapid rate of forgetting (●- - - -●, controls). (From Huppert & Piercy, 1979.)

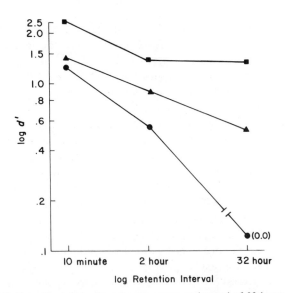

Figure 6.5. Forgetting of simple sentences across an interval of 32 hours by patient N.A. (■———■), patients with Korsakoff syndrome (▲———▲), and patients receiving bilateral ECT (●———●). All patients viewed the material for 8 seconds. N.A. and patients with Korsakoff ($N = 7$) syndrome forgot at a normal rate. Patients receiving ECT ($N = 9$) forgot more rapidly. (From Squire, 1981.)

may hold for monkeys with medial temporal lesions and monkeys with diencephalic lesions (Zola-Morgan & Squire, 1982). The neuropsychological evidence just reviewed suggests that diencephalic and medial temporal amnesia differ in some respects. The next section considers additional neuropsychological data that bear on the nature of the impairment in these amnesias.

IV. WHAT HAS HUMAN DIENCEPHALIC AND MEDIAL TEMPORAL AMNESIA TAUGHT US ABOUT THE NATURE OF THE IMPAIRMENT?

From the earliest reports of the amnesic syndrome, there has been interest in understanding which aspects of memory are affected. One approach to this problem has been to consider amnesia as a disorder at some particular stage of memory formation or information processing, and some progress has been made in understanding amnesia by experiments framed around constructs such as encoding, consolidation, and retrieval (for reviews, see Butters & Cermak, 1980; Cermak, 1982; Squire, Cohen, & Nadel, 1983). Another approach, which will be discussed in this section, has been to recognize that memory is not a monolithic entity, and to ask whether all kinds of memory are affected in amnesia, or whether some kinds are spared.

A. Preserved Learning Capacity in Human Amnesia

Amnesic patients can, under some circumstances, exhibit good learning and good retention across long intervals. The best known examples of this observation come from the learning of perceptual–motor skills. Case H.M., for example, exhibited progressive learning of mirror tracing, rotary pursuit, and bimanual tracking across several days of testing (Corkin, 1968; Milner, 1962), despite reporting on each day that he had no memory of having performed the task before. Day to day learning of the hand–eye coordination skills needed for the pursuit rotor task also occurred at a normal, or near-normal rate in patients with Korsakoff syndrome (Brooks & Baddeley, 1976; Cermak, Lewis, Butters, & Goodglass, 1973; Cohen, 1981), postencephalitic patients (Brooks & Baddeley, 1976), patients receiving bilateral ECT (Cohen, 1981), and patient N.A. (Cohen, 1981). Amnesic patients have also been reported to improve gradually their solution time for the adult version of the Porteus maze and for a 12-piece jigsaw puzzle (Brooks & Baddeley, 1976).

In the last few years, testing procedures that are less clearly perceptual motor have been identified that can also elicit signs of retention in patients who are by other indications profoundly amnesic. One example of good performance is the ability of amnesic patients to benefit from previous exposure to a group of pictures as demonstrated by their recognition of fragmented drawings of these pictures (Milner, Corkin, & Teuber, 1968; Warrington & Weiskrantz, 1968).

Another example is the ability of patients with Korsakoff syndrome to learn a rule permitting them to generate the successive integers in a Fibonacci number series (Wood, Ebert, & Kinsbourne, 1982). Still other examples based on less formal observations have also been catalogued recently (Weiskrantz, 1978).

One view of these data has been that amnesia is a retrieval deficit that can be overcome by favorable testing procedures (Weiskrantz, 1978; Weiskrantz & Warrington, 1979; see Warrington & Weiskrantz [1982] for a discussion of amnesia as a disconnection syndrome rather than a retrieval deficit). By this view, amnesic patients do not have access to their memories, in other words, they cannot reflect their memory in verbal report, but it is nevertheless possible with appropriate methods to demonstrate that learning and memory have occurred.

An alternative view has been that amnesia is essentially a disorder in the formation of memory (Milner, 1966; Squire, 1982). This view recognizes that amnesic patients may sometimes perform normally, but takes that observation to mean that some dimension of memory is organized so differently that it lies outside the limits of the amnesic syndrome. Thus, the brain regions damaged in amnesia, though necessary for many kinds of learning and memory, are not involved in certain other kinds. It has been suggested that the sparing of the perceptual–motor skills in amnesia, as described above, might be viewed in this sort of way (Corkin, 1968; Milner, 1966).

However, it is now clear that the domain of information processing that is spared in amnesia is broader than perceptual motor skills. Recent work has resulted in a formulation of spared functions which seems to encompass the available examples of good learning by amnesic patients and which also helps to understand the important observation that patients can sometimes demonstrate memory without being able to access it via verbal report. This work was guided by the demonstration that normal subjects can learn to read geometrically inverted or otherwise transformed text and can retain such pattern-analyzing skills for months (Kolers, 1976, 1979). In considering this ability, Kolers distinguished the acquisition of pattern-analyzing operations or encoding procedures (". . . that are directed at the surface lexical features of the text [Kolers, 1979, p. 374]") from specific memory for the results or outcomes of these operations (". . . the semantic or other grammatical content of text that is the subject of most contemporary studies [Kolers, 1979, p. 374]").

The usefulness of this distinction in understanding amnesia has been demonstrated by a study of mirror reading. Amnesic patients (case N.A., patients with Korsakoff syndrome, and patients receiving ECT) and control subjects were asked to read sets of words that were reversed by a mirror. The amnesic patients improved their skill at mirror reading at a normal rate over a 3-day period and then retained the skill at a normal level 3 months later. This occurred despite amnesia for aspects of the testing situation and despite profound amnesia for the specific words that had been read (Cohen & Squire, 1980) (Figure 6.6).

B. A Framework for Understanding Preserved Learning Capacity

This finding has suggested a distinction, developed in more detail elsewhere (Cohen, 1981; Squire & Cohen, 1983), between information based on procedures and information based on specific facts or data. Thus amnesic patients can learn the procedures needed for the acquisition and retention of mirror-reading skills, but cannot remember the specific data, that is, the words, that ordinarily result from applying these procedures. By this formulation, the mirror-reading skill, and other examples of preserved learning in amnesia, including the ability to learn the solution to certain puzzles (Cohen, 1981) as well as the ability to acquire perceptual-motor skills, belong to a class of memory operations that are rule based or procedure based. Procedural learning is considered by current thinking in cognitive psychology (Cohen, 1981; Rumelhart, 1981; Rumelhart & Norman, 1978) to result in the modification of tuning of existing schemata (Bartlett, 1932), where schemata are mental processes specialized for the interpretation of environmental events and for operating in the world. In contrast, information based on specific facts or data is considered to be represented as new data structures that reflect the outcomes of applying particular procedures or that reflect particular instances of their application.

This distinction is reminiscent of the classical distinction between "knowing how" and "knowing that" and seems to capture in important ways the dissociation among memory systems suggested by other earlier writers, such as Bergson (1910) (habit memory versus pure memory), Bruner (1969) (memory without record versus memory with record), and Kolers (1975) (operational memory versus semantic memory). A similar distinction has also appeared more recently in the artificial intelligence literature under discussions of "procedural" versus "declarative" knowledge (Winograd, 1975). The evidence from amnesic patients learning to mirror read suggests that such a distinction is honored by the nervous system. Thus acquisition of specific facts (e.g., the specific words that were read) is normally dependent on the diencephalic and bitemporal brain structures damaged in amnesia, whereas the acquisition of skills (e.g., the ability to mirror read) appears to be independent of these brain structures. Two other proposed dissociations among memory systems that have been related to the amnesic syndrome are the semantic–episodic distinction (Kinsbourne & Wood, 1975; Schacter & Tulving, 1982) and the working memory versus reference memory distinction (Olton, Becker, & Handelmann, 1979). We take these distinctions to be different than the one presented here in the sense that amnesia

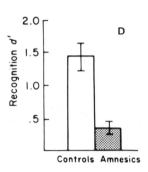

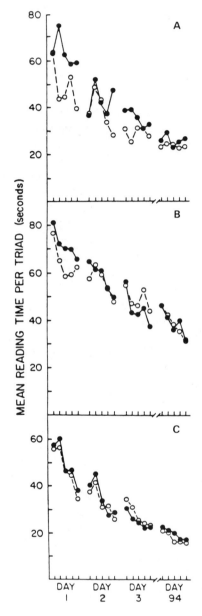

Figure 6.6. Acquisition of a mirror-reading skill (e.g., *capricious–bedraggle–grandiose*) by (A) patient N.A. (●——●), (B) patients with Korsakoff syndrome (●——●), and (C) patients receiving bilateral ECT (●——●). The ability to mirror read unique (nonrepeated) words, shown here, was acquired at a normal rate. Controls (○——○) for (A) and (B), $N = 6$, for (C) $N = 3$. (D). Despite their normal ability to acquire this skill amnesic patients ($N = 9$; controls, $N = 15$) could not remember the specific words they had read, as assessed by a recognition memory test given at the end of the third day of testing. (From Cohen & Squire, 1980.)

impairs more than what is included in episodic memory or working memory (Squire, 1982a; Squire & Cohen, 1983).

Importantly, the formulation presented here accounts for the ability of amnesic patients to learn and remember certain skills despite their inability to reflect that experience in verbal report. Skill-based knowledge is considered by its nature to be implicit, accessible only by engaging in or applying the procedures in which the knowledge is contained. Many skills, such as playing golf or tennis, proceed despite poor access to "the specific instances that led to the perfection of the [skill]." Thus these instances "change the rules by which [one] operates, but are virtually inaccessible in memory as specific encounters [Bruner, 1969, p. 254]." The critical idea here is that there can develop in memory a representation based on experience that changes the way an organism responds to the environment, but this representation by its nature does not afford access to the specific instances that led to the change. For example, even if an experience of a particular face left no neural trace that could aid later in recognition of the same face as having been seen previously, it could nevertheless tune or modify existing neural mechanisms (schemata) specialized for the analysis of faces.

In normal subjects, the capacity for skill learning is supplemented by a record of the acquired information, which affords the basis for specific recognition and recall of the acquired information, and which is directly accessible to verbal report. In amnesic patients the ability to form such a record is impaired, but skill learning proceeds in a normal way. The importance of the observation that amnesic patients can sometimes learn and remember without being able to access their memory through verbal report has been appreciated by Weiskrantz (1978), who suggested that amnesic patients have a deficit in monitoring their memory or in gaining access to it. The view presented here, and in more detail elsewhere (Cohen, 1981; Squire & Cohen, 1983), that amnesia is a deficit in the acquisition of a data-based representation, accounts for this observation without postulating a specific deficit in accessing memory.

The notion of amnesia as a selective deficit in the acquisition of facts or data-based knowledge is meant to apply to the diencephalic as well as to the medial temporal forms of the amnesic syndrome. If diencephalic and medial temporal amnesia are distinct entities, however, it is reasonable to suppose that the two affected brain regions might contribute in different ways to the acquisition of memory. This idea has been developed in detail elsewhere (Squire, 1982a; Squire & Cohen, 1983).

This section concludes our discussion of those neuropsychological features of human amnesia which form a background for work with monkeys. Obviously, the fact that there is a domain of memory that is spared in human amnesia has considerable relevance to work with monkeys, as it should help identify the kinds of memory tasks suitable for detecting amnesia. The next section considers a final body of information relevant to work with monkeys: cliniconeuropathological data from human amnesia concerning which specific brain regions are affected.

V. WHAT HAS HUMAN DIENCEPHALIC AND MEDIAL TEMPORAL AMNESIA TAUGHT US ABOUT THE BRAIN REGIONS THAT ARE AFFECTED?

In considering the neuropathology of amnesia, it has been an attractive and simplifying assumption to suppose that amnesia results when damage occurs to one of a group of anatomically related structures (e.g., the hippocampal formation of the medial temporal region and the mammillary bodies in the diencephalon, which are connected by the fornix) (Figure 6.7). However, three separate considerations concerning anatomy and the effects of fornix section suggest that this functional link may not be so obligatory as once thought. First, in the rhesus monkey a substantial projection from the subicular region of the hippocampal formation is directed caudally to a variety of cortical and subcortical structures (Rosene & Van Hoesen, 1977). Knowing of this projection, one need not expect that damage to another efferent pathway from the hippocampal formation, the fornix, should necessarily mimic the effects of hippocampal damage. Second, in fifty cases of fornix damage that could be found in the neurological literature, only three involved memory loss (Squire & Moore, 1979). Moreover, the best known and most carefully studied of the three positive cases (Sweet, Talland, & Ervin, 1959) had a relatively mild amnesia.

A final reason for relaxing the functional link between these anatomically related structures is that bilateral fornix lesions in the monkey do affect behavior, but not in the way that would be expected from our knowledge of human amnesia. For example, fornix section facilitated performance in an object reversal task (Zola & Mahut, 1973). Moreover, when monkeys with fornix section were impaired at relearning a previously acquired object discrimination, performance was poorer after a 1-hour interval than after a 24-hour interval (Mahut, Moss, & Zola-Morgan, 1981). Although fornix transection in a group of three monkeys has been reported to produce a memory deficit (Gaffan, 1974), the majority of studies have indicated that fornix section is without effect. For example, they are not deficient in tasks of associative memory (Gaffan, 1974).

In addition, on three tasks where monkeys with fornix section and monkeys with hippocampal damage have been compared, only monkeys with hippocampal damage exhibited impairment. Monkeys with fornix section were not impaired on (a) delayed retention of object discriminations (Mahut, Moss, & Zola-Morgan, 1981), (b) concurrent discrimination learning (Moss, Mahut, &

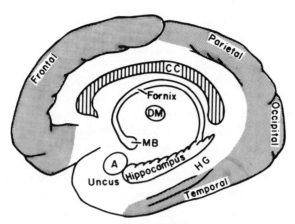

Figure 6.7. Schematic drawing of the medial surface of one hemisphere, showing the hippocampus, fornix, mammillary bodies (MB), and some other structures implicated in the amnesic syndrome. A, amygdala; DM, dorsomedial nucleus of thalamus; HG, hippocampal gyrus. (From Penfield and Jasper, 1954.)

Zola-Morgan, 1982) and (c) delayed non-matching-to-sample (Mahut, Zola-Morgan, & Moss, 1982).

These considerations tend to relax the functional link often presumed to connect the medial temporal and diencephalic regions involved in amnesia, and they are entirely consistent with the neuropsychological evidence that amnesia comes in two forms. With this in mind, we now review what human amnesia has suggested about the specific structures involved in each region.

A. Diencephalic Amnesia

This topic has been reviewed (Brierley, 1977; Mair, Warrington, & Weiskrantz, 1979; Markowitsch, 1982; Squire, 1980b, 1982a) and will only be summarized here. Although damage to the mammillary bodies is invariably associated with Korsakoff syndrome, the best studied of the diencephalic amnesias, there is uncertainty as to whether damage to this structure is responsible for the amnesia. Some have favored the view that damage to the dorsal medial thalamic nucleus correlates best with amnesia (Victor *et al.*, 1971), and a crucial role for this region is also supported by the finding that case N.A. has a lesion there (Squire & Moore, 1979).

Two thoroughly studied cases that have been described (Mair *et al.*, 1979) had bilateral subcortical damage limited to the mammillary bodies and to a site between the third ventricle and the closely adjacent dorsal medial nucleus. Uncertainty about nomenclature and the indistinct boundaries of the dorsal medial nucleus were considered to preclude a definitive statement about the role of that structure.

The available evidence leads to no easy conclusion at this time about the relative importance of the mammillary bodies and the dorsal medial nucleus. Indeed, it may be incorrect to suppose that one structure or the other is the critical one. Other neuropathological data suggest that amnesia can occur when lesions are present in the mammillary bodies, but not the dorsal medial nucleus (Brion & Mikol, 1978), or when lesions are present in the dorsal medial nucleus but not the mammillary bodies (Mills & Swanson, 1978). Perhaps combined damage to both structures would cause more severe amnesia than when either structure is damaged alone, but quantitative data are not yet available to permit a test of this idea.

The time is clearly ripe for some of these ideas to be tested in a rigorous way in monkeys, but to date only a few studies of diencephalic amnesia have been accomplished. We know of no studies that have investigated the effects of mammillary body lesions on memory in monkeys. The few studies reported for other species suggest that global deficits in learning and memory do not occur (Dahl, Ingram, & Knott, 1962; Kim, Chang, & Chu, 1967; Ploog & MacLean, 1963; Woody & Ervin, 1966). Exceptions may be certain kinds of avoidance tasks (Kreickhaus, 1967) and tasks that are distinctly spatial in nature (Rosenstock, Field, & Green, 1977).

A few studies have investigated the effects of dorsal medial nucleus damage in monkeys. Performance was unimpaired in delayed alternation, delayed response, and visual discrimination tasks (Chow, 1954; Peters, Rosvold, & Mirsky, 1956; Rosvold, Mishkin, & Schwartcbart, 1958; R. Thompson & Myers, 1971). However, the lesions to dorsal medial nucleus in these studies were made electrolytically and typically involved only 20–30% of the nucleus (Chow, 1954; Peters et al., 1956). Two studies have shown that larger lesions of the dorsal medial nucleus can impair performance. Schulman (1964) used stereotaxic implants of radioactive yttrium-90. Destruction of dorsal medial nucleus was complete in three of the nine monkeys tested, and these three performed poorly when retested on two preoperatively trained tasks: delayed response and a two-choice conditional brightness discrimination task. It should be cautioned though that all nine monkeys suffered damage to structures in addition to dorsal medial nucleus, including the habenular nuclei and the habenulopeduncular tract, and that the three monkeys just described had, in addition to dorsal medial nucleus lesions, bilateral destruction of nuclei ventralis anterior and lateralis. More circumscribed lesions involving 44% of the dorsal medial nucleus impaired performance on delayed alternation and delayed response tasks (Isseroff, Rosvold, Galkin, and Goldman-Rakic, 1982). The degree of impairment was correlated with the extent of damage to the posterior portion of the nucleus.

The remainder of this chapter takes up the topic of medial temporal amnesia, as it is this form of amnesia that has been used as the starting point for nearly all efforts to establish the syndrome in monkeys.

B. Medial Temporal Amnesia

Most of what is known about the neuropathology of medial temporal amnesia comes from surgical cases in which portions of the temporal lobes have been removed in an effort to relieve severe epilepsy or severe psychotic symptoms. In the 1950s, 30 such cases were described in which the surgical removal extended bilaterally for various distances from the tips of the temporal lobes and posteriorly along their medial surface (Scoville & Milner, 1957). The noted case H.M., an epileptic patient, was one of two patients who sustained the most extensive of these resections: the posterior limit of the removal was 8 cm from the temporal poles, and it included uncus, amygdala, and the anterior two-thirds of the hippocampus and hippocampal gyrus. H.M. and the other patient (case M.B. who was severely psychotic) exhibited profound and persistent anterograde amnesia following surgery. Neuropsychological assessment was also carried out for seven other patients in this series who were sufficiently cooperative to be tested. In six of these cases where bilateral resections extended posteriorly 4.5–6 cm so as to include uncus, amygdala, and anterior hippocampus, five exhibited a moderately severe memory deficit that was less severe than in case H.M. In the remaining case (D.C., a paranoid schizophrenic), where the resection had extended 5.5 cm posteriorly, the memory deficit was considered to be as severe as in case H.M. Finally, in one case (I.S., a paranoid schizophrenic) where the resection extended posteriorly only 4 cm and was limited to the uncus and amygdala, no memory deficit was reported. Taken together, this group of surgical cases indicated that a memory deficit occurred when and only when resection included portions of the hippocampus and hippocampal gyrus.

Two other cases (P.B. and F.C.) sustained left unilateral resections of the temporal lobe, extending posteriorly so as to involve the hippocampus and hippocampal gyrus (Penfield & Milner, 1958). These two patients also exhibited severe global memory deficits after their surgery, which resembled the effects of bilateral resection of the medial temporal region. It was presumed that these two patients had pre-existing pathology in the right temporal lobe, and for one of these patients (case P.B.) this point was subsequently confirmed at autopsy (Penfield & Mathieson, 1974). Finally for cases of left or right unilateral temporal resection who have material-specific deficits in verbal or nonverbal memory, respectively, it has been possible to correlate the severity of the memory deficit with the extent of involvement of the hippocampal zone (Milner, 1974).

A separate reason for supposing that damage to the hippocampal formation is responsible for the amnesic effects of medial temporal resections is the neuropsychological findings from patients sustaining left or right amygdalotomy (Andersen, 1978). These findings are relevant, as the amygdala was included in the medial temporal resections described above. However the patients with selective amygdala damage (Andersen, 1978) scored normally on tests of delayed recall and did not appear to have material-specific deficits in verbal or nonverbal memory.

In addition to these surgical cases which undoubtedly established the foundation for the view that the hippocampal formation is the critical brain region in medial temporal amnesia, it is worth noting that the neuropathological findings from other examples of amnesia are also entirely consistent with this position. Thus case studies of encephalitis (Drachman & Adams, 1962), dementing disorders such as Alzheimer's disease (Corsellis, 1970), infarctions of the posterior cerebral artery (Benson, Marsden, & Meadows, 1974), and anoxic encephalopathy (Gilman, 1965), all of which are associated with memory impairment, also involve bilateral damage to the hippocampal region.

Despite all this evidence converging on the hippocampal region, it must be pointed out that there has not yet been a reported case of well-documented amnesia in man with bilateral damage limited to the hippocampal formation. Nevertheless, a natural result of all this clinical and neuropathological material was that investigators attempted to reproduce the syndrome in experimental animals by making selective lesions of the hippocampus. There is an extensive and controversial literature reporting these efforts in a number of species, and much of it has been reviewed (see Douglas, 1967; Horel, 1978; Isaacson, 1972; Kimble, 1968; O'Keefe & Nadel, 1978; Zola & Mahut, 1973). Section VI reviews those studies that report the behavioral effects of bilateral hippocampal lesions in monkey.

VI. STUDIES OF MONKEYS WITH HIPPOCAMPAL LESIONS

We have reviewed 20 published studies involving approximately 80 monkeys that describe the behavioral effects of selective damage to the hippocampus. The majority of these studies used a ventral approach to the hippocampus that would have also involved hippocampal gyrus, i.e., subiculum, portions of area TH–TF, entorhinal cortex, and sometimes inadvertent damage to area TE (refer to Figure 6.15). Figure 6.8 shows the findings with a wide range of behavioral tasks, and with assessments of postoperative retesting of preoperative learning as well as assessments of postoperative learning. An examination of Figure 6.8 does not lead immediately to any easy generalization about the effects of hippocampal damage on memory.

There seem to be three kinds of difficulties. (1) As can be seen from Figure 6.8, different studies using nominally the same task have often reported contradictory findings (e.g., two-choice discrimination tasks). (2) Among the so-called delay tasks, which should be particularly sensitive to memory impairment, some reveal an impairment (e.g., delayed retentions of object discrimination, delayed non-matching-to-sample) whereas others do not (e.g., delayed response and delayed matching-to-sample). (3) Finally, among the reversal tasks and the alternation tasks, certain ones that would seem to require memory to the same extent do not yield the same results following hippocampal damage (e.g., impairment on spatial reversals, but not object reversals; impairment in delayed alternation, but not nonspatial, go–no-go alternation). Each of these points will be discussed in turn.

A. Contradictory Findings

As shown in Figure 6.8, when the same tasks have been used by different investigators, the results have often been contradictory. For instance, of seven studies investigating the effects of hippocampal damage on postoperative learning of two-choice pattern discrimination (e.g., □ versus +), three found impaired performance and four found performance to be normal. The results are similarly mixed for brightness and color discrimination tasks. The legend of Figure 6.8, however, indicates that there are often methodological differences between these studies (e.g., one-stage versus two-stage surgery or the use of different surgical approaches which affect the size and extent of the lesion). In pattern, color, and brightness discriminations, for example, the contradictory reports may well be a result of the extent of damage to extrahippocampal tissue. Specifically, in many of the studies we reviewed, the surgical approach to the hippocampus resulted in damage to the adjacent inferotemporal cortex (area TE). Thus of the seven separate studies reporting a deficit in discrimination performance, all but one (group HT in Moss et al., 1981) involved area TE to some extent in addition to hippocampus. In that study, monkeys without TE damage were normal on two out of three discrimination tasks. Conversely, of the seven separate studies reporting histology and including more than two animals, only two involved area TE (Mahut et al., 1981; group HA in Moss et al., 1981). Since it is now well known that tasks involving the discrimination of two-dimensional patterns, or discriminations of color or brightness, are especially sensitive to damage of area TE (Gross, 1973), impairment on such tasks in monkeys with hippocampal damage may largely be attributable to TE damage. In a later section, we also suggest that monkeys without TE damage can be mildly impaired on discrimination tasks, especially when the tasks are the kind that can be learned by normal monkeys in relatively few trials. In summary, monkeys with hippocampal damage show only mild deficits or no deficits on visual discrimination tasks (Figure 6.9).

B. Tasks Incorporating a Delay

A difficulty also arises with the so-called delay tasks, which yield inconsistent results, but should be expected to be particularly sensitive to memory impairment. In the case of human amnesia, tasks which measure delayed recall have long been considered to be particularly sensitive indices of impairment, and case H.M. (Figure 6.10) as well as the other kinds of patients described above

TASK	HIPPOCAMPUS				AMYGDALA			
	POSTOPERATIVE RETEST OF PREOPERATIVE LEARNING		POSTOPERATIVE LEARNING		POSTOPERATIVE RETEST OF PREOPERATIVE LEARNING		POSTOPERATIVE LEARNING	
	DEF.	NO DEF.	DEF.	NO DEF.	DEF.	NO DEF.	DEF.	NO DEF.
TWO CHOICE SIMULTANEOUS DISCRIMINATION								
PATTERN:	12[b], 24[b,f], 26[b]		11[ø], 27[b], 28[b,g]	11, 17[m], 18[t], 19[q]	2	29[b,c]	12[o], 18[b,f,o], 24[b,c,o,g]	1, 4[o,b], 11, 12[y], 35[r]
OBJECTS:				16, 21[b], 22[q,r], 28[q,r]			36, 18[b,f]	
BRIGHTNESS:	26[b]	24[f], 28[b,g]	28[b,g,o]	18[t], 19[q], 27[b,n]			16[b,f]	28[q,m], 33, 35
COLOR:	26[b]	24[f]	18[o], 28[b,g,o]	19[q], 27[b]			18[b,f,o]	
DELAYED RESPONSE	24[b,f,o]	26[b,c]	26[b,g,u]	8[o,g], 18, 26[b,g,u]		29[b,c]		18[b,f], 24[b,g]
ALTERNATION								
SPATIAL DELAYED ALTERNATION:	43		18, 28[q]				18[b,f]	28[q,m]
NONSPATIAL GO-NO-GO:				18				18[b,f]
REVERSAL LEARNING								
SPATIAL:			16, 18, 22[q,r]	19[q]			16[b], 18[b,f]	
PATTERN:			12[m], 38[b,s]				3[z], 12[o], 37[b,z], 41[m], 42[m,z]	12[y]
OBJECT:				16, 18, 19[q], 22[q,r]			16[b], 36, 22	
CONCURRENT LEARNING			27[b], 27[b,r]					
MATCHING TO SAMPLE								
DELAYED MTS.:	39[m,o,**]	7[q]			7[b,o], 39[**]			
DELAYED NMTS.	25[m,o]	10[m]	25[m,o], 23[o]		25[m,o]		25[m,o]	
GO-NO-GO MTS.:								
DELAYED RETENTION OF OBJECT DISCRIMINATION			21[q,r], 21[q,r]					

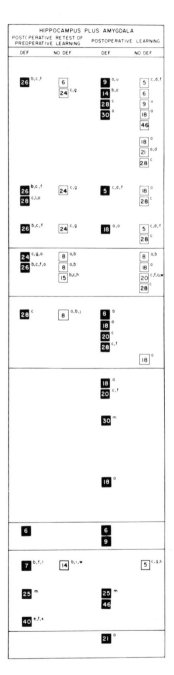

Figure 6.8. Behavioral findings for monkeys with medial temporal lesions. The numbers enclosed in the box are study numbers as follows: 1, Bagshaw & Benzies (1968); 2, Bagshaw & Pribram (1965); 3, Barrett (1969); 4, Brown (1963); 5, Cordeau & Mahut (1964); 6, Correll & Scoville (1965a); 7, Correll & Scoville (1965b); 8, Correll & Scoville (1967); 9, Correll & Scoville (1970); 10, Delacour (1977); 11, Douglas, Barrett, Pribram, & Cerny (1969); 12, Douglas & Pribram (1966); 13, Douglas & Pribram (1969); 14, Drachman & Ommaya (1964); 15, Jacobsen & Elder (1936); 16, Jones & Mishkin (1972); 17, Kimble & Pribram (1963); 18, Mahut (1971); 19, Mahut (1972); 20, Mahut & Cordeau (1963); 21, Mahut, Moss, & Zola-Morgan (1981); 22, Mahut & Zola (1973); 23, Mahut, Zola-Morgan, & Moss (1982); 24, Mishkin (1954); 25, Mishkin (1978); 26, Mishkin & Pribram (1954); 27, Moss, Mahut, & Zola-Morgan (1981); 28, Orbach, Milner, & Rasmussen (1960); 29, Pribram & Bagshaw (1953); 30, Pribram, Douglas, & Pribram (1969); 31, Riopelle, Alper, Strong, & Ades (1953); 32, Schwartzbaum (1960a); 33, Schwartzbaum (1960b); 34, Schwartzbaum (1964); 35, Schwartzbaum (1965); 36, Schwartzbuam & Poulous (1965); 37, Semmes, Mishkin, & Deue (1969); 38, Shapiro, Gol, & Kellaway (1965); 29, Spiegler & Mishkin (1981); 40, Stepien, Cordeau, & Rasmussen (1960); 41, Stamm & Knight (1963); 42, Stamm & Rosen (1971); 43, Waxler & Rosvold (1973); 44, Weiskrantz (1965); 45, Zola-Morgan, Mahut, & Moss (1982); 46, Zola-Morgan, Squire, & Mishkin (1982). Key to notation: a, Incomplete lesion; a significant portion of the target structure(s) spared; b, significant involvement of other structures; c, two-stage surgery; d, longer than usual surgery-to-testing interval; e, correction procedure used; f, only two animals; g, only one animal; h, additional testing during interoperative period; i, tested within 7 days of surgery; j, tested for 200 (trials) at each of four delays (15–60 seconds); k, distraction used between sample and match or during delay; l, the preoperative scores of these animals were among the worst of all preoperatively trained animals; m, no histology; n, mild impairment, not statistically significant; o, mild impairment, statistically significant; p, impaired on initial learning of problem; q, electrolytic lesion, incomplete; r, both visual and tactile modalities tested; s, auditory modality tested; t, of four operated animals, two had extensive damage to other than target tissue and are not considered here; u, unimpaired at the shorter interval, impaired at longer; v, impaired on internally sequenced task, unimpaired on externally sequenced task; w, impaired at 5-second intervals, unimpaired at 10–12 seconds; x, visual size discrimination: positive stimulus rewarded 70% of time, negative 30% of time; y, unimpaired on first 8 of 15 reversals by one response measure; z, tactile modality; ø, one rewarded stimulus, two to four unrewarded stimuli; #, trial unique matching and nonmatching to sample.

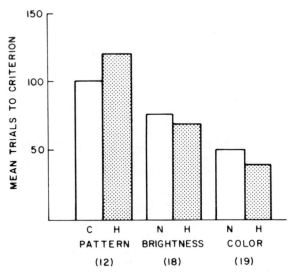

Figure 6.9. Visual discrimination performance on three kinds of tasks by monkeys with bilateral hippocampal lesions and minimal damage to area TE. Performance on these tasks was unimpaired or mildly impaired. Numbers in parentheses refer to references in Figure 6.8. N, normal; C, operated controls; H, hippocampal.

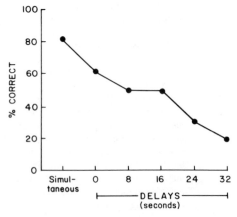

Figure 6.10. Delayed matching-to-sample for ellipses by patient H.M. (Adapted from Sidman, Stoddard, & Mohr, 1968.)

are deficient in tests of delayed recall (Cohen & Squire, 1981; Milner, 1972; Sidman, Stoddard, & Mohr, 1968). Of the delay tasks, perhaps the best known is delayed response. Here one of two food wells is baited as the monkey watches. Both wells are then covered in the same way, and after a delay during which the food wells are hidden by a screen, the monkey is given a choice between the two covered food wells. If findings for a single animal are excluded (Mishkin & Pribram, 1954), delayed-response performance by monkeys with hippocampal damage was unimpaired in three studies and mildly impaired in one study (Figure 6.8). For example, in monkeys with single-stage, bilateral removals of hippocampus, postoperative learning of delayed response with delays of up to 5 seconds was normal (Mahut, 1971). The lack of effect of hippocampal damage on delayed-response performance has been established for delays up to 10 seconds (Mishkin & Pribram, 1954). The one study reporting a mild deficit (Mishkin, 1954) was based on two animals, both of which had extensive damage to area TE and ventral temporal cortex including entorhinal cortex.

In matching-to-sample, another commonly used delay task, the monkey first responds to a single stimulus object presented alone and then after a delay makes a choice between two objects: the original one and another one. For delayed matching-to-sample the monkey learns to find food under the same object that was presented originally; for delayed non-matching-to-sample the monkey learns to find food under the novel object. In the traditional version of these tasks, the same two objects are used throughout testing and on each trial one of them is randomly selected as the sample. In a newer, trial-unique version of these tasks (Gaffan, 1974; Mishkin & Delacour, 1975), a new pair of objects is used on every trial. In four separate studies of hippocampal lesions and matching-to-sample or non-matching-to-sample, two involved delays of 5 or 10 seconds (Correll and Scoville, 1965b; Delacour, 1977), and two included delays of up to 2 minutes (Mishkin, 1978; Mahut, Zola, Morgan, & Moss, 1982). The last three studies cited in this group employed the trial-unique testing method. At delays of 5 or 10 seconds, there was no impairment in monkeys with hippocampal lesions. In the two studies employing longer delays, the operated monkeys were impaired. Specifically, at a delay of 2 minutes, normal monkeys and monkeys with hippocampal lesions scored 98 and 91% correct, respectively (Mishkin, 1978) or 95 and 78% correct, respectively (Mahut et al., 1982). In both studies the differences between normal and operated groups, though small, were statistically significant (Figure 6.11).

These findings might at first seem difficult to reconcile with the findings in humans if it is assumed that a deficit should appear after hippocampal lesions in any delay task regardless of the length of the delay. However, the data from human amnesia indicate that a delay of 5 to 10 seconds between a learning and retention trial is not sufficient to yield a reliable memory impairment. Thus H.M. matched ellipses at an 8-second delay (Sidman et al., 1968) and made same–

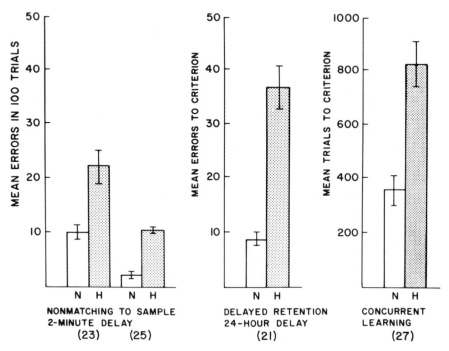

Figure 6.11. Performance by monkeys on three tasks sensitive to the effects of hippocampal lesions. H, hippocampus; N, normal. Numbers in parentheses refer to references in Figure 6.8.

different judgments between auditory and visual stimuli at a 15-second delay (Prisko, 1963) nearly as well as when there was no delay at all. The same was true for alcoholic Korsakoff patients recognizing nonsense shapes after a 10-second delay (Cermak, Reale, & DeLuca, 1977). Accordingly, the good performance of operated monkeys with delays up to seconds is entirely consistent with the findings in human amnesia. It is less clear how to interpret the finding that monkeys with hippocampal lesions were only mildly impaired at delays of 2 minutes (Mishkin, 1978; Mahut *et al.*, 1982). Does this finding reflect such good performance that the impairment of monkeys with hippocampal lesions cannot be considered to model human medial temporal amnesia or is this level of performance reconcilable with the facts of human amnesia?

If their deficit is to resemble human medial temporal amnesia, it might be expected that monkeys with hippocampal lesions should have a rather severe deficit whenever the delay in a matching or nonmatching task is as long as 2 minutes. Patient H.M., after all, failed to match ellipses after a delay of only 32 seconds (Sidman *et al.*, 1968); was deficient at comparing clicks, visual shapes, and other stimuli after a delay of 60 seconds (Prisko, 1963); and was deficient at matching nonsense shapes tactually after a delay of 30 seconds (Milner & Taylor, 1972). However, H.M. provides an uncertain standard against which to judge the performance of monkeys. First, monkeys with hippocampal lesions and H.M. have not yet been tested on any of the same matching tasks. Second, more needs to be known about what normally occurs during the sample–match interval in both monkeys and humans. When H.M. was able to rehearse and was not distracted, he maintained perfect performance on consonant trigrams up to delays of 40 seconds (Sidman et al., 1968) and was able to retain a three-digit number perfectly for at least 15 minutes (Milner, 1959). Although intertrial mental activity (e.g., rehearsal) has traditionally been discussed primarily in the context of verbal tasks, the concept may also be relevant to nonverbal tasks. For patients with surgical lesions of the right medial temporal lobe, performance was worse on a nonverbal task when distraction was interposed between learning and retention than when it was not (Milner, 1972). The concept of rehearsal may also be useful in understanding the representational capacity of experimental animals (Wagner, Rudy, & Whitlow, 1973).

For these reasons, it is difficult to judge the demands of the nonmatching task used with monkeys, which involves easily discriminable objects and no distraction between sample and match. Perhaps the operated monkeys would exhibit a severe deficit if a distracting task were interposed during the 2-minute interval, or if the task involved similarly shaped ellipses or other of the stimuli that H.M. could not match at a 2-minute delay. In short, the performance of operated monkeys at the 2-minute delay may be better than expected, but more needs to be known before their performance on this task can be satisfactorily interpreted.

On another kind of delay task (delayed retention of object discrimination) it is clear that hippocampal lesions can exert a marked effect. In this task monkeys are first taught an easy, simultaneous object discrimination to a criterion of nine correct responses in ten trials. After some interval, they are retrained again to criterion using the same pair of objects. Monkeys with hippocampal lesions readily learned these discriminations, but were impaired at retention intervals of 1 hour or 24 hours (Mahut et al., 1981) (Figure 6.11). This impairment was observed in both a visual and a tactual version of the task, a finding that parallels the modality-general nature of human amnesia (Milner, 1966, 1968). Another task in which hippocampal lesions exert a marked effect is the learning of concurrent discriminations (Moss et al., 1981; Figure 6.11). Here monkeys learned simultaneously eight different object discriminations, and the delay between trials with the same pair of objects averaged about 3 minutes. The impairment in the concurrent learning task was also observed in both the visual and tactual mode.

C. Impairment in Spatial Tasks

A final difficulty in interpreting the effects of hippocampal lesions is that certain tasks that would appear to involve memory to the same extent are not affected by hippocampal lesions in the same way. Thus operated monkeys are impaired in the spatial delayed alternation task, but not in a go–no-go, nonspatial version of delayed alternation (Figure 6.8). In the spatial delayed alternation task, as used in these studies, monkeys learn to alternate their choices between two identically covered food wells, with a delay of 10 seconds or less between each trial. In the nonspatial version of this task, monkeys learn to alternate responding and nonresponding to the same, covered food well, with a delay of 10 seconds or less between each trial. Since the requirement for memory appears similar in each task, the finding that hippocampal damage selectively impairs spatial delayed alternation (Mahut, 1971) implies that it is the spatial aspect of the task that is crucial. Similarly, the finding that hippocampal damage impairs spatial reversal tasks, but not object reversal tasks, also suggests a special role for a spatial factor (Mahut, 1971).

Importantly, the effects of hippocampal lesions on these tasks cannot be explained by supposing that the tasks which operated monkeys are deficient at are simply the more difficult ones, and that they are therefore more sensitive indices of brain damage. Spatial delayed alternation is easier for normal monkeys to learn than go–no-go alternation (Mahut, 1971), and spatial reversals are easier for normal monkeys to accomplish than object reversals (Mahut & Zola, 1973; Zola & Mahut, 1973) (Figure 6.12).

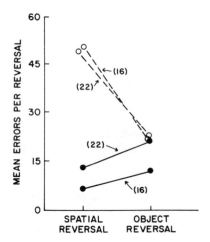

Figure 6.12. Performance of monkeys with hippocampal lesions (○- -○) on two kinds of reversal tasks. Although the object reversal task is the more difficult for normal monkeys (●- -●), operated monkeys are impaired on only the spatial reversal task. Numbers in parentheses refer to references in Figure 6.8.

D. Hippocampal Lesions in Monkeys: Lack of Correspondence with the Human Data

Having considered the findings reported in Figure 6.8 together with various difficulties that arise when attempting to interpret them, we would summarize the behavioral effects of hippocampal lesions in monkeys as follows. The ability to acquire two-choice, simultaneous discrimination tasks is mildly or not at all affected. On so-called delay tasks, performance is essentially normal when the delay does not exceed 10 seconds. On delayed non-matching-to-sample with delays up to 2 minutes performance is impaired. Note, however, that in the only 2 studies using delays as long as 2 minutes, the impairment was not severe. On delayed retention of object discriminations with delays of 1 or 24 hours, performance is impaired. There is also impairment on certain tasks that involve a spatial factor. Finally, there is substantial impairment in a concurrent discrimination task (Moss et al., 1981). This task, like tasks involving delays, is of particular interest because human amnesic patients are impaired on analogous tasks of associative learning (Oscar-Berman & Zola-Morgan, 1980b; Squire, Slater, & Chace, 1976). One of these studies (Oscar-Berman & Zola-Morgan, 1980b) tested concurrent learning in patients with Korsakoff syndrome, using a format nearly identical to that used in monkeys.

Because of the difficulty in producing lesions of hippocampus without damaging adjacent structures, a final question must be raised as to whether damage to other structures might account for the findings reviewed here. Of the two surgical approaches to hippocampus, lateral and ventral, the former necessarily damages some temporal neocortex (usually area TE and underlying white matter), and the latter necessarily damages area TH–TF and sometimes entorhinal cortex and area TE. Several investigators have suggested that temporal neocortex damage might in fact be responsible for the effects of surgery in the medial temporal region (Horel, 1978; Iversen, 1976; Weiskrantz, 1971). Moreover, lesions of entorhinal cortex are known to impair performance on at least one task affected by hippocampal lesions (Moss et al., 1981).

Nevertheless, consideration of the studies that demonstrated clear impairment on memory tasks following hippocampal lesions suggests that damage to hippocampus alone is responsible for the impairment, and not the additional involvement of temporal neocortex, underlying white matter, area TH–TF, or entorhinal cortex. First, the deficit in concurrent learning (Moss et al., 1981) and in delayed non-matching-to-sample with 2-minute delays (Mahut et al., 1982) occurred in monkeys operated on by a ventral approach, and these monkeys did not sustain bilateral damage to entorhinal cortex. Two of six monkeys in one study (Mahut et al., 1982) sustained unilateral damage. Second, four of the eight monkeys exhibiting a deficit in delayed retention of object discriminations sustained electroytic lesions of hippocampus and did not have entorhinal TH–TF, or inferotemporal cortex damage (Mahut *et al.*, 1981). Third, for the delayed retention tasks two monkeys who sustained some damage to area TH–TF but not to hippocampus performed like normal animals, unlike monkeys with lesions that also involved hippocampus (Mahut *et al.*, 1981). Finally, unless the ventricle is crossed, damage to underlying temporal lobe white matter is unlikely in the ventral approach to hippocampus. This possibility has been specifically evaluated (Moss *et al.*, 1981; Mahut *et al.*, 1982; Zola-Morgan *et al.*, 1982), and there was no damage to this region. The possible effects on memory of direct damage to temporal lobe white matter have recently been the subject of a great deal of discussion and will be considered again later.

Although this review has helped to identify a pattern of behavioral effects that can be attributed to lesions of the hippocampus, this pattern nevertheless fails in three respects to reveal a global disorder of memory as we might expect it from our understanding of human amnesia. First, it is not clear why monkeys with hippocampal damage are so mildly impaired or unimpaired on tasks such as two-choice discrimination problems which take many sessions to learn and which therefore require retention of information from one day to the next. Second, a deficit as severe as what might be expected from the findings in human amnesia has not yet been demonstrated at long delays in matching-to-sample or non-matching-to-sample tasks. Third, it is not clear why impairment is observed on certain spatial tasks, but not on nonspatial versions of the same tasks. Each of these points will be addressed subsequently in later sections of this chapter.

Others who have reviewed this body of work in the past decade have also pointed out that the literatures of human and nonhuman research are not in good correspondence (Douglas, 1967; Horel, 1978; Iversen, 1976; O'Keefe & Nadel, 1978; Rozin, 1976; Weiskrantz, 1971). The various explanations offered to account for this state of affairs have usually taken one of three forms: (1) The functional organization of the hippocampus is different in humans than in nonhuman species. That is, phylogenetically, the hippocampus has undergone a change in function such that its removal in humans has a different effect than its removal in monkeys. (2) The brain regions involved in human global amnesia have been misidentified to some extent, so that emphasis on hippocampus in monkey studies has been misplaced. (3) The behavioral tests used with monkeys have not been comparable to those used in the analysis of the human amnesic syndrome. For example, hippocampal damage might not produce impairment in monkeys if the tasks used are ones that human amnesic patients could succeed at. In the remainder of this chapter we consider explanations (2) and (3) and suggest that therein lie the clues for bringing the human and nonhuman literature into congruence.

VII. THE BRAIN REGIONS CRITICAL TO AMNESIA: TWO HYPOTHESES

Two different hypotheses have been advanced regarding which brain regions must be damaged to produce an animal model of human global amnesia. One hypothesis is that the hippocampus is involved in human global amnesia, but that this amnesia depends crucially on there being additional damage to amygdala (Mishkin, 1978, 1982; Mishkin, Spiegler, Saunders, & Malamut, 1982). This argument begins with a reminder that the medial temporal surgery which patient H.M. received did include both these structures. Such an argument is consistent with two facts about amnesia: (1) A clear case of human amnesia with lesions restricted to the hippocampal formation has not been reported and (2) amygdala lesions in man do not cause noticeable memory impairment (Andersen, 1978; Andy, Jurko, & Hughes, 1975; Narabayashi, Nagao, Saito, Yoshida, & Nagahata, 1963; Vaernet, 1972). These facts have ordinarily been interpreted to mean that the hippocampus is therefore the critical structure in medial temporal surgery and that its damage is responsible for amnesia. But the same facts are equally consistent with the hypothesis that amnesia depends on conjoint damage to the hippocampus and amygdala. We will shortly consider the data relevant to this hypothesis.

A second hypothesis has been that the critical brain region in human global amnesia is not the hippocampus at all, but the temporal stem or albal stalk which lies adjacent to the hippocampus just above the lateral ventricle (Horel, 1978). As the result of a thorough review of human and monkey data, Horel suggested that the amnesic syndrome is due to the cutting of some of the fiber connections of the temporal lobe contained within the temporal stem. It was argued that its position relative to the hippocampus makes it vulnerable to the anterior surgical approach used in human medial temporal surgery (Figure 6.13). When medial temporal lesions were made in monkeys in the same way they were made in humans, inadvertent damage to the temporal stem did occur along with the intended damage to amygdala and hippocampus (Correll & Scoville, 1965a). To evaluate this hypothesis, we will shortly evaluate the relevant data in monkeys with damage to the temporal stem.

A. The Hippocampus–Amygdala Hypothesis: Relevant Data

Three bodies of data are relevant to this hypothesis. Of these, the behavioral effects of separate lesions of hippocampus have already been reviewed. We now consider the behavioral effects of separate amygdala lesions and then the behavioral effects of conjoint lesions of the hippocampus and amygdala.

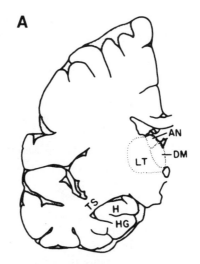

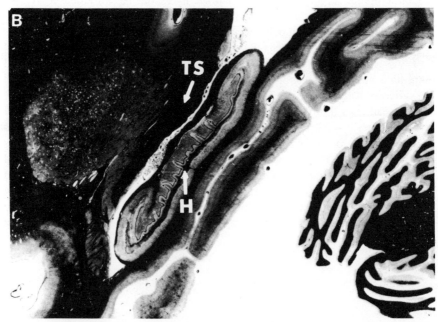

Figure 6.13. (A) Diagram of a frontal section through the right hemisphere showing how the position of the temporal stem makes it vulnerable to an anterior surgical approach to the hippocampus. H, hippocampus; HG, hippocampal gyrus; TS, temporal stem; DM, dorsomedial nucleus of thalamus; AN, anterior nucleus of thalamus; LT, lateral thalamus. (From Penfield & Roberts, 1959.) (B) The same point made in a saggital section. H, hippocampus; TS, temporal stem. (From DeArmand, Fusco & Dewey, 1976.)

1. Studies of Monkeys with Amygdala Lesions

We have reviewed 23 studies involving approximately 50 monkeys which describe the behavioral effects of selective damage to the amygdala. The majority of these studies used a medial approach through the frontal–temporal junction that would necessarily have involved the surrounding anterior and medial temporal cortex, and sometimes white matter situated lateral to the amygdala (Figure 6.15). Figure 6.8 shows the findings with the same behavioral tasks considered in our review of hippocampal lesions. Before considering these findings it should be emphasized that bilateral removal of the amygdala has profound effects on social and affective behavior (Downer, 1961; Goddard, 1964; Rosvold, Mirsky, & Pribram, 1954), which will not be reviewed here.

For the tasks that have been used, the results are reasonably clear. In the case of two-choice visual discrimination learning, nine of thirteen separate studies found no impairment following amygdala lesions. Not counting a study based on a single animal, there are only three studies reporting impairment. One (Douglas & Pribram, 1966) required monkeys to discriminate between two circles (diameters of ¾ versus ½ inch). This is an unusually difficult task for normal monkeys, compared to most of the other visual discrimination tasks reviewed in Figure 6.8. In the other two positive studies the lesions were larger than those in the nine negative studies, and included damage to structures other than amygdala. In one the temporal pole was intentionally removed together with the amygdala, and there was also damage to the anterior region of the temporal stem (Jones & Mishkin, 1972). In the other there was inadvertent damage to portions of temporal pole, the temporal stem region, and the tip of the hippocampus (Mahut, 1971). It is difficult to know whether the relatively greater additional damage in these two studies might account for the oberved impairment because we are unable to determine accurately which of these additional areas might also have been damaged in those studies reporting no impairment. Nevertheless, it is known that lesions of temporal white matter, including temporal stem, can impair visual discrimination performance (Horel & Misantone, 1976). In summary, the lack of effect of amygdala lesions on visual discrimination learning is rather clear, particularly when one considers those studies with minimal damage to adjacent tissue.

In the case of reversal learning, the results are even clearer. Of eight studies, involving both the visual and tactual modality, seven found an impairment in reversal of object, pattern, or spatial discriminations. The exception (Douglas & Pribram, 1966) involved a unique procedure, employed throughout original learning and the subsequent reversals, whereby choice of the positive stimulus was rewarded on 70% of the trials and the negative on 30% of the trials. Thus the conventional reversal task is uniformly difficult for monkeys with amygdala lesions, and this difficulty, contrary to what was observed in the case of hippocampal lesions, extends beyond spatial reversal tasks to include object and pattern reversal tasks as well.

Despite the reasonably clear findings for discrimination and reversal learning, the effects of amygdala lesions on memory are not yet as clear as one might wish them to be. Tasks that would most inform us about memory (e.g., tasks involving delays or other tasks that have clear counterparts in human neuropsychological testing) have been given only rarely to monkeys with amygdala lesions. In the five available studies of so-called delay tasks, amygdala lesions produced either no impairment [delayed response to 5 seconds, (Mahut, 1971; Mishkin, 1954; Pribram & Bagshaw, 1953)] or mild impairment [delayed matching-to-sample to 5 seconds (Correll & Scoville, 19565b); delayed non-matching-to-sample to 2 minutes (Mishkin, 1978)]. The mild nature of this impairment, even at delays as long as 2 minutes, can be appreciated by noting that normal monkeys scored 98% correct and that monkeys with amygdala lesions scored 94% correct (Mishkin, 1978).

One exception to this pattern of findings comes from a task that combined the matching-to-sample and non-matching-to-sample procedures (Spiegler & Mishkin, 1981). Three monkeys with lesions of hippocampus and hippocampal gyrus were mildly impaired. Because this kind of task has not yet been given to human patients, and because patients with bilateral amygdala lesions are not amnesic, it is difficult to know what this impairment means about memory functions. However, this finding is intriguing, as it raises the possibility that amygdala lesions produce an impairment that affects memory in a specific or selective way.

The behavioral effects of amygdala lesions in monkeys can be summarized in three statements: (1) The ability to acquire visual discriminations is largely unaffected. (2) Reversal learning is impaired whether performance is based on discrimination between objects, patterns, or spatial positions. (3) Performance on delay tasks up to 2 minutes is not affected or only mildly affected. Together, these results provide little evidence for memory impairment, and in this sense they conform to the expectation based on human neuropsychological studies. With the exception of the study that combined matching-to-sample and non-matching-to-sample procedures (Spiegler & Mishkin, 1981), the only clear and consistent example of behavioral impairment comes from reversal performance, which is an uncertain index of memory dysfunction. In the only reported study of reversal learning in patients that has used a format based on monkey studies (Oscar-Berman & Zola-Morgan, 1980a), amnesic patients with Korsakoff syndrome differed from monkeys with amygdala lesions. For example, monkeys were impaired on each of a series of 15 successive reversals (Barrett, 1969), but the patients performed normally on six of nine such reversals.

Although there is little evidence for memory impairment in monkeys with amygdala lesions, we must emphasize that this operated group has not yet been evaluated with tasks involving delays longer than 2 minutes or with other tasks sensitive to human amnesia. The next section turns to the final and critical body of data relevant to the hippocampal–amygdala hypothesis: the effects of conjoint damage to both structures.

2. Studies of Monkeys with Combined Hippocampal–Amygdala Lesions

We have reviewed 17 published studies involving approximately 100 monkeys that describe the behavioral effects of conjoint damage to hippocampus and amygdala. Two different surgical approaches have been used in these studies. The first and most common approach was designed to reproduce the surgical procedure that had been described for patient H.M. (Figure 6.14). In H.M. the surgery included amygdala, uncus, hippocampal gyrus, and the anterior two-thirds of hippocampus. In the monkey the amygdala is approached frontally through the frontotemporal junction, and the excision continues caudally to the posterior curve of the hippocampus. In this way, the removal typically extends to the posterior extent of the lateral geniculate, sparing approximately the posterior third of the hippocampus. This approach also results in removal of uncus and variable amounts of hippocampal gyrus and causes damage to portions of temporal pole and frequently to temporal stem. Area TE, which lies more laterally, is usually spared by this approach.

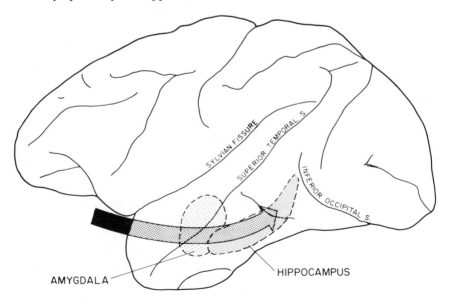

Figure 6.14. Lateral view of the left hemisphere of monkey showing the surgical approach that was designed to reproduce the medial temporal resection sustained by patient H.M. The hippocampus and amygdala were removed together in a single-opening frontal approach.

The second approach uses four separate entries, two on each side of the brain (Figure 6.15). Removal of the amygdala is accomplished by the approach just described, through the fronto-temporal junction. However, the lesion is not extended posteriorly through this opening. Instead, a second opening on each side is made to approach the hippocampus through the ventromedial surface of the temporal lobe at the level of area TH–TF and the entorhinal cortex. Hippo-campal tissue is removed in the anterior direction until the uncus is removed and the first opening is visualized. In the posterior direction the lesion is continued to approximately the posterior curve of the hippocampus. It seems likely that these lesions might extend somewhat more posteriorly than the lesions resulting from the frontal approach. This method of approaching the medial temporal region, like the frontal approach just described, will also result in some damage to temporal pole and variable amounts of hippocampal gyrus. Compared to the frontal approach, however, this method is less likely to damage temporal stem, which lies across the lateral ventricle from the hippocampus, and is more likely to damage area TE, which lies just lateral to the intended point of entry.

Figure 6.8 shows the findings with the same behavioral tasks considered previously. The available findings permit no simple or definitive generalization about the effects of conjoint hippocampus–amygdala damage on memory. The data do contain, however, some support for the notion that damage to both structures can mimic features of the human amnesic syndrome.

In the case of visual discrimination performance there have been ten sepa-rate studies involving a total of 25 discrimination tasks. In one study which investigated performance on three visual discrimination tasks (Mishkin & Pri-bram, 1954), the two monkeys with hippocampal–amygdala lesions had intended and additional damage to area TE and will not be considered here. Altogether, for 19 out of the 22 remaining tasks, performance on visual discrimi-nation tasks by the operated group was mildly impaired or unimpaired. Two of the three tasks in which this group exhibited a more severe impairment were based on data from only two monkeys (Cordeau & Mahut, 1964). The remaining task for which an impairment was observed as a postoperatively administered pattern discrimination, and the four monkeys who had difficulty with this task were nonetheless entirely normal at postoperative acquisition of brightness and color discrimination habits (Orbach, Milner, & Rasmussen, 1960). Taken to-gether, the weight of evidence is similar to the findings for hippocampal lesions and suggests that visual discrimination performance in monkeys with hippocam-pal–amygdala lesions is typically normal or mildly impaired.

In the case of reversal learning tasks, four different studies, involving reversals of spatial, pattern, or object discrimination habits, reported that monkeys with conjoint hippocampal–amygdala lesions were impaired. This re-sult is not surprising, considering that amygdala lesions alone impair perfor-mance on these same reversal tasks (Figure 6.8). In the case of spatial delayed

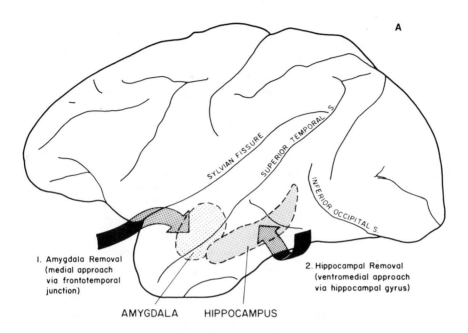

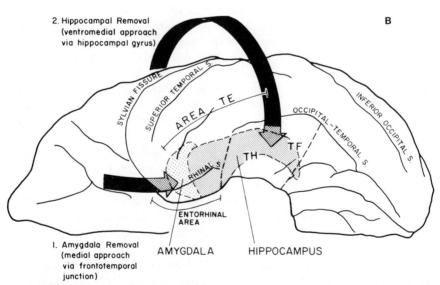

Figure 6.15. Lateral (A) and ventral (B) views of the left hemisphere of monkey showing the two-opening approach for producing conjoint hippocampal–amygdala lesions. The same two approaches have also been used separately to produce selective lesions of hippocampus or amygdala. Areas TE, and TH–TF as described by von Bonin and Bailey (1947).

alternation, the results are similar to the effects of separate hippocampal lesions. Monkeys with combined hippocampal–amygdala lesions were impaired in spatial delayed alternation, but not in go–no-go, nonspatial alternation. Since the go–no-go task is more difficult for normal monkeys and since the two tasks are otherwise rather similar, the findings suggest that the combined lesions, like separate hippocampal lesions, produce a spatial deficit (Mahut, 1971).

On the so-called delay tasks, the results are rather clear. Delayed response performance with delays up to 10 seconds was unimpaired in five studies and only mildly impaired in two. Of the two studies reporting a mild impairment (Mishkin, 1954; Mishkin & Pribram, 1954), the former involved one animal and the latter involved two animals. Delayed matching-to-sample has been studied with delays up to 12 seconds. In one study (Drachman & Ommaya, 1964), retention of preoperatively acquired matching-to-sample was normal in monkeys with combined hippocampal–amygdala damage. In another (Correll & Scoville, 1965b), involving only two monkeys and a maximum 5-second delay, performance was impaired. However, these two monkeys performed by far the worst of all animals during preoperative training, and they both sustained damage to temporal neocortex. Finally, on a variation of the matching-to-sample task, involving same and different judgments, operated monkeys were normal at delays up to 5 seconds (Cordeau & Mahut, 1964).

Delayed non-matching-to-sample has been tested in two studies at delays up to 2 minutes (Mishkin, 1978), and up to 10 minutes (Zola-Morgan *et al.*, 1982). Monkeys with conjoint damage to hippocampus and amygdala were severely impaired and performed close to chance at the long delays. In the study by Mishkin (1978), the performance of the group with combined lesions was considerably poorer than the performance of monkeys sustaining separate lesions of hippocampus or amygdala. Thus, whereas the average score at the 2-minute delay for monkeys with combined damage was 60%, the monkeys with separate hippocampal or amygdala damage scored 91 and 94%, respectively (Figure 6.16).

On other tasks which can be regarded as sensitive to memory impairment, monkeys with combined damage were also severely impaired. They were poor at delayed retention of object discriminations (Mahut *et al.*, 1981), and poor at concurrent learning tasks, where discriminations between two, three, or six pairs of stimuli must be acquired simultaneously (Correll & Scoville, 1965a, 1970). This deficit was particularly clear when discrimination habits were learned simultaneously for six different pattern pairs.

The experimental findings reviewed here provide clear evidence that monkeys with hippocampal–amygdala lesions are impaired on certain tasks known to be sensitive to human amnesia. The best examples of this impairment are delayed non-matching-to-sample with 2-minute delays, 24-hour retention of object discriminations, and concurrent learning. However, the hypothesis that a

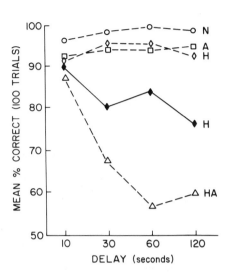

Figure 6.16. Delayed non-matching-to-sample performance for normal monkeys (N), monkeys with hippocampal lesions (H), amygdala lesions (A), or conjoint removal of both structures (HA). Monkeys with HA lesions performed worse than monkeys with separate H or A lesions. Closed symbols from Mahut, Zola-Morgan, & Moss (1982); open symbols from Mishkin (1978), and Saunders & Mishkin, unpublished data.

severe amnesia can be produced only by conjoint lesions of hippocampus and amygdala, and not by lesions limited to hippocampus, demands more than the observation that conjoint lesions can cause impairment on certain tasks. It is also critical that the deficit following combined lesions is more severe than the deficit following selective hippocampal lesions. On this point, there is supporting data, but several questions remain.

There have been only two studies comparing directly the effects of hippocampal lesions and hippocampal–amygdala lesions on the sorts of tasks just described, which are believed to be sensitive to human amnesia. In delayed non-matching-to-sample, with 2-minute delays (Mishkin, 1978), monkeys with hippocampal lesions scored 91% correct and monkeys with combined lesions scored 60%. The results of this study therefore provide support for the hypothesis that amnesia occurs only after conjoint lesions. However, there is some uncertainty about the 91% score obtained by the monkeys with hippocampal lesions. First, no histological reconstructions of these lesions are available. It will become clear shortly that there is a special reason for raising this issue (see Section VII,B). Second, six monkeys with verified hippocampal lesions have been studied on the same delayed non-matching-to-sample task (Mahut *et al.*, 1982). Their average score was 78% correct, significantly worse than the 91% score of the three monkeys studied by Mishkin (1978). Of course, it is also true that this result is still supportive of the conjoint lesion hypothesis in the sense that 78% is significantly better than the 60% score obtained by monkeys in Mishkin's (1978) study with the combined lesion (Figure 6.16). However, this comparison is complicated by the fact that prior to obtaining their 78% delayed non-matching-to-sample score, the six monkeys studied by Mahut *et al.* (1982) had 5 years of extensive postoperative testing experience which might possibly have benefited them on this task. In short, a comparison between monkeys with hippocampal and hippocampal–amygdala lesions is not yet available for the delayed non-matching-to-sample task where (a) histological reconstructions of the lesions are available, and (b) the two groups have similar testing histories.

In the second study that has afforded the needed comparison (Mahut *et al.*, 1981) eight monkeys with hippocampal lesions and four monkeys with combined hippocampal–amygdala lesions were tested for reversal or retention of simple object discriminations in an alternating sequence (Day 1: learn A+B−; Day 2: learn A−B+; Day 3: retain A−B+; Day 4: learn A+B−; Day 5: retain A+B−). For the retention sessions, monkeys with hippocampal lesions averaged 91 errors, and monkeys with combined lesions averaged 171 errors (Figure 6.17). These scores were significantly worse than those of 13 operated control animals, who averaged 37 errors. Although these results give the impression of greater impairment in the combined lesion group, the difference between this group and the group with hippocampal damage was not significant. The error

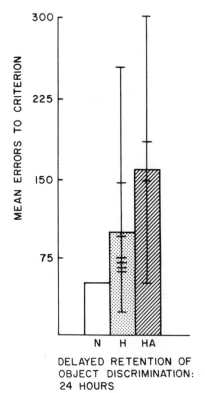

DELAYED RETENTION OF OBJECT DISCRIMINATION: 24 HOURS

Figure 6.17. Retention of object discriminations 24 hours after learning by normal monkeys (N), monkeys with hippocampal lesions (H), and monkeys with combined hippocampal–amygdala lesions (HA). Retention tests alternated with reversals of the discriminations. Both operated groups were impaired, but the deficit was as severe in the H group as in the HA group. Hash marks show individual scores for monkeys in the two operated groups. (Adapted from Mahut, Moss, & Zola-Morgan, 1981.)

scores in the combined lesion group ranged from 53 to 301, and the scores in the hippocampal lesion group ranged from 22 to 257. Unfortunately, this critical comparison is in the end complicated by the fact that the monkeys with combined lesions had less complete hippocampal damage (i.e., lesions confined to anterior hippocampus) than the monkeys with lesions restricted to hippocampus.

In summary, these two studies together provide limited support for the idea that combined lesions cause greater impairment than hippocampal lesions alone; however because of uncertainty about histology and other factors, the case is not yet a strong one. It is also worth emphasizing that, on some tasks that seem suitable for assessing memory, the impairment can be quite severe following hippocampal lesions alone. Thus the impairment was marked for delayed retention of visual and tactile object discriminations (Mahut et al., 1981), for delayed retention under the alternating reversal-retention procedure just described (Mahut et al., 1981), and for concurrent learning of object discriminations (Moss et al., 1981). It will obviously be important to obtain direct comparisons between hippocampal-damaged monkeys and monkeys with the combined lesion in these tasks, which bring out such a clear impairment in hippocampal-damaged monkeys.

B. A Precaution Concerning the Extent of Hippocampal Damage

One precaution that will need to be taken in all such comparisons is that there must be equivalence between the extent of the hippocampal lesions in the monkeys with the lesion restricted to the hippocampus and in the monkeys with the combined lesion. The possibility that these lesions could be of different size seems to have been recognized first by Orbach et al. (1960) in their early attempt to study the effects of medial temporal removals in the monkey. Their monkeys with combined hippocampal–amygdala lesions sustained "nearly complete removals sparing only the [posterior aspect beyond the] hippocampus-fornix confluence," whereas for the monkeys sustaining separate hippocampal removal "the anterior poles of the hippocampus were spared [Orbach et al., 1960, p. 237]." Later this same point was made by Correll and Scoville (1965b), who found bilateral large lesions of hippocampus in their monkeys with combined damage. However in their monkeys with selective hippocampal lesions they found the "hippocampus intact anterior to the lateral geniculate and complete destruction confined to an area between the midlateral geniculate and the posterior curve . . . the uncus sustained no damage [Cornell and Scoville, 1965b, p. 361]." By this description the monkeys were left with approximately the anterior one-third of the target structure intact.

Based on the comments that these early investigators have made about their lesions, we have reviewed all available studies of monkeys that involved either conjoint hippocampal–amygdala lesions ($N = 17$) or separate hippocampal lesions ($N = 20$) in an effort to determine the status of the anterior hippocampus in each case (Table 6.2). Of 17 studies of the combined lesion, we found that the anterior hippocampus was definitely included in the removal in 11, and likely to have been included in three. No histology was available for the remaining three. Of 20 studies of the hippocampal lesion, we found that the anterior hippocampus was definitely included in the removal in only three, and likely to have been included in an additional two. No histology was available for three studies. Thus, of studies presenting histology, the anterior hippocampus appears to have been removed in 14 of 14 studies of the combined lesion, and in only five of 17 studies of the single lesion. For the 12 studies of the single lesion in which sparing of anterior hippocampus occurred, we estimated that the sparing would have amounted to 20–30% of the extent of the hippocampus.

A review of the surgical procedure used to prepare these two operated groups allows us to understand how anterior sparing might result. For preparing combined lesions of hippocampus–amygdala, the approach is either frontal, in which case the hippocampal removal begins at its anterior aspect and moves caudally; or it is done through two entries, in which case the hippocampal excision is extended anteriorly to join the posterior limit reached during amygdala removal (Figure 6.15). In either case, the anterior hippocampus is consistently included in the lesion. However, for preparing lesions restricted to hippocampus, the approach is ventral, and the rostral extent of the removal is made with caution so as to avoid amygdala damage. The possibility that anterior hippocampus might sometimes be spared is obviously relevant to interpreting the studies in monkeys and especially relevant to making inferences about the human surgical cases. Case H.M., for example, was said to have developed profound amnesia following a removal that included the anterior two-thirds of the hippocampus. Studies with monkeys derived from this paradigmatic case and designed to test the hypothesis that the hippocampus itself is the critical structure would be of uncertain validity if the lesions spared the anterior third of the hippocampus.

Recent anatomical findings indicate why the extent of the lesion is of considerable importance. A lesion which spared the anterior third of hippocam-

TABLE 6.2
Was the Anterior Hippocampus Included in the Lesion?

	Definitely included	Likely included	Definitely spared	No histology
Conjoint hippocampal–amygdala lesion (17 studies)	11	3	0	3
Separate hippocampal lesion (20 studies)	3	2	12	3

pus would not entirely de-afferent and de-efferent this structure. It is now known that there are two distinct afferent and efferent systems of the hippocampal formation. The first is the subicular cortex of the hippocampal formation, the major target of the hippocampus proper, which lies adjacent to the hippocampus along its anterior–posterior extent. It receives a host of cortical inputs arising from a large expanse of temporal cortex medial and lateral to the rhinal sulcus (entorhinal cortex, areas TG, TE, TH–TF) (Van Hoesen, Rosene, & Mesulam, 1979). Subicular output reciprocates many of these projections (Rosene & Van Hoesen, 1977), and in addition substantial projections from the subiculum are directed toward a variety of other cortical and subcortical structures, including the frontal cortex, posterior cingulate cortex, and amygdala (Kosel & Van Hoesen, 1980; Rosene & Van Hoesen, 1977). The anterior portion of the hippo-campus in particular, via the adjacent portion of the subiculum, has substantial projections to entorhinal cortex, medial frontal cortex, and amygdala (Rosene & Van Hoesen, 1977). Accordingly, a lesion which spared the anterior third of the hippocampus would leave intact this anterior portion of its afferent and efferent system.

The second system, the fornix fimbria, has its origin in the subiculum of the hippocampal formation. The fibers contributing to this system emanate from the entire rostral–caudal extent of the subiculum, travel caudally, and then gather at the posterior end of the hippocampus. They then arch under the splenium of the corpus callosum and travel forward to their points of termination (see Figure 6.7). The fornix connects the hippocampus reciprocally with several areas of the septal complex, the hypothalamus, and the brainstem (DeVito, 1980; Poletti & Creswell, 1977; Swanson & Cowan, 1979; Valenstein & Nauta, 1959). Because these fibers gather together at the posterior end of the hippocampus, a lesion that spared the anterior third of the structure would nevertheless disrupt most if not all of these subcortical reciprocal connections. With these anatomical relationships in mind, it is clear that sparing the anterior third of the hippocampus would leave intact much of the subicular–cortical system but not the fornix–fimbria system.

In summary, the hypothesis that combined hippocampal–amygdala damage produces more severe deficits than hippocampal damage on certain tasks suitable for the study of amnesia has some evidence to support it. Yet direct comparisons are still needed in which histological reconstruction can verify the equivalence of the hippocampal removals in each group. Finally, it must be admitted that the pattern of behavioral effects associated with hippocam-pal–amygdala damage raises some of the same questions that were raised earlier in our review of the effects of hippocampal lesions. First, why do monkeys with combined damage perform so well on two-choice, visual discrimination prob-lems which take many sessions to learn and which therefore require retention of information from one day to the next? Second, why is impairment observed especially on certain spatial tasks and not on nonspatial versions of the same tasks? We will return to each of these points subsequently when we consider the problem of how amnesia should be assessed in monkeys.

C. The Temporal-Stem Hypothesis: Relevant Data

There are two kinds of evidence that could bear on this hypothesis. The first is evidence regarding the extent of temporal-stem damage in monkeys with other lesions that seem to affect memory. The second is evidence regarding the direct effects on behavior of selective damage to the temporal stem.

Evidence of the first kind became especially relevant to this issue after Horel (1978) pointed out that the temporal stem can be inadvertently included in lesions directed at the medial temporal region. Two studies have now specifically considered this question. In one, monkeys with hippocampal lesions without accompanying damage to the temporal stem, exhibited a severe impairment on concurrent discrimination learning (Moss et al., 1981). In a second, monkeys with hippocampal lesions and no temporal-stem damage exhibited an impairment in delayed, non-matching-to-sample with delays of 2 minutes (Mahut et al., 1982). These two studies make it clear that deficits in tasks considered sensitive to human amnesia can occur following lesions to the medial temporal region that spare the temporal stem.

Evidence of the second kind comes from two studies, which have assessed the behavioral effects of selective damage to temporal stem (Horel & Misantone, 1976; Zola-Morgan, Squire, & Miskin, 1982). In the first study lesions of the stem, without accompanying damage to hippocampus, severely impaired the ability of monkeys to relearn a preoperatively acquired visual discrimination, and the degree of impairment correlated with the extent of the lesion (Figure 6.18).

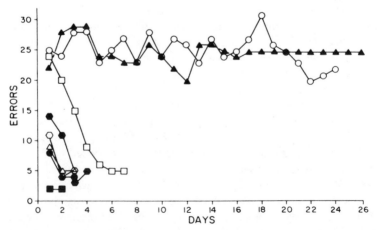

Figure 6.18. Postoperative relearning of various visual discrimination tasks by eight monkeys with lesions of temporal stem. The two monkeys with the most extensive lesions (▲——▲, ○——○) were unable to relearn. (From Horel & Misantone, 1976.)

However, this observation constitutes no real support for the hypothesis that temporal-stem damage causes amnesia. Monkeys exhibiting a visual discrimination deficit need not be considered amnesic. Failure on the visual discrimination task can reflect a visual information processing deficit, rather than amnesia, and has been taken as diagnostic of damage to area TE (Gross, 1973; Milner, 1954). This behavioral impairment need not be global like amnesia in that it can be restricted to the visual modality (Gross, 1973). The temporal stem contains both afferent and efferent TE connections. The second study (Zola-Morgan, *et al.*, 1982) was undertaken as a direct test of the temporal stem hypothesis, and it is described in the next section.

D. Temporal Stem versus Hippocampus–Amygdala: An Experiment

Monkeys with selective damage to the temporal stem, normal monkeys, and monkeys with conjoint damage to hippocampus–amygdala were first tested on a trial-unique, delayed non-matching-to-sample task, using well-spaced delays: 8 seconds, 15 seconds, 60 seconds, and 10 minutes. Figure 6.19 illustrates the intended surgical removals for each group. Representative lesions from the two operated groups have been described (Zola-Morgan *et al.*, 1982; Zola-Morgan & Squire, 1983). The temporal-stem lesion was made by removing part of the upper bank of the superior temporal sulcus to gain access to the white matter underlying the crux of the sulcus. The temporal stem was aspirated for

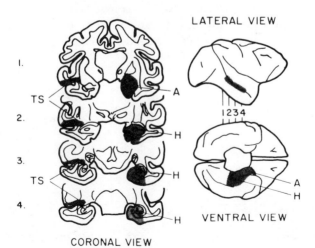

Figure 6.19. Temporal stem versus hippocampus–amygdala. Three views of the monkey brain illustrating the intended lesions. In the coronal views, the left side shows the temporal stem lesion and the right side shows the hippocampal–amygdala lesions. The lateral view shows the anterior–posterior extent of the temporal stem lesion. The levels of the coronal sections correspond to those indicated in the lateral and ventral views. TS, temporal stem; H, hippocampus; A, amygdala.

10–15 mm in its anterior–posterior extent using the lateral ventricle as a visual guide. Since the ventricle was not crossed, the hippocampus was left entirely intact.

The combined hippocampal–amygdala lesions were done in a single procedure, using two approaches on each side (Figure 6.15). The amygdala was removed by an approach through the frontal–temporal junction. The hippocampus was removed by a ventral approach that permitted excision of its anterior poles, the uncus, and the body of the hippocampus caudally to the region of the posterior curve. This approach to hippocampus spared the temporal stem because the lateral ventricle was not crossed during the operative procedure.

Two months following surgery, testing began by training monkeys (temporal stem, $N = 5$; hippocampus–amygdala, $N = 4$; normals, $N = 3$) to perform delayed nonmatching to sample with a delay of 8 seconds. All monkeys learned this task to a criterion of 90 correct responses in 100 consecutive trials. Following completion of training on this phase, the delay between sample and choice was lengthened in stages to 15 seconds, then to 60 seconds, and finally to 10 minutes, each stage tested for 100 trials.

Figure 6.20 shows that, as progressively longer delays were interposed between sample and choice, the performance of monkeys with hippocampal–amygdala lesions gradually deteriorated until at the 10-minute delay they were performing at chance. The animals with temporal stem damage, by contrast, scored 74% correct at the 10-minute delay, almost identical to the 79% score of normal animals. The same results were observed in the second phase of the study when the delays (8 seconds, 15 seconds, 60 seconds, or 10 minutes) were presented in a randomly mixed fashion during each daily session until monkeys had accumulated 50 trials at each delay (Figure 6.20).

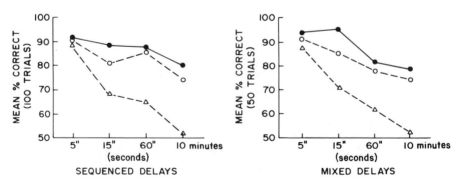

Figure 6.20. Trial-unique non-matching-to-sample. Normal monkeys (●——●), monkeys with temporal stem lesions (○- -○), and monkeys with conjoint hippocampal–amygdala lesions (△- -△) were tested on progressively longer delays presented in sequence from 8 seconds to 10 minutes (left) and then on the same delays presented in a mixed order (right). The HA group was severely impaired. The TS group was normal.

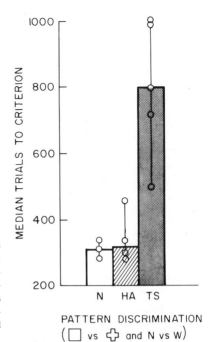

Figure 6.21. Average score for two pattern discrimination tasks by normal monkeys (N), monkeys with temporal stem lesions (TS), and monkeys with conjoint hippocampal–amygdala lesions (HA). Circles show individual scores for all monkeys. The TS group was impaired. The HA group was normal as measured by trials to criterion and mildly impaired as measured by errors to criterion.

In order to understand clearly this behavioral difference between monkeys with hippocampal–amygdala lesions and monkeys with temporal-stem lesions, it is essential to know that the difference is a specific one (i.e., that the deficit in monkeys with hippocampal–amygdala lesions is not a nonspecific result of brain damage or that the normal performance by temporal-stem animals is not due simply to the relatively small size of the lesions). One way to make this point is to demonstrate a "double dissociation" of symptoms (Teuber, 1955), whereby one lesion causes a clear impairment in Task A but not in Task B and a second lesion causes the reverse effect.

We chose pattern discrimination learning as Task B. The performance of the three groups on acquisition of two separate, two-dimensional pattern discrimination problems (□ versus + and N versus W) is shown in Figure 6.21. The group with temporal-stem lesions required a median of 800 trials to learn these tasks, significantly worse than the 310 trials required by the normal group. The temporal-stem group was also significantly poorer than the group of monkeys with hippocampal–amygdala lesions, who required a median of 345 trials. Relative to normal monkeys, the hippocampal–amygdala group was mildly impaired (significantly impaired in errors to criterion, 110 versus 99, $U = 0$, $p < .05$, but not in trials to criterion).

These results, taken together, provide a clear basis for rejecting the hypothesis that temporal-stem damage causes amnesia. Lesions of this region caused no discernible impairment of memory on a task that reliably reveals an impairment in human amnesic patients. The lesions did, however, disrupt visual information processing, presumably as a result of damage to afferents and efferents of area TE. By contrast, monkeys with conjoint hippocampal–amygdala lesions were markedly impaired on a task sensitive to human amnesia, confirming previous observations with this operated group using the same task (Mishkin, 1978). As discussed above (Sections VII,A & B) it is not yet clear whether hippocampal lesions themselves cause the greater part of this impairment or whether amygdala damage contributes to it in a crucial way.

Whereas the effects of medial temporal lesions described here do suggest an impairment such as that present in human amnesia, an important question remains. If poor performance by monkeys in delayed nonmatching to sample denotes impaired memory of the sort exhibited in human amnesia, how are we to understand the rather good memory exhibited by the same monkeys during day-to-day acquisition of visual discrimination? It is this question to which we turn next, as we consider the general issue of what kinds of tasks, among those given to monkeys, should be expected to be sensitive to the human amnesic syndrome.

VIII. THE BEHAVIORAL TASKS USED TO STUDY MEMORY IN MONKEYS: SOME ARE SENSITIVE TO HUMAN AMNESIA, BUT OTHERS ARE NOT

In previous sections we have seen that selective bilateral damage to the medial temporal region in monkeys impairs performance on certain tasks that would appear to be rather good indicators of the ability to learn and remember. Thus monkeys with hippocampal lesions and monkeys with conjoint damage to hippocampus and amygdala are consistently impaired in concurrent learning tasks, delayed retention of object discriminations, and also in delayed non-matching-to-sample when the delay is sufficiently long (Figure 6.22). This impairment seems similar to the memory impairment observed in human amnesia, since patient H.M. also failed matching-to-sample tasks (Milner & Taylor, 1972; Sidman et al., 1968) as well as other tasks that involved delays between learning and retention (Milner, 1972). Moreover, alcoholic Korsakoff patients were impaired on the concurrent learning task (Oscar-Berman & Zola-Morgan, 1980b), though other kinds of amnesic patients have not yet been given this task. These facts notwithstanding, monkeys with medial temporal lesions can do well on visual discrimination tasks. Indeed, their success on this particular task has been a reason for supposing that the behavioral impairment in monkeys with medial temporal lesions cannot be reconciled with the results for man (Orbach et al., 1960).

In this section, we argue that a *rapprochement* is now possible between these two bodies of data. We suggest that the neuropsychological facts of human

TASK	HIPPOCAMPUS				AMYGDALA				HIPPOCAMPUS PLUS AMYGDALA			
	POSTOPERATIVE RETEST OF PREOPERATIVE LEARNING		POSTOPERATIVE LEARNING		POSTOPERATIVE RETEST OF PREOPERATIVE LEARNING		POSTOPERATIVE LEARNING		POSTOPERATIVE RETEST OF PREOPERATIVE LEARNING		POSTOPERATIVE LEARNING	
	DEF	NO DEF	DEF	NO DEF	DEF	NO DEF	DEF	NO DEF	DEF	NO DEF	DEF	NO DEF
CONCURRENT LEARNING			27 [b]								6 [ ]	
			27 [b,r]								9 [ ]	
DELAYED RETENTION			21 [q,r]								21 [o]	
			21 [q,r]									
NONMATCHING-TO-SAMPLE (TWO MINUTE DELAYS)	25 [o,m]		25 [o,m]		25 [o,m]		25 [o,m]		25 [m]		25 [m]	
			23 [o]								46 [m]	

Figure 6.22. Performance by monkeys with medial temporal lesions on the tasks sensitive to human amnesia. Numbers enclosed in boxes are the reference numbers. See Figure 6.8 for a complete list of references. The letter notation used is the same as in Figure 6.8.

amnesia, as we now understand them, provide an account of memory impairment in man that is entirely consistent with the findings in monkey. Human amnesia is now known to be a selective impairment, in the sense that it does not encompass all forms of learning and memory. Thus not only is the capacity to acquire motor skills spared in the amnesic syndrome, as previously described by Milner (1962) and Corkin (1968), there is also preservation of the ability to acquire a range of cognitive skills including mirror reading and the solution to certain puzzles (Cohen, 1981; Cohen & Squire, 1980). These findings have led to a distinction between memory based on skills or procedures, which is spared in amnesia, and memory based on specific facts or data, which is impaired (Cohen, 1981; Cohen & Squire, 1980).

We believe that this distinction has useful application to the study of monkeys with medial temporal lesions. Specifically, when the tasks used to assess memory in monkeys are scrutinized with this distinction in mind, it is clear that some of them should be exquisitely sensitive to amnesia, whereas others would be expected to reveal either a mild memory impairment or none at all. Here we apply the distinction between kinds of memory to the learning of visual discrimination tasks, then to delayed retention of object discriminations, concurrent learning, and delayed matching and non-matching-to-sample.

The idea that the behavioral tasks used with brain-damaged monkeys might not always be sensitive to human amnesia has been recognized previously (Gaffan, 1974; Iversen, 1976), and has been discussed in the specific context of the visual discrimination task: "Until it is clear that visual discrimination learning involves the kind of mnemonic processing we have seen in humans after medial temporal lesions, it is premature to accept the task as a crucial test of memory function in the monkey. . . . In everyday human learning there are no strict counterparts of discrimination tasks in which the same piece of information is repeated *ad nauseam*. In humans, motor learning perhaps comes closest to this . . . [Iversen, 1976, pp. 15–16]."

A. The Visual Discrimination Task

This view can be developed further by asking whether the visual discrimination learning in monkeys might involve to a considerable extent what we have termed skill-based or procedural learning. According to many theories of simultaneous discrimination learning, two processes are involved in learning: the animal must come to attend to the appropriate stimulus dimension (e.g., brightness, orientation, or hue), and the animal must learn which of the two stimuli is rewarded. Often these ideas have been expressed as explicitly two-stage, attentional theories of learning, whereby an animal gradually (i.e., trial by trial) attends to the appropriate stimulus dimension and also increases the associative strength of the stimulus which is rewarded (Lovejoy, 1968; Sutherland & Mack-

intosh, 1971; Zeaman & House, 1963). Other accounts of discrimination learning, though explicitly one stage, nevertheless include a stimulus-specific learn-
ing-rate parameter to allow for the importance of both attention and increments in
associative strength (e.g., Mackintosh, 1975). In the case of pattern discrimination tasks, we will suggest that the process of tuning in the correct stimulus
dimension provides a clear example of skill learning. This process modifies the
pattern-analyzing operations themselves, changing the rules by which an animal
interprets the environment.

Stimulus dimensions, and the procedures involved in tuning them in, are
taken to be rather specific to individual discrimination tasks. To the extent that
stimulus dimensions are general (e.g., attend to the pattern, not to its color),
there should be considerable positive transfer between successive pattern discrimination tasks. Yet in the study described in Section VII, normal monkeys
exhibited no positive transfer between the two tasks (first task: $\bar{X} = 340$ trials, 91
errors; second task: $\bar{X} = 300$ trials, 96 errors; also see Figure 6.23). Indeed, it is
a common finding that monkeys do not show positive transfer from one visual
discrimination problem to the next (Harlow, 1944; Schrier & Harlow, 1957).
Accordingly, whereas the learning of a pattern discrimination may well include
the acquisition of some general procedures (e.g., the relevant dimension is the
pattern, not the color), the major work of the task would seem to be the selecting
or tuning in of features specific to the stimuli to be discriminated (e.g., □ versus

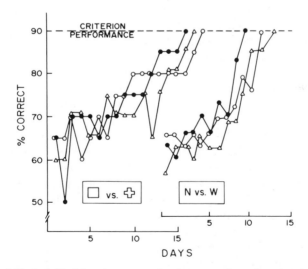

Figure 6.23. Individual learning curves for three normal monkeys learning two pattern
discrimination tasks in succession. For the first task, 20 trials were given each day. For the second
task, 30 trials were given each day. Although the second task was learned in fewer daily sessions than
the first, learning nevertheless required a similar number of trials and errors.

+, or N versus W). The idea that such procedures can be quite specific is also developed by Kolers (1975) in his work on reading skills with human subjects.

In contrast to learning the stimulus dimension, learning which stimulus is correct would appear to be a relatively minor component of the pattern discrimination task. Moreover, this information appears to be different than the information stored implicitly in altered pattern-analyzing operations. It constitutes specific knowledge about the world that is acquired through the use of these operations. It is a fact, an outcome, a proposition that is acquired as a result of operating upon the environment. We suggest that, at least in the initial phase of learning, knowledge of which stimulus is correct is represented explicitly in a directly accessible form.

This view supposes that pattern discrimination learning in monkeys is largely unaffected by medial temporal lesions because this learning is like skill learning in humans and lies outside the bounds of the amnesic syndrome. If this view is correct, then pattern discrimination learning should exhibit some of the same features exhibited by skill learning in humans. For example, learning should be gradual, just as the acquisition of mirror reading occurs slowly through practice. This expectation is confirmed in the individual learning curves of three normal monkeys learning two different pattern discriminations in succession (Figure 6.23), as described in Section VII (and in Figure 6.21). The gradual increment in performance exhibited by these monkeys has no clear counterpart in human discrimination learning. Human visual discrimination learning occurs typically in an almost all-or-none fashion, moving quickly from chance to perfect performance as soon as the appropriate stimulus dimension is discovered (Oscar-Berman & Zola-Morgan, 1980a, and personal communication).

Another feature of discrimination learning in monkeys that should parallel the findings for mirror reading in humans is that any portion of the learning thought to depend on a data-based, explicit representation should be susceptible to amnesia. Learning to mirror read unique sets of words proceeded normally in amnesic patients, and there was no forgetting between sessions (Figure 6.6). In the same study, however, amnesic patients learned to mirror read repeated words at a slower rate than control subjects and exhibited marked forgetting between sessions (Cohen & Squire, 1980). It was argued that the control subjects were advantaged in learning to read repeated words because in addition to acquiring a procedure for mirror reading (as the amnesic patients did), the control subjects benefited by recognizing the specific words that they were reading. Indeed, in the format of this study, whereby subjects saw words in sets of 3, control subjects were often able to say the final two words of each set in the repeated condition, as soon as they recognized the first word of the set. This kind of information is difficult for amnesic patients to acquire and is readily forgotten. By analogy, it is hypothesized that remembering which stimulus is correct during the course of pattern discrimination learning cannot be learned as a skill. Information about which stimulus is correct should therefore reveal some degree of forgetting from session to session in monkeys with medial temporal lesions.

This expectation is confirmed by the performance of four monkeys with hippocampal-amygdala lesions and three normal monkeys (Figure 6.24) during acquisition of the pattern discrimination tasks described in the preceding section. The mild deficit exhibited by the operated monkeys was accounted for entirely by their poor performance on the first five trials of each testing day (operated versus control monkeys, $t = 2.5$, $p < 0.05$). On the remaining trials of each testing day the operated monkeys performed like normal monkeys ($t = 1.2$, $p > 0.10$). These data indicate that the operated monkeys tended to forget some of what they had learned during each previous day. After 4–8 days of testing this overnight forgetting was no longer apparent.

These findings in monkeys, together with a consideration of the neuro-psychological facts of human amnesia, provide a way of understanding why visual discrimination learning can be largely spared in monkeys with medial temporal lesions. As we have seen, the case rests largely on the suggestion that visual discrimination learning in monkeys is fundamentally similar to motor-skill learning and cognitive-skill learning in man.

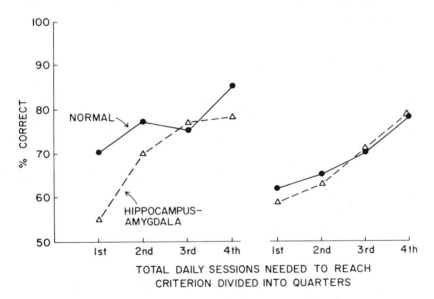

Figure 6.24. Monkeys with hippocampal–amygdala lesions ($N = 4$) and normal monkeys ($N = 3$) learned two pattern discriminations in succession. For each animal the number of daily sessions needed to reach criterion was determined, and the data were plotted to show acquisition performance during the first, second, third, and fourth quarters of training. The left panel shows average performance for the first five trials of daily sessions. The right panel shows average performance for the remaining trials of daily sessions.

The same neuropsychological perspective considered above can also be applied to delayed retention of object discriminations, a task that reveals a clear impairment in monkeys with medial temporal lesions. In the case of the two-dimensional pattern discrimination, which requires hundreds of trials to learn, we have suggested that performance depends largely on skill learning, which is not affected by medial temporal lesions. Discriminations between three-dimensional objects, however, can be learned more quickly, and when pairs of objects are specially selected for their discriminability (Mahut et al., 1981), monkeys can learn to discriminate between them in fewer than 50 trials. The increase in discriminability in such a task should greatly reduce the demand for skill learning (i.e., the gradual tuning in of the relevant stimulus dimension). When the discriminability between objects becomes so great that the task can be acquired in just 20 or 30 trials, instead of several hundred trials, it seems reasonable to suppose that the role of data-based, explicitly presented information (e.g., which stimulus is correct) would play a proportionally larger role. By this formulation, an object discrimination that takes 20–30 trials to learn should be expected to be more sensitive to the effects of medial temporal lesions than a pattern discrimination that takes 200–300 trials to learn. This expectation is confirmed by the impairment in delayed retention of simple object and tactile discriminations in monkeys with hippocampal or conjoint hippocampal–amygdala lesions (Mahut et al., 1981).

Based on the findings for our two pattern discrimination tasks (Figure 6.24) and the findings just cited for object discriminations (Mahut et al., 1981), we reviewed all available studies of monkeys that involved either separate hippocampal lesions or conjoint hippocampal–amygdala lesions. Together these studies report the findings for the acquisition of 48 different two-choice discrimination tasks, and 46 present numerical data. These 46 tasks were identified as either ones that could be learned by normal monkeys in no more than 80 trials ($N = 21$ tasks, average number of trials to criterion is 40) or ones that could be learned by normal monkeys in no fewer than 90 trials ($N = 25$ tasks, average number of trials to criterion is 200). Of the 21 tasks that could be learned in about 40 trials, 10 yielded a mild or severe impairment, whereas only 4 of the 25 tasks which took longer to learn yielded any sign of impairment ($\chi^2 = 4.0, p < 0.05$). Furthermore, as might be expected, impairment in the former group of tasks was even more noticeable when only those tasks were included in which acquisition required the bridging of at least one overnight interval. Thus, when 12 tasks that could be learned in a single session were excluded, the percentage of tasks yielding an impairment increased from 48 to 67%.

Altogether, this analysis provides support for the expectation that discrimination tasks requiring few trials to learn should bring out an impairment in monkeys with medial temporal lesions more reliably than discrimination tasks that require many trials to learn. Accordingly, the deficit associated with medial temporal lesions cannot be attributed to task difficulty or task complexity. We suggest that the impairment appears because the importance of skill learning in the quickly learned task has been decreased by simplifying the skill component (i.e., by increasing the distinctiveness of the discriminanda). In keeping with this idea, we have demonstrated impaired retention of easily learned visual discrimination tasks in monkeys with medial temporal lesions and in human amnesic patients (Zola-Morgan & Squire, 1983).

B. The Concurrent Learning Task

Another way to increase the importance of data-based learning would be to require the monkey to learn concurrently several different discriminations between pairs of objects. In such a task, monkeys must remember day-to-day a substantial amount of information concerning which objects are rewarded. By the formulation developed here, this requirement should increase the demand for data-based learning, and the concurrent learning task should be more sensitive to amnesia than the conventional discrimination task based on any one of the object pairs. The data are consistent with this point of view. Patients with Korsakoff syndrome were deficient in learning concurrent discriminations, though normal at learning a conventional discrimination task (Oscar-Berman & Zola-Morgan, 1980, 1980b). For monkeys, the concurrent task is one of the best for demonstrating an impairment following hippocampal lesions (Moss et al., 1981) or conjoint hippocampal–amygdala lesions (Correll & Scoville, 1965a, 1970).

C. Matching-to-Sample Tasks

Of all the tasks studied, those that have received the most parallel attention in monkey and human work are delayed matching and non-matching-to-sample. In this task training is first given at a short delay, from 0 to 10 seconds. Then after some performance criterion is reached, the interval between sample trial and test trial may be extended to assess the ability to perform across considerably longer delays. There is good agreement that, provided the delay is sufficiently long, these tasks are sensitive to both human amnesia and to the effects of medial temporal lesions in monkey. The distinction between kinds of memory that has been applied to visual discrimination and concurrent learning tasks can also be applied to initial acquisition of delayed matching and non-matching-to-sample at short delays and to tests given at long delays.

Skill learning embraces not only the specific pattern-analyzing abilities needed to acquire a new visual discrimination, or mirror-reading, but also the more general features of a task (i.e., testing habits or the rules of the game). H.M., for example, was able to remember testing habits over the course of separate experimental sessions (Corkin, 1968). In the case of matching-to-sample, the testing habits would include information that reward is sometimes under the objects, that the familiar object in any pair is rewarded, and that the un-familiar object is not. Presumably, these aspects of a task can be learned by amnesic patients and by monkeys with medial temporal lesions. This ability, together with the ability of patients to hold information in immediate memory, would explain how initial acquisition can occur at short delays. Since training on the matching task is often begun at a 0-second delay, it is easy to see under these circumstances how H.M. (Milner & Taylor, 1972; Prisko, 1963; Sidman *et al.*, 1968) and monkeys with medial temporal lesions (Cordeau & Mahut, 1964; Correll & Scoville, 1965b) are unimpaired and how they can remain unimpaired subsequently when the delay is increased to a few seconds.

Sometimes, however, monkeys in these tasks are trained postoperatively beginning at delays of 8 or 10 seconds (Mahut *et al.*, 1982; Zola-Morgan *et al.*, 1982) (as described in sections VI,B and VII), and in this case monkeys learn more slowly than normal. For example, in our study (Zola-Morgan *et al.*, 1981) normal monkeys required a mean of 140 trials to learn the task initially, and monkeys with conjoint hippocampal–amygdala lesions required 790 trials. This result can be understood if it is supposed that operated monkeys are disadvan-taged in this task by not being able to depend from the outset on an explicit, data-based record of which object is rewarded on each sample trial. Instead, they need to engage or develop specific skills of paying strict attention and avoiding dis-traction, so that they can maintain information in memory. Presumably, the same is true for normal monkeys, who are typically taught matching-to-sample at a delay of 0 seconds or a few seconds, and who, after this delay is gradually increased, are able to perform well at delays of 2 minutes (Mahut *et al.*, 1982; Mishkin, 1978; Zola-Morgan *et al.*, 1982).

This point is easiest to understand by analogy to human amnesia. Whereas H.M. can recall perfectly verbal material such as consonant trigrams (Sidman *et al.*, 1968) or three-digit numbers (Milner, 1959) for many seconds or minutes by engaging in rehearsal, there is no reason to think that he should be able to do this from the outset; or at all, until he knows that the task is to remember the material. Then he could engage in or develop "rehearsing procedures." To put it differ-ently, we predict that if H.M. were given no verbal instructions and began the automated matching-to-sample task used by Sidman *et al.* (1968) at a delay of 10 seconds or longer, he would be impaired relative to normal subjects. His perfor-mance should reach a normal level on this task only after he learned to direct his attention and to engage in rehearsal. By contrast normal subjects should perform better than H.M. at the outset, because they can draw on an explicit record of recent information, and for a 10-second delay would not need to engage in special techniques to achieve successful performance.

For delays exceeding 10 seconds, the situation is different. Whereas am-nesic patients and monkeys with medial temporal lesions are capable of remem-bering information for short intervals, they fail altogether at longer intervals.

Thus, except when he could employ verbal rehearsal and avoid distraction, H.M. performed poorly at delayed matching-to-sample at delays longer than 10–15 seconds (Milner & Taylor, 1972; Sidman *et al.*, 1968). Similarly, on the delayed non-matching-to-sample task the performance of monkeys with conjoint hippo-campal–amygdala lesions was near 60% at delays of 1 minute and was no better than chance at delays of 10 minutes (Mishkin, 1978; Zola-Morgan *et al.*, 1982).

We suggest that this deficit at long delays occurs because matching-to-sample and non-matching-to-sample are particularly clear examples of tasks that depend on an explicit record in memory. To perform well on these tasks after a long delay requires the ability to recognize a stimulus object as one that was seen recently, or as one seen in a particular time and place. By the view developed here, memory for the sample stimulus is ordinarily represented as a fact, a specific item in memory that results from having applied a particular procedure.

This same analysis helps us understand why amnesic patients are impaired not only on the delayed matching-to-sample problem, but on other kinds of recognition memory tasks as well (Huppert & Piercy, 1978; Squire, Wetzel, & Slater, 1978). That is, not only is there a failure to remember specifically when and where something was seen, as the delayed matching-to-sample impairment might suggest, but there is a deficit in yes–no recognition tasks and multiple-choice tasks where memory for time and place would not appear to play an important role.

The view that amnesia reflects a deficiency in acquisition of specific facts and data seems to account for this kind of deficit. This kind of memory includes representation of time and place and also representation of specific data in a way that permits later recall and recognition, independent of time and place information. This claim is supported by the fact that low-frequency events have not been shown to advantage disproportionately the recognition ability of amnesic patients. Unlike high-frequency events, which occur both inside and outside the experimental setting, memory for low-frequency events should place minimal burden on the need for information about time and place. Accordingly, if the deficit in amnesia were limited to memory for when and where an event occurred, then recognition memory for low-frequency events (not depending as much on that sort of information) might be unusually good in amnesic patients. However, there is little evidence that any kind of recognition task can benefit amnesic patients disproportionately (Squire & Cohen, 1983).

At the same time, the view that skill learning is preserved in amnesia suggests that recognition-like tasks might nevertheless be constructed in which amnesic patients would be advantaged (see Mandler, 1980, for a review of recognition memory germane to this issue). Thus, if the operations used to encode new material are themselves preserved, then in addition to demonstrating access to these encoding procedures through skill learning, an amnesic patient might also demonstrate retention of them under certain other testing conditions.

For example, upon seeing two pictures (one of which had been presented before), he might show differential behavior toward them if he were asked a
question directed at the encoding procedures rather than at the data that results
from these procedures. For example, one might ask the patient to judge which of
these pictures he preferred (see Kunst-Wilson & Zajonc, 1980, for a demonstration of the effects of experience on preference judgments in the absence of
recognition of familiarity).

D. Spatial Tasks

A final point about the tasks used to study amnesia in monkeys concerns
the finding that their behavioral impairment appears to include a spatial factor
(Figure 6.12). Even more evidence for a spatial factor has accumulated from the
behavioral study of hippocampal lesions in rats and from the findings of single
cell recordings in freely moving rats. Indeed, these observations and a monu-
mental review of the available data have recently formed the basis of a proposal
about hippocampal function whose central theme is that the hippocampus forms
and stores a map of an animal's spatial environment (O'Keefe & Nadel, 1978).

A literal interpretation of this proposal does not fit well either the findings
from humans with known damage to the hippocampal region (Squire, 1979) or
the findings from operated monkeys as reviewed here. The human cases seem to
have amnesia rather than an impairment that is in any sense restricted to spatial
operations. For example, patients with medial temporal resections of the right
hemisphere have difficulty in image-mediated verbal learning (Jones-Gotman &
Milner, 1978) and facial recognition (Milner, 1968), and the severity of these
deficits correlates with the extent of hippocampal removal. Moreover, the amnesia associated with bilateral medial temporal damage (e.g., case H.M.) certainly includes the spatial domain but is not limited to it. H.M. has difficulty
learning mazes, finding his way around, and reproducing a floor plan of his
house (Milner, Corkin, & Teuber, 1968), but he also has difficulty remembering
other things, such as colors, sounds, and tactual impressions. Even if one keeps
in mind the uncertainty as to whether hippocampal damage alone or damage to
hippocampus plus amygdala causes amnesia in man, patients with brain damage
involving hippocampus appear to have a memory impairment that includes spatial information rather than an impairment that is primarily spatial.

For the most part, the same can be said for monkeys with hippocampal
lesions. The deficit that occurs in tasks such as delayed matching-to-sample,
concurrent learning, and delayed retention of object discriminations (Figure
6.11) is not spatial in any obvious way. We have suggested here that the deficit
exhibited in these three tasks parallels the human findings and reflects a loss of
the ability to acquire a particular kind of memory. One might envision a concept
of space that is more abstract so that it somehow encompasses image-mediated
learning, faces, and the variety of things that amnesic patients cannot remember.

However, at this level of abstraction a spatial hypothesis becomes difficult to distinguish from a memory hypothesis.

The idea that the role of the hippocampus extends beyond strictly spatial operations has also been raised in the context of studies with rat and rabbit (Berger, Clark, & Thompson, 1980; Hirsch, 1974; Kesner, 1980; Moore, 1979; Olton et al., 1979; Solomon, 1979). Yet the view that the deficit following hippocampal lesions extends beyond spatial operations does not help us understand why in monkeys it seems to include a spatial factor, particularly if one holds that the deficit is to be explained in terms of memory dysfunction. Perhaps there are differences between rats, monkey, and man that explain why a spatial factor emerges more clearly in one species than another.

Before considering such differences however, more needs to be known about the deficit. First, the evidence for a spatial factor in monkey is based entirely on the findings for reversal tasks and spatial alternation (Figure 6.8). If the deficit following medial temporal lesions were spatial in any important way, it should be worthwhile to look for it in rigorous comparisons between delayed response and delayed matching-to-sample, or in other comparisons pitting memory for position against memory for objects. Second, in amnesic patients it should be worthwhile to search deliberately for evidence of greater impairment in the retention of spatial information relative to other kinds of information. For patients with medial temporal lesions, we know of no data bearing on this issue. Patients with Korsakoff syndrome, whose visual and spatial discrimination reversal learning has been compared in one study, were equivalently impaired in each task (Oscar-Berman & Zola-Morgan, 1980a).

However we come to understand the way that space is involved in the effects of medial temporal lesions, it should be emphasized that it is difficult to separate entirely discussion of space from discussion of memory. Thus one might speak of a spatial mapping system that provides a framework for embedding memory (Nadel & Willner, 1980). In any case, given the findings for amnesic patients and the similar findings in monkeys with medial temporal lesions, it seems reasonable to begin these discussions with an hypothesis of memory impairment. The available data for different species may reflect differences in what animals best remember or in which schemata or frameworks are best suited for embedding memory, rather than reflecting fundamental differences in brain organization or differences in the function of specific brain regions. Rats, for example, depend heavily on spatial information to learn about their environment, whereas humans have access to diverse modes of information storage.

IX. SUMMARY

The purpose of this chapter has been to consider the neurology of memory in the light of attempts to establish a model of human amnesia in the monkey. These attempts began when well-studied surgical cases of human amnesia drew attention to the medial temporal region of the brain, and particularly to the hippocampal formation. For the most part, efforts to reproduce the human amnesic syndrome in monkeys have had a mixed success. The main point of this chapter is the proposition that the monkey and human data can now be brought into good correspondence. This proposition is based largely on new information about (1) which brain regions are critically involved in memory functions and (2) the nature of the deficit in human amnesia, which helps to identify the behavioral tasks appropriate for studying amnesia in monkeys.

In the case of the brain regions that are involved, there has been uncertainty whether amnesia depends on damage to the hippocampus, on conjoint damage to the hippocampus and amygdala, or on damage to temporal-lobe white matter (e.g., temporal stem). The possibility that temporal-stem damage causes amnesia can now be ruled out by the data. The possibility that conjoint damage to hippocampus and amygdala is needed to produce amnesia, rather than the more traditional view that only hippocampal damage is required, must be regarded as an important new hypothesis regarding the neurology of memory. This proposal remains tentative, however, because (1) there have been only two direct comparisons between monkeys with hippocampal lesions and monkeys with combined hippocampal–amygdala lesions involving any of the three critical tasks that we have identified as sensitive to human amnesia, and the combined lesion group was more impaired in only one of these compairsons; (2) when all studies of monkeys with hippocampal lesions and monkeys with combined hippocampal–amygdala lesions are considered together, there has been a decided tendency for the anterior third of the hippocampus to be spared in monkeys with lesions of the hippocampus and for it to be included in monkeys with the combined lesion. This difference could give the impression of there being greater amnesia in the group with the combined lesion even if the hippocampus itself were the critical structure.

In the case of the behavioral tasks used to study memory in the monkey, it is now clear that they vary in how relevant they are to the human amnesic syndrome. A proposal founded in studies of human amnesia has been developed to account for the fact that the human amnesic syndrome is selective and spares some forms of learning and memory such as motor learning and cognitive-skill learning. This formulation distinguishes between skills and the facts or data obtained by engaging in skills (i.e., between changes in processing systems and the outcomes of using these systems). These ideas lead to framework for understanding those tasks at which human amnesic patients can and cannot succeed. In this chapter, we have attempted to apply this distinction to the tasks used in studies with monkeys and to show that this distinction helps the human work and the monkey work to be brought into correspondence. An important part of this argument is the contention that visual discrimination learning in monkey resembles in many respects motor learning and cognitive skill learning in humans and should therefore not be severely affected by medial temporal lesions.

It seems fair to say that it has been uncertainty about which tasks are appropriate to detect amnesia, more than any other factor, that has thwarted attempts to establish an animal model of human global amnesia. The understanding that can now be brought to this problem is cause for optimism. With the group of tasks identified here, which seems entirely appropriate for studying amnesia in both humans and monkey, it will be possible to address the questions that remain about the neurology of medial temporal amnesia and to extend the same analysis to diencephalic amnesia. The answers are close at hand. The promise of an animal model of human global amnesia is an exciting one, as a model should open the way to a wide variety of neurobiological studies that will have rich functional significance.

ACKNOWLEDGMENTS

We thank Lynn Nadel, Neal Cohen, and Helen Mahut for their comments on various sections of this chapter, and Elizabeth Statzer for preparing the manuscript.

REFERENCES

Andersen, R. Cognitive changes after amygdalotomy. *Neuropsychologia*, 1978, *16*, 439–451.
Andy, O. J., Jurko, M. F., & Hughes, J. R. Amygdalotomy for bilateral temporal lobe seizures. *South Medical Journal*, 1975, *68*, 743–748.
Baddeley, A. Implications of neuropsychological evidence for theories of normal memory. In D. E. Broadbent & L. Weiskrantz (Eds.), *Philosophical Transactions of the Royal Society of London*, pp. 59–72. London: The Royal Society, 1982.
Bagshaw, M. H., & Benzies, S. Multiple measures of the orienting reaction and their dissociation after amygdalectomy in monkeys. *Experimental Neurology*, 1968, *20*, 175–187.
Bagshaw, M. H., & Pribram, K. H. Effects of amygdalectomy on transfer of training in monkeys. *Journal of Comparative and Physiological Psychology*, 1965, *59*, 118–121.
Barrett, T. W. Studies of the function of the amygdaloid complex in *Macaca mulatta*. *Neuropsychologia*, 1969, *7*, 1–12.
Bartlett, F. C. *Remembering*. London & New York: Cambridge University Press, 1932.
Bechterew, W. W. von Demonstration eines gehirns mit zerstorung der vorderen und inneren theile der Hirnrinde beider Schlafenlappen. *Neurologisches Centralblatt*, 1900, *19*, 990.
Benson, D. F., Marsden, C. D., & Meadows, J. C. The amnesic syndrome of posterior cerebral artery occlusion. *Acta Neurologica Scandinavica*, 1974, *50*, 133–145.
Berger, T. W., Clark, G. A., & Thompson, R. F. Learning-dependent neuronal responses recorded from limbic system brain structures during classical conditioning. *Physiological Psychology*, 1980, *8*, 155–167.
Bergson, H. L. *Matter and memory* (authorized translation by Nancy M. Paul & W. Scott Palmer). London: Allen, 1910.
Brierley, J. B. Neuropathology of amnesic states. In C. W. M. Whitty & O. L. Zangwill (Eds.), *Amnesia* (2nd ed., pp. 199–223). London: Butterworth, 1977.
Brierley, J. B., & Beck, E. The effects upon behavior of lesions in the dorsomedial and anterior thalamic nuclei of cat and monkey. Experimental lesions in thalamic nuclei. *Neurological Basis of Behavior, Ciba Foundation Symposium, 1957*, 1958, 90–104.
Brion, S., & Mikol, J. Atteinte du noyau lateral dorsal du thalamus et syndrome de Korsakoff alcoolique. *Journal of Neurosciences*, 1978, *38*, 249–261.

Brooks, D. N., & Baddeley, A. What can amnesic patients learn? *Neuropsychologia,* 1976, *14,* 111–112.

Brown, T. S. Olfactory and visual discrimination in the monkey after selective lesions of the temporal lobe. *Journal of Comparative and Physiological Psychology,* 1963, *56,* 764–768.

Bruner, J. S. Modalities of memory. In G. A. Talland & N. C. Waugh (Eds.), *The pathology of memory* (pp. 253–259). New York: Academic Press, 1969.

Butters, N., & Cermak, L. S. *Alcoholic Korsakoff's syndrome: An information processing approach to amnesia.* New York: Academic Press, 1980.

Cermak, L. S. (Eds.) *Human Memory and Amnesia.* Hillsdale, New Jersey: Lawrence Erlbaum Associates, 1982.

Cermak, L. W., Lewis, R., Butters, N., & Goodglass, H. Role of verbal mediation in performance of motor tasks by Korsakoff patients. *Perceptual and Motor Skills,* 1973, *37,* 259–262.

Cermak, L. S., Reale, L., & DeLuca, D. Korsakoff patients' nonverbal vs. verbal memory: Effects of interference and mediation on rate of information loss. *Neuropsychologia,* 1977, *15,* 303–310.

Chow, K. L. Lack of behavioral effects following destruction of some thalamic association nuclei in monkey. *AMA Archives of Neurological Psychiatry,* 1954, *71,* 762–791.

Cohen, N. J. *Neuropsychological evidence for a distinction between procedural and declarative knowledge in human memory and amnesia.* Doctoral thesis, University of California, San Diego, 1981.

Cohen, N. J., & Squire, L. R. Preserved learning and retention of pattern-analyzing skill in amnesia: Dissociation of knowing how and knowing that. *Science,* 1980, *210,* 207–210.

Cohen, N. J., & Squire, L. R. Retrograde amnesia and remote memory impairment. *Neuropsychologia,* 1981, *19,* 337–356.

Cordeau, J. P., & Mahut, H. Some long-term effects of temporal lobe resections on auditory and visual discrimination in monkeys. *Brain,* 1964, *87,* 177–188.

Corkin, S. Acquisition of motor skill after bilateral medial temporal-lobe excision. *Neuropsychologia,* 6, 1968, 225–265.

Correll, R. E., & Scoville, W. B. Effects of medial temporal lesions on visual discrimination performance. *Journal of Comparative and Physiological Psychology,* 1965, *60,* 175–181. (a)

Correll, R. E., & Scoville, W. B. Performance on delayed match following lesions of medial temporal lobe structures. *Journal of Comparative and Physiological Psychology,* 1965, *60,* 360–367. (b)

Correll, R. E., & Scoville, W. B. Significance of delay in the performance of monkeys with medial temporal lobe resections. *Experimental Brain Research,* 1967, *4,* 85–96.

Correll, R. E., & Scoville, W. B. Relationship of ITI to acquisition of serial visual discriminations following temporal rhinencephalic resection in monkeys. *Journal of Comparative and Physiological Psychology,* 1970, *70,* 464–469.

Corsellis, J. A. N. The limbic areas in Alzheimer's disease and in other conditions associated with dementia. *Alzheimer's Disease and Related Conditions, Ciba Foundation Symposium, 1969,* 1970, 34–50.

Dahl, D., Ingram, W. R., & Knott, J. R. Diencephalic lesions and avoidance learning in cats. *Archives of Neurology (Chicago),* 1962, *1,* 314–319.

DeArmand, S. J., Fusco, M. M., & Dewey, M. M. *Structure of the human brain* (2nd ed.). London & New York: Oxford University Press, 1976.

Delacour, J. Role of temporal lobe structures in visual short-term memory, using a new test. *Neuropsychologia,* 1977, *15,* 681–684.

DeVito, J. L. Subcortical projections to the hippocampal formation in squirrel monkey (Saimiri Sciureus). *Brain Research Bulletin,* 1980, *3,* 285–289.

Douglas, R. J. The hippocampus and behavior. *Psychological Bulletin,* 1967, *67,* 416–442.

Douglas, R. J., Barrett, T. W., Pribram, K. H., & Cerny, M. C. Limbic lesions and error reduction. *Journal of Comparative and Physiological Psychology*, 1969, *68*, 437–441.

Douglas, R. J., & Pribram, K. H. Learning and limbic lesions. *Neuropsychologia*, 1966, *4*, 197–220.

Douglas, R. J., & Pribram, K. H. Distraction and habituation in monkeys with limbic lesions. *Journal of Comparative and Physiological Psychology*, 1969, *69*, 473–480.

Downer, J. L. de C. Changes in visual gnostic functions and emotional behavior following unilateral temporal pole damage to the "split-brain" monkey. *Nature (London)*, 1961, *191*, 50–51.

Drachman, D. A., & Adams, R. D. Acute herpes simplex and inclusion body encephalitis. *Archives of Neurology (Chicago)*, 1962, *7*, 45–63.

Drachman, D. A., & Ommaya, A. K. Memory and the hippocampal complex. *Archives of Neurology (Chicago)*, 1964, *10*, 411–425.

Gaffan, D. Recognition impaired and association intact in the memory of monkeys after transection of the fornix. *Journal of Comparative Physiological Psychology*, 1974, *86*, 1100–1109.

Gilman, S. Cerebral disorders after open-heart operations. *New England Journal of Medicine*, 1965, *272*, 489–498.

Goddard, G. V. Functions of the amygdala. *Psychological Bulletin*, 1964, *62*, 89–109.

Gross, C. G. Inferotemporal cortex and vision. In E. Stellar & J. M. Sprague (Eds.), *Progress in physiological psychology* (Vol. 5). New York: Academic Press, 1975.

Harlow, H. F. Studies in discrimination learning by monkeys. I. The learning of discrimination series and the reversal of discrimination series. *Journal of General Psychiatry*, 1944, *30*, 3–12.

Hawkins, R. D., Abrams, T. W., Carew, T. J., Kandel, E. R. A cellular mechanism of classical conditioning in Aplysia: activity-dependent amplification of presynaptic facilitation. *Science*, 1983, *219*, 401–404.

Hirsch, R. The hippocampus and contextual retrieval of information from memory: A theory. *Behavioral Biology*, 1974, *12*, 421–444.

Hirst, W. The amnesic syndrome: descriptions and explanations. *Psychological Bulletin*, 1982, *91*, 435–460.

Horel, J. A. The neuroanatomy of amnesia: a critique of the hippocampal memory hypothesis. *Brain*, 1978, *101*, 403–445.

Horel, J. A., & Misantone, L. J. Visual discrimination impaired by cutting temporal lobe connections. *Science*, 1976, *193*, 336–338.

Huppert, F. A., & Piercey, M. Dissociation between learning and remembering in organic amnesia. *Nature (London)*, 1978, *275*, 317–318.

Huppert, F. A., & Piercy, M. Normal and abnormal forgetting in organic amnesia: Effects of locus of lesion. *Cortex*, 1979, *15*, 385–390.

Inglis, J. Shock, surgery, and cerebral symmetry. *British Journal of Psychiatry*, 1970, *117*, 143–148.

Isaacson, R. L. Hippocampal destruction in man and other animals. *Neuropsychologia*, 1972, *10*, 47–64.

Isseroff, A., Rosvold, H. E., Galkin, T. W., and P. S. Goldman-Rakic. Spatial memory impairments following damage to the mediodorsal nucleus of the thalamus in Rhesus monkeys. *Brain Research*, 1982, *232*, 97–113.

Iversen, S. D. Do hippocampal lesions produce amnesia in animals? *International Review of Neurobiology*, 1976, *19*, 1–49.

Jacobsen, C. F., & Elder, J. H., II The effect of temporal lobe lesions on delayed response in monkeys. *Comparative Psychological Monographs*, 1936, No. 3 (Whole No. 63).

Jones, B., & Mishkin, M. Limbic lesions and the problem of stimulus-reinforcement associations. *Experimental Neurology*, 1972, *36*, 362–377.

Jones-Gotman, M., & Milner, B. Right temporal-lobe contribution of image-mediated verbal learning. *Neuropsychologia*, 1978, *16*, 61–71.

Kandel, E. R. *Cellular basis of behavior*. New York: Freeman Press, 1976.

Kandel, E. R., & Schwartz, J. H. Molecular biology of learning: modulation of transmitter release.
Science, 1982, *218*, 433–443.

Kaushall, P. I., Zetin, M., & Squire, L. R. A psychosocial study of chronic, circumscribed amnesia.
Journal of Nervous and Mental Disease, 1981, *169*, 383–389.

Kesner, R. P. An attribute analysis of memory: The role of hippocampus. *Physiological Psychology*,
1980, *8*, 189–197.

Kim, C., Chang, H. K., & Chu, J. W. Consequences of ablating mammillary bodies in dogs.
Journal of Comparative and Physiological Psychology, 1967, *63*, 469–476.

Kimble, D. P. Hippocampus and internal inhibition. *Psychological Bulletin*, 1968, *70*, 285–295.

Kimble, D. P., & Pribram, K. H. Hippocampectomy and behavioral sequences. *Science*, 1963, *139*,
824–825.

Kinsbourne, M., & Wood, F. Short-term memory processes and the amnesic syndrome. In D.
Deutsch & J. A. Deutsch (Eds.), *Short-term memory* (pp. 43–63). New York: Academic Press,
1975.

Kolers, P. A. Specificity of operations in sentence recognition. *Cognitive Psychology*, 1975, *7*,
289–306.

Kolers, P. A. Pattern-analyzing memory. *Science*, 1976, *191*, 1280–1281.

Kolers, P. A. A pattern-analyzing basis of recognition. In L. S. Cermak & F. I. M. Craik (Eds.),
Levels of processing in human memory (pp. 363–384). Hillsdale, NJ: Lwarence Erlbaum
Associates, 1979.

Korsakoff, S. S. Distrubance of psychic function in alcoholic paralysis and its relation to the
distrubance of the psychic sphere in multiple neuritis of non-alcoholic origin. *Vestnik
Psichiatril*, 1887, *4*, fasc. 2.

Kosel, K. C., & Van Hoesen, G. W. Extrahippocampal cortical projections from the entorhinal
cortex in the rat and monkey. *Society for Neuroscience Abstracts, 10th Annual Meeting, Cincin-
nati, Ohio*, 1980, *6*, 504.

Kreickhaus, E. E. The mammillary bodies: The function and anatomical connections. *Acta Biologiae
Experimentalis (Warsaw)*, 1967, *27*, 319–337.

Kunst-Wilson, W. R., & Zajonc, R. B. Affective discrimination of stimuli that cannot be recognized, *Science*, 1980, *207*, 557–558.

Lhermitte, F. & Signaret, J-L. Analyse neuropsychologique et differenciation des syndromes am-
nesique. *Revue Neurologique Paris*, 1972, *126*, 161–178.

Lovejoy, E. *Attention in discrimination learning*. San Francisco: Holden-Day, 1968.

Lund, R. D. *Development and plasticity of the brain*. London & New York: Oxford University Press,
1978.

Lynch, G., & Schubert, P. The use of in vitro brain slices for multidisciplinary studies of synaptic
function. *Annual Review of Neuroscience*, 1980, *3*, 1–22.

Mackintosh, N. J. A theory of attention: Variations in the associability of stimuli with reinforcement.
Psychological Review, 1975, *82*, 276–298.

Mahut, H. Spatial and object reversal learning in monkeys with partial temporal lobe ablations.
Neuropsychologia, 1971, *9*, 409–424.

Mahut, H. A selective spatial deficit in monkeys after transection of the fornix. *Neuropsychologia*,
1972, *10*, 65–74.

Mahut, H., & Cordeau, J. P. Spatial reversal deficit in monkeys after amygdalohippocampal ablations. *Experimental Neurology*, 1963, *7*, 426–434.

Mahut, H., Moss, M., & Zola-Morgan, S. Retention deficits after combined amygdalo-hippocampal
and selective hippocampal resections in the monkey. *Neuropsychologia*, 1981, *19*, 201–225.

Mahut, H., & Zola, S. M. A non-modality specific impairment in spatial learning after fornix lesions in monkeys. *Neuropsychologia,* 1973, *11,* 255–269.

Mahut, H., Zola-Morgan, S., & Moss, M. Hippocampal resections impair associative learning and recognition memory in the monkey. *Journal of Neuroscience,* 1982, *2,* 1214–1229.

Mair, W. G. P., Warrington, E. K., & Weiskrantz, L. Memory disorder in Korsakoff's psychosis: A neuropathological and neuropsychological investigation of two cases. *Brain,* 1979, *102,* 749–783.

Mandler, G. Recognizing: The judgment of previous occurrence. *Psychological Review,* 1980, *87,* 252–271.

Marslen-Wilson, W. D., & Teuber, H.-L. Memory for remote events in anterograde amnesia: Recognition of public figures from newsphotographs. *Neuropsychologia,* 1975, *13,* 353–364.

Mills, R. P., & Swanson, P. D. Vertical oculomotor apraxia and memory loss. *Annals of Neurology,* 1978, *4,* 149–153.

Milner, B. Intellectual function of the temporal lobes. *Psychological Bulletin,* 1954, *51,* 42–62.

Milner, B. Memory defect in bilateral lesions. *Psychiatric Research Reports,* 1959, *11,* 43–52.

Milner, B. Les troubles de la mémoire accompagnant des lésions hippocampiques bilatérales. In *Physiologie de l'Hippocampe.* Paris: Centre National de la Rechezche Scientifique, 1962.

Milner, B. Amnesia following operation on the temporal lobes. In C. W. M. Whitty & O. L. Zangwill (Eds.), *Amnesia* (pp. 109–133). London: Butterworth, 1966.

Milner, B. Disorders of memory after brain lesions in man. Preface: Material-specific and generalized memory loss. *Neuropsychologia,* 1968, *6,* 175–179.

Milner, B. Memory and the medial temporal regions of the brain. In K. H. Pribram & D. E. Broadbent (Eds.), *Biology of memory* (pp. 29–50). New York: Academic Press, 1970.

Milner, B. Disorders of learning and memory after temporal lobe lesions in man. *Clinical Neurosurgery,* 1972, *19,* 421–446.

Milner, B. Hemispheric specialization: Scope and limits. In F. O. Schmitt & F. G. Worden (Eds.), *The Neurosciences: Third Study Program* (pp. 75–89). Cambridge, MA: MIT Press, 1974.

Milner, B., Corkin, S., & Teuber, H.-L. Further analysis of the hippocampal amnesic syndrome: 14-year follow-up study of H.M. *Neuropsychologia,* 1968, *6,* 215–234.

Milner, B., & Taylor, L. Right hemispheric superiority in tactile pattern recognition after cerebral commissurotomy: Evidence for nonverbal memory. *Neuropsychologia,* 1972, *10,* 1–15.

Mishkin, M. Visual discrimination performance following partial ablations of the temporal lobe. II. Ventral surface vs. hippocampus. *Journal of Comparative and Physiological Psychology,* 1954, *47,* 187–193.

Mishkin, M. Memory in monkeys severely impaired by combined but not by separate removal of amygdala and hippocampus. *Nature (London),* 1978, *273,* 297–298.

Mishkin, M. A memory system in the monkey. In D. E. Broadbent & L. Weiskrantz (Eds.), *Philosophical Transactions of the Royal Society of London, B.* London: The Royal Society, 1982, 298, 85–95.

Mishkin, M., & Delacour, J. An analysis of short-term visual memory in the monkey. *Journal of Experimental Psychology: Animal Behavior Processes.* 1975, *1,* 326–334.

Mishkin, M., & Pribram, K. H. Visual discrimination performance following partial ablations of the temporal lobe. I. Ventral vs. lateral. *Journal of Comparative Physiological Psychology,* 1954, *47,* 14–20.

Mishkin, M., Spiegler, B. J., Saunders, R. C., & Malamut, B. J. An animal model of global amnesia. In S. Corkin, K. L. Davis, J. H. Growdon, E. Usdin, & R. J. Wurtman (Eds.), *Toward a treatment of Alzheimer's disease.* New York: Raven Press, pp. 235–247 1982.

Moore, J. W. Information processing in space-time by the hippocampus. *Physiological Psychology,* 1979, *1,* 224–232.

Moscovitch, M. Multiple dissociations of function in the amnesic syndrome. In L. S. Cermak (Ed.),

Human memory and amnesia (pp. 337–370). Hillsdale, NJ: Lawrence Erlbaum Associates, 1982.

Moss, M., Mahut, H., & Zola-Morgan, S. Concurrent discrimination learning of monkeys after hippocampal, entorhinal, or fornix lesions. *Journal of Neuroscience*, 1981, *1*, 227–240.

Nadel, L., Willner, J. Context and conditioning: A place for space. *Physiological Psychology*, 1980, *8*, 218–228.

Narabayashi, H., Nagao, T., Saito, Y., Yoshida, M., & Nagahata, M. Stereotaxic amygdalotomy for behavior disorders. *Archives of Neurology (Chicago)*, 1963, *9*, 11–26.

O'Keefe, J., & Nadel, L. *The hippocampus as a cognitive map*. London & New York: Oxford University Press, 1978.

Olton, D. S., Becker, J. T., & Handelmann, G. E. Hippocampus space, and memory. *Behavioral and Brain Sciences*, 1979, *2*, No. 4.

Orbach, J., Milner, B., & Rasmussen, T. Learning and retention in monkeys after amygdala-hippocampus resection. *Archives of Neurology (Chicago)*, 1960, *3*, 230–251.

Oscar-Berman, M. Neuropsychological consequences of long-term chronic alcoholism. *American Scientist*, 1980, *68*, 410–419.

Oscar-Berman, M., & Zola-Morgan, S. M. Comparative neuropsychology and Korsakoff's syndrome. I. Spatial and visual reversal learning. *Neuropsychologia*, 1980, *18*, 499–512. (a)

Oscar-Berman, M., & Zola-Morgan, S. M. Comparative neuropsychology and Korsakoff's syndrome. II. Two-choice visual discrimination learning. *Neuropsychologia*, 1980, *18*, 513–525. (b)

Papez, J. W. A proposed mechanism of emotion. *Archives of Neurological Psychiatry*, 1937, *38*, 725–743.

Penfield, W. W., & Jasper, H. *Epilepsy and the functional anatomy of the human brain*. Boston, MA: Little, Brown, 1954.

Penfield, W. W., Mathieson, G. Memory: Autopsy findings and comments on the role of hippocampus in experiential recall. *Archives of Neurology (Chicago)*, 1974, *31*, 145–154.

Penfield, W. W., Milner, B. Memory deficit produced by bilateral lesions in the hippocampal zone. *AMA Archives of Neurology and Psychiatry*, 1958, *79*, 475–497.

Penfield, W. W., & Roberts, L. *Speech and brain mechanisms*. Princeton, NJ: Princeton University Press, 1959.

Peters, R. H., Rosvold, H. E., & Mirsky, A. F. The effect of thalamic lesions upon delayed response-type tests in the Rhesus monkey. *Journal of Comparative and Physiological Psychology*, 1956, *49*, 111–116.

Ploog, D. W., & MacLean, P. O. On functions of the mammillary bodies in the squirrel monkey. *Experimental Neurology*, 1963, *7*, 76–85.

Poletti, C. E., & Creswell, G. Fornix system efferent projections in the squirrel monkey: An Experimental degeneration study. *Journal of Comparative Neurology*, 1977, *175*, 101–128.

Pribram, K. H., & Bagshaw, M. H. Further analysis of the temporal lobe syndrome utilizing frontotemporal ablations. *Journal of Comparative Neurology*, 1953, *99*, 347–375.

Pribram, K. H., Douglas, R. J., & Pribram, B. J. The nature of nonlimbic learning. *Journal of Comparative Physiological Psychology*, 1969, *69*, 765–772.

Prisko, L. Short term memory in cerebral damage. Unpublished Ph.D. thesis for McGill University, 1963.

Riopelle, A. J., Alper, R. G., Strong, P. N., & Ades, H. W. Multiple discrimination and patterned string performance of normal and temporal-lobectomized monkeys. *Journal of Comparative Physiological Psychology*, 1953, *46*, 145–149.

Rosene, D. L., & Van Hoesen, G. Hippocampal efferents reach widespread areas of cerebral cortex and amygdala in the Rhesus monkey. *Science*, 1977, *198*, 315–317.

Rosenstock, J., Field, T. D., & Greene, E. The role of mammillary bodies in spatial memory. *Experimental Neurology*, 1977, *55*, 340–352.

Rosenzweig, M. R., & Bennett, E. L. (Eds.). *Neural mechanisms of learning and memory.* Cambridge, MA: MIT Press, 1976.

Rosvold, H. E., Mirsky, A. F., & Pribram, K. H. Influence of amygdalectomy on social behavior in monkeys. *Journal of Comparative and Physiological Psychology*, 1954, *47*, 173–178.

Rosvold, H. E., Mishkin, M., & Schwartcbart, M. K. Effects of subcortical lesions in monkeys on visual-discrimination and single-alternation performance. *Journal of Comparative and Physiological Psychology*, 1958, *51*, 437–444.

Rozin, P. The psychobiological approach to human memory. In M. R. Rosenzweig & E. L. Bennett (Eds.), *Neural mechanisms of learning and memory* (pp. 3–48). Cambridge, MA: MIT Press, 1976.

Rumelhart, D. E. Schemata: The building blocks of cognition. In R. Spiro, B. Bruce, & W. Brewer (Eds.), *Theoretical issues in reading comprehension*. Hillsdale, NJ: Lwarence Erlbaum Associates, 1981.

Rumelhart, D. E., & Norman, D. A. Accretion, tuning and restructuring: Three modes of learning. In J. W. Cotton & R. Klatzky (Eds.), *Semantic factors in cognition*. Hillsdale, NJ: Lawrence Erlbaum Associates, 1978.

Schacter, D. L., & Tulving, E. Memory, amnesia and the semantic/episodic distinction. In R. L. Isaacson and N. E. Spear (Eds.) *Expression of Knowledge*, pp. 33–65. New York: Plenum Press, 1982.

Schrier, A. M., Harlow, H. F. Direct manipulation of the relevant cue and difficulty of discrimination. *Journal of Comparative and Physiological Psychology*, 1957, *50*, 576–592.

Schulman, S. Impaired delayed response from thalamic lesions. *Archives of Neurology (Chicago)*, 1964, *11*, 477–499.

Schwartzbaum, J. S. Changes in reinforcing properties of stimuli following ablation of the amygdaloid complex in monkeys. *Journal of Comparative and Physiological Psychology*, 1960, *53*, 388–395. (a)

Schwartzbaum, J. S. Response to changes in reinforcing conditions of bar-pressing after ablation of the amygdaloid complex in monkeys. *Psychological Representative*, 1960, *6*, 215–221. (b)

Schwartzbaum, J. S. Visually reinforced behavior following ablation of the amygdaloid complex in monkeys. *Journal of Comparative and Physiological Psychology*, 1964, *57*, 340–347.

Schwartzbaum, J. S. Discrimination behavior after amygdalectomy in monkeys: Visual and somesthetic learning and perceptual capacity. *Journal of Comparative and Physiological Psychology*, 1965, *60*, 314–319.

Schwartzbaum, J. S., & Poulos, D. A. Discrimination behavior after amygdalectomy in monkeys: Learning set and discrimination reversals. *Journal of Comparative and Physiological Psychology*, 1965, *60*, 320–328.

Scoville, W. B., & Milner, B. Loss of recent memory after bilateral hippocampal lesions. *Journal of Neurology, Neurosurgery and Psychiatry*, 1957, *20*, 11–21.

Semmes, J., Mishkin, M., & Deuel, R. K. Somesthetic discrimination learning after partial nonsensorimotor lesions in monkeys. *Cortex*, 1969, *5*, 331–350.

Shapiro, M. M., Gol, A., & Kellaway, P. Acquisition, retention, and discrimination reversal after hippocampal ablation in monkeys. *Experimental Neurology*, 1965, *13*, 128–144.

Sidman, M., Stoddard, L. T., & Mohr, J. P. Some additional quantitative observations of immediate memory in a patient with bilateral hippocampal lesions. *Neuropsychologia*, 1968, *6*, 245–254.

Solomon, P. R. Temporal versus spatial information processing theories of hippocampal function. *Psychological Bulletin*, 1979, *86*, 1272–1279.

Spiegler, B. J., & Mishkin, M. Evidence for the sequential participation of inferior temporal cortex and amygdala in the acquisition of stimulus-reward associations. *Behavioral Brain Research,* 1981, *3,* 303–317.

Squire, L. R. The hippocampus, space and human amnesia. *Behavioral and Brain Sciences,* 1979, *2,* 514–515.

Squire, L. R. Specifying the defect in human amnesia: Storage, retrieval and semantics. *Neuropsychologia,* 1980, *18,* 368–372. (a)

Squire, L. R. The anatomy of amnesia. *Trends in Neuroscience,* 1980, *3,* 52–54. (b)

Squire, L. R. Two forms of human amnesia: an analysis of forgetting. *Journal of Neuroscience,* 1981, *1,* 635–640.

Squire, L. R. The neuropsychology of human memory. *Annual Review of Neuroscience,* 1982, *5,* 241–273. (a)

Squire, L. R. Comparisons between forms of amnesia: some deficits are unique to Korsakoff syndrome. *Journal of Experimental Psychology: Learning, Memory, and Cognition,* 1982, *8,* 560–571. (b)

Squire, L. R. Neuropsychology of ECT. In W. B. Essman & R. Abrams (Eds.), *Electroconvulsive therapies: Biological foundations and clinical applications.* New York: Spectrum Publications, 1982, 169–186. (c)

Squire, L. R., & Cohen, N. J. Remote memory, retrograde amnesia, and the neuropsychology of memory. In L. Cermak & L. Erlbaum (Eds.), *Human memory and amnesia* (pp. 275–303). Hillsdale, N.J.: Lawrence Erlbaum Associates, 1983.

Squire, L. R. & Cohen, N. J. Human memory and amnesia. In J. McGaugh, G. Lynch, & N. Weinberger (Eds.), *Proceedings of the Conference on the Neurobiology of Learning and Memory,* New York: Guilford Press, 1983, in press.

Squire, L. R., & Moore, R. Y. Dorsal thalamic lesion in a noted case of chronic memory dysfunction. *Annals of Neurology,* 1979, *6,* 503–506.

Squire, L. R., & Slater, P. C. Anterograde and retrograde memory impairment in chronic amnesia. *Neuropsychologia,* 1978, *16,* 313–322.

Squire, L. R., Cohen, N. J., & Nadel, L. The medial temporal region and memory consolidation: a new hypothesis. In H. Weingartner & E. Parker (Eds.), *Memory Consolidation,* Hillsdale, New Jersey: Lawrence Erlbaum Associates, 1983, in press.

Squire, L. R., Slater, P. C., & Chace, P. Anterograde amnesia following electroconvulsive therapy: No evidence for state-dependent learning. *Behavioral Biology,* 1976, *17,* 31–41.

Squire, L. R., Wetzel, D., & Slater, P. C. Anterograde amnesia following ECT: An analysis of the beneficial effect of partial information. *Neuropsychologia,* 1978, *16,* 339–347.

Stamm, J. S., & Knight, M. Learning ⁻ᶠ visual tasks by monkeys with epileptogenic implants in temporal cortex. *Journal of Comparative and Physiological Psychology,* 1963, *56,* 254–260.

Stamm, J. S., & Rosen, S. C. Learning on somesthetic discrimination and reversal tasks by monkeys with epileptogenic implants in anteromedial temporal cortex. *Neuropsychologia,* 1971, *9,* 185–194.

Stepien, L. S., Cordeau, J. P., & Rasmussen, T. The effect of temporal lobe and hippocampal lesions on auditory and visual recent memory in monkeys. *Brain,* 1960, *83,* 470–489.

Stern, L. D. A review of theories of human amnesia. *Memory and Cognition,* 1981, *9,* 247–262.

Stone, C. P. Losses and gains in cognitive functions as related to electroconvulsive shock. *Journal of Abnormal Social Psychology,* 1947, *42,* 206–214.

Sutherland, N. S., & Mackintosh, N. J. *Mechanisms of animal discrimination learning.* New York: Academic Press, 1971.

Swanson, L. W., & Cowan, W. M. The connections of the septal region in the rat. *Journal of Comparative Neurology,* 1979, *186,* 621–656.

Sweet, W. H., Talland, G. A., & Ervin, F. R. Loss of recent memory following section of fornix. *Transactions of the American Neurological Association,* 1959, *84,* 76–82.

Talland, G. A. *Deranged memory*. New York: Academic Press, 1965.

Teuber, H.-L. Physiological psychology. *Annual Review of Psychology*, 1955, *6*, 267–296.

Teuber, H.-L., Milner, B., & Vaughan, H. G. Persistent anterograde amnesia after stab wound of the basal brain. *Neuropsychologia*, 1968, *6*, 267–282.

Thompson, R., & Myers, R. E. Brainstem mechanisms underlying visually guided responses in the Rhesus monkey. *Journal of Comparative and Physiological Psychology Monograph*, 1971, *74*, 479–512.

Vaernet, K. Stereotaxic amygdalotomy in temporal lobe epilepsy. *Confinia Neurologica*, 1972, *34*, 176–180.

Valenstein, E. S., & Nauta, W. J. H. A comparison of the distribution of the fornix system in the rat, guinea pig, cat and monkey. *Journal of Comparative Neurology*, 1959, *3*, 337–363.

Van Hoesen, G. W., Rosene, D. L., & Mesulam, M. M. Subicular input from temporal cortex in the rhesus monkey. *Science*, 1979, *205*, 608–610.

Victor, M., Adams, R. D., & Collins, G. H. In F. Plum & F. H. McDowell (Eds.), *The Wernicke-Korsakoff syndrome*. Philadelphia: F. A. Davis, 1971.

Von Bonin, G., & Bailey, P. *The neocortex of Macaca mulatta*. Urbana: University of Illinois Press, 1947.

Wagner, A. R., Rudy, J. W., & Whitlow, J. W. Rehearsal in animal conditioning. *Journal of Experimental Psychology Monograph*, 1973, *97*, 407–426.

Warrington, E. K., & Weiskrantz, L. A new method of testing long-term retention with special reference to amnesic patients. *Nature (London)*, 1968, *217*, 972–974.

Warrington, E. K., & Weiskrantz, L. Amnesia: a disconnection syndrome? *Neuropsychologia*, 1982, *20*, 233–248.

Waxler, M., & Rosvold, H. E. Delayed alternation in monkeys after removal of the hippocampus. *Neuropsychologia*, 1973, *8*, 137–146.

Weiskrantz, L. Behavioral changes associated with ablation of the amygdaloid complex in monkeys. *Journal of Comparative and Physiological Psychology*, 1956, *49*, 381–391.

Weiskrantz, L. Comparison of amnesic states in monkey and man. In L. E. Jarrard (Ed.), *Cognitive processes of nonhuman primates* (pp. 25–46). New York: Academic Press, 1971.

Weiskrantz, L. A comparison of hippocampal pathology in man and other animals. *Ciba Foundation Symposium*, 1978, *58*, 373–406.

Weiskrantz, L. Comparative aspects of studies of amnesia. In D. E. Broadbent & L. Weiskrantz (Eds.), *Philosophical Transactions of the Royal Society of London, B*, London: The Royal Society, 1982, *298*, 97–109.

Weiskrantz, L., & Warrington, E. K. The problem of the amnesic syndrome in man and animals. In R. L. Isaacson & K. H. Pribram (Eds.), *The hippocampus* (pp. 411–428). New York: Plenum, 1975.

Weiskrantz, L., & Warrington, E. K. Conditioning in amnesic patients. *Neuropsychologia*, 1979, *17*, 187–194.

Winograd, T. Frame representations and the declarative-procedural controversy. In D. G. Bobrow & A. M. Collins (Eds.), *Representation and understanding: Studies in cognitive science*. New York: Academic Press, 1975.

Wood, F., Ebert, V., & Kinsbourne, M. The episodic-semantic memory distinction in amnesia: clinical and experimental observations. In L. Cermak (Ed.) *Human Memory and Amnesia*, 167–193, Hillsdale, New Jersey: Lawrence Erlbaum Associates, 1982.

Woody, C. D., & Ervin, F. R. Memory function in cats with lesions of the fornix and mammillary bodies. *Physiology and Behavior*, 1966, *1*, 273–280.

Zangwill, O. L. The amnesic syndrome. In C. W. M. Whitty & O. L. Zangwill (Eds.), *Amnesia* (2nd ed.). London: Butterworth, 1977.

Zeaman, D., & House, B. J. The role of attention in retardate discrimination learning. In N. R. Ellis

(Ed.), *Handbook of mental deficiency: Psychological theory and research.* New York: McGraw-Hill, 1963.

Zola, S. M., & Mahut, H. Paradoxical facilitation of object reversal learning after transection of the fornix in monkeys. *Neuropsychologia,* 1973, *11,* 271–284.

Zola-Morgan, S., & Oberg, R. G. Recall of life experience in an alcoholic Korsakoff patient: A naturalistic approach. *Neuropsychologia,* 1980, *18,* 549–557.

Zola-Morgan, S. & Squire, L. R. Two forms of amnesia in monkeys: rapid forgetting after medial temporal lesions but not diencephalic lesions. *Society for Neuroscience Abstracts,* 1982, *8,* 24.

Zola-Morgan, S., & Squire, L. R. Towards an animal model of human amnesia: resolution of anomalous findings with visual discrimination tasks. Submitted for publication, 1983.

Zola-Morgan, S., Squire, L. R., & Mishkin, M. The neuroanatomy of amnesia: amygdala-hippo-campus versus temporal stem. *Science,* 1982, *218,* 1337–1339.

Zola-Morgan, S., Dabrowska, J., Moss, M., & Mahut, H. Enhanced preference for perceptual novelty in the monkey after fornix sections but not after hippocampal ablations. *Neuropsychologia,* in press, 1982.

CHAPTER

7

SELF-STIMULATION[1]

C. R. GALLISTEL
Department of Psychology
University of Pennsylvania
Philadelphia, Pennsylvania

[1]The expenses of preparing this chapter were defrayed by NIH Grant NS14935 to C. R. Gallistel, P. Hand, and M. Reivich. This grant also supported the autoradiographic research and the pimozide research conducted in the author's laboratory and here summarized.

I. INTRODUCTION

A. A Nerve–Memory Preparation

The self-stimulating rat is a nerve–memory preparation. Electrical stimulation of a neural pathway (in the basolateral diencephalon) yields a propagated nerve signal that eventuates in a memory. This memory for the stimulation-produced experience may direct the animal's behavior in the indefinite future. An experiment by Gallistel, Stellar, and Bubis (1974) demonstrates the dependence of self-stimulation behavior on a memory of the stimulation received for past performance. They plotted the trial by trial change in the rat's running speed in an alley following an alteration in the magnitude of the brain stimulation that rewarded each run. There was a 10-minute interval between trials. They found learning curves (Figure 7.1, dashed lines). The change in performance consequent upon a shift in reward developed over trials. The change was not complete by the fifth trial, 50 minutes after the shift in stimulation magnitude. The trial-dependent (rather than time-dependent) character of the change in performance indicates what is perhaps obvious anyway—the reinforcing effect of brain stimulation reward (BSR) is mediated by a memory of the stimulation received as a reward for earlier performance. One way to think of this aspect of self-stimulation is to imagine that the stimulation generates an experience of some kind, or, at least, the neural code for an experience. The knowledge thus gained, that is the record of the experience in memory, plays a role in orienting the animal's subsequent behavior. What the nature of the experience is and how the memory of it may orient subsequent behavior are questions we will turn to in a moment.

B. A Nerve–Motivation Preparation

The self-stimulating rat is also a nerve–motivation preparation. The stimulation engenders a transient but powerful motivational signal. A motivational signal is a signal that selectively potentiates several complex units of behavior having a common or coherent function and depotentiates other, competing units of behavior (Gallistel, 1980a, 1980b). The potentiated behaviors are easily elicited and vigorously performed; the depotentiated behaviors may be elicited with difficulty or not at all and are slowly and hesitantly performed. The effect of this selective potentiation of functional cohesive complex behaviors is to give the animal's behavior a goal-directed quality, the quality that leads us to say that the animal wants or desires something. In the case of the motivational signal engendered by rewarding brain stimulation, the potentiated behaviors are those that produce the BSR. In short, therefore, we say that rewarding brain stimulation engenders a transient desire for more stimulation.

The transient character of the animal's desire for more stimulation is palpable when you pull a vigorously self-stimulating rat away from the lever. At first,

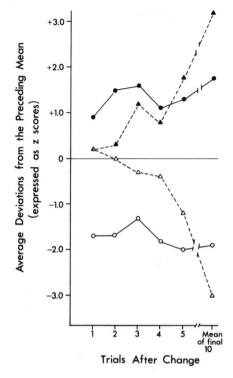

Figure 7.1. Change in runway performance as a function of the number of trials since a change in the amount of stimulation. When the change is an increase (▲--▲) or decrease (△--△) in the amount of stimulation that rewards performance, then the change in performance traces out a learning curve. When the change is an increase (●--●) or decrease (○--○) in the pretrial stimulation used to prime performance, then the change in performance is immediate. [From Gallistel, Stellar, & Bubis (1974), Figure 3, by permission of the American Psychological Association.]

the animal struggles to return to the lever. As you hold it, you can feel it relaxing. If you hold it for a minute and then release it, the rat may not return to the lever at all, or, if it does, it returns in a casual manner that is in marked contrast to the frantic efforts it makes immediately after stimulation has been interrupted. In other words, the strong drive to obtain more stimulation subsides rapidly.

The selective potentiating property of the transient drive state produced by rewarding stimulation is most clearly demonstrated in an experiment by Deutsch, Adams, and Metzner (1964). They ran thirsty rats on choice trials in a T maze with a water reward in one goal arm and BSR in the other. The rats were "primed" before each trial, that is, they were given free noncontingent BSR by the experimenter while they were in a holding box outside the T maze. The time between the priming and the start of a choice trial was varied. When trials began immediately after priming, the rats almost always chose BSR, no matter how thirsty they were. The longer the interval between priming and the start of a trial (in the range of 5–60 seconds), the less often the rats chose BSR. The thirstier the rats were, the more likely they were to shift their preference from BSR to water as the delay between priming and choice was increased (Figure 7.2). Thus,

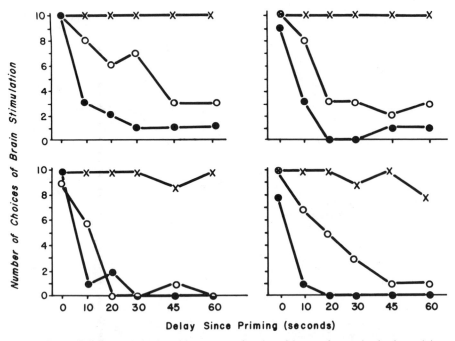

Figure 7.2. Choice behavior of four rats as a function of degree of water deprivation and time since priming with BSR. The more thirsty the rats and the longer the time elapsed since priming, the more likely rats were to choose water in preference to BSR. Zero hours thirst, X—X; 5 hours thirst, ○—○; 22 hours thirst, ●—●. [Reproduced from Deutsch, Adams, & Metzner (1964), Figure 1, by permission of the authors and the American Psychological Association.]

priming selectively increases the potential for responses directed toward obtaining BSR, just as thirst selectively increases the potential for responses directed toward obtaining water. The priming effect decays in a few seconds to at most a few minutes.

The transient motivating effect (the priming effect) is not mediated by a memory. There is no learning involved. Altering the magnitude of pretrial priming stimulation in the runway paradigm produces an immediate complete change in the vigor of performance (Figure 7.1, solid lines).

C. The Minimal Model

These simple facts about the self-stimulation phenomenon seem to require the minimal neurobiological model portrayed in Figure 7.3. This extremely schematic model is minimal because it does not address itself to any of the hard questions. It does not specify the natural functions of the neural systems underlying the reinforcing (memory-producing) and motivating effects of the stimula-

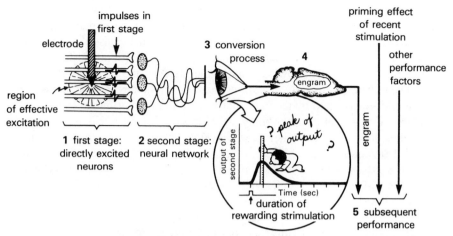

Figure 7.3. A minimal model of the self-stimulation phenomenon. The stages by which the reinforcing effect is realized in performance are numbered: (1) Stimulating pulses produce successive volleys of impulses in reward-relevant axons. (2) A postsynaptic network of unknown complexity carries out temporal and spatial summation. (3) The transient output of this network is seen by a conversion process, represented by the homunculus, which translates some aspect of this signal (e.g., its peak) into an engram—a record of the reward. (4) This record is the reinforcing effect. It, together with the priming effect of recent stimulation and innumerable other factors, determines the speed (vigor, rate, etc.) of subsequent performance (the fifth stage). For diagrammatic simplicity, the priming pathway is not shown. It would be represented by a directly stimulated first stage and an integrator, but no engram forming stage. [From Gallistel *et al.* (1981), Figure 2, with permission of the American Psychological Association.]

tion. It does not identify these neural systems anatomically, neurophysiologically, or neurochemically, and so on. These knotty questions are to be dealt with later. The minimal model is used as a framework for organizing the discussion of these questions.

The minimal model assumes that the substrates that carry the reinforcing and motivating signals may be divided into neurons that are directly excited by the electrode current and neurons that are indirectly excited by means of impulses relayed to them across one or more synapses. The directly driven neurons will be termed the *first-stage* neurons. Since the trade-off data to be reviewed give reason to believe that the first stage consists primarily of a bundle of axons coursing past the electrode, the first stage is also termed *the cable*. The neurons that are excited transynaptically, regardless of how remotely, are called the *second stage*.

The reinforcing effect in self-stimulation is an enduring record of the magnitude of the transient neural signal engendered by the stimulation in the reinforcing pathway. Hence, the second stage of the substrate for reinforcement must terminate at a *conversion process*. The conversion process, represented by the homunculus in Figure 7.3, converts the transient signal into an engram. The output of the second stage of the reinforcing pathway is by definition the input to the conversion process. In other words, it is the proximal cause of the engram. The engram may serve to orient subsequent behavior. The engram is the physical embodiment of the rat's knowledge about the effect of the stimulation.

The extent to which the engram is manifest in the direction of subsequent behavior depends in part on the momentary strength of the priming signal. When the potentiating effect of the priming signal is strong, behavior directed toward producing more stimulation is likely to occur and likely to be vigorously performed. Competing behaviors are correspondingly less likely and less vigorous. In other words, when the priming effect of stimulation is strong, the behavior that is directed by the engram has high potential for activation, while competing behaviors have low potential for activation. The output of the second stage of the priming pathway is the signal that exerts these selective potentiating and depotentiating effects on the circuits that coordinate the behavior patterns.

As already noted, the effect of priming stimulation (pretrial stimulation) is not mediated by a memory. When the magnitude of pretrial stimulation is changed, the resulting change in the vigor of self-stimulation behavior is immediate. Thus, the systems mediating the priming (potentiating) and reinforcing (engram-generating) effects of the stimulation must diverge at some point. They may have one and the same first stage, however, and much of the second stage may also be common to both. The minimal model makes no assumption on this point. The first and second stages of the priming pathway are not shown in Figure 7.3, because (a) their schematic structure duplicates that of the reinforcing pathway and (b) it is not clear whether they should be shown as distinct from or identical with the corresponding stages of the reinforcing pathway.

If we know what the nerve is in our nerve–memory preparation, then we may be able to follow it to the place where the transient signal is converted into a permanent record, that is, into knowledge. Likewise, for the motivational signal, we may be able to follow the nerve to the place where the signal exerts its potentiating effects on the circuits that pattern behavior. In short, identifying the neural substrate for the self-stimulation phenomenon may put us in a position to study the neurophysiological processes underlying motivation and memory formation. This chapter is primarily concerned with attempts to identify the neural systems that carry these reinforcing and motivating signals. First, however, let us consider what the natural functions of these systems may be.

II. THE NORMAL FUNCTION OF THE NEURAL SUBSTRATE FOR SELF-STIMULATION OF THE MFB

For reasons to be explained, this chapter focuses on self-stimulation of the medial forebrain bundle (MFB), which is one of the principal axon systems interconnecting the midbrain, hypothalamus, and forebrain. The MFB runs through the lateral hypothalamus between the lateral preoptic area and the ventral tegmentum. It has long been recognized as the system in which intense self-stimulation behavior is most readily obtained.

Self-stimulation of the MFB is the combined result of the reinforcing and motivating effects of brain stimulation reward. Given the twofold character of the effect of stimulation on behavior, there are three sorts of questions that can be asked about the normal functions of the neural system mediating self-stimulation of the MFB:

1. What is the normal function of the neural system whose excitation leads to the reinforcing effect?
2. What is the normal function of the neural system whose excitation leads to the priming effect?
3. What is the relation between these systems? To what extent are they one and the same? Is the activation of one a secondary consequence of activating the other? Can either be activated without activating the other? How do the functions of the two systems intermesh?

A. Theoretical Perspectives

The answers offered to the above questions depend on the theoretical framework within which one thinks about learning and motivation. Answers deriving from three different frameworks will be considered. I will call these frameworks the Hullian, the Aristotelian, and the cognitive–ethological. The three frameworks differ in their conception of what the reinforcing effect of a reward is. From this difference in conception, most other differences flow.

1. Hullian

The Hullian framework conceives of reinforcement as the stamping in of new sensory–motor connections. In the Hullian view, the co-occurrence of a sensory configuration and a response sets up within the nervous system the potential for the creation of a new sensory–motor linkage. Whether the potential linkage is converted to an actual linkage or not depends on whether or not the reinforcement process is activated by a reward during a brief period following the co-occurrence. The reinforcement process stamps in (strengthens and makes permanent) the linkage between the sensory input and the response (S–R), so that future occurrences of the sensory input tend to evoke that response.

Within this conceptual framework, the normal function of the substrate for the reinforcing effect in self-stimulation seems obvious. The electrode must be stimulating neurons that carry the signals that initiate the stamping in process (Huston, 1983). The strengthened S–R linkage left behind when these signals have done their work is the engram in Figure 7.3. Whether the signals initiating the stamping in also give rise to a pleasurable experience is irrelevant. Indeed, whether and in what sense the signal could be said to give rise to any sort of experience is irrelevant. The engram is the altered S–R linkage. It is not the record of an experience, whatever that might be. However, within this framework, one might be tempted to invoke an accompanying evanescent pleasurable experience as the basis for the priming effect, that is, for the transient prepotence of that particular S–R bond over most if not all of its competitors.

2. Aristotelian

The second view of reinforcement in self-stimulation, by far the most widely held, comes from a conception of the wellsprings of motivated behavior that dates back at least to Aristotle. Aristotle argued that behavior is motivated by the pursuit of pleasure. In modern terms, this is the incentive–motivational view of reinforcement. According to this view, certain kinds of experience are accompanied by an experience of pleasure. The experience of eating is accompanied, at least in a hungry animal, by the further experience of pleasure. The experience of copulation is accompanied by this same, further experience, namely, pleasure. Animals are assumed to make a record of the sequences of experiences they have had. Among these recorded experiences there are pleasure experiences. The pleasure experiences in memory broadcast a siren's song. This siren song lures the animal into repeating the behavior sequences that lead to the pleasure experience.

Within this framework, the normal function of the substrate for the reinforcing effect in self-stimulation is again obvious: It carries the signals that give rise to or code for the pleasure experience. The record of the pleasure experience thus generated is the engram underlying self-stimulation (see Figure 7.3). For an unusually explicit statement that this is the normal function of the neural system that mediates the reinforcing effect in self-stimulation, see Wise (1980). Lenzer (1972), Milner (1970), Olds (1976), Rolls (1975, 1976), and Stein (1964) have made similar suggestions. Bindra (1978) has championed this general view of learning and motivation. He has attempted to spell out the mechanisms by which the memories of past pleasure recruit pleasure-directed learned behavior.

A problem with which the unadorned Aristotelian conception must cope is this: Why does the animal abandon a pleasure-generating behavior in favor of something else? Why does it quit eating in order to copulate, and vice versa? In view of the intensity of the pleasure produced by copulation (assuming human testimony to be a reliable index), why do animals, even humans, spend so much time doing other things, things that generate less intense pleasure? The common first answer to this question, because the behavior when done without interruption ceases to generate pleasure, only gets one onto another horn of a dilemma. According to this answer, the most recent record one has should always indicate the experience X is no longer accompanied by the pleasure experience. If we stop eating pumpkin pie at the end of the Thanksgiving feast because eating it no longer gives pleasure, why are we keen to eat it when Christmas comes? The most recent experience of pumpkin pie in memory is not associated with pleasure!

The usual response to this last conundrum is to suppose that the record of a pleasure in memory is associated with a record of the internal state that accompanied its occurrence. The record of the pleasure experienced at table is associated with a record of the hunger state. It is further supposed that the hunger state gates the siren call of the pleasure memory (cf. Bindra, 1978; Milner, 1970). Thus, the memory of the pleasure of pumpkin pie only lures us if we are hungry.

This last assumption undermines the unitary conception of the pleasure experience and blurs the distinction between this view and the cognitive view. One no longer has to do with pleasure pure and simple but rather with distinct pleasures—the pleasure of eating, the pleasure of copulating, etc. In this form of the incentive-motivational view, pleasure-independent motivational processes (hunger, thirst, sexual drive, etc.) assume most of the burden for explaining why the animal does what when. Now, in the incentive–motivational view, hunger determines when the memory of the pleasure of food will organize the animal's behavior in a food-directed manner. It is therefore unclear what the motivating function of the pleasure memory itself is. The hunger drive has usurped the motivating function of pleasure. The difference between this and the cognitive–ethological view, in which the hunger drive organizes food-seeking behavior, becomes elusive.

3. Cognitive–Ethological View

This view assumes that Aristotle got cause confused with effect. Aristotle assumed that the experience of pleasure preceded and gave rise to motivation. The cognitive–ethological view assumes that motivation precedes and makes possible pleasurable experience. In this view, pleasure is not an experience in its own right. "Pleasure" designates a category of distinct experiences. The experiences belonging to this category have nothing in common except that they are all pertinent to the terminal or consummatory experiences in motivated behavioral sequences. There is no pleasure experience per se, only pleasurable experiences. Whether an experience will be pleasurable at any given time depends on the motivational state of the animal. Different motivational states (different drives) make different experiences pleasurable. The drive that makes eating pleasurable is the drive that selectively potentiates food-directed behavior. A different drive potentiates water-directed behavior and makes drinking pleasurable, and so on. Eating is pleasurable only when the appropriate drive is aroused.

The role of motivational states in this view comes directly from ethological conceptions of drives. Drives are internal processes that organize behavior by selectively raising the potential for the occurrence of functionally complementary units of behavior, while lowering the potential for the occurrence of functionally antagonistic units (see Gallistel, 1980a, for book-length elaboration).

The cognitive aspect of this view assumes that higher animals form and record representations of their experiences. These representations have no motivational consequences. The animal's drive state determines which of these representations will be used to control behavioral output at any given time (see Deutsch, 1960, for elaboration). Within this framework, the normal function of the substrate for the reinforcing effect in self-stimulation is to carry signals that code for certain kinds of situations or experiences, situations or experiences that constitute or are pertinent to the terminal events in one or more motivated behavior sequences (Deutsch, 1960, 1963; Deutsch & Howarth, 1963; Gallistel, 1972). The resulting record is the engram in Figure 7.3.

Viewpoints other than the cognitive–ethological have seldom dealt explicitly with the normal function of the substrate for the priming effect. They have tended to assume that a transient heightening of incentive appeal was a normal consequence of the pleasurable experience. That is, they have assumed that the activation of the substrate for the priming effect was secondary to the activation of the substrate for the reinforcing effect, and they have assumed that the normal function of this secondarily activated system was to mediate the "salted-peanut" effect of incentives—the transient, as opposed to the enduring, effect of an incentive on subsequent behavior. In the cognitive–ethological view, on the other hand, the function of the substrate for the priming effect belongs in a different category from the function of the substrate for the reinforcing effect. The normal function of the substrate for priming is to mediate the selective potentiating effects of internal states. Selective potentiating effects are the means by which motivational states determine the direction of ongoing behavior (Deutsch, 1960; Gallistel, 1980a). The function of the substrate for the reinforcing effect, by contrast, is to convey information about events to memory, where that information is recorded for possible use in the future. While it is possible to assume, within this cognitive–ethological framework, that the priming effect is secondary to the reinforcing effect, the usual assumption is that two so functionally disparate effects derive from the direct activation of two distinct substrates.

In the cognitive–ethological view, unlike the two previous views, neither the reinforcing nor the motivating effect of stimulation is likely to be the same from one stimulation site to the next, or even for different current levels at one and the same site. This view takes it as a premise that in any animal species there are many different kinds of reinforcing (sequence terminating) events and as many different motivational states. It further assumes that: (1) the codes for distinct reinforcing events (or distinct aspects of reinforcing events) are distinguished within the nervous system by the pathways over which they are reported—an extension of the doctrine of specific nerve energies; (2) different

motivational states potentiate and depotentiate functionally complementary combinations of behavioral units by way of different neural pathways (specific nerve
energies in a motivational context). In other words, this view inclines toward an
extreme position on the question of whether neurons in the MFB have differentiated and specific functions. It inclines to the view that, upon close analysis, the
function of every neuron can be distinguished from the function of every other
neuron.

It is therefore natural within the cognitive–ethological view to seek a more
differentiated assessment of function within the general category of the reinforcing function and likewise within the category of the motivating (priming) function. It is appropriate to ask what spectrum of reinforcing experiences is generated by stimulating at a given site with a given current intensity. It is also
appropriate to ask what the spectrum of selective potentiating (motivating) effects is. These daunting questions do not arise within the "reinforcement-as-
pure-pleasure" view, which may help explain the appeal of this view. While it
may be simpler to think of reinforcement as synonymous with the experience of
pure pleasure, it is far from clear that this long-held view will ever succeed in
doing justice to the facts of animal behavior.

B. Pertinent Findings

Which, if any, of the perspectives on the normal function of self-stimulation tissue eventually prevails is likely to depend more on the evolution of ideas
in the field of learning and motivation than on findings about self-stimulation per
se. In recent years, most experimental work has been directed to establishing the
characteristics of the tissue itself rather than to establishing a conception of the
function of this tissue in normal behavior. What follows, therefore, should be
regarded as an update that gives the relatively few pertinent experimental findings that have emerged since an earlier review of this literature (Gallistel, 1972).

1. Is Priming Secondary to Reinforcement?

An earlier review (Gallistel, 1972) argued from refractory period data that
the priming effect was not secondary to the reinforcing effect of the stimulation.
On the basis of studies by Deutsch (1964) and Gallistel, Rolls, and Greene
(1969), it appeared that the first-stage neurons for the two effects had distinct
refractory periods. It was later pointed out, however, that the seeming difference
in refractory periods could be an artifact of the input–output paradigms used in
these early studies (cf. Gallistel, 1975, Figure 8 and accompanying discussion).
A subsequent experiment, using the trade-off paradigm, found no difference
between the refractory periods for the two effects (see Gallistel, Shizgal, &
Yeomans, 1981), which removes some of the empirical basis for the earlier
argument that priming was a direct and independent effect of rewarding stimulation of the MFB.

However, pharmacological experiments have supplied a new basis for this argument. Pimozide blocks the reinforcing effect of MFB stimulation but not the priming effect (Wasserman, Gomita, & Gallistel, 1982; see Figure 7.22). This result seems to rule out the thesis that the priming effect is a secondary consequence of the reinforcing effect. Unlike the refractory period data, however, it does not rule out the hypothesis that the substrates for the two effects share a common first stage or stages. It is possible that both behavioral effects derive from the direct electrical excitation of one and the same population of axons. Experiments aimed at detecting differences in the quantitative characteristics of the first stages have so far failed (see Gallistel *et al.*, 1981, for review).

2. Do Naturally Reinforcing Events Have a Priming Effect?

There has been a tendency to try to conceptualize the self-stimulation phenomenon entirely in terms of reinforcement. The notion that the phenomenon depended on a bipartite effect of the stimulation has been resisted in several ways. One way has been to question the existence of the phenomena that indicate the presence of a transient motivational effect or to suggest that these phenomena were artifacts of some motivation-irrelevant aspect of self-stimulation testing. The phenomena in question indicate that an animal's tendency to seek further stimulation wanes rapidly following the receipt of its most recent stimulation. The rapid waning of the motivation to seek more stimulation is manifest in several ways:

1. The longer the intertrial interval, the slower rats run for BSR. The decline in motivation in the first minute accounts for most of this effect. Variations in intertrial interval beyond 1 minute have little effect. Kent and Grossman (1969) claimed that his often verified effect of intertrial interval was only present in some rats. However, a subsequent collaborative study (Reid, Hunsicker, Kent, Lindsay, & Gallistel, 1973) found the effect to be present to varying degrees in all rats.

2. Performance at the start of each day's session (after about 24 hours without stimulation) is slow. Kornblith and Olds (1968) showed that one could nonetheless get rats to learn a T maze for BSR, giving only 1 trial per day. They downplayed the fact that they had to use an unusual maze configuration—one with a large open start area. Such a start box would, by itself, encourage rats to seek the safety of the small arms, in one of which they also received BSR. No such configuration is necessary when conditions are such that the rats receive stimulation (whether contingent or noncontingent) shortly before each trial.

3. The cessation of responding when responses no longer yield stimulation is unusually rapid, at least in comparison to the extinction of food rewarded responding. More importantly, the number of responses to cessation depends strongly on whether or not the rat has been receiving stimulation just before

extinction testing begins (Howarth & Deutsch, 1962). A naturally arising hunger drive eliminates this difference between extinction performance for food and extinction performance for BSR (Deutsch & DiCara, 1967). Gibson, Reid, Sakai, and Porter (1965) suggested that these unusual aspects of the extinction of responding for BSR were an artifact of the manner in which BSR is given to the animal. The receipt of BSR is immediately contiguous with the response; whereas, with food and water, rats are usually made to collect the reward from a dispenser after making the reinforced response. Quartermain and Webster (1968), however, made the conditions for the receipt of a water reward comparable to the conditions for the receipt of BSR, and still they found that delaying the onset of extinction testing greatly reduced responding for BSR but not for water. Whether extinction for BSR is slower or faster than extinction for natural reinforcement depends no doubt on which natural reinforcer one has in mind. There is no reason to believe that the rate of extinction is independent of the kind of reinforcement (cf. Hogan & Roper, 1978). The peculiar property of "extinction" for BSR is that the rate of "extinction" depends strongly on the simple recency of the last stimulation, independent of how many nonreinforced responses have or have not been made in the interim. This aspect of "extinction" for BSR is no doubt due to loss of desire (decay of the priming effect) rather than to extinction in the ordinary sense (loss of hope).

Katz (1979, 1980, 1981), studying the patterns of behavior in rats given 24-hour a day access to brain stimulation reward, has also obtained data indicating the operation of two distinct processes, a priming process that keeps responding going at a high level once a bout of responding has been initiated and a reinforcing (or, as he terms it, an incentive) process that determines whether the animal will initiate a bout. He found (Katz, 1981) that the priming (bout-maintenance) process dissipated within a few minutes of the termination of stimulation, whereas the effects of the reinforcement process were evident for many days after the termination of stimulation.

4. Partial reinforcement schedules, which require the animal to continue responding for some time after each stimulation before getting another stimulation, do not work as well with BSR as with food (compare Keesey & Goldstein, 1968, with Hodos & Kalman, 1963). Pliskoff and Hawkins (1967) increased the number of trains constituting a reward from the usual 1 to between 10 and 100. They found that under these conditions, they got good responding on schedules with long interstimulation intervals. They argue that the incentive from the usual single train is simply inadequate. Gallistel (1969a), however, showed that the incentive of one train is usually asymptotic. He showed that the effect of multiple trains was to prolong the motivational aftereffect (the priming effect).

The above phenomena are often cited as evidence that brain stimulation reinforcement is different from other reinforcement. This way of putting the matter is misleading. If one views these phenomena as evidence that the pursuit of BSR depends on a drive state of some kind, which, like all drive states, varies over time, then BSR is no different from any other known reward. There is no reward whose capacity to control behavior does not vary as a function of fluctuation in drive states. BSR differs from other rewards only in that the same stimulation that produces the reinforcing effect also engenders a transient drive state directed toward that kind of reinforcement. One is led to ask whether at least some natural reinforcers might not also do this.

For a full answer to this question, one should consult Hogan and Roper's (1978) lengthy comparison of the results obtained in traditional learning paradigms using different kinds of reinforcers and different animal species. There are some clear examples of naturally reinforcing events or situations that prime behavior directed toward that kind of reinforcement. Aggressive interactions in many species of fish are an example. The opportunity to make aggressive displays is something Siamese fighting fish will actively seek. They will learn some kinds of appetitive behaviors (e.g., swimming a runway) for this kind of reinforcement. Furthermore, giving them this kind of reinforcement transiently arouses an aggressive drive, so that the fish perform the task more readily when primed by a previous presentation of the display arousing situation [another male fish or a mirror that reflects the fish's own image back to it (Hogan & Bols, 1980)].

Sexual reinforcement also primes further sexual behavior under some conditions. When male rats run an alley for the opportunity to mount and penetrate a female rat, they show markedly slower performance on the first trial of a day's session than on subsequent trials (Beach & Jordan, 1956), just as do rats running for BSR. The sexual encounter on the first trial transiently arouses the male sex drive, thereby priming subsequent sexually oriented behavior.

Both sex and aggression are nonhomeostatic drives. The factors arousing these drives are, to varying degrees in varying species and sexes, external rather than internal. By contrast with reinforcements pertinent to these drives, reinforcements pertinent to homeostatic drives, such as thirst and hunger, do not usually have pronounced priming effects. Priming effects in homeostatic "behavior systems" (cf. Hogan & Roper, 1978) would set up a positive-feedback process antithetical to the regulatory function of these systems. Certainly, with food reinforcement, a priming effect has been hard to find, at least in the rat. A dozen experiments, conducted over a span stretching back 60 years, all show that when rats run an alley or maze for food, either intertrial interval makes no difference or longer intertrial intervals promote faster performance (Cotton & Lewis, 1957; Lashley, 1918; Mayer & Stone, 1931; and references therein). However, van der Kooy and Hogan (1978) have succeeded in demonstrating a priming effect from food reinforcement in the hamster. They used a square maze, with each corner functioning as a goal box on one run and a start box on the next. It is not clear to what extent their success was due to the choice of hamsters or the unusual maze. In any event, it is clear that a priming effect from food is a fragile phenomenon, at least in the rat. With water reinforcement, results conflict: Gallistel (1967) found no systematic effect of intertrial interval on water-rein-forced performance in an experiment designed to compare water-reinforced per-formance with performance reinforced by BSR. Hunsicker & Reid (1974), in a similar experiment, found that longer intertrial intervals produced slower water-reinforced performance. Van der Kooy and Hogan (1978) also found a priming effect from water, using hamsters in their square maze. The reasons for the discrepancy between the outcomes of the experiments are unclear.

In short, the answer to the question of whether natural reinforcers have a priming effect is that it depends on the type of natural reinforcer, the species and the sex of the animals tested, and the precise conditions of testing. As Hogan and Roper (1978) point out, this is what one expects if one views the problem of learning and motivation from an ethological perspective. The ethological per-spective eschews the universality assumptions in traditional theories of learning and motivation. It assumes that there are no or very few laws of learned perfor-mance that hold across reinforcers and species. It assumes that a reinforcer operates within a behavior system more or less specific to that kind of reinforce-ment and that species. How performance is affected by such things as the in-tertrial interval, the schedule of reinforcement, the delay of reinforcement, and so on, varies from one behavior system to the next (cf. Rozin & Kalat, 1971).

Viewed from this perspective, the peculiarities of performance for BSR are not embarrassments to be explained away. On the contrary, they are clues that may some day lead us to an understanding of the natural function of the neural tissue whose stimulation yields the self-stimulation phenomenon. To a suffi-ciently educated eye, these peculiarities, and others that could no doubt be uncovered by appropriately contrived experiments, may indicate which behavior systems we are dealing with. That eye has not so far been cast on these data.

3. Does the Reinforcing Experience Differ from Site to Site within the MFB?

An earlier review (Gallistel, 1972) cited a number of studies (e.g., Deutsch & Howarth, 1962; Hoebel, 1968) reporting that the effect of manipulating natu-ral drives on self-stimulation performance depended on the site of stimulation within the MFB. These and other results suggest that different sites of stimula-tion provide different kinds of reinforcing experiences, or, in Hogan and Roper's (1978) terms, experiences pertinent to different behavior systems. Gallistel and Beagley (1971) provide a further demonstration that this is so. They worked with rats with two self-stimulation electrodes at different sites in the MFB. Using either a T maze or an automated analog thereof, they arranged a lever in one arm to deliver stimulation to one electrode and a lever in the other arm to deliver stimulation to the other electrode. They adjusted the parameters of stimulation so

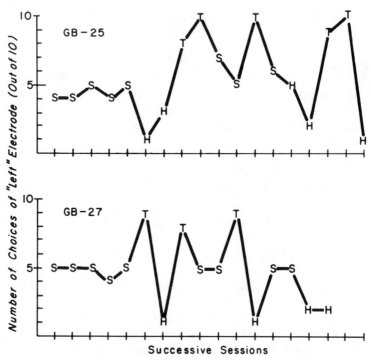

Figure 7.4. The session-by-session results from rats GB-25 and GB-27 indicate the stability and repeatibility of drive-induced changes in electrode preference. H indicates the rat was hungry; T, thirsty; S, satiated. (The "left" electrode was the electrode activated by the left-hand lever. It was not necessarily in the left side of the diencephalon.) [From Gallistel & Beagley (1971), Figure 2, with permission of the American Psychological Association.]

that each rat chose each lever approximately equally often when satiated. Then, they manipulated the natural drive states from day to day. Some days the rats were thirsty (T on Figure 7.4), some days hungry (H), and some days satiated (S). In seven of eight rats, electrode preference varied with drive state. In some rats, only thirst affected preference; in some, only hunger did; in some, both drives mattered. Results from the two most interesting subjects are shown in Figure 7.4. In these two subjects, hunger caused a preference for one electrode, while thirst caused a preference for the other electrode.

It would seem that the spectrum of experiences coded for by the stimulation-produced neural signals differs from one site of stimulation to the next within the MFB. It would further seem that these experiences are at least in part pertinent to the homeostatic hunger and thirst behavior systems. Gallistel and Beagley could not detect any systematic pattern relating site of stimulation to the kind of drive that favored that site. The 2-DG technique (see Section III,A) was not then available. The use of 2-DG autoradiography in conjunction with an experiment of this type might reveal some differences in pattern of activation, differences systematically related to the effects of drive states on preference.

4. Does the Motivating Effect Differ from Site to Site and Is It Interchangeable with One or Another Natural Drive State?

In Deutsch's (1960) formulation of what I have called the cognitive–ethological theory, it was assumed that electrodes at different sites would tap into reinforcing and motivating pathways for different behavior systems. An electrode at one site might stimulate the code for food and also make the animal transiently hungry. An electrode at another site might stimulate the code for water and also make the rat transiently thirsty, and so on.

If this formulation were true in a simple way, then the motivating effect from stimulation at one site would not be appropriate to the reinforcement provided by stimulation at another site. Further, the natural drive states that would interchange with the priming effect would differ from site to site. Finally, the interchanging of priming and natural drives ought to be symmetrical. If hunger could substitute for priming in potentiating the pursuit of BSR at some site, then priming at that site should substitute for hunger in potentiating the pursuit of food reinforcement.

Tests of these predictions have yielded a puzzling pattern—partially confirmatory, partially disconfirmatory. As already shown, natural drive states can substitute for priming in selectively increasing the potential for behavior directed toward BSR, with different drive states favoring different sites of BSR (Gallistel & Beagley, 1971). In a runway, hunger increases performance for BSR. As with priming, the effect of hunger is immediately evident in performance (compare Figure 7.5 with Figure 7.1). The effect of hunger on performance for BSR does not develop over trials as it would if hunger changed the incentive value of the BSR. The effects of changing from the hungry state to the satiated state and vice versa are present on the first trial of testing, just as are the effects of changing from pretrial priming to no pretrial priming, or vice versa.

The disconfirmatory and puzzling findings come when one tests for the symmetry of the interchange between hunger and priming. Priming, even on an electrode that produces stimulation bound eating, does not substitute for hunger in potentiating behavior directed toward food reward. Stellar and Gallistel (1975) tested 13 electrodes in four rats and found that in all but two cases priming the rats with brain stimulation before each trial reduced the speed with which hungry rats ran for a food reward (in the other two cases, there was no effect of priming). In a follow-up study, Stellar and Heard (1976) showed that pretrial priming with BSR increased the latency at which hungry rats initiated the eating of food when placed in a familiar environment containing foods (15 electrodes, five rats). Priming with BSR (outside the food environment) inhibited eating even when the food was highly palatable. In short, priming with BSR potentiates the pursuit of a

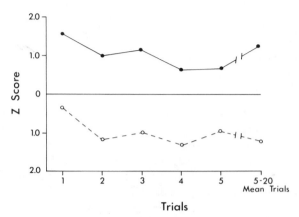

Figure 7.5. The trial-by-trial course of the change in running speed after food deprivation (upper) and after the return to satiation (lower). As in Figure 7.1, the deviations from the pretransition mean performance are plotted in Z score units for each of the first five trials after the change in drive state. Note that the change in performance consequent on a change in the hunger state is immediate and complete on the first test trial. It does not depend on learning. The same is true when the pretrial priming is changed (cf. Figure 7.1). [From Stellar & Gallistel (1975), Figure 4, with permission of the American Psychological Association.]

BSR reinforcement but depotentiates the pursuit of food reinforcement. Hunger, on the other hand, usually potentiates both pursuits.

Further puzzlement comes from testing the interchangeability of priming effects at different sites. The formulation that envisages many anatomically separate two-component behavior systems predicts that priming at one site (in one behavior system) should often fail to potentiate responding for BSR at another site (in a different behavior system). This is not what one finds (Gallistel, 1969b). In general, priming at a different anatomical site from the site to which the reward is delivered is as good or even better than priming at the site that serves for reward.

In sum, the priming effect is a motivating effect. It selectively raises the potential for behavior directed toward BSR, and it does so in a way that does not depend on learning. What the natural motivating function of the underlying neural tissue may be is obscure at present. It will remain obscure until we discover what kinds of natural reinforcers must be used and under what kinds of conditions in order that priming with BSR potentiate rather than depotentiate the naturally reinforced behavior.

C. Summary

Rewarding stimulation of the MFB produces both a reinforcing and a motivating effect. The usual frantic self-stimulation behavior is the combined result of these two effects. The tendency to seek more BSR depends strongly on the recency of the last stimulation, because the motivating effect decays rapidly when stimulation ceases. The motivating effect is not a secondary consequence of the reinforcing effect, because the motivating effect is still present in full force when the reinforcing effect has been blocked by pimozide. This does not, however, rule out the hypothesis that the neural systems mediating the two effects may have a common first stage or stages.

The way in which one conceives of these two effects depends on one's general perspective on the nature of reinforcement. The Hullian perspective conceives of reinforcement as the stamping in of S–R connections. The incentive–motivational view conceives of reinforcement as the experience of pleasure. The cognitive–ethological view conceives of reinforcement as the experience of sensations or events or situations pertinent to the terminal phases of motivated behavioral sequences. The author is partial to this last perspective. In this perspective, the reinforcing effect alters the animal's knowledge of its behavioral options—its act-outcome expectancies (Irwin, 1971). This knowledge becomes a determining factor in the genesis of behavior when and if the animal desires that outcome, to put the matter cognitively (Irwin, 1971). In ethological terms, this knowledge is expressed in the animal's behavior when and if its drive state selectively potentiates behaviors that tend toward that outcome.

A more narrow psychological specification of the reinforcing and motivating effects has so far eluded us. It appears that the reinforcing experiences are often relevant to the basic drives most often studied by physiological psychology—hunger, thirst, and sex. The relation between these natural drives and the drive induced by priming is, however, obscure. Stimulation at different sites in the MFB appears to produce different kinds of experience, as indicated by the effects of natural drives on electrode preference. However, priming at any site motivates the pursuit of a reward from any other site but does not motivate the pursuit of a food reward.

Although we are far from understanding the natural function of the neural systems whose stimulation gives rise to the self-stimulation phenomenon, the self-stimulating rat nonetheless seems a good preparation in which to approach the problem of the neurobiology of knowledge formation and motivation in higher vertebrates. As emphasized in the minimal model (Figure 7.3), the electrical stimulation gives rise to a transient reinforcing signal (the action potentials in the reward pathway). Somewhere in the brain, this signal is converted into a reinforcing effect—the engram. This engram is the neurophysiological basis of the rat's new knowledge, its knowledge about the outcome of the stimulation-producing behavior. If we could identify the neural system that carries the reinforcing signal, we ought to be in a position to study the neurophysiological processes by which the information in transient signals is converted to enduring records. To put it baldly, if we can find the nerve in our nerve-memory preparation, we ought to be able to follow it to where the memory is made. A similar argument may be made regarding the motivating effect, the effect that makes the animal temporarily desire more stimulation. If we could find the nerve, we ought to be able to follow it to the circuits subjected to selective potentiation.

The advantages of this preparation are, first, the initial neural events are produced by a readily controllable electrical stimulus, whose action on neural tissue is well understood, and, second, the resulting mnemonic and motivational effects can dominate the animal's behavior for hours on end. These two advantages make it possible to conduct behavioral experiments designed to reveal neurophysiological, neuroanatomical, and neuropharmacological properties of the neural systems mediating self-stimulation. By means of these properties we may hope to identify the systems.

III. IDENTIFYING THE SUBSTRATE

In setting out to find the neural substrate for self-stimulation, we must ask how we will know when we have found it. What properties must a neural system possess in order to be regarded as the substrate for self-stimulation? The most obvious property is that it must be driven by the stimulation. We may narrow our search immediately to those systems that are so driven.

A. Activated Systems: 2DG Autoradiography

Until recently, the knowledge that the system we are looking for must be one of the systems driven by the stimulation was an advantage more in theory than in practice, because there was no way to identify the systems driven by the stimulation. The sampling problem rendered any attempt to do this electrophysiologically more or less hopeless. The advent of 2-deoxyglucose (2DG) autoradiography (Sokoloff, Reivich, Kennedy, & Des Rosiers, 1977), however, makes it possible to specify what systems are driven by the stimulation. We have recently used this technique to map the neural systems driven by rewarding stimulation either in the MFB or well outside the MFB in the locus coeruleus or the medial prefrontal cortex (Yadin, Guarini & Gallistel, 1983).

Rats with electrodes at one or another of these sites were trained to press a lever for 0.5-second trains of 0.1-msec pulses at 100 pulses per second. They were repeatedly tested at randomly chosen current intensities until stable rate–intensity curves were obtained. They were then set to responding for a current that yielded a rate three-fourths maximal and injected with a dose of [^{14}C]2DG. The rats continued self-stimulating for 45 minutes, while the radioactive 2DG was incorporated into the neurons (and other cells of the body). At the end of the 45 minutes the rats were sacrificed, their brains removed and sliced, and the slices exposed to X-ray film. The resulting images were analyzed by a computer-assisted image analyzing system (Gallistel, Piner, Allen, Adler, Yadin, & Negin, 1982).

There were no obvious bilateral effects of the stimulation. The detection and verification of subtle bilateral effects pose several methodological problems. Therefore, we focused our initial analysis on the unilateral effects of the stimulation, that is, on the detection of those systems that were more (or less) activated on the stimulated side of the brain than on the unstimulated side.

In the brains from rats with electrodes in or near the locus coeruleus, the only signs of activation we could detect were in the locus coeruleus itself and, occasionally, in the overlying cerebellum. The neural system showing the strongest and most reliable activation from the other three sites of stimulation are shown in Figure 7.6.

Electrodes in or near the MFB, whether anteriorly at the level of the lateral preoptic area or posteriorly at or slightly anterior to the level of the mammillary bodies, reliably and strongly activated the nucleus of the diagonal band of Broca near the anterior end of the MFB (PMFB, I and AMFB, I in Figure 7.6) and the anterior ventromedial tegmentum, particularly the medial portions of A-9 and the interfascicular portion of A-10 (PMFB, V–VI and AMFB, V–VI). Usually, the MFB was activated all along its course between these two sites (PMFB, II–IV and AMFB, II–IV). In some animals with electrodes near the mammillary origins of the fornix, the fornix was the focus of activation rather than the MFB, although fibers in the medial part of the MFB adjacent to the fornix may have been activated. The nucleus of the diagonal band and the anterior ventromedial tegmentum were activated regardless of whether the MFB or the fornix was the focus of activation at intermediate levels. Although some of the midbrain areas where the dopamine projection systems originate (A-8, A-9, A-10) were strongly and reliably activated, there was no reliable activation of any of the dopaminergic terminal fields.

There was no discernible overlap between the neural systems activated by rewarding MFB stimulation and the neural systems activated by rewarding stimulation of the medial prefrontal cortex. In addition to the medial cortex itself (MPFC, I), the stimulation reliably activated the rhinal cortex (MPFC, II), the claustrum (MPFC, II–VI), and the basolateral amygdaloid nucleus (MPFC-IV). It usually activated in addition a small part of the extreme dorsolateral septum (MPFC, II) and the anterior part of the medial thalamic nucleus (MPFC, III).

One might hope that there would be a neural system activated in common by stimulation at all the sites where the self-stimulation phenomenon may be produced. Such a system would be a likely candidate for the substrate of self-stimulation. However, autoradiographic analysis has not yet revealed a common system. Of course, there is no necessity for unilateral stimulation to cause only unilateral activity. It is possible that unilaterally generated signals from all the sites diverge bilaterally to activate some common and essential system equally on

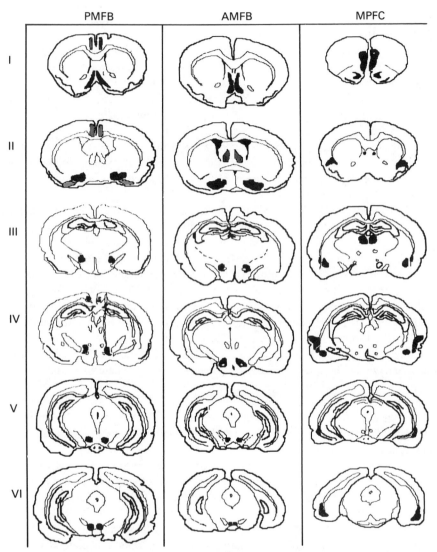

Figure 7.6. Neural systems unilaterally activated by self-administered rewarding stimulation at three different sites: posterior medial forebrain bundle (PMFB), anterior medial forebrain bundle (AMFB), and medial prefrontal cortex (MPFC). The areas in which activity on the stimulated side was greater than activity on the unstimulated side are blacked out bilaterally. The drawings were made during analysis with a computer-assisted image-processing system . [Gallistel, Piner, Allen, Adler, Yadin, & Negin (1982).] The activated region was highlighted with a color window. This region and the corresponding region on the other side of the section were outlined and filled in, using a cursor to draw and paint on the TV monitor of the system, where the image of the autoradiograph was displayed. Then the histological image was superimposed on the autoradiographic image. The cursor was used to outline the section and prominent structures within the section. When the drawing

both sides of the brain. No such bilaterally activated system is obvious upon simple visual comparison of autoradiographs from stimulated and unstimulated brains. A search for subtle bilateral effects using computer-assisted image analysis is now under way. The limits of the 2DG techniques are at present poorly understood, so one cannot rule out the possibility of a common unilaterally activated area that was not detected by this method for one reason or another. Nonetheless, the autoradiographic data suggest that there is no single neural substrate for self-stimulation.

It has often been remarked that rats self-stimulating at sites outside the MFB do not look like rats self-stimulating at MFB sites, suggesting that upon closer analysis these might be shown to be behaviorally distinct phenomena whose similarity is an artifact of the constrictions imposed by the Skinner box paradigm. Data from paired-pulse experiments indicate that self-stimulation at sites outside the MFB has little in common with MFB self-stimulation. The refractory periods obtained with electrodes in the medial prefrontal cortex and the cingulate cortex are much longer than those obtained with MFB electrodes (Silva, Vogel, & Corbett, 1982; Schenk & Shizgal, 1982). Refractory periods in the periaquaductal gray are slightly longer than MFB refractory periods but shorter than medial prefontal refractory periods (Bielajew, Jordan, Fermi-Enright, & Shizgal, 1981). There is little or no summation of rewarding effectiveness when stimulation is applied concurrently to the MFB and the medial prefrontal cortex (Schenk & Shizgal, 1982), whereas there is strong summation when two MFB sites are used, one in the lateral hypothalamus and one in the ventral tegmentum (Bielajew & Shizgal, 1982). Lesioning the MFB has no effect on medial prefrontal self-stimulation, whereas transection of efferents to sulcal cortex abolishes it (Corbett, Laferriere, & Milner, 1982). Lesioning the projection from the locus coeruleus to the MFB does not disrupt self-stimulation on electrodes in or near the locus coeruleus (Corbett, Skelton, & Wise, 1980). In short, self-stimulation at sites outside the MFB does not look much like MFB self-stimulation; data on refractory periods and the degree of summation between MFB and extra-MFB stimulation indicate that different, nonconverging substrates are involved; and lesions that interupt communication between the MFB and the extra-MFB sites do not interfere with self-stimulation at the extra-MFB sites. It is hard to avoid the conclusion that self-stimulation at extrahypothalamic sites has little in common with self-stimulation in the MFB, which is what one would conclude from the autoradiographic data as well.

---

was complete, the system removed the images from the screen and converted the drawing to a black on white image that was photographed. Level I corresponds to Figure 14 in the Paxinos & Watson (1982) atlas of the rat brain, Level II to their Figure 15, Level III to their Figure 20, Level IV to their Figure 22, Level V to their Figure 25, and Level VI to their Figure 26. [This figure is based on work reported in Yadin, Guarini, & Gallistel (1983).]

On the other hand, there are many reasons to think that within the MFB we are dealing with a coherent phenomenon. Electrodes anywhere along the MFB from the lateral preoptic area into the ventral tegmentum yield similar patterns of autoradiographic activation. Shizgal, Bielajew, Corbett, Skelton, and Yeomans (1980; see also Bielajew & Shizgal, 1982) have shown that two self-stimulation electrodes arrayed unilaterally along the MFB commonly excite overlapping sets of reward-relevant axons. Hence, there would appear to be a common substrate mediating self-stimulation of the MFB. The substrate for MFB self-stimulation, which is what we will be primarily concerned with, is presumably one or more of the neural systems whose activation is revealed in Panels PMFB and AMFB of Figure 7.6. The problem now is how to sort the wheat from the chaff, the systems relevant to self-stimulation from those that are irrelevant.

B. Quantitative Properties

Being driven by the stimulation is a necessary property of the substrate for the mnemonic and motivating effects of rewarding stimulation, but it is hardly sufficient. Most of the systems driven by the stimulation may have nothing to do with these effects. If activation by the stimulation is the only known property of what we are looking for, then we will never know whether or not we have found it. We must first use self-stimulation behavior to determine the neurophysiological, neuroanatomical, and neuropharmacological properties of the neural systems mediating the reinforcing and motivating effects, and then determine which of the systems revealed by autoradiography has the requisite properties. But how can we do this? What properties of the substrate can be made to show through in the behavior and how?

In tackling this question, we may turn for guidance to two of the best established linkage hypotheses in behavioral neurobiology: (1) the hypothesis that links the action potential (an electrophysiologically defined phenomenon) to the concept of conducted excitation in nerve (a behaviorally defined phenomenon) and (2) the hypothesis that links the isomerization of rhodopsin (a photochemically defined phenomenon) to the experience of seeing dim lights (a behaviorally defined phenomenon). Both of these neurobehavioral linkage hypotheses were established in large part by behavioral trade-off experiments.

A behavioral trade-off experiment is an experiment that determines those combinations of two stimulus parameters that yield a constant behavioral effect. For example, the shock-strength versus shock-duration experiment determines those combinations of pulse duration and current intensity that yield a muscle twitch of constant magnitude when pulses are applied to the nerve of a nerve-muscle preparation. Data from such experiments led to the resistance–capacitance model of the neuronal membrane (Lapicque, 1907). The fact that the electrical response of the neuronal membrane exhibits the same trade-off as one sees in the muscle-twitch data is part of the justification for equating the electrical response of the neuronal membrane with the concept of excitation in nerve.

For further example, the scotopic spectral sensitivity curve is determined by finding those combinations of wavelength and light intensity that yield the same frequency of "yes, I see it" responses when a dark-adapted human observer is shown dim flashes of light. The congruence between this behavioral trade-off function and the action spectrum of rhodopsin is the principal justification for regarding the isomerization of rhodopsin as the first stage in scotopic vision.

Behavioral trade-off functions play a unique and ubiquitous role in establishing neurobehavioral linkage hypotheses, because the behaviorally determined function propagates backward through the chain of underlying physiological mechanisms. The same trade-off relation that is manifest at the behavioral level must also be manifest in the output from any physiological stage that mediates between the stimulus and the resulting behavior. Conversely, trade-off experiments make quantitative properties of the neurophysiological substrate show through the behavior. They make manifest in the behavioral data properties of the substrate that may be measured by electrophysiological and anatomical techniques.

The realization of the power of trade-off experiments has motivated an extensive series of such experiments designed to determine quantitative properties of the neural substrate for the self-stimulation phenomenon. A recent review of these experiments (Gallistel *et al.*, 1981) forms the basis for the summary below.

1. Properties of the First Stage

In their review of the experiments that have determined quantitative properties of the substrate for self-stimulation, Gallistel *et al.* (1981) draw the following conclusions about the first stage.

1. The first stage is composed of long axons that course the length of the MFB and into the tegmentum.
2. These axons are myelinated.
3. Most of them have absolute refractory periods in the range 0.5–1.2 msec.
4. Following the refractory period, there supervenes a period of hyperexcitability, which is most evident in the period 2.0–5.0 msec after an impulse.
5. The axons conduct impulses at velocities of 2–8 m per second.
6. On the basis of the values for refractory period and conduction velocity, the diameter of these axons is probably 0.5–2 μm.

7. The orthodromic direction of conduction is rostrocaudal.
8. Local nonconducted potentials produced in these axons by extracellular stimulation decay in an approximately exponential manner with a time constant of 0.1 msec.
9. The interval over which axons in the cable integrate current is exceptionally long. When a steady cathodal current is applied, the number of firings it produces continues to increase for up to 15 msec after current onset.
10. These axons accommodate slowly to an anodal (hyperpolarizing) pulse. They fire on the offset of an anodal pulse, but only if the pulse is 5 msec or more in duration.
11. These axons cannot be any of the known monoamine projections, because the axons comprising these projections have the wrong properties: They are unmyelinated, have refractory periods greater than 1.5 msec, conduction velocities less than 1.5 m per second, and normally conduct caudorostrally.
12. This description applies to the first stage for reward, and to the first stage for priming as well, implying that these two first stages are either very similar or one and the same.

The experimental bases for these conclusions are elaborated in the sections that follow.

a. Paired-Pulse Experiments. Conclusions (1)–(6), (8), and (11) derive from experiments in which the stimulation is a train of paired pulses. When a pair of pulses falls upon a bundle of axons, both pulses fire the axons, unless the second pulse (called the T pulse) comes too close to the first (C pulse), in which case it finds some or all of the axons refractory to reexcitation. The extent to which the T pulse is or is not effective at various intervals after the C pulse may be estimated by varying the C–T interval and compensating for the resulting changes in stimulation efficacy by increasing or decreasing the total number of pairs. Suppose that we use a train of 20 evenly spaced pulses as a standard of comparison. When the second pulse in a pair of pulses is fully as effective as the first, then a train with 10 pairs will be just as effective as the standard. When the second pulse is completely ineffective, each pair fires the axons but once, and 20 pairs are required to bring the effectiveness of the train up to standard.

From this line of reasoning, Yeomans (1975) derived a formula for paired-pulse effectiveness

$$[N(\text{standard})/N(\text{C–T})] - 1$$

where $N(\text{standard})$ is the number of pulses in the brain of evenly spaced pulses and $N(\text{C–T})$ is the number of pairs required to achieve equivalent efficacy at a given C–T interval. This statistic goes from 0 to 1 as the effectiveness of the

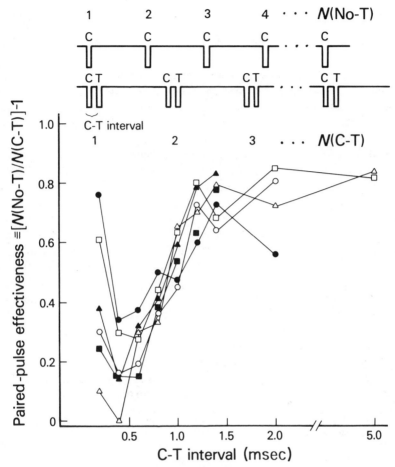

Figure 7.7. Paired-pulse effectiveness as a function of C–T interval. Data from six different electrodes in five different rats. The letters to the left of each curve identify the rat and electrode placement. The effectiveness statistic is based on the ratio between the required number of evenly spaced pulses, N(No–T), and the required number of pulse pairs, N(C–T). When a pair is no more effective than a single pulse, the statistic is zero. When a pair is as effective as two evenly spaced pulses, the statistic is one. The cartoon of the stimulating train at the top of this and all subsequent trade-off figures indicates the two parameters that are being traded against one another, in this case, N(C–T) and the C–T interval. [From Gallistel *et al.* (1981), Figure 3B with permission of the American Psychological Association, based on work reported in Yeomans (1975).]

second pulse goes from nothing to equivalence with effectiveness of the first pulse. Yeomans (1975) used rate of bar pressing as the behavioral variable and plotted paired-pulse effectiveness as a function of C–T interval (Figure 7.7). The curves in Figure 7.7 have two phases: As the C–T interval increases from 0 to 0.5 msec, paired-pulse effectiveness decreases; as the C–T interval increases beyond 0.5 msec, paired-pulse effectiveness increases. Following Deutsch (1964), who first conceived of measuring the refractory period of the first stage neurons using trains of paired pulses, Yeomans attributed the decline in paired-pulse effectiveness over the interval 0–0.5 msec to decreasing local potential summation. He attributed the recovery of effectiveness at intervals beyond 0.5 msec to recovery from refractoriness. Local potential summation occurs in axons lying just outside the region in which the C pulse fires axons. The axons in this subliminal fringe are depolarized, but not fired. The sub-threshold depolarization decays rapidly, but if a T pulse comes close on the heels of the C pulse, its depolarizing effect builds on the residual from the C pulse, so that together the pair of pulses fire more axons than either acting alone.

In a series of experiments. Yeomans and his collaborators have verified and extended this interpretation of the data in Figure 7.7 (see Gallistel et al., 1981, for review). From these experiments one may conclude that the first stage axons that account for at least 80% of the reinforcing effect of MFB stimulation have refractory periods in the range from 0.5 to 1.2 msec [conclusion (3) in the above list of conclusions]. This range of refractory periods suggests that one has to do with myelinated axons [conclusion (2)], since small (0.5–2 μm diameter) myelinated axons typically have refractory periods in this range [conclusion (6)], while unmyelinated axons, and particularly the monoaminergic axons [conclusion (11)], have much longer refractory periods (see below).

The above conclusions are buttressed by two-electrode paired-pulse experiments done by Shizgal, Bielajew, Corbett, Skelton, and Yeomans (1980). They used rats with two self-stimulation electrodes, one in the MFB at the level of the lateral hypothalamus and one in the ipsilateral tegmental extension of the MFB. Lucas (1913) realized that two-electrode paired-pulse experiments provide a means of estimating the conduction velocity of a signal that passes from one electrode to the other along a bundle of axons. He showed that the recovery from refractoriness in the two-electrode case was delayed relative to the one-electrode case by an amount equal to the time it took the action potential to travel from one electrode to the other.

When an axon is stimulated, impulses propagate both orthodromically ("downstream," toward the synapse) and antidromically ("upstream," away from the synapse). When the axon is stimulated more or less simultaneously at two sites, the impulse propagating orthodromically from the upstream electrode collides with the impulse propagating antridromically from the downstream electrode and both extinguish. Only the orthodromic impulse from the downstream electrode reaches the synapse. In order for impulses from both electrodes to reach the synapse, the C and T pulse must be separated by an interval sufficient (a) to allow an impulse from one electrode to propagate past the other and (b) to allow the membrane under the second electrode then to recover from refractoriness. Hence, the delay required for a T pulse to be effective in the two-electrode case is equal to the delay required in the one-electrode case [(b) above] plus the propagation time between the electrodes [(a) above].

Lucas, who worked with the nerve-muscle preparation, knew that both his electrodes excited one and the same axons at two different points. In the self-stimulation preparation, on the other hand, it was an open question whether one and the same first stage axons were being excited by two electrodes 3–4 mm apart, one in the lateral hypothalamus and one in the ventral tegmentum. In this preparation, the two-electrode paired-pulse experiment takes on added importance. If one finds a recovery from refractoriness effect in a plausible range of C–T intervals and if the effect is temporally symmetric, that is, independent of which electrode gets the C pulse and which the T, then one has evidence that a common set of self-stimulation relevant axons links the two sites [conclusion (1)].

Figure 7.8 shows the data from Shizgal, Bielajew, Corbett, Skelton, and Yeomans (1980). There was a recovery from refractoriness effect when the electrodes were ipsilateral, and it was temporally symmetric. There was no effect when the electrodes were contralateral. These results are to be expected if one assumes that ipsilateral sites are likely to be linked by axons running rostrocaudal or caudorostral and that contralateral sites are not likely to be so linked.

By subtracting the earliest interval evidencing recovery in the one-electrode case from the corresponding interval in the two-electrode case, Shizgal, Bielajew, Corbett, Skelton, and Yeomans obtained an estimate of conduction time (see, also, Bielajew & Shizgal, 1982). Dividing that by the distance between the electrodes yielded estimates of conduction velocity in the range 2–8 m per second [conclusion (5)]. This conduction velocity is characteristic of small myelinated axons, so these data reinforce the conclusions drawn from the one-electrode experiment [i.e., conclusions (2), (6), and (11)].

b. Pulse Strength versus Pulse Duration.   Conclusions (9) and (10)—the long interval over which current is integrated, the slow accommodation, and the firing upon the offset of a prolonged anodal pulse—derive from work by Matthews (1977) on the trade-off between pulse duration and required current intensity.

The integration interval of any system (neuron, synapse, neural circuit, etc.) is the interval over which output continues to increase in response to a sustained (step) input. In the case of an axon bundle subjected to a constant current, this means the interval after the onset of the current during which the total number of firings continues to increase. If individual axons within the bundle fire repetitively and unceasingly in response to a steady current, then the integration interval is infinite. However, axons seldom do this. Usually, they fire from one to, say, half-dozen spikes, and then cease firing. When the axons cease

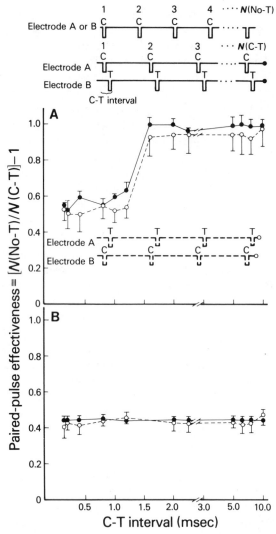

Figure 7.8. (A) Electrodes ipsilateral. Paired-pulse effectiveness as a function of C–T interval when the C and T pulses are delivered via separate electrodes arrayed unilaterally along the MFB and its ventral tegmental extension. The baseline, N(No–T), is an average of the number of pulses required when either electrode alone gets evenly spaced pulses. (B) Same experiment but with contralateral electrodes. [From Gallistel, Shizgal, & Yeomans (1981), Figure 7, with permission of the American Psychological Association, based on work reported in Shizgal, Bielajew, Corbett, Skelton, & Yeomans (1980).]

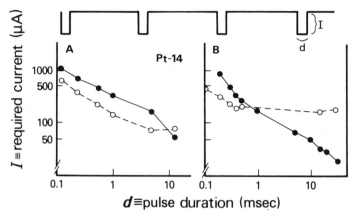

Figure 7.9. (A) Pulse strength (I) as a function of pulse duration (d) in the production of equivalent rewarding effects. Closed circles and solid lines are for anodal pulses. Open circles and dashed lines are for cathodal pulses. (B) Similar data for the motor twitch elicited via the same electrode. [From Gallistel, Shizgal, & Yeomans (1981), Figure 12, with permission of the American Psychological Association, based on work reported in Matthews (1977).]

to fire, the interval of integration is at an end; one has got all the firings one can get from a single pulse at that current level.

The interval of integration is reflected in the trade-off between pulse duration and required current. So long as pulse duration is less than the interval, increasing pulse duration increases the number of firings produced by a given current. Hence, increasing pulse duration reduces required current. As pulse duration approaches the limit of integration, increments in pulse duration purchase ever smaller reductions in required current. The required current approaches a constant value, called the rheobase.

Figure 7.9A shows representative strength–duration data for the reinforcing effect of cathodal and anodal pulses. Figure 9B shows representative data for the motor twitch produced by the rewarding stimulation, probably through excitation of motor fibers in the nearby internal capsule. Note that the limit of integration of cathodal current for the fibers that mediate the twitch is considerably shorter than for the fibers that mediate the reinforcing effect, which is to say that the cathodal strength–duration curve for the twitch levels off much sooner than does the corresponding curve for the reinforcing effect. A common measure of the rapidity with which a strength–duration curve approaches its rheobase is the chronaxie, the pulse duration at which the required current is twice the rheobase. Chronaxies for the reinforcing effect range from 0.7 to 3.0 msec with a mean of about 1.5 msec, whereas chronaxies for the motor twitch range from 0.15 to 0.48 msec (Matthews, 1977). Clearly, the manner in which fibers mediating the reinforcing effect integrate cathodal current distinguishes them from the fibers which mediate motor effects.

Accommodation is a change in axonal excitability in response to a prolonged change in membrane polarization. In response to prolonged or intense
depolarization, the axons become inexcitable. This accommodation determines
the limits of temporal integration; it terminates firing in axons subjected to
prolonged cathodal current. When subjected to prolonged anodal (hyperpolarizing) current, axons undergo the opposite change; they become hyperexcitable.
When the anodal current ceases, the return to normal membrane polarization in
axons become hyperexcitable may initiate a spike. This phenomenon, known
since the nineteenth century, is called firing on break (see Matthews, 1978). In
looking at the anodal strength–duration curves in Figure 7.9, one notes that they
parallel the cathodal curves at shorter pulse durations, then dip toward or below
them at longer durations. This dip comes much sooner in the motor effect data
than in the reward data. Matthews (1977) gives strong reasons for believing that
the dip marks the onset of the firing at break phenomenon. The fact that it occurs
only at lengthy pulse durations in the reward data is an indication that the reward-
relevant axons accommodate slowly. The unusually long interval of integration
for cathodal current, as already indicated, implies the same conclusion—slow
accommodation.

At short pulse durations anodal pulses are only about half as effective as
cathodal pulses, that is, they require twice the current to achieve the same level
of reinforcement. Because anodal current hyperpolarizes rather than depolarizes
the neuronal membranes in the immediate vicinity of the electrode, it is hardly
surprising that it is less effective. What is surprising is that short anodal pulses
are as effective as they are. The fact that they are effective at all is presumably
due to remote exit currents. Hyperpolarizing current entering an axon at the
electrode tip must be balanced by a depolarizing current exiting elsewhere,
which causes the firing. This remote exit current will be more effective if the
depolarizing flux is not spread out along the axonal membrane but confined
instead to a few sites. A myelin sheath would have this effect; it would confine
the exit current to the nodes of Ranvier. Thus, the surprising effectiveness of
short anodal pulses again suggests that one has to do with myelinated axons.

  c. *The Direction of Normal Conduction.*   Stimulation pulses falling upon
the relevant axons excite action potentials propagating both orthodromically
(toward the synapse) and antidromically (away from the synapse). Presumably,
only the orthodromically conducted pulses impulses are behaviorally relevant.
Shizgal, Bielajew, and Kiss (1980) and Bielajew and Shizgal (in preparation,
1983) did a two-electrode strength–duration experiment to determine the
orthodromic direction of conduction. The experiment rests on another nineteenth
century discovery, called Pflügers law, to the effect that "descending current is
more effective than ascending current." A descending current is one in which the
cathode lies closer to the synapse than the anode. Because the cathode depolarizes while the anode hyperpolarizes, the cathode is the site of origin for action

potentials. When the cathode lies closer to the synapse than the anode, the orthodromic impulses propagate from the cathode unhindered to the synapse. When, however, the anode lies between the cathode and the synapse, the impulses must propagate through the region of hyperpolarization around the anode. Some of the impulses do not get through this region (anodal block), which is why this configuration (anode downstream from cathode) is less effective than the reverse configuration (anode upstream). The anodal-blocking effect is only found when longer pulses are used, because with shorter pulses the hyperpolarization at the anode has disappeared (the stimulating pulse has ended) before the impulses from the cathode arrive beneath the anode. Bielajew and Shizgal worked with preparations in which they had already demonstrated collision between the impulses produced by a lateral hypothalamic electrode and the impulses produced by a ventral tegmental electrode (see Figure 7.8 and accompanying discussion). They compared the data from four different strength–duration experiments. In the two control conditions, the anode was an indifferent electrode on the skull away from the path of impulse flow. In the test conditions, strength–duration curves were obtained using either the lateral hypothalamic electrode as the cathode and the ventral tegmental electrode as the anode or the reverse configuration. The curve obtained with the cathode in the ventral tegmentum and the anode in the lateral hypothalamus looked like the corresponding control curve; there was no anodal blocking effect with this configuration. The curve obtained with the reverse configuration departed upwards from the control curve at longer pulse durations—the anodal blocking effect. From this, it may be concluded that the orthodromic direction of conduction is rostrocaudal, from the hypothalamus to the ventral tegmentum [conclusion (7)].

2. Properties of the Second Stage

One property of the first stage was not mentioned above because it only emerges in connection with experiments designed primarily to reveal properties of the second stage. It appears that when short (0.1 msec) pulses are used, the number of first-stage axons fired by a pulse is a linear function of current intensity. This conclusion emerges from experiments that study the temporal and spatial integrating properties of the second stage by trading the number of pulses in a train of fixed duration against current intensity. As Figure 7.10 shows, the required current is a linear function of the reciprocal of the number of pulses.

The surprisingly simple relation between the required current and the number of pulses in a train of fixed duration may be explained by three intertwined assumptions:

1. Each 0.1-msec pulse fires one and only one action potential in every axon within the radius of effective excitation.
2. The number of relevant axons fired by a pulse increases as a linear function of current intensity.

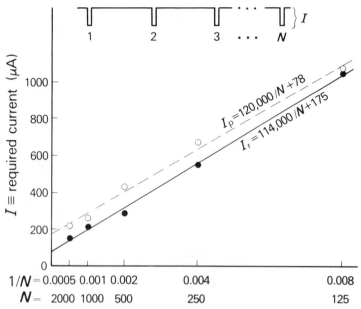

Figure 7.10. Required current, I, as a function of the reciprocal of the number, N, of pulses in a train. Closed circles are data for rewarding effect; open circles for priming effect in same rat. Train duration in both experiments was 10 seconds. Unweighted linear regressions, I_r and I_p, account for 99.7% of variance in case of reward, and 99.3% in case of priming. [Modified from Gallistel, Shizgal, & Yeomans (1981).]

3. When train duration is fixed and the strength of stimulation constant throughout a train, then the reinforcing effect is determined solely by the number of action potentials in the first-stage axons, not by their temporal or spatial distribution.

These three assumptions and their tight interrelation are discussed at greater length in Gallistel *et al.* (1981). The first assumption—that very short pulses fire only one action potential—was implicitly assumed in interpreting all of the paired-pulse data. It is justified by all the electrophysiological data of which I am aware (e.g., Matthews, 1978). It implies that the number of action potentials in the first-stage axons, that is, the amount of initial excitation or, put another way, the magnitude of the first-stage signal, is directly proportional to the number of pulses in a train of fixed duration. This gives one a powerful angle of attack on the problem of scaling the effects of other variables, such as current intensity, or even drugs and lesions (see Sections III,C,D,&F).

The second assumption—that the number of first-stage axons fired increases linearly with current intensity—follows from the first and third assumptions and the linear trade-off between current and the reciprocal of the number of

Stimulation

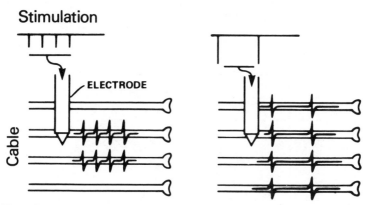

Figure 7.11. The "counter" model of the integrator assumes that the above two inputs from the cable yield the same output from the integrator, despite the difference in the spatiotemporal distribution of the spikes. [Reproduced from Gallistel, Shizgal, & Yeomans (1981), Figure 15, by permission of the American Psychological Association.]

pulses. An extensive theoretical discussion of the relation between current intensity, the region of effective excitation, and the number of axons fired is given by Shizgal, Howlett, and Corbett (1979).

The third assumption is illustrated in Figure 7.11. It may be called the "integrator as counter" assumption. It says that when train duration is fixed the reinforcement-relevant aspect of integrator output depends only on the number of action potentials it receives as input. The integrator would not have this property if the synaptic processes that determine its summation characteristics showed appreciable accommodation or facilitation. Suppose, for example, that there were appreciable temporal facilitation, meaning that spikes arriving soon after preceding spikes had a bigger than usual effect. Then, high-frequency, low-current stimulation should be more effective than high-current, low-frequency stimulation. Conversely, suppose there were accommodation, meaning that spikes arriving soon after preceding spikes were less effective than usual. Then, high-current, low-frequency stimulation should be more effective. In neither case would one expect a simple linear trade-off between required current and the reciprocal of the number of pulses.

The counterlike behavior of the second stage obtains only so long as one is discussing trains that have the same duration. When the overall duration of the train is allowed to vary, the total number of first-stage action potentials required to produce a given level of reward also varies. One way to interpret this fact is by assuming that the integrator is a leaky one: When its input is more spread out in time, the effects of initial impulses have decayed to a greater extent by the time the effects of final pulses are felt, so there is less summation between initial and final effects. Hence, longer train durations require more total input to reach a

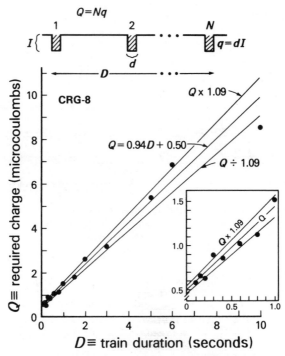

Figure 7.12. Required charge (Q) as a function of train duration (D). The required charge is Nq, where q is the charge per pulse and N is the number of pulses. The center line, labeled $Q = 0.94D + 0.50$, represents the best fitting (weighted) linear regression. Most of the points fall within a factor of 1.09 of this regression (upper and lower lines). [Modified from Gallistel, Shizgal, and Yeomans (1981).]

given level of summated effect. Because the summation between initial and final effects is more complete in trains of short duration, they require less total input. However, they must build up a given level of summed effect in a shorter time, so they must deliver more input per unit time, that is, the strength of the input must be greater in shorter inputs.

In order to measure the temporal integrating characteristics of the integrator, Gallistel (1978) determined required charge (charge per second × train duration) at various train durations. He found that required charge increased as a linear function of train duration (Figure 7.12). This means that the required strength of stimulation is a hyperbolic function of train duration (Figure 7.13).

If this integration is correctly conceived as an instance of leaky integration, then the limits of temporal integration may be estimated from the strength–duration plots in Figure 7.13. As duration becomes longer and longer, the degree of summation between the effects of initial and final pulses becomes less and less. When there is no appreciable summation between the effects of initial and

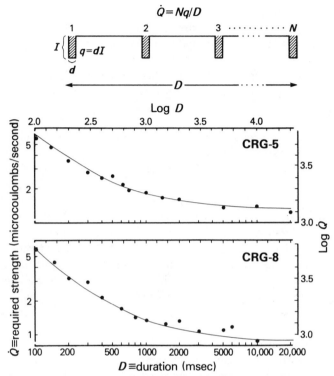

Figure 7.13. Required train strength ($\dot{Q}$ is the charge per second) as a function of train duration. The data in the lower panel are the same data as in Figure 7.12, but replotted in strength–duration form. The solid line is calculated from a hyperbolic strength–duration function using a representative value for the chronaxie (0.5 second). Slightly better fits are obtained using differing values of chronaxie for each data set—0.35 second for the CRG-5 (upper panel), and 0.53 second for the CRG-8 (lower panel). [Reproduced from Gallistel, Shizgal, & Yeomans (1981), Figure 17, by permission of the American Psychological Association.]

final pulses, the leaky integrator is losing as much per unit time as it gains from continued stimulation, hence there is no further reduction in required strength. This asymptotically low strength is called the rheobase. One sees in Figure 7.13 that the required strength of stimulation is very near the rheobase when train duration reaches 2.0 seconds. We may take this as approximately the limit of temporal integration.

Another way to characterize the rate at which a hyperbolic strength–duration function approaches rheobase is by its chronaxie. The chronaxie is the duration at which the required strength is twice the rheobase. The chronaxie of the train-strength-versus-train-duration functions for both the reinforcing and priming effects of MFB stimulation are about 0.5 second. Huston, Mills, and

Huston (1972) also determined the trade-off between train duration and train strength, using 100-Hz sine wave stimulation and a Skinner box paradigm. They, too, obtained linear charge– duration functions (hyperbolic strength– duration functions), but the functions they obtained had chronaxies almost an order of magnitude shorter (around .06 second). The reasons for this large and puzzling discrepancy are at present obscure. The matter would repay further investigation.

3. Summary

Long thin myelinated axons coursing through the MFB into the ventral tegmentum constitute the first stage. They have refractory periods of 0.5–1.2 msec and conduction velocities of 2–8 m per second. The number of these axons fired is a linear function of current intensity when brief cathodal pulses are used. The postsynaptic processes that integrate the temporally and spatially dispersed action potentials from the first-stage axons care only about the number of spikes, provided train duration is fixed and the strength of stimulation is constant throughout the train. This makes it unlikely that these integrating processes manifest noticeable facilitation or accommodation. These integrating processes may have the characteristics of a leaky integrator. This would explain why the required strength of stimulation approaches an asymptotic minimum (rheobase) as train duration is increased. If this leaky-integrator interpretation is correct, then the limit of temporal integration is on the order of two seconds.

The conclusion that the first stage axons, the axons in the MFB whose stimulation gives rise eventually to the reinforcing and motivating effects, are descending myelinated axons accords well with the autoradiographic data. Nieuwenhuys, Geeraedts, and Veening (1982) have published an excellent atlas of the MFB in the rat, in which they divide the MFB into various compartments, in part based on the diameters of the descending myelinated axons. We have reanalyzed the autoradiographs in Gomita and Gallistel (1982) to see how the activation in those autoradiographs corresponds to these compartments (un-published analysis). At the anterior end of the optic chiasm (Figure 4 in the Nieuwenhuys *et al.* atlas), the activation is primarily in the DBB (nucleus of the diagonal band of Broca) and not in the more lateral and ventral compartment ''a,'' where the large-diameter (2–8 μm) fibers run. At a midchiasmatic level, the activation is primarily in the compartments they label ''APM'' (anterior medial preoptic area) and ''b,'' the compartments where the thin- to medium-diameter (0.5–2 μm) myelinated fibers are found. As one moves caudally back through the hypothalamus, the activation is primarily in their compartments ''e'' and ''c'' in the dorsal part of the MFB. Again, these are the compartments where the 0.5–2 μm descending myelinated axons are found. When it is borne in mind that the conclusions from the behavioral data regarding myelination, axon diameter, and direction of conduction antedate the anatomical specification of these charac-teristics by Nieuwenhuys *et al.*, the correspondence between these conclusions, and the anatomical/autoradiographic data is both startling and gratifying. Further substantiation of these conclusions comes from the electrophysiological data of Shizgal, Kiss, and Bielajew (1982), who showed that the compound action potential evoked in the MFB by stimulation from a rewarding electrode is carried by axons with refractory periods and conduction velocities matching those inferred from the behavioral data. Thus, autoradiographic and electrophysiological data testify to the plausability of the inference that the first stage axons are thin myelinated axons descending via the MFB into the ventral tegmentum.

4. Adaptation Rather Than Leaky Integration?

Deutsch, Chisholm, and Mason (1980) have argued that the leveling off of the train-strength versus train-duration function reflects a process of adaptation rather than leaky integration. Their adaptation model assumes, first, that "the instantaneous values of the reward signals, above a certain threshold, are summed," and, second, that "the value of a constant signal fed in declines as a function of time from the beginning of the signal" (Deutsch, Chisholm, & Mason, 1980, p. 360). The idea is that the magnitude of the reward signal generated by a constant strength of stimulation declines with time. The reinforcing effect is the integral of the function obtained by subtracting a constant function (the threshold) from this decreasing reward signal.

The puzzling thing about the Deutsch adaptation model is that the second assumption, adaptation of the reward signal, takes back what is gained by the first assumption. The first assumption, that the integrator sums the reward signal above some threshold level without temporal leakage, means that the reinforcing effect of a constant suprathreshold reward signal increases linearly and indefinitely. If this were true and if the strength of the rewarding signal generated by constant rewarding stimulation remained constant over time, then one would get a hyperbolic strength–duration function

$$\dot{Q} = K_1/D + K_2 \qquad (1)$$

where $\dot{Q}$ is the strength of stimulation (charge per second), D is train duration, K_1 is a constant proportional to the reinforcement required for a given level of performance, and K_2 is a constant proportional to the threshold level above which the reward signal is integrated. Thus, the first assumption, by itself, explains the precise form of the train-strength versus train-duration function, which is something the leaky integrator model does not do. However, the first assumption yields a hyperbolic strength–duration function only so long as one assumes the negation of the second assumption—only so long as one assumes that the reward signal does not adapt.

Why, then, do Deutsch et al. (1980) assume adaptation? In order, I think, to explain why the rats have little or no preference between a 1-second train and a 2-second train of the same strength, whereas they (can) have a marked preference between a 0.5-second train and a 1.0-second train (Deutsch, Roll, & Wetter, 1976). If we make the perhaps unlikely assumption that the reinforcing effects of reward signals may increase without limit, then the nonleaky integration model predicts that the reinforcing effects differ by the same ratio in both cases,

$$R(2.0)/R(1.0) = R(1.0)/R(0.5) \tag{2}$$

where $R(2.0)$ is the magnitude of the reinforcing effect produced by a 2-second train, and so on.

Deutsch et al. (1980) seem to assume implicitly that the equality of reinforcement ratios implies an equality in the rat's preferences. They seem to assume that from Eq. (2) we must infer that the rat's preference for $R(2.0)$ over $R(1.0)$ is the same as its preference for $R(1.0)$ over $R(0.5)$. No such inference is in fact required, and, upon study, I think one can see that such an inference would be implausible.

Deutsch et al. find that for a relatively weak strength of stimulation, $P[R(1.0), R(0.5)]$ is only slightly greater than 1, where $P[R_1,R_2]$ is the ratio of choices of R_1 to choices of R_2, that is, the rats have only a slight preference for the 1.0-second train over the 0.5-second train when the stimulation is weak. When the stimulation is stronger, however, they find that the preference for the 1.0-second train is more marked. That is, $P[R(1.0), R(0.5)]$ is considerably greater than 1. They argue that the leaky integrator model must predict the same preference in both cases.

The Deutsch et al. argument rests on implicit assumptions about the form of the preference function $P[R_1, R_2]$, the processes that translate different magnitudes of reinforcement into choice ratios. Figure 7.14 shows the outputs of an illustrative leaky integrator for two pairs of inputs. The reinforcing effects are assumed to be proportional to the peak values of these outputs. Since the integrator is assumed to behave as a linear system, increasing the strength of stimulation by a common factor (a factor of 2 in Figure 7.14) must increase the peak outputs by the same factor. If we double the strength of both the short and long trains, then the peak response must double in both cases. Hence the difference in their reinforcing value must also double (assuming always that the reinforcing effect may increase without limit).

If we assume that the preference $P[R_1, R_2]$ depends solely on this difference, $R_1 - R_2$, then the leaky integrator model predicts just what Deutsch et al. (1980) in fact found. The solid lines in Figure 7.15 plot the preference for one reinforcement over another reinforcement on the assumption that preference is proportional to the difference between the reinforcements.

If, on the other hand, we assume that the preference depends solely on the ratio R_1/R_2, then we get the result that Deutsch et al. (1980) erroneously assume the leaky integrator model must predict: the preference is unaffected by increasing the strength of both trains by a common factor (dashed lines in Figure 7.15).

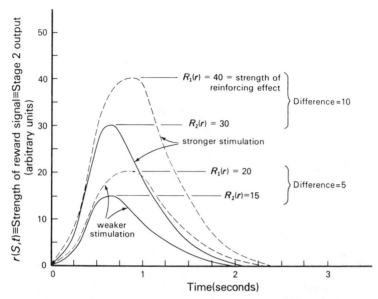

Figure 7.14. Hypothetical outputs, $r(S, t)$, from a linear leaky integrator given inputs of two different durations (solid line, 0.5-second train; dashed line, 1.0-second train) at two different strengths. In a linear system, increasing the strength of an input by a factor necessarily increases peak output by the same factor. Hence, doubling the strength of both trains doubles the difference in the peak values of the outputs. The reinforcing effect, $R(r)$, of a rewarding signal is assumed to be proportional to the peak value of $r(S, t)$. The notation $r(S, t)$ expresses the fact that the reward signal, r, depends on the parameters of the stimulation, S, and on the passage of time, t. The notation $R(r)$ expresses the fact that the reinforcing effect, R, depends on the rewarding signal, r. In this figure, it is assumed to depend on the peak of r. In the model proposed by Deutsch, Chisolm, and Mason (1980), it is assumed to depend on the integral with respect to time of $r(S, t) - k$ where k is a constant.

In fact, neither of these assumptions seems plausible. They both assume that the absolute values of R_1 and R_2 have no effect on the preference. The first assumption means, to use monetary rewards for illustration, that the preference for $10.00 over $5.00 is the same as the preference for $1,000,000 over $999,995. The second assumption means that the preference for $10.00 over $5.00 is the same as the preference for $1,000,000 over $500,000. We do not know what the true preference function looks like. The important point is that the outcome of the Deutsch *et al.* (1980) experiment neither supports nor contradicts any prediction from the leaky integrator model.

The Deutsch *et al.* (1980) paper illustrates the importance of adhering to two conceptual guidelines in trying to derive quantitative characteristics of the substrate for self-stimulation:

1. Distinguish carefully between the following three functions: $r(S, t) \equiv$ the function that translates stimulation (S) into a rewarding signal (r) that fades as

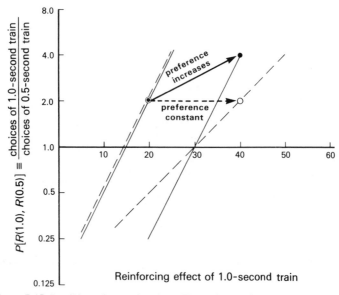

Figure 7.15. Possible preference functions. The preference for a 1.0-second train over a 0.5-second train is plotted as a function of the reinforcing value of the 1.0-second train. A different plot is required for each value of the comparison reinforcement (the reinforcement provided by the 0.5-second train). The axis of no preference is the horizontal line at $P[R(1.0), R(0.5)] = 1$. The rightmost pair of lines, which intersect this axis at 30, are for the strong stimulation case, where the reinforcing value of the 0.5-second train is assumed to be 30. The left-most pair, which intersect at 15, are for the weak stimulation case, where the reinforcing value of the 0.5-second train is assumed to be 15. The solid parallel lines represent the hypothesis that preference depends on the difference between two reinforcements. On this hypothesis, the leaky integrator model predicts what Deutsch *et al.* found, namely, that increasing the strength of both trains by the same factor increases the preference for the longer train. The dashed divergent lines represent the implicit hypothesis of Deutsch *et al.*, that preference depends on the ratio between two reinforcements. Either an increase, no change, or decrease in preference is consistent with the leaky-integrator model, depending on the manner in which preference is assumed to vary as the two reinforcements vary.

a function of time (t) when stimulation ceases. (Equivalent to the signal in the reward pathway in Figure 7.3 and to the signals whose time course is plotted in Figure 7.14.) $R(r) \equiv$ the function that converts the rewarding signal (r) into a reinforcing effect (R) which is a time-independent variable. (Equivalent to the conversion process in Figure 7.3.) $P(R) \equiv$ the function that translates a given reinforcement (or pair of reinforcements) into a performance (e.g., running speed, bar pressing rate) or preference (choice ratio). Equivalent to Stage 4 in Figure 7.3)

2. In deriving the characteristics of $r(S, t)$, rely only on trade-off data. Relying on differences in performance, as Deutsch *et al.* (1980) do, confounds all three functions, permitting no inferences to be drawn about any of them.

As a rule, it is difficult to draw any conclusions about the outcome of trade-off experiments from the outcome of input–output experiments, such as the Deutsch *et al.* (1980) experiment. Deutsch *et al.* suppose that their data imply that the chronaxies of train-strength versus train-duration functions derived from different levels of performance would not be the same. Their data do not in fact imply this, nor is it empirically true. Edmonds, Stellar, and Gallistel (1974) call attention to the fact that running-speed versus current intensity functions are approximately parallel when plotted on semilog paper, which means that the form of the trade-off functions is independent of the level of performance used in deriving the trade-off. This parallelism was strikingly apparent in Gallistel's (1978) experiment (see Figure 7.16). The parallelism seen in Figure 7.16 means

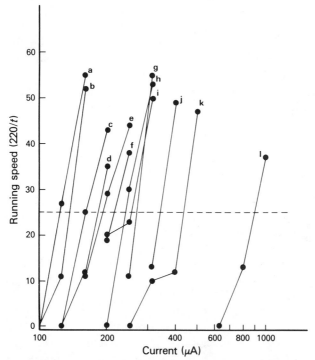

Figure 7.16. Running speed as a function of reward current at different train durations (*D*, msec) and pulse frequencies (N). The current axis is logarithmic. The strength–duration function for CRG-5 in Figure 7.13 was derived from these data (and others not shown), using the criterion shown (dashed line). The plots of performance as a function of log current at different train durations and pulse frequencies are parallel. Therefore, the form of the trade-off function is independent of the performance criterion used to derive it. Functions derived from different criteria differ only by a multiplicative constant. (a) $D = 20,000, N = 2,001$; (b) $D = 10,000, N = 1,001$; (c) $D = 2000, N = 201$; (d) $D = 1000, N = 101$; (e) $D = 700, N = 71$; (f) $D = 620, N = 63$; (g) $D = 300, N = 31$; (h) $D = 400, N = 41$; (i) $D = 500, N = 51$; (j) $D = 200, N = 21$; (k) $D = 140, N = 15$; (l) $D = 70; N = 8$.

that the chronaxies of strength–duration functions derived from these data using different levels of performance (different criteria) all have about the same value.

In sum, changes in the preference between two trains of different durations when their strengths are varied by a common factor do not provide evidence against the leaky-integrator model or for the adaptation model. On the other hand, the perfect integration above a threshold assumption would explain the hyperbolic form of the strength–duration function. This assumption ought to be tested further. The fact that neither preference nor speed of performance is altered much by increasing train duration beyond 2 seconds is not a decisive objection to the perfect-integration model, since this fact may be accommodated by assuming that the integrator has a limited capacity. When the integrator is filled to capacity, the maximum possible reinforcement has been generated. Upon reflection, it may seem likely that increasing the magnitude of a reward beyond some limit has no further influence on its reinforcing effect. For a rat, one silo full of corn may have the same reinforcing effect as would all the corn in Kansas. If a 2-second train of stimulation at just above the threshold of integration generates the maximum possible reinforcement, then prolonging stimulation beyond 2 seconds will be pointless. It will not result in any appreciable reduction in the required strength of stimulation and longer trains will not be preferred over a 2-second train.

5. Can the Substrates for Priming and Reinforcements Be Distinguished on the Basis of Their Quantitative Properties?

Experiments on the quantitative properties of the substrate for self-stimulation were originally undertaken in the hope of revealing distinct properties for the two effects of the stimulation. The first experiments (Deutsch, 1964; Gallistel *et al.*, 1969), which did not rely on trade-off functions, found seeming differences in the refractory periods for priming and reinforcement. However, Gallistel (1975) and Yeomans (1975) called attention to the possibility that these differences were artifactual. When the experiment was repeated using the trade-off methodology, no difference was found (Gallistel *et al.*, 1981). Also, Rompré and Miliaressis (1980) found that the recovery from refractoriness for the active exploration elicited by continuous rewarding stimulation was identical to the recovery for self-stimulation (using same electrodes for both behaviors). The exploratory behavior may be another manifestation of the priming effect. It has also been found that the two substrates, if two there be, yield identical pulse-strength versus pulse-duration functions with both cathodal and anodal pulses (Matthews, 1977). One also finds the same linear relation between the required current and the reciprocal of the number of pulses in a train of fixed duration and the same hyperbolic relation between the required strength of stimulation and the train duration (Liran, 1981).

In short, the quantitative properties of the substrates for the priming and reinforcement are very similar, if not identical. The most parsimonious interpretation is that the two behavioral effects of the stimulation derive from the stimulation of one and the same neural system. We will see, however, that the two effects may be dissociated pharmacologically. One can find drugs that block one effect but not the other. It may be, therefore, that the priming and reinforcing effects of MFB stimulation derive from the excitation of two distinct neural substrates that happen to have similar quantitative properties.

In any event, the determination of the trade-offs between various parameters of the stimulation has revealed a number of quantitative properties of the substrate for self-stimulation. These results in turn help answer the question of how we may know whether or not, in the course of electrophysiological and autoradiographic experiments, we have found the substrate for the motivating and reinforceing effects of stimulation. The force of these behavioral data will be evident when we come to consider electrophysiological data.

C. Pharmacological Properties

Behavioral pharmacology may add to the list of characteristics by which we may establish the anatomical and electrophysiological identity of the substrate for self-stimulation. Given an appropriate set of experiments in the behavioral pharmacology of self-stimulation, we may ask of a given neural system not only whether it manifests the right refractory periods, condution velocities, etc., but also whether its output is blocked or enhanced by drugs known to have such actions on the substrate for self-stimulation.

Wise (1978; 1982) and Fibiger (1978) have extensively reviewed the large literature on the pharmacology of self-stimulation, focusing particularly on the question of whether catecholaminergic neurons constitute a crucial part of the substrate for self-stimulation. In this chapter I confine myself to experiments reported since those reviews, particularly those that bear on what Wise and many others have pointed to as a central problem in this literature.

The problem is to determine whether drugs that attentuate or abolish self-stimulation behavior do so by blocking the reinforcing and/or motivating effect of the stimulation. There are innumerable other neurobehavioral functions that if pharmacologically interfered with would cause attenuated or nonexistent self-stimulation behavior. Curare, which blocks nerve-muscle transmission; methocarbamol, which is a spinally acting paralytic; and Chloropent, a general anaesthetic used by veterinarians, have all been shown to attentuate self-stimulation behavior in a dose-dependent fashion (Edmonds & Gallistel, 1974; Gallistel, Boytim, Gomita, & Klebanoff, 1982). No one supposes, however, that these drugs block the reinforcing or motivating effects of brain stimulation. The same problem arises with drugs that enhance self-stimulation. They may do so either by a specific effect on the reinforcing and motivating functions or by a general effect on one or more of the unspecifiably large number of neurobehavioral functions pertinent to self-stimulation performance.

Unless it can be convincingly shown that certain drugs act specifically on the motivating and reinforcing functions, data on the pharmacology of self-stimulation behavior will be of little use in establishing the identity of the neural substrate. Establishing the functional specificity of drug effects in self-stimulation requires behavioral controls that rule out nonspecific functions.

Two often-employed controls are to examine the rat for obvious signs of general debility and/or to show that its performance on some other task is unimpaired by doses of the drug that attentuate self-stimulation performance. Both of these controls are widely recognized to be inadequate. The first assumes that any effect of a drug on functions other than reinforcement and motivation will show up as a general behavioral debility, obvious upon casual inspection. The second assumes that if the impairment of a given nonspecific function shows up in the performance of one task then it must show up in the performance of another task. Neither of these assumptions seems defensible. Both may be shown to be wrong when picrotoxin is used (see below).

Convincing behavioral controls must focus on behavioral phenomena that constitute a signature of the reinforcing (or motivating) function—a signature that cannot readily be counterfeited by other neurobehavioral functions. Two sets of experiments have recently been done that focus on these sorts of signatures. Both lead to the conclusion that the neuroleptic, pimozide, which blocks dopamine receptors, blocks the reinforcing effect of MFB stimulation.

1. Extinction Experiments

The first set of experiments focuses on the extinctionlike change in performance that should be seen if a drug blocks reinforcement. If an animal has been trained to perform a task and the reinforcing effect of the reward is then blocked, the animal ought to start out at the predrug level of performance, then exhibit a trial by trial decrease in performance, as it finds the results of previous experience contradicted by present experience.

Liebman and Butcher (1973) were the first to report an extinctionlike change in self-stimulation performance in rats treated with pimozide. Their result has repeatedly been confirmed and extended (e.g., Fouriezos & Wise, 1976). Figure 7.17 compares the decline in speed of runway performance in pimozide-treated rats with the decline shown by the untreated animal when the experimenter disconnects the reward stimulation. The drug-induced "extinction" closely parallels genuine extinction. In either case, rats perform at normal speed on the first one or two trials, then more hesitantly on the next several trials, ceasing entirely to perform after somewhere between 6 and 50 trials.

The fact that the rat's performance is normal on the first few trials rules out

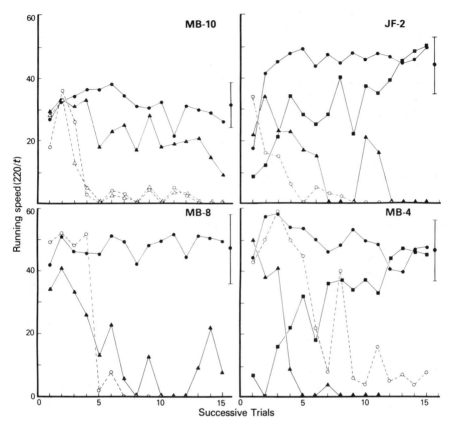

Figure 7.17. The trial by trial running speeds of four rats (identified by letter number combinations) over the first 15 trials of a session, under control conditions (normal reward, ●——●, mean of four), with no reward (○--○), or after treatment with pimozide (▲——▲, 0.5 mg/kg; △--△, 0.75 mg/kg) or Chloropent (■——■). Rats run under pimozide extinguish, just like rats run with no reward. Rats treated with Chloropent increase their speed from trial to trial. (Control, mean ± SD is indicated at far right of each graph, I.) [Reproduced from Gallistel, Boytim, Gomita, & Klebanoff (1982), Figure 2, by permission of ANKHO International (PB&B).]

a large class of nonspecific functions. The impairment of most functions other than reinforcement would be manifest at the outset of testing. (The results in Figure 7.17 cannot be attributed to a gradual time-dependent onset of drug action because the same result was obtained when testing began anywhere between 3.5 and 4.5 hours after injection.)

One must, however, worry about a class of nonspecific effects that could produce pseudo-extinction. Suppose, for example, that a drug made the rat exceptionally prone to fatigue. The rat might stop running after a few trials because it was too tired rather than because it no longer expected reinforcement.

Gallistel, Boytim, Gomita, and Klebanoff (1982) demonstrated pseudo-extinction using picrotoxin. Picrotoxin in doses of 2–4 mg/kg does not produce any obvious debilitation in rats, and it does not impair performance on a task that requires pressing a lever to escape footshock (Kent & Fedinets, 1976). It does, however, increase rats' susceptibility to the seizure-producing effects of stimulation of the MFB. After some number of trials in a runway or some minutes in a Skinner box, self-stimulating rats treated with picrotoxin often show signs of seizure activity. In some cases, however, these signs are slight. They are only seen if the rats are carefully observed. The decline in performance, which can look a lot like extinction (Figure 7.18), follows the appearance of this seizure activity, at least in our experience.

The results with picrotoxin illustrate the inadequacy of the controls most commonly employed to demonstrate the specificity of a drug's action on the reinforcement process. Picrotoxin does not produce any obvious debility by itself, nor does it interfere with performance on a task such as pressing a lever to escape footshock. The debility is the result of an interaction between the drug and a peculiarity of the brain stimulation task—the potentially epileptigenic stimulation. While the debilitating consequences of this interaction are obvious in some rats, they are not obvious in others. In fact, Kent and Fedinets (1976) reported "observation of the animal's behavior showed no evidence of seizure activity or other abnormal behavior [p. 631]." More generally, one cannot safely assume that a debility that hinders performance on a self-stimulation task will necessarily be evident in a rat's general behavior or that it will necessarily hinder performance on other tasks. Indeed, there is no reason why a debility might not be specific to a particular site of self-stimulation and/or a particular self-stimulation task. In fact, Annau (1977) found that hypoxia had a greater effect on the performance of rats with lateral hypothalamic electrodes pressing at high rates on an FR5 schedule of reinforcement than it did on the performance of rats with septal electrodes pressing at lower rates for continual reinforcement—a superb confusion of variables if ever there was one (see also the evidence for site-specific performance deficits from a dorsal pontine lesion, below).

However, normal performance by a drugged animal on the first few trials of a test proves that the drug does not by itself produce any performance-hindering debility. In dealing with drugs that do produce an extinctionlike change in performance, we can concentrate on devising controls that rule out pseudo-extinction. Gallistel, Boytim, Gomita, and Klebanoff (1982) devised two such controls in their attempt to determine whether pimozide in fact blocks the reinforcing effect of MFB stimulation.

In one control, they tested for an extinctionlike decline in runway perfor-mance after having the pimozide-treated rats run in a running wheel while receiv-ing brain stimulation. Even though the rats ran farther in the running wheel and received more brain stimulation than would ordinarily be the case in the course of

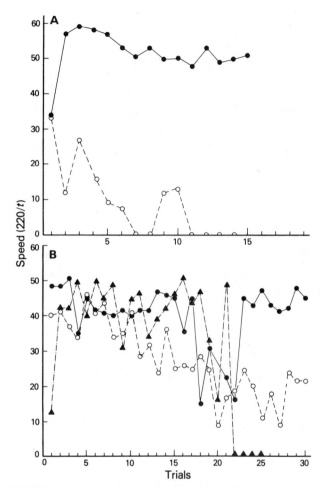

Figure 7.18. Trial by trial running speeds in two rats (A and B) under control (normal reward, ●———●) conditions or after treatment with picrotoxin (○--○, 2 mg/kg; ▲–·–▲, 4 mg/kg). The extinction-like declines in performance were correlated with the appearance of seizure activity. [Reproduced from Gallistel, Boytim, Gomita, and Klebanoff (1982), Figure 3, by permission of ANKHO International.]

extinction, they nonetheless performed at the normal level on the first one or two trials in the runway and then showed the usual trial-dependent decline in performance. This control proves that pimozide treatment plus running plus brain stimulation does not result in a performance-hindering debility. This control, it should be noted, did distinguish between pimozide and picrotoxin. Picrotoxin-treated rats given the running wheel plus brain stimulation were then unable or unwilling to perform on the first trial in the runway test.

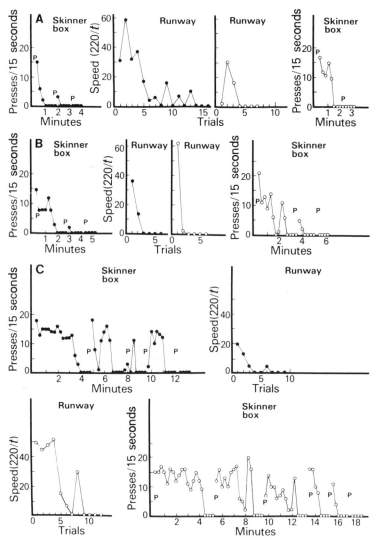

Figure 7.19. Performance of three rats (A, B, and C) 4 hours after pimozide injection (0.75 mg/kg) in a Skinner box followed by a runway (closed circles), or vice versa (open circles). A *P* indicates that the rat was primed with 10 trains of stimulation outside the Skinner box, then returned to it. [Reproduced from Gallistel, Boytim, Gomita, and Klebanoff (1982), Figure 6B, with permission of ANKHO International.]

The reinforcement-specific effect of pimozide was established perhaps even more convincingly in a second control, which tested for the task specificity of the extinction seen under pimozide. Rats trained in both a Skinner box and a runway were treated with pimozide and tested first in the Skinner box, then in the runway, or vice versa. Whenever a rat ceased pressing in the Skinner box, it was removed, given priming stimulation, and replaced. Only when the rat refused to reume pressing upon being replaced was it shifted to the runway. As may be seen in Figure 7.19, pimozide-treated rats that have completely extinguished in the Skinner box nonetheless resume responding for brain stimulation when shifted to the runway, then show extinction all over again. The same result is obtained when the runway is used first followed by the Skinner box. This task-specific decline in performance is what one sees under normal extinction, that is, with the reward stimulation disconnected. Task specificity is not seen when the rats are treated with picrotoxin.

Franklin and McCoy (1979) provided another demonstration that the extinctionlike decline in performance under pimozide is not due to the progressive onset of a performance debility. They showed that lever pressing in a Skinner box was temporarily reinstated when the experimenter reintroduced a tone that had been associated with reinforcement. Gallistel, Boytim, Gomita, and Klebanoff (1982) also showed that doses of pimozide 5 to 10 times greater than that required to cause extinction nonetheless left many rats capable of normal performance on the first one or two trials in a runway. In sum, the extinction paradigm with suitable controls for pseudo-extinction, gives strong evidence that pimozide blocks the reinforcing effect of MFB stimulation. This conclusion is strengthened by confirmatory evidence from a different paradigm, the curve-shift paradigm.

2. The Curve-Shift Paradigm

The curve-shift paradigm looks for drug-induced lateral shifts in the curve relating rate of performance to amount of stimulation. This curve rises steeply from negligible rates to near maximal rates (Figure 7.20). Most of the rise occurs within a twofold change in the amount of stimulation (number of pulses) in a train of fixed duration. The curve-shift paradigm assumes that this steep rise and fairly abrupt leveling off reflect the rapid growth and saturation of the reinforcing effect of the stimulation. If this assumption is correct, then the only way to change the range of stimulation magnitudes over which this rise occurs is by altering the reinforcing efficacy of the stimulation.

To see why, let us return to the notation introduced earlier, where $r(S)$ represents the function (process) that translates a given amount (S) of stimulation into a time-varying rewarding signal (r), $R(r)$ represents the conversion process that converts the rewarding signal into a reinforcing effect (R), and $P(R)$ represents the unknowably large number of processes that translate the reinforcing

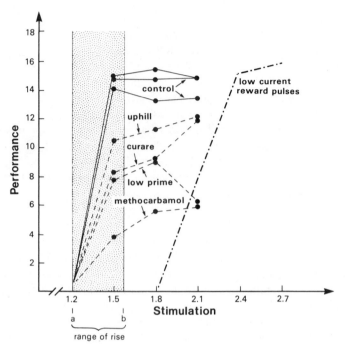

Figure 7.20. The function, $P(S)$, gives performance, P (in this case, running speed), as a function of the amount of stimulation, S (in this case, log N where N = number of pulses). When $S <$ a, $P(S) \simeq 0$; when $S > b$, $P(S) \simeq k$, a constant asymptotically high level of performance. Manipulations not specific to reinforcement—curare, methacarbamol, low priming, making rat run uphill—alter $P(S)$ but they do not alter the fact that $P(S)$ exhibits its steep rise over the range $a < S < b$. Reducing the reinforcing efficacy of the stimulation, by contrast, shifts the range over which the steep rise occurs (low current reward). [Modified from Edmonds & Gallistel (1974).]

effect into a rate of performance or preference, that is, into a measurable behavior. These functions are compoundable, that is, $r(S)$ is the argument of (input to) $R(r)$, which is in turn the argument of (input to) $P(R)$. By compounding $R(r)$ and $r(S)$, we get

$$R[r(S)] = R(S)$$

the function that translates a given amount of stimulation into a reinforcing effect. By compounding this function with $P(R)$, we get

$$P[R(S)] = P(S)$$

the function that specifies the level of performance for a given amount of stimulation. $P(S)$ is the only function we can directly determine experimentally.

We observe (Figure 7.20) that the function $P(S)$ rises steeply only within a narrow range. The level of performance is nearly constant for amounts of stimulation greater than the upper limit of that range. We assume this reflects similar properties in the underlying, unobservable function $R(S)$. That is, we assume that $R(S)$ rises steeply over the range $a \leq S \leq b$ and then saturates, so that for $S > b$, $R(S) \simeq k$, where k is a constant.

If this assumption is correct, then no alteration of the performance function, $P(R)$ can alter the range of the steep rise in $P(S)$. Outside the range $a \leq S \leq b$, $R \simeq k$ and R is the argument of (input to) P. No matter how we alter the processes that translate a given reinforcing effect into a performance, it will still be the case that constant levels of reinforcement yield constant levels of performance. If any amount of stimulation greater than some value b yields the maximum possible reinforcement, then all amounts of stimulation greater than b will yield the same asymptotic performance. Changes in the performance function, $P(R)$, will alter what this level is; they may raise or lower asymptotic performance, as witness Figure 7.20, but they will not alter the amount of stimulation at which the asymptotic level is attained.

On the other hand, reducing the reinforcing efficacy of the stimulation, for example, by reducing the current intensity, will increase the amount of stimulation required to generate any given level of reinforcement. Thus, the range over which $P(S)$ rises will shift laterally toward higher values of S, as indeed it does (Figure 7.20). In short, a drug that does not act specifically on the processes that convert stimulation into a reinforcing effect, but does reduce the rat's capacity or inclination to perform the reinforced behavior will lower the observable function $P(S)$ but will not shift it laterally. A drug that reduces the reinforcing efficacy of stimulation will shift the function laterally.

Pimozide and its fellow neuroleptics shift the entire $P(S)$ function laterally toward higher values of S, whether one measures running speed in an alley (Figure 7.21) or bar-pressing rate in a Skinner box (Zarevics & Setler, 1979). One is again led to the conclusion that these known dopamine receptor blockers can reduce or abolish the reinforcing effect of MFB stimulation.

The two tests for reinforcement specificity, curve shifts and extinction, rest on different lines of reasoning. That two so different experimental paradigms lead to the same conclusion strengthens one's confidence in the conclusion.

Neuroleptics may block the reinforcing effect either by reducing the rewarding signal [they may alter the function $r(S)$] or by reducing the reinforcing effect of a given rewarding signal [acting on the function $R(r)$]. The simplest hypothesis would be that the first stage neurons (see Figure 7.3) were dopaminergic and that dopamine receptor blockers affected $r(S)$ by reducing the signal transmitted from first stage to the second stage of the reward pathway. This hypothesis gains credibility from the fact that there is a very close correlation between the loci of dopaminergic neurons and the loci of good self-stimulation electrodes throughout the ventral tegmentum and MFB (Corbett & Wise, 1980). [There is not, by contrast, a close correlation between the loci of noradrenergic

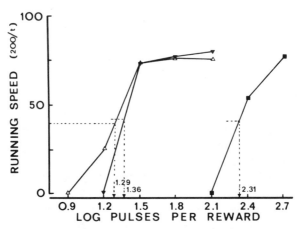

Figure 7.21. The effect of pimozide on the reward summation function, the curve relating performance (in this case, running speed in an alley) to the number of pulses in the train of reinforcing stimulation. At a dose of 0.2 mg/kg, the range of steep rise is shifted by 1.0 log units (a 10-fold change) to the right of its normal locus, with no decline in the asymptotic level of performance. This indicates that the drug reduced the reinforcing efficacy of the stimulation without impairing the innumerable other processes that translate a reinforcing effect into an observable behavior (compare Figure 7.20). (△——△, Vehicle; ▼——▼, 0.1 mg/kg pimozide; ■——■, 0.2 mg/kg pimozide.) [Reproduced from Franklin (1978), Figure 7, by permission of the author and ANKHO International.]

neurons and the loci of good self-stimulation electrodes in the dorsal brainstem (Corbett & Wise, 1979).]

As we will see when we come to consider relevant electrophysiological evidence, the difficulty with the hypothesis that the first-stage neurons are dopaminergic is that the quantitative properties of the dopaminergic neurons (their refractory periods and conduction velocities) do not match the properties of the first-stage neurons inferred from behavioral trade-off functions (Shizgal, Bielajew, Corbett, Skelton, & Yeomans, 1980).

Rejecting the hypothesis that the first-stage neurons are dopaminergic leads one to consider the hypothesis that some component of the second-stage neural network is dopaminergic. This hypothesis could explain the fact that neuroleptics apparently block the reinforcing effects of stimulation from electrodes in the dorsal brainstem remote from the dopaminergic neural systems (Liebman & Butcher, 1974; Phillips, Brooke & Fibiger, 1975). Under this hypothesis the correlation between the loci of dopaminergic neurons and the loci of good self-stimulation electrodes in the ventral tegmentum arises only because the descending myelinated axons are converging on the dendrites and soma of the dopamine neurons.

One might expect, on this hypothesis, to find in autoradiographic mapping studies an area activated from electrodes in the MFB and electrodes in the dorsal brainstem. This area would be the second stage common to both systems. So far, we have not found such an area.

If one rejects the notion that the neural systems mediating self-stimulation at diverse loci share a common dopaminergic second stage, then one is led to consider the hypothesis that dopamine receptor blockers interfere with the process by which a reward signal is converted into a reinforcing effect (Stage 3 in Figure 7.3), that is, that the drugs act on the function $R(r)$. Gomita and Gallistel (1982) used 2DG autoradiography to determine how reinforcement-blocking doses of pimozide altered the pattern of neural activation in rats given rewarding stimulation via electrodes in the posterior MFB. The pattern of activation along the MFB from the diagonal band of Broca to the anterior ventral tegmentum was the same in the pimozide-treated rats as in untreated rats self-stimulating via similar placements. Surprisingly, there was no clear effect of the pimozide in any of the telencephalic terminal fields of the dopamine neurons. There was only one clear autoradiographic effect of the pimozide, a very strong activation of the lateral two-thirds of the lateral habenula, an effect seen both in pimozide-treated rats that were not given the rewarding stimulation as well as in those given the brain stimulation. The lateral habenula receives a modest dopaminergic projection from the anterior ventral tegmentum (Phillipson & Griffith, 1980) and sends a nondopaminergic projection back to this same area (Herkenham & Nauta, 1979). The lateral habenula is also where some of the strongest autoradiographic effects of amphetamine are seen. Amphetamine has the opposite effect from pimozide both autoradiographically and behaviorally; it reduces 2DG uptake in the lateral habenula (Wechsler, Savaki, & Sokoloff, 1979) and increases reinforcing efficacy (Cassens & Mills, 1973; Esposito, Perry, & Kornetsky, 1980). One is naturally led to wonder whether the effect of dopaminergically active drugs on reinforcing efficacy is mediated by the lateral habenula. Because lesioning the lateral habenula improves MFB self-stimulation (Sutherland & Nakajima, 1981), it seems unlikely that the pathways linking the tegmentum and the lateral habenula form part of the second stage of the reward pathway. Rather, one is inclined to think that neuroleptic-induced signals in these pathways may block the conversion of the rewarding signal into a reinforcing effect.

Regardless of which hypothesis one favors, it would seem that the study of the dopaminergic systems in the brain is likely to aid and abet the process of identifying the substrate for the reinforcing effect of MFB stimulation.

3. Pharmacological Dissociation of the Priming and Reinforcing Effects

Franklin (1978) observed that rats treated with reinforcement-blocking doses of pimozide seemed nonetheless to be sensitive to the priming effect of this stimulation. Katz (1981), using his continuous access paradigm, also concluded that neuroleptics blocked reinforcement but not priming. Wasserman, Gomita, and Gallistel (1982) put this conclusion to direct test. In predrug control sessions, they ran rats in an alley with and without pretrial priming stimulation. The priming was 10 trains of stimulation, identical in all respects to the 1 train the rat received as a reward for pressing the goal lever. The priming stimulation, however, was not contingent on anything the rat did. It was given automatically a few seconds before each trial, while the rat was in a separate priming box beside the runway. Strong stimulation was used because this maximizes the difference between primed and unprimed performance.

When numerous control sessions had established the normal ranges of primed and unprimed performance, each rat was tested on several drug sessions, separated from each other by at least 48 hours. In some of these drug sessions, the pimozide-treated rat was given pretrial priming; in others, it was not.

Results were unequivocal: On initial trials, the pimozide-treated rats, like undrugged rats, showed much faster performance when primed than when not primed. Performances with and without priming generally fell within the rat's normal ranges of primed and unprimed performance. Pimozide did not block the priming effect of the stimulation, even though it did block the reinforcing effect, as shown by the fact that the normal performance on the first few trials soon gave way to extinction (Figure 7.22).

Next, Wasserman et al. tested to see whether the behavior-directing effect of priming was also unaffected by pimozide. They replicated the earlier experiment of Deutsch et al. (1964), using a T maze with water as the reward on one side and brain stimulation as the reward on the other. Like Deutsch et al., they found that when thirsty rats were primed before a choice trial, they preferred the brain stimulation reward to the water reward. When unprimed, they preferred the water. This effect of priming on preference was still observed after the rats were treated with extinction-producing doses of pimozide. In short, pimozide does not block either manifestation of the selective potentiating (priming) effect of rewarding stimulation. In pimozide-treated rats, pretrial stimulation invigorates subsequent performance for a stimulation reward, and it does so selectively, that is, it causes performance of the stimulation-directed behavior to occur in preference to performance directed to other sorts of reward.

These results have theoretical import: They rule out any theory of the priming effect that makes it a secondary consequence of the reinforcing effect. They also encourage the hope that the substrate for the reinforcing effect may be distinguished from the substrate for the priming effect on the basis of its pharmacological properties, if not on the basis of its quantitative properties.

D. Effects of Lesions

Studies of the effects of lesions ought to help identify the substrates for the reinforcing and motivating effects of the stimulation. As with pharmacological

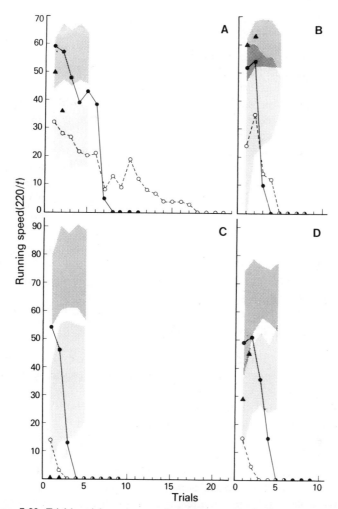

Figure 7.22. Trial-by-trial running speeds for four rats (A, B, C, and D) under pimozide, with (●———●) and without (○--○) pretrial priming. (A and B, 0.5 mg/kg pimozide; C and D, 0.75 mg/kg pimozide.) The shaded areas indicate the range (mean ± two standard deviations) of performance under control (no drug) conditions. Darker shading is primed, lighter is not. Only the first two trials are plotted from the high dose test (▲, 5 mg/kg). [Reproduced from Wasserman, Gomita, & Gallistel (1982), Figure 1, by permission of ANKHO International.]

studies, however, the help offered by lesion studies depends on the development of behavioral methods that distinguish between the effects of lesions on the reinforcing or motivating functions and the effects of lesions on the multitudinous other processes that influence performance on a given self-stimulation task. Since relatively little attention has been paid to this central methodological problem, it is perhaps not surprising that there is contradiction and confusion in the lesion literature. The conclusion that lesions remote from the site of self-stimulation seldom completely abolish self-stimulation continues to hold (e.g., Clavier & Corcoran, 1976; Farber, Ellman, Mattiace, Holtzmann, Ippolito, Halperin, & Steiner, 1976; Robinson & Bloom, 1978; see Gallistel, 1972, for review of earlier lesion studies). Stellar, Iles and Mills (1982) have shown that ablating the entire forebrain on the side of stimulation not only leaves self-stimulation performance in the runway intact, it also has no effect on the charge–duration function nor on the number–current function!

It would seem that the methods applicable in the pharmacological case could also be applied in the case of lesions. Suppose a rat is trained to self-stimulate on a given electrode and then subjected to a lesion that destroys the reward pathway. When subsequently tested, it should begin performing at the prelesion level and then extinguish. Also, a lesion that reduced the number of functioning axons in the reward pathway ought to shift the reward summation function to the right. It should require more stimulating pulses to generate any given level of reinforcement, since these pulses now fall upon fewer reward-relevant axons then they did prior to the lesion (see Stellar & Neely, 1982).

The extinction paradigm has not been used in connection with lesions, but the curve-shift paradigm has, sometimes wittingly (Stellar & Neely, 1982), sometimes unwittingly, as when Robinson and Bloom (1978) produced unilateral damage to the lateral aspect of the frontoparietal cortex by ligating the medial cerebral artery. Their subjects had self-stimulation electrodes bilaterally in or near the MFB at the level of the posterior hypothalamus. Curves showing rate of pressing as a function of current intensity were obtained both preoperatively and at several intervals after the cortical lesions. The lesions had a unilateral biphasic effect on self-stimulation performance (Figure 7.23). In the first 2–5 days, the rate versus current function for the electrode on the side of the lesion was lowered and shifted slightly ($\approx 12\%$) to the right (Figure 7.23A), while the function for the electrode contralateral to the lesion was unperturbed (Figure 7.23B). By 8 days, postlesion, the function for the ipsilateral electrode was elevated and shifted slightly to the left (Figure 7.23A). It returned to its prelesion position by 20 days after the lesion.

Robinson and Bloom take both the changes in elevation and the lateral shifts in the rate versus current functions to indicate changes in the reinforcing effectiveness of the stimulation, because general appetitive behaviors (food and water intake) were unperturbed and because there were no changes in the functions for the contralateral electrodes. The first of these arguments assumes that the neurobehavioral processes pertinent to the performance of lever pressing for brain stimulation are the same as the neurobehavioral processes pertinent to eating and drinking, except for only the reinforcing process. It assumes that if the depression or elevation of self-stimulation performance were due to anything

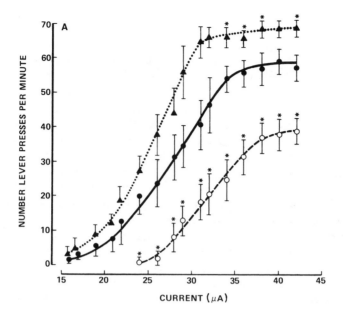

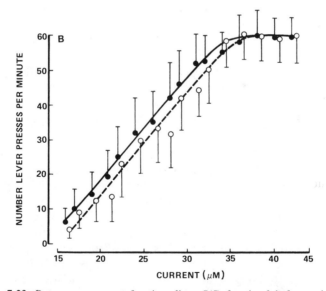

Figure 7.23. Rate versus current functions [i.e., *P(S)* functions] before and at various intervals after lateral frontoparietal infarctions. (A) Electrodes ipsilateral to the coritical damage. Note the absence of any clear lateral shift. (B) Electrodes contralateral to the damage. (●——●, Preoperative; ○--○, 5 days postoperative; ▲···▲, 8 days postoperative; *, *p* < .05) [Reproduced from Robinson & Bloom (1978) Figures 3 and 4, by permission of the senior author and the American Psychological Association.]

other than an effect on reinforcement, then there would necessarily be a depression or elevation in eating and drinking as well. Such an assumption hardly seems warranted, particularly in the light of the task-specific performance deficits produced by a drug such as picrotoxin (see Section III,C).

The second argument—the lack of any effect of the lesion on responding for contralateral stimulation—assumes that there can be no such thing as a unilateral performance deficit (or enhancement). It assumes that there is nothing that can prevent just one side of the brain from efficiently reading out a reinforcing effect into an observable behavior. This hardly seems warranted. One would not be surprised, I think, to find that unilateral spreading depression, unilateral hypoxia, or any number of other general unilateral insults interfered with a hemisphere's ability to generate some particular piece of self-stimulating behavior, but did not interfere with the production of a reinforcing effect of brain stimulation somewhere within that hemisphere.

The depressions and elevations in the rate-versus-current function in Figure 7.23A are the sort of changes one sees when performance variables (non-reinforcement-specific variables) are manipulated (see Figure 7.20). A depression or elevation of the performance-versus-stimulation function is not what one sees when one unequivocally and selectively reduces the reinforcing efficacy of the stimulation (by, for example, reducing pulse frequency), rather, one sees lateral shifts. The lateral shifts in the Robinson and Bloom curves are so small as to be equivocal. Most of the rise in the control curves occurs in the range from 20 to 36 μA. The same is true for both the depressed and elevated curves. Close approximations to both the lower and upper curves can be made by vertically compressing or vertically expanding the control curve, without any lateral shifting. Lateral shifts are unequivocal only when the new range of steep rise lies completely outside the old range, as in Figures 7.20 and 7.21 (see also Edmonds & Gallistel, 1977).

In summary, there are no compelling reasons to believe that Robinson and Bloom's cortical infarcts altered the reinforcing efficacy of stimulation from electrodes ipsilateral to the infarcts. Indeed, it seems extremely unlikely given that Stellar, Iles, and Mills (1982) found no effect when they ablated the entire ipsilateral forebrain. It has been demonstrated that the sorts of vertical shifts they observed can be produced by performance variables, such as general health, curarization, partial anaesthetization, low level seizure activity, and so on. Since the number of these potentially intrusive variables is unspecifiably large, and since a lesion might bring on the intrusion of any one of these largely unknown possibilities, there would appear to be no way of ruling out nonspecific effects, so long as one observes primarily elevations or depressions in the rate-versus-current curve. On the other hand, there are theoretical arguments why unequivocal lateral shifts could not be produced by changes in nonspecific variables, and there are empirical demonstrations that such shifts are not in fact produced by manipulating performance variables. So, an unequivocal lateral shift in the $P(S)$ function following a lesion would be good evidence that the lesion had destroyed reward fibers. Stellar and Neely (1982) found such shifts when they lesioned at or posterior to an MFB electrode but not when they lesioned anterior to the electrode.

Farber *et al.* (1976) reported that lesions of the dorsal hindbrain in and around the locus coeruleus had a greater effect on the reinforcing efficacy of stimulation at sites in the fields of Forel than at sites in the MFB. They, too, report rate-versus-current functions (Figure 7.24). In their functions, as in Robinson and Bloom's, the shifts are primarily vertical not lateral. They are not the kinds of shifts that would be produced by such unequivocally reinforcement-specific manipulations as reducing pulse frequency. They are the kinds of shifts that are produced by changes in performance variables.

If I correctly interpret the Farber *et al.* data as showing only performance effects, then the primary interest of their study lies in the demonstration that lesions may produce performance debilities that are more marked in the performance for stimulation at one site than in the performance for stimulation at another site. A similar argument may apply to the results of Clavier and Corcoran (1976). Site-specific attenuation of self-stimulation would be obtained with picrotoxin if stimulation at one site were more prone to induce seizure activity than was stimulation of another site. This highlights once more the need to use behavioral methods that have been shown to discriminate between effects on performance and effects on reinforcement. The fact that a deficit in performance is specific to a particular site of stimulation is no proof that the deficit is due to a decline in the reinforcing effect of stimulation at that site.

E. Electrophysiological Data

Recordings by means of microelectrodes give direct and unequivocal evidence for the activity of individual neurons. The problem is to determine what the neurons one is recording from have to do with the neurobehavioral function one is interested in. A cursory perusal of literature that seeks to link electrophysiological data to behavioral phenomena will show that this is no small problem.

The kinds of psychophysical, pharmacological, and lesion data reviewed up to this point constitute, I believe, an indispensable background for any successful attempt to link electrophysiological and anatomical data to behavioral phenomena. These behavioral data generate or can generate a list of properties that a neural system must possess if it is to be regarded as the substrate for a neurobehavioral function such as the reinforcing or motivating function in self-stimulation. Given such a list, one can proceed to check, by electrophysiological experiments and anatomical observations, whether a given neural system has the

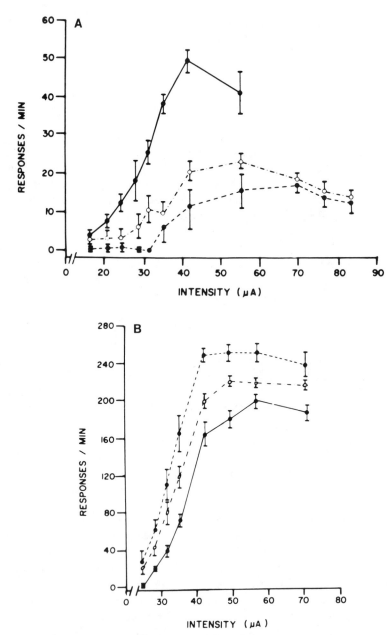

Figure 7.24. Lesions in the vicinity of the locus coeruleus depress self-stimulation at sites in the fields of Forel (A) more than at sites in the MFB (B). The depressions in both cases look like performance effects (cf. Fig. 7.20). ●——●, Prelesion baseline; ○--○, postlesion baseline; ●--●, recovery check; I, S.E.M.) [Reproduced from Farber, Ellman, Mattiace, Holtzmann, Ippolito, Halperin, & Steiner (1976) Figure 3 by permission of the authors and Elsevier.]

right properties. In this way, one may build a case for or against each neural system one investigates. In the absence of a list of required properties, it is not clear how to build a case either for or against any given neural system.

The force of this approach may be illustrated by considering electrophysiological data on the two catecholaminergic neural systems that have figured prominently among the suggested substrates for self-stimulation. The catecholaminergic neural systems consist of those neurons in the central nervous system that use either dopamine or norepinephrine as a transmitter substance. The cell bodies of these neurons lie in a number of discrete loci in the midbrain and hindbrain. They send long axons to a variety of areas in the forebrain (Lindvall & Björklund, 1974; Ungerstedt, 1971). The properties of these catecholaminergic axons, as established by electrophysiological and anatomical measurements, do not tally with the properties of the first-stage axons in self-stimulation, as established by behavioral data (data on the trade-off between the intrapair interval and the number of pulse pairs required to generate a given level of performance) as was first pointed out by Shizgal, Bielajew, Corbett, Skelton, and Yeomans (1980).

Faiers and Mogenson (1976) recorded from neurons in the locus coeruleus of the rat, a site where many of the cell bodies of noradrenergic neurons lie. Although there are nonnoradrenergic neurons in the locus coeruleus (Shimizu & Imamoto, 1970), the neurons reported by Faiers and Mogenson were presumed to be noradrenergic, because they could be antidromically driven from one or more of the sites to which the noradrenergic cells in the locus coeruleus send their axons—the supracallosal bundle, the olfactory bulb, the MFB, and the dorsal noradrenergic bundle at the level of the midbrain. The conduction velocities of action potentials in these axons were determined by noting the latency between stimulus pulses and the appearance of an antidromically conducted spike at the locus coeruleus, then dividing this latency by the estimated distance traveled between the site of stimulation and the locus coeruleus. The estimates of conduction velocity were about the same (0.4–0.6 m per second) whether the site of stimulation was in the dorsal noradrenergic bundle at the level of the midbrain, about 4 mm from the locus coeruleus, or in the supracallosal bundle, about 18 mm from the locus coeruleus along the looping route taken by the noradrenergic axons. This conduction velocity is considerably slower than the value that the behavioral data give for the first-stage axons in MFB self-stimulation (2–8 m per second, see Section III,B,1).

Faiers and Mogenson (1976) also determined the refractory periods of these axons, that is, they determined the least interval at which a second stimulating pulse could elicit a second antidromic spike. Here, their results varied from site to site: When stimulating the supracallosal bundle, they found refractory periods ranging from 8 to 20 msec, with a mean of 15 msec (35 units in all). When stimulating the dorsal midbrain site, the mean was 6.0 msec (4 units in all). When stimulating the MFB, the mean was 10 msec (4 units in all). One thing is clear: No matter where they stimulated, the refractory periods were nowhere near the values required by the behavioral data. In the monkey, however, there is some evidence that neurons recorded in the vicinity of the locus coeruleus have the "right" refractory periods (German & Fetz, 1976), although it was not established that these neurons were noradrenergic.

The Faiers and Mogenson data are inconsistent with the hypothesis that the dorsal noradrenergic bundle constitutes the first stage in the substrate for self-stimulation of the MFB. They are also inconsistent with the hypothesis that these neurons are the first stage in the substrate for self-stimulation of the locus coeruleus itself. Abou-Hamed, Schmitt, and Karli (1977) determined the refractory period of these first-stage neurons by the input–output method. That is, they plotted bar-pressing rate as a function of the intrapair interval in trains of paired pulses. While their failure to use a trade-off method makes it impossible to compare in detail their data with data from other sites of self-stimulation, it is nonetheless clear that the predominant refractory period of the neurons mediating self-stimulation in the vicinity of the locus coeruleus lies in the range from 0.6 to 1.2 msec (Figure 7.25).

1. The Noradrenergic Hypothesis

There is now overwhelming evidence against the hypothesis that the direct electrical stimulation of the noradrenergic neurons originating in the locus coeruleus is the first step in the neurophysiological events underlying self-stimulation. First, when care is taken in determining the locus of self-stimulation electrodes relative to the locus of noradrenergic neurons, there is a poor correlation (Amaral & Routtenberg, 1975; Corbett & Wise, 1979; Simon, Le Moal, & Cardo, 1975). Second, self-stimulation at sites along the dorsal noradrenergic bundle is not lastingly impaired by electrolylic or neurotoxic lesions that destroy the majority of the noradrenaline-containing neurons and radically reduce the forebrain norepinephrine content (Clavier & Fibiger, 1977; Clavier, Fibiger, & Phillips, 1976; Clavier & Routtenberg, 1976; Corbett, Skelton, & Wise, 1977; van der Kooy, 1979). Third, the axons of the noradrenergic projection have the wrong conduction velocity and the wrong refractory periods. In short, psychophysical data, pharmacological data, lesion data, and electrophysiological data combine to rule out noradrenergic neurons as the first-stage neurons, and these data make it unlikely that noradrenergic neurons play a role at any stage in the realization of the motivating and reinforcing effects of the stimulation.

2. The Dopaminergic Hypothesis

The pharmacological evidence (see above) and the strong correlation between the locus of good electrodes and the locus of the dopaminergic neurons in the ventral tegmentum and MFB (Corbett & Wise, 1980) encourage the hypothesis that dopaminergic neurons are the first-stage neurons in self-stimulation of

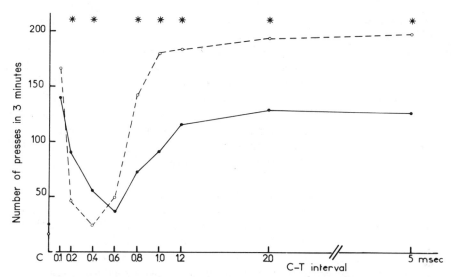

Figure 7.25. Bar-pressing rate (number of presses in 3 minutes) as a function of the intrapair (C–T) interval in a group of rats with electrodes in the cerebellum (O––O) and a group of rats with electrodes in the dorsal pontine tegmentum, in or near the locus coeruleus (●——●). The asterisks indicate points at which the differences between the two curves are statistically significant. [Reproduced from Abou-Hamed, et al. (1977) Figure 4, by permission of the authors and Pergamon Press.]

the MFB. The dopaminergic neurons in question originate in the substantia nigra [Area A-9, in the terminology of Ungerstedt (1971)] and the ventral tegmental area of Tsai (A-10) and send axons through the MFB to the caudate, putamen, globus pallidus, thalamus, nucleus accumbens, medial and sulcal frontal cortex, entorhinal cortex, and cingulate cortex. Unfortunately, electrophysiological ex- periments indicate that these neurons do not have the properties required by the behavioral trade-off data.

Guyenet and Aghajanian (1978) recorded from spontaneously active cells in the rat substantia nigra. They found two types of neurons. The first type were mainly in the pars compacta. They could be antidromically driven from various sites along the nigrostriatal projection (the MFB, the caudate–putamen, and the globus pallidus) but not from the ventromedial thalamus nor several other areas where dopaminergic axons do not go. The antidromic driving of these neurons was blocked by microinfusion of 6-hydroxydopamine (6-OHDA) (a neurotoxin relatively specific for catecholamine-containing neurons) into the MFB. The spontaneous firing of these neurons (with the animal under chloral hydrate anaes- thesia) was slow (0.5–8 spikes per second) and the action potentials were wide (4–5 msec). The spontaneous firing rates of these neurons were dramatically reduced by intravenous infusions of the dopamine agonist, apomorphine (the dose required for 50% inhibition was 9.3 μg/kg), and by the iontophoretic application of either dopamine or γ-aminobutyric acid (GABA).

Substantia nigra neurons of the second type were predominantly in the pars reticulata. They could be antidromically activated not only from the MFB, but also from the ventral thalamus where dopaminergic axons are not found. Antidromic driving of these neurons was not blocked by microinfusions of 6-OHDA into the MFB. These neurons had higher rates of spontaneous activity (up to 60 spikes per second) and a narrower action potential (2–3 msec). Their activity was not inhibited by intravenous apomorphine (doses up to 20 μg/kg or higher) or by iontophoretically applied dopamine, but it was inhibited by iontophoresed GABA.

Guyenet and Aghajanian (1978) concluded that neurons of the first type were dopaminergic, while the neurons of the second type were not. They determined the conduction velocity of both types of neurons by plotting antidromic spike latency as a function of the distance between the recording and stimulating electrodes. The first type (dopaminergic) had a conduction velocity of 0.58 m per second, while the second type (nondopaminergic) had a conduction velocity of 2.8 m per second. The velocity of the second type is consistent with the Shizgal, Bielajew, Corbett, Skelton, and Yeomans (1980) values for the first-stage neurons in MFB self-stimulation; the velocity of the first type—the putative dopamine neurons—is not. The slow velocity is, however, what one would expect from anatomical studies, since the dopaminergic axons have been observed to be of small diameter (< 0.5 μm) and unmyelinated.

Guyenet and Aghajanian's (1980) findings have been confirmed and extended to neurons in the A-10 region by Yim and Mogenson (1980); German, Dalsass, and Kiser (1980); and Grace and Bunney (1980). The second of these studies also reported the refractory periods of the putative dopamine neurons— 2.2 ± 0.3 msec. This value is not consistent with the value for the first-stage neurons in self-stimulation, as determined by behavioral methods. It is much too long.

3. Other Systems

There is no dearth of axons in the MFB with the properties implied by the behavioral paired-pulse experiments. Szabó, Lénard, and Kosaris (1974) studied the MFB under both the light and electron microscope and found it rich in small 0.6–3.0 μm myelinated axons, whose conduction velocities and refractory periods might be expected to have approximately the values obtained in the behavioral experiments. The autoradiographic activation from rewarding stimulation reported by Yadin, Guarini, and Gallistel (1983) and by Gomita and Gallistel (1982) is concentrated in the areas where Nieuwenhuys, Geeraedts, and Veening (1982) report concentrations of thin myelinated fibers 0.5–2 μm in diameter. Shizgal, Kiss, and Bielajew (1982) and Deutsch (see Deutsch & Deutsch, 1966)

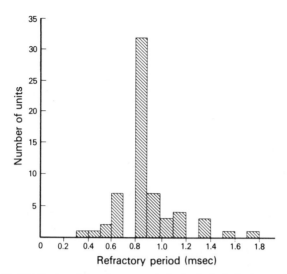

Figure 7.26. Distribution of the refractory periods of units in the brainstem directly driven by rewarding stimulation of the MFB (62 directly excited units). The majority of units fall within the range required by behavioral data on MFB self-stimulation. [Redrawn from Rolls (1971), Figure 2A, by permission of the author and Elsevier.]

have recorded the compound action potentials that propagate up and down the MFB and shown that the axons making the predominant contribution to these potentials have the right conduction velocities and refractory periods. Guyenet and Aghajanian's (1978) Type II (nondopaminergic) neurons had axons in the MFB with the right conduction velocities. Rolls (1971) recorded from a great many neurons in the brainstem that could be directly driven by rewarding stimulation of the MFB or nucleus accumbens septi. These units had refractory periods in just the range demanded by the behavioral data (Figure 7.26). The latencies of the spikes in these units (1–3 msec over distances of 3–4 mm) indicate that their conduction velocities were also appropriate. Rolls and Cooper (1973, 1974) also found many neurons in the sulcal and medial frontal cortex directly driven by rewarding stimulation of the MFB or dorsal pontine tegmentum, but having refractory periods longer than required by the behavioral data for MFB self-stimulation (Figure 7.27). These refractory periods are, however, in the range indicated by behavioral data on frontal cortex self-stimulation (Schenk & Shizgal, 1982; Silva, Vogel, & Corbett, 1982).

In short, electrophysiological experiments demonstrate that there are axons coursing through the MFB and the ventral tegmentum that have the conduction velocities and refractory periods required by the behavioral data, but these are not the dopaminergic axons. The dopaminergic axons have conduction velocities that are too slow and refractory periods that are too long. The long refractory

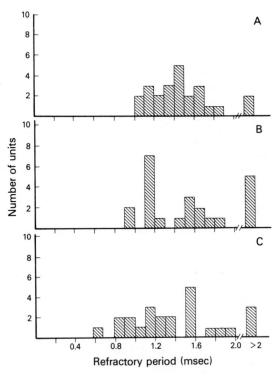

Figure 7.27. The refractory periods of the majority of directly driven units in the frontal cortex lie outside the range required by the behavioral data on MFB self-stimulation (0.5–1.2 msec) but inside the range required by behavioral data on frontal cortex self-stimulation (1.2–5.0 msec). (A) Absolute refractory periods for 24 units recorded in the sulcal prefrontal cortex and directly driven by rewarding stimulation of the MFB at the level of the lateral hypothalamus (7 rats). (B) Absolute refractory periods of 23 units recorded in the medial frontal cortex and directly driven by rewarding stimulation of the MFB at the level of the lateral hypothalamus (9 rats). (C) Absolute refractory periods of 24 units recorded in the sulcal prefrontal cortex and directly driven by rewarding stimulation in the vicinity of the locus coeruleus (4 rats). [A & B Redrawn from Rolls & Cooper (1973), Figures 3B and 5B, by permission of the authors and Elsevier. C redrawn from Rolls & Cooper (1974), Figure 4, by permission of the authors and Academic Press.]

periods and slow conduction velocities found in the electrophysiological experiments are what one would expect from anatomical studies, which indicate the dopaminergic axons, like the noradrenergic axons, are unmyelinated and of small diameter (Andén, Dahlström, Fuxe, Larrson, Olson, & Ungerstedt, 1966). Also the dopamine system conducts caudorostrally, while recent anodal block experiments by Shizgal, Bielajew, and Kiss (1980) and Bielajew and Shizgal (1983, in preparation) show that the orthodromic direction of conduction in the first-stage self-stimulation axons is rostrocaudal.

4. Behavioral Correlates of Unit Activity

If and when we can establish that an anatomically and electrophysiologically specifiable set of neurons constitute either the first or second stage of either the reward or priming pathways, it will be exceedingly interesting to determine the behavioral correlates of activity in these neurons. To make such determinations, one must record from individual neurons while the animal is free to behave in tasks where events and objects have motivational significance and reinforcing effects. Work by Rolls and his collaborators demonstrates the technical feasibility of such experiments (Burton, Rolls, & Mora, 1976; Mora, Mogenson, & Rolls, 1977; Mora, Rolls, & Burton, 1976; Rolls, 1972, 1974, 1975, 1976, 1979; Rolls, Burton, & Mora, 1976; Rolls & Rolls, 1977; Rolls, Sanghera, & Roper-Hall, 1979). This work has not focused on the problem of establishing whether the neurons recorded from were in fact part of the substrate for either reinforcement or priming, but the results are nonetheless sufficiently intriguing to warrant review here. The experiments by Rolls and his collaborators have been conducted for the most part with alert monkeys (rhesus and squirrel) in a restraining chair. The experiments reveal a population of neurons in the lateral hypothalamus and adjacent substantia innominata that have a hunger-modulated response to either the sight or the taste of palatable foods (but not both) and that are transsynaptically driven by rewarding stimulation from at least one self-stimulation site. Often these neurons may be driven by stimulation from two or more disparate self-stimulation sites (lateral hypothalamus, orbital frontal cortex, nucleus accumbens, amygdala). The effect of rewarding electrical stimulation on the firing of these neurons may be monophasically excitatory, monophasically inhibitory, or multiphasic. The effects of either the sight or the taste of food upon the firing rate may also be either excitatory or inhibitory. In either case, the effect is observed only when the monkey is hungry and willingly accepts the liquid food, which is forced into its mouth. The spontaneous firing rate of these neurons is not affected by the transition from hunger to satiety, only the response to food stimuli. The response to food stimuli does not appear to be a secondary consequence of the motor reaction because it precedes and predicts the reaction (acceptance or rejection).

The units responding to taste and the units responding to the sight of food form mutually exclusive populations. In many cases, the units responding to the sight of food also develop responses to the sight of nonfood visual stimuli when the presentation of the nonfood stimulus is repeatedly associated with the presentation of food reward. These conditioning-dependent responses are also modulated by hunger.

The neurons responding to the sight or taste of food together constitute a small percentage (14%) of the lateral hypothalamic neurons driven by rewarding stimulation (under, of course, the unknown sampling bias imposed by the particular recording procedures). It was sometimes (but not always) possible to obtain self-stimulation at low-current intensities at sites where these units had been found. In such cases, hunger sometimes (but again, not always) modulated the rate of self-stimulation and the current required to sustain a given rate.

The properties of these neurons are interesting. However, are these the properties that neurons carrying the reinforcing or motivating signals in self-stimulation must possess? Could a system of neurons in which neither the individual neurons nor the system as a whole had any of these properties nonetheless be the system that carried the reinforcing and/or motivating signal from one or even all of the self-stimulation sites? Is there anything in the behavioral data on self-stimulation in the monkey that requires (or suggests) that neurons carrying the reinforcing or motivating signals have the properties that these neurons have? I pose these rhetorical questions to emphasize once again the importance of having behavioral data that impose constraints on the underlying neural systems. Such data are lacking in the monkey. In their absence, it is hard to see how one could go about falsifying the hypothesis that any given population of stimulation-driven neurons carried the reinforcing and motivating signals. Until it is possible to falsify linkage hypotheses of this kind, it will remain impossible to support them with strong arguments.

F. Summary

All the technical and methodological tools that we need to find the neural substrate for the reinforcing and motivating effects of brain stimulation appear to be at hand. When the phenomenon of self-stimulation was first discovered, most of these tools were not at hand. The technique of 2DG autoradiography was unknown; the application of trade-off methods in electrical stimulation of the CNS was unheard of; and the technique of recording from single units in behaving animals was in its infancy. We were looking for a needle in a haystack under three disheartening handicaps—we did not know where the haystack was; we did not know what a needle looked like; and we could not properly examine a needle if we somehow managed to find one. Now, 2DG autoradiography tells us where the haystack is, trade-off experiments tell us what the needle looks like, and modern single unit techniques permit us to record from the needle under semi-natural circumstances.

It appears that the self-stimulation phenomenon is not the same at disparate sites of stimulation. Rats with electrodes in the medial frontal cortex or in the vicinity of the locus coeruleus are much harder to train than rats with placements in the MFB, and they do not exhibit the intense excitement seen in MFB self-stimulation. Paired-pulse experiments show that the directly stimulated neurons mediating frontal cortex self-stimulation and those mediating dorsal raphe self-stimulation differ from the first-stage neurons for MFB self-stimulation, and they differ from one another. Autoradiographic mapping of the activity produced by rewarding stimulation at these diverse sites does not reveal a common second-order system, a system activated transsynaptically from all self-stimulation sites (which might, of course, be attributed to some insensitivity in the technique rather than to the absence of such a common postsynaptic system). In short, it appears that self-stimulation of the MFB may differ from self-stimulation of other sites, both at the behavioral and at the neural level of analysis. For that reason, this chapter focuses on self-stimulation of the MFB.

Autoradiography shows that the neural systems manifesting ipsilateral elevation of activity in response to ipsilateral rewarding stimulation of the MFB are confined to the diencephalon and immediately contiguous portions of the telencephalon and mesencephalon. The areas that appear excited regardless of placement within the MFB appear to be primarily the MFB itself (or, sometimes, fibers in or adjacent to the fornix), the nucleus of the diagonal band of Broca in the forebrain, and the ventromedial areas of the anterior tegmentum in or near the origins of the dopaminergic neurons. There is a good correspondence between the foci of autoradiographic activation and the compartments of the MFB where the thin myelinated axons run.

Experiments that trade the number of pulse pairs against the intrapair interval implicate small myelinated axons, coursing the length of the MFB and into the ventral tegmentum, with conduction velocities of 2–8 m per second and refractory periods of 0.5–1.2 msec. These are the characteristics of the first-stage elements, the elements whose direct excitation by the electrode current eventuates in the reinforcing and motivating effects. Experiments that trade pulse intensity against pulse duration indicate that these axons accommodate slowly, firing on the break of anodal pulses only when those pulses last at least 5 msec.

All of these data are consistent with the suggestion of Arbuthnott (1980) that the first-stage axons are among the fibers he and his collaborators have traced. Arbuthnott, Mitchell, Tulloch, and Wright (1976) traced the efferent fibers from self-stimulation sites in the posterior lateral hypothalamus by injecting tritiated leucine. The caudal terminations of the fibers revealed by subsequent autoradiography correspond closely with what we have obtained by 2DG autoradiography. There was a notable concentration of terminals in and around the pars compacta of the substantia nigra (Ungerstedt's A-9). Whether these were myelinated fibers is not stated, but, if they were, they may be the first-stage neurons in self-stimulation.

The behavioral data on refractory periods, conduction velocity, and direction of conduction seem to rule out the hypothesis that the dopaminergic neurons themselves constitute the first stage. The pharmacological data, on the other hand, strongly suggest that dopaminergic neurons constitute part or all of the second stage, or that they carry a signal that can competitively alter the reinforcing effect of the reward signal. Thus, we are looking for a neural system whose first stage consists of small myelinated nondopaminergic fibers that descend from the basolateral diencephalon by way of the MFB to interact directly or indirectly with dopaminergic neurons originating in the midbrain.

Behavioral data tell us something about the temporal and spatial integrating characteristics of the second (postsynaptic) stage of this system. The required current intensity in a train of fixed duration is a linearly increasing function of the reciprocal of the number of pulses. This implies (1) that the second stage basically counts arriving action potentials and (2) that the number of first-stage axons fired by brief cathodal pulses is a linear function of current intensity. To say that the second stage counts arriving impulses is to say that there is no spatial or temporal nonlinearity in the summation of the first-stage impulses by the second stage. There is neither synaptic facilitation nor synaptic accommodation. The output for a train with a fixed duration and a strength that does not vary in the course of that duration depends only on the total number of spikes generated in the first-stage axons.

When train duration is varied (while pulse frequency is held constant), the required current decreases hyperbolically as train duration increases, or, expressing the same data in another way, the total charge required is a linearly increasing function of train duration. Gallistel (1978) suggested a leaky integrator model to account for these data, with the reinforcing effect of the signal depending on the peak of the integrator output. Another possibility is that the integration is perfect, but only that part of the signal strength that exceeds some threshold contributes to the integral. The first possibility, while it can be made to account for the linear charge-duration function, does so by ad hoc assumptions about the form of the impulse response of the leaky integrator. A linear charge-duration function is an immediate consequence of the second model.

Attempts to determine the pharmacological characteristics of the substrate for self-stimulation have been bedeviled by the problem of distinguishing between drug-induced alterations in the reinforcing and motivating effects of the stimulation, on the one hand, and drug-induced alterations in other processes pertinent to performance, on the other hand. What is needed are signature paradigms—paradigms that focus on changes in performance of a kind that can only be produced by changes in reinforcement or motivation.

One test of a signature paradigm is to give the rats drugs, such as Chloropent and curare, whose effects on performance are almost certainly not due to effects on reinforcement (or motivation). These nonspecific drugs should not be able to duplicate at any dose the effects used to index reinforcement (or, motivation). Measures of performance vigor (bar-pressing rate, running speed) do not pass the signature test. The only two paradigms that have been shown to pass the test are the extinction paradigm and the curve-shift paradigm. Both paradigms have been employed with pimozide, leading to the conclusion that this drug blocks the reinforcing effect of MFB stimulation. It does not block the motivating effect of the stimulation, however, even at doses 10 times greater than required to block reinforcement.

Attempts to block the propagation of the reinforcing or motivating signals by lesions have not been very successful. The methodological problem that bedevils the pharmacological experiments is also an issue in lesion experiments. One must use behavioral paradigms capable of distinguishing effects on reinforcement or motivation from effects on other performance-relevant processes. Both the extinction and the curve-shift paradigm could be used.

The curve-shift paradigm seems particularly promising (see Stellar & Neely, 1982). It offers the possibility of measuring the percent of reinforcement-relevant axons destroyed by a lesion. The use of the curve-shift paradigm in lesion and pharmacological work may be thought of as an extension of the trade-off method. One compensates for the drug- or lesion-induced impairment in signal transmission by increasing the number of stimulus pulses in the reward. With train duration held constant, the percentage increase in the required number of pulses measures the magnitude of the impairment produced by a drug or a lesion. If half the reinforcement-relevant fibers excited by a given reward current are destroyed by a lesion, then the number of pulses required to produce the same level of reinforcement should double. The reinforcement before the lesion was produced by a barrage of action potentials whose total number was Nx, where N is the number of pulses in the train of stimulation and x is the number of reward axons fired by a pulse. If a lesion reduces x by a factor of 2 (or 3, or 4, etc.), increasing N by the same factor should restore the reward signal to its prelesion value. The validity of these measures hangs on the argument that temporal and spatial facilitation or accommodation are negligible.

Behavioral experiments are painting a detailed portrait of the substrates for the reinforcing and motivating effects of the stimulation. This portrait is the key to the anatomical and electrophysiological identification of that substrate. Once the identification has been made, recordings from single units in behaving animals may increase our understanding of the normal function of this neural system. The identification of this substrate should also provide us with a preparation in which to study some of the neurophysiological events and processes underlying motivational and learning phenomena in a mammal.

IV. CONCLUSIONS

Electrical stimulation of the MFB generates neural signals that code for motivationally pertinent experiences of some kind. This code is converted to a memory. At the same time, by way of the same or different neural tissue, the stimulation produces transient motivating signals. These signals, while they last, selectively raise the potential for behavior directed toward obtaining the artificially induced experience. The self-stimulation behavior, which results from the combined operation of these two effects, is extraordinarily intense and persistent.

The self-stimulation phenomenon lends itself to experiments of a psychophysical character, in which one determines the trade-offs between various parameters of the electrical stimulation. These trade-off experiments reveal distinctive quantitative and pharmacological characteristics of the neural tissue whose stimulation yields the behavioral phenomenon. By means of these characteristics, it may be possible to identify the relevant neural systems at the electrophysiological and anatomical level. Such an identification would enable us to study the neurophysiological events underlying learning and motivation in a mammal.

Simple observation gives no reason to suppose that rats self-stimulating at sites outside the MFB, such as the frontal cortex, the vicinity of the locus coerulues, or the dorsal raphe, are having experiences similar to those produced by MFB stimulation. Nor does stimulation at these sites usually have the potent motivating effect of MFB stimulation. Analysis by 2DG autoradiography of the neural systems excited by stimulation at these diverse sites does not encourage the assumption that the self-stimulation phenomenon results from the activation of any single system. Refractory period studies imply that the quantitative characteristics of the directly stimulated neural systems differ from site to site. In short, there are many reasons to suppose that self-stimulation at sites outside the MFB has little if anything to do with self-stimulation in the MFB.

In the MFB, on the other hand, collision experiments (double-electrode refractory period experiments) show that self-stimulation electrodes several millimeters apart may stimulate many of the same reward and/or motivation-relevant axons. Self-stimulation throughout the MFB is highly motivated, intense, and persistent. Self-stimulation anywhere along the MFB may be seen by 2DG autoradiography to activate systems within the MFB all the way from the ventral tegmental part of the anterior midbrain to the diagonal band of Broca in the forebrain. In short, there are many reasons to think that self-stimulation throughout the MFB depends on the activation of interrelated neural systems. The stimulation may evoke a spectrum of interrelated experiences and drive states, probably those experiences and drive states that are more or less immediately related to the animal's fundamental biological concerns—homeostasis, social interaction, defense, and reproduction.

The problem of determining the natural function of the neural substrate for self-stimulation of the MFB is both conceptually and experimentally difficult. The difficulties revolve around our uncertain and inadequate conceptualizations of the processes of motivation and reinforcement. Really decisive progress on this question may have to await the emergence of more satisfactory conceptualizations in the general field of learning and motivation. The identification of the neural substrate, however, could hardly fail to shed some light on the normal function of this substrate, since it will then be possible to record from it and see the conditions under which it becomes active.

Identification of the substrate would amount to finding the nerve in a nerve–memory preparation and a nerve–motivation preparation. By following these nerves through the brain, we may arrive at sites where deeply interesting neurophysiological events occur, namely, the events underlying the laying down of memories and the motivation of behavior. It may well prove possible to study these events neurophysiologically, even in the absence of any clear understanding of how these events achieve their behavioral effects. The molecular biologists study the molecular basis of genetic information transfer in the absence of any clear understanding of how this information achieves phenotypic expression. It may be possible for physiological psychologists to do the same with regard to the neurophysiological bases of motivation and memory. They may be able to study the neurophysiological and/or biochemical bases of memory in the absence of a clear understanding of how memories achieve behavioral expression.

ACKNOWLEDGMENTS

The computer-assisted image analysis was done at the Computer Image Processing and Pattern Recognition Facility at Drexel University. I am grateful to the past and present Directors of this facility (Michael Negin and Oleh Tretiak, respectively) for their aid and support in developing the analyzing software.

REFERENCES

Abou-Hamed, H., Schmitt, P., & Karli, P. Charactéristiques de l'autostimulation au niveau de tegmentum pontin dorsal et du cervelet. *Physiology and Behavior*, 1977, *19*, 753–759.

Amaral, D. G., & Routtenberg, A. Locus coeruleus and intracranial self-stimulation: A cautionary note. *Behavioral Biology*, 1975, *13*, 331–338.

Andén, N.-E., Dahlström, A., Fuxe, K., Larrson, K., Olson, L., & Ungerstedt, U. Ascending monoamine neurons to the telencephalon and diencephalon. *Acta Physiological Scandinavica*, 1966, *67*, 313–326.

Annau, Z. Comparison of septal and hypothalamic self-stimulation during hypoxia. *Physiology and Behavior*, 1977, *18*, 735–737.

Arbuthnott, G. W. The dopamine synapse and the notion of 'pleasure centres' in the brain. *Trends in Neuroscience*, 1980, *3*, 199–200.

Arbuthnott, G. W., Mitchell, M. J., Tulloch, I. F., & Wright, A. K. Efferent pathways from lateral hypothalamic neurons. *Journal of Physiology (London)*, 1976, *263*, 131P–132P.

Beach, F. A., & Jordan, L. Effects of sexual reinforcement upon the performance of male rats in a straight runway. *Journal of Comparative and Physiological Psychology*, 1956, *49*, 105–110.

Bielajew, C., Jordan, C., Fermi-Enright, J., & Shizgal, P. Refractory periods and anatomical linkage of the substrates for lateral hypothalamic and periaqueductal gray self-stimulation. *Physiology and Behavior*, 1981, *27*, 95–104.

Bielajew, C., & Shizgal, P. Behaviorally derived measures of conduction velocity in the substrate for rewarding medial forebrain bundle stimulation. *Brain Research*, 1982, *237*, 107–119.

Bielajew, C., & Shizgal, P. The normal direction of conduction in the axons mediating self-stimulation of the MFB. In preparation, 1983.

Bindra, D. How adaptive behavior is produced: A perceptual-motivational alternative to response-reinforcement. *Behavioral and Brain Sciences*, 1978, *1*, 41–91.

Burton, M. J., Rolls, E. T., & Mora, F. Effects of hunger on the responses of neurons in the lateral hypothalamus to the sight and taste of food. *Experimental Neurology*, 1976, *51*, 669–677.

Cassens, G. P., & Mills, A. W. Lithium and amphetamine. Opposite effects on the threshold of reinforcement. *Psychopharmacologia,* 1973, *30,* 283–290.

Clavier, R. M., & Corcoran, M. E. Attenuation of self-stimulation from substantia nigra but not dorsal tegmental noradrenergic bundle by lesions of sulcal prefrontal cortex. *Brain Research,* 1976, *105,* 325–332.

Clavier, R. M., & Fibiger, H. C. On the role of ascending catecholaminergic projections in intracranial self-stimulation of substantia nigra. *Brain Research,* 1977, *131,* 271–286.

Clavier, R. M., Fibiger, H. C., & Phillips, A. G. Evidence that self-stimulation of the region of the locus coeruleus in rats does not depend upon noradrenergic projections to the telencephalon. *Brain Research,* 1976, *113,* 71–81.

Clavier, R. M., & Routtenberg, A. Brain stem self-stimulation attenuated by lesions of medial forebrain bundle but not by lesions of locus coeruleus or caudal ventral norepinephrine bundle. *Brain Research,* 1976, *101,* 251–271.

Corbett, D., Laferriere, A., & Milner, P. M. Elimination of medial prefrontal cortex self-stimulation following transection of efferents to the sulcal cortex in the rat. *Physiology and Behavior,* 1982, *29,* 425–431.

Corbett, D., Skelton, R. W., & Wise, R. A. Dorsal bundle lesions fail to disrupt self-stimulation from the region of the locus coeruleus. *Brain Research,* 1977, *133,* 37–44.

Corbett, D., & Wise, R. A. Intracranial self-stimulation in relation to the ascending noradrenergic fiber systems of the pontine tegmentum and caudal midbrain: A moveable electrode mapping study. *Brain Research,* 1979, *177,* 423–436.

Corbett, D., & Wise, R. A. Intracranial self-stimulation in relation to the ascending dopaminergic systems of the midbrain: A moveable electrode mapping study. *Brain Research,* 1980, *185,* 1–15.

Cotton, J. W., & Lewis, D. J. Effects of intertrial interval on acquisition of a running response. *Journal of Experimental Psychology,* 1957, *54,* 15–20.

Deutsch, J. A. *The structural basis of behavior.* Chicago: University of Chicago Press, 1960.

Deutsch, J. A. Learning and self-stimulation of the brain. *Journal of Theoretical Biology,* 1963, *4,* 193–214.

Deutsch, J. A. Behavioral measurement of the neural refractory period and its application to intracranial self-stimulation. *Journal of Comparative and Physiological Psychology,* 1964, *58,* 1–9.

Deutsch, J. A., Adams, D. W., & Metzner, R. J. Choice of intracranial stimulation as a function of delay between stimulations and strength of competing drive. *Journal of Comparative and Physiological Psychology,* 1964, *57,* 241–243.

Deutsch, J. A., Chisholm, D., & Mason, P. A. Adaptation to rewarding brain stimuli of differing amplitude. *Behavioral and Neural Biology,* 1980, *29,* 359–364.

Deutsch, J. A., & Deutsch, D. *Physiological psychology.* Homewood, IL: Dorsey Press, 1966.

Deutsch, J. A., & DiCara, L. Hunger and extinction in intracranial self-stimulation. *Journal of Comparative and Physiological Psychology,* 1967, *63,* 344–347.

Deutsch, J. A., & Howarth, C. I. Evocation by fear of a habit learned for electrical stimulation of the brain. *Science,* 1962, *136,* 1057–1058.

Deutsch, J. A., & Howarth, C. I. Some tests of a theory of intracranial self-stimulation. *Psychological Review,* 1963, *70,* 444–460.

Deutsch, J. A., Roll, P. L., & Wetter, F. Choice between rewarding brain stimuli of differing length. *Behavioral Biology,* 1976, *18,* 369–377.

Edmonds, D. E., & Gallistel, C. R. Reward vs. performance in self-stimulation: Electrode-specific affects of α-methyl-*p*-tyrosine on reward in the rat. *Journal of Comparative and Physiological Psychology,* 1977, *91,* 962–974.

Edmonds, D. E., & Gallistel, C. R. Parametric analysis of brain stimulation reward in the rat. III. The effect of performance variables on the reward summation function. *Journal of Comparative and Physiological Psychology,* 1974, *87,* 876–884.

Edmonds, D. E., Stellar, J. R., & Gallistel, C. R. Parametric analysis of brain stimulation reward in the rat. II. Temporal summation in the reward system. *Journal of Comparative and Physiological Psychology,* 1974, *87,* 860–870.

Esposito, R. U., Perry, W., & Kornetsky, C. Effects of *d*-amphetamine and naloxone on brain stimulation reward. *Psychopharmacology,* 1980, *69,* 187–191.

Faiers, A. A., & Mogenson, G. J. Electrophysiological identification of neurons in locus coeruleus. *Experimental Neurology,* 1976, *53,* 254–266.

Farber, J., Ellman, S. J., Mattiace, L. A., Holtzmann, A., Ippolito, P., Halperin, R., & Steiner, S. S. Differential effects of unilateral dorsal hindbrain lesions on hypothalamic self-stimulation in the rat. *Brain Research,* 1976, *112,* 148–155.

Fibiger, H. D. Drugs and reinforcement mechanisms: A critical review of the catecholamine theory. *Annual Review of Pharmacology and Toxicology,* 1978, *18,* 37–56.

Fouriezos, G., & Wise, R. A. Pimozide-induced extinction of intracranial self-stimulation. Response patterns rule out motor or performance deficits. *Brain Research,* 1976, *103,* 377–380.

Franklin, K. B. J. Catecholamines and self-stimulation: Reward and performance effects dissociated. *Pharmacology, Biochemistry and Behavior,* 1978, *9,* 813–820.

Franklin, K. B. J., & McCoy, S. N. Pimozide-induced extinction in rats: Stimulus control of responding rules out motor deficit. *Pharmacology, Biochemistry and Behavior,* 1979, *11,* 71–75.

Gallistel, C. R. Intracranial stimulation and natural rewards: Differential effects of trial spacing. *Psychonomic Science,* 1967, *9,* 167–168.

Gallistel, C. R. The incentive of brain stimulation reward. *Journal of Comparative and Physiological Psychology,* 1969, *69,* 713–721. (a)

Gallistel, C. R. Self-stimulation: Failure of pretrial stimulation to affect rats' electrode preference. *Journal of Comparative and Physiological Psychology,* 1969, *69,* 722–729. (b)

Gallistel, C. R. Self-stimulation: The neurophysiology of reward and motivation. In J. A. Deutsch (Ed.), *The physiological basis of memory.* New York: Academic Press, 1972.

Gallistel, C. R. Motivation as central organizing process: The psychophysical approach to its functional and neurophysiological analysis. *Nebraska Symposium on Motivation,* 1975, *22,* 183–250.

Gallistel, C. R. Self-stimulation in the rat: Quantitative characteristics of the reward pathway. *Journal of Comparative and Physiological Psychology,* 1978, *92,* 977–998.

Gallistel, C. R. *The organization of action: A new synthesis.* Hillsdale, NJ: Lawrence Erlbaum Associates, 1980. (a)

Gallistel, C. R. From muscles to motivation. *American Scientist,* 1980, *68,* 398–409. (b)

Gallistel, C. R., & Beagley, G. Specificity of brain stimulation-reward in the rat. *Journal of Comparative and Physiological Psychology,* 1971, *76,* 199–205.

Gallistel, C. R., Boytim, M., Gomita, Y., & Klebanoff, L. Does pimozide block the reinforcing effect of brain stimulation? *Pharmacology, Biochemistry and Behavior,* 1982, *17,* 769–781.

Gallistel, C. R., Piner, C., Allen, T. O., Adler, N. T., Yadin, E., & Negin, M. Computer-assisted analysis of 2-DG autoradiographs. *Neuroscience and Biobehavioral Reviews,* 1982, *6,* 409–420.

Gallistel, C. R., Rolls, E. T., & Greene, D. Neuron function inferred by behavioral and electrophysiological measurement of refractory period. *Science,* 1969, *166,* 1028–1030.

Gallistel, C. R., Shizgal, P., & Yeomans, J. S. A portrait of the substrate for self-stimulation. *Psychological Review,* 1981, *88,* 228–273.

Gallistel, C. R., Stellar, J. R., & Bubis, E. Parametric analysis of brain stimulation reward in the rat. I. The transient process and the memory-containing process. *Journal of Comparative and Physiological Psychology,* 1974, *87,* 848–860.

German, D. C., Dalsass, M., & Kiser, R. S. Electrophysiological examination of the ventral tegmental area in the rat. *Brain Research,* 1980, *181,* 191–197.

346   **C. R. Gallistel**

German, D. C., & Fetz, E. E. Responses of primate locus coeruleus and subcoeruleus neurons to stimulation at reinforcing brain sites and to natural reinforcers. *Brain Research*, 1976, *109*, 497–514.

Gibson, W. E., Reid, G. D., Sakai, M., & Porter, P. B. Intracranial reinforcement compared with sugar water reinforcement. *Science*, 1965, *148*, 1357–1359.

Gomita, Y., & Gallistel, C. R. Effects of reinforcement-blocking doses of pimozide on neural systems driven by rewarding stimulation of the MFB: A ^{14}C-2-deoxyglucose analysis. *Pharmacology, Biochemistry, and Behavior*, 1982, *17*, 841–845.

Grace, A. A., & Bunney, B. S. Nigral dopamine neurons: Intracellular recording and identification with L-Dopa injection and histofluorescence. *Science*, 1980, *210*, 654–656.

Guyenet, P. G., & Aghajanian, G. K. Antidromic identification of dopaminergic and other output neurons of the rat substantia nigra. Brain Research, 1978, *150*, 69–84.

Herkenham, M., & Nauta, W. J. H. Efferent connections of the habenular nuclei in the rat. *Journal of Comparative Neurology*, 1979, *187*, 19–48.

Hodos, W., & Kalman, G. Effects of increment size and reinforcer volume on progressive ratio performance. *Journal of the Experimental Analysis of Behavior*, 1963, *6*, 387–392.

Hoebel, B. G. Inhibition and disinhibition of self-stimulation and feeding: Hypothalamic control and post-ingestional factors. *Journal of Comparative and Physiological Psychology*, 1968, *66*, 89–100.

Hogan, J. A., & Bols, R. J. Priming of aggressive motivation in *Betta Splendens*. *Animal Behaviour*, 1980, *28*, 135–142.

Hogan, J. A., & Roper, T. J. A comparison of the properties of different reinforcers. *Advances in the Study of Behavior*, 1978, *8*, 155–255.

Howarth, C. I., & Deutsch, J. A. Drive decay: The cause of fast "extinction" of habits learned for brain stimulation. *Science*, 1962, *137*, 35–36.

Hunsicker, J. P., & Reid, G. D. Priming effect in conventionally reinforced rats. *Journal of Comparative and Physiological Psychology*, 1974, *87*, 618–621.

Huston, J. P. Searching for the neural mechanism of reinforcement (of "stamping-in"). In B. G. Hoebel & D. Novin (Eds.), *The neural basis of feeding and reward*. Brunswick, ME: Haer Co., 1982.

Huston, J. P., Mills, A. W., & Huston, R. Strength–duration function of hypothalamic self-stimulation. *Behavioral Biology*, 1972, *7*, 383–390.

Irwin, F. W. *Intentional behavior and motivation: A Cognitive Theory*. Philadelphia: Lippincott, 1971.

Katz, R. J. The temporal structure of reinforcement: An analysis of brain-stimulated reward. *Behavioral and Neural Biology*, 1979, *26*, 416–430.

Katz, R. J. The temporal structure of motivation. II. Determinants of reinforcement patterns in the local organization of intracranial reward. *Behavioral and Neural Biology*, 1980, *28*, 463–472.

Katz, R. J. The temporal structure of motivation. IV. A reexamination of extinction effects in intracranial reward. *Behavioral and Neural Biology*, 1981, *32*, 191–200.

Keesey, R. E., & Goldstein, M. D. Use of progressive fixed-ratio procedures in the assessment of intracranial reinforcement. *Journal of the Experimental Analysis of Behavior*, 1968, *11*, 293–301.

Kent, E. W., & Fedinets, P. Effects of GABA blockade on lateral hypothalamic self-stimulation. *Brain Research*, 1976, *107*, 628–632.

Kent, E. W., & Grossman, S. P. Evidence for a conflict interpretation of anomalous effects of rewarding brain stimulation. *Journal of Comparative and Physiological Psychology*, 1969, *69*, 381–390.

Kornblith, C., & Olds, J. T-maze learning with one trial per day using brain stimulation reinforcement. *Journal of Comparative and Physiological Psychology*, 1968, *66*, 488–492.

Lapicque, L. Recherches quantitatives sur l'excitation électrique des nerfs traitée comme une polarisation. *Journal de Physiologie et de Pathologie Generale*, 1907, *9*, 620–635.

Lashley, K. S. A simple maze: With data on the relation of distribution of practice to rate of learning. *Psychobiology*, 1918, *1*, 353–367.

Lenzer, I. I. Differences between behavior reinforced by electrical stimulation of the brain and conventionally reinforced behavior: An associative analysis. *Psychological Bulletin*, 1972, *78*, 103–118.

Liebman, J. M., & Butcher, L. L. Effects on self-stimulation behavior of drugs influencing dopaminergic neural transmission mechanisms. *Naunyn-Schmiederbergs Archives of Pharmacology*, 1973, *277*, 305–318.

Liebman, J. M., & Butcher, L. L. Comparative involvement of dopamine and noradrenaline in rate-free self-stimulation in substantia nigra, lateral hypothalamus, and mesencephalic central gray. *Naunyn-Schmiederbergs Archives of Pharmacology*, 1974, *284*, 167–194.

Lindwall, O., & Björklund, A. The organization of the ascending catecholamine neuron systems in the rat brain as revealed by the glyoxylic acid fluorescence method. *Acta Physiologica Scandinavica, Supplementum*, 1974, *412*.

Liran, J. Parametric analysis of the neural substrate(s) mediating the priming and the rewarding effects in MFB self-stimulation. Ph.D. thesis, University of Pennsylvania, 1981.

Lucas, K. The effect of alcohol on the excitation, conduction, and recovery process in nerve. *Journal of Physiology (London)*, 1913, *46*, 470–505.

Matthews, G. Neural substrate for brain stimulation reward in the rat. Cathodal and anodal strength-duration properties. *Journal of Comparative and Physiological Psychology*, 1977, *91*, 858–874.

Matthews, G. Strength-duration properties of single units driven by electrical stimulation of the lateral hypothalamus in rats. *Brain Research Bulletin*, 1978, *3*, 171–174.

Mayer, B. A., & Stone, C. P. The relative efficiency of distributed and massed practice in maze learning by young and adult albino rats. *Journal of Genetic Psychology*, 1931, *39*, 28–48.

Milner, P. *Physiological psychology*. New York: Holt, Rinehart, & Winston, 1970.

Mora, F., Mogenson, G. J., & Rolls, E. T. Activity of neurones in the region of the substantia nigra during feeding. *Brain Research*, 1977, *133*, 267–276.

Mora, F., Rolls, E. T., & Burton, M. J. Modulation during learning of the responses of neurones in the lateral hypothalamus to the sight of food. *Experimental Neurology*, 1976, *53*, 508–519.

Nieuwenhuys, R., Geeraedts, L. M. G., & Veening, J. G. The medial forebrain bundle of the rat. I. General introduction. *Journal of Comparative Neurology*, 1982, *206*, 49–81.

Olds, J. Reward and drive neurons: 1975. In A. Wauguier & E. T. Rolls (Eds.), *Brain-stimulation reward* (pp. 1–27). New York: American Elsevier, 1976.

Paxinos, G., & Watson, C. The rat brain in stereotaxic coordinates. New York: Academic Press, 1982.

Phillips, A. G., Brooke, S. M., & Fibiger, H. C. Effects of amphetamine isomers and neuroleptics on self-stimulation from the nucleus accumbens and dorsal noradrenergic bundle. *Brain Research*, 1975, *85*, 13–22.

Phillipson, O. T., & Griffith, A. C. The neurones of origin for the mesohabenular dopamine pathway. *Brain Research*, 1980, *197*, 213–218.

Pliskoff, S. S., & Hawkins, T. D. A method for increasing the reinforcement magnitude of intracranial stimulation. *Journal of the Experimental Analysis of Behavior*, 1967, *10*, 281–289.

Quartermain, D., & Webster, D. Extinction following intracranial reward: The effect of delay between acquisition and extinction. *Science*, 1968, *159*, 1259–1260.

Reid, L. D., Hunsicker, J. P., Kent, E. W., Lindsay, J. G., & Gallistel, C. R. Incidence and magnitude of the "priming effect" in self-stimulating rats. *Journal of Comparative and Physiological Psychology*, 1973, *82*, 286–293.

Robinson, R. G., & Bloom, F. E. Changes in posterior hypothalamic self-stimulation following experimental cerebral infarction in the rat. *Journal of Comparative and Physiological Psychology*, 1978, *92*, 969–976.

Rolls, E. T. contrasting effects of hypothalamic and nucleus accumbens septi self-stimulation on brain stem single unit activity and cortical arousal. *Brain Research*, 1971, *31*, 275–285.

Rolls, E. T. Activation of amygaloid neurones in reward, eating and drinking elicited by electrical stimulation of the brain. *Brain Research*, 1972, *45*, 365–381.

Rolls, E. T. The neural basis of brain-stimulation reward. *Progress in Neurobiology*, 1974, *3*, 71–160.

Rolls, E. T. *The brain and reward.* Oxford: Pergamon, 1975.

Rolls, E. T. The neurophysiological basis of brain-stimulation. In A. Wauquier & E. T. Rolls (Eds.), *Brain-stimulation reward* (pp. 65–87). Amsterdam: North-Holland Publ., 1976.

Rolls, E. T. Activity of hypothalamic and related neurons in the alert animal. In P. J. Morgane & J. Panksepp (Eds.), *Handbook of the hypothalamus.* New York: Dekker, 1979.

Rolls, E. T., Burton, M. J., & Mora, F. Hypothalamic neuronal responses associated with the sight of food. *Brain Research*, 1976, *111*, 53–66.

Rolls, E. T., & Cooper, S. J. Activation of neurons in the prefrontal cortex by brain-stimulation reward in the rat. *Brain Research*, 1973, *60*, 351–368.

Rolls, E. T., & Cooper, S. J. Connection between the prefrontal cortex and pontine brain-stimulation reward sites in the rat. *Experimental Neurology*, 1974, *42*, 687–699.

Rolls, E. T., & Rolls, B. J. Activity of neurons in sensory, hypothalamic and motor areas during feeding in the monkey. In Y. Oomura (Ed.), *Food intake and chemical senses.* Tokyo: Tokyo University Press, 1977.

Rolls, E. T., Sanghera, M. K., & Roper-Hall, A. The latency of activation of neurones in the lateral hypothalamus and substantia innominata during feeding in the monkey. *Brain Research*, 1979, *164*, 121–135.

Rompré, P.-P., & Miliaressis, E. A comparison of the excitability cycles of the hypothalamic fibers involved in self-stimulation and exploration. *Physiology and Behavior*, 1980, *24*, 995–998.

Rozin, P., & Kalat, J. W. Specific hungers and poison avoidance as adaptive specializations of learning. *Psychological Review*, 1971, *78*, 459–487.

Schenk, S., & Shizgal, P. The substrates for lateral hypothalamic and medial pre-frontal cortex self-stimulation have different refractory periods and show poor spatial summation. *Physiology and Behavior*, 1982, *28*, 133–138.

Shimizu, N., & Imamoto, K. Fine structure of the locus coeruleus in the rat. *Archivum Histologicum Japonicum*, 1970, *31*, 229–246.

Shizgal, P., Bielajew, C., Corbett, D., Skelton, R., & Yeomans, J. S. Behavioral methods for inferring anatomical linkage between rewarding brain stimulation sites. *Journal of Comparative and Physiological Psychology*, 1980, *94*, 227–237.

Shizgal, P., Bielajew, C., & Kiss, I. Anodal hyperpolarization block technique provides evidence for rostro-caudal conduction of reward signals in the medial forebrain bundle. *Society for Neuroscience Abstracts*, 1980, No. 147, 19.

Shizgal, P., Howlett, F., & Corbett, D. *Current-distance relationships in rewarding stimulation of the medial forebrain bundle.* Paper presented at the meeting of the Canadian Psychological Association, Quebec City, June, 1979.

Shizgal, P., Kiss, I., & Bielajew, C. Psychophysical and electrophysiological studies of the substrate for brain-stimulation reward. In B. G. Hoebel & D. Novin (Eds.) *The neural basis of feeding and reward.* Brunswick, ME: Haer Co., 1982.

Silva, L. R., Vogel, J. A., & Corbett, D. Frontal cortex self-stimulation: Evidence for independent substrates within areas 32 and 24. *Neuroscience Abstracts*, 1982.

Simon, H., Le Moal, M., & Cardo, B. Self-stimulation in the dorsal pontine tegmentum in the rat. *Behavioral Biology*, 1975, *13*, 339–347.

Sokoloff, L., Reivich, M., Kennedy, C., & Des Rosiers, M. The ^{14}C-deoxyglucose method for measurement of local cerebral glucose utilization. Theory, procedure, and normal values in the conscious and anesthetized albino rat. *Journal of Neurochemistry,* 1977, *28,* 897–916.

Stein, L. Reciprocal action of reward and punishment. In R. G. Heath (Ed.), *The role of pleasure in behavior* (pp. 113–139). New York: Harper (Hoeber), 1964.

Stellar, J. R., & Gallistel, C. R. Runway performance of rats for brain-stimulation or food reward: Effects of hunger and priming. *Journal of Comparative and Physiological Psychology,* 1975, *89,* 590–599.

Stellar, J. R., & Heard, K. Aftereffects of rewarding lateral hypothalamic brain stimulation and feeding behavior. *Physiology and Behavior,* 1976, *17,* 865–867.

Stellar, J. R., Iles, J., & Mills, L. E. Role of ipsilateral forebrain in lateral hypothalamic stimulation reward in rats. *Physiology and Behavior,* 1982, *29,* 1089–1097.

Stellar, J. R., & Neeley, S. P. Reward summation function measurements of lateral hypothalamic stimulation reward: Effects of anterior and posterior medial forebrain bundle lesions. In B. G. Hoebel & D. Novin, (Eds.), *The neural basis of feeding and reward.* Brunswick, ME: Haer Co., 1982.

Sutherland, R. J., & Nakajima, S. Self-stimulation of the habenular complex in the rat. *Journal of Comparative and Physiological Psychology,* 1981, *95,* 781–791.

Szabó, I., Lénard, L., & Kosaris, B. Drive decay theory of self-stimulation: Refractory periods and axon diameters in hypothalamic reward loci. *Physiology and Behavior,* 1974, *12,* 329–343.

Ungerstedt, U. Stereotaxic mapping of the monoamine pathways in the rat brain. *Acta Physiologica Scandinavica, Supplementum,* 1971, *367,* 1–47.

van der Kooy, D. An analysis of the behavior elicited by stimulation of the dorsal pons in rat. *Physiology and Behavior,* 1979, *23,* 427–432.

van der Kooy, D., & Hogan, J. A. Priming effects with food and water reinforcers in hamsters. *Learning and Motivation,* 1978, *9,* 332–346.

Wasserman, E. M., Gomita, Y., & Gallistel, C. R. Pimozide blocks reinforcement but not priming from MFB stimulation in the rat. *Pharmacology, Biochemistry and Behavior,* 1982, *17,* 783–787.

Wechsler, L. R., Savaki, H. E., & Sokoloff, L. Effects of *d*- and *l*-amphetamine on local cerebral glucose utilization in the conscious rat. *Journal of Neurochemistry,* 1979, *32,* 15–22.

Wise, R. A. Catecholamine theories of reward: A critical review. *Brain Research,* 1978, *152,* 215–247.

Wise, R. A. The dopamine synapse and the notion of 'pleasure centers' in the brain. *Trends in Neuroscience,* 1980, *3,* 91–95.

Wise, R. A. Neuroleptics and operant behavior: The anhedonia hypothesis. *Behavioral and Brain Sciences,* 1982, *5,* 39–87.

Yadin, E., Guarini, V., & Gallistel, C. R. Unilaterally activated systems in rats self-stimulating at sites in the medial forebrain bundle, medial prefrontal cortex, or locus coeruleus. *Brain Research,* 1983, *266,* 39–50.

Yeomans, J. S. Quantitative measurement of neural poststimulation excitability with behavioral methods. *Physiology and Behavior,* 1975, *15,* 593–602.

Yim, C. Y., & Mogenson, G. J. Electrophysiological studies of neurons in the ventral tegmental area of Tsai. *Brain Research,* 1980, *181,* 301–313.

Zarevics, P., & Setler, P. E. Simultaneous rate-independent and rate-dependent assessment of intracranial self-stimulation: Evidence for the direct involvement of dopamine in brain reinforcement mechanisms. *Brain Research,* 1979, *169,* 499–512.

CHAPTER

8

ELECTROCONVULSIVE SHOCK AND MEMORY[1]

ALLEN M. SCHNEIDER
Department of Psychology
Swarthmore College
Swarthmore, Pennsylvania

MARY PLOUGH[2]
Department of Psychology
Swarthmore College
Swarthmore, Pennsylvania

[1]Preparation of this chapter was supported by Grant BNS-7924072 from the National Science Foundation.
[2]Present address: School of Medicine, University of Miami, Miami, Florida 33136.

THE PHYSIOLOGICAL BASIS OF MEMORY
351

I. INTRODUCTION

It is generally accepted by memory researchers that short-term memory (i.e., memory of recent events) is more vulnerable to interference than long-term memory. Short-term memory in humans, for instance, is often disrupted by drugs and by certain neurological disorders that have relatively little effect on long-term memory. Similarly a number of studies with laboratory animals have shown that simply by varying the amount of time between training and neural trauma, it is possible to vary the amnesic effects of the trauma. Animals given electroconvulsive shock (ECS) 0.5 second after training, for instance, show amnesia the following day; whereas, animals administered ECS 30 seconds later show retention (Chorover & Schiller, 1965).

The literature reporting these and similar effects expands almost on a monthly basis. Nevertheless, the research can generally be organized in terms of two basic concerns. First, what is it about short-term memory that makes it more vulnerable than long-term memory? Is it a matter of storage or retrieval? Second, what is the origin of this difference? Is it physiological or environmental? We shall examine experiments concerned with both issues, limiting our attention principally to studies that have used ECS as the amnesic agent. We feel that much of the current research can be presented within this context even though we cannot arrive at definitive conclusions at many of the choice points.

II. AMNESIC EFFECTS OF ECS

The literature does not lack for theories to account for the differential effect that ECS has on short-term and long-term memory. These theories, generally speaking, fall into one of two groups: nonassociative and associative. The nonassociative theories center on disruption of sensory and motor capacities—the so-called performance effects. The associative theories focus on disruption of storage and retrieval. Today it is pretty much taken for granted that ECS disrupts associative processes, but this was not always the case. The nonassociative interpretations, however, are reviewed elsewhere (Lewis, 1969), and therefore we shall consider only two of the more recent proposals here.

A. Nonassociative Factors

One nonassociative theory attributes the time-dependent effects of ECS to altered brain states (Thompson & Neely, 1970) or, as we interpret it, to altered stimulus states. According to this theory, the amnesic effects of ECS delivered

0.5 seconds after training differ from the amnesic effects of ECS delivered 30 seconds after training because the stimulus state of the animal is different in each case. Immediately after training the animal is presumably in the process of storing memory, and the stimulus state created by ECS becomes a conditioned stimulus for that memory; later when the animal is tested, the stimulus state has worn off, and in the absence of the conditioned stimulus the animal shows no retention. However, 30 seconds after training, the animal has presumably completed the storage of memory, and thus the stimulus state created by ECS does not become a conditioned stimulus for that memory.

The theory is easy to test. If ECS produces amnesia because during storage it produces a stimulus state that is different from the stimulus state during testing, then making the stimulus state the same during storage and testing should prevent amnesia. To accomplish this, researchers administered ECS twice, once shortly after training (i.e., during storage) and once again before testing. The results are mixed. Thompson and Neely (1970) found that the added ECS before testing prevented amnesia, while Zornetzer and McGaugh (1969) found that it did not. The only reasonable conclusion then is that if ECS produces amnesia by altering the stimulus state, it does so in a limited and unpredictable way.

Another nonassociative interpretation, one which we proposed several years ago (Schneider & Sherman, 1968), is that ECS produces aftereffects which linger in the nervous system and disrupt the animal's ability to perform the conditioned response the next day. To account for why ECS delivered 0.5 seconds after training produces amnesia while ECS delivered 30 seconds after training does not, we proposed a theory that links amnesia not only to ECS but to an increase in neural arousal produced during the training itself and the aftereffects produced by this increase. In our view, animals that have just been trained (i.e., animals that have just learned to avoid shock) are in a state of arousal and, thus when given ECS, overreact and experience prolonged neural aftereffects. On the other hand, animals that have been trained and allowed to rest for 30 seconds before being given ECS are no longer in a state of arousal, do not overreact to ECS, and thus do not experience prolonged neural aftereffects.

Support for this hypothesis came from a study in which we trained animals to avoid footshock and then, 1 hour later, gave them either a noncontingent footshock followed by ECS or ECS alone. The next day we tested the animals for retention. Reinstatement of footshock before ECS was designed to induce neural arousal and, consistent with the aftereffects hypothesis, it also induced amnesia.

Soon after these results appeared, Misanin, Miller, and Lewis (1968) reported similar results but with a different procedure and a different interpretation. In the Misanin *et al.* study, animals were given tone paired with footshock during training and then, 24 hours later, were divided into two groups and were given either ECS alone or tone followed by ECS. The next day the animals were tested for retention of conditioned fear to the tone. The results indicated that the animals that received the tone followed by ECS showed amnesia, while the animals that received ECS alone did not.

Misanin *et al.* took an entirely different view of their results from us. Rather than proposing that the tone produces arousal which potentiates the after-effects of ECS, as we might have, Misanin *et al.* proposed that the reinstatement of the tone reactivates a memory trace which is then disrupted by ECS. In other words, what we would have taken as a strong case for an aftereffects theory, Misanin *et al.* took as evidence for vulnerability of a retrieved memory. It remained for a study by Robbins and Meyer (1970) to settle the issue.

Robbins and Meyer trained rats on a series of three discrimination tasks. Although the three tasks were different, two of the tasks were acquired under the same motivational state, that is, two of the tasks were acquired while the animals were motivated by footshock or in other cases by hunger. The animals were given ECS immediately after the third task and then, the next day, were tested for retention of either the first or second task. The results were surprising. Electroconvulsive shock disrupted retention of one of the two tasks, the one acquired under the same motivational state that prevailed during the third task. For example, if the third task were footshock-motivated, ECS disrupted retention of the previous footshock-motivated task; if the third task were hunger-motivated, ECS disrupted retention of the previous hunger-motivated task.

The aftereffects hypothesis cannot account for these data. If aftereffects were indeed the source of disruption, we would expect the amnesic effects of ECS to be general and to disrupt retention of all the tasks regardless of their motivational state. On the other hand, the retrieval hypothesis can account for the data. If retrieval were, in fact, the source of disruption, we would expect the amnesic effects of ECS to be selective, and would expect ECS to disrupt retention of only those tasks acquired and later retrieved under the same motivational state.

In any event if it is difficult to interpret these results, the results themselves are clear enough. The amnesic effects of ECS are not as circumscribed as originally thought: ECS produces amnesia when delivered shortly after newly acquired memories (i.e., shortly after training), and it produces amnesia when delivered shortly after reinstated memories. Moreover, recent studies, not using ECS, indicate that the vulnerability of the two memories is remarkably similar: the vulnerability in both cases is time dependent and in both cases is modifiable by drugs (Gordon & Spear, 1973) or by brain stimulation (DeVietti & Kirkpatrick, 1976).

The interpretation of these data is difficult. On the one hand, since the vulnerability of the two memories is so similar, it is tempting to argue that the mechanisms underlying the vulnerability are also similar, and indeed this is precisely the case presented by Lewis (1979). According to Lewis, the feature shared by newly acquired and reinstated memories is that both are active memories and, in Lewis' view, active memories are vulnerable memories. On the other hand, recent data indicate that the two memories may not be as similar as originally thought. The data indicate that newly acquired memories remain vulnerable for a longer period of time than reinstated memories (Gordon, 1977) and, once disrupted, are less likely to recover (Judge & Quartermain, 1982; Mactutus, Riccio, & Ferek, 1979). Whether these data should be taken as evidence that different mechanisms underlie the vulnerability of the two memories or whether, as some have argued (e.g., Judge & Quartermain, 1982), the same mechanism is involved to different degrees remains a topic for future research.

Less tentative is our feeling about nonassociative factors in general. Although we considered only two nonassociative hypotheses, we see no reason to continue since the pattern of results has been the same. For every positive claim in the literature there has usually been a corresponding refutation. Thus, we shall assume that the time-dependent effects of ECS represent disruption of an associative process and that what remains to be determined is the precise nature of that process.

B. Associative Factors

Retention depends on two associative processes. One is storage, the process by which learned information endures over time. The other is retrieval, the process by which learned information is accessed during recall. In the event that either process (storage or retrieval) is disrupted, retention is lost, but the loss is different in each instance. When storage is disrupted, the loss is permanent (nonrecoverable); when retrieval is disrupted, the loss is temporary (recoverable). It is true of course that the line between disruption of storage and retrieval is not a sharp one, for we can never be certain that nonrecoverable losses, under some unforeseen circumstances, will not become recoverable losses.

Workers of a traditional bent have argued that the time-dependent effects of ECS reflect changes in memory storage (Hebb, 1949; McGaugh, 1966). In their estimation the difference between short-term and long-term memory is the state of storage. Short-term memory, they argue, is stored in a vulnerable state, long-term memory is stored in a resistant state. The process that mediates the transformation from one state to the other is referred to as memory consolidation. Views differ as to precisely how the consolidation process works, but it is generally agreed that there is a brief period shortly after training in which memory storage is fragile and open to interference by ECS (Gold & McGaugh, 1975). This assumption is the key to the consolidation position, and it is this assumption that has come under serious attack. Two problems have been raised.

First, results indicate that the time-dependent effects of ECS are highly variable. For example, Alpern & McGaugh (1968) found that as the duration of ECS is increased from 0.2 to 0.8 seconds, the time in which ECS can be delivered after training and still produce amnesia increased from roughly 10 seconds to 3 hours. How can the same memory take 10 seconds to consolidate one time and 3 hours another? The simplest explanation has been to assume that neither length of time, 10 seconds or 3 hours, represents the true consolidation period. Rather even after 3 hours, consolidation may not be entirely completed, but may be nearly completed, to the extent that intense disruption, such as 0.8-seconds ECS, can interfere with the process.

The other problem, and in some ways the more serious one, centers on the processes that underlie the time-dependent effects of ECS: whether they reflect changes in memory storage or memory retrieval? What makes this question so important today is that recent studies have shown that the amnesic effects of ECS on short-term memory are not as permanent as originally thought. The results indicate that animals made amnesic for memory of a learned response can be prompted to recall that memory if given reminder stimuli (i.e., fragments of the original training experience). These results seem to offer persuasive evidence for the notion that ECS does indeed disrupt a retrieval process, but closer evaluation of the results has raised some serious doubts. In the remainder of this section we shall present an encapsulation of the debate and then describe some experiments that may help resolve the issue.

C. Reminder Effect

Generally speaking, when we refer to the reminder effect, we are referring to several observations, all of which indicate basically the same phenomenon: ECS-treated animals recover from amnesia when given fragments of the original training experience. A study by Quartermain, McEwen, and Azmitia (1972) provides one of the more complete accounts of the effect. Quartermain et al. found that animals given passive-avoidance training (i.e., footshock for stepping from a small to large compartment) and ECS 1 second later could be induced to recover retention of the avoidance response if they were given reminder stimuli. The animals recovered when given repeated test trials (i.e., when given repeated opportunity to step from the small to large compartment without footshock), and they recovered when given a single test trial plus reminder shock (i.e., a footshock outside the training apparatus). They also recovered when given intense reminder shock alone (Miller & Springer, 1972a).

There have been two interpretations of these data. The original view was that memory storage is present all along and that what is missing is the ability to access that memory (Miller & Springer, 1973; Quartermain et al., 1972). Presumably, then, the reminder stimuli, by producing retrieval, restore the accessing ability. The other view is that memory storage is present all along, but that what is missing is strength of memory (Gold, Haycock, Macri, & McGaugh, 1973). In this instance the reminder stimuli, by producing learning, restore that strength.

In deference to earlier work, it should be noted that researchers were not oblivious to the possibility that the success of reminder stimuli in restoring retention depends on their acting as a learning experience. This possibility was ruled out, however, once it was found that reminder stimuli did not produce retention-like performance in naive animals (Quartermain et al., 1972). However, proponents of the learning theory have countered with the argument that for reminder stimuli to produce retention the stimuli must be given to animals that have a weak memory to begin with. According to the theory, amnesic animals have that memory but naive animals do not (Gold & King, 1974).

Therefore, in summary, the two theories agree that memory storage survives the amnesic effects of ECS, but the theories disagree as to why that enduring memory does not produce retention. According to the retrieval theory, the problem is one of accessing. According to the learning theory, the problem is one of strength. Gold et al. (1973) tested the learning theory as it applies to recovery produced by reminder shock, and we tested the theory as it applies to recovery produced by reminder shock (Schneider, 1979) and repeated test trials (Schneider, Tyler, & Jinich, 1974). Let us look at the work of Gold et al. first.

Gold et al. found that the reminder shock effect is selective and that recovery occurs only if reminder shock is given to animals that show partial amnesia following ECS. Gold et al. concluded that to benefit from reminder shock animals must have a weak memory, and they took the data as evidence for the learning theory. Others have countered with the claim that the Gold et al. results are incomplete—that reminder shock, given that it is of sufficient intensity, is just as apt to produce recovery in animals that show complete amnesia as in animals that show partial amnesia (Miller & Springer, 1974). There is no denying that these data raise serious questions regarding the validity of the argument of Gold et al. At the same time they do not constitute evidence against the learning theory per se. It is true that the learning theory assumes that animals must have a weak memory to benefit from reminder shock, but it is also true that animals can have that weak memory and still appear to be completely amnesic. Recently we offered some speculations about circumstances under which this might occur (Schneider, 1979).

Let us look first at the literature. Most ECS experiments in the animal literature have been concerned with the effects of ECS on retention of avoidance behavior. A few experiments, however, have also measured the effects of ECS on the autonomic behavior that normally accompanies avoidance behavior. Hine and Paolino (1970), for example, compared the effects of ECS on avoidance behavior with the effects of ECS on conditioned heart rate changes. Animals in their experiment were given punishing footshock for stepping from a small to large compartment; immediately after footshock, they were given ECS. The next day the animals were divided into two groups and were tested for retention of either the avoidance or autonomic behavior. As expected, the group tested for retention of avoidance behavior showed no overt signs of remembering the punishment, and immediately stepped into the large compartment. Surprisingly, however, the group tested for retention of autonomic behavior showed internal signs of remembering the punishment, that is, they showed a decrease in heart rate.

The connection between the decreased heart rate and the reminder effect was made soon after in a study from our laboratory (Schneider et al., 1974). We took the decreased heart rate as an indication that memory survives the disruptive effects of ECS. Accordingly, we focused on how reminder stimuli transformed that memory into retention of the avoidance response. Consistent with the learning theory, we identified the problem as one of strength. The enduring memory, in our view, was too weak to produce retention of the avoidance response. The reminder stimuli, on the other hand, by producing learning, offset that weakness. We had no problem explaining how reminder shock could do this: the shock produces conditioned fear that generalizes to the test apparatus and summates with the enduring memory (Schneider, 1979; see Gold & King, 1974, for a similar explanation). We had no problem confirming the hypothesis: Confining animals to the reminder apparatus after reminder shock, a manipulation designed to extinguish the conditioned fear, extinguished the reminder shock effect (Schneider, 1979).

However, more elusive was the repeated test trial effect. How can a trial in which there is no footshock produce learning of avoidance behavior? The plausibility of our argument (Schneider et al., 1974) rested on the following set of assumptions: First, we assumed that during passive avoidance training, when the animal steps from the small to large compartment and is punished, two memories are formed, one memory is of the contingency between response and punishment (commonly referred to as instrumental conditioning), the other memory is of the association between the large compartment and punishment (commonly referred to as classically conditioned fear). Second, we assumed that ECS affects the two memories differently, ECS disrupts the response memory but does not disrupt the fear memory. Finally, we assumed that the fear memory is not sufficient to produce retention of the avoidance response, at least initially, but is necessary in promoting later recovery during repeated test trials. Specifically, during the initial test trial when the amnesic animal steps from the small to large compartment, we assumed that the animal is punished by the conditioned fear which presumably survives the disruptive effects of ECS. The conditioned fear, in turn, works in the same way as, but perhaps to a lesser extent than, the footshock during training to recondition the avoidance response.

These assumptions led to a simple prediction. If reminder stimuli produce recovery by producing learning, then manipulations that weaken learning should weaken recovery. To test this hypothesis, we gave amnesic animals repeated test trials with one added feature. We confined the animals to the large compartment of the training apparatus for 8 minutes after the first test trial. Confinement was designed to produce extinction of the conditioned fear, and consistent with the learning theory, it also prevented recovery.

These data notwithstanding, one might argue that the learning theory is not general enough to account for the pervasiveness of the reminder effect. The reminder effect, after all, occurs with appetitive (Miller, Ott, Berk, & Springer, 1974) as well as aversive conditioning. There is no conflict. Weak memories can endure with appetitive as well as aversive conditioning, and learning can be produced by appetitive as well as aversive reminder stimuli.

Finally, to dispel any ambiguities concerning our view of ECS in general, it should be emphasized that we are not denying the possibility that ECS disrupts retrieval. It may indeed disrupt retrieval, but in our estimation recovery produced by reminder stimuli is not evidence. Recovery produced by pharmacological manipulations, however, may be evidence, and it is to these studies which we now turn.

D. Drug and Hormone Effects

A number of studies have demonstrated that a variety of drugs or hormones, among them scopolamine, strychnine, amphetamine, ACTH, and vasopressin, have the capacity to reverse the amnesic effects of ECS, but a number of questions remain unanswered.

First of all, neither the strychnine (Duncan & Hunt, 1972) nor the scopolamine effects (Davis, Thomas, & Adams, 1971) have proved readily reproducible (Lewis & Bregman, 1972; Miller & Springer, 1972b). Second, the procedure used in the ACTH (Rigter & van Riezen, 1975) and vasopressin (Pfeifer & Bookin, 1978) studies (the hormones were administered 1 hour before testing) leaves open the possibility that the effect may have more to do with the animal's ability to perform than with its ability to retrieve the conditioned response.

The amphetamine results, too, are open to question. The problem is that amphetamines reverse the amnesia produced by ECS delivered 15 seconds after training, but they do not reverse amnesia produced by ECS delivered 4 seconds after training (Mah & Albert, 1974). One explanation of these results is that ECS disrupts both storage and retrieval, but at different time intervals—storage 4 seconds after training, retrieval 15 seconds after training—and that amphetamines reverse the latter but not the former.

E. Summary

In summary the major purpose of this section was to examine a series of experiments concerned with determining the effects of ECS on associative processes. The pattern has been one of give and take between data and theory. The initial observation was that the amnesic effects of ECS are time dependent, and the theory proposed to explain this result was that ECS disrupts memory storage. It was then discovered that the amnesic effects of ECS are temporary, and the theory proposed to explain these data was that ECS disrupts memory retrieval. It was then reported that the recovery effect is spurious, that the reminder data on which it is based is a learning effect, and that no conclusion could be drawn from these data regarding disruption of storage or retrieval. Finally, an alternative approach was considered. It consisted of pharmacological studies, and it suggested that ECS disrupts both storage and retrieval processes.

Given the lack of evidence, it is prudent to reserve judgment on the storage and retrieval issue until more data become available. However, our reservations on this issue have little to do with our views concerning the time-dependent effects of ECS in general. In our estimation the time-dependent effects clearly indicate that ECS disrupts a consolidation process, be it storage, retrieval, or both. In Section III we shall consider some of the more promising possibilities concerning the nature of the consolidation process.

III. THE CONSOLIDATION PROCESS

The process of consolidation, how the brain converts short-term memory to long-term memory, is an obviously complex process and a process whose physiological mechanisms are still very much a mystery. Nevertheless, progress has been made, and we now have an idea of some of the mechanisms of control at the physiological and environmental levels. The purpose of this section is not to review the extensive literature on these mechanisms but to describe experiments which are representative of our current knowledge, staying within the context of ECS experiments when possible.

A. Neural Arousal

Early work focused on the assumption that consolidation depends on neural arousal. The test of this hypothesis was sought through studies using neural stimulants as means of modifying the consolidation process. The expectation was that if the level of neural arousal plays a role in consolidation, then stimulating neural activity should facilitate the process.

The hypothesis has been tested extensively, beginning with a series of studies by McGaugh (1973). McGaugh did not use ECS but instead used only stimulants and found that the sooner after training an animal is injected with picrotoxin or strychnine, the greater the facilitatory effect on subsequent retention. This result, of course, is precisely what one would expect if drugs do indeed affect consolidation because it is immediately after training that consolidation should be in its most active form.

But there is one obvious problem with using drugs such as strychnine and picrotoxin to study consolidation. The problem is the indiscriminate effect of these drugs on the nervous system. Working with these agents makes it impossible to implicate any one or, for that matter, any group of neurochemicals or anatomical sites in the consolidation process. This is why experimenters, attempting to circumvent this problem, have begun to study the consolidation process using other techniques, such as discrete brain stimulation or drugs with known neurochemical effects.

Although far from complete, the picture that has emerged is perfectly consistent with the arousal hypothesis. Drugs or brain stimulation procedures that increase or decrease neural arousal have a corresponding effect on strength of retention. When amphetamines are administered immediately after training, they facilitate retention; when the drugs are delayed, they have no effect (McGaugh, 1973). The same pattern holds for norepinephrine (Gold & van Buskirk, 1975) and for stimulation of the reticular formation (Bloch, 1976), and the same pattern holds for drugs that deplete norepinephrine (Randt, Quartermain, Goldstein, & Anagnosti, 1971), except that the effect of these drugs is to impair rather than facilitate retention. Moreover, the impairment in this case is reversible (Botwinick & Quartermain, 1974), a result implicating disruption of retrieval as the source of amnesia.

If arousal is the means by which the nervous system produces memory consolidation, it is reasonable to ask what normally produces the arousal. What stimulates the reticular formation to activate the brain, and what produces the release of norepinephrine? The answer is twofold. On the one hand, it seems reasonable to assume that arousal is produced by the learning experience itself. Indeed Kety (1976) and Gold and McGaugh (1975) have made a strong case for such a proposition. On the other hand, there is evidence that arousal is produced from within the brain itself when the animal is sleeping (Bloch, 1976). Sleep is cyclical, consisting of paradoxical and slow-wave stages, and recent experiments have implicated the paradoxical stage as a major source of arousal. Let us now consider the studies that have examined this phenomenon.

B. Paradoxical Sleep

The impression that we have given thus far is that there is a well-defined period of consolidation beginning immediately after training and ending a short time later. This is accurate only up to a point. Bloch (1976) proposed that consolidation is not complete during this period, but that it recurs at least one more time during sleep, specifically during paradoxical sleep. He based this conclusion on the following results:

First, animals deprived of paradoxical sleep for 2 days after training and then given ECS show amnesia, while nondeprived animals given ECS 2 days after training show no effect (Fishbein, McGaugh, & Swarz, 1971). Apparently without paradoxical sleep memory remains in an unconsolidated fragile state.

Second, there is a relation between the amount of information that has been learned and the amount of time spent in paradoxical sleep. When learning is in progress, paradoxical sleep increases; when learning is complete, paradoxical sleep returns to normal (Smith, Kitahama, Valatx, & Jouvet, 1974).

Finally, it appears that the function served by paradoxical sleep in the consolidation process is to provide neural arousal. Animals stimulated in the reticular formation immediately after training and thus given supplementary arousal before they fall asleep, do not show the typical increase in paradoxical sleep (Bloch, Hennevin, & Leconte, 1977). Apparently, stimulation of the reticular formation immediately after training satisfies a need for arousal that is normally satisfied by paradoxical sleep.

C. Environmental Factors

Central to the consolidation theory is the idea that neural arousal underlies the transformation of short-term memory into long-term memory. This assumption explains why agents that stimulate the nervous system, drugs or electrical stimulation of the reticular formation or paradoxical sleep, strengthen retention. However, there appears to be another factor, apart from neural arousal, that contributes to the consolidation process. It is possible, for instance, that even if the nervous system is in an optimal state of arousal immediately after training, consolidation will not occur unless appropriate environmental conditions are also present. Evidence for this hypothesis comes from studies by Lewis (1976) and his colleagues.

In these experiments Lewis, Miller, and Misanin showed that an animal's environmental experience before or after training goes a long way to determine the animal's reaction to the amnesic effects of ECS. They found, for instance, that they could intensify the amnesia by inserting a flashing light between training and ECS (Miller, Misanin, & Lewis, 1969), but they could also weaken the amnesia by familiarizing the animals with the learning environment before training and ECS (Lewis et al., 1968). To account for this relationship between environmental experience and the amnesic effects of ECS, Lewis et al. proposed that after training, animals engage in a process similar to rehearsal (see Wagner, Rudy & Witlow, 1973, for an analysis of rehearsal in lower animals). The flashing light, in the view of Lewis et al., disrupts the rehearsal process, and familiarization facilitates it.

It is easy to understand how an intrusive light could interfere with rehearsal. Understanding how familiarization facilitates rehearsal, however, calls for clarification. Lewis (1976) proposed that during familiarization the animal builds an elaborately connected system of memories for details of the environment. Later, when trained, the animal need only establish and integrate the one memory of the punishing footshock into this preexisting context. This integration occurs almost instantaneously and so is completed before ECS. Animals not familiarized with the apparatus, on the other hand, must establish memories of the learning environment as well as the punishing shock. This takes time, too much time to be completed before ECS, and so these animals are amnesic.

Convincing as Lewis' explanation may seem, it is not without problems. For one thing the data have not proved readily reproducible, although this may have more to do with the procedure than with the phenomenon itself (Dawson & McGaugh, 1969; Galosy & Thompson, 1971; Sara & Lefevre, 1973). Studies that have not successfully reproduced the familiarization effect have typically used different training or ECS procedures from Lewis but have not used different amounts of familiarization and, according to Lewis (1976), what works for one procedure may not work for another. Consistent with this hypothesis, Miller (1970) found that if the learning environment were increased in complexity, a longer period of familiarization was required to produce the attenuation effect.

IV. CONCLUDING REMARKS

In summary, the data suggest that memory consolidation is rooted in two mechanisms, rehearsal and arousal, and two processes, storage and retrieval. However, the chief question here is how the processes and the mechanisms are related. Our explanation is a relatively simple one. We suggest that the two mechanisms serve different functions: rehearsal, producing memory storage, and arousal, producing memory retrieval. This would explain why amnesia produced by norepinephrine depletion (i.e., by disruption of arousal) can be reversed by restoring norepinephrine before testing. Furthermore, on the assumption that rehearsal precedes arousal, this theory would also explain why amphetamines cannot reverse amnesia produced by ECS delivered 4 seconds after training (i.e., by disruption of rehearsal) but can reverse amnesia produced by ECS delivered 15 seconds after training (i.e., by disruption of arousal).

It would be misleading to imply that the theory we have outlined here is new. The possibility that neural trauma disrupts both storage and retrieval has been proposed by others (e.g., Kapp & Schneider, 1971; Kesner, 1973). What we have done, then, is to reevaluate the theory in light of new data and to reaffirm the importance of linking disruption of storage and retrieval to underlying mechanisms. The data are limited, however, and any attempt to define more precisely the relation between process and mechanism remains a challenge for future research.

REFERENCES

Alpern, H. P., & McGaugh, J. L. Retrograde amnesia as a function of duration of electroshock stimulation. *Journal of Comparative and Physiological Psychology*, 1968, *65*, 265–269.

Bloch, V. Brain activation and memory consolidation. In M. R. Rosenzweig & E. L. Bennett (Eds.), *Neural mechanisms of learning and memory*. Cambridge, MA: MIT Press, 1976.

Bloch, V., Hennevin, E., & Leconte, P. Interaction between post-trial reticular stimulation and subsequent paradoxical sleep in memory consolidation processes. In R. R. Drucker-Colin & J. L. McGaugh (Eds.), *Neurobiology of sleep and memory*. New York: Academic Press, 1977.

Botwinick, C. Y., & Quartermain, D. Recovery from amnesia induced by pretest injections of monoamine oxidase inhibitors. *Pharmacology, Biochemistry and Behavior*, 1974, *2*, 375–379.

Chorover, S. L., & Schiller, P. H. Short-term retrograde amnesia in rats. *Journal of Comparative and Physiological Psychology*, 1965, *59*, 73–78.

Davis, J. W., Thomas, R. K., & Adams, H. E. Interactions of scopolamine and physostigmine with ECS and one trial learning. *Physiology and Behavior*, 1971, *6*, 219–222.

Dawson, R. G., & McGaugh, J. L. Electroconvulsive shock-produced retrograde amnesia: Analysis of the familiarization effect. *Communications in Behavioral Biology*, 1969, *4*, 91–95.

DeVietti, T. L., & Kirkpatrick, B. R. The amnesia gradient: Inadequate as evidence for a memory consolidation process. *Science*, 1976, *194*, 438–439.

Duncan, N., & Hunt, E. Reduction of ECS produced retrograde amnesia by post-trial introduction of strychnine. *Physiology and Behavior*, 1972, *9*, 295–300.

Fishbein, W., McGaugh, J. L., & Swarz, J. R. Retrograde amnesia: Electroconvulsive shock effects after termination of rapid eye movement sleep deprivation. *Science*, 1971, *172*, 80–82.

Galosy, R. A., & Thompson, R. W. Further investigation of familiarization effects on ECS produced retrograde amnesia. *Psychonomic Science*, 1971, *22*, 147–148.

Gold, P. E., Haycock, J. W., Macri, J., & McGaugh, J. L. Retrograde amnesia and the "reminder effect": An alternative interpretation. *Science*, 1973, *180*, 1199–1200.

Gold, P. E., & King, R. A. Retrograde amnesia: Storage failure versus retrieval failure. *Psychological Review*, 1974, *81*, 465–469.

Gold, P. E., & McGaugh, J. L. A single-trace, two-process view of memory storage process. In D. Deutsch & J. A. Deutsch (Eds.), *Short-term memory*. New York: Academic Press, 1975.

Gold, P. E., & van Buskirk, R. B. Facilitation of time-dependent memory processes with post-trial epinephrine injections. *Behavioral Biology*, 1975, *13*, 145–153.

Gordon, W. C. Similarities between recently acquired and reactivated memories with production of memory interference. *American Journal of Psychology*, 1977, *90*, 231–242.

Gordon, W. C., & Spear, N. E. The effect of strychnine on recently acquired and reactivated passive avoidance memories. *Physiology and Behavior*, 1973, *10*, 1071–1075.

Hebb, D. O. *The organization of behavior*. New York: Wiley, 1949.

Hine, B., & Paolino, R. W. Retrograde amnesia: Production of skeletal but not cardiac response gradient by electroconvulsive shock. *Science*, 1970, *169*, 1224–1226.

Judge, M. E., & Quartermain, D. Characteristics of retrograde amnesia following reactivation of memory in mice. *Physiology and Behavior*, 1982, *28*, 585–590.

Kapp, B. S., & Schneider, A. M. Selective recovery from retrograde amnesia produced by hippocampal spreading depressing. *Science*, 1971, *173*, 1149–1151.

Kesner, R. A neural system analysis of memory storage and retrieval. *Psychological Bulletin*, 1973, *80*, 177–203.

Kety, S. S. Biological concomitants of affective states and their possible role in memory processes. In M. R. Rosenzweig & E. L. Bennett (Eds.), *Neural mechanisms of learning and memory*. Cambridge, MA: MIT Press, 1976.

Lewis, D. J. Sources of experimental amnesia. *Psychological Review*, 1969, *76*, 461–472.

Lewis, D. J. A cognitive approach to experimental amnesia. *American Journal of Psychology*, 1976, *89*, 51–80.

Lewis, D. J. Psychobiology of active and inactive memory. *Psychological Bulletin*, 1979, *86*, 1054–1083.

Lewis, D. J., & Bregman, N. J. The cholinergic system, amnesia and memory. *Physiology and Behavior*, 1972, *8*, 511–514.

Lewis, D. J., Miller, R. R., & Misanin, J. R. Control of retrograde amnesia. *Journal of Comparative and Physiological Psychology*, 1968, *66*, 48–52.

Mactutus, C. F., Riccio, D. C., & Ferek, J. M. Retrograde amnesia for old (reactivated) memory: Some anomalous characteristics. *Science*, 1979, *204*, 1319–1320.

Mah, C. J., & Albert, D. J. Reversal of ECS-induced amnesia by post-ECS injections of amphetamine. *Pharmacology, Biochemistry and Behavior*, 1974, *3*, 1–5.

McGaugh, J. L. Time dependent processes in memory storage. *Science*, 1966, *153*, 1351–1358.

McGaugh, J. L. Drug facilitation of learning and memory. *Annual Review of Pharmacology*, 1973, *13*, 220–241.

Miller, R. R. Effects of environmental complexity on amnesia induced by electroconvulsive shock in rats. *Journal of Comparative and Physiological Psychology*, 1970, *71*, 267–275.

Miller, R. R., Misanin, J. R., & Lewis, D. J. Amnesia as a function of events during the learning-ECS interval. *Journal of Comparative and Physiological Psychology*, 1969, *67*, 145–148.

Miller, R. R., Ott, C. A., Berk, A. M., & Springer, A. D. Appetitive memory and restoration after ECS in the rat. *Journal of Comparative and Physiological Psychology*, 1974, *87*, 717–723.

Miller, R. R., & Springer, A. D. Induced recovery of memory in rats following electroconvulsive shock. *Physiology and Behavior*, 1972, *8*, 645–651. (a)

Miller, R. R., & Springer, A. D. Effects of strychnine on ECS-induced amnesia in the rat. *Psychonomic Science*, 1972, *26*, 289–290. (b)

Miller, R. R., & Springer, A. D. Amnesia, consolidation, and retrieval. *Psychological Review*, 1973, *80*, 69–79.

Miller, R. R., & Springer, A. D. Implications of recovery from experimental amnesia. *Psychological Review*, 1974, *81*, 470–473.

Misanin, J. R., Miller, R. R., & Lewis, D. J. Retrograde amnesia produced by electroconvulsive shock after reactivation of a consolidated memory trace. *Science*, 1968, *160*, 554–555.

Pfeifer, W. D., & Bookin, H. B. Vasopressin antagonizes retrograde amnesia in rats following electroconvulsive shock. *Pharmacology, Biochemistry and Behavior*, 1978, *9*, 261–263.

Quartermain, D., McEwen, B. S., & Azmitia, E. C., Jr. Recovery of memory following amnesia in the rat and mouse. *Journal of Comparative and Physiological Psychology*, 1972, *79*, 360–370.

Randt, C. T., Quartermain, D., Goldstein, M., & Anagnosti, B. Norepinephrine biosynthesis inhibition: Effects on memory in mice. *Science*, 1971, *172*, 498–499.

Rigter, H., & van Riezen, H. Anti-amnesic effect of ACTH 4–10: Its independence of the nature of the amnesic agent and the behavioral test. *Physiology and Behavior*, 1975, *14*, 563–566.

Robbins, M. J., & Meyer, D. R. Motivational control of retrograde amnesia. *Journal of Experimental Psychology*, 1970, *84*, 220–225.

Sara, S. J., & Lefevre, D. A reexamination of the role of familiarization (FAM) in retrograde amnesia. *Journal of Comparative and Physiological Psychology*, 1973, *84*, 361–364.

Schneider, A. M. Recovery from retrograde amnesia: A behavioral analysis. In M. A. B. Brazier (Ed.), *Brain mechanisms in memory and learning: From the single neuron to man*. New York: Raven Press, 1979.

Schneider, A. M., & Sherman, W. Amnesia: A function of the temporal relation of footshock to electroconvulsive shock. *Science*, 1968, *159*, 219–221.

Schneider, A. M., Tyler, J., & Jinich, D. Recovery from retrograde amnesia: A learning process. *Science*, 1974, *184*, 87–88.

Smith, C., Kitahama, K., Valatx, J. L., & Jouvet, M. Increased paradoxical sleep in mice during acquisition of a shock avoidance task. *Brain Research*, 1974, *77*, 221–230.

Thompson, C. I., & Neely, J. E. Dissociated learning in rats produced by electroconvulsive shock. *Physiology and Behavior*, 1970, *5*, 783–786.

Wagner, A., Rudy, J., & Whitlow, J. Rehearsal in animal conditioning. *Journal of Experimental Psychology*, 1973, *97*, 407–426.

Zornetzer, S., & McGaugh, J. L. Effects of electroconvulsive shock upon inhibitory avoidance: The persistance and stability of amnesia. *Communications in Behavioral Biology*, 1969, *3*, 173–180.

CHAPTER

9

THE CHOLINERGIC SYNAPSE AND THE SITE OF MEMORY

J. ANTHONY DEUTSCH

Department of Psychology
University of California, San Diego
La Jolla, California

I. INTRODUCTION

The idea that learning and memory are due to some form of change of synaptic conductance is very old, having been suggested by Tanzi in 1893. It is a simple idea and in many ways an obvious one. However, the evidence that learning is due to changes at the synapse has hitherto been meager (Sharpless, 1964). Though changes do occur at spinal synapse as a result of stimulation, there is no evidence that the changes are those utilized in the nervous system for information storage. To use an analogy, if we pass large amounts of current across resistors in a computer, temporary increases in temperature and perhaps even permanent increases in resistance occur. However, such an experiment shows only that the computer could store information by using "poststimulation" alterations in its resistors, but not that this is the actual way in which the computer does store information. Furthermore, Sharpless (1964) has pointed out that learning is not due to simple use of stimulation of a pathway, and he therefore questions whether the phenomena studied by Eccles (1961, 1964) have anything to do with learning as observed in the intact organism. Nevertheless, this does not mean that learning is not due to synaptic changes of some sort. It means only that a different experimental test of the possibility must be devised.

In designing our experimental approach to this problem, clues from human clinical evidence were used. After blows to the head sustained in accidents, events which occurred closest in time prior to the accident cannot be recalled (retrograde amnesia). [This generalization, known as Ribot's law, is based upon clinical observation, but its correctness has been strikingly confirmed by Squire, Slater, and Chace (1975) by the use of an ingenious experimental paradigm.] Such patches of amnesia may cover days, or even weeks. The lost memories tend to return, with those most distant in time from the accident becoming available first (Russell & Nathan, 1946). In the Korsakoff's syndrome (Talland, 1965), retrograde amnesia may gradually increase until it covers a span of many years. An elderly patient may end up remembering only his youth, while there is no useful memory of the more recent intervening years. From such evidence concerning human retrograde amnesia we may conclude that the changes that occur in the substrate of memory take a relatively long time and are measurable in hours, days, and even months. If we suppose from this that the substrate of memory is synaptic, and that it is slowly changing, then it may be possible to follow such synaptic, and that it is slowly changing, then it may be possible to follow such synaptic changes using pharmacological methods. If the same dose of a synaptically acting drug has different effects on remembering, depending on the age of the memory (and this can be shown for a number of synaptically acting drugs), we may assume that there has been a synaptic alteration as a function of time since learning, and we may infer that such a synaptic change underlies memory.

Pharmacological agents are available that can either increase or decrease the effectiveness of neural transmitters (Goodman & Gilman, 1965). For instance, anticholinesterase and anticholinergic drugs affect transmission at synapses utilizing the transmitter acetylcholine. During normal transmission, acetylcholine is rapidly destroyed by the enzyme cholinesterase. Anticholinesterase drugs, such as physostigmine and diisopropyl fluorophosphate (DFP), inactivate cholinesterase and so indirectly prevent the destruction of acetylcholine. In submaximal dosage these drugs inactivate not all but only a part of the cholinesterase present and, hence, only slow down but do not stop the destruction of acetylcholine. The overall effect at such submaximal levels of anticholinesterase is to increase by some constant the lifetime of any acetylcholine emitted into the synapse and to increase, thereby, the acetylcholine synaptic concentrations resulting from a given rate of emission. Up to a certain level, the greater this concentration the greater is the efficiency of transmission, that is, the conduction across the synapse. Above that level, which is set by the sensitivity of the postsynaptic membrane, any further increase in acetylcholine concentration produces a synaptic block (Feldberg & Vartiainen, 1934; Goodman & Gilman, 1965; Volle & Koelle, 1961). Thus the application of a given dosage of anticholinesterase will (by protecting acetylcholine from destruction) have different effects on the efficiency of synaptic conduction depending on the rate of acetylcholine emission during transmission and on the sensitivity of the postsynaptic membrane. At low levels of emission of acetylcholine or low sensitivity of the postsynaptic membrane, an application of anticholinesterase will render transmission more efficient. Such a property is used to good effect in the treatment of myasthenia gravis. In the treatment of this disorder, anticholinesterase is used to raise the effective concentration of acetylcholine at the neuromuscular junction and so to reduce apparent muscular weakness. On the other hand, the same dose of anticholinesterase that caused muscular contraction in the myasthenic patient produces paralysis in a man with normal levels of function at the neuromuscular junction.

If there are changes with time after learning in the level of acetylcholine emitted at the modified synapse, then such a synapse should show either facilitation or block depending on when in time after learning we inject the same dose of anticholinesterase. A similar argument with regard to the action of anticholinesterase can be applied if we assume that instead of a presynaptic increment in transmitter, it is the postsynaptic membrane which becomes more sensitive to transmitter as a function of time after learning. However the use of an anticholinesterase does not allow us to decide which of these alternative versions of the hypothesis of the increment of synaptic conductance actually holds for the learning situation. Later, however, I shall indicate how the use of other types of drugs, such as the cholinomimetics, allows us to surmise that postsynaptic sensitization is the more likely mechanism.

The first two experiments (Deutsch, Hamburg, & Dahl, 1966; Deutsch & Leibowitz, 1966) show that facilitation or block of a memory can be obtained with the same dose of anticholinesterase simply as a function of time of injection since original learning, as might be expected if synaptic change formed the substrate of memory.

II. EXPERIMENTAL INVESTIGATIONS

In the first experiment, rats were trained on a simple task.[1] Then an intracerebral injection of anticholinesterase was made at different times after initial training, the time being varied from one group of subject to another. After

[1]The rats were Sprague-Dawley males approximately 350 grams at the start of the experiment.

injection, all rats, irrespective of the group to which they were assigned, were retested 24 hours after injection. Thus, what was varied was the time between training and injection. The time between injection and retest was kept constant. Any difference in remembering between groups was therefore due to the time between initial training and injection.

Rats were placed on an electrified grid in a Y maze. The lit arm of the Y was not electrified, and its position was changed randomly from trial to trial. The rats therefore learned to run into the lit arm. The criterion of learning was met when they had chosen the lit arm 10 trials in succession, whereupon training was concluded.

Then, at various times after training, the rats were injected intracerebrally with DFP dissolved in peanut oil.[2] This dose did not increase the number of trials to criterion in a naive group of rats, thus showing that learning capacity during training was not affected by the drug in the amounts used. At 24 hours after injection, the rats were retrained to the same criterion of 10 successive trials correct. The number of trials to criterion in this retraining session represented the measure of retention.

The first group was injected 30 minutes after training. Its retention was significantly worse than that of a control group injected only with peanut oil.[3] By contrast, a group injected with DFP 3 days after training showed the same amount of retention as did the control group. Thus, up to this point, it seems that memory is less susceptible to DFP the older it is. In fact, a subsidiary experiment (Deutsch & Stone, unpublished) has established that injections of DFP on habits 1 and 2 days old have no effect, showing that the initial stage of vulnerability lasts less than 1 day. Beyond 3 days, however, the situation seems to reverse itself: the memory is more susceptible to DFP the older it is because a DFP group injected 5 days after training showed only slight recollection at retest, and a further group injected 14 days after training showed complete amnesia. The score of the group trained 14 days before injection was the same as the score of the previously mentioned naive group which has not been trained before but had simply been injected with DFP 24 hours prior to testing. The amnesia of the DFP group trained 14 days before injection was not due to normal forgetting, since other controls showed almost perfect retention over a 15-day span. Similar results have been obtained by Hamburg (1967) with intraperitoneal injections of

---

[2] The subjects were placed in a stereotaxic instrument under nembutal anesthesia. They were intracerebrally injected in two symetrically placed bilateral loci. The placements were: anterior 3, lateral 3, vertical +2, and anterior 3, lateral 4.75, vertical −2, according to the atlas of DeGroot (1957). 0.01 ml of peanut oil containing 0.1 of diisopropyl fluorophosphate (DFP) was injected in each locus.

[3] Except as otherwise stated, the results quoted are significant beyond the 1% level. The tests used were the t-test, Mann-Whitney U test, and analysis of variance.

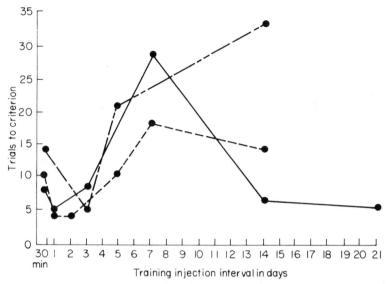

Figure 9.1. The effect of anticholinesterase injection on memories of different age, shown in three separate experiments. Trials to criterion during retest are plotted against the time which elapsed between retest and original learning. A larger number of trials to criterion during retest signifies a greater amnesia. The time between injection and retest was constant. The differences past the 7-day point probably present differing rates of forgetting in the three situations. (●——●, DFP appetitive; ●--●, DFP escape; ●---●, physostigmine escape.) The three experiments are Deutsch, Hamburg, and Dahl (1966), Hamburg (1967), and Wiener and Deutsch (1968).

the anticholinesterase physostigmine, using the same escape habit. Biederman (1970) confirmed the shape of the amnesic function with physostigmine in an operant situation. He used a latency measure of forgetting and a bar-press response.

To make sure that we were not observing some periodicity in fear or emotionality interacting with the drug, another experiment employing an appetitive rather than an escape task was conducted. The rats were taught to run a reward of sugar water, the position of which always coincided with the lit arm of a Y maze (Wiener & Deutsch, 1968). As seen in Figure 9.1, the results when compared to the maze results from the preceding experiments show a very similar pattern of amnesia as a function of time of learning before injection. It is therefore most likely that we are, in fact, studying memory. The divergences in the curves after 7 days are probably due to differences in rates of forgetting among the three groups. These basic effects have now been observed a number of times (Biederman, 1970, 1974; Puerto, Molina, Rogers, & Moss, 1976; Squire, 1970; Stanes, Brown, & Singer, 1976). An impressive series of experiments on primates has been reported by Bartus (1980).

In this first set of experiments which dealt with the effects of the anticholinesterases DFP and physostigmine on habits which are normally well retained, the effects of these drugs were to decrease the retention of a habit, depending on its age. Thus, one of the predicted effects of an anticholinesterase was verified. However, the other predicted effect, facilitation, was not shown. The reason for this is that the habit which was acquired was so well retained without treatment over 14 days that one could not, on methodological grounds, show any improvement of retention subsequent to injection of the drug. It may be the case that 1-, 2-, and 3-day-old habits were facilitated instead of merely being unaffected, but the design of the experiment would not allow us to detect this because there is an effective ceiling on performance. Therefore, an attempt was made to obtain facilitation where it was methodologically possible to detect it, namely, where retention of the habit by a control group was imperfect. For example, it was found that 29 days after learning, the escape habit described above was almost forgotten by a group of animals injected with peanut oil only 24 hours before. On the basis of this observation, a second kind of experiment was devised.

Rats were divided into four groups. The first two groups were trained 14 days before injection, the second two groups 28 days before injection. One of the 28-day and the 14-day groups were injected with the same dose of DFP, the remaining 28-day and 14-day groups were injected with the same volume of pure peanut oil instead. The experimental procedure and dosage were exactly the same as previously described.

On retest, poor retention was exhibited by the 14-day DFP group and 28-day peanut oil group. By contrast, the 28-day DFP group and the 14-day peanut oil group exhibited good retention. The results of anticholinesterase injection show a large and clear facilitation of an otherwise almost forgotten 28-day-old habit while they confirm the obliteration of an otherwise well-remembered 14-day-old habit already demonstrated in the previous experiments (Figure 9.2A). The same facilitation of a forgotten habit was shown by Wiener and Deutsch (1968) using an appetitive habit and by Squire (1970) using physostigmine-injected mice. Biederman (1970) showed an improvement in memory in pigeons when physostigmine is injected 28 days after a line tilt discrimination was partly learned. A well-learned color discrimination acquired by the same subjects showed no such improvement under the same conditions. Similar facilitation of memory when tested in a delayed-response situation has been shown by Alpern and Marriott (1973). Physostigmine produced increasing facilitation of memory with time as the same memory became poorer in control animals. Such effects were observed with a 25-minute delay interval, suggesting cholinergic storage even at very short times after learning. Thus, these results also lend strong support to the notion that forgetting is due to a reversal of the change in syanptic conductance which underlies learning (Figure 9.2B). It must be emphasized,

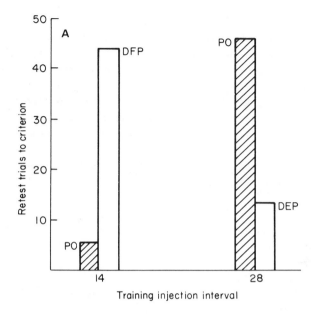

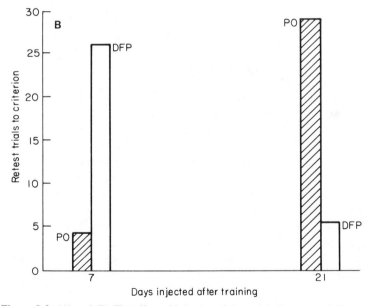

Figure 9.2. (A) and (B) The effect of injection of the anticholinesterase DFP (diisopropyl fluorophosphate) and PO (peanut oil) the drug vehicle on well retained or almost forgotten habits. Trials to criterion are plotted against time between retest and original training. It can be seen that when controls remember well, DFP injected animals forget. When controls forget, DFP injected animals remember well. (From Deutsch & Leibowitz, 1966; Wiener & Deutsch, 1968.)

however, that both the block and facilitation of a memory are temporary, wearing off as the injected drug wears off (Deutsch, 1966; Signorelli, 1976).

So far it has been shown that the anticholinesterase drugs DFP and physostigmine have different effects on memories of different age. Though their actions on memory are consistent with and plausibly interpreted by their anticholinesterase action, some other property besides their indirect action on acetylcholine could, in some unknown manner, produce the same results. It was, thus, desirable to conduct an independent check on the hypothesis that the effects observed are due to an effect on acetylcholine. This check can be provided by the use of an anticholinergic drug. An anticholinergic drug (such as atropine or scopolamine) reduces the effective action of a given level of acetylcholine at the synapse without actually changing the level itself. It does this apparently by occupying some of the receptor sites on the postsynaptic membrane without producing depolarization. It thus prevents acetylcholine from reaching such receptor sites and so attenuates the effectiveness of this transmitter. We would therefore expect an anticholinergic to block conduction at a synapse where the postsynaptic membrane is relatively insensitive, while simply diminishing conduction at synapses where the postsynaptic membrane is highly sensitive. If the interpretation of the effects of DFP is correct, we would then expect the reverse effect with the administration of an anticholinergic drug. That is, we would expect the greatest amnesia with anticholinergics precisely where the effect of anticholinesterase was the least, and we would predict the least effect where the effect of anticholinesterase on memory was the largest. It will be recalled that the least effect of anticholinesterase was on habits 1 to 3 days of age.

In a third set of experiments (Deutsch & Rocklin, 1967; Wiener & Deutsch, 1968) the anticholinergic agent employed was scopolamine, and it was injected using exactly the same amount of oil and location as in the previous experiments using DFP.[4] The same experimental procedure was also used. A group injected 30 minues after training showed little if any effect of scopolamine. However, a group injected 1 and 3 days after training showed a considerable degree of block. Groups injected 7 and 14 days after training showed little if any effect. The results from the appetitive and escape situations were very similar.

As far as the experimental methodology will allow us to discern, the effect, then, of an anticholinergic is the mirror-image of the anticholinesterase effect (Figure 9.3). There is an increase of sensitivity between 30 minutes and 1 to 3 days, followed by a decrease of sensitivity. This further confirms the notion that

---

[4]Deutsch and Rocklin used an injection of scopolamine at the same loci as in footnote 3. Peanut oil (0.01 ml) containing 0.58% of scopolamine was injected in each placement. Wiener and Deutsch used only the first locus, but doubled the amount injected at that site (both of scopolamine and DFP).

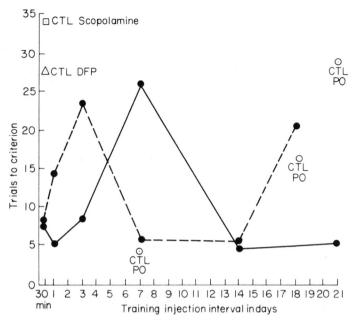

Figure 9.3. The effects of the injection of the anticholinergic scopolamine (●--●) compared with that of the anticholinesterase DFP (●——●) and control injections of PO (peanut oil) on the retention of an appetitive task at various times after original learning. The time between injection and retest was constant. Also indicated are the number of trials to criterion when rats were injected with scopolamine (CTL scopolamine) or DFP (CTL DFP) before original learning to give an estimate of actual amount of amnesia produced. (From Wiener & Deutsch, 1968.)

there are two phases present in memory storage. Finally, it is of interest to note that amnesia can result in man from anticholinergic therapy (Cutting, 1964).

The experiments already outlined support the idea that at the time of learning some unknown event stimulates a particular group of synapses to alter their state and to increase their conductivity. At this point we may ask why such an increase in synaptic conductivity does not manifest itself with the passage of time when no drugs are injected. Why has it not been noted that habits are better remembered a week after initial learning than, say, 3 days after such learning? There are various possible answers. One is that the phenomena we have described are some artifact of drug injection. Another is that animal training has, in general, stretched over days in other studies, blurring in time the initiation of a memory. In addition, and partly as a consequence of the foregoing, it is difficult to find studies where the age of the habit, measured in days, has been used as an independent variable in studies of retention. However, should we not have seen such an improvement in recall in our control groups? This would have been unlikely for the methodological reasons that our animals were trained to the very high criterion of 10 out of 10 trials correct. Given a score which was initially almost perfect, it was thus well nigh impossible to observe any subsequent improvement in retention that might in fact actually exist. To rid ourselves of this methodological limitation, we devised a study in which rats were initially under-trained using escape from shock. The rats were given 15 trials. We then waited to see how many trials it would take these rats on some subsequent day to reach our strict criterion (Huppert & Deutsch, 1969). No drugs were used. We found that the rats took only about half the number of trials to reach criterion when they waited 7 or 10 days than when they waited 1 or 3 days (Figure 9.4). F. A. Huppert (personal communication) has now shown an analogous improvement using an appetitive task. Finally, Dr. J. L. McGaugh has pointed out that there are old animal studies which purport to find similar effects (Anderson, 1940; Bunch & Lang, 1939; Bunch & Magdsick, 1933). This shows that our conclusions about the varying substrate of memory were not due to some pharmacological artifact.

A similar variation in memory strength can be observed with the use of a very different experimental paradigm. The rat is placed in a lit compartment, and there is an entrance available into the dark compartment. When the rat steps into the dark compartment it is given an electric shock. When it is again placed in the lit compartment, the latency of step-through into the dark compartment is grossly increased. The increase in latency of step-through into the dark compartment can be used as an index of the strength of memory of the shock. (The task is called one-trial step-through passive avoidance.) The data of Rogers (published in Deutsch & Rogers, 1978) show clearly that there are large fluctuations in latency of step-through over 50 days as if the memory of the shock changed over such a period. The experiment is especially interesting because the effects of physostigmine (0.5 mg/kg) injected before retest were measured in the same experiment. It is interesting to note that the better the memory of control rats, the worse the recall of physostigmine-injected controls, and vice versa. As might be expected, the temporal parameters for recall of the one-trial passive avoidance habit differ from discrimination tasks employing many trials. Mean recall 3 days after training is less than optimum but improves steadily to reach good performance by 21 days. On the other hand, the performance of physostigmine-injected rats decreases steadily from Day 3 and reaches significant impairment by 21 days.

As we have seen above there are differences in susceptibility to cholinergic agents as functions of time since learning and behavioral task. Stanes et al. (1976) have shown the existence of another factor, namely, speed of initial learning. They have reported that fast learners and slow learners differ in the time it takes to produce a maximum of amnesia with physostigmine. Using an appetitive Y maze light discrimination task, they found that rats which learned the discrimination task quickly were maximally susceptible to the amnesic effects of physostigmine approximately 4 days after initial learning, whereas slow learners

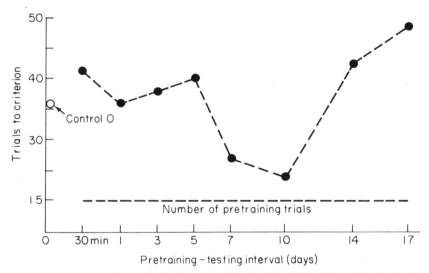

Figure 9.4. The effects of delay between original partial training (15 trials) and subsequent training to criterion. Plotted are trials to criterion in subsequent training against time since original partial training. Control O indicates the number of trials to criterion taken by a group which received its training all in one session.

were maximally affected about 7 days after initial learning. It also seems that slow learners do not reach the same high level of synaptic transmission as is attained by fast learners if we use susceptibility to memory block by the same dose of physostigmine as the index. [However, such a conclusion could be due to the small number of time interval sampled in the study (4, 7 and 35 days) or a larger variability in the maxima attained by the slow learners.]

We may now ask ourselves whether the inferred modification of a synapse represents an all-or-none or a graded process. In other words, can a synapse be modified only once during learning, or does a repetition of the same learning task after some learning has already occurred further increase conductance at a single synapse. If we postulate an all-or-none process then how, according to such a model, can we explain empirical increases in "habit strength" with increased training? Possibly they are due to a progressive involvement of fresh synapses and a spread involving more parallel connections in the nervous system. In support of a graded process, we may hypothesize that successive learning trials modify the same synapses in a cumulative way by producing an increase in the rate at which conductance increases, or in the upper limit of such conductance, or both.

There are tests of these two alternatives. If, with increased training, a synapse becomes more conductive, then a habit should become increasingly more vulnerable to anticholinesterase with increased training. Furthermore, the memory of the same habit should be facilitated when its level of training is very low. In other words, we should be able to perform the same manipulations of memory by varying the level of training as we were already able to perform when we varied time since training.

If, on the other hand, increases in training simply involve a larger number of synapses but no increase in the level of transmitter at any one synapse, then increases in training should not lead to an increased vulnerability of a habit to anticholinesterase. Rather, the opposite should be the case. As the number of synapses recruited is increased, some of the additional synapses will, by chance variation, be less sensitive to a given level of anticholinesterase. Thus, a larger number of synapses should be left functional after anticholinesterase injection when we test an overtrained habit. Three experiments (Deutsch & Leibowitz, unpublished; Deutsch & Lutzky, 1967; Leibowitz, Deutsch, & Coons, unpublished) show a large and unequivocal effect. Poorly learned habits are enormously facilitated and well-learned habits are blocked (Figure 9.5). This supports the hypothesis that a set of synapses underlying a single habit remains restricted, and each synapse within such a set simply increases in conductance as learning proceeds.

So far the results presented have been interpreted in terms of the action of drugs on synapses which alter their conductance as a function of time since training and amount of training. We can use the model we have developed to generate a somewhat different kind of prediction. An anticholinesterase in submaximal concentrations simply slows down the rate of destruction of acetylcholine. Since we have hypothesized that amnesia is due to a block resulting from an acetylcholine excess, we should predict no amnesia if we spaced our trials so that all or most of the acetylcholine emitted on the previous trial is destroyed by the time the next trial comes along. It has been shown by Bacq and Brown (1937) that (with an intermediate dose of anticholinesterase) block at a synapse occurred only when the intervals between successive stimuli were shortened. Accordingly, an experiment was performed where we varied the interval during retest between 25 and 50 seconds (Deutsch & Rocklin, 1972). Using a counterbalanced design it was found that rats tested under physostigmine at 25-second intervals showed amnesia for the original habit. Those tested at a 50-second intertrial interval under physostigmine showed no amnesia.

In a second experiment the rats during retest had to learn an escape habit reverse of the one they had learned during training. Therefore, to escape shock during retest they had to learn not only to run to the dark alley but also to inhibit the original learning of running to the lit alley. Thus, provided that the original habit was remembered at the time the reversal was being learned, the time to learn the reversal should take longer than the time to learn the original habit. However if the original habit was not remembered, there should be no difference in trials to criterion between original learning and retest. The results showed that

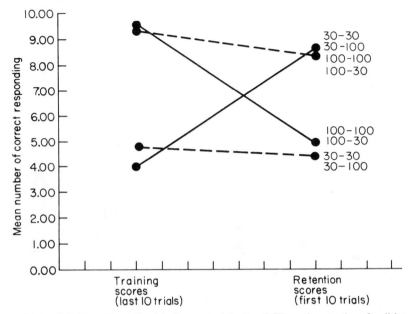

Figure 9.5. The effects of anticholinesterase injection (DFP) on the retention of well-learned and poorly learned habits. The mean number of correct responses of the last 10 of 30 trials for two groups are shown on the left. One group had to learn to run to alley illuminated by bulb with 30-V; the other had to learn the same task except that the bulb had 100 V across it. As can be seen from the last 10 trials, the dim light of the 30-V group posed a difficult task which produced little learning by the end of the 30 trials. The group learning the brighter cue (100 V) displayed excellent acquisition. Because of the different rates of acquisition of the 100- and 30-V habits, half of each group was shifted to retest on the other brightness and half was retrained on the same brightness (30–30, 100–100 retested on the same brightness, 30–100 trained on 30, retested on 100, 100–30 trained on 100, retested on 30). The scores of animals trained on the same brightness are combined. Half the animals were injected with DFP, the other half with peanut oil (PO). There is little change in the scores of the peanut oil animals. However, there is a complete crossover of the drug-injected animals, showing block of the well-learned habit and facilitation of the poorly learned habit.

at 50 seconds between trials animals in both the physostigmine and the saline control groups took almost twice as long to reverse as it took them to learn the original habit, indicating in fact that they remembered the original habit (Figure 9.6). At 25 seconds between trials, the physostigmine animals learned the reversal as quickly as the original habit, whereas the saline animals again took much longer. This second experiment shows that the amnesia of the 25-second physostigmine group in the first experiment is not due to disorientation or an incapacity to perform or learn, but to an amnesia. We might explain the high relearning scores of the same habit of the rats run at 25-second intervals under physostigmine by saying that the rats were somehow incapacitated by the physostigmine if they had to run at 25-second intervals. However, it is difficult to see

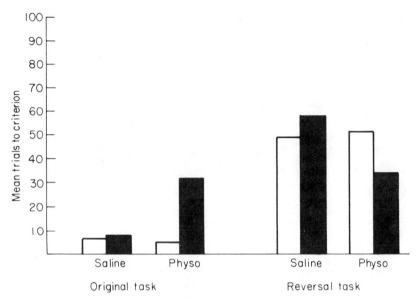

Figure 9.6. The effect of massing and spacing trials during retest on anticholinesterase-induced amnesia. On the left, retest consisted of relearning the original habit (run to light, avoid dark). On the right, retest consisted of unlearning the original habit. On retest the animal had to learn to run to dark and avoid light (reversal). (Physo, physostigmine.)

how such incapacitation could produce abnormally low learning scores of the reversal habit. This dependence of the amnesia on the precise interval of trials during retest should of course not be seen with anticholinergics or cholinomimetics, but only with anticholinesterases. This further prediction from the hypothesis should be tested.

So far, then, it seems that the drugs we are using to block or facilitate memory have their effect on synaptic conductance. However, what is it that changes when synaptic conductance alters? As mentioned previously, the two main hypotheses are (1) that the amount of transmitter emitted at the presynaptic ending increases or (2) that the postsynaptic ending increases in its sensitivity to transmitter. To test this idea, carbachol (carbamylcholine) was injected before retest. This drug is a cholinomimetic. It acts on the postsynaptic membrane much like acetylcholine. However, it is not susceptible to destruction by the enzyme acetylcholinesterase. Therefore, by injecting this drug, we can test the sensitivity of the postsynaptic membrane. It seems that 7-day-old habits are blocked by a dose of this cholinomimetic which leaves a 3-day-old habit unaffected (Table 9.1). This would indicate that it is probably the postsynaptic membrane that has increased its sensitivity and so increased synaptic conductance. A finding of possible relevance to this conclusion has been reported by Bradley and Horn

TABLE 9.1

The Effect of Carbachol Injection on Recall of Habits
That Were 3 and 7 Days Old[a,b]

Treatment	Medium number of trials to criterion	
	3 days	7 days
Carbachol	6.0 (15)	20 (15)[a]
Saline	4.0 (8)	0 (7)

[a]Criterion was 7 correct trials in succession.
[b]Numbers in parentheses indicate number of rats tested.
[c]$p < 0.01$ compared with saline, Mann-Whitney U test.

(1981) who studied cholinergic receptor sites in the chick brain as a function of imprinting.

One of the questions that often arises is why it is that we do not block all cholinergic synaptic activity with the drugs we use. As was seen above, rats learn appetitive tasks at a normal rate under doses of drug that under some circumstances produce complete amnesia. There is very little in the overt behavior of the rat to indicate that it has been drugged. The doses of drugs used produce no apparent malaise or incoordination. Clearly, the dose we use only seems to affect what one might call the "memory" synapses. It would therefore seem that these are more sensitive to our drugs. Such an abnormal sensitivity may be more apparent than real. We know that there are some levels of training and times after training where a habit is unaffected by the dosage of drug we use, and this shows that "memory" synapses are not always affected. It therefore seems more plausible to think of the "memory" synapses as traveling through a much larger range of postsynaptic sensitivity, while normal synapses remain fixed somewhere in the middle of the range of sensitivity variation of the memory synapse. In other words, the "memory" synapse has to swing from extreme insensitivity to transmitter to extreme sensitivity in order to manifest those changes in conductance that we have demonstrated. It will therefore be much more susceptible to anticholinergic agents when conductance is low and to anticholinesterases and cholinomimetics when conductance is high. In the middle of the range, sensitivity to all agents will resemble that of a normal synapse, and only grossly toxic doses will affect memory. This speculation, of course, will have to be further tested. The experiments so far reported implicate the cholinergic system in memory. It is, of course, possible that other systems such as the adrenergic will also turn out to have a similar function, and this, too, we hope to test.

When an animal is rewarded for performing a habit such a habit will be learned or acquired. However, when the habit is no longer rewarded, the animal will cease to perform the habit. Another kind of learning takes place, and this is called extinction. If initial learning consists of the formation of some synaptic (or other) connection, does extinction consist of the weakening or uncoupling of this connection? Or is it the formation of some other connection which then works to oppose the effects of the first (''learning'') connection? If extinction consists of weakening the connection set up in original learning, then an extinguished habit should be similar to a forgotten habit pharmacologically. We have already shown that an almost forgotten habit is facilitated by anticholinesterase. We would, then, on the ''weakening'' hypothesis of extinction, expect an injection of an anticholinesterase to produce less amnesia of an extinguished habit than of the same unextinguished habit. If, on the other hand, during extinction there is another habit acquired that inhibits the expression of the original habit, another pattern of results should be discernible after injection with an anticholinesterase. If original learning occurs 7 days before anticholinesterase injection and retest, there should be amnesia for the original habit. If extinction of the habit is given close in time to its acquisition, there should be amnesia for both the original learning and extinction. If, however, original learning is 7 days before injection and retest, the extinction is 3 days before injection and retest; the original habit should be lost but the extinction habit retained. (As we noted above, 3-day-old habits are unaffected by our dose of anticholinesterase.) When extinction was given to rats close in time to the original training, both the original training and extinction were blocked by physostigmine (Deutsch & Wiener, 1969). These rats took the same number of trials to relearn as control animals, which were trained, not extinguished, and then drugged. However, when extinction was placed 3 days before injection and retest, it took the rats approximately twice as many trials during retest after drug injection to learn as control animals (unextinguished and drugged), showing that extinction has been retained while the original habit was blocked (Figure 9.7). This supports the idea that extinction is the learning of a separate habit opposing the performance of the initially rewarded habit.

It has also been suggested (Carlton, 1969) that different systems, such as excitatory or inhibitory systems, are subserved by different transmitters. Habits acquired during extinction have been viewed as inhibitory. However, the last experiment we have outlined also shows that extinction placed close to original learning is equally as vulnerable to anticholinesterase as original learning. Habits can probably not be classified into synaptically inhibitory and excitatory on the basis of behavioral excitation or inhibition. However, as all habits compete for behavioral expression, there must be excitation and reciprocal inhibition connected with all habits.

The manipulation of memory with cholinergic agents turns out to have clinical implications. It has been possible to mimic some of the cognitive deficits found in aging by the administration of anticholinergics to young human subjects (Drachman, 1977; Drachman & Leavitt, 1974; Drachman & Sahakian, 1979).

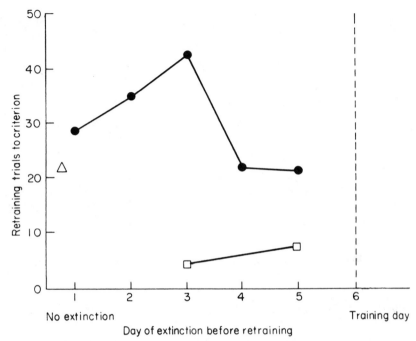

Figure 9.7. The effect of physostigmine on retraining after extinction. The time between original learning and retraining is the same for all groups. When time of extinction is close to original learning, there is amnesia but no difference from the group receiving no extinction. At extinction 3 days before learning, the number of trials to relearn is almost double (☐———☐, scores of controls injected with saline; ●———●, scores of animals injected with physostigmine.)

Cholinergic abnormalities in senile dements (Bartus, Dean, Beer & Lippa, 1982) and aged rats have been found (Lippa, Pelham, Beer, Critchette, Dean, & Bartus, 1980; Strong, Hicks, Hsu, Bartus, & Enna, 1980). An interesting theoretical interpretation of such correlations has been presented by Blass and Gibson (1979). The whole area has been ably reviewed by Squire and Davis (1981) and by Bartus, Dean, Beer and Lippa (1982).

III. CONCLUSIONS

A simple hypothesis can explain the results obtained to date if we disregard those results when we wait 30 minutes after original learning to inject. The hypothesis is that, as a result of learning, the postsynaptic endings at a specific set of synapses become more sensitive to the transmitter. This sensitivity increases with time after initial learning and then declines. The rate at which such sensitivity increases depends on the amount of initial learning. If the curve of

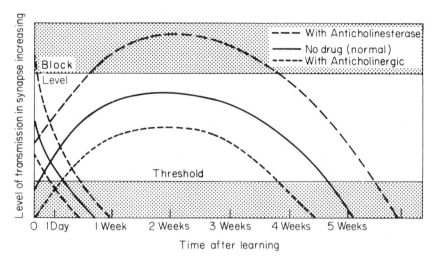

Figure 9.8. The hypothesized changes in "memory" synapses with time after training and with pharmacological intervention.

transmission plotted against time is displaced upward with anticholinesterases, then the very low portions will show facilitation and the high portions will cause block (Figure 9.8). The middle portions will appear unaffected (unless special experimental tests are made). If the curve of transmission is displaced down with anticholinergics, then the middle portion will appear unaffected and only the very early or late components will show block.

Taken together, then, the results that have been obtained are evidence that synaptic conductance alters as a result of learning. So far it seems (1) that cholinergic synapses are modified as a result of learning and that it probably is the postsynaptic membrane that becomes increasingly more sensitive to acetylcholine with time after learning up to a certain point. (2) After this point, sensitivity declines, leading to the phenomena of forgetting. (3) There is also good evidence that there is an initial phase of declining sensitivity to cholinesterase or increasing sensitivity to anticholinergics. This could reflect the existence of a parallel set of synapses with fast decay serving as short-term store. (4) Increasing the amount of learning leads to an increase in conductance in each of a set of synapses without an increase in their number. (5) Both original learning and extinction are subserved by cholinergic synapses.

REFERENCES

Alpern, M. P., & Marriott, J. G. Short-term memory: facilitation and disruption with cholinergic agents. *Physiology and Behavior*, 1973, *11*, 571–576.

Anderson, A. C. Evidences of reminiscence in the rat in maze learning. *Journal of Comparative Psychology*, 1940, *30*, 399–412.

Bacq, Z. M., & Brown, G. C. Pharmacological experiments on mammalian voluntary muscle in relation to the theory of chemical transmission. *Journal of Physiology (London)*, 1937, *89*, 45–60.

Bartus, R. T. In L. W. Poon (Ed.), *Aging in the 1980's: Psychological issues*, (pp. 163–180), Washington, D.C.: American Psychological Association, 1980.

Bartus, R. T., Dean, R. L., Beer, B., & Lippa, A. S. The cholinergic hypothesis of geriatric memory dysfunction. *Science*, 1982, *217*, 408–417.

Biederman, G. B. Forgetting of an operant response: physostigmine-produced increases in escape latency in rats as a function of time of injection. *Quarterly Journal of Experimental Psychology*, 1970, *22*, 384–388.

Biederman, G. B. The search for the chemistry of memory: recent trends and the logic of investigation in the role of cholinergic and adrenergic transmitters. *Progress in Neurobiology (Oxford)*, 1974, *2*, 289–307.

Blass, J. P., & Gibson, G. E. In K. L. Davis & P. A. Berger (Eds.), *Brain Acetylcholine and Neuropsychiatric Disease*, (pp. 215–236). New York: Plenum, 1979.

Bradley, P., & Horn, G. Imprinting, a study of cholinergic receptor sites in parts of the chick brain. *Experimental Brain Research*, 1981, *41*, 121–123.

Bunch, M. E., & Lang, E. S. The amount of transfer of training from partial learning after varying intervals of time. *Journal of Comparative Psychology*, 1939, *27*, 449–459.

Bunch, M. E., & Magdsick, W. K. The retention in rats of an incompletely learned maze solution for short intervals of time. *Journal of Comparative Psychology*, 1933, *16*, 385–409.

Carlton, P. L. In J. T. Tapp (Ed.), *Reinforcement and Behavior*. New York: Academic Press, 1969.

Cutting, W. C. *Handbook of pharmacology . . . The actions and uses of drugs*. New York: Appleton-Century-Crofts, 1964.

DeGroot, J. The rat forebrain in stereotaxic coordinates. *Verhandelingen der Koninklijke Nederlandse Akademie van Wetenschappen, Afdeling Natuurkunde, Reeks 2*, 1957, *52*, 1–40.

Deutsch, J. A. Substrates of learning and memory. *Diseases of the Nervous System*, 1966, *27*, 20–24.

Deutsch, J. A., Hamburg, M. D., & Dahl, H. Anticholinesterase induced amnesia and its temporal aspects. *Science*, 1966, *151*, 221–223.

Deutsch, J. A., & Leibowitz, S. F. Amnesia or reversal of forgetting by anticholinesterase depending simply on time of injection. *Science*, 1966, *153*, 1017.

Deutsch, J. A., & Lutzky, H. Memory enhancement by anticholinesterase as a function of initial learning. *Nature (London)*, 1967, *213*, 742.

Deutsch, J. A., Rocklin, K. Amnesia induced by scopolamine and its temporal variations. *Nature (London)*, 1967, *216*, 89–90.

Deutsch, J. A., & Rocklin, R. Anticholinesterase amnesia as a function of massed or spaced retest. *Journal of Comparative and Physiological Psychology*, 1972, *81*, 64–68.

Deutsch, J. A., & Rogers, J. B. In K. L. Davis & P. A. Berger (Eds.), *Brain acetylcholine and neuropsychiatric disease*, (pp. 175–204). New York: Plenum, 1978.

Deutsch, J. A., & Wiener, N. I. Analysis of extinction through amnesia. *Journal of Comparative and Physiological Psychology*, 1969, *69*, 179–184.

Drachman, D. A. Memory and cognitive function in man: does the cholinergic system have a specific role? *Neurology*, 1977, *27*, 783–790.

Drachman, D. A., & Leavitt, J. Human memory and the cholinergic system: a relationship to aging. *Archives of Neurology (Chicago)*, 1974, *30*, 113–121.

Drachman, D. A., & Sahakian, B. J. *Nutrition and the Brain*, 1979, *5*, 351–366.

Feldberg, W., & Vartiainen, A. Further observations on the physiology and pharmacology of a sympathetic ganglion. *Journal of Physiology (London)*, 1934, *83*, 103–128.

Goodman, L. S., & Gilman, A. (Eds.), *The pharmacological basis of therapeutics* (3rd ed.). New York: Macmillan, 1965.

Hamburg, M. D. A retrograde amnesia produced by intraperitoneal injections of physostigmine. *Science*, 1967, *156*, 973–974.

Hubbert, H. B. The effect of age on habit formation in the albino rat. *Behavior Monograph*, 1915, *2*, No. 6.

Huppert, F. A., & Deutsch, J. A. Improvement in memory with time. *Quarterly Journal of Experimental Psychology*, 1969, *21*, 267–271.

Lippa, A. S., Pelham, R. W., Beer, B., Critchette, D. J., Dean, R. L., & Bartus, R. T. Brain cholinergic dysfunction and memory in aged rats. *Neurobiology of Aging*, 1980, *1*, 13–19.

Perry, E. K., Tomlinson, B. E., Blessed, G., Bergmann, K., Gibson, P. H., & Perry, R. H. *British Medical Journal*, 1978, *2*, 1457–1459.

Puerto, A., Molina, F., Rogers, J. B., & Moss, D. E. Physostigmine-induced amnesia for an escape response 12 to 72 hours after training. *Behavioral Biology*, 1976, *16*, 85–91.

Russell, W. R., & Nathan, P. W. Traumatic amnesia. *Brain*, 1946, *69*, 280–300.

Sharpless, S. K. Reorganization of function in the nervous system—use and disuse. *Annual Review of Physiology*, 1964, *26*, 357–388.

Signorelli, A. Influence of physostigmine upon consolidation of memory in mice. *Journal of Comparative and Physiological Psychology*, 1976, *90*, 658–664.

Squire, L. R. Physostigmine: effects on retention at different times after brief training. *Psychonomic Science*, 1970, *19*, (1), 49–50.

Squire, L. R., & Davis, H. P. The pharmacology of memory: a neurobiological perspective. *Annual Review of Pharmacology and Toxicology*, 1981, *21*, 323–356.

Squire, L. R., Slater, P. C., & Chace, P. M. Retrograde amnesia: temporal gradient in very long-term memory following electroconvulsive therapy. *Science*, 1975, *187*, 77–79.

Stanes, M. D., Brown, C. P., & Singer, G. Effect of physostigmine on Y-maze discrimination retention in the rat. *Psychopharmacologia* 1976, *46*, 269–276.

Strong, R., Hicks, P., Hsu, L., Bartus, R. T., & Enna, S. J. Age-related alterations in the rodent brain cholinergic system and behavior. *Neurobiology of Aging*, 1980, *1*, 59–63.

Talland, G. A. *Deranged memory*. New York: Academic Press, 1965.

Tanzi, E. I fatti e le induzioni nella odierna istologia del sistema nervoso. *Rivista Sperimentale di Freniatria e Medicina Legale delle Alienazioni Mentali*, 1893, *19*, 419–472.

Volle, R. L., & Koelle, G. B. The physiological role of acetylcholinesterase (ACHE) in sympathetic ganglia. *Journal of Pharmacology and Experimental Therapeutics*, 1961, *133*, 223–240.

Wiener, N. I., & Deutsch, J. A. Temporal aspects of anticholinergic and auticholinesterase-induced amnesia for an appetitive habit. *Journal of Comparative and Physiological Psychology*, 1968, *66*, 613–617.

CHAPTER

10

THE ROLE OF CATECHOLAMINES IN MEMORY PROCESSING[1,2,3]

DAVID QUARTERMAIN

Departments of Neurology, Physiology, and Biophysics
New York University School of Medicine
New York, New York

I. INTRODUCTION

Current research into the role of catecholamines (CAs) in memory processes developed out of the general interest in the biogenic amines and behavior

[1]This chapter is dedicated with appreciation to Neal E. Miller.

[2]Supported by Grant NS-12633 from the National Institute of Neurological and Communicative Disorders and Stroke.

[3]I thank Drs. Lewis Freedman and Kenneth Bonnet for comments on the manuscript and Dr. Eric Stone for advice on neuropharmacology.

THE PHYSIOLOGICAL BASIS OF MEMORY   387

that followed the discovery of the antipsychotic properties of reserpine and chlorpromazine. Specific interest in memory can be traced to Seymour Kety's (1971) hypothesis on the role of the catecholamines in memory consolidation. According to this hypothesis, CAs released during affective states promote consolidation of learning by stimulating protein synthesis or modulating other trophic processes at synapses of recently activated neuronal populations. This hypothesis has stimulated a considerable number of experiments over the last decade, and it still provides the theoretical basis of much contemporary research. The experimental evidence to date indicates that the CAs are involved in memory processing, but the exact nature of this participation remains to be determined. Most of the evidence implicating CAs in memory comes from pharmacological studies, and interpretation of many of these findings is not straightforward because of the complex side effects of many of the drugs that are used to manipulate CA activity. Carefully designed studies are necessary to rule out the influence of nonspecific drug effects on memory processes.

II. METHODOLOGICAL CONSIDERATIONS

A. Pharmacological Techniques

Since the 1960s significant advances in the field of biogenic amine biochemistry and pharmacology have provided researchers with a wide spectrum of pharmacological agents that influence pre- and postsynaptic neuronal events. Most of these agents have complex effects on CA metabolism and behavior, and detailed dose and time response studies are usually necessary to reveal the range of effects that a particular drug may exert on memory processes.

It is convenient to classify agents that influence CAs into two broad classes, those that increase and those that decrease CA activity (Gorelick, Bozewicz, & Bridger, 1975). This classification will be adopted to provide a framework for both a description of the drugs that have been used to investigate CA involvement in memory processes and a discussion of the behavioral data. As most of the pharmacological agents discussed in this section have well-established and documented modes of action, primary sources have not been referenced. The interested reader is referred to Goodman and Gilman (1978) for more detailed information.

1. Agents That Decrease CA Activity

a. Synthesis Blockers. Inhibition of the CA biosynthetic enzymes, tyrosine hydroxylase (TH) and dopamine-β-hydroxylase (DBH), can result in marked but acute disruption of CA neuronal systems. The initial rapid inhibition of TH and DBH that turns off norepinephrine (NE) and/or dopamine (DA) synthesis has two functionally important consequences: (1) the decrease in availability of newly synthesized CAs that are preferentially released and (2) the subsequent depletion of tissue stores of NE and/or DA. Tyrosine hydroxylase, TH, which catalyzes the first step in the biosynthesis of both NE and DA by the conversion of tyrosine to dihydroxyphenylalanine (DOPA), can be inhibited by α-methyl-*p*-tyrosine (AMPT). Inhibition of TH does not in itself differentiate between the relative roles 'of NE and DA unless the inhibitor is specifically injected into a noradrenergic or dopaminergic pathway. Dopamine-β-hydroxylase, which catalyzes the conversion of DA and NE in mainly noradrenergic nerve terminals, can be inhibited by a variety of drugs [diethyl dithiocarbamate (DEDTC), bis(4-methyl-1-homopiperazinylthiocarbonyl)disulphide (FLA-63), and fusaric acid], most of which act by chelating the copper that is necessary for the catalytic activity of the enzyme. These agents although potent DBH inhibitors suffer from the fact that all copper-containing enzymes are inhibited. Nonspecific action of these inhibitors have been maximized by the relatively high doses that have been used to induce memory disruption (cf. DEDTC 500–1200 mg/kg).

b. Storage Blockers. Inhibition of CA uptake into storage vesicles by such drugs as reserpine or tetrabenazine can also result in marked depletion of tissue stores of CAs. However, these drugs lack specificity in that NE, DA, and serotonin (5-HT) systems are all depleted. Some pharmacological differention between CA and 5-HT can be obtained by attempting to reverse the reserpine-induced behavioral effects by use of the CA precursor L-DOPA or the 5-HT precursor 5-hydroxytryptophan (5-HTP). It should be noted that the time course of action of the storage blockers is complex; there is an initial release of stored biogenic amines, a subsequent depletion of amine stores, and a later repletion of amines often followed by overshoot.

c. Chronic depletion by Administration of Neurotoxins. Long-term depletion of CAs can be achieved by intraventricular administration of the neurotoxin 6-hydroxydopamine (6-OHDA). This agent can be used to deplete both NE and DA simultaneously or the individual amines selectively (Breese & Traylor, 1971). Application of 6-OHDA typically results in widespread destruction of CA neurons throughout the brain. More selective destruction of CA systems can be achieved by the microinjection of the neurotoxin into specific CA pathways (Ungerstedt, 1971). For example, 6-OHDA injected into the dorsal bundle or locus coeruleus results in NE depletion throughout the forebrain. Similarly, 6-OHDA injected into the nigrostriatal pathway or directly into the substantia nigra results in DA depletion in the striatum.

d. Receptor Blockers. Disruption of CA neurotransmission can also be achieved by the pharmacological blockade of CA receptors. Three types of CA antagonists have been employed in memory research: NE blockers, such as phentolamine and phenoxybenzamine; β NE blockers, propranolol and alprenolol; and DA blockers, pimozide and haloperidol. Because of the structural similarity between NE and DA none of these agents is extremely specific. α-Blockers and propranolol can block DA receptors and some β blockers can also stimulate adrenergic receptors. In addition it has been reported that CA antagonists can block acetycholine and histamine receptors in the peripheral nervous system (Furchgott, 1972).

2. Agents That Increase CA Activity

a. Drugs That Stimulate CA Release. Amphetamine and methylpheni-date are the prototypic compounds in this category. These agents are nonspecific in that they release both NE and DA. Doses of amphetamine above 5.0 mg/kg can also release 5-HT (Fuxe & Ungerstedt, 1970). Although amphetamine has been one of the most widely used drugs in pharmacological investigations of memory, it suffers from the disadvantage that it increases CA activity by many different mechanisms (Biel & Bopp, 1978), so that its usefulness as an analytical tool is limited.

b. Drugs That Block Reuptake. Blocking reuptake of CAs into the cell body is another means by which the action of the biogenic amines can be potentiated. Most commonly used agents in memory research have been the tricyclic antidepressants, imipramine, and desimipramine. Although these com-pounds also block 5-HT uptake mechanism, some specificity can be achieved by selection of the appropriate drug. For example, benztropine is a much more potent inhibitor of DA than NE uptake while desipramine (DMI) is a more potent NE uptake blocker. Serotonin reuptake can be most potently blocked by chlorimipramine.

c. Drugs That Block the Inactivation of CAs. Catecholamine activity can be potentiated by inhibiting the action of two enzymes, catechol-*O*-meth-yltransferase (COMT) and monoamine oxidase (MAO), that normally degrade NE and DA. The most widely used agents in behavioral research have been the MAO inhibitors, pheniprazine, pargyline, and iproniazid. These agents lack specificity and will increase intraneuronal levels of NE, DA, and 5-HT.

c. Drugs That Stimulate Postsynaptic Receptors. A number of agents are available that stimulate NE and DA receptors. In the NE system clonidine (α) and isoproterenol (β) agonists have been used to study the effects of enhanced adrenergic activity on retention (e.g., Quartermain, Freedman, Botwinick, & Gutwein, 1977). As these drugs are becoming more widely used, unsuspected actions and side effects are becoming increasingly revealed. For example, al-though standard doses of clonidine stimulate postsynaptic receptors to enhance NE activation, low doses can stimulate presynaptic "auto receptors" that result in decreased NE release. In addition clonidine may stimulate DA receptors, as its action can be partially blocked by pimozide (Lenard & Beer, 1975). In the DA system apomorphine and piribedil (ET-495) are regarded as fairly specific DA agonists. Additional evidence indicates that there may be different types of DA receptors, and these may be differentially activated by DA agonists (Cools & Van Rossum, 1976).

3. Use of Drug Combinations to Study CA Involvement in Memory

Most studies usually employ more than one of these pharmacological tools simultaneously. For example, impairment in retention resulting from inhibition of CA synthesis induced by DEDTC has been reversed by administration of dihydroxyphenylserine (DOPS), an NE precursor (Hamburg & Kerr, 1976); NE by itself (Stein, Belluzi, & Wise, 1975); and the NE agonist clonidine (Freedman, Backman, & Quartermain, 1979). Typically the depleting agent is given before or immediately after training and the recovery agents are administered either after training or before testing, depending on whether the investigator is interested in preventing the development of amnesia or studying processes involved in memory retrieval. Similarly, the effects of receptor stimulators are usually used in combination with several blocking agents in order to determine whether the agonists are exerting their behavioral effect via specific receptors (Quartermain et al., 1977). The use of such a research strategy provides a greater degree of pharmacological specificity than can be obtained by the use of a single agent. Such strategies are nevertheless not without interpretative difficulties and require carefully designed behavioral controls before valid conclusions are possible.

B. Behavioral Controls

The need for carefully designed control groups to evaluate the many nonspecific side effects of pharmacological agents that influence CA metabolism is of paramount importance in studies of memory. The absence of such controls has prevented an unambiguous interpretation of many of the behavioral findings. The most obvious way of assessing the role of nonspecific drug effects is to employ several agents whose mode of action is similar but whose side effects are unlikely to be so. For example, inhibition of NE synthesis can be achieved by the use of several DBH inhibitors, such as DEDTC, FLA-63, and fusaric acid. If all of these agents induce similar disruption of memory, it can be fairly safely concluded that the behavioral effect is the result of inhibition of NE biosynthesis due to blocking of the DBH enzyme and not to other effects of the compounds.

More refined behavioral controls are usually necessary to evaluate the role of CAs in memory processes. A question that frequently arises when determining whether a particular drug impairs retention is whether the observed performance deficit is a true loss of memory or a generalized impairment of performance due to sickness or loss of motor control. Most of the compounds that influence CA metabolism produce profound changes in activity. They are also frequently administered in such large doses that the health of the animal at the time of testing or training is called into question. Some of these problems can be circumvented by administering the agent immediately posttraining and testing the animal several days later when the drug has been metabolized. It is however not known what effect posttraining sickness may have on memory storage processes, and when large doses are administered after training there is still the problem of determining whether the amnesia resulted from interference with CA metabolism or from some other effect of the drug.

In designs where animals are tested shortly after training it is particularly important to be able to evaluate the contribution of nonspecific factors. Tasks that employ behavioral suppression as an index of retention are particularly susceptible to contamination by nonspecific side effects, especially if drugs are administered prior to training and performance is tested shortly after. Inability to inhibit responding may mean an absence of memory, but it may also reflect increase in activity, disorientation, or loss of the capacity to inhibit all responses. Independent assessment of these possibilities is necessary before any conclusions can be drawn on the effects of a particular agent on memory. The analytical power of avoidance procedures can be enhanced by employing both an active and a passive test of retention. For example, Quartermain and Judge (1982a) showed that pretraining reserpine treatment resulted in faster response latencies (relative to vehicle controls) when a passive test was used and slower latencies when an active measure was the index of retention. These findings strengthen the conclusion that reserpine is disrupting memory processes.

Many of the problems inherent in single trial inhibitory avoidance tasks can be circumvented by employing tests of memory that include a discrimination component. For example, Gibbs and Barnett (1976) used a task in which chicks were trained to avoid a red bead by coating it with methyl anthranilate. The drug was injected before the learning trial, and retention was tested at various times up to 24 hours posttraining. Birds were presented with a red and a blue bead on the retention test. Pecking on the red bead was an index of the level of retention and pecking on the blue bead measured the nonspecific effects of the treatment on performance. The employment of such experimental designs would simplify the interpretation of many studies in the CA literature.

Additional difficulties of interpretation are encountered with inhibitory avoidance tasks when pharmacological agents are administered prior to testing in an attempt to restore memory following induction of amnesia. In such experiments it is difficult to distinguish recovery of memory from nonspecific depressant effects, and absence of recovery may be masked by increases in general activity or arousal when agents such as amphetamine are employed. In some cases the behavior of the animals can provide important clues. For example, recovery of memory in cycloheximide (CXM)-treated mice following pretest treatment with MAO inhibitors was accompanied by autonomic signs of fear, such as piloerection, urination, and defecation (Botwinick & Quartermain, 1974). This finding makes it more plausible to conclude that the suppression of responding was the result of recovery of memory of footshock rather than a general depression of activity. In avoidance procedures the use of both active and passive tests of retention can also simplify the interpretation of drug-induced enhancement of retention. A good example is a recent study by Quartermain and Judge (1982a). In this experiment mice were treated with reserpine prior to Pavlovian fear conditioning. In an attempt to alleviate the resultant amnesia the mixed dopamine–serotonin agonist lisuride was given prior to testing. Lisuride increased latencies in animals tested with the passive procedure and decreased latencies in mice given the active test. This pattern of results suggests lisuride was influencing memory processes.

The most satisfactory solution to this problem is usually the use of a noncontingent control group. This group is treated identically to the experimental group, except that the footshock is given in a different apparatus. If pharmacological agents that induced recovery (i.e., enhanced suppression) in the experimental animals produce the same effect in the noncontingent control group, it can be safely concluded that the effect is due to general depression of performance. This control is conspicuous by its absence in most studies in which attempts at restoration of memory are made in single trial inhibitory avoidance tasks.

In contrast to single trial inhibitory avoidance tasks, discrimination procedures contain a built in control for nonspecific effects of drugs (Quartermain, 1976). Following the induction of amnesia, animals can be tested on either the response to which they were trained or on the opposite response. If drug-treated animals show poor performance relative to controls when tested on the original discrimination, but better performance when tested on the reversal, it can be concluded that the deficit is a specific memory loss rather than a general nonspecific disruption of performance. This control is additionally useful in the interpretation of drug-induced alleviation of amnesia. In these studies it is important to determine whether the improved performance of amnestic animals is the result of recovery of the specific memory or a reflection of a general facilitation of performance. The use of this control is illustrated in a recent study designed to determine whether amnesia induced by DEDTC treatment could be alleviated by the NE α receptor agonist clonidine (Freedman et al., 1979). In this experiment clonidine, administered pretesting, facilitated performance if the mice were tested on the original discrimination, but if mice were tested on a reversal, their performance was significantly impaired and comparable to saline-treated mice who had not been made amnestic. This finding suggests that clonidine was inducing a recovery of a specific memory rather than generally facilitating performance.

The fact that overtraining inoculates animals against the disrupting effects of most amnestic agents can be used as a control for certain side effects of drugs that influence CA metabolism. For example, it has been shown that DEDTC induces a conditioned aversion in certain behavioral situations (Roberts & Fibiger, 1976). This finding raises the possibility that the effects of this drug on behavior, especially in tasks involving appetitive motivation, may be more appropriately attributed to aversion than to memory loss. One way to evaluate this issue is to use a group that is overtrained prior to drug administration. Because overtraining should increase the opportunity for conditioned aversion but decrease the likelihood of amnesia, the outcome of such an experiment should provide a decisive test. This experiment has been carried out, and the results indicate that the amnesias induced by both DEDTC and AMPT cannot be accounted for in terms of conditioned aversion (Quartermain & Botwinick, 1975a).

Because many of the agents that influence CA metabolism have been shown to exert differential effects on retention of strong and weak habits (e.g., Gold & Van Buskirk, 1978b; Hall, 1969), it is important that habit strength is adequately sampled if the full range of effects of a particular drug are to be revealed. This requires that at least two shock levels be employed in inhibitory avoidance studies and two or three different numbers of trials (or reinforcements) in discrimination tasks (Quartermain & Botwinick, 1975a).

III. CATECHOLAMINES AND MEMORY PROCESSING

The following sections provide a critical review of selected studies that investigate the role of CAs in memory processes. The experiments are discussed under two broad categories based on the procedures employed to manipulate CAs, which have been described in Section II.

A. Effects of Reductions in CA Activity

1. Depletion of CAs by Inhibition of Tyrosine Hydroxylase

Several studies have indicated that blocking the synthesis of CAs by inhibiting tyrosine hydroxylase (TH) can disrupt retention performance. For example, Quartermain and Botwinick (1975a) have shown that 50 mg/kg AMPT injected 60 minutes prior to training on a food-motivated spatial discrimination task produced amnesia 24 hours later. The same study also showed that the amnesic effect of AMPT could be antagonized by increasing the number of training trials. Hall and Mayer (1975) have also reported that the effects of AMPT on retention depend on strength of learned response. They showed that 35 mg/kg AMPT administered 4 hours pretraining induced amnesia for a single trial inhibitory avoidance response if the level of training footshock was 1.6 mA, but facilitated retention if footshock intensity was 0.16 mA. Posttaining injections were ineffective. Orsingher and Fulginiti (1971) showed that the amnestic effects of AMPT could be potentiated by amphetamine administered before training and that this amnesia could be partially reversed by L-DOPA. Fulginiti, Molina, and Orsingher (1976) have demonstrated amnesia in rats following AMPT administration in both active and passive avoidance learning. Immediate posttraining injections of 60 mg/kg AMPT resulted in amnesia 5 days following two-way active avoidance training. This amnesia could be reversed by L-DOPA administered up to 2 hours after training. AMPT also blocked retention of a passive avoidance response, but only in female rats. Haycock, Van Buskirk, and McGaugh (1977) have shown that pre- but not posttraining AMPT treatment produced amnesia for a one trial inhibitory avoidance in Swiss Webster mice.

These results indicate that the AMPT administered prior to training can disrupt retention performance. However, the failure to find disruption with posttraining treatment weakens the argument that the drug is influencing memory storage processes. It is possible that the AMPT-induced disruption is the result of state-dependent learning. Most studies have not tested for this possibility, although two were designed specifically to test the state dependency hypothesis. Zornetzer, Gold, and Hendrickson (1974), using Swiss Webster mice and AMPT at 100 mg/kg, demonstrated a significant state dependence in a single trial inhibitory avoidance task. On the other hand, Hall and Mayer (1975) using the same task but C57BL/6J mice failed to demonstrate state-dependent effects. Altman and Quartermain (1982) have recently demonstrated asymmetrical state dependence with doses of AMPT from 60 to 250 mg/kg, using Swiss Webster mice in a multiple trial shock motivated brightness discrimination task. These studies suggest that AMPT can induce state-dependent learning, and this finding, in conjunction with the failure of posttraining treatment to induce amnesia, weakens the argument that inhibition of TH synthesis with AMPT blocks memory storage.

2. Depletion of NE by Inhibition of Dopamine-β-Hydroxylase (DBH)

Inhibition of CA biosynthesis at the DBH step blocks the synthesis of NE without affecting dopamine and thus provides a useful technique for investigating the specific role played by norepinephrine in memory processes. A large number of studies have utilized this technique, and the results indicate that inhibition of NE biosynthesis may impair, enhance, or have no effect on retention depending upon the particular training parameters that are employed. The first demonstration that depletion of NE may impair memory was a study by Krantz and Seiden (1968). In this study rats were trained in a one-way avoidance task until they had achieved a criterion of 90% avoidance. Following this they were given an additional 20 "overtraining" trials, and 24 hours later they were injected with different doses of the DBH inhibitor DEDTC. Retention was tested 6, 24, and 48 hours following drug treatment. Results indicated that 250 and 500 mg/kg of DEDTC disrupted retention when animals were tested 6 hours following drug treatment but not at longer times. Absence of control groups to evaluate possible nonspecific effects of DEDTC prevents an unambiguous interpretation of this finding. Randt, Quartermain, Goldstein, and Anagnoste (1971) examined the effects of DEDTC on retention of single trial inhibitory avoidance in C57BL/6J mice. In one experiment, mice were injected 30 minutes before training and different groups were tested 1 and 5 minutes and 1, 6, and 24 hours later. Significant amnesia was present in groups tested 1, 6, and 24 hours posttraining. In a second experiment, DEDTC was injected at various times before and after training and retention was tested 24 hours later. Results showed that amnesia was present when DEDTC was injected 30 minutes before training and immediately after training, but not when it was injected 2 hours posttraining. Amnesia also occurred when the drug was administered 30 minutes before testing, indicating an effect of NE depletion of retrieval processes. A more recent study (Haycock, Van Buskirk, Gold, & McGaugh, 1978) has demonstrated that DEDTC can induce amnesia in rats for a one trial inhibitory avoidance habit when it is injected as long as 24 hours (but not 72 hours) posttraining. In the same study it was shown that DEDTC could also disrupt retention if it was administered up to 10 days prior to training. Animals were amnestic when tested 30 minutes posttraining, whereas rats injected 1 day prior to training showed normal retention at 30 minutes and an amnesia 24 hours after training. This finding indicates that DEDTC injected 10 days before learning may have impaired acquisition processes and suggests the existence of slowly developing nonspecific effects of the drug, which complicates the interpretation of retention data. A number of studies using single trial inhibitory tasks have confirmed the Randt et al. (1971) finding that DEDTC can induce amnesia when administered before or shortly after training (e.g., Hamburg & Cohen, 1973; Haycock, Van Buskirk, & McGaugh, 1977; Stein, et al., 1975). The finding that DEDTC can in addition disrupt retrieval has also been confirmed. Hamburg and Cohen (1973) showed that rats tested 24, 48, 72, and 96 hours after training all showed retention deficits when DEDTC was administered 30 minutes prior to testing. A recent study by Izquierdo, Beamish, and Anisman (1979) investigated the amnestic effects of FLA-63 (40 mg/kg) on four different avoidance tasks in mice. Results showed that pre- but not posttraining treatment resulted in amnesia in three of the four tasks. The drug did not disrupt retention of a task requiring immobility to avoid shock. No effects on acquisition were observed, and there was not any evidence of state-dependent learning. This experiment confirms several findings reported by Botwinick, Quartermain, Freedman, and Hallock (1977).

Amnesia has also been induced by DBH inhibitors for multiple trial approach and avoidance discrimination tasks (e.g., Botwinick et al., 1977; Quartermain & Bostwinick, 1975a; Spanis, Haycock, Handwerker, Rose, & McGaugh, 1977). In these tasks the effect of DBH inhibition on retention is determined to a large degree by the strength of the learned response. Increasing the number of training trials has been shown to antagonize the amnestic effects of both DEDTC and FLA-63 (Botwinick *et al.*, 1977; Hall, 1976; Quartermain, 1976; Quartermain & Botwinick, 1975a). It is possible that the weak and inconsistent amnestic effect frequently encountered with DBH inhibition may be the result of incomplete blocking of NE synthesis. Some support for this comes from a recent study by Flood, Smith, and Jarvik (1979). They showed that posttraining injections of DEDTC (250 mg/kg) did not induce amnesia for a weakly learned discriminated avoidance habit unless it was administered in combination with other pharmacological agents that enhanced NE depletion, such as imipramine, amphetamine, cocaine, and ouabain.

The behavioral effects of DBH inhibition on retention are complicated by several reports of facilitation of retention following DEDTC treatment (Danscher & Fjerdingstad, 1975; Hall, 1977; Haycock, Van Buskirk, & McGaugh, 1976). In the Haycock *et al.* study mice were injected with either 100, 300, or 900 mg/kg DEDTC immediately following 50 training trials on a shuttle avoidance response. A 7-day retention test showed a dose-related enhancement of performance. It is possible that this enhancement of retention may be a consequence of the transient increase of DA levels that accompanies DBH inhibition. However, the multitude of side effects that accompany high doses of DEDTC make this hypothesis difficult to evaluate. Haycock *et al.* suggest that DEDTC may be enhancing performance by virtue of its effects on reducing nonspecific pituitary–adrenal responses to the training situation, which may have exceeded optimal levels. If DEDTC was influencing retention via its effects on nonspecific hormonal responses NE inhibition might be expected to disrupt retention of mildly stressful or weakly learned responses and improved retention of tasks that employed prolonged and stressful training procedures. These predictions are not borne out by Hall (1977) in a study that examined the effects of differences in response strength on magnitude of DEDTC-induced amnesia. Hall showed that in a passive avoidance task DEDTC disrupted retention if mice were trained with 1.6 mA footshock but enhanced performance if 0.1 mA foot shock was employed. In a second experiment DEDTC disrupted retention of a brightness discrimination if mice were given 15 training trials, but enhanced performance if only five training trials were employed.

The biochemical specificity of DBH inhibitors requires special comment. Most of the studies that have investigated the effect of inhibition of NE on memory have used DEDTC as the pharmacological agent, and the possibility that the behavioral effects of this compound are due to other side effects have frequently been raised, especially because large doses are required to produce amnesia. In order to investigate the role of nonspecific effects of DBH inhibition,

Haycock, Van Buskirk, and McGaugh (1978) tested the effects of four agents known to inhibit DBH centrally and one agent with peripheral actions only. Mice were injected either 30 minutes before or immediately after one trial inhibitory avoidance training with DEDTC, FLA-63, U 14,624, fusaric acid (FA), and the peripheral inhibiting agent benzyloxyamine. FLA-63 and U 14,624 are structural analogs of disulfiram which is converted by ascorbic acid to DEDTC. These agents inhibit DBH by the chelation of copper. Fusaric acid, which is more potent and selective than the other agents, inhibits DBH by competing with the ascorbic acid cofactor to DBH rather than by chelating copper. The results indicated that all of the centrally acting DBH inhibitors disrupted retention when administered before training, but only DEDTC produced amnesia with posttraining administration. Benzyloxyamine was without behavioral effect. Haycock *et al.* (1978) conclude that the effects on retention were therefore probably not the result of inhibition of NE, but may have related to the known effects of DEDTC on heavy metal staining or amino acid metabolism. However, using rats as subjects, Haycock *et al.* (1978) showed that posttraining administration of both DEDTC (690 and 1340 mg/kg) and FA (66 and 99 mg/kg) did disrupt the retention of an inhibitory avoidance response. In addition to decreased NE levels in brain and adrenal gland, DEDTC was also shown to result in bleaching of Timm's staining in the hippocampus and changes in electrographic activity in the amygdala and hippocampus. Fusaric acid, on the other hand, reduced central and peripheral NE levels but did not alter other measures. The authors conclude on the basis of the FA data that inhibition of DBH activity is probably the basis of the amnestic effects of both FA and DEDTC, although specific effects cannot be conclusively ruled out.

The specificity of the DEDTC-induced amnesia to NE depletion is suggested by the finding that posttraining intracerebral administration of NE prevents the development of amnesia. Stein *et al.* (1975) showed that NE, administered intraventricularly immediately after training, abolished the amnestic effect of pretraining DEDTC treatments. Similarly, Meligeni, Ledergerber, and McGaugh (1978) showed that amnesia induced by DEDTC could be reversed by posttraining injections of either centrally of peripherally administered NE. Furthermore, this study showed that reversal of amnesia depends upon the intensity of the training footshock. Low doses of NE (0.01 μg) attenuated amnesia if training was conducted under high (2.0 mA) footshock but not with low (0.5 mA). Subcutaneously administered NE (5.0 μg) also blocked amnesia only if animals were trained with high footshock. Under conditions of low footshock high doses of NE (50 μg/kg) were necessary to alleviate the amnesia. These results emphasize the importance of peripheral CAs on memory processing by showing that low doses of NE, which do not readily pass the blood-brain barrier, can alter retention performance. The pattern of results in this study suggest that adrenal CAs released by footshock combine with exogenous NE to either influence the CNS directly or to produce cardiovascular changes that alter CNS activity.

The amnestic effects of DEDTC have also been reversed by administration of NE precursors. Hamburg and Kerr (1976) showed that retention deficits induced by administration of DEDTC 30 minutes before training and deficits in retrieval induced by DEDTC administered 30 minutes prior to testing could both be alleviated if the NE precursor DL-DOPS was injected 60 minutes prior to DEDTC treatment. Haycock, Van Buskirk, and McGaugh (1977) however report that neither DOPA nor DOPS in doses as high as 400 mg/kg reversed the amnestic effect of DEDTC. The amnestic effects of DEDTC have also been reversed by direct NE receptor stimulation with clonidine (Freedman et al., 1979). While these data are consistent with the claim that inhibition of NE synthesis is the mechanism underlying DEDTC-induced memory disruption, they are not conclusive. The demonstration that NE can reverse a behavioral deficit does not necessarily imply that the deficit was the result of a reduction in NE. As it has been shown that centrally administered NE can facilitate retention in nondepleted animals, it is difficult to separate the effects of exogenous NE as replacement from the direct enhancing effects of the amine itself. It is also possible that the exogenous NE may stimulate DA receptors directly. At the present time NE replacement studies provide only weak evidence that DBH inhibitors disrupt retention because they inhibit NE synthesis.

Spontaneous recovery following amnesia induced by DBH inhibition has been reported in several studies and has failed to occur in others. Botwinick et al. (1977) showed that amnesia for a multiple trial spatial discrimination task induced by FLA-63 was present 24 hours after training, but full recovery of memory occurred at 48 hours. Similar recovery occurred when amnesia was induced in the same task by DEDTC (Freedman et al., 1979). Spontaneous recovery following DBH inhibition does not appear to occur in single trial inhibitory avoidance tasks. A study by Hamburg and Cohen (1973) failed to show spontaneous recovery 7 days after pretraining DEDTC treatment. Quinton and Bloom (1977) also report a study in which no spontaneous recovery occurred by 3 days in mice that had been treated with DEDTC prior to training. Absence of spontaneous recovery does not necessarily indicate that memory storage was blocked by NE depletion. The memory may be present but inaccessible to retrieval mechanisms. Quinton and Bloom (1977) have recently shown that administration of d-amphetamine 30 minutes before testing induces recovery of memory in DEDTC-treated mice who had failed to show spontaneous recovery of a single trial inhibitory avoidance. The fact that the same dose of d-amphetamine failed to recover memory in mice pretreated with cycloheximide suggests that the increased latencies in the DEDTC mice were unlikely to be due to nonspecific effects of the amphetamine. It should be noted however that a recent study failed to demonstrate a reversal of DEDTC-induced amnesia when

amphetamine was injected prior to the retention test (Freedman *et al.*, 1979).
Most of the studies that have attempted to antagonize the effects of NE depletion
by treatment with NE or agents that stimulate NE metabolism have generally
administered the agents around the time of training and have ignored possible
effects on retrieval. For example, the Stein, *et al.* (1975) study cited above
showed that DEDTC-induced amnesia in rats could be counteracted by intraventricularly administered NE immediately and 1 hour after training. More recent studies have indicated that stimulation of CA metabolism can reverse DE-
DTC-induced amnesia both shortly after training and before testing. For
example, Freedman *et al.* (1979) showed that DEDTC-induced amnesia for a
spatial discrimination task could be reversed if the α-adrenergic agonist clonidine
was administered immediately and 1 and 2 hours but not 3 hours posttraining,
and also 3 and 1 hours before testing.

These data suggest that two types of amnesia can be induced by inhibition
of DBH; a transient amnesia, which spontaneously recovers 48–72 hours following training (Botwinick *et al.*, 1977; Freedman *et al.*, 1979; Quartermain &
Botwinick, 1975a), and amnesias that are durable for up to 1 week and longer
(Hamburg & Cohen, 1973; Haycock, Van Buskirk, & McGaugh, 1977; Quinton
& Bloom, 1977). Both types of amnesias can be alleviated by pretesting administration of adrenergic stimulants. The interpretation of this recovery is controversial. One possibility is that inhibition of NE biosynthesis prevents the normal
operation of retrieval processes but does not block the formation of the memory
trace. Another is that NE depletion allows the consolidation of a weak, partially
formed memory that is facilitated by the stimulants. At present there does not
appear to be any obvious methodological procedure available to distinguish
between these two possibilities.

3. Depletion of CAs by Disruption of Storage Mechanisms

Positive evidence of a role for CAs in memory comes from studies in
which central stores of the biogenic amines are depleted by reserpine treatment.
Dismukes and Rake (1972) trained DBA/2J mice for 30 trials in a one-way
avoidance task and injected reserpine either 1 minute or 24 hours following
training. Retention tests 5 days later revealed a significant retention decrement in
the group treated with reserpine 1 minute after training. Results also indicated
that the decrement could be reversed by posttraining treatment with L-DOPA.
Similar findings were reported by Rake (1973) using a single trial inhibitory
avoidance task. Kurtz and Palfai (1978) have recently reported a study on the
effects of reserpine on the retention of discriminated escape learning. They
showed that reserpine administered 2 hours before and up to 1 hour after training
produced a dose-dependent retention deficit 10 days later. In addition they
showed that reserpine also disrupted memory retrieval. These retention deficits

could be ameliorated by treatment with the biogenic amine precursors L-DOPA and DL-5-hydroxytryptophan (DL-5-HTP). The results of this study suggest that reserpine may block both the storage of information and its retrieval. As reserpine depletes both NE and DA, no information on the role of specific CAs can be obtained from this study. The demonstration that treatment with 5-HTP alleviated retention deficits indicates that serotonin may play a role in memory processing.

Ambiguity regarding the mechanism of reserpine-induced amnesia is introduced in a recent study by Palfai, Brown, and Walsh (1978). Using gas chromatography mass spectrometry techniques they were unable to show any correlation between retention performance and levels of NE and DA in the brain. Neither were they able to demonstrate any changes in NE or DA levels as a result of doses of L-DOPA and 5-HTP which successfully attenuated the amnesia. Interpretation of this finding is not straightforward. Changes in levels is the least sensitive indicator of alterations in functional activity of neurotransmitters. Since newly synthesized CAs are preferentially released, the result of precursor treatments might influence behavior without being reflected in increased levels of the biogenic amines. Changes in release may have been a more appropriate neurochemical measure with which to examine the effects of the precursors on biogenic amine activity. Brown, Palfai, and Wichlinski (1981) administered amnestic doses of reserpine, guanethidine, and syrosingopine to mice and measured whole brain levels of CAs 2 or 24 hours after training. Reserpine reduced brain levels of NE and DA at both times, while the other two agents were without effect. Since all three drugs disrupted retention, these findings indicate that brain levels of CAs at time of training do not predict amnesia. The mechanism underlying the effect of reserpine on memory in unclear. It is possible as indicated above that alterations in other parameters of central CA metabolism such as turnover may be involved or alternatively that other transmitter systems (e.g., serotonin) may be more important. Another possibility is that peripheral CA mechanisms mediate the behavioral effect. The role of peripheral CA systems in memory processing is reviewed in Section III, D.

Walsh and Palfai (1979) have suggested that reserpine amnesia is qualitatively different from memory loss induced by peripheral CA depleting agents such as syrosingopine. They have shown that while amnesia produced by syrosingopine was attenuated by repeated exposures to the training apparatus, reserpine amnesia remained permanent. They suggest that reserpine may disrupt storage processes while peripheral agents impair retrieval. The results of an experiment by Quartermain and Judge (1982a) show that memory loss resulting from pretraining reserpine can be alleviated by the DA–5-HT agonist lisuride administered before testing. This result indicates that some information remains in storage following reserpine treatment.

4. Depletion of CA's by Destruction of DA and NE Neurons

Effects of 6-OHDA Treatment.   Although this procedure produces the most drastic and durable effects on CA metabolism few studies have employed the technique to directly investigate retention processes. In one study (Rainbow, Adler, & Flexner, 1976) the amnestic effects of 6-OHDA, were compared to those induced by the protein synthesis inhibitor cycloheximide (CXM). Mice were injected intraventricularly with 6-OHDA 2 weeks prior to training in a single trial passive avoidance task. Retention was tested 6 and 24 hours posttraining. The results indicated that whereas CXM induced amnesia at both retention intervals, 6-OHDA-treated mice were amnestic only at the 24 hour test. These results suggest that chronic depletion of the CAs disrupts long-term memory. The fact that retention was unimparied 6 hours after training reduces the likelihood that the treatment disrupted acquisition. Little can be concluded however about the specificity of the effect because 6-OHDA treatment depleted NE by 83% and DA by 71%.

A second study by this group (Rainbow & Flexner, 1978) used 6-OHDA to test the hypothesis that CXM-induced transient amnesia was the result of disruption of adrenergic mechanisms. Mice were injected intraventricularly with 6-OHDA and subsequently trained in a Y maze shock discrimination task. Animals showed amnesia at 24 hours but spontaneous recovery occurred by 72 hours. Thus, despite substantial and persistent depletion of both NE and DA, normal retention was possible. If however TH was inhibited with AMPT immediately after training, no spontaneous recovery was observable, suggesting that residual CA neurons may have mediated the spontaneous recovery. This study suggests that chronic depletion of the CAs by 6-OHDA results in only a temporary loss of memory. Palfai and Walsh (1980) have recently investigated the effects of peripherally administered 6-OHDA on retention of passive avoidance in mice. Their results indicated that despite significant depletion of peripheral CAs no impairment in retention was evident. This finding casts some doubt on the critical importance of peripheral CA depletion for amnesia, although it is possible that compensatory changes in medullary CA synthesis could have counteracted the effects of the 6-OHDA.

5. Specific 6-OHDA Lesions of NE Pathways

Attempts have been made to evaluate the contribution of specific CAs to behavior by making discrete 6-OHDA lesions in both DA and NE pathways. Crow and Wendlandt (1976) examined the effects of depletion of hippocampal and forebrain NE on retention by injecting 6-OHDA bilaterally into the locus coeruleus. Rats were subsequently trained on a passive avoidance task and tested for retention immediately and 72 hours posttraining. Acquisition and immediate retention was normal, but significant retention defects were apparent at the 72-

hour retention interval. The authors interpret these results as supporting the hypothesis that cortical NE is necessary for transmission between short- and long-term memory to take place. This finding has not been confirmed by other studies. Mason and Fibiger (1978b) injected 6-OHDA into the dorsal NE bundle and trained and tested rats on a passive avoidance response. They showed that acquisition and retention was normal. However, in repeated extinction tests, the lesioned rats showed a slightly slower rate of extinction. Increased resistance to extinction appears to be the most conspicuous behavior sequela of depletion of forebrain NE (Mason, 1979). Data from runway extinction studies also fail to support the notion that long-term consolidation of memory is impaired in animals depleted of hippocampal and cortical NE. Mason and Iversen (1977) have shown that, in repeated daily extinction sessions, lesioned animals and nontreated controls have comparable running speeds at the beginning of each day; only intra-session runway speeds are significantly slower for NE-depleted animals. This suggests that long-term storage is normal. The possibility that forebrain NE may be important for spatial memory is suggested by a recent study by Mason and Fibiger (1978a). 6-Hydroxydopamine-treated rats were trained to alternate in a T maze to obtain food rewards. A constant intertrial interval (ITI) of 15 seconds was employed. Control rats reached 90% correct by the seventh training day, but lesioned animals failed to progress beyond 75% level after 19 days of training. Mason and Fibiger state that the defect may reflect an impairment of spatial memory, but they prefer an explanation based on disruption of attentional mechanisms. One way of distinguishing between these two possibilities, would have been to vary the ITI. If performance of the lesioned animals was better at shorter than at longer delays an explanation in terms of memory would become more plausible. This study does not demonstrate that the deficit in spatial performance is specifically due to depletion of NE. From the available evidence it appears that lesions to a variety of inputs to the hippocampus can result in a disruption of spatial memory. Similar findings may occur following depletion of any neurotransmitter system that disrupts the normal functioning of the hippocampus.

6. Specific 6-OHDA Lesions of DA Systems

Several studies have investigated the role of the DA system in memory processes. Fibiger, Phillips, and Zis (1974) showed that rats lesioned after acquisition of an active avoidance response showed significantly poorer retention than untreated controls. The magnitude of the difference was small, but this might have been because animals were considerably overtrained prior to lesioning. More convincing evidence of a role for DA in memory comes from a recent study by Fibiger and Phillips (1976). They showed that stimulation of the substantia nigra (SN) with 10 μA–60 Hz current impaired long-term retention of a passive avoidance habit, thus confirming an earlier report by Routtenberg and Holzman (1973). Fibiger and Phillips showed that a prior ipsilateral lesion of the

DA nigro–striatal bundle blocked the impairment of memory induced by SN electrical stimulation, suggesting that the memory deficit is mediated by the nigro–striatal pathway. That this DA system is not an essential neural structure for memory processing is indicated by their finding that bilateral lesions of the bundle did not disrupt retention of passive avoidance learning. This suggests that the critical site is one of the projection areas of the nigro–striatal bundle. Fibiger and Phillips hypothesize that stimulation of the SN might disrupt retention by causing an excess release of DA in the caudate–putamen. This is an interesting hypothesis for which there is some supporting evidence. It is known that SN stimulation increases the release of DA in the neostriatum (von Voiglander & Moore, 1971), and there is evidence that posttraining electrical stimulation of the caudate disrupts retention (Wyers, Deadwyler, Hirasuna, & Montgomery, 1973). In support of this hypothesis Kim and Routtenberg (1976) have shown that posttraining injections of DA into the striatum disrupted the retention of a passive avoidance response in rats. Further support for a role for DA in retention of passive avoidance is provided by the demonstration that 6-OHDA injected into the substantia nigra 5 minutes after passive avoidance learning caused a marked disruption of retention (Routtenberg & Kim, 1978). There are also a number of studies showing that electrolytic lesions of the DA neostriatal system cause amnesia for passive avoidance learning (e.g., Mitcham & Thomas, 1972; Prado-Alcala, Grinberg, Arditti, Garcia, Prieto, & Brust-Carmona, 1975). Taken together, these findings suggest that DA systems in the neostriatum may play a role in mediating retention of passive avoidance learning.

7. Effects of Electrolytic Lesions of the Locus Coeruleus (LC)

The consensus from a number of studies on the effects of LC lesions on learning is that depletion of forebrain NE induced by this procedure does not generally impair the acquisition of instrumental responding (Mason, 1979). However, recent work by Zornetzer and his colleagues indicates that these lesions may influence memory processes. Zornetzer and Gold (1976) showed that unilateral but not bilateral posttraining LC lesions extended the gradient of susceptibility to electroconvulsive shock (ECS)-induced amnesia to 48 hours and in a later study, out as far as 7 but not 14 days (Zornetzer, Abraham, & Appleton, 1978). If the lesions were delayed for 6 hours posttraining no enhancement of ECS susceptibility was apparent. More recently, de Carvelho and Zornetzer (1981) have reported that mice sustaining unilateral lesions made 2 or 14 days before training showed significant amnesia if ECS was administered 24 hours and 14 days posttraining. Although bilateral lesions did not enhance susceptibility to ECS, they produced an accelerated rate of forgetting 15 days after training. These findings are presently difficult to integrate into a coherent framework. It is not clear why enhanced susceptibility occurs only with unilateral lesions. De Carvalho and Zornetzer review studies that suggest that unilateral lesions may result in alterations in CA metabolism different from those that follow bilateral LC destruction. It is possible that these changes may be related to the behavioral consequences of bilateral lesions. Until this is determined it is difficult to relate these findings to current ideas about the role of NE in memory processing.

8. Effects of CA Receptor Blockade on Retention

If normal levels of transmission in adrenergic pathways are necessary for memory processing then blockade of postsynaptic receptors should result in memory deficits similar to those produced by CA synthesis inhibition. Available evidence suggests that this is the case. Cohen and Hamburg (1975) investigated the effects of the β adrenergic antagonist propranolol on retention of a passive avoidance response in rats. In one experiment, propranolol injected 5 minutes posttraining induced an amnesia when rats were tested 1, 3, and 7 days later. Retention up to 6 hours was unaffected. In a second experiment propranolol was injected 1 day or 3 days posttraining, and retention tested 2 hours later. In both cases, a significant retention decrement occurred. These findings were identical to those reported for the NE synthesis inhibitor DEDTC by the same authors. Haycock, Van Buskirk, and McGaugh (1977) failed to confirm these findings. Using mice as subjects they were unable to demonstrate amnesia with either pre- or posttraining administration of propranolol. However, several other reports have confirmed the finding that blockade of β adrenergic receptors disrupts retention. For example, Hess (1977) has shown that short-term retention measured in a single alternation paradigm is disrupted by pretraining propranolol treatment if the ITI is 30 seconds, but performance is unaffected when the ITI is 3 seconds. A recent study has shown that micro-injections of both dl-propranolol and another β antagonist, dl-alprenolol, into the amygdala immediately after training disrupted retention of a passive avoidance response in rats (Gallagher, Kapp, Musty, & Driscoll, 1977). Dismukes and Rake (1972) report a study in which another β antagonist dichloroisoproterenol (DCI) disrupted retention of a multiple trial active avoidance response in mice. These findings are complicated by two reports that propranolol may enhance retention. Merlo and Izquierdo (1971) demonstrated that posttraining injection of propranolol facilitated retention of and active avoidance response in rats. A second study from this group (Izquierdo, Fabian, & Chemerinski, 1974) showed that pretraining administration of both d- and l-propranolol enhanced retention of a passive avoidance response in mice. These studies suggest that β-adrenergic blockade may both disrupt storage and retrieval and also facilitate retention. The exact behavioral conditions under which these diverse effects occur has yet to be specified.

Gold and Sternberg (1978) have recently demonstrated that the α NE antagonist phenoxybenzamine (PBZ) administered before passive avoidance training blocked the amnestic effects of electroconvulsive shock, electrical stimulation of the brain, metrazol, DEDTC, and CXM treatments. This finding suggests that some common adrenergic mechanisms may underlie most experimentally induced retrograde amnesias. In a recent report Sternberg, Gold, and McGaugh (1982) have demonstrated that centrally administered CA antagonists failed to alleviate amnesia induced by electrical stimulation of the frontal cortex. This finding suggests that the amnesia-attenuating effect of pretraining antagonists may be mediated by peripheral adrenergic responses to the treatments. The basis of the phenomenon of amnesia blockade by pretraining treatment with CA antagonists is unclear. Gold and Sternberg suggest that the common factor underlying these amnesias may be a release of NE induced by stress of the treatment. This suggestion is based on a previous finding (see below) in which a 40% decrease in brain NE levels was correlated with poor retention. Another possibility is that PBZ has turned on synthesis and release of NE via receptor-mediated feedback mechanisms. This hypothesis is consistent with the finding that the NE α agonist clonidine blocks CXM-induced amnesia when it is administered up to an hour before training (Quartermain et al., 1977). Further research will be necessary to reveal the nature of the mechanism underlying this phenomenon.

Blockade of DA receptors with haloperidol does not appear to disrupt either short-term memory in monkeys (Bartus, 1978) or retention of passive avoidance responding in mice (Haycock, Van Buskirk, & McGaugh, 1977). One positive finding has been reported by Gozzani and Izquierdo (1976) who showed that haloperidol administered posttraining disrupted retention of a shuttle box avoidance response.

B. Effects of Increased CA Activity on Memory Processes

1. Effects of Enhanced CA Release

Amphetamine has been the most widely employed CA releasing agent in memory studies. Like other CA agents, this compound has been shown to exert both facilitating and disrupting effects on retention (e.g., Doty & Doty, 1966; Evangelista & Izquierdo, 1971; Hall, 1969; Krivanek & McGaugh, 1969; McGaugh, 1966). Facilitation occurs with doses ranging from 0.25 to 2.0 mg/kg, but usually not with higher doses. The posttraining temporal gradient is relatively steep, with no facilitation usually occurring with training to injection intervals of longer than 1 or 2 minutes (Krivanek & McGaugh, 1969). Disruption of retention has been reported with posttraining amphetamine administration using passive avoidance tasks (Bovet, Robustelli, & Bignami, 1965; Weissman, 1967), and Crabbé and Alpern (1973) have shown that a series of amphetamine injections begun 24 hours after appetitive discrimination training disrupts retention in mice. A more recent study by these authors indicates that d-amphetamine may both impair and enhance retention of an appetitively motivated brightness discrimination (Crabbé & Alpern, 1975). They showed that an injection of 2.0 mg/kg d-amphetamine for 5 days impaired retention when it was administered following 2 days of training on a thirst-motivated successive brightness discrimination task. The same dose-facilitated performance in mice who had received no initial maze training before drug treatment. This finding suggests that amphetamine treatment can also disrupt an established memory. James (1975) has recently reported a study which shows that d-amphetamine administered intravenously immediately following footshock in a one trial passive avoidance task disrupts retention tested 1 and 4 days later. Training to treatment delays of longer than 90 seconds eliminated the amnesia. A similar injection following one trial appetitive learning failed to alter retention.

These findings are difficult to organize into a coherent generalization. Posttraining amphetamine can both impair and facilitate retention, but the conditions that determine these effects have not been specified. Task, training, and motivational conditions appear to be important determinants of the effects of amphetamine. For example, amphetamine has been shown to disrupt retention of shock-induced lick suppression if mice are given four adaptation sessions prior to shock, although the same dose will facilitate retention if animals are adapted to drinking for 7 days (Haycock, Van Buskirk, & Gold, 1977). Similarly the facilitation of retention usually observed when amphetamine is administered following discrimination training can be eliminated if the task is too simple (Hall, 1969). James (1975) has suggested that amphetamine-induced disruption of retention occurs only when behavior is under aversive motivational control. This generalization is contradicted by the results of the Crabbé and Alpern studies, which showed disruption of the retention of an appetitive discrimination habit. However, this disruption was induced by repeated amphetamine treatment over 5 days. Some of the ambiguity surrounding these studies may result from the fact that d-amphetamine releases both NE and DA, and these amines may interact differentially with different tasks and motivational conditions. Some clarity could be introduced by determining which CA is mediating the enhanced or impaired retention performance. This could be achieved by using amphetamine in combination with NE and DA receptor blocking agents and synthesis inhibitors.

Additional evidence that amphetamine-induced release of CAs influence memory processes is obtained from studies that show that this agent can reverse experimentally induced amnesias. Several studies have shown that amphetamine administered shortly after training can alleviate amnesias induced by protein synthesis inhibition (Barondes & Cohen, 1967; Flood, Jarvik, Bennett, Orme, & Rosenzweig, 1977; Hall, 1976; Serota, Roberts, & Flexner, 1972). One interpretation of this finding is that amphetamine increases the strength and duration of a short-term memory process that supports the trace until protein synthesis recovers from inhibition. There is no direct evidence to support this hypothesis.

Amphetamine can also reverse amnesias when it is administered prior to the retention test. Quartermain and Botwinick (1975a) showed that amnesia induced by CXM for a spatial discrimination habit could be reversed if amphetamine was administered 30 minutes before testing. This effect of amphetamine could not be attributed to nonspecific influences on test performance because amphetamine-treated mice performed poorly if they were tested using a reversal procedure. These findings suggest that amnesias induced by protein synthesis inhibitors can be attenuated by increasing CA release either after training of before testing. The effectiveness of pretesting treatment suggests the possibility that amphetamine may directly facilitate retrieval mechanisms.

Squire (1979) has also shown that d-amphetamine facilitates retention following CXM-induced amnesia. However, he attributes the enhanced performance to accelerated relearning rather than to facilitated retrieval. Squire suggests that the difference between this result and that reported by Quartermain and Botwinick (1975a) may be due to differences in durability of the amnesia between the two studies. In the Quartermain and Botwinick study CXM induced an amnesia that spontaneously recovered 48 hours after training, while in the Squire experiment the amnesia was permanent. This possibility was tested in a recent experiment by Quartermain & Altman (1982). Amnesia was produced by injecting mice with the protein synthesis inhibitor anisomycin (ANI) immediately following training in a lick suppression task. This treatment results in an amnesia that does not show spontaneous recovery. Mice treated with d-amphetamine before the retention test showed a strong restoration of the avoidance response. Mice given noncontingent shocks did not suppress drinking following amphetamine, indicating that nonspecific behavioral suppression was not an adequate explanation for the findings. Agents that induced arousal and nonspecific fear failed to mimic the effects of amphetamine. This suggests that the faciliated avoidance was unlikely to be the result of enhanced motivation. The findings are more consistent with the notion that amphetamine facilitates retrieval of stored memories. Squire's hypothesis that amphetamine facilitates relearning rather than retrieval is inconsistent with the results of some recent studies. Meyer and Meyer (1977) showed that rats amnestic following posterior cortical lesions showed immediate improvement following amphetamine treatment, a result that would not be expected if amphetamine was facilitating relearning. Similarly, Sara and DeWeer (1982) have shown that amphetamine alleviated forgetting when it was administered before the retention test, but had no effect when it was administered early in acquisition when the level of performance was comparable to that existing prior to testing. Further evidence for an effect on retrieval processes comes from a recent experiment by Quartermain (1982). In this study, forgetting of a two lever spatial discrimination habit measured under extinction conditions was alleviated by d-amphetamine (1.0 mg/kg) administered 30 minutes before testing. The drug-treated mice showed increased presses on the previously rewarded lever but not on the lever not reinforced during training. This pattern of results suggests an effect on memory retrieval.

There is also evidence that d-amphetamine can alleviate forgetting following a long retention interval. In the Sara and DeWeer (1982) study described above forgetting was produced by a 3-week training to test interval, and Quartermain and Judge (1982b) showed that forgetting of fear conditioning produced by a 1-month retention interval could be alleviated by amphetamine administered before the test. These studies indicate that amphetamine can facilitate retention when forgetting is induced by both an amnestic agent and by a long retention interval.

The effects of amphetamine on amnesias induced by inhibition of catecholamine synthesis are equivocal. Quinton and Bloom (1977) have shown that amnesias induced by DEDTC and CXM respond differently to posttraining and pretesting amphetamine treatment. Posttraining but not pretesting amphetamine reversed CXM-induced amnesias, while pretesting but not posttraining amphetamine alleviated amnesias induced by DEDTC. These results have not been confirmed by other studies. As indicated above, several experiments have shown that amphetamine injected before testing can attenuate amnesias induced by protein synthesis inhibitors (Quartermain & Altman, 1982; Quartermain & Botwinick, 1975a). The effect of pretest administration of d-amphetamine on DEDTC-induced amnesia was not confirmed in a recent study by Freedman et al. (1979). They showed that under conditions where clonidine produced recovery, amphetamine failed to reverse the amnesia. In fact, amphetamine tended to exacerbate the retention deficit in many animals, suggesting that depletion of NE consequent on the release of the amine may have exaggerated the effect of DEDTC.

Further support for the suggestion that amphetamine may stimulate memory retrieval processes comes from studies that show that loss of retention of a brightness discrimination resulting from bilateral posterior cortical ablations can be overcome by amphetamine administered before retention testing (Meyer & Meyer, 1977). It is worth noting that the effective doses of amphetamine used in these experiments do not facilitate original learning. It has also been shown that loss of retention of a shuttle box avoidance habit, induced by posttraining decortication, can be overcome by amphetamine treatment (Meyer & Beattie, 1977). Taken together with the data from drug-induced amnesias, these studies suggest that one of the functions of amphetamine in memory processing may be to permit the restablishment of access to memory traces that would otherwise remain inaccessible. Another possibility is that amnestic agents and lesions result in the storage of a weak habit that is strengthened by the amphetamine. This latter interpretation cannot easily account for some of the findings from the lesion studies. For example, Meyer and Meyer (1977) note that when decorticate rats are treated with amphetamine they almost immediately begin avoiding in the shuttle box after having failed to do so for many hundred trials. This behavior suggests that amphetamine is allowing reestablishment of access to an intact memory trace. A similar, though perhaps less compelling, interpretation can be made for amphetamine-induced recovery from amnesia induced by protein synthesis inhibition. Quartermain and Altman (1982) have shown that anisomycin injected following training on a sbock-induced lick suppression task results in a robust amnesia that does not spontaneously recover. If amphetamine (2.0 mg/kg) is given 30 minutes before the retention test, animals exhibit levels of suppression equal to those of mice that had never received the amnestic agent. The results of noncontingent control groups indicate that amphetamine does not induce suppression in animals not trained in the test apparatus. When the mice are retested 48 hours later without amphetamine, a significant number of them relapse into amnesia that can be alleviated by a second injection of amphetamine. It is not possible to conclude from this observation alone that amphetamine is permitting retrieval of an intact memory rather than temporarily strengthening a weak habit. Such a conclusion is however encouraged by the finding that amphetamine-treated animals show a complete recovery of conditioned suppression exhibiting test latencies indistinguishable from non-amnestic mice.

2. Effect of Reuptake Blockade

Agents that block reuptake potentiate the effect of the CAs by preventing their removal by uptake mechanisms. It might therefore be expected that such agents would facilitate retention, especially under conditions where the habit is relatively weak. This expectation is confirmed in a recent study by Flood et al. (1979). They showed that blockade of NE uptake with desipramine (50 mg/kg), administered immediately after weak training in a shock avoidance discrimination task, significantly improved retention performance measured 7 days later. A more detailed experimental analysis by Leftoff (1973) revealed that blockade of reuptake with imipramine can also alter memory retrieval. Leftoff trained rats in a shock escape brightness discrimination task to a criterion of 10 consecutively correct response and then tested groups 1, 7, 14, or 28 days later. Animals were treated with imipramine directly preceding retraining. Results showed that imipramine disrupted retention only when the task was normally well retained (habits of intermediate age); recently acquired and old habits were not affected. The failure to demonstrate the predicted facilitation of retrieval of the oldest habit may have been due to insufficient forgetting in the 28-day group.

Reuptake blockade has also been employed to potentiate tissue depletion of CAs induced by synthesis inhibition. Flood et al. (1979) have shown that DEDTC and AMPT produce amnesia when injected in combination with imipramine but fail to do so when administered alone. These studies indicate that potentiating the synaptic effects of released CAs by reuptake blockade enhance retention of weak habits but disrupt retention of well-learned habits. This effect on well-learned responses is the opposite of that usually found with the administration of CA depleting agents where increases in training strength typically result in attenuation of the amnesia.

3. Effect of Inhibition of Enzymes That Inactivate CAs

Effects of inhibition of MAO on retention has been investigated in two experimental situations. First, it has been shown that posttraining administration of the MAO inhibitor pheniprazine enhances retention of a poorly learned habit (Flood et al., 1979). This finding would be expected based on the results from release and reuptake blocking experiments. Second, administration of MAO inhibitors prior to retention testing have been shown to result in the amelioration of retrograde amnesia (Botwinick & Quartermain, 1974; Quartermain & Botwinick, 1975a, 1975b). These findings are consistent with the notion that increases in intraneuronal levels of CAs can facilitate retention.

4. Effect of Direct Receptor Stimulation

The influence of CA agonists on retention is difficult to interpret because of the complex concentration and time-dependent effects these agents exert on CA metabolism. For example, clonidine, an α NE agonist, stimulates presynaptic receptors at high doses and probably both pre- and postsynaptic receptors at high doses. . Low doses of clonidine would therefore be expected to directly inhibit NE, whereas at high doses the agonist should act like released NE. The behavioral effects of clonidine on retention are somewhat paradoxical in that this agonist has been shown to induce amnesias at the same doses that it can alleviate them. Gozzani and Izquierdo (1976) report that clonidine (0.1 mg/kg) disrupted retention of shuttle box performance and that the amnesia could be blocked by phentolamine. On the other hand, it has been shown that clonidine can reverse amnesias induced by both protein and CA synthesis inhibition. Amnesia induced by CXM can be reversed if clonidine (0.5 mg/kg) is administered prior to training and CXM treatment, up to 1 hour posttraining and up to 3 hours prior to testing (Quartermain et al., 1977). The β NE agonist isoproterenol also reversed CXM-induced amnesia. Clonidine administered both posttraining and pretesting reversed amnesia induced by DEDTC (Freedman et al., 1979).

Recent experiments indicate that agents that directly stimulate DA receptors may also facilitate retention. Quartermain, Judge, and Friedman (1982) have shown that pretest administration of the DA agonist lisuride can alleviate amnesia induced by protein synthesis inhibition, reduce forgetting after a long training to test interval, and improve retention of inhibitory avoidance in senescent mice. It has also been demonstrated that dopamine and lisuride, admin-

istered intracerebroventricularly, can alleviate amnesia induced by protein synthesis inhibition. These findings suggest that dopamine may play a role in the
retention of inhibitory avoidance learning.

C. Changes in Brain Norepinephrine Levels as a Result of Training and Hormone-Treatments

Further support for the importance of NE in memory storage processes is
provided by studies showing that changes in levels of brain NE correlate with
degree of retention of an avoidance response. Research by Gold and his associates has indicated that hormone responses activated by the training experience
may modulate retention performance (Gold & McGaugh, 1977). In a series of
studies these authors have shown that posttraining injections of epinephrine,
norepinephrine, and ACTH facilitate retention of a weak avoidance response in a
time-dependent manner. Epinephrine and ACTH administered posttraining can
also produce retrograde amnesia for a strong avoidance response. Gold believes
that these hormonal influences on retention may be mediated by brain NE. In a
series of experiments (Gold and Van Buskirk (1978a) trained rats with either
high (2.0 mA for 1 second) or low (0.7 mA for 0.4 second) shock and injected
different doses of either ACTH or epinephrine immediately following training.
Brain NE levels were examined 10 minutes following training. Brain NE levels
were examined 10 minutes following training. The results showed that the high
footshock level (which produced good retention) resulted in a 20% decrease in
brain NE concentrations. The low shock level, which produced poor retention,
did not result in a significant decline in NE. When, however, low shock was
combined with an immediate injection of ACTH or epinephrine, good retention
occurred and brain levels of NE showed a 20% decrease. When epinephrine was
injected immediately following training with high shock a 40% decrease in NE
concentrations resulted. This is the training condition in which posttraining epinephrine treatment results in amnesia. These findings suggest that changes in
concentrations of brain NE can predict retention performance.

D. Role of Central and Peripheral CAs in Memory Processing

Recent evidence indicates that peripheral CAs play a significant role in
modulating storage processes. Studies by Gold and McGaugh (1978) have shown
that epinephrine and norepinephrine injected peripherally posttraining can both
impair and enhance retention performance. Since these amines have difficulty in
penetrating into the brain it seems likely that their effects are mediated principally by peripheral CA mechanisms. This conclusion is supported by studies
showing that plasma epinephrine and NE levels are elevated following intensities
of footshock that result in good retention of inhibitory avoidance (Gold &

McCarty, 1981). Furthermore, it has been shown that an injection of epinephrine, which enhances retention of a weak shock, results in plasma epinephrine levels similar to that observed following strong shock (McCarty & Gold, 1981). In addition, there is evidence that the amphetamine analog, 4-hydroxyamphetamine, which does not readily enter the brain, can facilitate retention when it is administered immediately posttraining (Martinez, Jensen, Messing, Vasquez, Soumireu-Mourat, Geddes, Liang, & McGaugh, 1980). These results suggest that endogenous peripheral CA responses to training play an important role in memory storage.

There is also evidence indicating that peripheral CAs are important in the etiology of retrograde amnesia. It has been shown that high doses of epinephrine produce amnesia in rats and mice (Gold & Van Buskirk, 1975, 1978b) and that guanethidine and syrosingopine, two CA-depleting agents that do not readily enter the brain, can cause forgetting of a passive avoidance response (Palfai & Walsh, 1980; Walsh & Palfai, 1979). In addition, it has been demonstrated that α-adrenergic antagonists (Sternberg et al., 1982) and d-amphetamine (Martinez, Vasquez, Rigler, Messing, Jensen, Liang, & McGaugh, 1980) can attenuate amnesia if they are administered peripherally but not centrally around the time of training.

While these findings suggest that peripheral CA systems have a function in storage processes there are some contradictory findings. For example, Palfai and Walsh (1980), have shown that the peripherally administered neurotoxin 6-OHDA failed to induce amnesia for passive avoidance learning. Also Sternberg (1982) has shown that adrenalectomy sometimes fails to affect amnesia, and Sternberg, Gold, and McGaugh (1982) have recently reported that bretylium, a drug that blocks release from sympathetic nerve endings, does not alter memory itself nor does it attenuate the amnesia induced by electrical stimulation of the frontal cortex. These findings suggest that alterations in peripheral CAs may not always be sufficient to influence memory processes.

Considerably less research has been devoted to the investigation of the relative roles of central and peripheral CAs in retrieval processes. The available information suggests that peripheral CAs may have a more important function in modulating storage processes than in mediating retrieval. This generalization is based on studies that have shown that (a) d-amphetamine administered before testing attenuates amnesia, but 4-hydroxyamphetamine is without effect (Quartermain & Altman, 1982); (b) both d-amphetamine and the dopamine agonist lisuride can facilitate retention when administered directly into the brain (Altman & Quartermain, 1982); and (c) the attenuation of amnesia induced by pretest administration of the MAO inhibitor pheniprazine is blocked by reserpine but not by the peripheral depleting agent syrosingopine (Quartermain & Botwinick, 1975a). Taken together, these findings suggest that central CAs are involved in mediating retrieval processes.

E. Conclusions

1. Effects on Storage and Retrieval Processes

Research reviewed in the preceding sections has shown that agents that alter CA transmission can influence memory processing when they are administered both at training and before testing. These findings suggest that CA systems may participate in both the storage and the retrieval of information. The means by which they influence storage processes is not known. CAs released at training may prime the CNS to promote efficient storage by controlling arousal levels and focusing attention. They may also influence memory storage by facilitating poststimulus processing operations, which serve to associate the target memory with contextual stimuli in the training environment. The regional distribution and anatomical characteristics (see below) of CA systems suggest that they are more likely to modulate memory storage processes than they are to directly participate in the encoding of specific information.

An important role for the CAs in mediating retrieval processes is becoming increasingly well established. It has been shown that the inhibition of NE synthesis before testing can disrupt retrieval of inhibitory avoidance learning, and numerous studies have shown that forgetting induced by a wide variety of sources can be alleviated by pretest treatment with CA-stimulating agents. These findings suggest that increased activity in CA systems may underlie the retrieval of information from storage. Mechanisms by which the CAs could fulfill this function remain speculative. It is possible that increased CA activity may reinstate internal cues that were present during training, thereby making the conditions at retrieval more comparable to those existing at the time of encoding. It has been shown that similarity between conditions at encoding and retrieval enhance retention performance (Spear, 1978; Tulving & Thomson, 1973). Another possibility is that CA stimulants may facilitate retrieval by enhancing selective attention, thus making retrieval cues more discriminable at time of testing. The suggestion that CAs may be involved in the effects of retrieval cues on memory receives some support from a study by Cassens, Roffman, Kurac, Orsulak, and Shildkraut (1980). These authors showed that contextual cues, which had previously been associated with shock, released NE in the brain when animals were returned to the training apparatus for testing under extinction conditions. This finding suggests the possibility that release of NE may mediate the effects of retrieval cues on memory. The efficacy of CA stimulants in facilitating retrieval processes following forgetting may provide clues for the treatment of memory disorders in man.

2. Involvement of NE in Memory

Research reviewed in the preceding sections suggest that while most of the individual studies do not provide unambiguous support for adrenergic involvement in memory, the collective evidence favors a significant role for NE. The major support for such a conclusion comes from the following sources:

1. The numerous studies that have demonstrated that inhibition of NE at the DBH step disrupts both memory storage and retrieval. This evidence is not conclusive principally because of the complex side effects that accompany DBH inhibition. However, the demonstration that several classes of inhibitors that have different side effects produce amnesia in several learning situations encourages the the belief that inhibition of NE synthesis disrupts retention.

2. The demonstration that amnesias induced by a number of agents can be alleviated by both pre- and posttraining and pretesting administration of NE, NE precursors, and NE receptor stimulators.

3. The observation by Gold and his associates that brain levels of NE are accurate predictors of degree of retention. Additional related support comes from a study in humans in which degree of memory impairment in patients with Korsakoff's syndrome was shown to be highly correlated with the reduction in concentration of the primary brain metabolites of NE (McEntee & Mair, 1978).

The major evidence against a role for NE is the absence of retention impairments after forebrain NE depletion induced by 6-OHDA injections into the dorsal bundle. Despite a greater than 90% NE depletion in cortex, hippocampus, and amygdala the retention of most learned responses is normal. It is difficult to reconcile this finding with the positive effects of acute and chronic (intraventricular 6-OHDA) pharmacological treatments reviewed earlier. In a recent review of the dorsal bundle lesion literature Mason (1979) argues that NE plays no significant role in learning or memory and that the positive findings from the pharmacological studies are probably the results of side effects of the drugs. This conclusion should be viewed with extreme caution. Negative results from chronic lesion studies are notoriously difficult to interpret. Because a period of at least 2 weeks elapses before animals are tested following surgery, ample time is available for functional compensatory changes to occur. A number of possibilities for compensation exist. For example, retention may be maintained by postsynaptic supersensivity to small quantities of NE remaining after the lesion or by increased turnover in remaining NE nerve terminals. Another possibility is that receptors may become sensitive to other amines, such as tyramine or octopamine, or to other neurotransmitters, such as serotonin. Absence of a behavioral effect following a chronic lesion is not conclusive evidence that the lesioned system plays no role in the behavior. In order to resolve the discrepancy between the acute pharmacological and chronic lesion findings, it will be necessary to carry out experiments in which dorsal bundle lesioned animals can be tested before any functional compensatory changes can occur. This has been done in the dopamine system by Ranje and Ungerstedt (1977) in animals with 6-OHDA degeneration of the ascending DA bundle. These authors showed that lesioned rats could be tested as soon as 48 hours following surgery if learning was studied in a swim maze, a situation in which lesioned animals can overcome their akinesia.

3. Possible Modes of Action of Norepinephrine

Some suggestion on the possible function of NE in memory processing can be gained from recent studies of the ultrastructural features of adrenergic neurons and their biophysical properties. It is now well documented that there are two major NE neuron systems in the brain that have extensive projections throughout the CNS [see Moore and Bloom (1979) for an up-to-date and detailed account of the anatomy and physiology of these two systems]. One is the locus coeruleus system, which originates in that nucleus and innervates wide areas of the cortex, hippocampus, amygdala, cerebellum, lateral geniculate, hypothalamus, and thalamus. The other, the lateral tegmental NE system has its origin in diffuse cell groups in the medulla and projects to spinal cord, brainstem, and hypothalamus. The principal target of this system is the medial hypothalamus where NE innervation plays an important role in hormone regulation. The fibers that make up these systems are thin and unmyelinated and project diffusely over wide areas of the nervous system with no significant topographic organization. Detailed radioautographic studies of NE axons from the frontal parietal cortex of the rat have revealed new information of the ultrastructure properties of NE neurons (Beaudet & Descarries, 1978; Descarries, Watkins, & Lapierre, 1977). These workers labeled NE axons and terminals by topical application of tritiated NE and then fixed them with glutaraldehyde for autoradiography and examination by the electron microscope. Analysis of this material revealed that the nerve endings consisted of widely dispersed thin unmyelinated fibers bearing varicosities containing large granular vesicles spaced $1-3$ μm apart. The most striking feature was the finding that less than 5% of these axonal varicosities made synaptic contact with post-synaptic elements compared with more than 50% of nonlabeled terminals. The NE labeled varicosities failed to show the close cellular apposition and postsynaptic membrane thickening usually seen in electron micrographs of classic synapses. This implies that the released NE may diffuse over long distances to receptors that are remote from the varicosities, suggesting a function more like neuroendocrine secretion than classic synaptic transmission. This organization suggests that NE may function to modulate ongoing activity over widely dispersed neuronal populations for relatively long time periods rather than exerting a direct one-to-one influence on individual postsynaptic cells (Dismukes, 1977).

Recent electrophysiological evidence suggests a similar role (Woodward, Moises, Waterhouse, Hoffer, & Freedman, 1979). Studies have shown that iontophoretic application of NE to Purkinje cell membranes results in a distinctly different electrophysiological effect from those of a classic inhibitory neurotransmitter such as α-aminobutyric acid (GABA). Whereas GABA results in a hyperpolarization with an increase in membrane ionic conductance, applied NE produced either no change or a decrease in membrane conductance. Similar results have been shown with stimulation of the locus coeruleus and with application of cAMP. Detailed electrophysiological investigations of the basis of NE-induced depression of Purkinje cell activity suggest that applied NE differentially suppresses background activity induced by afferent input with a resulting enhancement of the evoked excitation. Norepinephrine appeared to increase signal-to-noise ratio rather than merely uniformly to inhibit activation. Similar findings are reported for NE neurons in the cerebral cortex, hippocampus, and lateral geniculate. Woodward *et al.* conclude that the term ''neuromodulatory'' is an appropriate description for these actions of NE in that synaptic inputs are improved independent of any effects on spontaneous activity.

The results of these anatomical and physiological studies provide some clues to the possible role that NE might play in memory processing. They suggest that the function of NE is to modulate the activity of synaptic inputs over widespread brain regions rather than to transmit detailed local information on a moment to moment basis. How this modulation of neuronal activity influences information processing is not known. One suggestion from the electrophysiological studies is that NE released during states of arousal could promote learning and facilitate retrieval by suppressing irrelevant background information, while simultaneously amplifying inputs from significant environmental stimuli. The improved signal-to-noise ratio that would result from such a screening function may provide the basis for the influence of NE on both encoding and retrieval processes.

4. Dopamine and Memory

Only a few of the pharmacological studies reviewed in the preceding sections have directly examined the role of DA in memory processes. While there is some evidence that DA injected into the brain can enhance the retention of a passive avoidance response, too few experiments have been conducted with specific DA agonists and antagonists to evaluate the significance of this amine. The demonstrations that amnesias can be produced by low level electrical stimulation of areas rich in DA neurons indicates that DA may play a more significant role in memory processing then is suggested by pharmacological studies.

Additional studies have indicated that DA may have a significant role in the retrieval of inhibitory avoidance learning. Quartermain *et al.* (1982) have shown that the exaggerated forgetting of lick suppression seen in senescent mice can be alleviated by pretesting treatment with the DA agonist lisuride. Similarly forgetting of lick suppression induced in young animals by protein synthesis inhibition can also be attenuated by DA and DA agonists injected directly into the brain (Altman & Quartermain, 1982). More studies will be necessary to determine whether these drug effects are due to actions on the nigrostriatal DA system.

REFERENCES

Altman, H. J., & Quartermain, D. State dependent learning induced by α-methyl-*p*-tyrosine in a brightness discrimination. 1982, in preparation.

Altman, H. J., & Quartermain, D. Facilitation of memory retrieval by centrally administered catecholamine stimulating agents. *Behavioral Brain Research*, 1982, in press.

Barondes, S. H., & Cohen, H. D. Delayed and sustained effect of acetoxycycloheximide on memory in mice. *Proceedings of the National Academy of Sciences of the U.S.A.*, 1967, *58*, 157–164.

Bartus, R. T. Short-term memory in the rhesus monkey: Effects of dopamine blockade via acute haloperidol administration. *Pharmacology, Biochemistry and Behavior*, 1978, *9*, 254–260.

Beaudet, A., & Descarries, L. The monoamine innervation of rat cerebral cortex: Synaptic and nonsynaptic axon terminals. *Neuroscience*, 1978, *3*, 851–860.

Biel, J. H., & Bopp, B. A. Amphetamines: Structure activity relationship. In L. L. Iversen, S. D. Iversen & S. H. Snyder (Eds.), *Handbook of pharmacology (Vol. 2)*. New York: Plenum, 1978.

Botwinick, C. Y., & Quartermain, D. Recovery from amnesia induced by pre-test injections of monoamine oxidase inhibitors. *Pharmacology, Biochemistry and Behavior*, 1974, *2*, 375–379.

Botwinick, C. Y., Quartermain, D., Freedman, L. S., & Hallock, M. F. Some characteristics of amnesia induced by FLA-63 an inhibitor of dopamine beta hydroxylase. *Pharmacology, Biochemistry and Behavior*, 1977, *6*, 487–491.

Bovet, D., Robustelli, F., & Bignami, G. Etude du conditionnement inhibiteur chez le rat. Action de l'amphetamine, de la chlorpromazine et des agents cholinergiques. *Compte Rendu Hebdomadaires des Seances de l'Academie des Sciences*, 1965, *260*, 4641–4645.

Breese, G. R., & Traylor, T. D. Depletion of brain noradrenaline and dopamine by 6-hydroxydopamine. *Britian Journal of Pharmacology*, 1971, *42*, 88–93.

Brown, O. M., Palfai, T., & Wichlinski, L. Effect of an amnesic dose of reserpine, syrosingopine or guanethidine on the levels of whole brain norepinephrine in the mouse. *Pharmacology, Biochemistry and Behavior*, 1981, *15*, 911–914.

Cassens, G., Roffman, M., Kurac, A., Orsulak, P., Shildkraut, J. Alterations in brain norepinephrine metabolism induced by environmental stimuli previously paired with inescapable shock. *Science*, 1980, *209*, 1138–1140.

Cohen, R. P., & Hamburg, M. D. Evidence for adrenergic neurons in a memory access pathway. *Pharmacology, Biochemistry and Behavior*, 1975, *3*, 519–523.

Cools, A. R., & Van Rossum, J. M. Excitation-mediating and inhibition mediating dopamine receptors. A new concept towards a better understanding of electrophysiology, biochemistry, pharmacology, functional and clinical data. *Psychopharmacologia*, 1976, *45*, 243–254.

Crabbé, J. C., & Alpern, H. P. Facilitation and disruption of the long-term store of memory with neural excitants. *Pharmacology, Biochemistry and Behavior*, 1973, *1*, 197–202.

Crabbé, J. C., & Alpern, H. P. *d*-Amphetamine: Disruptive effects on the long-term store of memory and proactive facilitatory effects on learning in inbred mice. *Pharmacology, Biochemistry and Behavior*, 1975, *3*, 647–652.

Crow, T. J., & Wendlandt, S. Impaired acquisition of a passive avoidance response after lesions induced in the locus coeruleus by 6-OH-dopamine. *Nature (London)*, 1976, *258*, 42–44.

Danscher, G., & Fjerdingstad, E. J. Diethyldithiocarbamate (Antabuse): Decrease of brain heavy metal staining pattern and improved consolidation of shuttle box avoidance in goldfish. *Brain Research*, 1975, *83*, 143–155.

Descarries, L., Watkins, D. C., & Lapierre, Y. Noradrenergic axon terminals in the cerebral cortex of the rat. III. Toponetric ultrastructural analysis. *Brain Research*, 1977, *133*, 197–222.

Dismukes, E. K. New look at the aminergic nervous system. *Nature (London)*, 1977, *269*, 557–558.

Dismukes, R. K., & Rake, A. V. Involvement of biogenic amines in memory formation. *Psychopharmacologia*, 1972, *35*, 17–25.

Doty, B., & Doty, L. Facilitating effects of amphetamine on avoidance conditioning in relation to age and problem difficulty. *Psychopharmacologia*, 1966, *9*, 136–142.

Evangelista, A. M., & Izquierdo, I. The effect of pre and post-trial amphetamine injections on avoidance responses in rats. *Psychopharmacologia*, 1971, *20*, 325–350.

Fibiger, H. C., & Phillips, A. G. Retrograde amnesia after electrical stimulation of the substantia nigra: Mediation by the dopaminergic nigro-neostriatal bundle. *Brain Research*, 1976, *116*, 23–33.

Fibiger, H. C., Phillips, A. G., & Zis, A. P. Deficits in instrumental responding after 6-hydroxydopamine lesions of the nigro-neostriatal dopaminergic projection. *Pharmacology, Biochemistry and Behavior*, 1974, *2*, 212–216.

Flood, J. F., Jarvik, M. E., Bennett, E. L., Orme, A. E., & Rosenzweig, M. R. The effect of stimulants, depressants, and protein synthesis inhibition on retention. *Behavioral Biology*, 1977, *20*, 168–183.

Flood, J. F., Smith, G. E., Jarvik, M. E. Catecholamine neuro-transmitter-receptor interaction and its effects on long term memory processing. 1979, in preparation.

Freedman, L. S., Backman, M. Z., & Quartermain, D. Clonidine the amnesia induced by dopamine β-hydroxylase inhibition. *Pharmacology, Biochemistry and Behavior*, 1979, *11*, 259–263.

Fulginiti, S., Molina, V. A., & Orsingher, O. A. Inhibition of catecholamine biosynthesis and memory processes. *Psychopharmacology (Berlin)*, 1976, *51*, 65–69.

Furchgott, R. F. The classification of adrenoceptors (adrenergic receptors) An evaluation from the standpoint of receptor theory. *Handbuch der Experimentellen Pharmacologie*, 1972, *33*, 283–335.

Fuxe, K., & Ungerstedt, U. Histochemistry, biochemistry, and functional studies on central monoamine neurons after acute and chronic amphetamine administration. In E. Costa & S. Garattini (Eds.), *Amphetamines and related compounds*. New York: Raven Press, 1970.

Gallagher, M., Kapp, B. S., Musty, R. E., & Driscoll, P. A. Memory formation: Evidence for a specific neurochemical system in the amygdala. *Science*, 1977, *198*, 423–425.

Gibbs, M., & Barnett, E. L. Effects of amphetamine on short-term protein independent memory in day-old chickens. *Pharmacology, Biochemistry and Behavior*, 1976, *4*, 305–309.

Gold, P. E., & McCarty, R. Plasma catecholamines: Changes after foot shock and seizure-producing frontal cortex stimulation. *Behavioral and Neural Biology*, 1981, *31*, 247–260.

Gold, P. E., & McGaugh, J. L. Endogenous modulators of memory storage processes. *Behavioral Biology*, 1977, *20*, 329–334.

Gold, P. E., & McGaugh, J. L. Endogenous modulators of memory storage processes. In L. Carenza, P. Pancheri and L. Zichella (Eds.), *Clinical Psychoneuroendocrinology in Reproduction*, 25–46. New York: Academic Press, 1978.

Gold, P. E., & Sternberg, D. B. Retrograde amnesia produced by several treatments: Evidence for a common neurobiological mechanism. *Science*, 1978, *201*, 367–368.

Gold, P. E., & Van Buskirk, R. B. Facilitation of time-dependent memory storage processes with posttrial epinephrine injections. *Behavioral Biology*, 1975, *13*, 145–153.

Gold, P. E., & Van Buskirk, R. B. Posttraining brain norepinephrine concentrations: Correlation with retention performance of avoidance training and with peripheral epinephrine modulation of memory processing. *Behavioral Biology*, 1978, *23*, 252–258. (a)

Gold, P. E., & Van Buskirk, R. B. Effects of alpha- and beta-adrenergic receptor antagonists on posttrial epinephrine modulation of memory: Relationship to posttraining brain norepinephrine concentrations. *Behavioral Biology*, 1978, *24*, 168–184. (b)

Goodman, L. S., & Gilman, A. (Eds.). *The pharmacological basis of therapeutics* (5th ed.). New York: Macmillan, 1978.

Gorelick, D. A., Bozewicz, T. R., & Bridger, W. H. The role of catecholamines in animal learning and memory. In A. J. Friedhoff (Ed.), *Catecholamines and behavior* (Vol. 2). New York: Plenum, 1975.

Gozzani, J. L., & Izquierdo, I. Possible peripheral adrenergic and central dopaminergic influences in memory consolidation. *Psychopharmacology (Berlin)*, 1976, *49*, 109–111.

Hall, M. E. Effects of posttrial amphetamine and strychinine on learning as a function of task difficulty. *Communications in Behavioral Biology*, 1969, *4*, 171–175.

Hall, M. E. The effects of norepinephrine biosynthesis inhibition on the consolidation of two discriminated escape responses. *Behavioral Biology*, 1976, *6*, 145–163.

Hall, M. E. Enhancement of learning by cycloheximide and DDC: A function of response strength. *Behavioral Biology*, 1977, *21*, 41–51.

Hall, M. E., & Mayer, M. A. Effects of α-methyl-*p*-tyrosine on the recall of a passive avoidance response. *Pharmacology, Biochemistry and Behavior*, 1975, *3*, 579-582.

Hamburg, M. D., & Cohen, R. P. Memory access pathway: Role of adrenergic versus cholinergic neurons. *Pharmacology, Biochemistry and Behavior*, 1973, 275–300.

Hamburg, M. D., & Kerr, A. DDC-induced retrograde amnesias prevented by injections of Dl-DOPS. *Pharmacology, Biochemistry and Behavior*, 1976, *5*, 499–501.

Haycock, J. W., Van Buskirk, R., Gold, P. E. Effects on retention of post training amphetamine injections in mice. Interactions with pre training experience. *Psychopharmacology (Berlin)*, 1977, *54*, 21–24.

Haycock, J. W., Van Buskirk, R., Gold, P. E., & McGaugh, J. L. Effects of diethyldithiocarbamate and fusaric acid upon memory storage processes in rats. *European Journal of Pharmacology*, 1978, *51*, 261–273.

Haycock, J. W., Van Buskirk, R., & McGaugh, J. L. Facilitation of retention performance in mice by posttraining diethyldithiocarbamate. *Pharmacology, Biochemistry and Behavior*, 1976, *5*, 525–528.

Haycock, J. W., Van Buskirk, R., & McGaugh, J. L. Effects of catecholaminergic drugs upon memory storage processes in mice. *Behavioral Biology*, 1977, *20*, 281–310.

Hess, H. *Effects of propranolol on short term memory in rats.* Paper presented at the Eastern Psychological Association Annual Conference, April 1977.

Izquierdo, I., Beamish, D. G., & Anisman, H. Effect of an inhibitor of dopamine-β-hydroxylase on the acquisition and retention of four different avoidance tasks in mice. *Psychopharmacology (Berlin)*, 1979, *63*, 174–179.

Izquierdo, J. A., Fabian, H. L., & Chemerinski, L. Effects of *d*- and *l*-propranolol on spontaneous mobility and retention in male mice. *Acta Physiologica Latino Americana*, 1974, *24*, 669–670.

James, D. T. D. Posttrial *d*-amphetamine sulfate and one-trial learning in mice. *Journal of Comparative and Physiological Psychology*, 1975, *89*, 626–635.

Kety, S. S. The biogenic amines in the central nervous system: Their possible roles in arousal, emotion, and learning. In F. O. Schmitt (Ed.), *The neurosciences: Second study program*. New York: Rockefeller University Press, 1971.

Kim, H. J., & Routtenberg, A. Retention deficit following posttrial dopamine injection into rat neostriatum. *Neuroscience Abstracts*, 1976(6), 2(1), 445.

Krantz, K. D., & Seiden, L. Effects of diethyldithiocarbamate on the conditioned avoidance response of the rat. *Journal of Pharmacy and Pharmacology*, 1968, *20*, 343–348.

Krivanek, J., & McGaugh, J. L. Facilitating effects of pre- and posttrial amphetamine administration on discrimination learning in mice. *Agents and Actions*, 1969, *1*, 12–16.

Kurtz, P., & Palfai, T. Effects of reserpine on retention of escape reversal in mice: Absence of state-dependent learning. *Journal of Comparative and Physiological Psychology*, 1978, *91*, 393–406.

Leftoff, S. *Time-dependent, memory retrieval effects following peripheral* and *hippocampal treatments to increase synaptic biogenic amines*. Doctoral dissertation, New York University, 1973.

Lenard, L. G., & Beer, B. Modification of avoidance behavior in 6-hydroxydopamine-treated rats by stimulation of central noradrenergic and dopaminergic receptors. *Pharmacology, Biochemistry and Behavior*, 1975, *3*, 121–127.

Martinez, J. L., Jr., Jensen, R. A., Messing, R. B., Vasquez, B. J., Soumireu-Mourat, B., Geddes, D., Liang, K. C., & McGaugh, J. L. Central and peripheral actions of amphetamine on memory storage. *Brain Research*, 1980, *183*, 157.

Martinez, J. L., Jr., Vasquez, B. J., Rigter, H., Messing, R. B., Jensen, R. A., Liang, K. C., & McGaugh, J. L. Attenuation of amphetamine-induced enhancement of learning by adrenal demedullation. *Brain Research*, 1980, *195*, 433.

Mason, S. T. Noradrenaline: Reward or extenction? *Neuroscience and Biobehavioral Reviews*, 1979, *3*, 1–11.

Mason, S. T., & Fibiger, H. C. 6-OHDA lesions to the dorsal noradrenergic bundle alters extinction of passive avoidance. *Brain Research*, 1978, *152*, 209–214. (a)

Mason, S. T., & Fibiger, H. C. Noradrenaline and spatial memory. *Brain Research*, 1978, *156*, 382–386. (b)

Mason, S. T., & Iversen, S. D. Effects of selective forebrain noradrenaline loss on behavioral inhibition in the rat. *Journal of Comparative and Physiological Psychology*, 1977, *91*, 373–379.

McCarty, R., & Gold, P. E. Plasma catecholamines: Effects of footshock level and hormonal modulators of memory storage. *Hormones and Behavior*, 1981, *15*, 168–182.

McEntee, W. J., & Mair, R. G. Memory impairment in Korsakoff's psychosis: A correlation with brain noradrenergic activity. *Science*, 1978, *202*, 905–907.

McGaugh, J. L. Time-dependent processes in memory storage. *Science*, 1966, *153*, 1351–1358.

Meligeni, J. A., Ledergerber, S. A., & McGaugh, J. L. Norepinephrine attenuation of amnesia produced by diethydithiocarbamate. *Brain Research*, 1978, *149*, 155–164.

Merlo, A. B., & Izquierdo, J. A. Effect of post-trial injection of beta adrenergic blocking agents on a conditioned reflex in rats. *Psychopharmacologia*, 1971, *22*, 342–346.

Meyer, D. R., & Beattie, M. S. Some properties of substrates of memories. In L. Miller, C. Sandman, & A. Kastin (Eds.), *Neuropeptide influences in the brain and behavior*. New York: Academic Press, 1977.

Meyer, D. R., & Meyer, P. Dynamics and bases of recoveries of functions after injuries to the cerebral cortex. *Physiological Psychology*, 1977, *5*, 133–165.

Mitcham, J. C., & Thomas, R. K. Effects of substantia nigra and caudate nucleus lesions on avoidance learning in rats. *Journal of Comparative and Physiological Psychology*, 1972, *81*, 101–107.

Moore, R. Y., & Bloom, F. E. Central catecholamine neuron systems: Anatomy and physiology of the norepinephrine and epinephrine system. *American Review of Neuroses*, 1979, *2*, 113–168.

Orsingher, O. A., & Fulginiti, S. Effects of α-methyltyrosine and adrenergic blocking agents on the facilitating action of amphetamine and nicotine on learning in rats. *Psychopharmacology (Berlin)*, 1971, *19*, 231–240.

Palfai, T., Brown, O. M., & Walsh, T. J. Catecholamine levels in the whole brain and the probability of memory formation are not related. *Pharmacology, Biochemistry and Behavior*, 1978, *8*, 717–721.

Palfai, T., & Walsh, T. J. Comparisons of the effects of guanethidine, 6-hydroxydopamine and diethyldithiocarbamate on retention of passive avoidance. *Pharmacology, Biochemistry and Behavior*, 1980, *13*, 805–809.

Prado-Alcala, R. A., Grinberg, Z. J., Arditti, L. L., Garcia, M. M., Prieto, H. G., & Brust-

Carmona, H. Learning deficits produced by chronic and reversible lesions of its corpus striatum in rats. *Physiology and Behavior*, 1975, *15*, 283–287.

Prado de Carvalho, L., & Zornetzer, S. F. The involvement of the locus coeruleus in memory. *Behavioral and Neural Biology*, 1981, *31*, 173–186.

Quartermain, D. The influence of drugs on learning and memory. In M. R. Rosenweig & E. L. Bennett (Eds.), *Neural mechanisms of learning and memory*. Cambridge, MA: MIT Press, 1976.

Quartermain, D. 1982, in preparation.

Quartermain, D., & Altman, H. J. Facilitation of retrieval by *d*-amphetamine following anisomycin-induced amnesia. *Physiological Psychology*, 1982, in press.

Quartermain, D., & Botwinick, C. Y. Role of the biogenic amines in the reversal of cycloheximide-induced amnesia. *Journal of Comparative and Physiological Psychology*, 1975, *88*, 386–401. (a)

Quartermain, D., & Botwinick, C. Y. Effects of age of habit on susceptibility to cycloheximide-induced amnesia in mice. *Journal of Comparative and Physiological Psychology*, 1975, *89*, 803–809. (b)

Quartermain, D., Freedman, L. S., Botwinick, C. Y., & Gutwein, B. M. Reversal of cycloheximide-induced amnesia by adrenergic receptor stimulation. *Pharmacology, Biochemistry and Behavior*, 1977, *7*, 259–267.

Quartermain, D., & Judge, M. E. Recovery of memory following forgetting induced by depletion of biogenic amines. 1982, submitted for publication. (a)

Quartermain, D., & Judge, M. E. Amphetamine alleviates forgetting of fear conditioning induced by a long retention interval. 1982, in preparation. (b)

Quartermain, D., Judge, M. E., & Friedman, E. The role of lisuride and other dopamine agonists in memory retrieval processes. In D. B. Calne, R. Horowski, R. J. McDonald, W. Wuttke (Eds.), *Lisuride and other dopamine agonists*. New York: Raven Press, 1982 in press.

Quinton, E. E., & Bloom, A. S. Effects of *d*-amphetamine and strychnine on cycloheximide and diethyldithiocarbamate-induced amnesia in mice. *Journal of Comparative Physiological Psychology*, 1977, *91*, 1390–1398.

Rainbow, T. C., Adler, J. E., & Flexner, L. B. Comparison in mice of the amnestic effects of cycloheximide and 6-hydroxydopamine in a one-trial passive avoidance task. *Pharmacology, Biochemistry and Behavior*, 1976, *4*, 347–349.

Rainbow, T. C., & Flexner, L. B. Studies on memory: Spontaneous return of memory in 6-hydroxydopamine-treated mice and its relation to cycloheximide-induced transient amnesia. *Pharmacology, Biochemistry and Behavior*, 1978, *8*, 1–7.

Rake, A. V. Involvement of biogenic amines in memory formation: The central nervous system indole amine involvement. *Psychopharmacologia*, 1973, *29*, 91–100.

Randt, C. T., Quartermain, D., Goldstein, M., & Anagnoste, B. Norepinephrine biosynthesis inhibition: Effects of memory in mice. *Science*, 1971, *172*, 498–499.

Ranje, C., & Ungerstedt, U. Lack of acquisition in dopamine denervated animals tested in an underwater Y-maze. *Brain Research*, 1977, *134*, 95–111.

Roberts, D. C. S., & Fibiger, H. C. Conditioned taste aversion induced by diethyldithiocarbamate (DDC). *Neuroscience Letters*, 1976, *2*, 349–352.

Routtenberg, A., & Holzman, N. Memory disruption by electrical stimulation of substantia nigra pars compacta. *Science*, 1973, *181*, 83–89.

Routtenberg, A., & Kim, H. J. The substantia nigra and neostriatum: Substrates for memory consolidation. In L. Butcher (Ed.), *Cholinergicmonoaminergic interactions in the brain*. New York: Academic Press, 1978.

Sara, S. J., & DeWeer, B. Memory retrieval enhanced by amphetamine after a long retention interval. *Behavioral and Neural Biology*, 1982, in press.

Serota, R. G., Roberts, R. B., & Flexner, L. B. Acetoxycycloheximide-induced transient amnesia: Protective effects of adrenergic stimulants. *Proceedings of the National Academy of Sciences of the U.S.A.*, 1972, *69*, 340–342.

Spanis, C. W., Haycock, J. W., Handwerker, M. H., Rose, R. P., & McGaugh, J. L. Impairment of retention of avoidance responses in rats by posttraining diethyldithiocarbamate. *Psychopharmacology (Berlin)*, 1977, *53*, 213–215.

Spear, N. E. *The processing of memories: Forgetting and retention*. Hillsdale, NJ: Lawrence Erlbaum Associates, 1978.

Squire, L. R. Cerebral protein synthesis inhibition and discrimination training: effects of d-amphetamine. *Brain Research*, 1979, *177*, 401–406.

Stein, L., Belluzzi, J. D., & Wise, C. D. Memory enhancement of central administration of norepinephrine. *Brain Research*, 1975, *84*, 329–335.

Sternberg, D. B. The role of catecholamines in memory modulation. *Dissertation Abstracts International*, 1982, in press.

Sternberg, D. B., Gold, P. E., & McGaugh, J. L. Noradrenergic sympathetic blockade: Lack of effect on memory or retrograde amnesia. 1982, submitted for publication.

Tulving, E., & Thomson, D. M. Encoding specificity and retrieval processes in episodic memory. *Psychological Review*, 1973, *80*, 352–373.

Ungerstedt, U. Histochemical studies of intracerebral and intraventricular injections of 6-Hydroxydopamine in the rat brain. In T. Malmfors & H. Thoenen (Eds.), *6-Hydroxydopamine and catecholamine neurons*. New York: American Elsever, 1971.

von Voiglander, P. F., & Moore, K. E. The release of H³-dopamine from cat brain following electrical stimulation of the substantia nigra and caudate nucleus. *Neuropharmacology*, 1971, *10*, 733–741.

Walsh, T. J., & Palfai, T. Memory storage impairment or retrieval failure: Pharmacologically distinguishable processes. *Pharmacology, Biochemistry and Behavior*, 1979, *11*, 453–456.

Weissman, A. Drugs and retrograde amnesia. *International Review of Neurobiology*, 1967, *10*, 167–197.

Woodward, D. J., Moises, H. C., Waterhouse, B. D., Hoffer, B. J., & Freedman, R. Modulatory actions of norepinephrine in the central nervous system. *Federation Proceedings, Federation of American Societies for Experimental Biology*, 1979, *38*, 2109–2116.

Wyers, E. J., Deadwyler, S. A., Hirasuna, N., & Montgomery, D. Passive avoidance retention and caudate stimulation. *Physiology and Behavior*, 1973, *111*, 809–819.

Zornetzer, S. F., Abraham, W. C., & Appleton, R. Locus coeruleus and labile memory. *Pharmacology, Biochemistry and Behavior*, 1978, *9*, 227–234.

Zornetzer, S. F., Gold, P. E. The locus coeruleus: Its possible role in memory consolidation. *Physiology and Behavior*, 1976, *16*, 331–336.

Zornetzer, S. F., Gold, M. S., & Hendrickson, J. α-Methyl-*p*-tyrosine and memory: State dependency and memory failure. *Behavioral Biology*, 1974, *12*, 135–141.

INDEX

84-4345/mcl

QP
406
.P49   The Physiological
1983   basis of memory